The Works of John Owen

VOLUME XV

The Works of
JOHN OWEN

EDITED BY

William H. Goold

VOLUME XV

The Banner of Truth Trust

This Edition of
THE WORKS OF JOHN OWEN
first published by Johnstone & Hunter, 1850–53

Reprinted by
THE BANNER OF TRUTH TRUST
3 Murrayfield Road, Edinburgh EH12 6EL
PO Box 621, Carlisle, Pennsylvania 17013, USA

VOLUME XV

1965
Second printing 1976
Third printing 1983
ISBN 0 85151 130 9

Reprinted by photolithography in Great Britain by
Fletcher & Son Ltd, Norwich
Bound by Richard Clay (The Chaucer Press) Ltd,
Bungay, Suffolk

CONTENTS OF VOL. XV.

CHAPTER VI.

CHAPTER VII.

CHAPTER VIII.

CHAPTER IX.

CHAPTER X.

A DISCOURSE CONCERNING EVANGELICAL LOVE, CHURCH PEACE, AND UNITY.

CHAPTER I.

CHAPTER II.

CONTENTS.

V

CHAPTER III.

Page

Nature of the catholic church—The first and principal object of Christian love—Differences among the members of this church, of what nature, and how to be managed—Of the church catholic as visibly professing—The extent of it, or who belong unto it—Of union and love in this church-state—Of the church of England with respect hereunto—Of particular churches; their institution; corruption of that institution—Of churches diocesan, etc.—Of separation from corrupt particular churches—The just causes thereof, etc. . . . 77

CHAPTER IV.

Want of love and unity among Christians justly complained of—Causes of divisions and schisms—1. Misapprehensions of evangelical unity—Wherein it doth truly consist—The ways and means whereby it may be obtained and preserved—Mistakes about both—2. Neglect in churches to attend unto known gospel duty—Of preaching unto conversion and edification—Care of those that are really godly—Of discipline: how neglected, how corrupted—Principles seducing churches and their rulers into miscarriages: 1. Confidence of their place; 2. Contempt of the people; 3. Trust unto worldly grandeur—Other causes of divisions—Remainders of corruption from the general apostasy—Weakness and ignorance—Of readiness to take offence—Remedies hereof—Pride—False teachers . . 104

CHAPTER V.

Grounds and reasons of nonconformity 141

AN INQUIRY INTO THE ORIGINAL, NATURE, INSTITUTION, POWER, ORDER, AND COMMUNION OF EVANGELICAL CHURCHES.

Prefatory Note by the Editor 188
To the Reader 189

THE PREFACE.

An Examination of the general principles of Dr Stillingfleet's Book of the Unreasonableness of Separation 193

CHAPTER I.

Of the original of churches 223

CHAPTER II.

The especial original of the evangelical church-state 230

CHAPTER III.

The continuation of a church-state and of churches unto the end of the world—What are the causes of it, and whereon it depends 247

CHAPTER IV.

The especial nature of the gospel church-state appointed by Christ . . . 261

AN ANSWER TO DR STILLINGFLEET'S BOOK OF THE UNREASONABLENESS OF SEPARATION.

A BRIEF INSTRUCTION IN THE WORSHIP OF GOD AND DISCIPLINE OF THE CHURCHES OF THE NEW TESTAMENT.

A DISCOURSE

CONCERNING

LITURGIES, AND THEIR IMPOSITION.

PREFATORY NOTE.

IT deserves attention that this pamphlet, with its humble title, "A Discourse concerning Liturgies," etc., and printed anonymously in 1662, contains the judgment of our author in regard to measures which gave rise to most important events in the ecclesiastical history of England. It is an argument against the liturgy, the imposition of which obliged nearly two thousand clergy of the Church of England to resign their livings rather than sacrifice a good conscience.

On the Restoration, the Book of Common Prayer had been resumed in the royal chapel at Whitehall; it was ordained to be read in the House of Peers; and before the year closed, some of the parochial clergy, who scrupled to use it, were prosecuted according to the laws in force before the civil war.

As many leading Presbyterians, however, had been favourable to the Restoration, the Court could not afford at first to come to an open rupture with them, and accordingly, in 1661, a conference was appointed between twelve bishops and an equal number of Presbyterian ministers, with instructions to revise the Book of Common Prayer, so as to bring it into conformity with the religious convictions of both parties, and establish peace and unity in the church. This conference, however, after long and keen debate, broke up without any good results.

The Convocation was then ordered to revise the liturgy. The changes made on it were not such as to relieve the consciences of the Presbyterians; but, nevertheless, as revised by the Convocation, it was adopted by Parliament, and ratified by the Act for Uniformity in the Prayers and Ceremonies of the Church of England. This act, designed, according to Burnet, to make the terms of conformity stricter than before, passed the House of Commons by a majority of 186 to 180. The House of Lords endeavoured to abate the stringency of some of its provisions, but, supported by the Court, the majority in the Lower House effectually resisted the modifications proposed. The bill passed the House of Peers by a small majority, and received the royal assent on 19th May 1662. The act required all ministers to announce publicly their adherence to the liturgy, and to subscribe a declaration that it was unlawful, upon any pretence, to take arms against the king, or to endeavour any change in the government of church or state. No person, moreover, according to the act, could hold a benefice or administer the Lord's supper unless he was episcopally ordained. Fines, imprisonment, and the forfeiture of their livings, were the penalties to be inflicted on those who could not yield compliance with the law. The act took effect on the 24th of August, and nearly two thousand devout and faithful pastors were then expelled from the Church of England.

The chief merit of the following tract can only be understood in the light of these exciting events. From some expressions in it, it must have been written while the contest prevailed, and before the liturgy was actually imposed; and yet the whole argument is conducted in perfect temper, and the readers of Owen might fail to bear in mind that he is discussing a question which was stirring English society to its depths, and involved consequences unparalleled in English history. The treatise has all the weight and gravity of a judicial decision. The author, rising above petty details, expends his strength in proof that the *imposition* of a liturgy by civil enactment is an interference with the authority of Christ; and, unwilling to heighten the asperities of the prevailing controversy, he excludes from discussion the character of the English liturgy, and confines himself to the abstract question, as to the lawfulness of enforcing it on the conscience as essential to divine worship. It is the more honourable to Owen that he should have exerted himself against the imposition of the liturgy, when it is remembered that as at this time he held no living in the church, he could not suffer under the Act of Uniformity, and the measures of the Court were directed against the Presbyterians rather than the Independents. Orme remarks of this production and its subject, "The principle which these forms of human composition involve is of vast importance; and I know not where, in so small a compass, this principle is so well stated and so ably opposed as in this work."—ED.

A DISCOURSE

LITURGIES, AND THEIR IMPOSITION.

CHAPTER I.

The state of the Judaical church—The liberty given by Christ; 1. From the arbitrary impositions of men; 2. From the observances and rites instituted by Moses—The continuance of their observation, in the patience and forbearance of God—Difference about them stated—Legal righteousness and legal ceremonies contended for together—The reason of it.

ALTHOUGH our present inquiry be merely after one part of instituted worship under the gospel, and the due performance of it according to the mind of God, yet, there being a communication of some light to be obtained from the turning over of that worship from the Mosaical to the care and practice of the evangelical church, we shall look a little back unto it as therein stated; hoping thereby to make way for our clearer progress. What was the state of the church of God amongst the Jews as to instituted worship, when our blessed Saviour came to make the last and perfect discovery of his mind and will, is manifest both from the appointment of that worship in the law of Moses, and the practice of it remarked in the gospel. That the rites and ordinances of the worship in the church observed, were from the original in their nature *carnal*, and for the number *many*, on both accounts *burdensome* and grievous to the worshippers, the Scripture frequently declares. Howbeit, the teachers and rulers of the church, being grown wholly carnal in their spirits, and placing their only glory in their yoke, not being able to see to the end of the things that were to be done away, had increased those institutions, both in number and weight, with sundry inventions of their own; which, by their authority, they made necessary to be observed by their disciples. In an equal practice of these divine institutions and human inventions did our Lord Jesus Christ find the generality of

the church at his coming in the flesh. The former, being to continue in force until the time of reformation, at his resurrection from
the dead, should come, both by his practice and his teaching, as a
minister of Circumcision, he confirmed and pressed frequently on the
consciences of men, from the authority of the Law-maker. The latter
he utterly rejected, as introduced in a high derogation from the perfection of the law, and the honour of Him whose prerogative it is to
be the sole lawgiver of his church,—the only fountain and disposer
of his own worship. And this was the first dawning of liberty that,
with the rising of this Day-star, did appear to the burdened and lan-
guishing consciences of men. He freed them, by his teaching, from
the bondage of Pharisaical, arbitrary impositions, delivering their consciences from subjection to any thing in the worship of God but his
own immediate authority. For it may not be supposed that, when
he recommended unto his hearers an attendance unto the teaching
of the scribes and Pharisees, with an injunction to obey their directions, that he intended aught but those commands which they gave
from Him, and according to his mind, whose fear they did outwardly
profess; seeing that, both in general and particular, he did himself
condemn their traditions and impositions, giving out a rule of liberty
from them unto others in his own constant practice. Yea, and whereas he would do *civil* things in their own nature indifferent, whereunto he was by no righteous law obliged, to avoid the offence of any
which he saw might follow, Matt. xvii. 27, yet would he not practise
or give countenance unto, nay, nor abstain from condemning of, any
of their ecclesiastical self-invented observances, though he saw them
offended and scandalized at him, and was by others informed no less,
chap. xv. 12–14; confirming his practice with that standing rule concerning all things relating to the worship of God, " Every plant which
my heavenly Father hath not planted shall be rooted up." But he
is yet farther to carry on the work of giving liberty to all the disciples, that he might take them into a subjection to himself and his
own authority only. The Aaronical priesthood being the hinge on
which the whole ceremonial worship turned, so that upon a change
thereof the obligation of the law unto that worship, or any part of
it, was necessarily to cease, our blessed Saviour, in his death and obla-
tion, entering upon the office, and actually discharging the great
duty of his priesthood, did virtually put an end to the whole obligation of the first institution of Mosaical worship. In his death was
the procurement of the liberty of his disciples completely finished, as
unto conscience; the *supposed* obligation of men's traditions, and the
real obligation of Mosaical institutions, being by him (the first as a
prophet in his teaching, the last as a priest in his offering) dissolved
and taken away. From that day all the disciples of Christ were

taken under his immediate lordship, and made free to the end of the world from all obligations in conscience unto any thing in the worship of God but what is of his own institution and command.

This dissolution of the obligation of "the law of commandments contained in ordinances," being declared by his apostles and disciples, became a matter of great difference and debate amongst the Jews, to whom the gospel was first preached. Those who before had slain him, in pursuit of their own charge, that he would bring in such an alteration in the worship of God as was now divulged, were many of them exceedingly enraged at this new doctrine, and had their prejudices against him and his way much increased,—hating indeed the light, because their deeds were evil. These being obstinately bent to seek after righteousness (as it were, at least) by the works of the law, contended for their ceremonial works as one of the best stakes in their hedge, in whose observance they placed their chiefest confidence of their acceptance with God. But this is not all: many who, falling under powerful convictions of his doctrine and miracles, believed on him, did yet pertinaciously adhere to their old ceremonial worship. Partly for want of clear light and understanding in the doctrine of the person and office of the Messiah; partly through the power of those unspeakable prejudices which influenced their minds in reference to those rites which, being from of old observed by their forefathers, derived their original from God himself (much the most noble pleas and pretences that ever any of the sons of men had to insist upon for a subjection to such a yoke as indeed had lost all power to oblige them); they were very desirous to mix the observance of them with obedience unto those institutions which they, through the Lord Jesus, had superadded to them.

Things being thus stated amongst the Jews, God having a great work to accomplish among and upon them in a short time, would not have the effect of it turn upon this hinge merely; and therefore, in his infinite wisdom and condescension, waived the whole contest for a season. For whereas, within the space of forty years or thereabout, he was to call and gather out from the body, by the preaching of the gospel, his remnant according to the election of grace, and to leave the rest inexcusable,—thereby visibly glorifying his justice in their temporal and eternal ruin,—it pleased him, in a way of connivance and forbearance, to continue unto that people an allowance of the observation of their old worship until the time appointed for its utter removal and actual casting away should come. Though the original obligation on conscience, from the first institution of their ceremonies, was taken away, yet hence arose a new necessity of the observation of them, even in them who were acquainted with the dissolution of that obligation,—namely, from the offence and scandal of them to whom their observance was providentially indulged. On this account the disciples of Christ (and the apostles themselves) continued in a promiscuous observation of Mosaical institutions with the rest of the body of that people, until the appointed season of the utter rejection and destruction of the apostate churches was come. Hence many of the ancients affirm that James the Less, living at Jerusalem in great reputation with all the people for his sanctity and righteousness, was not, to the very time of his martyrdom, known to be a Christian; which had been utterly impossible had he totally abstained from communion with them in legal worship. Neither had that old controversy about the feast of the passover any other rise or spring than the mistake of some, who thought John had observed it as a Christian, who kept it only as a Judaical feast among the Jews: whence the tradition ran strong that he observed it with them on the fourteenth day of the month; which precise time others, turning it into a Christian observation, thought meet to lay aside.

Things being thus stated, in the connivance and forbearance of God, among the Jews, some of them, not contented to use the indulgence, granted to them in mere patience, for the ends before mentioned, began sedulously to urge the Mosaical rites upon all the Gentiles that were turned unto God; so making, upon the matter, the preaching of the gospel to be but a new way of proselyting men unto Judaism. For the most part, it appears that it was not any mistake or unacquaintedness with the liberty brought in by Christ that made them engage in this quarrel for Moses; but that indeed, being themselves carnal, and, notwithstanding the outward name of Christ, seeking yet for righteousness by the law, they esteemed the observation of the ceremonies indispensably necessary unto salvation. This gave occasion unto Paul, unto whom the apostleship of the Gentiles was in a special manner committed, to lay open the whole mystery of that liberty given by Christ to his disciples from the law of Moses; as also the pernicious effects which its observance would produce, upon those principles which were pressed by the Judaical zealots. Passing by the peculiar dispensation of God towards the whole nation of the Jews, wherein the Gentile believers were not concerned; as also that determination of the case of scandal made at Jerusalem, Acts xv., and the temporary rule of condescension as to the abridgment of liberty in some particulars agreed unto thereupon; he fully declares that the time of the appointment was come, that there was no more power in the law of their institutions to bind the consciences of men, and that it was not in the power of all the men in the world to impose the observation of them, or any like unto them, upon any one, though the meanest of the disciples of Jesus Christ. The mind of Christ in this matter being fully made known, and the liberty of his disciples vindicated, various effects in the minds of men ensued thereupon. Those who were in their inward principle themselves carnal, notwithstanding their outward profession of the gospel, delighting in and resting on an outward ceremonious worship, continued to oppose him with violence and fury. Those who with the profession of the Lord Christ had also received the Spirit of Christ, and were by him instructed, as in the perfection of righteousness, so in the beauty and excellency of the worship of the gospel, rejoiced greatly in the grace and privilege of the purchased liberty. After many contests, this controversy was buried in the ruins of the city and temple, when the main occasion of it was utterly taken away.

By these degrees were the disciples of Christ put into a complete actual possession of that liberty which he had preached to them, and purchased for them. Being first delivered from any conscientious subjection to the institutions of men, and then to the temporary institutions of God which concerned them not, they were left in a dependence on and subjection unto himself alone, as to all things concerning worship; in which state he will assuredly continue and preserve them to the end of the world, under the guidance and direction of those rules for the use of their liberty which he has left them in his word. But yet the principle of the difference before mentioned, which is fixed in the minds of men by nature, did not die together with the controversy that mainly issued from it. We may trace it effectually exerting itself in succeeding ages. As ignorance of the righteousness of God, with a desire to establish their own, did in any take place, so also did endeavours after an outward, ceremonious worship: for these things do mutually further and strengthen each other; and commonly proportionable unto men's darkness in the mystery of the righteousness of God in Christ is their zeal for a worldly sanctuary and carnal ordinances. And such hath been the force and efficacy of these combined principles in the minds of carnal men, that, under the profession of Christianity, they reduced things (in the Papacy) to the very state and condition wherein they were in Judaism at the time of reformation; the main principle in the one and the other church, in the apostasy, being legal righteousness and an insupportable yoke of ceremonious observances in the worship of God. And generally, in others the same principles of legal righteousness and a ceremonious worship have their prevalency in a just proportion, the latter being regulated by the former; and where by any means the former is everted, the latter for the most part falls of its own accord; yea, though rivetted in the minds of men by other prejudices also. Hence when the soul of a sinner is effectually wrought upon, by the preaching of the gospel, to renounce himself and his own righteousness, and, being truly humbled for sin, to receive the Lord Christ by faith, as " made unto him of God wisdom, righteousness, sanctification, and redemption," there needs, for the most part, little arguing to dissuade him from resting in or laying weight upon an outside, pompous worship; but he is immediately sensible of a delivery from its yoke, which he freely embraceth. And the reason hereof is, because that good Spirit by whom he is enabled to believe and receive the Lord Jesus Christ, gives him also an acquaintance with, and an experience of, the excellency, glory, and beauty of that spiritual communion with God in Christ whereunto believers are called in the gospel; which discovers the emptiness and uselessness of all which before, perhaps, he admired and delighted in : for " where the Spirit of Christ is, there is liberty." And these things,—of seeking a righteousness in Christ alone, and delighting in spiritual communion with God, exercising itself only in the ways of his own appointment,—do inseparably proceed from the same Spirit of Christ, as those before mentioned from the same principle of self and flesh.

CHAPTER II.

The disciples of Christ taken into his own disposal—General things to be observed about gospel institutions—Their number small—Excess of men's inventions—Things instituted brought into a religious relation by the authority of Christ—That authority is none other—Suitableness in the matter of institutions, to be designed to their proper significancy—That discoverable only by infinite wisdom—Abilities given by Christ for the administration of all his institutions—The way whereby it was done, Eph. iv. 7, 8—Several postulata laid down—The sum of the whole—State of our question in general.

WE have brought unto and left the disciples of Jesus Christ in the hand and sole disposal of him, their Lord and Master, as to all things which concern the worship of God; and how he hath disposed of them we are in the next place to consider. Now, he being the Head, Lord, and only Lawgiver of his church, coming from the bosom of his Father to make the last revelation of his mind and will, was to determine and appoint that worship of God in and by himself which was to continue to the end of the world. It belongeth not unto our purpose to consider distinctly and apart all the several institutions which by him were ordained. We shall only observe some things concerning them in general, that will be of use in our progress, and so proceed to the consideration of that particular about which we are in disquisition of his mind and will. The worship of God is either moral and internal, or external and of sovereign or arbitrary institution. The former we do not now consider; nor was the ancient, original, fundamental obligation unto it altered or dissolved in the least by the Lord Christ. It was as unto superadded institutions of outward worship, which have their foundation and reason in sovereign will and pleasure, that he took his disciples into his own disposal, discharging them from all obligations to aught else whatever but only what he should appoint. Concerning these, some few considerations will lead us to what in this discourse we principally intend. And the first is, *That they were few, and easy to be observed.* It was his will and pleasure that the faith and love of his disciples should, in some few instances, be exercised in a willing, ready subjection to the impositions of his wisdom and authority; and their service herein he doth fully recompense, by rendering those his institutions blessedly useful to their spiritual advantage. But he would not burden them with observances, either for nature or number, like or comparable unto them from which he purchased them liberty. And herein hath the practice of succeeding ages put an excellent lustre upon his love and tenderness. For whereas he is the Lord of his church, to whom the consciences of his disciples are in an unquestionable subjection, and who can give power and efficacy to his institutions to make them useful to their souls, yet when some of their fellow-servants came, I know not how, to apprehend themselves enabled to impose arbitrarily their appointments, for reasons seeming good to their wisdom, they might have been counted moderate if they had not given above ten commandments for his one. Bellarmine tells us, indeed, that the laws and institutions of the church that absolutely bind all Christians, so that they sin if they omit their observation, are upon the matter but four,— namely, to observe the fasts of Lent and Ember-weeks, to keep the holy days, confession once a year, and to communicate at Easter, De Rom. Pontif., lib. iv. cap. 18. But whereas they double the number of the sacred ceremonies instituted by Christ, and have every one of them a greater number of subservient observations attending on them, so he must be a stranger to their councils, canon-laws, and practices, that can believe his insinuation.

Again: as the institutions and ordinances of Christ in the outward worship of God, whose sole foundation was in his will and pleasure, were few, and easy to be observed, being brought into a relation of worship unto God by virtue of his institution and command, without which no one thing in their kind can do so more than another; so they were, for the matter of them, such as he knew had *an aptness to be serviceable unto the significancy* whereunto they were appointed by him, which nothing but infinite wisdom can judge of. And this eternally severs them from all things of men's invention, either to the same purpose, or in the same way to be used. For as whatever they shall appoint in the worship of God can have no significancy at all, as unto any spiritual end, for want of a Christ-like authority in their institution, which alone can add that significancy to them which in themselves, without such an appointment, they have not; so they themselves, want wisdom to choose the things which have any fitness or aptitude to be used for that end, if the authority were sufficient to introduce with them such a significancy. There is nothing they can in this kind fix upon, but as good reason as any they are able to tender, for the proof of their expedience unto the end proposed to them, will be produced to prove them meet for a quite other signification and purpose, and the contrary unto them, at least things diverse to them, be asserted with as fair pretences, as meet to be used in their place and room.

But that which we principally shall observe, in and about Christ's institutions of gospel worship, is the provision that he made for the administration of it acceptably unto God. It is of the instituted worship of his public assemblies that we treat. The chiefest acts and parts thereof may be referred to these three heads:—*preaching of the word, administration of the sacraments, and the exercise of discipline;* all to be performed with prayer and thanksgiving. The rule for the administration of these things, so far as they are purely of his institution, he gave his disciples in his appointment of them. Persons, also, he designed to the regular administration of these his holy things in the assemblies of his saints,—namely, pastors and teachers,—to endure to the end of the world, after those of an extraordinary employment under him were to cease. It remaineth, then, to consider how the persons appointed by him unto the administration of these holy things in his assemblies, and so to the discharge of the whole public worship of God, should be enabled thereunto, so as the end by him aimed at, of the edification of his disciples and the glory of God, might be attained. Two ways there are whereby this may be done: First, By such spiritual abilities for the discharge and performance of this whole work as will answer the mind of Christ therein, and so serve for the end proposed. Secondly, By the prescription of a form of words, whose reading and pronunciation in these administrations should outwardly serve as to all the ends of the prayer and thanksgiving required in them, which they do contain. It is evident that our Saviour fixed on the former way; what he hath done as to the latter, or what his mind is concerning it, we shall afterward inquire.

For the first, as in many other places, so signally in one, the apostle acquaints us with the course he has taken, and the provision that he hath made—namely, Eph. iv. 7, 8, 11–13: "Unto every one of us is given grace, according to the measure of the gift of Christ. Wherefore he saith, When he ascended up on high, he led captivity captive, and gave gifts unto men. And he gave some, apostles; and some, prophets; and some, evangelists; and some, pastors and teachers; for the perfecting of the saints, for the work of the ministry, for the edifying of the body of Christ: till we all come in the unity of the faith, and of the knowledge of the Son of God, unto a perfect man, unto the measure of the stature of the fulness of Christ," etc. The thing aimed at is, the bringing of all the saints and disciples of Christ, the whole church, to that measure and perfection of grace which Christ hath assigned to them in this world, that they may be meet for himself to receive in glory. The means whereby this is to be done and effected is, the faithful, regular, and effectual discharge of the work of the ministry; unto which the administration of all his ordinances and institutions doth confessedly belong. That this work may be discharged in an orderly manner to the end mentioned, he has granted unto his church the offices mentioned, to be executed by persons variously called thereunto, according to his mind and will.

The only inquiry remaining is, how these persons shall be enabled for the discharge of their office, and so accomplishment of the work of the ministry? This, he declares, is by the communication of grace and spiritual gifts from heaven unto them by Christ himself. Here lieth the spring of all that followeth,—the care hereof he hath taken upon himself unto the end of the world. He that enabled the shoulders of the Levites to bear the ark of old, and their arms to slay the sacrifices, without which natural strength those carnal ordinances could not have been observed (nor was the ark to be carried for a supply of defect of ability in the Levites), hath, upon their removal, and the institution of the spiritual worship of the gospel, undertaken to supply the administrators of it with spiritual strength and abilities for the discharge of their work, allowing them supply of the defect of that which he hath taken upon himself to perform. I suppose, then, that these ensuing will seem but reasonable postulata:—

1. That the means which Jesus Christ hath appointed for the attaining of any end, is every way sufficient for that purpose whereunto it is so appointed. His wisdom exacts our consent to this proposition.

2. That what he hath taken upon himself to perform unto the end of the world, and promised so to do, that he will accomplish accordingly. Here his faithfulness requires our assent.

3. That the communication of spiritual gifts and graces to the ministers of the gospel, is the provision that Christ hath made for the right discharge of the work of their ministry, unto the edification of his body. This lies plain in the text.

4. That the exercise and use of those gifts, in all those administrations for which they are bestowed, are expected and required by him. The nature of the thing itself, with innumerable testimonies, confirm this truth also.

5. That it is derogatory to the glory, honour, and faithfulness of the Lord Jesus Christ, to affirm that he ceaseth to bestow gifts for the work of the ministry, whilst he continueth and requireth the exercise and discharge of that work. What hath befallen men, or doth yet befall them, through the wretched sloth, darkness, and unbelief, which their wilful neglect of dependence on him, or of stirring up or improving of what they do receive from him, and the mischiefs that have accrued to the church by the intrusion of such persons into the place and office of the ministry as were never called nor appointed by him thereunto, are not to be imputed unto any failing on his part, in his promise of dispensing the gifts mentioned to the end of the world. Of which several positions we shall have some use in our farther progress.

Our Lord Jesus Christ, then, having delivered his disciples from the yoke of Mosaical institutions, which lay upon them from of old; as also from being entangled in their consciences by or from any inventions of men imposed on them; giving them rules for the practice of the liberty whereunto by him they were vindicated, taking them for the future into his own sole disposal in all things concerning the worship of God, he appoints, in his sovereign authority, both the ordinances which he will have alone observed in his church, and the persons by whom they are to be administered; [and] furnishing them with spiritual abilities to that end and purpose, promising his presence with them to the end of the world, commands them to set such, in his name and strength, in the way and unto the work that he hath allotted to them.

That, now, which on this foundation we are farther to inquire into is, whether, over and above what we have recounted, our Saviour hath appointed, or by any ways given allowance unto, the framing of a stinted form of prayers and praises, to be read and used by the administrators of his ordinances in their administration of them? or whether the prescription and imposing of such a form or liturgy upon those who minister in the church, in the name and authority of Christ, be not contrary to his mind, and cross to his whole design for perpetuating of his institutions to the end of the world, in due order and manner? And this we shall do, and withal discover the rise and progress which such liturgies have had and made in the church of God.

CHAPTER III.

Of the Lord's prayer, and what may be concluded from thence as to the invention and imposition of liturgies in the public worship of God—The liberty whereunto Christ vindicated and wherein he left his disciples.

THE first plea used to give countenance unto the composing and imposing of liturgies is taken from that act of our Saviour himself, who, upon the request of his disciples, composed for them a form of prayer; which, being recorded in the gospel, is said to have the force of an institution, rendering the observation or use of that form a necessary duty unto all believers to the end of the world. And this plea is strengthened by a discovery which some learned men say they have made,—namely, that our blessed Saviour composed this form, which he delivered to his disciples, out of such other forms as were then in ordinary use among the Jews; whereby, they say, he confirmed that practice of prescribing forms of prayer among them, and recommended the same course of proceeding, by his so doing, unto his disciples. Now, though it be very hard to discover how, upon a supposition that all which is thus suggested is the very truth, any thing can be hence concluded to the justification of the practice of imposing liturgies, now inquired into; yet, that there may be no pretence left unto a plea, though never so weak and infirm, of such an extract as this lays claim unto, it will be necessary to consider the severals of it. It is generally apprehended that our Saviour, in his prescription of that form of prayer unto his disciples, did aim at two things:—1. That they might have a summary symbol of all the most excellent things they were to ask of God in his name, and so a rule of squaring all their desires and supplications by. This end all universally concur in; and therefore Matthew, considering the doctrinal nature of it, gives it a place in the first recorded sermon of our Saviour, by way of anticipation, and mentions it not when he comes to the time wherein it was really first delivered by him. 2. For their benefit and advantage, together with other intercessions that they should also use the repetition of those words, as a prescript form wherein he had comprised the matter of their requests and petitions. About this latter all men are not agreed in their judgments, whether indeed our Saviour had this aim in it or no. Many learned men suppose that it was a supply of a rule and standard of things to be prayed for, without prescribing to them the use or rehearsal of that form of words, that he aimed at. Of this number are Musculus, Grotius, and Cornelius à Lapide, with many others; but it may suffice to intimate, that some of all sorts are so minded. But we shall not, in the case in hand, make use of any principle so far obnoxious unto common prejudice as experience proves that opinion of these learned men to be. Let it, therefore, be taken for granted that our Saviour did command that form to be repeated by his disciples, and let us then consider what will regularly ensue thereupon. Our Saviour at that time was minister of the Circumcision, and taught the doctrine of the gospel under and with the observation of all the worship of the Judaical church. He was not yet glorified, and so the Spirit was not as yet given; I mean that Spirit which he promised unto his disciples to enable them to perform all the worship of God by him required at their hands, whereof we have before spoken. That, then, which the Lord Jesus prescribed unto his disciples, for their present practice in the worship of God, seems to have belonged unto the economy of the Old Testament. Now, to argue from the prescription of, and outward helps for, the performance of the worship of God under the Old Testament, unto a necessity of the like or the same under the New, is upon the matter to deny that Christ is ascended on high, and to have given spiritual gifts unto men eminently distinct from and above those given out by him under the Judaical pedagogy. However, their boldness seems unwarrantable, if not intolerable, who, to serve their own ends, upon this prescription of his, do affirm that our Lord Jesus composed this form out of such as were then in common use among the Jews. For as the proof of their assertion which they insist on,—namely, the finding of some of the things expressed in it, or petitions of it, in the writings of the Jews, the eldest whereof is some hundreds of years younger than this prayer itself,—is most weak and contemptible; so the affirmation itself is exceeding derogatory to the glory and honour of his wisdom, assigning unto him a work so unnecessary and trivial as would scarce become a man of ordinary prudence and authority. But yet, to carry on the work in hand, let it be supposed that our Saviour did command that form of prayer out of such as were then customarily used among the Jews (which is false, and asserted without any colour of proof); also, that he prescribed it as a form to be repeated by his disciples (which we have shown many very eminently learned men to deny); and that, though he prescribed it as a minister to the Judaical church, and to his disciples whilst members of that church, under the economy of the Old Testament, not having as yet received the Spirit and gifts of the New, yet that he did it for the use and observance of his disciples to the end of the world, and that not as to the objective regulation of their prayers, but as to the repetition of the words; yet it doth not appear how, from all these concessions, any argument can be drawn to the composition and imposition of liturgies, whose rise and nature we are inquiring after: for it is certain that our Saviour gives this direction for the end which he intends in it, not primarily as to the public worship of the assemblies of his disciples, but as to the guidance of every individual saint in his private devotion, Matt. vi. 6–8. Now, from a direction given unto private persons, as to their private deportment in the discharge of any religious duty, to argue unto a prescription of the whole worship of God in public assemblies is not safe. But, that we may hear the argument drawn from this act of our Saviour speak out all that it hath to offer, let us add this also to the fore-mentioned presumptions, that our Saviour hath appointed and ordained, that in the assemblies of his disciples, in his worship by him required, they who administer in his name in and to the church should repeat the words of this prayer, though not peculiarly suited to any one of his institutions: what will thence be construed to ensue? Why, then, it is supposed that this will follow,—That it is not only lawful, but the duty of some men to compose other forms, a hundred times as many, suited in their judgment to the due administration of all ordinances of worship in particular, imposing them on the evangelical administrators of those ordinances to be read by them, with a severe interdiction of the use of any other prayers in those administrations. Bellarmine, De Pont. Rom., lib. iv. cap. 16, argues for the necessity of the observation of rites indifferent, when once commanded by the church, from the necessity of the observation of baptism, in itself a thing indifferent, after it was commanded by Christ. Some think this is not to dispute, but blaspheme. Nor is the inference before mentioned of any other complexion. When it shall be made to appear, that whatever it was lawful for the Lord Christ to do and to prescribe to his church and disciples, in reference to the worship of God, the same, or any thing of the like nature, it is lawful for men to do, under the pretence of their being invested with the authority of the church, or any else whatever, then some colour will be given to this argument; which being raised on the tottering suppositions before mentioned, ends in that which seems to deserve a harder name than at present we shall affix to it.

And this is the state and condition wherein the disciples of Christ were left by himself, without the least intimation of any other impositions in the worship of God to be laid upon them. Nor in any thing, or by any act of his, did he intimate the necessity or lawful use of any such liturgies as these which we are inquiring after, or prescribed and limited forms of prayers or praises, to be used or read in the public administration of evangelical institutions; but indeed made provision rendering all such prescriptions useless, and (because they cannot be made use of but by rejection of the provision by himself made) unlawful.

CHAPTER IV.

Of the worship of God by the apostles—No liturgies used by them, nor in the
churches of their plantation—Argument from their practice—Reasons pleaded
for the use of liturgies: disabilities of church officers for gospel administration to the edification of the church; uniformity in the worship of God—
The practice of the apostles as to these pretences considered—Of other impositions—The rule given by the apostles—Of the liturgies falsely ascribed
unto some of them.

OUR next inquiry is after the practice of the apostles,—the best interpretation of the mind of the Lord Jesus Christ as to the " agenda"
of the church, or what he would have done therein in the worship
of God, and how. That one end of their being furnished with the
Spirit of Christ, was the right and due administration of his ordinances in his church, to the edification of his disciples, I suppose will
not be denied. By virtue of his assistance, and the gifts from him
received, they discharged this part of their duty accordingly. That
they used any liturgies in the church-worship, wherein they went at
any time before the disciples, cannot with any colour of proof be
pretended. The Scripture gives us an account of many of their
prayers,—of none that were a repetition of a form. If any such
were used by them, how came the memory of them utterly to perish
from off the earth? Some, indeed, of the ancients say that they
used the Lord's prayer in the consecration of the eucharist; which
by others is denied, being in itself improbable, and the testimonies
weak that are produced in behalf of its assertion. But, as hath
been showed, the use of that prayer no way concerns the present
question. There are no more Christs but one: " To us there is one
Lord Jesus Christ." For him who hath affirmed that it is likely
they used forms of prayer and homilies composed for them by
St Peter, I suppose he must fetch his evidence out of the same
authors that he used who affirmed that Jesus Christ himself went
up and down singing mass!

The practice, then, of the apostles is not, as far as I know, by any
sober and learned persons controverted in this matter. They administered the holy things of the gospel by virtue of the holy gifts
they had received. But they were apostles. The inquiry is, what
directions and commands they gave unto the bishops or pastors of
the churches which they planted, that they might know how to behave themselves in the house and worship of God. Whatever they
might do in the discharge of their duty, by virtue of their extraordinary gifts, yet the case might be much otherwise with them who
were intrusted with ordinary ministerial gifts only. But we do not

find that they made any distinction in this matter between themselves and others; for as the care of all the churches was on them, the duties whereof they were to discharge by virtue of the gifts they had received, according to their commission empowering them thereunto, so to the bishops of particular churches they gave charge to attend unto the administration of the holy things in them, by virtue of the gifts they had received to that purpose, according to the limits of their commission. And upon a supposition that the apostles were enabled to discharge all gospel administrations to the edification of the church, by virtue of the gifts they had received, which those who were to come after them in the performance of the same duties should not be enabled unto, it cannot be imagined but that they would have provided a supply for that want and defect themselves, and not have left the church halt and maimed to the cure of those men whose weakness and unfitness for the duty was its disease. So, then, neither did the apostles of our Lord Jesus Christ use any liturgies, in the sense spoken of, in their administration of the worship instituted by him in his church, nor did they prescribe or command any such to the churches, or their officers that were planted in them; nor by any thing intimate the usefulness of any such liturgy, or form of public worship, as after ages found out and used.

Thus far, then, is the liberty given by Christ unto his church preserved entire; and the request seems not immodest that is made for the continuance of it. When men cry to God for the liberty in his worship which was left unto them by Christ and his apostles, he will undoubtedly hear, though their fellow-servants should be deaf to the like requests made unto them; and truly they must have a great confidence in their own wisdom and sufficiency, who will undertake to appoint, and impose on others, the observation of things in the worship of God which neither our Lord Jesus nor his apostles did appoint or impose.

Two things are principally pretended as grounds of the imposition of public liturgies:—First, The disability of the present ministers of the churches to celebrate and administer the ordinances of the gospel, to the honour of God and edification of the church, without the use of them. Secondly, The great importance of uniformity in the worship of God, not possibly to be attained but by virtue of this expedient. I desire to know whether these arguments did occur to the consideration of the apostles or no. If they shall say they did, I desire to know why they did not make upon them the provision now judged necessary; and whether those that so do, do not therein prefer their wisdom and care for the churches of God unto the wisdom and care of the apostles. If it shall be said, that the bishops or pastors of the churches in their days had abilities for the dis-

charge of the whole work of the ministry without this relief, so that
the apostles had no need to make any such supply, I desire to know
from whom they had these abilities. If it be said that they had
them from Jesus Christ, I then shall yet also farther ask, whether
ordinary bishops or pastors had any other gifts from Jesus Christ
but what he promised to bestow on ordinary bishops and pastors of
his churches? It seems to me that he bestowed no more upon them
than he promised to bestow,—namely, gifts for the work of the
ministry, with an especial regard to that outward condition of his
churches whereunto by his providence they were disposed. It will,
then, in the next place, be inquired whether the Lord Jesus Christ
promised to give any other gifts to the ordinary bishops and pastors
of the churches in those days than he promised to all such officers
in his church to the end of the world? If this appear to be the state
of things, that the promise by virtue whereof they received those
gifts and abilities for the discharge of their duty which rendered the
prescription of liturgies needless, as to the first ground of them pretended, did and doth equally respect all that succeed in the same
office and duty, according to the mind and will of Christ, unto the
end of the world, is not the pretended necessity derogatory to the
glory of the faithfulness of Jesus Christ, as plainly intimating that
he doth not continue to fulfil his promise; or at least a full declaration of men's unbelief, that they do not nor will depend upon him
for the accomplishment of the same? Thus the first pretended
ground of the necessary use of such liturgies as we speak of endeth
in a reflection upon the honour of our Lord Jesus, or a publication
of their own unbelief and apostasy.

The second is like the former. It will not, I suppose, be denied
but that the apostles took care for the unity of the churches, and for
that uniformity in the worship of God which is acceptable unto him.
Evidence lies so full unto it in their writings that it cannot be denied.
Great weight everywhere they lay upon this duty of the churches,
and propose unto them the ways whereby it may be done, with multiplied commands and exhortations to attend unto them. Whence
is it, then, that they never once intimate any thing of that which is
now pressed as the only medium for the attaining of that end? It
cannot but seem strange to some, that this should be the only expedient for that uniformity which is acceptable unto God, and yet
not once come into the thoughts of any of the apostles of Christ, so
as to be commended unto the churches for that purpose. Considering the many treacheries that are in the hearts of men, and the
powerful workings of unbelief under the most solemn outward professions, I fear it will appear at the last day, that the true rise of
most of the impositions on the consciences of men, which on various

pretences are practised in the world, is from the secret thoughts that either Christ doth not take that care of his churches, nor make that supply unto them of spiritual abilities for the work of the ministry, which he did in the days of old; or that men are now grown wiser than the apostles, and those who succeeded them in the administration of the things of God, and so are able to make better provision for attaining the end they professedly aimed at than they knew how to do.

The heathen, I confess, thought forms of prayer to be a means of preserving a uniformity in their religious worship. Hence they had a solemn form for every public action; yea, for those orations which the magistrates had unto the people. So Livius informs us, that when Sp. Posthumius the consul was to speak unto the people about the wickednesses that were perpetrated by many under the pretence of some Bacchanalian superstition, he gave them an account of the usefulness of the " solenne precationis carmen," which he had recited to keep out and prevent such differences about their religion as were then fallen out, lib. xxxix. 15 : " Concione advocata cum solenne carmen precationis, quod præfari, priusquam populum alloquantur, magistratus solent, peregisset consul, ita cœpit: ' Nulli unquam concioni, Quirites, tam non solum apta, sed etiam necessaria, hæc solennis Deorum comprecatio fuit, quæ nos admoneret, hos esse Deos, quos colere, venerari, precarique majores vestri instituissent, non illos,'" etc. But I hope we shall not prefer their example and wisdom before that of our Lord Christ and his apostles.

Were prejudices removed, and self-interests laid out of the way, a man would think there were not much more necessity for the determination of this difference. Christ and his apostles, with the apostolical churches, knew no such liturgies. At least it seems, as was said, not an unreasonable request, to ask humbly and peaceably at the hands of any of the sons of men, that they would be pleased to allow unto ministers of the gospel that are sound in the faith, and known so to be, who will willingly submit the trial of their ministerial abilities to the judgment of any who are taught of God, and enabled to discern of them aright, that liberty in the worship of God which was confessedly left unto them by Christ and his apostles. But the state of things is altered in the world. At a convention of the apostles and others, wherein the Holy Ghost did peculiarly preside, when the question about impositions was agitated, it was concluded that nothing should be imposed on the disciples but what was necessary for them to observe antecedently to any impositions, Acts xv. 28, 29; necessary, though not in their own nature, yet in the posture of things in the churches; necessary to the avoidance of scandal, whereby the observation of that injunction was to be regulated. Nor was there among the things called necessary the imposition of any one thing positively to be practised by any of the disciples in the worship of God, but only an abridgment of their liberty in some few external things, to which it did really extend. But that spirit of wisdom, moderation, and tenderness, whereby they were guided, being rejected by men, they began to think that they might multiply impositions as to the positive practice of the disciples of Christ in the worship of God at their pleasure, so that they could pretend that they were indifferent in themselves before the imposition of them; which gives, as they say, a necessity to their observation: which proceeding must be left to the judgment-seat of Jesus Christ, Matt. xxv. 45.

It is not worth our stay to consider what is pretended concerning the antiquity of liturgies, from some yet extant that bear the names of some of the apostles or evangelists. There is one that is called by the name of James, printed in Greek and Latin; another ascribed unto Peter, published by Lindanus; one also to Matthew, called the Ethiopic; another to Mark; which are in the Bible[1] P. P. And pains have been taken by Santesius, Pamelius, and others, to prove them genuine; but so much in vain as certainly nothing could be more. Nor doth Baronius in their Lives dare ascribe any such thing unto them. We need not any longer stay to remove this rubbish out of our way. They must be strangers to the spirit, doctrine, and writings of the apostles, who can impose such trash upon them as these liturgies are stuffed withal. The common use of words in them not known in the ages of the apostles, nor of some of them ensuing; the parts in them whose contrivers and framers are known to have lived many ages after; the mentioning of such things in them as were not once dreamed of in the days whereunto they pretend; the remembrance of them in them, as long before them deceased, who are suggested to be their authors; the preferring of other liturgies before them when once liturgies came in use, with a neglect of them; with the utter silence of the first Christian writers, stories, councils, concerning them, do abundantly manifest that they are plainly suppositions of a very late fraud and invention. Yea, we have testimonies clear enough against this pretence in Gregor., lib. vii. epist. 63. Alcuinus, Amatorius, Rabanus, Lib. P. P. tom. x.; with whom consent Walafridus Strabo, Rupertus Titiensis, Berno, Radulphus Tangrensis, and generally all that have written any thing about liturgies in former days; many of whom show how, when, and by whom, the several parts of that public form which at length signally prevailed were invented and brought into use.

---

[1] So the words are given in the original and subsequent editions. The reference is to the "Bibliotheca Patrum," in the second volume of which the liturgies mentioned will be found.—Ed.

CHAPTER V.

The practice of the churches in the first three centuries as to forms of public worship—No set forms of liturgies used by them—The silence of the first writers concerning them—Some testimonies against them.

IT is not about stinted forms of prayer in the worship and service of God, by those who, of their own accord, do make use of that kind of assistance, judging that course to be better than any thing they can do themselves in the discharge of the work of the ministry, but of the imposition of forms on others who desire " to stand fast in the liberty with which Christ hath made them free," that we inquire. This freedom we have manifested to have been purchased for them by the Lord Jesus, and the use of it continued by the apostles in their own practice, and to the churches planted by themselves; and this will one day appear to have been a sufficient plea for the maintenance of that liberty to the end of the world. Now, though what is purely matter of fact among the succeeding churches be not so far argumentative as to be insisted on as a rule exactly binding us to the imitation of it, yet it is deservedly worthy of great consideration, and not hastily to be rejected, unless it be discovered to have been diverse from the word, whereunto we are bound in all things to attend. We shall, therefore, make some inquiry into the practice of those churches, as to this matter of prescribing of forms of prayer in public church administrations, so far as any thing thereof is, by good antiquity, transmitted unto us.

Our first inquiry shall be into the three first centuries, wherein, confessedly, the streams of gospel institutions did run more clear and pure from human mixtures than in those following, although few of the teachers that were of note do escape from animadversions from those that have come after them. It cannot be denied but that for the most part the churches and their guides, within the space of the time limited, walked in the paths marked out for them by the apostles, and made conspicuous by the footsteps of the first churches planted by them. It doth not, then, appear, for aught as I can yet discover, that there was any attempt to invent, frame, and compose any liturgies or prescribed forms of administering the ordinances of the gospel, exclusive to the discharge of that duty by virtue of spiritual gifts received from Jesus Christ, much less for an imposition of any such forms on the consciences and practice of all the ministers of the churches within the time mentioned. If any be contrary-minded, it is incumbent on them to evince their assertion by some instances of unquestionable truth. As yet, that I know of, this is not performed by any. Baronius, ad an. Christi 58, num. 102–104, etc., treating expressly of the public prayers of the ancient Christians, is wholly silent as to the use of any forms amongst them, though he contends for their worshipping towards the east: which custom, when it was introduced, is most uncertain; but most certain that by many it was immoderately abused, who expressly worshipped the rising sun: of which abominable idolatry among Christians Leo complains, Serm. vii. De Nativitate. Indeed, the cardinal, ad an. 63, 12, 17, faintly contends that some things in the liturgy of James were composed by him, because some passages and expressions of it are used by Cyril of Jerusalem in his Mystagog. v.; but whereas Cyril lived not within the time limited unto our inquiry, and those treatises are justly suspected to be suppositions, nor is the testimony of that liturgy once cited or mentioned by him, the weakness of this insinuation is evident. Yea, it is most probable, that whosoever was the composer of that forged liturgy, he took those passages out of those reputed writings of Cyril, which were known in the church long before the name of the other was heard of. I know no ground of expectation of the performance of that which, as yet, men have come short in,—namely, in producing testimonies for the use of such liturgies as we are inquiring after; considering the diligence, ability, and interest of those who have been already engaged in that inquiry. Now, the silence of those who, in all probability, would have given an account of them had any such been in use in their days, with the description they give us of such a performance of the worship of God in the assemblies of Christians as is inconsistent with, and exclusive of, such prescribed forms as we treat of, is as full an evidence in this kind as our negative is capable of. In those golden fragments of antiquity which we have preserved by Eusebius,—I mean the Epistles of the church of Smyrna about the martyrdom of Polycarpus, and of the churches of Vienne and Lyons concerning their persecution,—we have not the least intimation of any such forms of service. In the Epistle of Clemens, or the church of Rome to the church of Corinth, in those of Ignatius, in the writings of Justin Martyr, Clemens, Tertullian, Origen, Cyprian, and their contemporaries, there is the same silence concerning them. The pseudographical writings that bear the names of the men of those days, with any pretence of considerable antiquity, as the Canons of the Apostles, Quæstiones ad Orthodoxos, Dionysius Hierarch. Divin. Nom., will not help in the cause; for though in some of them there are prayers mentioned,—and that for and about such things as were not " in rerum natura" in the days wherein those persons lived unto whose names they are falsely ascribed,—yet they speak nothing to the point of liturgies as stated in our inquiry. Something, I confess, may be found in some of the writings of some one or two of those of the third century, intimating the use of some particular prayers in some churches. So Origen, Homil. xi. in Hierimea: "Ubi frequenter in oratione dicimus, ' Da omnipotens, da nobis partem cum prophetis, da cum apostolis Christi tui, tribue ut inveniamur ad vestigia unigeniti tui.'" But whether he speaks of a form or of the matter only of prayer, I know not. But such passages belong not unto our purpose. Those who deal expressly about the order, state, and condition of the churches, and the worship of God in them, their prayers and supplications, knew nothing of prescribed liturgies; yea, they affirm plainly that which is inconsistent with the use of them. The account given of the worship of the Christians in those days by Justin Martyr and Tertullian is known as having been often pleaded. I shall only mention it in our passage, and begin with the latter. " Illuc," saith he, (that is, towards heaven,) "suspicientes Christiani," (not like the idolaters, who looked on their idols and images,) "manibus expansis," (not embracing altars or images, as did the heathen,) "quia innocuis, capite nudo, quia non erubescimus, denique sine monitore, quia de pectore oramus," (not as they who repeat their prayers after their priests or sacrificers, but pouring out our prayers conceived in our breasts,) Apol., cap. xxx. And again, cap. xxxix.: " Corpus sumus de conscientia, religionis et disciplinæ unitate, et spei fœdere coimus in cætum et congregationem, ut ad Deum quasi vi facta precationibus ambiamus orantes. Hæc vis Deo grata est. Oramus etiam," etc. Whether this description of the public worship of the Christians in those days be consistent with the prescribed forms contended about, impartial men may easily discern.

The former treateth of the same matter in his Apology, in several places of it: Ἄθεοι μὲν οὖν ὡς οὐκ ἐσμέν, τὸν δημιουργὸν τῶν δὲ τοῦ παντὸς σεβόμενοι, ἀνενδεῆ αἱμάτων καὶ σπονδῶν καὶ θυμιάματων, ὡς ἐδιδάχθημεν λέγοντες, λόγῳ εὐχῆς καὶ εὐχαριστίας ἐφ' οἷς προσφερόμεθα πᾶσιν ὅση δύναμις αἰνοῦντες·—" Atheists," saith he, " we are not, seeing we worship the Maker of the world; affirming, indeed, as we are taught, that he stands in no need of blood, drink-offerings, or incense. In all our oblations we praise him according to our abilities, with " (or in the way of) " prayer and thanksgivings." This was, it seems, the liturgy of the church in the days of Justin Martyr; they called upon God with prayer and thanksgivings, according to the abilities they had received. The like account he gives of the prayers of persons converted, to prepare themselves for baptism; as also of the prayers of the administrators of that ordinance. Afterward, also, treating of the joining the baptized person unto the church, and the administration of the Lord's supper in the assembly, he adds: Μετὰ τὸ οὕτως λοῦσαι τὸν πεπεισμένον, καὶ συγκατατεθειμένον, ἐπὶ τοὺς λεγομένους ἀδελφοὺς ἄγομεν ἔνθα συνηγμένοι εἰσί, κοινὰς εὐχὰς ποιησόμενοι ὑπὲρ τε ἑαυτῶν, καὶ τοῦ φωτισθέντος, etc.;—" After the believer who is joined unto us is thus washed, we bring him to those who are called brethren" (that is, the body of the church), " thither where they are gathered together for to make their prayers and supplications for themselves, and him who is" (newly) " illuminated," etc. These prayers, he declares afterward, were made by him who did preside among the brethren in the assembly,—that is, the bishop or pastor; who, when he had finished his prayer, the whole people cried, Amen; which leaves small room for the practice of any liturgy that is this day extant, or that hath left any memory of itself in this world. These prayers and supplications, he addeth, the president of the assembly ὅση δύναμις αὐτῷ ἀναπέμπει, "poureth out according to his ability;" and ἐπὶ πολὺ ποιεῖται, he " doth this work at large," or continues long in his work (of praises unto God in the name of Jesus Christ). I know some have excepted against the usual interpretation of these words, Ὅση δύναμις, although they have not been able to assign any other tolerable sense unto them besides that which they would willingly oppose. But as the rendering of them " According to his ability," or, " As he is able," may not only be justified, but evinced to be the only sense the words are capable of, so the argument in hand doth not, as to its efficacy, depend on the precise signification of those two words, but on the whole contexture of the holy martyr's discourse; so relating to the worship of the churches in those days as to manifest that the use of prescribed forms of liturgies to be read in them was then utterly unknown.

I suppose it will be granted, that the time we have been inquiring into,—namely, the first three hundred years after Christ,—was the time of the church's greatest purity, though out of her greatest prosperity; that the union of the several churches was preserved beyond what afterward was ever in a gospel way attained, and the uniformity in worship which Christ requires observed amongst them; but all this while the use of these liturgies was utterly unknown: which makes the case most deplorable, that it should now be made the hinge whereon the whole exercise of the ministry must turn, it being a thing not only destitute of any warrant from Christ and his apostles, but utterly unknown to those churches whose antiquity gives them deservedly reverence with all; and so cannot claim its spring and original antecedent to such miscarryings and mistakes in the churches as all acknowledge to deserve a narrow and serious weighing and consideration. We may, then, I suppose, without giving occasion to the just imputation of any mistake, affirm, That the composing and imposition of liturgies, to be necessarily used or read in the administration of the ordinances of the gospel, is destitute of any plea or pretence, from Scripture or antiquity.

CHAPTER VI.

The pretended antiquity of liturgies disproved—The most ancient—Their variety —Canons of councils about forms of church administrations—The reasons pleaded in the justification of the first invention of liturgies answered—Their progress and end.

CONSIDERING with what confidence the antiquity of liturgies in the churches of Christ hath been pretended, it may seem strange to some that we should so much as attempt to divest them of that plea and pretence. But the love of the truth enforceth us to contend against many prejudices in this matter. May a denial of their antiquity, with the reasons of that denial tendered, provoke any to assert it by such testimonies as we have not as yet had the happiness to come to an acquaintance with, the advantage as well as the trouble will be theirs who shall so do. Only, in their endeavour to that purpose, I shall desire of them that they would not labour to impose on those whom they undertake to inform, by the ambiguous use of some words among the ancients; nor conclude a prescribed form of administration when they find mention of the administration itself; nor reckon reading of the Scriptures or singing of psalms as parts of the liturgy contended about; nor, from the use of some particular prayer by some persons, argue for the equity or necessity of composing such entire liturgies, or offices as they call them, for all evangelical administrators, and their necessary observation. So that these conditions be observed, I shall profess myself much engaged unto any one who shall discover a rise of them within the limits of the antiquity that hath been usually pretended and pleaded in their justification and practice. For my part, I know not any thing that ever obtained a practice and observation among Christians, whose springs are more dark and obscure than those of liturgies. They owe not their original to any councils, general or provincial; they were not the product of the advice or consent of any churches, nor was there any one of them at any time completed. No pleas can I as yet discover in them of old about uniformity in their use, or any consent in them about them. Every church seemeth to have done what seemed good in the church's own eyes, after once the way unto the use of them was opened. To whom in particular we are indebted for that invention, I know not; it may be those who are wiser do, and I wish they would value the thanks that they may have for the discovery when they shall be pleased to make it. They seem to me to have had but slender originals. One invented one form of prayer, or thanksgiving, or benediction; another added to what he had found out,—which was the easier task. Future additions gave some completeness to their beginners. Those in the

Greek church, which bear the names of Chrysostom and Basil, seem to be the first that ever extended themselves to the whole worship of the church. Not that by them whose names they bear they were composed as now they appear, unless we shall think that they wrote them after their decease; but probably they collected some forms into order that had been by others invented, making such additions themselves as they judged needful, and so commended the use of them to the churches wherein they did preside. The use of them being arbitrarily introduced was not, by any injunction we find, made necessary; much less did any one single form plead for a general necessity. In the Latin church, Ambrose used one form, Gregory another, and Isidore a third. Nor is it unlikely but the liturgies were as many as the episcopal churches of those days. Hence, in the beginning of the fifth century, in an African council, can. 70, which is the 103d in the Codex Can. African., it is provided that no prayers be read in the administration of the eucharist but such as have been approved in some council, or have been observed by some prudent men formerly; which canon, with some addition, is confirmed in the second Milevitan council, can. 12: and the reason given in both is, lest there should any thing contrary to the faith creep into their way of worship. But this, as I said, was in the beginning of the fifth century, after divers forms of administration of holy things in the church had by divers been invented. The finding out of this invention was the act of some particular men, who have not been pleased to acquaint us with the reason of their undertaking. As yet it doth not appear unto us that those reasons could possibly be taken from the word, the practice of the apostles, or the churches by them planted, or those which followed them for some generations, nor from any council held before their days; and so, it may be, we are not much concerned to inquire what they were. Yet what is at present pleaded in the behalf of the first composers of liturgies may, in the way, be chiefly considered. Necessity is the first thing usually pretended. Many men being put into the office of the ministry who had not gifts and abilities for the profitable discharge of the work of the ministry, unto the edification of the church, they who had the oversight of them, according to the custom of those days, were enforced to compose such forms for their use as they judged expedient; so providing for the edification of the church, which else would have suffered from their weakness and insufficiency. Besides, many parts of the world, especially the east, in those days swarmed with antitrinitarian heretics of sundry sorts, who, many of them, by unsuspected wiles and dissimulations, and subscriptions of confessions, endeavoured to creep into the office of the ministry of the church, partly out of blind zeal to diffuse the poison of their abominations, partly out of carnal policy to be made partakers of the advantages which for the most part attended the orthodox profession. This increased the necessity of composing such forms of public worship as, being filled with expressions pointed against the errors of the times, might be a means to keep seducers from imposing themselves on ecclesiastical administrations. Thus there is no ancient liturgy, but it is full of the expressions that had been consented upon in the councils that were convened for the condemnation of those errors which were in their days most rife and pernicious. On this ground do learned men of all sorts conclude the liturgy falsely ascribed to James to be younger than the Nicene and Ephesine councils, from the use of the words ὁμοούσιος and Θεοτόκος in it.

But it doth not yet appear that these reasons were sufficient to justify such an innovation in the churches of Christ; for supposing that there were such a decay of gifts and abilities among them that were called to the administration of gospel institutions, that they were not able to discharge their duty in that work to the edification of the church, in like manner as those had done who went before them, this must needs have come to pass, either because our Lord Jesus Christ did cease to give out his gifts to his church, as he had done in former days upon his usual terms, or that men were negligent and careless in the receiving of them from him,—either not seeking them at his hand, or not exercising and improving of them according to his will and command. Other reason of this decay that I know of cannot be assigned. To affirm the former, on any pretence whatever, is blasphemously to accuse our Lord Jesus Christ of breach of promise, he having solemnly engaged to be with his disciples, not for an age or two, but to the end of the world, and that by the graces and gifts of his Spirit. I know it is pretended, that when Christians were multiplied there was a necessity of appointing them officers who had not the gifts and qualifications that otherwise would have been esteemed necessary; but I know withal that it is impossible Christians should be multiplied in the way of Christ faster than he is ready to give out gifts for their edification. The latter reason above, then, must be granted to be the cause of the defect of abilities in church officers, pleaded in the justification of the introduction into the church of composed forms of administration to be read by them. I wish, then, we might, in the fear of the Lord, consider whether the remedy were well suited unto the disease. I suppose all impartial men will grant that there ought to have been a return unto Him endeavoured from whom they were gone astray; at least gospel means used for the obtaining of those gifts of Christ, and the improving of them being received. Finding themselves at the loss wherein they were, should they not have searched their hearts and ways, to consider wherefore it was that the presence of Christ was so withdrawn from them, that they were so left without the assistance which others ministering in their places before them had received? Should not they have pulled out their single talent, and fallen to trading with it, that it might have increased under their care? Was not this the remedy and cure of the breach made by them, that God and man expected from them? Was it just, then, and according to the mind of Christ, that, instead of an humble returnal unto a holy, evangelical dependence on himself, they should invent an expedient to support them in the condition wherein they were, and so make all such returnal for hereafter needless? Yet this they did in the invention of liturgies,—they found out a way to justify themselves in their spiritual negligence and sloth, and to render a dependence on the Lord Christ for supplies of his Spirit, to enable them unto gospel administrations, altogether needless; they had now provided themselves with an ability they could keep in the church, so that he might keep the furniture of his Spirit unto himself. And this quickly became the most poisonous ingredient in the apostasy of the latter times.

Nor is there any sufficient warrant for this invention in the second pretence. There were many antichrists in the apostles' time, yet they never thought of this engine for their discovery or exclusion out of the church. Confessions of faith, or acknowledged forms of wholesome words, with the care of the disciples of Christ, or his churches, which are enabled by him to judge and discern of truth and error, are the preservations against the danger intimated that the gospel hath provided.

This being the entrance that the liturgies inquired after made into the churches of God, we are not much concerned to inquire what was their progress. That in the western parts of the world they all at length centred in the Roman mass-book and rituals we know. Their beginnings were small, plain, brief; their use arbitrary; the additions they received were from the endeavours of private men in several ages, occasional for the most part; the number of them great, equal to the various denominations of the churches; until the papal authority growing absolute and uncontrollable, the Roman form was imposed on the world, that, by innumerable artifices in a long tract of ages, was subjected thereunto, and that contrary to the determination of former Roman bishops, who advised the continuance of the different forms of administration which were in use in several churches: " Mihi placet, ut sive in Romanis sive in Galliarum partibus, seu in quâlibet ecclesiâ aliquid invenisti quod plus omnipotenti Deo possit placere sollicitè eligas," Greg. Resp. ad Interrogat. August.

This being the state and condition, this the issue, that the invention of liturgies to be read in the worship of God was come unto before the Reformation, I shall briefly subjoin unto it an account of what was done in these kingdoms in reference unto it; which will make way to the clear stating of the question in particular that we are farther to speak unto. The history of our Reformation is known. I shall not speak any thing that may reflect with the least dishonour on the work or the workmen. We have abundant cause to bless the Lord continually for the one and the other. Yet still we must remember that our Reformers were men, and that the Reformation was a work performed by men. The former never claimed infallibility, nor the latter, that I know of, perfection; so that some things that were done by the one and in the other may admit of new considerations, without the reflection of any thing upon them that the one and the other would not readily and willingly admit. I shall therefore briefly give an account of that part of the work which concerns our business in hand. What was the state of this nation at the time of the Reformation, and what were the minds of the greater part of men in it in reference unto the work, is sufficiently declared in all the stories of those days. God having been pleased to send the saving light of the gospel into the minds and hearts of them in chief rule,—that is, King Edward and some of his counsellors,—they found no small difficulties to wrestle withal in dealing with the inveterate prejudices wherewith the generality of men were possessed against the work they intended. The far greater part of the clergy, true to their carnal present interest, with all their might and cunning opposed their endeavours. The greatest part of the nobility averse to their proceedings; the body of the people, blinded with superstition and profaneness, easily excited by the priests (whose peculiar concernment lay in keeping all things in their old channel and course) to make head against their proceedings ; foreign nations round about fomenting to the uttermost all home-bred discontents, and offering themselves, by the instigation of the pope, to hinder the work by all ways that possibly they could imagine;—amongst all these the body of the people, which are the king's most special care, as they are his strength and wealth, were looked on as most to be regarded, as without whose concurrence their discontents of all others were likely only to consume themselves. Now, the people being in those days very ignorant, and unacquainted with the doctrines of the Scripture, were very little or not at all concerned what persuasion men were of in religion, as to the articles of pure belief, so as they might retain the "agenda" in the worship of God which they had been accustomed unto. Hence it was that those prelates, who were the instruments of the papal persecution in this nation, wisely stated the whole cause of their cruelty to be the Mass, or the worship of the church, seldom, unless compelled by disputations, once mentioning of the articles of faith, which yet they knew to be the main foundation of the difference between themselves and the reformers; because in this particular they had the advantage of the popular favour, the people violently interposing themselves in the behalf of that part of the present religion wherein their only share did lie. Had they laid the reasons and grounds of their quarrel in the differences of opinions about the " credenda " of the gospel, they would scarcely have prevailed with the common people to carry fagot for the burning of their brethren for things whereof they understood little or nothing at all.

Our wise and provident reformers, considering this state of things and temper of the minds of men, however they resolvedly declared for the "credenda" of the gospel, and asserted the articles of faith from which the Roman church had most eminently apostatized, yet found it their concernment to attemper the way of public worship, as much as possible with consistency with the articles of the faith they professed, to that which the popularity had been inured unto. Observing plainly that all their concernment in religion lay in the outward worship whereunto they had been accustomed, having very confused apprehensions of the speculative part of it, it was easy for them to apprehend that if they could condescend to furnish them with such a way thereof as might comply in some reasonable manner with their former usage, these two things would ensue:—First, That the main reformation, in the doctrine, which alone would deliver the people from their prejudicate opinions about the worship of God, would be carried on with less noise and observation, and consequently less contest and opposition; for whilst they had a way and form of worship proposed to them wherewith they could be contented, those that were wiser might believe and teach what they pleased: which, in the providence of God, proved in a short time a blessed means of delivering them from their old entanglements and darkness. Secondly, That their priests, who were the chief instigators to all disorder and opposition to the whole work of reformation, finding a way proposed for their continuance in the possession of their places, and a worship prescribed which they could as easily perform and go through withal as what they had practised in former days, might possibly acquiesce in the proceedings of their betters, finding the temporal interest, which they chiefly respected, to be saved. And this afterward, accordingly, they did, reading the service-book instead of the mass; without which supply of such wants and defects in them as I shall not name, they would never have entertained any thoughts of owning the Reformation, nor of suffering the people to submit themselves thereunto. On these considerations, and for these ends, it is evident, from the story of those times, that our present liturgy was framed. Rejecting out of the offices before in use such things as were directly contrary to the articles of faith protested in the reformation in hand, translating of what remained into English, with such supplies and alterations as the rejection of those things before mentioned made necessary, the book mentioned, in some haste, and with some other disadvantages for such a work, was by our first reformers compiled. And, indeed, somewhat there was in this case not much unlike that insisted on in the entrance of this discourse between the believing Jews and Gentiles. Many of the Jews who were willing to receive Christ's reformation in point of faith and obedience, yet pertinaciously adhered to their old ceremonious worship, violently setting themselves against any that durst speak a word against its continuance. That there might not be an endless contest and strife about the matter, and so the progress of the gospel be hindered amongst the one sort and the other, the apostles taking in hand the old worship, as to the Gentile worshippers, whose case above came then under consideration, they reject and declare abrogate all such ceremonies whose necessary observation had an inconsistency with the doctrine of the gospel, proposing only some few things to be observed, which occasioned the greatest difference between the parties at variance.

Now, as this composition of that difference was accommodated to the present scandal, and the obligation unto its observation to be regulated thereby; so by the removal thereof, itself, as unto any use in the church of Christ, did expire. Not unlike unto this of the apostles seems the aim of our first reformers to have been; that they might win the people, who had been accustomed to the way of worship in use in the Papacy, unto a compliance with the doctrine of the gospel, and that there might not be endless contests about that which was presently to be practised,—which perhaps they thought of small importance in comparison of those weighty fundamental truths which they had endeavoured to acquaint them with, and bring them to the belief of,—they provided for the use of such parts of it and in such a manner as were not openly inconsistent with the truths which was in their hearts to communicate unto them. And it is not impossible but that this constitution might have had the same end with the other, if not of present use, being of things of another nature, yet of a timely expiration, when notoriously useless as to the main ends intended in it, had not the interest of some interposed for its continuance beyond the life and influence of all or any of those causes or occasions. And hence it is that those streams at this day run strongly and fiercely, by the addition and pouring into of adventitious rivulets, with showers or rather storms of temporal interest, whose springs are all utterly long since dried up.

The Book of Common Prayer being composed as hath been declared, became from its very cradle and infancy a bone of contention to the church of God in this nation. Many of the people and ministers, who seemed to be enlightened with a beam of truth of an equal lustre and brightness with that which shined in the minds of their brethren, wholly decried that prudential compliance with the people's ignorance and adherence to Popery, which was openly avowed in the composition and imposition of it, and called earnestly for a purer way of the administration of gospel ordinances, more agreeable to the word and primitive times, than they apprehended that prescribed form to contain and exhibit. Others, again, in the justification of that whereof themselves were the authors, laboured to recommend the book, not only as to truth, but as useful and very beneficial for the edification of the church. It is known, also, that the contests of men in this nation about this form of divine service were not confined to this nation, but were carried by them into other parts of the world. And should I pursue the suffrage that hath lain against it, from the first day of its composure to this wherein we live, never giving it a quiet possession in the minds and consciences of men, with the various evils that have all along attended its imposition, I suppose it might of itself prevail with sober men, who desire their moderation should be known to all, because the Judge standeth at the door, to take the whole matter of the imposition of this or the like form once more under a sedate consideration. And they may, perhaps, be the rather induced thereunto, if they will but impartially weigh that the opposition to the imposed liturgy hath increased daily, according to the increase of light and gospel gifts among men: so that there seems to be no way to secure its station but by an opposition unto them and extirpation of them; which is a sad work for any that are called Christians to engage into.

I presume the conscientious reader will be able to discover, from what hath been spoken, rules sufficient to guide his judgment in reference unto the use of prescribed liturgies. The story of their rise and progress is enough to plead for a liberty from an indispensable necessity of their observation. That which is of pure human invention, and comparatively of late and uncertain original, whose progress hath been attended with much superstition and persecution, stands in need of very cogent reasons to plead for its continuance; for others will not outbalance the evils that are asserted to flow from it. But it may be this will not suffice with some for a final decision and determination of this difference. I shall, therefore, briefly state the question about them, which only I shall speak unto, and try their use and usefulness by that infallible rule by which both we and they must be judged another day.

CHAPTER VII.

The question stated—First argument against the composing and imposing of liturgies—Arbitrary additions to the worship of God rejected—Liturgies not appointed by God—Made necessary in their imposition, and a part of the worship of God—Of circumstances of worship—Instituted adjuncts of worship
not circumstances—Circumstances of actions, as such, not circumstances of
worship—Circumstances commanded made parts of worship—Prohibitions
of additions produced, considered, applied.

To clear up what it is in particular that we insist upon, some few
things are to be premised:—First, then, I do not in especial intend
the liturgy now in use in England, any farther than to make it an
instance of such imposed liturgies, whereof we treat. I shall not,
then, at all inquire what footing it hath in the law, how nor when
established, nor what particular failings are pleaded to be in it, nor
what conformity it bears with the Roman offices, with the like things
that are usually objected against it. Nor, secondly, do I oppose the
directive part of this liturgy as to the reading of the Scripture, when
it requires that which is Scripture to be read, the administration of
the ordinances by Christ appointed, nor the composition of forms of
prayer suited to the nature of the institutions to which they relate,
so they be not imposed on the administrators of them to be read
precisely as prescribed. But, thirdly, this is that alone which I shall
speak unto,—the composing of forms of prayer in the worship of
God, in all gospel administrations, to be used by the ministers of the
churches, in all public assemblies, by a precise reading of the words
prescribed unto them, with commands for the reading of other things,
which they are not to omit, upon the penalty contained in the sanction of the whole service and the several parts of it. The liberty
which some say is granted for a man to use his own gifts and abilities
in prayer before and after sermons, will, I fear, as things now stand,
upon due consideration, appear rather to be taken than given. However, it concerns not our present question, because it is taken for
granted by those that plead for the strict observation of a book, that
the whole gospel worship of God, in the assemblies of Christians,
may be carried on and performed without any such preaching as is
prefaced with the liberty pretended.

These things being premised, I shall subjoin some of the reasons
that evidently declare the imposition and use of such a liturgy or
form of public words to be contrary to the rule of the word, and consequently sinful.

First, the arbitrary invention of any thing, with commands for its
necessary and indispensable use in the public worship of God, as a

part of that worship, and the use of any thing so invented and so commanded in that worship, is unlawful, and contrary to the rule of the word; but of this nature is the liturgy we treat of. It is an invention of men, not appointed, not commanded of God; it is commanded to be used in the public worship of God, by reading the several parts of it, according to the occasions that they respect, and that indispensably; and is made a part of that worship.

There are three things affirmed in the assumption concerning the liturgy:—*First,* That it is not appointed or commanded of God; that is, there is no command of God either for the use of this or that liturgy in particular, nor in general that any such should so be, and be so used as is pleaded. And this we must take for granted, until some instance of such command be produced. *Secondly,* That it is made necessary, by virtue of the commands of men, to be used in the public worship of God. About this there will be no difference. Let it be denied, and there is an end of all this strife. I shall not dispute about other men's practice. They who are willing to take it upon their consciences that the best way to serve God in the church, or the best ability that they have for the discharge of their duty therein, consists in the reading of such a book (for I suppose they will grant that they ought to serve God with the best they have), shall not by me be opposed in their way and practice. It is only about its imposition, and the necessity of its observance by virtue of that imposition, that we discourse. Now, the present command is, that such a liturgy be always used in the public worship of God, and that without the use or reading of it the ordinances of the gospel be not administered at any time, nor in any place, with strong pleas for the obligation arising from that command, making the omission of its observance to be sinful. It is, then, utterly impossible that any thing should be more indispensably necessary than the reading of the liturgy in the worship of God is. It is said, indeed, that it is not commanded as though in itself it were necessary, either a prescribed liturgy, or this or that, for then it were sin in any not to use it, whether it were commanded by the church or not; but for order, uniformity, conveniency, and the preventing of sundry evils that would otherwise ensue, it is commanded: which command makes the observation of it necessary unto us. But we are not as yet inquiring what are the reasons of its imposition; they may afterward be spoken unto. And time also may be taken to show that it were much more tolerable if men would plead for the necessity of the things which it seems good unto them to command, and on that ground to command their observance, than, granting them not necessary in themselves, to make them necessary to be observed merely by virtue of their commands, for reasons which they say satisfy themselves, but come short of giving satisfaction to them from whom obedience is required; for whereas the will of man can be no way influenced unto obedience but by mere acknowledged sovereignty, or conviction of reason in and from the things themselves, commands in and about things wherein they own not that the commanders have an absolute sovereignty (as God hath in all things, the civil supreme magistrate in things civil that are good and lawful), nor can they find the reasons of the things themselves cogent, are a yoke which God hath not designed the sons of men to bear. But it is concerning the necessary use of the liturgy in the worship of God that we are disputing; which, I suppose, will not be denied.

[Thirdly,] It remaineth, then, to consider whether the use of the liturgy as prescribed be made a part of the worship of God. Now, that wherewith and whereby God is commanded to be worshipped, and without which all observation or performance of his public worship is forbidden, is itself made a part of his worship. The command, "With this (or thus) shall you worship God," makes the observation of that command a part of God's worship. It is said that it is only a circumstance of worship, but no part of it. Prayer is the worship of God; but that *this prayer* shall be used and no other is only a circumstance of it: so that though it may be possibly accounted a circumstance or accidentary part of God's worship, yet it is not asserted to be of the substance of it. How far this is so, and how far it is otherwise, must be considered. Circumstances are either such as follow actions as actions, or such as are arbitrarily superadded and adjoined by command unto actions, which do not of their own accord, nor naturally nor necessarily attend them. Now, religious actions in the worship of God are actions still. Their religious relation doth not destroy their natural being. Those circumstances, then, which do attend such actions as actions not determined by divine institution, may be ordered, disposed of, and regulated by the prudence of men. For instance, prayer is a part of God's worship. Public prayer is so, as appointed by him. This, as it is an action to be performed by man, cannot be done without the assignment of time, and place, and sundry other things, if order and conveniency be attended to. These are circumstances that attend all actions of that nature, to be performed by a community, whether they relate to the worship of God or no. These men may, according as they see good, regulate and change as there is occasion; I mean, they may do so who are acknowledged to have power in such things. As the action cannot be without them, so their regulation is arbitrary, if they come not under some divine disposition and order, as that of time in general doth. There are also some things, which some men call circumstances, also, that no way belong of themselves to the actions whereof they are said to be the circumstances, nor do attend them, but are imposed on them, or annexed unto them, by the arbitrary authority of those who take upon them to give order and rules in such cases; such as to pray before an image or towards the east, or to use this or that form of prayer in such gospel administrations, and no other. These are not circumstances attending the nature of the thing itself, but are arbitrarily superadded to the things that they are appointed to accompany. Whatever men may call such additions, they are no less parts of the whole wherein they serve than the things themselves whereunto they are adjoined. The schoolmen tell us that that which is made so the condition of an action, that without it the action is not to be done, is not a circumstance of it, but such an adjunct as is a necessary part. But not to contend about the word, such additionals, that are called circumstantial, are made parts of worship as are made necessary by virtue of command to be observed. Sacrifices of old were the instituted worship of God. That they should be offered at the tabernacle or temple at Jerusalem, and nowhere else, was a circumstance appointed to be observed in their offerings; and yet this circumstance was no less a part of God's worship than the sacrifice itself. In the judgment of most men, not only prayer, and the matter of our prayer, is appointed by our Saviour in the Lord's prayer, but we are commanded also to use the very words of it. I desire to know whether the precise use of these words be not a part of God's worship? It seems that it is; for that which is commanded by Christ to be used in the worship of God is a part of God's worship. The case is the same here. Prayer is commanded, and the use of these prayers is commanded; the latter distinctly, as such, as well as the former, is made a part of God's worship. Nor is there any ground for that distinction of the circumstantial or accidentary part of God's worship, and worship substantially taken, or the substantial parts of it. The worship of God is either moral or instituted. The latter contains the peculiar ways and manner of exerting the former according to God's appointment. The actions whereby these are jointly discharged, or the inward moral principles of worship are exerted in and according to the outward institutions, have their circumstances attending them. These in themselves, nakedly considered, have in them neither good nor evil, nor are any circumstances in the worship of God, much less circumstantial parts of his worship, but only circumstances of those actions as actions whereby it is performed. And whatever is instituted of God in and about those circumstances is a substantial part of his worship.

Nor is the prescribing of such a form of prayer a regulation of those circumstances of public prayer, for decency, order, and uniformity, which attend it as a public action, but the superaddition of an adjunct condition, with which it is to be performed, and without which it is not to be performed as it is prayer, the worship of God. Of this nature was sacrificing of old on the altar at the tabernacle or temple, and there alone; and many more instances of the like nature may be given. Praising of God and blessing of the people were parts of the worship of God, appointed by himself to be performed by the priests under the law. In the doing thereof at certain seasons, they were commanded to use some forms of words prescribed unto them for that purpose. Not only hereby the praising and blessing of God, but the use of those forms in so doing, became a necessary part of the worship of God; and so was the use of organs and the like instruments of music, which respect that manner of praising him which God then required. The case is here no otherwise. Prayers and thanksgivings, in the administration of the ordinances of the gospel, are of the instituted worship of God. Unto these, as to the manner of their performance, is the imposition of the liturgical forms spoken of superadded, and their use made a necessary adjunct of the duty itself, so as that it may not be performed without them; which makes them a no less necessary part of the worship of God than any of his institutions of old were which related to the circumstances and the manner of his worship, as the temple, tabernacle, altar, forms of thanksgiving and confession, composed and prescribed by the Holy Ghost himself.

But I suppose this will not be much gainsaid; by some it is acknowledged in express terms. And for the matter of fact, we find that the reading of a book of service is with many taken not to be a part, but the whole of the worship of God, which if it be done, they suppose God is acceptably worshipped without more ado; and if it be omitted, whatever else be done in the room of it, that God is not worshipped at all.

Our inquiry, then, must be, whether such additions to or in the worship of God, besides or beyond his own institution and appointment, be allowable, or lawful to be practised. I shall first recite the words in general of some testimonies that lie against such a practice, and then consider what they most particularly speak unto. Of this sort are Exod. xx. 4, 5: " Thou shalt not make unto thee any graven image, or any likeness of any thing that is in heaven above, or that is in the earth beneath, or that is in the water under the earth; thou shalt not bow down thyself to them, nor serve them: for I the LORD thy God am a jealous God, visiting the iniquity of the fathers upon the children," etc. Deut. iv. 2: " Ye shall not add unto the word which I command you, neither shall ye diminish ought from it, that ye may keep the commandments of the LORD your God which I command you." Chap. xii. 32: " What thing soever I command you, observe to do it: thou shalt not add thereto, nor

diminish from it." Prov. xxx. 6: " Add not unto his words, lest he
reprove thee, and thou be found a liar." Jer. vii. 31: " They have
built the high places of Tophet, which is in the valley of the son of
Hinnom, to burn their sons and their daughters in the fire; which I
commanded them not, neither came it into my heart." Matt. xv. 9:
" In vain do they worship me, teaching for doctrines the commandments of men." Ver. 13: " Every plant which my heavenly Father
hath not planted, shall be rooted up." Also, Mark vii. 7, 8; Rev.
xxii. 18: " If any man shall add unto these things, God shall add
unto him the plagues that are written in this book." The mind
of God in these and the like prohibitions, the reader may find exemplified, Lev. x. 1–3, etc.; Josh. xxii. 10, etc.; Judges viii. 24, etc.;
2 Kings xvi. 11, 12; 1 Chron. xv. 13, and in other places.

Men who, having great abilities of learning, are able to distinguish
themselves from under the power of the most express rules and commands, should yet, methinks, out of a sense of their weakness (which
they are ready to profess themselves convinced of when occasion is
offered to deliver their thoughts concerning them), have compassion
for those who, being not able to discern the strength of their reasonings, because of their fineness, are kept in a conscientious subjection
to the express commands of God, especially conceiving them not
without some cogent cause reiterated.

But lest the present exasperation of the spirits of men should
frustrate that hope and expectation, let us consider what is the precise intendment of the testimonies produced, seeing we have reason
to look well to the justice of our cause in the first place; which
being cleared, we may the better be satisfied in coming short of
favour where it may not be obtained. The places of Scripture produced are taken partly out of the Old Testament, partly out of the
New. And I suppose it will be granted that there is an equal force
of rule in the one as in the other; for though these in the Old
Testament had their peculiar respect to the worship that was then instituted, yet they had [respect to it] not as then instituted, but as the
worship which God himself had appointed. And therefore their general force abides while God requires any worship at the hands of men,
unless it may be made appear that God hath parted with that prerogative of being the appointer of his own worship now under the
New Testament, which he so vindicated unto himself under the Old.
Take them, then, in their general aim and intention, that which
these and the like testimonies unanimously speak unto us is this,
That the will of God is the sole rule of his worship, and all the concernment of it, and that his authority is the sole principle and cause
of the relation of any thing to his worship in a religious manner;
and consequently, that he never did, nor ever will, allow that the

wills of his creatures should be the rule or measure of his honour or worship, nor that their authority should cause any thing to hold a new relation unto him, or any other but what it hath by the law of its creation. And this is the sum and substance of the second commandment, wherein so great a cloud of expositors do centre their thoughts, that it will not be easy for any to withstand them; so that the other texts produced are express to all the particulars of the assertion laid down may be easily evinced.

That the Lord asserts his own authority and will as the constituting cause and rule of all his worship was the first thing asserted. His repetition of " My words," " What I have commanded," and the like expressions, secure this enclosure. Unless men can pretend that there is the same reason of the words and commands of God himself, it is in vain for them to pretend a power of instituting any thing in the worship of God; for the formal reason of every such institution is, that the word of it is the word of God. It is enough to discard any thing from a relation to the worship of God, to manifest that the appointers of it were men, and not God. Nor can any man prove that God hath delegated unto them his power in this matter; nor did he ever do so to any of the sons of men,—namely, that they should have authority to appoint any thing in his worship, or about it, that seemeth meet unto their wisdom. With some, indeed, in former days, he intrusted the work of revealing unto his church and people what he himself would have observed; which dispensation he closed in the person of Christ and his apostles. But to intrust men with authority, not to declare what he revealed, but to appoint what seemeth good unto them, he never did it; the testimonies produced lie evidently against it. Now, surely, God's asserting his own will and authority as the only rule and cause of his worship, should make men cautious how they suppose themselves like or equal unto him herein, especially being destitute of warrant from the approved example or precedent of any that have gone before them. If the example of any one in the Old or New Testament could be produced, that of his own mind and authority made any such additions to the worship of God as that which we treat about, by virtue of any trust or power pretended from or under him, and found acceptance in his so doing, or that was not severely rebuked for his sin therein, some countenance would seem to be given unto those that at present walk in such paths; although I suppose it would not be easy for them to prove any particular instances, which might have peculiar exemption from the general law, which we know not, to be a sufficient warrant for their proceedings. But whereas God himself having instituted his own worship and all the concernments of it, doth also assert his own authority and will as the sole cause and rule of all the worship that he will accept, no instance being left on record of any one that ever made any additions to what he had appointed, on any pretence whatever, or by virtue of any authority whatever, that was accepted with him; and whereas the most eminent of those who have assumed that power to themselves, as also of the judgment of the reasons necessary for the exerting of it, as to matter and manner, have been given up, in the righteous judgment of God, to do things not convenient, yea, abominable unto him (as in the papal church),—it is not unlikely to be the wisdom of men to be very cautious of intruding themselves into this thankless office.

But such is the corrupt nature of man, that there is scarce any thing whereabout men have been more apt to contend with God from the foundation of the world. That their will and wisdom may have a share (some at least) in the ordering of his worship, is that which of all things they seem to desire. Wherefore, to obviate their pride and folly, to his asserting of his own prerogative in this matter, he subjoins severe interdictions against all or any man's interposing therein, so as to take away any thing by him commanded, or to add any thing to what is by him appointed. This also the testimonies recited fully express. The prohibition is plain, " Thou shalt not add to what I have commanded." Add not to his words, " That is, in his worship, to the things which by his word he hath appointed to be observed,—neither to the word of his institution nor to the things instituted." Indeed, adding things adds to the word; for the word that adds is made of a like authority with his. All *making to ourselves* is forbidden, though what we so make may seem unto us to tend to the furtherance of the worship of God. It is said men may add nothing to the substance of the worship of God, but they may order, dispose, and appoint the things that belong to the manner and circumstances of it, and this is all that is done in the prescription of liturgies. Of circumstances in and about the worship of God we have spoken before, and removed that pretence. Nor is it safe distinguishing in the things of God where himself hath not distinguished. When he gave out the prohibitions mentioned under the Old Testament, he was appointing or had appointed his whole worship, and all that belonged unto it, in matter and manner, way and order, substance and circumstance. Indeed, there is nothing in its whole nature, as it belongs to the general being of things, so circumstantial, but that if it be appointed by God in his worship, it becomes a part of the substance of it; nor can any thing that is not so appointed ever by any be made a circumstance of his worship, though many things are circumstances of those actions which in his worship are performed. This distinction, then, directly makes void the command, so that conscience cannot acquiesce in it. Besides, we have showed that liturgies prescribed and imposed are necessary parts of God's worship, and so not to be salved by this distinction.

Moreover, to testify what weight he laid on the observance of these general prohibitions, when men found out other ways of worship than what he had appointed, though the particulars were such as fell under other special interdictions, yet the Lord was pleased to place the great aggravation of their sin in the contempt of those general rules mentioned. This is that he urgeth them with, that they did things by him *not appointed;* of not observing any thing in religion but what he requires, that he presseth them withal. The command is general, " You shall add nothing to what I have instituted." And the aggravation of the sin pressed by him relates not to the particular nature of it, but to this general command or prohibition, "You have done what I commanded you not." That the particular evil condemned was also against other special commands of God, is merely accidental to the general nature of the crime they were urged withal. And whereas God hath given out these rules and precepts, " You shall do whatever I command you, and according as I command you; you shall add nothing thereunto, nor take any thing therefrom," can the transgression of this rule be any otherwise expressed but thus, " They did the thing which he commanded not, nor did it ever come into his heart?"

It is said, that the intention of these rules and prohibitions is only to prevent the addition of what is contrary to what God hath appointed, and not of that which may tend to the furtherance and better discharge of his appointments. The usual answer to this acceptation is, that whatever is added is contrary to what is commanded, though not in this or that particular command, yet to that command that nothing be added. It is not the nature of any particular that is condemned, but the power of adding, in those prohibitions. Let us see, then, whether of these senses has the fairest evidence with the evident purport and intention of the rules, precepts, and prohibitions under consideration.

Our Lord Jesus Christ directs his apostles to teach his disciples "to do and observe whatever he commanded them." Those who contend for the latter interpretation of those and the like precepts before mentioned, affirm that there is in these words a restriction of the matter of their commission to the express commands of Christ. What he commands, they say, they were to teach men to observe, and nothing else; nor will he require the observance of aught else at our hands. The others would have his intention to be, whatever he commanded, and whatever seemeth good to them to command, so it be not contrary unto what was by him commanded; as if he had said, "Teach men to observe whatever I command them; and command you them to observe whatever you think meet, so it be not contrary to my commands." Certainly this gloss at first view seems to defeat the main intendment of Christ, in that express limitation of their commission unto his own commands. So also under the Old Testament: giving order about his worship, the Lord lets Moses know that he must do all things according to what he should show and reveal unto him. In the close of the work committed unto him, to show what he had done was acceptable to God, it is eight or ten times repeated that he did all as the Lord commanded him; nothing was omitted, nothing added by him. That the same course might be observed in the following practice which was taken in the first institution, the Lord commands that nothing be added to what was so appointed by him, nothing diminished from it. The whole duty, then, of the church, as unto the worship of God, seems to lie in the precise observation of what is appointed and commanded by him. To assert things may be added to the worship of God not by him appointed, which, in the judgment of those that add them, seem useful for the better performance of what he hath appointed, so that they be not contrary unto them, seems to defeat the whole end and intention of God in all those rules and prohibitions, if either the occasion, rise, cause of them, or their commendable observance, be considered. On these and no better terms is that prescribed liturgy we treat of introduced and imposed. It comes from man, with authority to be added to the worship that Christ requires, and ventures on all the severe interdictions of such additions, armed only with the pretence of not being contrary to any particular command in the matter of it (which yet is denied), and such distinctions as have not the least ground in Scripture, or in the reason of the things themselves which it is applied unto. Might we divert into particulars, it were easy to demonstrate that the instances given in the Scripture of God's rejection of such additions do abundantly obviate all the pleas that are insisted on for the waiving of the general prohibition.

CHAPTER VIII.

Of the authority needful for the constituting and ordering of any thing that is to have relation to God and his worship—Of the power and authority of civil magistrates—The power imposing the liturgy—The formal reason of religious obedience—Use of the liturgy an act of civil, not religious obedience, Matt. xxviii. 20—No rule to judge of what is meet in the worship of God, but his word.

BESIDES the regulation of all our proceedings and actions in the worship of God by the command and prohibitions insisted on in the foregoing chapter, there are two things indispensably necessary to render the prescription of any thing in religious worship allowable or lawful to be observed, both pointed unto by the testimonies produced; and these are,—first, An *authority* to enjoin; and, secondly, A certain *rule* to try the injunction by.

The worship of God is of that nature that whatsoever is performed in it is an act of religious obedience. That any thing may be esteemed such, it is necessary that the conscience be in it subject to the immediate authority of God. His authority alone renders any act of obedience religious. All authority is originally in God, and there are two ways whereby he is pleased to exert it:—First, By a delegation of authority unto some persons for some ends and purposes; which they being invested withal, may command in their own names an observance of the things about which, by God's appointment, their authority is to be exercised. Thus is it with kings and rulers of the earth. They are powers ordained of God, having authority given them by him. And being invested with power, they give out their commands for the doing or performing of such or such things whereunto their authority doth extend. That they ought to be obeyed in things good and lawful, doth not arise from the authority vested in themselves, but from the immediate command of God that in such things they ought to be obeyed. Hence obedience in general unto magistrates is a part of our moral and religious obedience unto God, as it respects his command, whatever the nature and object of it be. But the performance of particular actions, wherein by their determination our obedience exerts itself, being resolved into that authority which is vested in them, is not religious but civil obedience, any otherwise than as in respect of its general nature it relates to the command of God in general. No act, I say, that we perform, whereof this is the formal reason, that it is appointed and commanded by man, though that man be intrusted with power from God to appoint and require acts of that nature, is an act of religious obedience unto God in itself, because it relates not immediately to his divine authority requiring that act.

Secondly, God doth exert his authority immediately, and that either directly from heaven, as in the giving of the law, or by the inspiration of others to declare his will; unto both which his word written answereth. Now, whatever is done in obedience to the authority of God thus exerting itself is a part of that religious duty which we owe to God, whether it be in his first institution and appointment, or any duty in its primitive revelation, or whether it be in the commands he gives for the observation of what he hath formerly appointed; for when God hath commanded any things to be observed in his worship, though he design and appoint men to see them observed accordingly, and furnish them with the authority of commanding to that purpose, yet the interposition of that authority of men, though by God's institution, doth not at all hinder but that the duty performed is religious obedience, relating directly to the will and command of God. The power commanding in the case we have in hand is man's, not that of the Lord; for though it be acknowledged that those who do command have their authority from God, yet unless the thing commanded be also in particular appointed by God, the obedience that is yielded is purely civil, and not religious. This is the state of the matter under consideration: The commanding and imposing power is variously apprehended. Some say it is the church that doth it, and so assert the authority to be ecclesiastical. "Every church," say they, "hath power to order things of this nature for order and decency's sake." When it is inquired what the church is that they intend, then some are at a loss, and would fain insinuate somewhat into our thoughts that they dare not openly assert and maintain. The truth is, the church in this sense is the king, or the king and parliament, by whose advice he exerts his legislative power. By their authority was the liturgy composed, or it was composed without authority; by their authority it must be imposed, if it be imposed. What is or was done in the preparation of it by others, unto their judgment, hath no more influence into the authoritative imposition of it than the act of a person learned in the law, drawing up a bill for the consideration of parliament, hath into its binding law-power when confirmed. In this sense we acknowledge the power ordaining and imposing this liturgy to be of God, to be good and lawful, to be obeyed unto the utmost extent of that obedience which to man can be due, and that upon the account of the institution and command of God himself; but yet, supposing the liturgy to fall within the precincts and limits of that obedience, the observance and use of it, being not commanded of God, is purely an act of civil obedience, and not religious, wherein the conscience lies in no immediate subjection to Jesus Christ. It is of the same general nature with the honest discharge of the office of a constable; and this seems inconsistent with the nature of the worship of God.

But whatever be the immediate imposing power, we have direction as to our duty in the last injunction of our blessed Saviour to his apostles, Matt. xxviii. 20, "Teaching them to observe all things whatsoever I have commanded." In things which concern the worship of God, the commanding power is Christ, and his command the adequate rule and measure of our obedience. The teaching, commanding, and enjoining of others to do and observe those commands, is the duty of those intrusted with Christ's authority under him.

Their commission to teach and enjoin, and our duty to do and observe, have the same rules, the same measure, bounds, and limits. What they teach and enjoin beyond what Christ hath commanded, they do it not by virtue of any commission from him; what we do beyond what he hath commanded, we do it not in obedience to him; —what they so teach, they do it in their own name, not his; what we so do, we do in our own strength, not his, nor to his glory. The answer of Bellarmine to that argument of the protestant divines from this place, against the impositions of his church, is the most weak and frivolous that I think ever any learned man was forced to make use of; and yet where to find better will not easily occur. Our Lord Jesus Christ saith, " Go and teach men to observe whatsoever I have commanded you; and, lo, I am with you alway;" to which he subjoins, " It is true, but yet we are bound also to obey them that are set over us,—that is, our church guides;" and so leaves the argument as sufficiently discharged! Now, the whole question is concerning what those church guides may teach and enjoin, where-unto we are to give obedience, which is here expressly restrained to the things commanded by Christ; to which the cardinal offers not one word. The things our Saviour treats about are principally the " agenda" of the gospel,—things to be done and observed in the wor-ship of God. Of these, as was said, he makes his own command the adequate rule and measure: " Teach men to observe" πάντα ὅσα " all whatsoever I command." In their so doing alone doth he promise his presence with them; that is, to enable them unto the discharge of their duty. He commands, I say, all that shall to the end of the world be called to serve him in the work of the gospel, to " teach." In that expression he compriseth their whole duty, as their whole authority is given them in this commission. In their teaching, indeed, they are to command with all authority; and upon the non-obedience of men unto their teaching, either by not receiving their word, or by walking unworthy of it when it is received in the profession of it, he hath allotted them the course of their whole pro-ceedings; but still requiring that all be regulated by what they are originally commissionated and enabled to teach and command. Let, then, the imposition of a liturgy be tried by this rule. It was never by Christ commanded to his apostles, cannot by any be taught as his command; and therefore men, in the teaching or imposing of it, have no promise of his presence, nor do they that observe it yield any obedience unto him therein. This, I am sure, will be the rule of Christ's inquiry at his great visitation at the last day,—the things which himself hath commanded will be inquired after, as to some men's teachings, and all men's observation, and those only. And I cannot but admire with what peace and satisfaction to their own souls men can pretend to act as by commission from Christ, as the chief administrators of his gospel and worship on the earth, and make it their whole business almost to teach men to do and observe what he never commanded, and rigorously to inquire after and into the observation of their own commands, whilst those of the Lord Jesus are openly neglected.

But let the authority of men for imposition be supposed to equal the fancy of any who through ignorance or interest are most devoted unto it, when they come to put their authority into execution, commanding things in and about the worship of God, I desire to know by what rule they are to proceed in their so doing. All the actions of men are or ought to be regular: good or evil they are, as they answer to or dissent from their proper rule. The rule in this matter must be the word of God, or their own prudence. Allow the former to be the rule,—that is, revealing what they ought to command,—and there is a total end of this difference. What a rule the latter is like to prove is easy to conjecture; but there is no need of conjectures where experience interposeth. The great philosopher is blamed by some for inserting the determination of men wise and prudent into his definition of the rule of moral virtue; for they say, "That cannot be certainly known whose rule and measure is fluctuating and uncertain." If there be ground for this assertion in reference to moral virtues, whose seed and principles are inlaid in the nature of man, how much more is that rule to be questioned when applied to things whose spring and foundation lies merely in supernatural revelation? How various, uncertain, and tumultuating, how roving this pretended rule is like to prove, how short it comes to any one single property of a sufficient rule, much more of all things that are necessary to complete a rule of prorocecome[1] in such cases, were easy to demonstrate. What good and useful place that is like to obtain in the worship of God, which, having its rise in the authority of man, is framed by the rule of the wisdom of man, and so wholly resolved into his will, I may say will be one day judged and determined, but that it is so already sufficiently in the word of truth.

CHAPTER IX.

Argument second—Necessary use of the liturgy exclusive of the use of the means appointed by Christ for the edification of his church.

WE proceed to some farther considerations upon the state of the question before laid down, and shall insist on some other arguments against the imposition pleaded for. We have spoken to the authority

---

[1] So the word is given in the first, and in Russell's edition. It seems a misprint for "procedure."—ED.

imposing; our next argument is taken from the thing or matter imposed, and the end of that imposition.

A human provision of means for the accomplishing of any end or ends in the worship of God for which Jesus Christ himself hath made and doth continue to make provision, to the exclusion of that provision so by him made, is not allowable. About this assertion I suppose we shall have no contention. To assert the lawfulness of such provisions is, in the first instance, to exalt the wisdom and authority of men above that of Christ, and that in his own house. This men will not nakedly and openly do, though by just consequence it be done every day. But we have secured our proposition by the plainness of its terms, against which no exception can lie. It remaineth, then, that we show that the things mentioned in it, and rejected as disallowable, are directly applicable to the imposition of liturgies contended about.

That the prescription of the liturgy, to be used as prescribed, is the provision of a means for the accomplishing of some ends in the worship of God, the judgment and the practice of those who contend for it do sufficiently declare. Those ends, or this end (to sum up all in one), is, that the ordinances and institutions of Christ may be quickly administered and solemnized in the church with decency and order, unto the edification of the assemblies wherein it is used. I suppose none will deny this to be the end intended in its imposition; it is so pleaded continually; nor is there any other that I know of assigned. Now, of the things mentioned it is the last that is the principal end, —namely, the edification of the church; which is aimed at for its own sake, and so regulates the whole procedure of mere mediums, and those that are so mediums as also to be esteemed subordinate ends. Such are decency and order, or uniformity. These have not their worth from themselves, nor do they influence the intention of the liturgists for their own sakes, but as they tend unto edification; and this the apostolical rule expressly requireth, 1 Cor. xiv. The prescription, then, of a liturgy is a provision for the right administration of the ordinances of the gospel unto the edification of the church. This is its general nature; and in the administration of the ordinances of the gospel consists the chief and main work of the ministry. That this provision is human hath been before declared. It was not made by Christ nor his apostles, but of men; and by men was it made and imposed on the disciples of Christ. It remaineth, then, that we consider whether Jesus Christ have not made provision for the same end and purpose,—namely, that the ordinances and institutions of the gospel may be administered to the edification of the church. Now, this the apostle expressly affirms, Eph. iv. 7–13, " Unto every one of us is given grace according to the measure of the gift of Christ. Wherefore he saith, When he ascended up on high, he led captivity captive, and gave gifts unto men. And he gave some, pastors and teachers; for the perfecting of the saints, for the work of the ministry, for the edifying of the body of Christ: till we all come in the unity of the faith, and of the knowledge of the Son of God, unto a perfect man, unto the measure of the stature of the fulness of Christ." The Lord Jesus, who hath appointed the office of the ministry, hath also provided sufficient furniture for the persons called according to his mind to the discharge of that office and the whole duty of it. That the administration of the ordinances of the gospel is the work of the ministry, I suppose will not be denied. Now, that this work of the ministry may be discharged to the edification of his body, and that to the end of the world, until all his people in every generation are brought unto the measure of grace assigned unto them in this life, is expressly affirmed. He hath given gifts for this end and purpose,— namely, that the work of the ministry may be performed to the edification of his body. To say that the provision he hath made is not every way sufficient for the attaining of the end for which it was made by him, or that he continueth not to make the same provision that he did formerly, are equally blasphemous; the one injurious to his wisdom, the other to his truth, both to his love and care of his church. For decency and uniformity in all his churches the Lord Jesus also hath provided. The administration of the same specifical ordinances in the assemblies of his disciples, convened according to his mind, according to the same rule of his word, by virtue of the same specifical gifts of the Spirit by him bestowed on the administrators of them, constitutes the uniformity that he requires, and is acceptable unto him. This was the uniformity of the apostolical churches, walking by the same rule of faith and obedience, and no other; and this is all the uniformity that is among the true churches of Christ that are this day in the world. To imagine that there should be a uniformity in words and phrases of speech, and the like, is an impracticable figment, which never was obtained, nor ever will be to the end of the world. And when men, by the invention of rites and orders, began to depart from this uniformity, how far they were from falling into any other is notorious from that discourse of Socrates on this matter, lib. v. cap. 21. For these, then, the Lord Christ hath made provision. And where there is this uniformity unto edification, let those things be attended unto which are requisite for the nature of assemblies meeting for such ends, as assemblies, and all the decency and order which Christ requireth will ensue. I suppose it will not be safe for any man to derogate from the sufficiency of this provision. If any shall say, that we see and find by experience that men called to be ministers are not so enabled to the work of the ministry as, by virtue of the gifts they have received, to administer the ordinances of the gospel unto the edification of the church, I shall desire them to consider whether indeed such persons be rightly called unto the ministry, and do labour aright to discharge their duty in that office; seeing that if they are so and do so, there seems to be a direct failure of the promise of Christ, which is blasphemy to imagine. And it may be considered whether this pretended defect and want do not, where it is in those who are indeed called to the work of the ministry, proceed from their neglect to stir up the gifts that they have received by the use and exercise of them; for which end alone they are intrusted with them. And it may be farther considered, whether their neglect hath not been occasioned greatly by some men's imposing of prescribed liturgies, and others trusting to their use in those things and for those ends for which men are intrusted with those gifts by Jesus Christ. And if this be so,—as indeed, upon due search, it will appear so to be,—then we have a secret inclusion of the provision made by Christ for the ends mentioned plainly intimated unto us, before we arrive at the express consideration of it.

But to proceed. The provision that Christ hath made for the discharge of the whole work of the ministry, in the administration of the ordinances of the gospel, unto the edification of his church, is his collation or bestowing of gifts on men rightly called to the office of the ministry, enabling them unto, and to be exercised in, that work. In the prescription and imposition of a liturgy, there is a provision made for the discharge of the work of the ministry, in the administration of the ordinances of the gospel, unto the edification of the church, in and by the precise reading and pronouncing of the words set down therein, without alteration, diminution, or addition. It remaineth, then, to consider whether this latter provision be not exclusive of the former, and whether the use of them both at the same time be not inconsistent. The administration of gospel ordinances consists in prayer, thanksgiving, instruction, and exhortations, suitably applied unto the special nature and end of the several ordinances themselves, and the use of them in the church. For the right performance of all these, Christ gives gifts unto ministers; the liturgy [gives] a certain number of words, to be read without addition or alteration, and this " toties quoties" as the ordinances are to be administered. Now, unless it can be made to appear that an ability to read the prescribed words of the liturgy be the gifts promised by Christ for the discharge of the work of the ministry, which cannot be done, it is most evident that there is an inconsistency between the use and actual exercise of these several provisions of mediums for the compassing of the same end; and, consequently, the necessary, indispensable use of the liturgy is directly exclusive of the use of the means provided by Christ, and for that end for which the liturgy is invented and imposed. What dismal effects have issued hereupon may be declared hereafter, if need be. Certainly more than one commandment of God, and more than one promise of Christ, have been made void by this tradition; and I desire that none would be offended if, as my own apprehension, I affirm that the introduction of liturgies was, on the account insisted on, the principal means of increasing and carrying on that sad defection and apostasy, in the guilt whereof most churches in the world have inwrapped themselves. Nor doth there lie at present any relief against this consideration from hence, that ministers are allowed the exercise of their gifts they have received in their preaching, and prayers before and after sermons. For, first, that indeed there is such a liberty allowed, if the present liturgy be so imposed as by some is pretended, is very questionable. Many that are looked on as skilled in that law and mystery of it do by their practice give another interpretation of the intendment of its imposition, making it extend to all that is done in the public worship, the bare preaching or reading of a sermon or homily excepted. Nor, secondly, is that the matter inquired into, whether ministers may at any time, or in any part of God's worship, make use of their gifts? but whether they may do it in all those administrations, for whose performance, to the edification of his body, they are bestowed on them by Jesus Christ? which, by the rule of the liturgy, we have showed they may not; and I doubt not but it will be granted, by those who contend for the imposition of the liturgy, that it extends to the principal parts, if not the whole, of the public worship of God in the church. Now, certainly, it is necessary that conscience be clearly satisfied that this prescription of a human provision of means for such ends in the worship of God as Christ hath made provision for, which is excluded thereby, be not against express rule of Scripture, Ezek. xliii. 8; Matt. xv. 9; Col. ii. 20–22; without precedent or example; derogatory to the glory of Christ, Heb. iii. 5, 6, and, in particular, of his truth, wisdom, and love of his church, as also to the perfection of the Scripture, 2 Tim. iii. 15, 16;—and whether it brings not the ministers of the gospel into open sin, Rom. xii. 6–8; 1 Cor. xii. 6–10; Eph. iv. 8, 11, 12; 1 Pet. iv. 10, 11; and so be an occasion of the wrath of God and ruin of the souls of men, before they admit of it or submit unto it.

CHAPTER X.

Other considerations about the imposition of liturgies.

FURTHERMORE, the great rule of gospel administrations is, that all things be done to edification. This is the main end of the ministry itself, in all the duties thereof that are purely evangelical. For this end was the office of the ministry instituted; for this end are ministerial gifts dispensed; for this end were the sacraments appointed, and all church assemblies, church power, and whatever else belongs to churches. It is all ordained for this end, that the body of Christ may be "edified" and "increased with the increase of God," Eph. iv. 7, 8, 11–15; Col. ii. 19; Acts ix. 31; Rom. xiv. 15, 19; 1 Cor. x. 23, xiv. 3–5, 12, 26; 2 Cor. xii. 19; 1 Tim. i. 4. The full and adequate rule of all church order and duties is, that all things be done to edification. It doth not hence ensue that whatever men shall judge to conduce to edification may be used by themselves or imposed on others in the worship of God. Christ himself, the only wise and competent judge in such cases, hath precisely himself determined what is conducing hereunto, having, as on other accounts, so on this also, limited men to his prescription, because nothing is effectual unto edification but by virtue of his blessing, which is annexed only to his own institutions. But this will undeniably hence ensue, that whatever is contrary unto or a hinderance of edification, ought not to be appointed or observed in the worship of God; for certainly whatever is a hinderance of that, in any kind, unto whose furtherance all things of that kind ought to contribute, their whole worth and virtue consisting in that contribution, can have no due place amongst them. If it appear that this is the state and condition of this imposed liturgy in church administrations, I presume it will be confessed that it ought not to obtain any place or room amongst them. The edification of the church depends principally on the blessing of God upon the exercise of those ministerial gifts which are bestowed on men for that end,—namely, that the church be edified. God supplying "seed to the sower" blesseth it with an increase in the field where it is sowed, 2 Cor. ix. 10. The gifts that are bestowed on ministers are their principal talents, that they ought to trade withal for the profit of their Master; that is, the building up of his house, wherein his wealth in this world doth lie. Yea, all the gifts that are bestowed by the Spirit of Christ on men are given them "to profit withal," 1 Cor. xii. 7; and they are required with them to act for God in the edification of the body of Christ, every one according to his measure, 1 Pet. iv. 10, 11. This, I suppose, will be granted. Moreover, that the gifts bestowed by Christ on the guides of his church, the ministers of the gospel, are proportioned and suited to the end which he aimeth to accomplish by them, as we have in part before declared, so it is evident from the infinite wisdom of him that bestows them. From both which it will undeniably follow, that on the due and regular use and employment of those gifts which men receive from Christ depends, and that solely, the edification of his church. I suppose this will not be denied, [that] where the gifts bestowed by the Spirit of Christ upon the ministers of his church are used and exercised in the work of the ministry, according to his mind and will, there, by his blessing, the edification which he doth intend will ensue. Let us, then, proceed. These gifts, as the Scripture witnesseth and experience convinceth, are bestowed in great variety and in several degrees. The greater and more excellent they are in any intrusted with them, the more excellent is the means of edification which the Lord affords unto his disciples by them. Edification, then, as in its general nature it depends on the gifts of Christ which he bestows on the officers of his church, so as to the degrees of it and its special furtherance, it depends on the degrees and special improvement of those gifts. For this cause all those to whom the work of the ministry is committed, as they ought to " desire spiritual gifts," 1 Cor. xiv. 1, that the church may be edified by them, so to " covet earnestly the best gifts," chap. xii. 31, that they may singularly edify the church; and also seek to excel in those gifts, chap. xiv. 20, that the same word of edification may be carried on to the utmost. It may, then, be inquired how these spiritual gifts,—which we must suppose all ministers of the gospel, in some measure, to have received,—may be improved, so that they may "excel to the edifying of the church," which is expressly required of them. We say, then, that the improvement and increase of spiritual gifts doth ordinarily and regularly depend on their due and holy exercise. He that had a talent and used it not, though he endeavoured to keep it safe, yet it did not increase, when every one that traded with the stock wherewith they were intrusted made a regular increase, according to the measure they had received. And in experience we daily see men napkining their talents until they are taken from them, whilst others receive additions to their store, at least such supplies as that their first provisions fail not. Hence, the great direction for the exercise of the work of the ministry is, to stir up the gift received; by a due performance whereof, in all persons intrusted with them, is the whole work of edifying the body of Christ, until it reach the measure appointed to every member, completed and finished. Edification, then, depends on the improvement of gifts, and the improvement of gifts on their due exercise according to the mind of Christ. The want, then, of that due exercise, either by the neglect of them on whom they are bestowed, or any hinderance of it put upon them by others, is the sole way of obstructing the improvement of spiritual gifts, and, by direct and immediate consequence, of the edification of the church. Now, this seems to be so much done by the prescription of the liturgy and imposition of it, that it is impossible for the wit of man to invent a more effectual expedient for the compassing of that evil end. The main exercise of spiritual gifts, on which their growth and improvement doth depend, lies in the administration of gospel ordinances; that is, the work of the ministry, for which they are bestowed.   To hinder, therefore, or forbid that exercise is directly to forbid the due, regular, appointed means of their increase; and so, also, of the edification of the body of Christ, the means indispensably necessary unto it being removed and taken away.   Now, this is openly and avowedly done in the imposed liturgy, if imposed.   It says expressly that the ministers of the gospel shall not use or exercise any spiritual gift in the administration of those ordinances for which provision is made in the book.

And as in this case the condition of the people, who are deprived of the means of their edification, is sad, so that of the ministers of the gospel is miserable and deplorable.   The Lord Jesus Christ bestows gifts upon them, requiring the use and exercise of them in the work of the ministry at their utmost peril; men, on the other side, forbid them that use and exercise, and that with such forcible prohibitions as threaten to bear down the whole public exercise of the ministry before them.   But the Lord knows how to deliver those that are his out of temptation.   It will be no relief against the force of this consideration, that there are some things left wherein ministers may exercise their gifts and trade with their talents; for as this is but pretended, so it is not in this or that part of their work, but in the whole of the ministry committed unto them, that Christ indispensably requires the guides of his church that they should trade with their talents and exercise their gifts; and accordingly are they to provide for their account at the last day.   By this one engine, then, at the same time, are the people deprived of the means of edification provided for them in the care, wisdom, and love of the Lord Christ, and ministers brought into a necessity of sinning, or foregoing the public exercise of their ministry.

Again, in particular, it is the work and duty of the ministers of the gospel to make application of the grace of Christ, whereof they are stewards, to the flocks committed to their charge, and that according to the especial state and condition of all especial wants which may any way be known unto them.   The way of their application of this grace lies principally in the administration of gospel ordinances. Therein are they to declare, unfold, tender, and apply the grace of Christ, according unto the wants of his disciples, the good of whose souls they watch for in particular.   These wants are very far from being the same, in the same degree, in and unto every congregation, or unto any one congregation at all times, or unto all persons in any congregation; which is easily discerned by a faithful and skilful guide.   The especial application, then, mentioned, according to the rule of the gospel, and special addresses unto God in the name of the flock, with respect to the especial wants of all or any of them, belong to that edification which Christ hath appointed for his church. Now, how this duty can be attended unto in the observance of a prescribed form of liturgy, from whence it is not lawful to digress, is beyond my understanding to apprehend. I confess, men who scoff at edification and deride spiritual gifts, who think all religion to consist in the observation of some carnal institution, who neither know nor care to come to an acquaintance with the spiritual wants of poor souls, nor do tremble at the threatenings of Christ pointed against their negligence and ignorance, Ezek. xxxiv. 4; that suppose the whole baptized world converted to God, and preaching itself, on that account, less necessary than formerly at the first plantation of the gospel; that esteem the doubts and temptations of believers as needless scruples, and their sedulous endeavours to grow in grace and the knowledge of our Lord Jesus Christ, labour lost in hypocrisy; that perhaps do envy at and are troubled with the light and knowledge of the people of God, and suppose they can discharge the duty of the ministry by a bare reading of the service-book to their parish, by themselves, or some hired by them so to do, without once inquiring into the spiritual condition of them the care of whose souls they plead to be committed to them,—may think light of this consideration: but those who know the terror of the Lord, and any thing of their own duty, will be otherwise minded. Yea, farther, there seems to be in the imposition of a liturgy, to be used always as a form in all gospel administrations, an unwarrantable abridgment of the liberty wherewith Christ hath made us free, and therefore sin in the imposition and use of it; for as it is a sin in others to abridge us of the liberty purchased for us by Jesus Christ, so it is in us to give it up, and not to suffer in our testimony for it. Now, of that liberty purchased for us by Jesus Christ, so far as it relates to the worship of God, there are two parts,—first, A freedom from those pedagogical institutions of God himself, which by his own appointment were to continue only to the time of reformation; secondly, A freedom from subjection to the authority of men as to any new impositions in or about the worship of God, 1 Cor. vii. 23. And the same rule is given out as to our duty and deportment in reference unto both these, Gal. v. 1; 1 Pet. ii. 16. Now, not to stand fast in the liberty for us purchased by Christ, is not to have that esteem of it as a privilege given us by his love we ought to have, nor that sense of it as a duty enjoined us by him which ought to be in us. I say, there is the same reason of both these in respect of liberty. As we are freed from Mosaical institutions, so that none can impose the observation of them upon us by virtue of their first appointment, so are we also from any succeeding impositions of men. Our liberty equally respects the one and the other. And as to those institutions, such was the tenderness of the Holy Ghost and the apostles of our Lord Jesus Christ, by his directions and guidance, that they would not (no, not for a season) enjoin the observance of any of them (no, not of those which put men on no positive duties, but were mere abridgments in point of some practices) upon the disciples of Christ, but only such whose observation for that season was made necessary by reason of scandals and offences before any such imposition of theirs, Acts xv. Nor, by a parity of reason, if regard be had to their example, can there any abridgment be lawfully made of the liberty of Christ's disciples by any imposition of things of the latter sort, unless it be as to the observation of some such things as are made necessary in case of scandal antecedent unto any such imposition. We grant, then, that there may be, yea, there ought "de facto" to be, an abridgment made of our liberty as to the performance of some things at some times, which in general we are made free unto, where that performance, in the use and exercise of our liberty, would prove a hinderance unto edification, the great end whereunto all these things are subservient. But then the case must be so stated antecedent to any imposition. First to impose that which is not necessary, and then to assert a necessity of its observation lest scandal should ensue, is a course that men are not directed unto by any gospel rule or apostolical practice. The sum is, That abridgment of the liberty of the disciples of Christ, by impositions on them of things which he hath not appointed, nor made necessary by circumstances antecedent unto such impositions, are plain usurpations upon the consciences of the disciples of Christ, destructive of the liberty which he hath purchased for them, and which, if it be their duty to walk according to gospel rule, is sinful to submit unto. That of this nature is the imposition of a liturgy contended about is evident. It hath no institution or appointment by Jesus Christ, it is wholly of men; there is nothing antecedent unto its imposition that should make it necessary to be imposed; a necessity of its observation is induced upon and by its imposition, which is directly destructive to our liberty in Jesus Christ. The necessity pretended from the insufficiency of ministers for the discharge of that which is their proper work hath in great part been caused by this imposition, and where it hath not, some men's sin is not to be made other men's punishment. Reasons pleaded for the imposition opposed shall be elsewhere considered.

A DISCOURSE

EVANGELICAL LOVE, CHURCH PEACE, AND UNITY;

WITH THE

OCCASIONS AND REASONS OF THE PRESENT DIFFERENCES AND DIVISIONS
ABOUT THINGS SACRED AND RELIGIOUS.

———

"Speciosum quidem nomen est pacis, et pulchra opinio unitatis; sed quis ambigat eam solam unicam
ecclesiæ pacem esse quæ Christi est?"—HILAR.

PREFATORY NOTE.

In 1672, the year in which this "Discourse concerning Evangelical Love, Church-Peace, and Unity" was published, an indulgence had been extended to Dissenters; and, encouraged by this capricious gleam of better feeling on the part of the Government, Dr Owen endeavours in the following discourse to exhibit the religious principles of his denomination, under a light fitted to disarm hostility and allay the rancour with which they had been long regarded.

He shows, Chap. I., that it was not from want of Christian love they continued in a state of separation from the Church of England. After illustrating the obligation of Christian love to all mankind in general, II., he proceeds to establish the claims of the Church of Christ on our affections, considering it first as the spiritual body of Christ, secondly, in regard to its outward profession, and, thirdly, as consisting of professors of the gospel ranged under particular churches. In a position of dissent from the Church of England, there is no repudiation of it as a true church of Christ, and no sin of schism from the church, viewed as catholic and *invisible*, or as *visibly professing* the fundamental truths of the gospel, III. The causes of schisms and divisions are specified, such as erroneous views of evangelical unity, and the neglect of various duties incumbent upon the churches for the preservation of order and purity, IV. In the last chapter the grounds and reasons of nonconformity are stated. He first proves that the imposition of terms of communion not required by divine law is inconsistent with the *rule of communion* established by Christ himself; secondly, with the *practice* of the apostles; thirdly, with the *doctrine* of Scripture on the duty of churches and the liberty of Christians in these matters; fourthly, with certain *special facts* in the history of the primitive churches; and, fifthly, he argues that if unscriptural terms of communion are allowed, it would follow that no rule of communion had been fixed by Christ himself,—an inference which would set aside the authority of Christ over the church. He next illustrates in what respects the terms of communion in the Church of England are unscriptural ;—in the subscription to the liturgy which is exacted; in the canonical submission required to the polity of the church; in the observance of unscriptural ceremonies; and in the oath of canonical obedience, which must be taken by its ministers. He shows farther, that in conforming to the usages and polity of the Established Church, consent would be given to the omission of sundry duties which Christ expressly enjoins,—such as the obligation of every minister of the gospel to take the *immediate care* of the flock whereof he is the overseer, and the responsibility under which he lies to admit to sacramental privileges those only who make "a credible profession of repentance, faith, and obedience." The scope of the argument is to produce the conviction that the guilt of schism rests not with those who refuse, but with those who exact compliance with unscriptural terms of communion.

Mr Orme states that this work of Owen, though very excellent, has not attained the celebrity and circulation of his other writings, "perhaps in consequence of its being without his name." He does not seem to have been aware that though the work on its first issue was anonymous, within a twelvemonth after its publication it was issued anew with the name of the author on the title-page. The value of this discourse would be less appreciated when the controversy between the Established Church and Dissenters assumed another phase. The charge of schism, with the refutation of which it is occupied, soon lost all power, when, in the course of discussion, it came to be felt that this question depended entirely on the validity of the grounds on which secession from any church took place. And to this change in the nature of the discussion, more than to the circumstance that the work was at first published anonymously, may be attributed the comparative neglect into which, in later times, the treatise had fallen. It contains, nevertheless, much important matter, and the spirit which it breathes throughout is admirable.—Ed.

A DISCOURSE

CHRISTIAN LOVE AND PEACE.

CHAPTER I.

Complaints of want of love and unity among Christians, how to be managed, and whence fruitless—Charge of guilt on some, why now removed, and for whose sakes—Personal miscarriages of any not excused—Those who manage the charge mentioned not agreed.

THE great differences that are in the world amongst professors of the gospel, about things relating to the worship of God, do exercise more or less the minds of the generality of men of all sorts; for, either in themselves or their consequences, they are looked on to be of great importance. Some herein regard principally that disadvantageous influence which they are supposed to have into men's spiritual and eternal concernments; others, that aspect which they fancy them to have upon the public peace and tranquillity of this world. Hence, in all ages, such divisions have caused "great thoughts of heart," Judges v. 15, especially because it is very difficult to make a right judgment either of their nature or their tendency. But generally by all they are looked on as evil;—by some, for what they are in themselves; by others, from the disadvantage which they bring (as they suppose) unto their secular interests. Hence there are amongst many great complaints of them, and of that want of love which is looked on as their cause. And, indeed, it seems not only to be in the liberty, but to be the duty of every man soberly to complain of the evils which he would but cannot remedy; for such complaints, testifying a sense of their evil and a desire of their cure, can be no more than what love unto the public good requireth of us. And if in any case this may be allowed, it must be so in that of divisions about sacred things or the worship of God, with their causes and manner of management amongst men: for it will be granted that the glory of God, the honour of Christ, the progress of the gospel, with the edification and peace of the church, are deeply concerned in them, and highly prejudiced by them; and in these things all men have, if not an equal, yet such a special interest as none can forbid them the due consideration of. No man, therefore, ought to be judged as though he did transgress his rule, or go beyond his line, who soberly expresseth his sense of their evil and of the calamities wherewith they are attended. Yet must it not be denied but that much prudence and moderation are required unto the due management of such complaints; for those which either consist in, or are accompanied with, invectives against the persons or ways of others, instead of a rational discourse of the causes of such divisions and their remedies, do not only open, inflame, and irritate former wounds, but prove matters of new contention and strife, to their great increase. Besides, in the manifold divisions and differences of this nature amongst us, all men are supposed to be under an adherence unto some one party or other. Herein every man stands at the same distance from others as they do from him. Now, all complaints of this kind carry along with them a tacit justification of those by whom they are made; for no man can be so profligate as to judge himself, and the way of religious worship wherein he is engaged, to be the cause of blamable divisions amongst Christians, and yet continue therein: reflections, therefore, of guilt upon others they are usually replenished withal. But if those are not attended with evident light and unavoidable conviction, because they proceed from persons supposed not indifferent, yea, culpable in this very matter more or less themselves, by them whom they reflect upon, they are generally turned into occasions of new exasperations and contests. And hence it is come to pass, that although all good men do on all occasions bewail the want of love, forbearance, and condescension that is found among professors of the gospel, and the divisions which follow thereon, yet no comfortable nor advantageous effects do thence ensue. Yea, not only is all expectation of that blessed fruit, which a general serious consent unto such complaints might produce, as yet utterly frustrated, but the small remainders of love and peace amongst us are hazarded and impaired, by mutual charges of the want and loss of them on the principles and practices of each other. We have, therefore, need of no small watchfulness and care, lest in this matter it fall out with us as it did with the Israelites of old on another occasion, 2 Sam. xix. 41–43. For when they had, by a sinful sedition, cast out David from amongst them, and from reigning over them, after a little while, seeing their folly and iniquity, they assembled together with one consent to bring him home again; but in the very beginning of their endeavours to this purpose, falling into a dispute about which of the tribes had the greatest interest in him, they not only desisted from their first design, but fell into another distemper of no less dangerous importance than what they were newly delivered from. It must be acknowledged that there hath been a sinful decay of love among professors of the gospel in this nation, if not a violent casting of it out, by such prejudices and corrupt affections as wherewith it is wholly inconsistent. And it would be a matter of no small lamentation if, upon the blooming of a design for its recovery and reduction, with all its train of forbearance, condescension, gentleness, and peace, if any such design there be, by contests about the occasions and causes of its absence, with too much fierceness in our own vindication, and pleas of a special interest in it above others, new distempers should be raised, hazarding its everlasting exclusion.

In this state of things we have hitherto contented ourselves with the testimony of our own hearts unto the sincerity of our desires, as to walk in love and peace with all men, so to exercise the fruits of them on all occasions administered unto us. And as this alone we have thus far opposed unto all those censures and reproaches which we have undergone to the contrary, so therewithal have we supported ourselves under other things which we have also suffered. Farther to declare our thoughts and principles, in and about the worship of God, than they are evidenced and testified unto by our practice, we have hitherto forborne, lest the most moderate claims of an especial interest in the common faith and love of Christians should occasion new contests and troubles unto ourselves and others. And we have observed, that sometimes an over-hasty endeavour to extinguish flames of this nature hath but increased and diffused them, when, perhaps, if left alone, their fuel would have failed, and themselves expired. Besides, a peaceable practice, especially if accompanied with a quiet bearing of injuries, gives a greater conviction to unprejudiced minds of peaceable principles and inclinations than any verbal declaration, whose sincerity is continually obnoxious to the blast of evil surmises. In a resolution, therefore, to the same purpose we had still continued, had we not so openly and frequently been called on either to vindicate our innocency or to confess and acknowledge our evil. One of these, we hope, is the aim and tendency of all those charges or accusations, for want of love, peaceableness, and due compliance with others, of being the authors and fomenters of schisms and divisions, that have been published against us, on the account of our dissent from some constitutions of the church of England: for we do not think that any good men can please themselves in merely accusing their brethren, whereby they add to the weight of their present troubles, and evidently expose them unto more; for every charge of guilt on

those who are already under sufferings gives new encouragement
and fierceness to the minds of them from whom they suffer.   And
as no greater encouragement can be given unto men to proceed in
any way wherein they are engaged than by their justification in
what they have already done; so the only justification of those who
have stirred up persecution against others consists in charging guilt
on them that are persecuted.   As, therefore, we shall readily acknowledge any evil in our persons, principles, or ways, which we are or
may be convinced of; so the sober vindication of truth and innocency,
that none of the ways of God be evil spoken of by reason of us, is a
duty in the care whereof we are no less concerned.   Yea, did we design and directly endeavour our own justification, we should do no
more than the prime dictates of the law of nature, and the example
of some of the best of men, will give us a sufficient warrant for.
Besides, the clearing of private persons, especially if they are many,
from undue charges and false accusations, belongs unto public good,
that those who have the administration of it committed unto them
may not be misled to make a wrong judgment concerning what they
have to do, as David was in the case of Mephibosheth, upon the
false suggestions of Ziba, 2 Sam. xvi. 4.   Neither could we be justly
blamed should we be more than ordinarily urgent herein, considering how prone the ears of men are to receive calumnious accusations
concerning such as from whom they expect neither profit nor advantage, and how slow in giving admittance to an address of the most
modest defensative.   But this is the least part of our present design.
Our only aim is, to declare those principles concerning mutual love
and unity among Christians, and practices in the worship of God,
wherein our own consciences do find rest and peace, and others
have so much misjudged us about.   This, therefore, we shall briefly
do, and that without such reflections or recriminations as may any
way exasperate the spirits of others, or in the least impede that re-
introduction of love and concord which it is the duty of us all to
labour in.   Wherefore we shall herein have no regard unto the revilings, reproaches, and threatenings of them who seem to have had
no regard to truth, or modesty, or sobriety, indeed to God or man,
in the management of them.   With such it is our duty not to strive,
but to commit our cause to Him that judgeth righteously, especially
with respect unto those impure outrages which go before unto judgment.   Furious persons, animated by their secular interests or desire
of revenge, unacquainted with the spirit of the gospel and the true
nature of the religion revealed by Jesus Christ, incompassionate towards the infirmities of the minds of men, whereof yet none in the
world give greater instances than themselves, who have no thoughts
but to trample under foot and destroy all that differ from them, we

shall rather pity and pray for, than either contend withal or hope to convince. Such they are, as, if outward prevalency were added to their principles and desires, they would render all Christians like the Moabites, Ammonites, and Edomites, who came out to fight against Judah, 2 Chron. xx. 23. The two greater parties, upon some difference or distaste, conspire at first to destroy the inhabitants of Seir, not doubting but that, when they had despatched them out of the way, they should accord well enough among themselves; but the event deceived their expectation,—their rage ceased not until issued in the mutual destruction of them all. No otherwise would it be with those who want nothing but force or opportunity to exterminate their next dissenters in matters of religion; for when they had accomplished that design, the same principle and rage would arm them to the wasting of the residue of Christians, or their own, for a conceit of the lawfulness hereof is raised from a desire of enlarging power and dominion, which is boundless. Especially is it so where an empire over the reason, faith, and consciences of men is affected; which first produced the fatal engine of papal infallibility, that nothing else could have strained the wit of men to invent, and nothing less can support. Unto such as these we shall not so much as tender satisfaction, until they are capable of receiving the advice of the apostle, Eph. iv. 31, " Let all bitterness, and wrath, and anger, and clamour, and evil speaking, be put away from you, with all malice ;" for until this be done, men are to be esteemed but as " raging waves of the sea, foaming out their own shame," whom it is to no purpose to seek to pacify, much less to contend withal.

It is for the sake of them alone who really value and esteem love, peace, and unity among Christians for themselves, that we here tender an account of our thoughts and principles concerning them; for even of them there are some who unduly charge us with owning of principles destructive unto Christian love and condescension, and suited to perpetuate the schisms and divisions that are amongst us. Whether this hath been occasioned by an over-valuation of their own apprehensions, conceiting that their judgments ought to give rule and measure to other men's; or whether they have been, it may be insensibly unto themselves, biassed by provocations, as they suppose, unjustly given them; we are not out of hopes but that they may be convinced of their mistakes. Upon their indications we have searched our consciences, principles, and practices, to find whether there be any such way of perverseness in them as we are charged withal; and may with confidence say that we have a discharge from thence, where we are principally concerned. Having, therefore, satisfied that duty which on this occasion was in the first place incumbent on us, we shall now, for their satisfaction and our own vindication with all impartial men, declare what are our thoughts and judgments, what are our principles, ways, and practices, in and about the great concerns of Christian love, unity, and peace, referring the final decision of all differences unto Him who " hath appointed a day, wherein he will judge the world in righteousness by the man whom he hath ordained."

This being our present design, none may expect that we should attempt to justify or excuse any of those miscarriages or failings that are charged on some or all of those professors of the gospel who at this day come not up unto full communion with the church of England; for we know that " no man liveth and sinneth not," yea, that " in many things we all offend." We all know but in part, and are liable to manifold temptations, even all such as are common unto men. Those only we have no esteem of who through the fever of pride have lost the understanding of their own weak, frail, and sinful condition. And we do acknowledge that there are amongst us " sins against the Lord our God," for which he might not only give us up unto the reproaches and wrath of men in this world, but himself also cast us off utterly and for ever. We shall not, therefore, in the least complain of those who have most industriously represented unto the public view of the world the weakness and miscarriages that have fallen out amongst some or more of them whose cause we plead, and discovered those corrupt affections from whence, helped on with variety of temptations, they might probably proceed; nor shall we use any reflections on them who have severely, and we fear maliciously, laid to their charge things which they knew not; as hoping that by the former the guilty may learn what to amend, now they are taught with such thorns and briers as are the scorns and reproaches of the world, and by the latter the innocent may know what to avoid. Such charges and accusations, therefore, we shall wholly pass over, with our hearty prayers that the same or worse evils may never be found amongst them by whom they are accused. Much less shall we concern ourselves in those reflections on them which are raised from the words, expressions, or actions of particular persons, as they have been reported and tossed up and down in the lips of talkers. The debate of such things tends only to mutual exasperations and endless strife. It may be, also, that for the most part they are false, or misreported invidiously, or misapplied; and, true or false, have been sufficiently avenged by severe retortions. And in such altercations few men understand the sharpness of their own words. Their edge is towards them whom they oppose; but when a return of the like expressions is made unto themselves, they are sensible how they pierce. So are provocations heightened, and the first intendment of reducing love ends in mutual defamatory contentions.   All things, therefore, of this nature we shall pass over, and help to bury by our silence.

The principal charge against us, and that whereinto all others are resolved, is *our nonconformity unto the present constitutions of the church of England;* for hence we are accused to be guilty of the want of Christian love and peaceableness, of schism, and an inclination to all sorts of divisions, contrary to the rules and precepts of the gospel.   Now, we think it not unreasonable to desire that those who pass such censures on us would attend unto the common known rule, whereby alone a right judgment in these cases may be made; for it is not equal that we should be concluded by other men's particular measures, as though by them we were to be regulated in the exercise of love and observance of peace.   And as we doubt not but that they fix those measures unto themselves in sincerity, according unto their own light and apprehension of things, so we are sure it will be no impeachment of their wisdom or holiness to judge that others who differ from them do with an equal integrity endeavour the direction and determination of their consciences in what they believe and practise; yea, if they have not pregnant evidence to the contrary, it is their duty so to judge.   A defect hereof is the spring of all that want of love whereof so great a complaint is made.   And rationally they are to be thought most sincere and scrupulous herein who take up with determinations that are greatly to their outward disadvantage; for unless it be from a conviction of present duty with respect unto God and their own eternal good, men are not easily induced to close with a judgment about sacred things and religious worship, which will not only certainly prejudice them, but endanger their ruin in things temporal.   It is ordinarily outward secular advantages, wherewith the minds of men are generally too much affected, that give an easy admission unto persuasions and practices in religion.   By these are men turned and changed every day from what before they professed, when we hear of no turnings unto a suffering profession but what arise from strong and unavoidable convictions.   Moreover, should we endeavour to accommodate ourselves to the lines of other men, it may make some change of the persons with whom we have to do, but would not in the least relieve us against the charges of guilt, of schism, and want of love, which we suffer under.   Some would prescribe this measure unto us: That we should *occasionally join with parish assemblies,* as now stated, in all their worship and sacred administrations, but will not require of us that we should absolutely forbear all other ways and means of our own edification.   Will this measure satisfy all amongst us? will it free us from the imputation we suffer under? shall we not be said any more to want Christian love, to be factious or guilty of schism?

It is known unto all how little it will conduce unto these ends, and how little the most will grant that church peace is preserved thereby. Yea, the difficulty will be increased upon us beyond what an ordinary ability can solve, though we doubt not but that it may be done, for if we can do so much, we may expect justly to be pressed severely to answer why we do no more; for others say immediately that our attendance on the public worship must be constant, with a forbearance of all other ways of religious worship beyond that of a family: yet this they would have us so to do, as in the meantime studiously to endeavour the reformation of what is judged amiss in the doctrine, discipline, and worship of the church. This is the measure which is prescribed unto us by some, and we know not how many censures are passed upon us for a nonconformity thereunto. Will, therefore, a compliance unto this length better our condition? will it deliver us from the severest reflections of being persons unpeaceable and intolerable? Shall we live in a perpetual dissimulation of our judgments as to what needeth reformation? will that answer our duty, or give us peace in our latter end? Shall we profess the persuasions of our minds in these things, and endeavour by all lawful means to accomplish what we desire? shall we then escape the severest censures, as of persons inclined to schisms and divisions? Yea, many great and wise men of the church of England do look on this as the most pernicious principle and practice that any can betake themselves unto; and in reporting the memorials of former times,[1] some of them have charged all the calamities and miseries that have befallen their church to have proceeded from men of this principle endeavouring reformation according unto models of their own without separation. And could we conscientiously betake ourselves to the pursuit of the same design, we should not, especially under present jealousies and exasperations, escape the same condemnation that others before us have undergone. And so it is fallen out with some; which might teach them that their measures are not authentic; and they might learn moderation towards them who cannot come up unto them, by the severity they meet withal from those that do outgo them. Shall we, therefore,— which alone seems to remain,—proceed yet farther, and, making a renunciation of all those principles concerning the constitution, rule, and discipline of the church, with the ways and manner of the worship of God to be observed in the assemblies of it, which we have hitherto professed, come over unto a full conformity unto the present constitution of the church of England, and all the proceedings of its rulers thereon? "Yea, this is that," say some, "which is required of you, and that which would put an end unto all our

_____
[1] Heyl. Hist. of Presb.

differences and divisions." We know, indeed, that an agreement in any thing or way, right or wrong, true or false, will promise so to do, and appear so to do for a season; but it is truth alone that will make such agreements durable or useful. And we are not engaged in an inquiry merely after peace, but after peace with truth. Yea, to lay aside the consideration of truth, in a disquisition after peace and agreement in and about spiritual things, is to exclude a regard unto God and his authority, and to provide only for ourselves. And what it is which at present lays a prohibition on our consciences against the compliance proposed shall be afterward declared. Neither will we here insist upon the discouragements that are given us from the present state of the church itself; which yet are not a few. Only, we must say, that there doth not appear unto us in many that steadiness in the profession of the truth owned amongst us upon and since the Reformation, nor that consent upon the grounds and reasons of the government and discipline in it that we are required to submit unto, which were necessary to invite any dissenters to a thorough conformity unto it. That there are daily inroads made upon the ancient doctrine of this church, and that without the least control from them who pretend to be the sole conservators of it, until, if not the whole, yet the principal parts of it are laid waste, is sufficiently evident, and may be easily proved. And we fear not to own that we cannot conform to Arminianism [and] Socinianism, on the one hand, or Popery on the other, with what new or specious pretences soever they may be blended. And for the ecclesiastical government, as in the hands of our mere ecclesiastical persons, when it is agreed among themselves whether it be from heaven or of men, we shall know the better how to judge of it. But suppose we should waive all such considerations, and come up to a full conformity unto all that is, or shall, or may be required of us, will this give us a universally pleadable acquitment from the charges of the guilt of want of love, schism, and divisions? We should, indeed, possibly be delivered from the noise and clamour of a few crying-out sectaries, fanatics, schismatics, church-dividers; but withal should continue under the censures of the great, and at present thriving church of Rome, for the same supposed crimes. And sure enough we are, that a compliance with them who have been the real causes and occasions of all the schisms and divisions that are amongst Christians almost in the whole world, would yield us no solid relief in the change of our condition; yet without this no men can free themselves from the loudest outcries against them on the account of schism. And this sufficiently manifests how little indeed they are to be valued, seeing, for the most part, they are nothing but the steam of interest and party. It is therefore apparent, that the accommodations of our judgments and

practices to the measures of other men will afford us no real advantage as to the imputations we suffer under, nor will give satisfaction
unto all professors of Christianity that we pursue love and peace in a
due manner: for what one sort requireth of us, another will instantly disallow and condemn; and it is well if the judgment of the
major part of all sorts be not influenced by custom, prejudices, and
secular advantages.   We have, therefore, no way left but that which,
indeed, ought to be the only way of Christians in these things,—
namely, to seek in sincerity the satisfaction of our own consciences,
and the approving of our hearts unto the Searcher of them, in a diligent attendance unto our own especial duty, according to that rule
which will neither deceive us nor fail us; and an account of what
we do herein we shall now tender unto them that follow truth with
peace.

CHAPTER II.

Commendations of love and unity—Their proper objects, with their general rules
    and measures—Of love toward all mankind in general—Allows not salvation
    unto any without faith in Christ Jesus—Of the differences in religion as to
    outward worship.

THE foundation of our discourse might be laid in the commendation of Christian love and unity, and thereon we might easily enlarge, as also abound in a collection of testimonies confirming our
assertions ; but the old reply in such a case,—" By whom ever were
they discommended?"—evidenceth a labour therein to be needless and
superfluous.   We shall therefore only say, that they are greatly mistaken who, from the condition whereinto at present we are driven
and necessitated, do suppose that we value not these things at as
high a rate as themselves, or any other professors of Christian religion in the world.   A greater noise about them may be made, possibly, by such as have accommodated their name and notion to their
own interests, and who point their pleas about them and their pretences of them to their own secular advantage; but as for a real
valuation of the things themselves, as they are required of us and
prescribed unto us in the gospel, we shall not willingly be found
to come behind any that own the name of Christ in the world.
We know that God hath styled himself the God of love, peace, and
order in the church, because they are eminently from him, and
highly accepted with him.   And as love is the new commandment
which Jesus Christ hath given unto his disciples, so he hath appointed it to be the bond of perfection unto them; which nothing
else will ever be, however *finely invented* for them, or *forcibly im-*

posed on them. Without this love, in what relates to church communion, whatever else we are, we are but as " sounding brass and
tinkling cymbals." And all unity or agreement in outward order
not proceeding from and animated by this love, are things wherein
neither Christ nor the gospel is much concerned. An endeavour
also after one mind and one judgment, Phil. ii. 2, 1 Cor. i. 10,
amongst all believers, for a help unto us to keep the " unity of the
Spirit in the bond of peace," we acknowledge to be indispensably
required of us. And, therefore, where any opinion or practice, in or
about religion or the worship of God, do apparently in themselves
impair the gracious, holy principles of love and peace, or obstruct
men in the exercise of any duties which those principles require or
lead unto, it is a great and weighty prejudice against their truth and
acceptation with God. As, therefore, we shall not boast of the prevalency of these principles in our minds, seeing that, though we
should know nothing to the contrary by ourselves, yet are we not therefore justified; so we are assured that none can justly condemn us for
the want of them, unless they can make good their charge by instances not relating to the peculiar differences between them and us,
for what doth so will neither warrant any to make such a judgment,
nor carry any conviction in it towards them that are judged. Upon
the whole matter, we shall not easily be diverted from pursuing our
claim unto an equal interest in these things with any other professors of the Christian religion, although at present we do it not by
enlarged commendations of them. Much less are we in the least
moved or shaken in our minds from the accusations of them who,
having the advantage of force and power, do make a compliance
with themselves, in all their impositions and self-interested conceptions, the sole measure of other men's exercise and actings of these
principles. We have a much safer rule whereby to make a judgment of them, whereunto we know " we shall do well to attend, as
unto a light shining in a dark place." But, now, whereas all these
things,—namely, love, peace, and unity,—are equally dear unto us,
yet there are different rules prescribed for the exercise and pursuit
of them. Our love is to be catholic, unconfined as the beams of the
sun, or as the showers of rain that fall on the whole earth. Nothing
of God's rational creation in this world is to be exempted from being
the object thereof. And where only any exception might seem to
be warranted by some men's causeless hatred, with unjust and unreasonable persecution of us, there the exercise of it is given us in
especial and strictest charge; which is one of the noble singularities
of Christian religion. But whereas men are cast into various conditions on account of their relation unto God, the actual exercise of
love towards them is required of us in a suitable variety; for it is

God himself, in his infinite excellencies, who is the first and adequate object of our love, which descends unto others according to their participation from him, and the especial relations created by his appointment; whereof we shall speak afterward. Our duty in the observance of peace is, as unto its object, equally extended; and the rule or measure given us herein is the utmost of our endeavours in all ways of truth and righteousness which are required or may have a tendency thereunto: for as we are commanded to " follow peace with all men," Heb. xii. 14, under the same indispensable necessity as to obtain and observe "holiness" in our own persons, "without which no man shall see the Lord;" so as to the measure of our endeavours unto this end, we are directed, " if it be possible, and as far as in us lieth, to live peaceably with all men," Rom. xii. 18. The rule for unity, as it is supposed to comprise all church-communion, falls under many restrictions; for herein the especial commands of Christ and institutions of the gospel committed unto our care and observance falling under consideration, our practice is precisely limited unto those commands and by the nature of those institutions.

These being the things we are to attend unto, and these being their general rules and measures, we shall, with respect unto the present state of religious affairs in the world amongst those who make profession of the Christian religion, plainly declare what are our thoughts and judgments, what we conceive to be our duty, and what is our practice; submitting them unto the present apprehensions of unprejudiced persons, leaving the final sentence and determination of our cause to the judgment-seat of Jesus Christ.

Love toward *all mankind in general* we acknowledge to be required of us, and we are debtors in the fruits of it to the whole creation of God: for he hath not only implanted the principles of it in that nature whereof we are in common partakers with the whole race and kind, whereunto all hatred and its effects were originally foreign, and introduced by the devil, nor only given us his command for it, enlarging on its grounds and reasons in the gospel; but in his design of recovering us out of our lapsed condition unto a conformity with himself, proposeth in an especial manner the example of his own love and goodness, which are extended unto all, for our imitation, Matt. v. 44, 45. His philanthropy and communicative love, from his own infinite self-fulness, wherewith all creatures, in all places, times, and seasons, are filled and satisfied, as from an immeasurable ocean of goodness, are proposed unto us to direct the exercise of that drop from the divine nature wherewith we are intrusted. " Love your enemies," saith our Saviour, " bless them that curse you, do good to them that hate you, and pray for them which despitefully use you, and persecute you; that ye may be the children of your Father which is in heaven: for he maketh his sun to rise on the evil and on the good, and sendeth rain on the just and on the unjust." Now, all mankind may be cast into two ranks or orders: for, first, there are those who are yet "without Christ, being aliens from the commonwealth of Israel, and strangers from the covenants of promise, having no hope, and without God in the world," Eph. ii. 12,—such, we mean, as are either negatively or privatively infidels or unbelievers, who have yet never heard the sound of the gospel, or do continue to refuse and reject it where it is proposed and tendered unto them; and there are those, secondly, who have in one way or other received the doctrine of the gospel, and do make profession thereof in the world. To both these sorts we do acknowledge that we owe the duty of love. Even towards the infidel, pagan, and Mohammedan world, Jews and Gentiles, we are debtors in this duty; and we desire to be humbled for it as our sin, wherein we are wanting in the discharge of it, or wherein the fruits of it do not abound in us to the praise of God. Now, love, in the first notion of it, is the willing of a wanted good unto the object of it, or those that are loved, producing an endeavour to effect it unto the utmost of the ability of them in whom it is. Where this absent good is of great importance, the first natural and genuine effect of love is *compassion*. This good, as unto all unbelievers, is whatever should deliver them from present or eternal misery,—whatever should lead, guide, or bring them unto blessedness in the enjoyment of God. Besides, the absence hereof is accompanied, even in this world, with all that blindness and darkness of mind, all that slavery unto sin and the devil, that can any way concur to make a rational being truly miserable. If we have not hearts like the flint or adamant, we cannot but be moved with compassion towards so many perishing souls, originally made like ourselves, in the image of God, and from whom that we differ in any thing is an effect of mere sovereign grace, and not the fruit of our own contrivance nor the reward of our worth or merit. And those who are altogether unconcerned in others are not much concerned in themselves; for the true love of ourselves is the rule of our love unto other men. Again, compassion proceeding from love will work by *prayer* for relief; for it is God alone who can supply their wants, and our only way of treating with him about it is by our humble supplications. And if herein also we should be found wanting, we should more judge ourselves to be defective in true Christian love and charity than we can for many of those mistakes which are charged on us in other things, were we convinced that such they are, which as yet we are not. It is therefore our continual prayer, that God would send out his light and his truth unto the utmost parts of the earth, to visit by them those dark places which are yet filled with habitations of cruelty; that he would remove the vail of covering which is yet on the face of many great and populous nations; that "the whole earth may be filled with the knowledge of the LORD, as the waters cover the sea;" even that, according to his promise, "he would turn to the people a pure language, that they may all call upon the name of the LORD, to serve him with one consent." And this we desire to be found doing, not in a formal or customary manner, but out of a sincere compassion for the souls of men, a deep sense of the interest herein of the glory of God, and a desire after the accomplishment of those prophecies and promises in the Scripture which speak comfortably towards an expectation of abundant grace to be manifested unto the residue of sinners, both Jews and Gentiles, in the latter days. Moreover, unto compassion and supplications, love requireth that we should add also all other possible *endeavours for their relief.* Herein consists that work and labour of love which are so much recommended unto us. But the actings of love in these most useful ways are, for the most part, obstructed unto us by the want of opportunities; which, under the guidance of divine Providence, are the rule of our call unto the duties wherein such endeavours consist, and whereby they may be expressed. Only, this at present we have to rejoice in, that, through the unwearied labours of some holy and worthy persons, sundry churches of Indians are lately called and gathered in America; wherein the natives of those parts of the world, who for so many generations sat in darkness and in the shadow of death, do, under the guidance of pastors and elders of their own, walk in the fellowship of the gospel, giving glory to God by Jesus Christ.[1] And let it not seem impertinent that we have given this account of our judgments concerning that love which we do and ought to bear unto all, even the worst of men; seeing those by whom our testimony is received will not, nay cannot, easily suppose that we would wilfully neglect the exercise of the same affections towards those concerning

---

[1] So early as 1556, some missionaries were sent to labour among the natives of America by the church of Geneva, and this is affirmed to have been the first protestant mission. In 1644, a petition was presented to the English parliament in favour of a similar mission to America, and an ordinance of the Lords and Commons was passed, authorizing the Earl of Warwick to take measures in furtherance of this object. "The Society for the Propagation of the Gospel in New England," was established in 1649, by the authority of parliament. Eliot distinguished himself as "the apostle of the Indians," and three authentic narratives were published, in 1653, 1655, and 1659, giving an account of the remarkable success which had attended his labours, containing several sermons by Indian converts, and mentioning several villages in which the inhabitants had wholly conformed to the principles and usages of Christianity. It is interesting to notice the germ of the vast system of modern missions; and when a disposition has been manifested to reproach our fathers for indifference to this great work, it is well to find that Owen was fully alive to its importance, and that the pressure of circumstances alone hindered British Christians in his day from engaging in it on a scale worthy alike of its momentous nature and their own eagerness to advance it.—ED.

whom our obligations thereunto are unspeakably greater and more excellent.

There is, indeed, another kind of pretended charity towards this sort of men, which we profess we have not for them, although we judge we do not want it; for there can be no want unto any of an error or mistake, wherein the charity intended doth consist. And this is the judgment of some, that they, or some of them, may attain salvation or eternal blessedness in the condition wherein they are, without the knowledge of Jesus Christ. This, we acknowledge, we neither believe nor hope concerning them; nor, to speak plainly, can desire it should be so, unless God had otherwise revealed himself concerning Jesus Christ and them than yet he hath done. And we are so far from supposing that there is in us, on this account, any blamable defect of charity, that we know ourselves to be freed by this persuasion from a dangerous error, which, if admitted, would both weaken our own faith and impair all the due and proper effects of charity towards others: for "though there be that are called gods, whether in heaven or in earth, (as there be gods many, and lords many,) yet to us there is but one God, the Father, of whom are all things, and we in him; and one Lord Jesus Christ, by whom are all things, and we by him," 1 Cor. viii. 5, 6. We know "there is no salvation in any other" but by Jesus Christ; and that "there is none other name under heaven given among men, whereby we must be saved," Acts iv. 12. Nor is this name given any otherwise amongst men but by the gospel; for it is not the giving of the person of Christ absolutely to be a mediator, but the declaration of his name by the gospel, as the means of salvation, that is intended. Hence our Lord Jesus Christ, giving that commission to his apostles to preach it, " Go ye into all the world, and preach the gospel to every creature," he adds unto it that decretory sentence concerning the everlasting condition of all men with respect thereunto, " He that believeth and is baptized shall be saved; but he that believeth not shall be damned," Mark xvi. 15, 16. As the preaching of the gospel, and the belief on Jesus Christ thereon, are the only means of obtaining salvation, so all those who are not made partakers of them must perish eternally. So when the apostle affirms that the Jews would have hindered them from preaching to the Gentiles "that they might be saved," 1 Thess. ii. 16, he plainly declares that without it they could not so be. Neither were any of them ever better, or in a better condition, than they are described by the same apostle, Eph. ii. 12, and in sundry other places, wherein he allows them no possibility of obtaining eternal blessedness. Neither do we in this matter consider what God can do, or what he hath done, to the communicating of grace and faith in Jesus Christ unto any particular persons at any time, or in any

place, in an extraordinary manner. We are not called to make a
judgment thereof, nor can any rule be hence collected to regulate
the exercise of our love: "Secret things belong to the LORD our God,
but revealed things to us and our children, that we may do his will."
When and where such grace and faith do manifest themselves by
their effects, we ought readily to own and embrace them. But the
only inquiry in this matter is, what those that are utterly destitute
of the revelation of Jesus Christ, either as made originally in the
promise or as explained in the gospel, may, under the mere conduct
of the light of nature, as consisting of the innate principles of reason,
with their improvement, or as increased by the consideration of the
effects of divine power and providence, by the strength and exercise
of their own moral principles, attain unto, as unto their present acceptance with God and future eternal salvation? That they may be
saved in every sect who live exactly according to the light of nature,
is a doctrine anathematized by the church of England, article xviii.;
and the reason given hereof is, because the Scriptures propose the
name of Jesus Christ alone whereby we may be saved. And if we
do believe that description which is given in the Scripture of men,
their moral abilities and their works, as they lie in the common state
of mankind since the entrance of sin, with respect unto God and
salvation, we shall not be able to be of another mind: for they are
said to be "blind," Luke iv. 18; yea, to be "darkness," to be "dead in
trespasses and sins," not to "receive the things of the Spirit of God,
because they are foolishness unto them," and their minds to be "enmity against God" himself, Acts xxvi. 18; Eph. ii. 1–3, iv. 18; Rom.
viii. 7. That there may be any just expectation concerning such persons, that they will "work out their salvation with fear and trembling,"
we are not convinced; neither do we think that God will accept of a
more imperfect obedience in them that know not Jesus Christ than
he requires of them who do believe in him, for then should he prove a
disadvantage unto them. Besides, all their best works are severely reflected on in the Scripture, and represented as unprofitable; for whereas
in themselves they are compared to evil trees, thorns, and briers, we
are assured they neither do nor can bring forth good grapes or figs.
Besides, in the Scripture the whole business of salvation, in the first
place, turns upon the hinge of faith supernatural and divine: for "without faith it is impossible to please God," and " he that believeth not
shall be damned;" " he that believeth not in the name of the Son of
God is condemned already;" for " neither circumcision availeth any
thing, nor uncircumcision, but faith which worketh by love;" and it is
"by faith that the just shall live," Heb. xi. 6, [Mark xv. 16,] John iii.
18, 36, Gal. v. 6, [Hab. ii. 4.] That this faith may be educed out of
the obediential principles of nature was, indeed, the opinion of Pelagius

of old; but it will not now, we hope, be openly asserted by any. Moreover, this faith is in the Scripture, if not limited and determined, yet directed unto Jesus Christ as its necessary peculiar object: "For this is life eternal, that we may know the only true God, and Jesus Christ, whom he hath sent." It seems, therefore, that the knowledge of the only true God is not sufficient to attain eternal life, unless the knowledge of Jesus Christ also do accompany it; for "this is the record, that God hath given to us eternal life, and this life is in his Son. He that hath the Son hath life; and he that hath not the Son of God hath not life," 1 John v. 11, 12; which is enough to determine the controversy. And those assertions, that "there is none other name given among men whereby they must be saved," and that "other foundation can no man lay than that is laid, which is Jesus Christ," Acts iv. 12, 1 Cor. iii. 11, are of the same importance; and it were needless to multiply the testimonies that are given us to that purpose elsewhere. Neither can it be made to appear that the concatenation of the saving means, whereby men that are adult are brought unto glory, is not absolutely universal; and amongst them there is vocation, or an effectual calling (Rom. viii. 29, 30) to the knowledge of Christ by the gospel. Neither will the same apostle allow a saving invocation of the name of God to any but those that are brought to believe by hearing the word preached, Rom. x. 13–15. It is said that God may, by ways secret and unknown to us, reveal Jesus Christ to them, and so by faith in him sanctify their natures and endow them with his Spirit; which things it is granted, we suppose, are indispensably necessary unto salvation. Those whom God thus deals withal are not Pagans but Christians, concerning whom none ever doubted but they might be saved. It is also granted that men may learn much of the power, wisdom, and goodness of God, which both require and teach many duties to be performed towards him; but withal, we believe that without the internal sanctification of the Spirit, communicated by and with the knowledge of Jesus Christ, no man can be saved. But we intend not here to dispute about these things. Instead of an effect of love and charity, it is manifest that the opinion which grants salvation unto the heathen, or any of them, upon the due improvement of their rational faculties and moral principles, ariseth from a want of due consideration of the true nature of sin and grace, of the fall of man and his recovery, of the law and gospel, and of the wisdom and love of God in sending Jesus Christ to make atonement for sinners, and to bring in everlasting righteousness. And not only so, but it evidently prepares the way unto those noxious opinions which at this day among many infest and corrupt Christian religion, and foment those seeds of atheism which spring up so fast as to threaten the overspreading of the whole field of Christianity; for hence it will follow, by an easy deduction, that every one may be saved, or attain unto his utmost happiness, in his own religion, be it what it will, whilst under any notion or conception he acknowledgeth a divine Being, and his own dependence thereon. And seeing that, on this supposition, it must be confessed that religion consists solely in moral honesty, and a fancied internal piety of mind towards the Deity (for in nothing else can a centring of all religions in the world unto a certain end be imagined), it follows that there is no outward profession of it indispensably necessary, but that every man may take up and make use of that which is best suited unto his interest in his present condition and circumstances And as this, being once admitted, will give the minds of men an indifferency as unto the several religions that are in the world, so it will quickly produce in them a contempt of them all. And, from an entertainment of, or an indifferency of mind about, these and the like noisome opinions, it is come to pass that the gospel, after a continued triumph for sixteen hundred years over hell and the world, doth at this day, in the midst of Christendom, hardly with multitudes maintain the reputation of its truth and divinity; and is by many, living in a kind of outward conformity unto the institutes of Christian religion, despised and laughed to scorn. But the proud and foolish atheistical opiniators of our days, whose sole design is to fortify themselves by the darkness of their minds against the charges of their own conscience upon their wicked and debauched conversations, do but expose themselves to the scorn of all sober and rational persons; for what are a few obscure, and, for the most part, vicious renegadoes, in comparison of those great, wise, numerous, and sober persons, whom the gospel, in its first setting forth in the world, by the evidence of its truth and the efficacy of its power, subdued and conquered? Are they as learned as the renowned philosophers of those days, who, advantaged by the endeavours and fruits of all the great wits of former ages, had advanced solid, rational literature to the greatest height that ever it attained in this world, or possibly ever will do so, the minds of men having now something more excellent and noble to entertain themselves withal? Are they to be equalled in wisdom and experience with those glorious emperors, senators, and princes who then swayed the sceptres and affairs of the world? Can they produce any thing to oppose unto the gospel that is likely to influence the minds of men in any degree comparably to the religion of these great, learned, wise, and mighty personages; which, having received by their fathers from days immemorial, was visibly attended with all earthly glories and prosperities, which were accounted as the reward of their due observance of it? And yet, whereas there was a conspiracy of all those persons, and this influenced by the craft of infernal powers, and managed with all that wisdom, subtlety, power, and cruelty that the nature of man is capable to exercise, on purpose to oppose the gospel, and keep it from taking root in the world; yet, by the glorious evidence of its divine extract and original wherewith it is accompanied, by the efficacy and power which God gave the doctrine of it in and over the minds of men, all managed by the spiritual weapons of its preachers, which were " mighty through God to the pulling down of those strongholds, casting down imaginations, and every high thing that exalted itself against the knowledge of God," 2 Cor. x. 4, 5, it prevailed against them all, and subdued the world unto an acknowledgment of its truth, with the divine power and authority of its Author. Certainly there is nothing more contemptible than that the indulgence of some inconsiderable persons unto their lusts and vices, who are void of all those excellencies, in notion and practice, which have already been triumphed over by the gospel when set up in competition with it or opposition unto it, should be once imagined to bring it into question or to cast any disreputation upon it. But to treat of these things is not our present design; we have only mentioned them occasionally, in the account which it was necessary we should give concerning our love to all men in general, with the grounds we proceed upon in the exercise of it.

CHAPTER III.

Nature of the catholic church—The first and principal object of Christian love—
Differences among the members of this church, of what nature, and how to
be managed—Of the church catholic as visibly professing—The extent of it,
or who belong unto it—Of union and love in this church-state—Of the church
of England with respect hereunto—Of particular churches; their institution;
corruption of that institution—Of churches diocesan, etc.—Of separation
from corrupt particular churches—The just causes thereof, etc.

IN the *second sort of mankind,* before mentioned, consists the visible kingdom of Christ in this world. This being grounded in his death and resurrection, and conspicuously settled by his sending of the Holy Ghost after his ascension, he hath ever since preserved in the world against all the contrivances of Satan or opposition of the gates of hell, and will do so unto the consummation of all things; for " he must reign until all his enemies are made his footstool." Towards these, on all accounts, our love ought to be intense and fervent, as that which is the immediate bond of our relation unto them and union with them. And this kingdom or church of Christ on the earth may be, and is generally, by all considered under a threefold notion:—FIRST, As therein, and among the members of it, is comprised that *real living and spiritual body of his*, which is firstly, peculiarly, and properly the *catholic church* militant in this world. These are his elect, redeemed, justified, and sanctified ones, who are savingly united unto their head by the same quickening and sancti-fying Spirit, dwelling in him in all fulness, and communicated unto them by him according to his promise. This is that catholic church which we profess to believe; which being hid from the eyes of men, and absolutely invisible in its mystical form, or spiritual saving rela-tion unto the Lord Christ and its unity with him, is yet more or less always visible by that profession of faith in him and obedience unto him which it maketh in the world, and is always obliged so to do: " For with the heart man believeth unto righteousness; and with the mouth confession is made unto salvation," Rom. x. 10. And this church we believe to be so disposed over the whole world, that wherever there are any societies or numbers of men who ordi-narily profess the gospel, and subjection to the kingly rule of Christ thereby, with a hope of eternal blessedness by his mediation, we no way doubt but that there are among them some who really belong thereunto. In and by them doth the Lord Christ continually fulfil and accomplish the promise of his presence by his Spirit with them that believe in his name; who are thereby interested in all the pri-vileges of the gospel, and authorized unto the administration and participation of all the holy ordinances thereof. And were it not that we ought not to boast ourselves against others, especially such as have not had the spiritual advantages that the inhabitants of these nations have been intrusted withal, and who have been ex-posed unto more violent temptations than they, we should not fear to say, that among those of all sorts who in these nations hold the Head, there is probably, according unto a judgment to be made by the fruits of that Spirit which is savingly communicated unto the church in this sense alone, a greater number of persons belonging thereunto than in any one nation or church under heaven. The charge therefore of some against us that we paganize the nation, by reason of some different apprehensions from others concerning the regular constitution of particular churches for the celebration of gos-pel worship, is wondrous vain and ungrounded. But we know that men use such severe expressions and reflections out of a discomposed habit of mind, which they have accustomed themselves unto, and not from a sedate judgment and consideration of the things themselves; and hence they will labour to convince others of that whereof, if they would put it unto a serious trial, they would never be able to convince themselves.

This, then, is that church which, on the account of their sincere

faith and obedience, shall be saved, and out of which, on the account
of their profession, there is no salvation to be obtained: which things
are weakly and arrogantly appropriated unto any particular church
or churches in the world; for it is possible that men may be members
of it, and yet not belong or relate unto any particular church on the
earth; and so it often falleth out, as we could manifest by instances,
did that work now lie before us.   This is the church which the
Lord Christ "loved and gave himself for; that he might sanctify
and cleanse it with the washing of water by the word, that he might
present it unto himself a glorious church, not having spot, or
wrinkle, or any such thing; but that it should be holy and without
blemish," Eph. v. 26, 27.   And we must acknowledge that in all
things this is the church unto which we have our first and principal
regard, as being the spring from which all other considerations of
the church do flow.   Within the verge and compass of it do we
endeavour to be found, the end of the dispensation of the gospel
unto men being that they should do so.   Neither would we, to save
our lives (which, for the members of this church and their good, we
are bound to lay down, 1 John iii. 16, when justly called thereunto),
wilfully live in the neglect of that love towards them or any of them
which we hope God hath planted in our hearts, and made natural
unto us, by that one and self-same Spirit, by whom the whole mystical body of Christ is animated.   We do confess, that, because the
best of men in this life do know but in part, all the members of
this church are in many things liable to error, mistakes, and miscarriages; and hence it is that, although they are all internally acted and
guided by the same Spirit in all things absolutely necessary to their
eternal salvation, and do all attend unto the same rule of the word,
according as they apprehend the mind of God in it and concerning
it, have all, for the nature and substance of it, the same divine faith
and love, and are all equally united unto their Head, yet, in the profession which they make of the conceptions and persuasions of their
minds about the things revealed in the Scripture, there are, and
always have been, many differences among them.   Neither is it
morally possible it should be otherwise, whilst in their judgment
and profession they are left unto the ability of their own minds and
liberty of their wills, under that great variety of the means of light
and truth, with other circumstances, whereinto they are disposed by
the holy wise providence of God.   Nor hath the Lord Christ absolutely promised that it shall be otherwise with them; but securing
them all by his Spirit in the foundations of eternal salvation, he
leaves them in other things to the exercise of mutual love and forbearance, with a charge of duty after a continual endeavour to grow
up unto a perfect union, by the improvement of the blessed aids and

assistances which he is pleased to afford unto them. And those who, by ways of force, would drive them into any other union or agreement than their own light and duty will lead them into, do what in them lies to oppose the whole design of the Lord Christ towards them and his rule over them. In the meantime, it is granted that they may fall into divisions, and schisms, and mutual exasperations among themselves, through the remainders of darkness in their minds and the infirmity of the flesh, Rom. xiv. 3; and in such cases mutual judgings and despisings are apt to ensue, and that to the prejudice and great disadvantage of that common faith which they do profess. And yet, notwithstanding all this (such cross-entangled wheels are there in the course of our nature), they all of them really value and esteem *the things wherein they agree* incomparably above those wherein they differ. But their valuation of the matter of their union and agreement is purely spiritual, whereas their differences are usually influenced by carnal and secular considerations, which have, for the most part, a sensible impression on the minds of poor mortals. But so far as their divisions and differences are unto them unavoidable, the remedy of farther evils proceeding from them is plainly and frequently expressed in the Scripture. It is love, meekness, forbearance, bowels of compassion, with those other graces of the Spirit wherein our conformity unto Christ doth consist, with a true understanding and the due valuation of the " unity of faith," and the common hope of believers, which are the ways prescribed unto us for the prevention of those evils which, without them, our unavoidable differences will occasion. And this excellent way of the gospel, together with a rejection of evil surmises, and a watchfulness over ourselves against irregular judging and censuring of others, together with a peaceable walking in consent and unity so far as we have attained, is so fully and clearly proposed unto us therein, that they must have their eyes blinded by prejudices and carnal interests, or some effectual working of the god of this world on their minds, into whose understandings the light of it doth not shine with uncontrollable evidence and conviction. That the sons or children of this church, of " Jerusalem which is above, and is the mother of us all," should, on the account of their various apprehensions of some things relating to religion or the worship of God, unavoidably attending their frail and imperfect condition in this world, yea, or of any schisms or divisions ensuing thereon, proceeding from corrupt and not thoroughly mortified affections, be warranted to hate, judge, despise, or condemn one another, much more to strive by external force to coerce, punish, or destroy them that differ from them, is as foreign to the gospel as that we should believe in Mohammed and not in Jesus Christ. Whatever share, therefore, we are forced to bear in differences with or divisions from the members of this church (that is, any who declare and evidence themselves so to be by a visible and regular profession of faith and obedience), as it is a continual sorrow and trouble unto us, so we acknowledge it to be our duty (and shall be willing to undergo any blame, where we are found defective in the discharge of it, unto the utmost of our power) to endeavour after the strictest communion with them in all spiritual things that the gospel doth require, or whereof our condition in this world is capable. In the meantime, until this can be attained, it is our desire to manage the profession of our own light and apprehensions without anger, bitterness, clamour, evil speaking, or any other thing that may be irregular in ourselves or give just cause of offence unto others. Our prayers are also continually for the spiritual prosperity of this church, for its increase in faith and holiness, and especially for the healing of all breaches that are among them that belong thereunto throughout the world. And were we not satisfied that the principles which we own about the right constitution of the churches of Christ, and the worship of God to be observed in them, are singularly suited to the furtherance and preservation of union and due order among all the members of this church, we should not need to be excited by any unto their renunciation. But our main design in all these things is, that both they and we with them may enjoy that peace which the Lord Christ hath bequeathed unto us, and walk in the way which he hath prescribed for us. And these things we mention, neither to boast of nor yet to justify ourselves, but only to acknowledge what is our conviction concerning our duty in this matter. And might there any sedate, peaceable, unprejudicate endeavours be countenanced and encouraged, for the allaying of all occasional distempers and the composing of all differences among them who belong to this church of Christ, so as that they might all of them (at least in these nations) not only " keep the unity of the Spirit in the bond of peace," but also agree and consent in all ways and acts of religious communion, we doubt not to manifest that no rigid adherence unto the practice of any conceptions of our own, in things wherein the gospel alloweth a condescension and forbearance, no delight in singularity, no prejudice against persons or things, should obstruct us in the promotion of it to the utmost of our power and ability. Upon the whole matter, we own it as our duty to follow and seek after peace, unity, consent and agreement in holy worship, with all the members of this church, or those who, by a regular profession, manifest themselves so to be; and will, with all readiness and alacrity, renounce every principle or practice that is either inconsistent with such communion, or directly or indirectly is in itself obstructive of it.

SECONDLY, The church of Christ may be considered with respect unto its *outward profession*, as constitutive of its being, and the formal reason of its denomination. And this is the church catholic visible, whereunto they all universally belong who profess the invocation of the name of our Lord Jesus Christ, their Lord and ours, under the limitations that shall be mentioned afterward. And this is the visible kingdom of Christ; which, on the account of its profession, and thereby, is distinguished from that world which lieth in evil and is absolutely under the power of Satan. And so in common use the church and the world are contradistinguished. Yet, on other accounts, many who belong unto this church, by reason of some kind of profession that they make, may justly be esteemed to be the world, or of it. So our Lord Jesus Christ called the generality of the professing church in his time. " The world," saith he, " hateth me," John xvii. 18, 19, 25. And that we may know that he thereby intended the church of the Jews, besides that the circumstances of the place evince it, he puts it out of question by the testimony which he produceth in the confirmation of his assertion concerning their unjust and causeless hatred,—namely, " It is written in their law, They hated me without a cause;" which, being taken out of the Psalms (Ps. xxxv. 19), was part of the law or rule of the Judaical church only. Now, he thus terms them, because the generality of them, especially their rulers, although they professed to know God, and to worship him according to his word and the tradition of their fathers, yet were not only corrupt and wicked in their lives, but also persecuted him and his disciples, in whom the power and truth of God were manifested beyond what they were able to bear. And hence a general rule is established: That what profession soever any men do make of the knowledge and worship of God, to what church soever they do or may be thought to belong, yet if they are wicked or ungodly in their lives, and persecutors of such as are better than themselves, they are really of the world, and with it will perish, without repentance. These are they who, receiving on them a form or delineation of godliness, do yet deny the power of it; from whom we are commanded to "turn away." But yet we acknowledge that there is a real difference to be made between them who in any way or manner make profession of the name of Christ, with subjection unto him, and that infidel world by whom the gospel is totally rejected, or to whom it was never tendered.

In this *catholic visible church*, as comprehensive of all who throughout the world outwardly own the gospel, there is an acknowledgment of " one Lord, one faith, one baptism:" which are a sufficient foundation of that love, union, and communion among them, which they are capable of, or are required of them; for in the joint pro-

fession of the same Lord, faith, and baptism, consists the union of
the church under this consideration,—that is, as catholic and visibly
professing,—and in nothing else.   And hereunto also is required, as
the principle animating that communion, and rendering it acceptable, mutual love with its occasional exercise, as a fruit of that love
which we have unto Jesus Christ, who is the object of our common
profession.   And setting aside the consideration of them who openly
reject the principal fundamentals of Christian religion (as denying
the Lord Christ to be the eternal Son of God, with the use and
efficacy of his death, as also the personal subsistence and deity of
the Holy Spirit), there is no known community of these professors in the world but they own so much of the truths concerning
" one Lord, one faith, and one baptism," as is sufficient to guide
them unto life and salvation.   And thereon we no way doubt but
that among them all there are some really belonging to the purpose
of God's election, who by the means that they do enjoy shall at
length be brought unto everlasting glory: for we do not think that
God, by his providence, would maintain the dispensation of the gospel in any place, or among any people, among whom there are none
whom he hath designed to bring into the enjoyment of himself; for
that is the rule of his sending and continuing of it, whereon he enjoined the apostle Paul to stay in such places where he had "much
people" whom he would have to be converted, Acts xviii. 9–11.
He would not continue from generation to generation to scatter his
pearls where there were none but rending swine, nor send fishers
unto waters wherein he knew there were nothing but serpents and
vipers.   It is true the gospel, as preached unto many, is only a testimony against them, Matt. xxiv. 14, leaving them without excuse,
and proves unto them " a savour of death unto death."   But the
first, direct, and principal design of the dispensation of it being the
conversion of souls and their eternal salvation, it will not probably be
continued in any place, nor is so, where this design is not pursued
nor accomplished towards any; neither will God make use of it anywhere merely for the aggravation of men's sins and condemnation;
nor would his so doing consist with the honour of the gospel itself, or
the glory of that love and grace which it professeth to declare.
Where it is indeed openly rejected, there that shall be the condemnation of men; but where it finds any admittance, there it hath somewhat of its genuine and proper work to effect.   And the gospel is
esteemed to be in all places dispensed and admitted, where, the
Scripture being received as the word of God, men are, from the light,
truth, and doctrine contained therein, by any means so far instructed
as to take upon them the profession of subjecting their souls to Jesus
Christ, and of observing the religious duties by him prescribed, in

opposition to all false religions in the world. Amongst all these the foundations of saving faith are at this day preserved; for they universally receive the whole canonical Scripture, and acknowledge it to be the word of God, on such motives as prevail with them to do so sincerely. Herein they give a tacit consent unto the whole truth contained in it, for they receive it as from God, without exception or limitation; and this they cannot do without a general renunciation of all the falsities and evils that it doth condemn. Where these things concur, men will not believe nor practise any thing in religion but what they think God requires of them and will accept from them. And we find it also in the event, that all the persons spoken of, wherever they are, do universally profess that they believe in the God and Father of our Lord Jesus Christ, and in his only and eternal Son. They all look, also, for salvation by him, and profess obedience unto him, believing that God raised him from the dead. They believe, in like manner, that the Holy Spirit is the Spirit of the Father and the Son, with many other sacred truths of the same importance; as also, that " without holiness no man shall see the Lord." However, therefore, they are differenced and divided among themselves, however they are mutually esteemed heretics and schismatics, however, through the subtlety of Satan, they are excited and provoked to curse and persecute one another with wonderful folly, and by an open contradiction unto other principles which they profess; yet are they all subjects of the visible kingdom of Christ, and belong all of them to the catholic church, making profession of the name of Christ in the world, in which there is salvation to be obtained, and out of which there is none.

We take not any consideration at present of that absurd, foolish, and uncharitable error, which would confine the catholic church of Christ unto a particular church of one single denomination, or, indeed, rather unto a combination of some persons in an outward mode of religious rule and worship; whereof the Scripture is as silent as of things that never were, nor ever shall be. Yea, we look upon it as intolerable presumption, and the utmost height of uncharitableness, for any to judge that the constant profession of the name of Christ made by multitudes of Christians, with the lasting miseries and frequent martyrdoms which for his sake they undergo, should turn unto no advantage, either of the glory of God or their own eternal blessedness, because in some things they differ from them. Yet such is the judgment of those of the church of Rome, and so are they bound to judge by the fundamental principles and laws of their church-communion. But men ought to fear lest they should meet with "judgment without mercy, who have shewed no mercy," James ii. 13. Had we ever entertained a thought uncharitable to such a prodigy of insolence, had we ever excluded any sort of Christians absolutely from an interest in the love of God or grace in Jesus Christ, or hope of salvation, because they do not or will not comply with those ways and terms of outward church-communion which we approve of, we should judge ourselves as highly criminal, in want of Christian love, as any can desire to have us esteemed so to be.

It is, then, the universal collective body of them that profess the gospel throughout the world which we own as the catholic church of Christ. How far the errors in judgment, or miscarriages in sacred worship, which any of them have superadded unto the foundations of truth which they do profess, may be of so pernicious a nature as to hinder them from an interest in the covenant of God, and so prejudice their eternal salvation, God only knows. But those notices which we have concerning the nature and will of God in the Scriptures, as also of the love, care, and compassion of Jesus Christ, with the ends of his mediation, do persuade us to believe that where men in sincerity do improve the abilities and means of the knowledge of divine truth wherewith they are intrusted, endeavouring withal to answer their light and convictions with a suitable obedience, there are but few errors of the mind of so malignant a nature as absolutely to exclude such persons from an interest in eternal mercy. And we doubt not but that men, out of a zeal to the glory of God, real or pretended, have imprisoned, banished, killed, burned others for such errors as it hath been the glory of God to pardon in them, and which he hath done accordingly. But this we must grant, and do, that those whose lives and conversations are no way influenced by the power of the gospel, so as to be brought to some conformity thereunto, or who, under the covert of a Christian profession, do give themselves up unto idolatry and persecution of the true worshippers of God, are no otherwise to be esteemed but as enemies to the cross of Christ; for as " without holiness no man shall see the Lord," so " no idolater or murderer hath eternal life abiding in him," Heb. xii. 14; Rev. xxi. 8; 1 John iii. 15.

With respect unto these things we look upon the church of England, or the generality of the nation professing Christian religion (measuring them by the doctrine that hath been preached unto them and received by them since the Reformation), to be as sound and healthful a part of the catholic church as any in the world; for we know no place nor nation where the gospel for so long a season hath been preached with more diligence, power, and evidence for conviction, nor where it hath obtained a greater success or acceptation. Those, therefore, who perish amongst us, do not do so for want of truth and a right belief, or miscarriages in sacred worship, but for their own personal infidelity and disobedience; for according to the rules before laid down, we do not judge that there are any such errors publicly admitted among them, nor any such miscarriages in sacred administration, as should directly or absolutely hinder their eternal salvation. That they be not any of them, through the ignorance or negligence of those who take upon them the conduct of their souls, encouraged in a state or way of sin, or deprived of due advantages to further their spiritual good, or led into practices in religion neither acceptable unto God nor tending to their own edification, whereby they may be betrayed into eternal ruin, is greatly incumbent on themselves to consider.

Unto this catholic church we owe all Christian love, and are obliged to exercise all the effects of it, both towards the whole and every particular member, as we have advantage and occasion. And not only so, but it is our duty to live in constant communion with it. This we can no otherwise do but by a profession of that faith whereby it becomes the church of Christ in the notion under consideration. For any failure herein we are not, that we know of, charged by any persons of modesty or sobriety. The reflections that have been made of late by some on the doctrines we teach or own, do fall as severely on the generality of the church of England (at least until within a few years last past) as they do on us; and we shall not need to own any especial concernment in them until they are publicly discountenanced by others. Such are the doctrines concerning God's eternal decrees, justification by faith, the loss of original grace, and the corruption of nature, the nature of regeneration, the power and efficacy of grace in the conversion of sinners, that we say not of the Trinity and satisfaction of Christ. But we do not think that the doctrines publicly taught and owned among us ever since the Reformation will receive any great damage by the impotent assaults of some few, especially considering their management of those assaults by tales, railing, and raillery, to the lasting reproach of the religion which themselves profess, be it what it will.

THIRDLY, The church of Christ, or the visible professors of the gospel in the world, may be considered as they are disposed of by providence, or their own choice, in *particular churches*. These at present are of many sorts, or are esteemed so to be; for whereas the Lord Christ hath instituted sundry solemn ordinances of divine worship to be observed jointly by his disciples, unto his honour and their edification, this could not be done but in such societies, communities, or assemblies of them to that purpose. And as none of them can be duly performed but in and by such societies, so some of them do either express the union, love, and common hope that is among them, or do consist in the means of their preservation. Of this latter sort are all the ways whereby the power of Christ is acted in the discipline of the churches. Wherefore, we believe that our Lord Jesus Christ, as the king, ruler, and lawgiver of his church, hath ordained that all his disciples, all persons belonging unto his church in the former notion of it, should be gathered into distinct societies, and become as flocks of sheep in several folds, under the eye of their great Shepherd and the respective conducts of those employed under him. And this conjunction of professors in and unto particular churches, for the celebration of the ordinances of sacred worship appointed by Christ, and the participation of his institutions for their edification, is not a matter of accident, or merely under the disposal of common providence, but is to be an act in them of choice and voluntary obedience unto the commands of Christ. By some this duty is more expressly attended unto than by others, and by some it is totally neglected; for neither antecedently nor consequentially unto such their conjunction do they consider what is their duty unto the Lord Christ therein, nor what is most meet for their own edification. They go on in these things with others, according to the customs of the times and places wherein they live, confounding their civil and spiritual relations. And these we cannot but judge to walk irregularly, through ignorance, mistakes, or prejudices. Neither will they in their least secular concernments behave themselves with so much regardlessness or negligence; for however their lot previously unto their own choice may be cast into any place or society, they will make an after-judgment whether it be to their advantage, according to the rules of prudence, and by that judgment either abide in their first station, or otherwise dispose of themselves. But a liberty of this nature, regulated by the gospel, to be exercised in and about the great concernments of men's souls, is by many denied and by most neglected. Hence it is come to pass that the societies of Christians are for the most part mere effects of their political distributions by civil laws, aiming principally at other ends and purposes. It is not denied but that civil distributions of professors of the gospel may be subservient unto the ends of religious societies and assemblies; but when they are made a means to take off the minds of men from all regard to the authority of the Lord Christ instituting and appointing such societies, they are of no small disadvantage unto true church communion and love.

The institution of these churches, and the rules for their disposal and government throughout the world, are the same,—stable and unalterable. And hence there was in the first churches, planted by the apostles, and those who next succeeded them in the care of that work, great peace, union, and agreement; for they were all gathered and planted alike, according unto the institution of Christ, all regulated and ordered by the same common rule. Men had not yet found out those things which were the causes of differences in after ages, and which yet continue so to be. Where there was any difference, it was for the most part on the account of some noisome, foolish, fantastical opinions, vented by impostors, in direct opposition to the Scripture; which the generality of Christians did with one consent abhor. But on various occasions, and by sundry degrees, there came to be great variety in the conceptions of men about these particular churches appointed for the seat and subject of all gospel ordinances, and wherein they were authoritatively to be administered in the name of Jesus Christ; for the church in neither of the former notions is capable of such administrations. Some, therefore, rested in particular assemblies, or such societies who did or might meet together under the guidance and inspection of their own elders, overseers, guides, or bishops, Acts xiv. 23, xx. 28; 1 Pet. v. 1–3; Acts xv. 2; Phil. i. 1. And hereunto they added the occasional meetings of those elders and others, to advise and determine in common about the especial necessities of any particular church, or the general concernments of more of them, as the matter might require. These in name, and some kind of resemblance, are continued throughout the world in parochial assemblies. Others suppose a particular church to be such a one as is now called diocesan, though that name in its first use and application to church affairs was of a larger extent than what it is now applied unto, for it was of old the name of a patriarchal church. And herein the sole rule, guidance, and authoritative inspection of many, perhaps a multitude of particular churches, assembling for sacred worship and the administration of gospel ordinances distinctly, is committed unto one man, whom, in contradistinction from others, they call the Bishop: for the joining of others with him, or their subordination unto him in the exercise of jurisdiction, hinders not but that the sole ecclesiastical power of the diocese may be thought to reside in him alone; for those others do either act in his name or by power derived from him, or have no pretence unto any authority merely ecclesiastical, however in common use what they exercise may be so termed. But the nature of such churches, with the rule and discipline exercised in them and over them, is too well known to be here insisted on. Some rest not here, but unto these diocesan add metropolitan churches; which also are esteemed particular churches, though it be uncertain by what warrant or on what grounds. In these one person hath in some kind of resemblance a respect unto and over the diocesan bishops, like that which they have over the ministers of particular assemblies. But these things being animated and regulated by certain arbitrary rules and canons, or civil laws of the nations, the due bounds and extent of their power cannot be taken from any nature or constitution peculiar unto them; and therefore are there, wherever they are admitted, various degrees in their elevation. But how much or little the gospel is concerned in these things is easy for any one to judge; neither is it by wise men pretended to be so, any farther than that, as they suppose, it hath left such things to be ordered by human wisdom for an expediency unto some certain ends. One or more of these metropolitan churches have been required, in latter ages, to constitute a church national: though the truth is, that appellation had originally another occasion, whereunto the invention of these metropolitan churches was accommodated; for it arose not from any respect unto ecclesiastical order or rule, but unto the supreme political power, whereunto the inhabitants of such a nation as gives denomination to the church are civilly subject. Hence, that which was provincial at the first erection of this fabric, which was in the Romish empire whilst the whole was under the power of one monarch, became national when the several provinces were turned into kingdoms, with absolute sovereign power among themselves, wholly independent of any other. And he who, in his own person and authority, would erect an ecclesiastical image of that demolished empire, will allow of such provincial churches as have a dependence upon himself, but cares not to hear of such national churches as in their first notion include a sovereign power unto all intents and purposes within themselves: so the church of England became national in the days of King Henry VIII., which before was but provincial.

Moreover, the consent of many had prevailed that there should be patriarchal churches, comprehending under their inspection and jurisdiction many of these metropolitical and provincial churches. And these also were looked on as particular; for, from their first invention, there having been four or five of them, no one of them could be imagined to comprise the catholic church, although those who presided in them, according to the pride and vanity of the declining ages of the church, styled themselves Œcumenical and Catholic. Things being carried thus far, about the fifth and sixth century of years after Christ, one owned as principal or chief of this latter sort set up for a church denominated Papal, from a title he had appropriated unto himself; for by artifices innumerable he ceased not from endeavouring to subject all those other churches and their rulers unto himself, and by the advantage of his pre-eminence over the other patriarchs, as theirs over metropolitans, and so downwards, whereby all Christians were imagined to be comprised within the precincts of some of them, he fell into a claim of a sovereignty over the whole body of Christianity, and every particular member thereunto belonging. This he could have had no pretence for, but that he thought them cast into such an order as that he might possess

them on the same grounds on which that order itself was framed;
for had not diocesan, metropolitical, and patriarchal churches made
way for it, the thought of a church papal, comprehensive of all believers, had never befallen the minds of men; for it is known that
the prodigious empire which the pope claimed and had obtained
over Christianity, was an emergency .of the contests that fell out
amongst the leaders of the greater sorts of churches about the rights,
titles, and pre-eminencies among themselves, with some other occasional and intestine distempers.   Only, he had one singular advantage for the promotion of his pretence and desire; for whereas this
whole contignation of churches into all these storeys, in the top
whereof he emerged and lifted up himself, was nothing but an accommodation of the church and its affairs unto the government of
the Roman empire, or the setting up of an ecclesiastical image and
representation of its secular power and rule, the centring therein of
all subordinate powers and orders in one monarch inclined the minds
of men to comply with his design as very reasonable.   Hence, the
principal plea for that power over the whole church which at present
he claims lies in this, that the government of it ought to be mon-
archical.   And therein consists a chief part of the mystery of this
whole work, that whereas this fabric of church rule was erected in
imitation of and compliance with the Roman empire, so that he
could never effect his sovereignty whilst that empire stood in its
strength and union, under the command of one or more emperors
by consent, yet when that empire was destroyed, and the provinces
thereof became parcelled out unto several nations, who erected absolute independent sovereignties among themselves, he was able, by
the reputation he had before obtained, so to improve all emergencies
and advantages as to gather all these new kingdoms into one religious empire under himself, by their common consent.   In the meantime, by the original divisions of the empire, and the revolutions that
happened afterward amongst the nations of the world, the greatest
number of Christians were wholly unconcerned in this new church-
sovereignty, which was erected in the western provinces of that empire.   So was the mystery of iniquity consummated; for whereas the
pope, to secure his new acquisitions, endeavoured to empale the title
and privileges of the catholic church unto those Christians which professed obedience unto himself, unto an exclusion of a greater number, there ensued such a confusion of the catholic and a particular
church, as that both of them were almost utterly lost.

Concerning these several sorts of conceited particular churches, it
is evident that some of them, as to their nature and kind, have no
institution in or warrant from the Scripture, but were prudential
contrivances of the men of the days wherein they were first formed;

which they effected by various degrees, under the conduct of an apprehension that they tended unto the increase of concord and order among Christians. Whether really and effectually they have attained that end, the event hath long since manifested. And it will be one day acknowledged that no religious union or order among Christians will be lasting, and of spiritual use or advantage unto them, but what is appointed and designed for them by Jesus Christ. The truth is, the mutual intestine differences and contests among them who first possessed the rule of such churches, about their dignities, pre-eminencies, privileges, and jurisdictions, which first apparently let in pride, ambition, revenge, and hatred into the minds and lives of church guides, lost us the peace of Christendom; and the degeneracy of their successors more and more into a secular interest and worldly frame of spirit, is one great means of continuing us at a loss for its retrieval.

How far any man may be obliged in conscience unto communion with these churches in those things wherein they are such, and as such behave themselves in all their rule and administrations, may be inquired into by them who are concerned. What respect we have unto them, or what duty we owe them, as they may in any place be established by the civil laws of the supreme magistrate, is not of our present consideration. But whereas, in their original and rise, they have no other warrant but the prudential contrivance of some men, who unquestionably might be variously influenced by corrupt prejudices and affections in the finding out and management of their inventions, what ground there is for holding a religious communion with them, and wherein such communion may consist, is not easy to be declared; for the notion that the church-communion of the generality of Christians and ministers consists only in a quiet subjection unto them who, by any means, may pretend to be set over them and claim a right to rule them, is fond and impious. In the meantime, we wholly deny that the mistakes or disorders of Christians in complying with or joining themselves unto such churches as have no warrantable institution ought to be any cause of the diminishing of our love towards them, or of withdrawing it from them: for, notwithstanding their errors and wanderings from the paths of truth in this matter, they do or may continue interested in all that love which is due from us unto the church of Christ upon the double account before insisted on; for they may be yet persons born of God, united unto Christ, made partakers of his Spirit, and so belong to the church catholic mystical, which is the first principal object of all Christian love and charity. The errors wherewith they are supposed to be overtaken may befall any persons under those qualifications, the admittance of them, though culpable, being not inconsistent with a state of grace and acceptation with God. And they may also, by a due profession of the fundamental truths of the gospel, evince themselves to be professed subjects of the visible kingdom of Christ in the world, and so belong to the church catholic visibly professing; under which notion the disciples of Christ are in the next place commended unto our love. And it is the fondest imagination in the world, that we must of necessity want love towards all those with whom we cannot join in all acts of religious worship, or that there need be any schism between them and us on the sole account thereof, taking schism in the common received notion of it. If we bear unkindness towards them in our minds and hearts; if we desire or seek their hurt; if we persecute them, or put them to trouble in the world for their profession; if we pray not for them; if we pity them not in all their temptations, errors, or sufferings; if we say unto any of them when naked, " Be thou clothed," and when hungry, " Be thou fed," but relieve them not according unto our abilities and opportunities; if we have an aversion to their persons, or judge them any otherwise than as they cast themselves openly and visibly under the sentence of natural reason or Scripture rule,—we may be justly thought to fail in our love towards them. But if our hearts condemn us not in these things, it is not the difference that is or may be between them and us about church-constitutions or order that ought to be a cause, or can be an evidence, of any want of love on our parts. There will, indeed, be a distinct and separate practice in the things wherein the difference lies; which in itself, and without other avoidable evils, need not on either side to be schismatical. If by censures, or any kind of power, such churches or persons would force us to submit unto or comply with such things or ways in religious worship as are contrary unto our light, and which they have no authority from the Lord Christ to impose upon us, the whole state of the case is changed, as we shall see afterward.

As for those particular churches, which in any part of the world consist of persons assembling together for the worship of God in Christ, under the guidance of their own lawful pastors and teachers, we have only to say, that we are full well assured that " wherever two or three are gathered together in the name of Christ," there he is present with them; and farther than this, there are very few concerning whom we are called to pass any other censure or judgment. So we hope it is with them, and so we pray that it may be. And therefore we esteem it our duty to hold our communion with all these assemblies, when called thereunto; which is required of any Christians in the like cases and circumstances. Unless we are convinced that, with respect unto such or such instances, it is the mind of Christ that neither among ourselves, nor in conjunction with others, nor for the sake of the present communion with them, we should observe them in his worship, we judge ourselves under an obligation to make use of their assemblies in all acts of religion unto our edification, as occasion shall require. But where the authority of Christ in the things of sacred worship doth intervene, all other considerations must be discarded; and a compliance therewith will secure us from all irregular events.

It must be acknowledged that many of these churches have wofully degenerated, and that any of them may so do, both from their primitive institution and also the sole rule of their worship. And this they may do, and have done, in such various degrees and ways as necessarily requires a great variety in our judgments concerning them and our communion with them. The whole Christian world gives us instances hereof at this day; yea, we have it confirmed unto us in what is recorded concerning sundry churches mentioned in the Scripture itself. They were newly planted by the apostles themselves, and had rules given by them to attend unto for their direction; and, besides, they were obliged in all emergencies to inquire after and receive those commands and directions, which they were enabled infallibly to give unto them. And yet, notwithstanding these great advantages, we find that sundry of them were suddenly fallen into sinful neglects, disorders, and miscarriages, both in doctrine, discipline, and worship. Some of these were reproved and reformed by the great apostle, in his epistles written unto them for that end; and some of them were rebuked and threatened by the Lord Christ himself immediately from heaven, Rev. ii., iii. That in process of time they have increased in their degeneracy, waxing worse and worse, their present state and condition in the world, or the remembrance of them which are now not at all, with the severe dealings of God with them in his holy, wise providence, do sufficiently manifest. Yea, some of them, though yet continuing under other forms and shapes, have, by their superstition, false worship, and express idolatry, joined with wickedness of life and persecution of the true worshippers of Christ, as also by casting themselves into a new worldly constitution, utterly foreign unto what is appointed in the gospel, abandoned their interest in the state and rights of the churches of Christ. So are sundry faithful cities become harlots; and where righteousness inhabited, there dwell persecuting murderers. Such churches were planted of Christ wholly noble vines, but are degenerated into those that are bitter and wild. Whatever our judgment may be concerning the personal condition of the members of such apostatized churches, or any of them, all communion with them, as they would be esteemed the seat of gospel ordinances, and in their pretended administration of them, is unlawful for us, and it is our indispensable duty to separate from them : for whatever indifferency many may be growing into in matter of outward worship,—which ariseth from ignorance of the respect that is between the grace and institutions of Christ, as that from an apprehension that all internal religion consists in moral honesty only,—yet we know not any other way whereby we may approve ourselves faithful in our profession but in the observance of all whatever Christ hath commanded, Matt. xxviii. 20, and to abstain from what he condemns; for both our faith and love, whatever we pretend, will be found vain if we endeavour not to keep his commandments, John xv. 10, 14.

Such was the state of things in the church of Israel of old, after the defection under Jeroboam. It was no more a true church, nor any church at all, by virtue of positive institution; for they had neither priests, nor sacrifices, nor any ordinances of public worship, that God approved of. Hence it was the duty of all that feared God in the ten tribes not to join with the leaders and body of the people in their worship; as also to observe those sacred institutions of the law which were forbidden by them, in the order that they should not go up to Jerusalem, but attend unto all their sacred solemnities in the places where the calves were set up, 1 Kings xii. xiii., 2 Chron. xi. xiii. Accordingly, many of the most zealous professors among them, with the priests and Levites, and with a great multitude of the people, openly separated from the rest, and joined themselves unto Judah in the worship of God continued therein. Others amongst them secretly, in the worst of times, preserved themselves from the abominations of the whole people. In like manner under the New Testament, when some have deserved the title of "Babylon," because of their idolatry, false worship, and persecution, we are commanded to " come out from among them," in an open, visible, professed separation, that we be not partakers of their sins and plagues. But this judgment we are not to make, nor do make concerning any, but such as among whom idolatry spreads itself over the face of all their solemn assemblies, and who join thereunto the persecution of them who desire to worship God in spirit and in truth. The constitution of such churches, as to their being acceptable assemblies of worshippers before God, is lost and dissolved; neither is it lawful for any disciple of Christ to partake with them in their sacred administrations, for so to do is plainly to disown the authority of Christ, or to set up that of wicked and corrupt men above it.

Yet all this hinders not but that there may in such apostatical churches remain a profession of the fundamental truths of the gospel. And by virtue thereof, as they maintain the interest of Christ's visible kingdom in the world, so we no way doubt but that there may be many amongst them who, by a saving faith in the truths they do profess, do really belong to the mystical church of Christ.

An instituted church, therefore, may, by the *crimes and wickedness of its rulers* and the generality of its members, and their idolatrous administrations in holy things, utterly destroy their instituted estate, and yet not presently all of them cease to belong unto the kingdom of Christ: for we cannot say that those things which will certainly annul church administrations, and render them abominable, will absolutely destroy the salvation of all individual persons who partake in them; and many may secretly preserve themselves from being defiled with such abominations. So in the height of the degeneracy and apostasy of the Israelitish church, there were seven thousand who kept themselves pure from Baalish idolatry, of whom none were known to Elijah. And therefore did God still continue a respect unto them as his people, because of those secret ones, and because the token of his covenant was yet in their flesh, affording unto them an extraordinary ministry by his prophets, when the ordinary by priests and Levites was utterly ceased. This we are to hope concerning every place where there is any profession made of the name of Christ, seeing it was the passion of Elijah which caused him to oversee so great a remnant as God had left unto himself in the kingdom of Israel. And from his example we may learn, that good men may sometimes be more severe in their censures for God than he will be for himself.

Moreover, such as were baptized in those churches were not baptized into them as particular churches, nor initiated into them thereby; but the relation which ensued unto them thereon was unto the catholic church visible, together with a separation from the infidel world, lying wholly in darkness and evil, by a dedication unto the name of Christ. Upon a personal avowment of that faith whereinto they were baptized, they became complete members of that church. Whatever state they are hereby admitted into, whatever benefit or privilege they are personally interested in, they lose them not by the miscarriage of that particular church whereunto they do relate; yea, losing the whole advantage of an instituted church-state, they may still retain whatever belongs unto their faith and profession. Were baptism only an institution into a particular church, upon the failure of that church, baptism, as to all its benefits and privileges, must cease also. We do therefore own, that amongst those whose assemblies are rejected by Christ, because of their false worship and wickedness, there may be persons truly belonging to the mystical church of God, and that also by their profession are a portion of his visible kingdom in the world. How far they do consent unto the abominations of the churches whereunto they do belong, how far they have light against them, how far they do bewail them, how far they repent of them, what God will bear withal in them, we know not, nor are called to judge. Our love is to be towards them as persons relating unto Jesus Christ in the capacity mentioned; but all communion with them in the acts of false worship is forbidden unto us. By virtue also of that relation in which they still continue unto Christ and his church, as believers, they have power, and are warranted (as it is their duty), to reform themselves, and to join together anew in church order, for the due celebration of gospel ordinances, unto the glory of Christ and their own edification; for it is fond to imagine, that by the sins of others any disciples of Christ, in any place of the world, should be deprived of a right to perform their duty towards him, when it is discovered unto them. And these are our thoughts concerning such churches as are openly and visibly apostatical.

Again, there are *corruptions* that may befall or enter into churches, that are not of so heinous a nature as those before insisted on, especially if, as it often falls out, the whole lump be not leavened; if the whole body be not infected, but only some part or parts of it, which others more sound do resist and give their testimony against. And these may have none of the pernicious consequences before mentioned. Thus, many errors in doctrines, disorders and miscarriages in sacred administrations, irregular walking in conversation, with neglect or abuse of discipline in rulers, may fall out in some churches, which yet may be so far from evacuating their church state, as that they give no sufficient warrant unto any person immediately to leave their communion or to separate from them. The instances that may be given of the failings of some of the primitive churches in all these things, with the consideration of the apostolical directions given unto them on such occasions, render this assertion evident and uncontrollable. Nor do we in the least approve of their practice (if any such there be that are considerable), who, upon every failing in these things in any church, think themselves sufficiently warranted immediately of their own minds to depart from its communion. Much more do we condemn them who suffer themselves in these things to be guided by their own surmises and misapprehensions; for such there may be as make their own hasty conceptions to be the rule of all church administrations and communion,—who, unless they are in all things pleased, can be quiet nowhere. Wherefore, when any church, whereof a man is by his own consent antecedently a member, doth fall, in part or in whole, from any of those truths which it hath professed, or when it is overtaken with a neglect of discipline or irregularities in its administration, such a one is to consider that he is placed in his present state by divine Providence, that he may orderly therein endeavour to put a stop unto such defections, and to exercise his charity, love, and forbearance towards the persons of them whose miscarriages at present he cannot remedy. In such cases there is a large and spacious field for wisdom, patience, love, and prudent zeal to exercise themselves. And it is a most perverse imagination, that separation is the only cure for church disorders. All the gifts and graces of the Spirit bestowed on church members, to be exercised in their several stations at such a season,—all instructions given for their due improvement unto the good of the whole,—the nature, rules, and laws of all societies,—declare that all other remedies possible and lawful are to be attempted before a church be finally deserted. But these rules are to be observed provided always that it be judged unlawful for any persons, either for the sake of peace, or order, or concord, or on any other consideration, to join actually in any thing that is sinful, or to profess any opinion which is contrary to sound doctrine or the form of wholesome words, which we are bound to hold fast on all emergencies. And farther: if we may suppose, as sure enough we may, that such a church, so corrupted, shall *obstinately persist* in its errors, miscarriages, neglects, and maladministrations; that it shall refuse to be warned or admonished, or being so, by any means, shall wilfully reject and despise all instruction; that it will not bear with them that are yet sound in it, whether elders or members, in peaceable endeavours to reduce it unto the order of the gospel, but shall rather hurt, persecute, and seek their trouble for so doing, whereby their edification comes continually to be obstructed, and their souls to be hazarded, through the loss of truth and peace;—we no way doubt but that it is lawful for such persons to withdraw themselves from the communion of such churches, and that without any apprehension that they have absolutely lost their church-state, or are totally rejected by Jesus Christ; for the means appointed unto any end are to be measured and regulated according unto their usefulness unto that end. And let men's present apprehensions be what they will, it will one day appear that the end of all church order, rule, communion, and administrations, is, not the grandeur or secular advantage of some few, not outward peace and quietness, unto whose preservation the civil power is ordained; but the edification of the souls of men, in faith, love, and gospel obedience. Where, therefore, these things are so disposed of and managed as that they do not regularly further and promote that end, but rather obstruct it, if they will not be reduced unto their due order and tendency, they may be laid aside and made use of in another way. Much more may any refuse the communion of such churches, if they *impose on them* their corruptions, errors, failings, and mistakes, as the condition of their communion; for hereby they directly make themselves lords over the faith and worship of the disciples of Christ, and are void of all authority from him in what they so do or impose. And it is so far [from being true], that any men's withdrawing of themselves from the communion of such churches, and entering into a way of reformation for their own good, in obedience to the laws of Christ, should infer in them a want of love and peaceableness, or a spirit of division, that to do otherwise were to divide from Christ, and to cast out all true Christian love, embracing a cloud of slothful negligence and carelessness in the great concernments of the glory of God and their own souls in the room thereof. We are neither the authors nor the guides of our own love: he who implants and worketh it in us hath given us rules how it must be exercised, and that on all emergencies. It may work as regularly by sharp cutting rebukes as by the most silken and compliant expressions,—by manifesting an aversation from all that is evil, as by embracing and approving of what is good. In all things and cases it is to be directed by the word. And when, under the pretence of it, we leave that rule, and go off from any duty which we owe immediately unto God, it is will, pride, and self-conceit in us, and not love. And among all the exhortations that are given us in the Scripture unto unity and concord, as the fruits of love, there is not one that we should agree or comply with any in their sins or evil practices. But as we are commanded in ourselves to abstain " from all appearance of evil," so are we forbidden a participation in the sins of other men, and all " fellowship with the unfruitful works of darkness." Our love towards such churches is to work by pity, compassion, prayer, instructions; which are due means for their healing and recovery;—not by consent unto them or communion with them, whereby they may be hardened in the error of their way, and our own souls be subverted: for if we have not a due respect unto the Lord Christ and his authority, all that we have, or may pretend to have, unto any church is of no value; neither ought we to take into consideration any terms of communion whose foundation is not laid in a regard thereunto.

Moreover (as hath been declared), there is no such society of Christians in the world, whose assemblies, as to instituted worship, are rejected by Christ so that they have a bill of divorce given unto them, by the declaration of the will of the Lord Jesus to that purpose in the Scripture, but that, until they are utterly also, as it were, extirpate by the providence of God (as are many of the primitive plantations), we are persuaded of them that there are yet some secret, hidden ones among them, that belong unto the purpose of God's grace; for we do judge that wherever the name of Jesus Christ is called upon, there is salvation to be obtained, however the ways of it may be obstructed unto the most by their own sins and errors. They may also retain that profession which distinguisheth them from the infidel world. In these things we are still to hold communion with them, and on these accounts is our love to be continued unto them. Some kind of communion we may hold with them that are of no instituted or particular churches, or whose church-state is rejected, even as a person excommunicated is to be admonished as a brother. And some kind of communion we may lawfully refuse with some true churches; instances whereof shall be given afterward.

There is, therefore, no necessity that any should deny all them to be true churches from whom they may have just reason to withdraw their communion; for such as are so may require such things thereunto as it is not lawful for them to accept of or submit unto. What assemblies of Christians we behold visibly worshipping God in Christ, we take for granted to be true visible churches. And when we judge of our own communion with them, it is not upon this question, *whether they are true churches or no*, as though the determination of our practice did depend solely thereon: for as we are not called to judge of the being of their constitution, as to the substance of it, unless they are openly judged in the Scripture, as in the case of idolatry and persecution persisted in; so a determination of the truth of their constitution, or that they are true churches, will not presently resolve us in our duty as to communion with them, for the reasons before given. But in such a case two things are by us principally to be considered:—1. That nothing *sinful* in itself, or unto us, be required of us as the condition of communion. 2. That we may in such churches obtain the *immediate end of their institution* and our conjunction with them; which is our edification in faith, love, and obedience.

And the things whereof we have discoursed comprise our thoughts concerning those societies of Christians whose degeneracy from their primitive rule and institution is most manifest and notorious. Whilst there is any profession of the gospel, any subjection of souls unto Jesus Christ avowed, or any expectation of help from him continued among them, we cannot but hope that there are, in all of them, at least some few names that are "written in the Lamb's book of life," and which shall be saved eternally: for as a relation unto a particular visible church, walking according to the order and rule of the gospel, is the duty of every believer to give himself up unto, as that which is a means appointed and sanctified to the furtherance of his edification and salvation; so where it cannot be obtained, through invincible outward impediments, or is omitted through ignorance of duty, or is on just causes refused where opportunities make a tender of it, or where the being and benefit of it are lost through the apostasy of those churches whereunto any persons did belong, the utter want of it, and that always, is not such as necessarily infers the eternal loss of their souls who suffer under it.

Other churches there are in the world, which are not evidently guilty of the enormities, in doctrine, worship, and discipline, before discoursed of. These all we judge to be true churches of Christ, and do hope that his promised presence is with them in their assemblies. Answerable hereunto is our judgment concerning their officers or rulers, and all their sacred administrations. It becomes us to think and believe that the one have authority from Christ, and that the other are accepted with him; for it is most unwarrantable rashness and presumption, yea, an evident fruit of ignorance, or want of love, or secular, private interest, when upon lesser differences men judge churches to be no true churches, and their ministers to be no true ministers, and, consequently, all their administrations to be invalid. So do some judge of churches, because they have bishops; and so do more of others because they have none. But the validity or invalidity of the ordinances of Christ, which are the means of union and communion with him unto all his disciples, depend not on the determination of things highly disputable in their notion, and not inconsistent with true gospel obedience in their practice. And we are unduly charged with other apprehensions. God forbid that any such thought should ever enter into our hearts, as though the churches constituted in all things according unto our light, and the rules we apprehend appointed in the Scripture for that purpose, should be the only true churches in the world. They do but out of design endeavour to expose us to popular envy and hatred who invent and publish such things concerning us, or any of us. But whatever be the judgment of others concerning us, we intend not to take from thence any such provocation as might corrupt our judgments concerning them, nor to relieve ourselves by returning the like censures unto them as we receive from them. Scripture rule and duty must in these matters regulate our thoughts on all occasions. And whilst we judge others to be true churches, we shall not be much moved with their judgment that we are none, because we differ from them. We stand to the judgment of Christ and his word. We cannot but judge, indeed, that many churches have missed, and do miss, in some things, the precise rules of their due constitution and walking; that many of them have added useless, superfluous rites to the worship of God among them; that there is in many of them a sinful neglect of evangelical discipline, or a carnal rule erected in the stead of it; that errors in doctrines of importance and danger are prevalent in sundry of them; that their rulers are much influenced by a spirit of bitterness and envy against such as plead for reformation beyond their measure or interest;—yet that hereupon they should all or any of them immediately forfeit their church-state, so as to have no lawful ministers nor acceptable sacred administrations, is in itself a false imagination, and such as was never by us entertained.

In particular, as to those churches in Europe which are commonly called Reformed, we have the same thoughts of them, the same love towards them, the same readiness for communion with them, as we would desire any disciples of Christ in the world to have, bear, or exercise towards ourselves. If we are found negligent in any office of love towards them or any of their members,—in compassion, help, or assistance, or such supplies in outward or inward things as we have opportunity or ability for,—we are willing to bear the guilt of it as our sin, and the reproach of it as our shame. And herein we desire to fulfil the royal law, according to the Scripture, "Thou shalt love thy neighbour as thyself." The same we say concerning all the churches in England of the same mould and constitution with them; especially if it be true, which some say, that parochial churches are under a force and power, whereby they are enjoined the practice of sundry things and forbidden the performance of others, wherein the compliance of some is not over-voluntary nor pleasing to themselves. Neither is there a nullity or invalidity in the ordinances administered in them, any otherwise than as some render them ineffectual unto themselves by their unbelief. And this is the paganizing of England which some of us are traduced for! We believe that, among the visible professors in this nation, there is as great a number of sincere believers as in any nation under heaven; so that in it are treasured up a considerable portion of the invisible mystical church of Christ. We believe that the generality of the inhabitants of this nation are, by their profession, constituted an eminent part of the kingdom of Christ in this world. And we judge not, we condemn not, those who, walking according to their light and understanding in particular rites, do practise such things in the worship of God as we cannot comply withal; for we do not think that the things wherein they fail, wherein they miss or outgo the rule, are in their own nature absolutely destructive of their particular church-state. And what more can reasonably be required of us, or expected from us, in this matter, we know not. The causes of the distance that doth remain between us and them shall be afterward inquired into. For our duty in particular presential communion, at the celebration of the same individual ordinances, with such churches as are remote from us, in Asia or Africa, we shall, we hope, be directed to determine aright concerning it when we are called thereunto. In the meantime, what are our thoughts concerning them hath been before declared: to love them as subjects of the kingdom of Jesus Christ in the world, to pray for them that they may have all needful supplies of grace and the Holy Spirit from above, that God would send out his light and truth to guide them in their worship and obedience, and to help them in things spiritual and temporal, as we have opportunity, is the sum of the duty which is required in us towards them. Those we are more concerned in who are within the lines of our ordinary communication, among whom we walk and converse in the world. Unto any of these it is in the liberty and power of every believer to join himself, by his own consent. And no more is required hereunto, in the present constitution of churches among ourselves, but that a man remove his habitation, to comply with his own desires herein: and this choice is to be regulated by a judgment how a man may best improve and promote his own edification. We see not, therefore, how any man, with the least pretence of sobriety or modesty, can charge us with the want of an esteem and valuation of evangelical unity; for we embrace it on all the grounds that it is in the gospel recommended unto us. And we do know within what narrow bounds the charity. and unity of some are confined, who yet advantage themselves by a noise of their pretence. But that we do not in the least disturb, break, or dissent from the catholic church, either as it is invisible, in its internal form, by faith and the renovation of the Holy Ghost, or as visibly professing necessary, fundamental truths of the gospel, we have sufficiently evinced. And the principles laid down concerning particular churches, congregations, assemblies, or parishes, have not as yet been detected by any to spring from want of love, or to be obstructive of the exercise of it. Having, therefore, thus briefly given some account of what we conceive to be our duty in relation unto the whole church of God, we can with confidence and much assurance of mind own as dear a valuation of love, unity, and peaceableness in the profession of the gospel as any sort of professors whatever. And we are persuaded that our principles do as much tend and conduce unto the improvement of them as any that are or can be proposed unto that end; for we either do or are in a readiness to embrace every thing or way that the Lord Christ hath appointed or doth bless thereunto.

We doubt not, as hath been before acknowledged, but that there have been many failings and sinful miscarriages among all sorts of professors, who *separate*, or are rather driven from, the present public worship. There is no question but that in them all there are some remainders of the bitter root of corrupt affections, which, under the various temptations and provocations they have been exposed unto, hath brought forth fruit of an unpleasant relish. It is no new thing that irregular prejudices should be found acting themselves in professors of the gospel; it hath been so among them from the beginning. And we hope that, where there is or hath been any guilt of this nature, the reproofs which have been publicly given unto it (with what spirit or intention soever managed) may be useful to the amendment of them who have offended. But for our own parts, we must bear this testimony unto our sincerity, that we not only condemn but abhor all evil surmises among professors, all rash and uncharitable censures, all causeless aversations of mind and affections, all strife, wrath, anger, and debate, upon the account of different apprehensions and practices in and about the concerns of religious worship. Much more do we cast out all thoughts of judging men's eternal state and condition with respect unto such differences; nor do we, nor dare we, give countenance unto any thing that is in the least really opposite to love, peace, unity, or concord, amongst the disciples of Christ. And as we shall not excuse any of those extravagancies and intemperate heats, in words or otherwise, which some it may be have been guilty of, who, until their repentance, must bear their own judgment; so we will not make a recharge on others who differ in persuasion from us of the same or the like crimes; nor indeed need we so to do, their principles and practices, contrary unto all Christian love and charity, being written as with the beams of the sun. And we do not complain of our lot in the world,—that the appearance of such things in any of us would be esteemed a scandalous crime, which others that condemn them in us indulge in themselves without the least check or control. The law of this condition is put upon us by the profession which we do avow. Only, we are not willing that any should make advantage against us by their pleas for love, unity, and concord; as if, indeed, they were for peace, but that we make ourselves ready for war. Could they convince us that we come behind them in the valuation and seeking after these things by all ways and means blessed by Christ to that purpose, we should judge ourselves with a severity at least commensurate to the utmost they are able to exercise against us, whilst free from malice and evil designs. Only we must add, that there is no true measure of love to be taken by the accessions that men can make towards them who depart from truth. If it were so, those must be judged to abound most with it who can most comply with the practices of the church of Rome. But we are persuaded that such discourses, with the application of them unto those who differ from their authors, do proceed from sincerity in them; only, as we fear, somewhat leavened with an apprehension that their judgments and practices, being according unto truth, ought to be the standard and measure of other men's, perhaps no less sincere and confident of the truth than themselves, though differing from them. And hence it is unhappily fallen out, that, in the reproofs which some do manage on the foundations mentioned, and in the way of their management, many do suppose that there is as great an appearance, if not evidence, of evil surmises, ungrounded, temerarious censures; of self-conceit and elation of mind; of hard thoughts of, undue charges on, and the contempt of others;

and in all of a want of real love, condescension, and compassion, as
in any things that are true and to be really found among professors
blamed by them: for these things, both as charged and recharged,
have a double appearance.   Those from whom they proceed look on
them in the light of that sincerity and integrity which they are conscious of to themselves, wherein they seem amiable, useful, and free
from all offence; whereas others, that are concerned, viewing of them
in the disordered reflections of their opposition unto them, and the
disadvantage which they undergo by them, do apprehend them quite
of another nature.   And it is a matter of trouble unto us to find
that when some are severely handled for those principles and ways
wherein they can and do commend their consciences unto God,—and
thereby apprehending that their intentions, purposes, principles, and
affections, are injuriously traduced and perverted,—they fall with an
equal severity on them by whom they are reproved; though their
reproofs proceed from an equal sincerity unto what themselves profess and expect to be believed in.   Especially are such mutual reflections grievous and irksome unto men, when they apprehend that in
them or by them professed friends do industriously expose them to
the contempt and wrath of professed adversaries.

CHAPTER IV.

Want of love and unity among Christians justly complained of—Causes of divisions and schisms—1. Misapprehensions of evangelical unity—Wherein it
doth truly consist—The ways and means whereby it may be obtained and
preserved—Mistakes about both—2. Neglect in churches to attend unto
known gospel duty—Of preaching unto conversion and edification—Care of
those that are really godly—Of discipline: how neglected, how corrupted—
Principles seducing churches and their rulers into miscarriages: 1. Confidence of their place; 2. Contempt of the people; 3. Trust unto worldly
grandeur—Other causes of divisions—Remainders of corruption from the
general apostasy—Weakness and ignorance—Of readiness to take offence—
Remedies hereof—Pride—False teachers.

UPON the whole matter, it is generally acknowledged that there
is a great decay of love, a great want of peace and unity, among professors of the gospel in the world.   And it is no less evident nor less
acknowledged that these things are frequently commanded and enjoined unto them in the Scripture.   Might they be obtained, it
would greatly further the ends of the gospel and answer the mind
of Christ; and their loss is obstructive unto the one, and no less dishonourable unto that profession which is made of the name of the
other: for the divisions of Christians (occasioned chiefly by false

notions of unity, and undue means of attaining it) are the chief cause of offences unto them who are yet strangers from Christianity. The Jews object unto us the wars among Christians, which they suppose shall have no place under the kingdom and reign of the true Messiah. And we have been reproached with our intestine differences by Gentiles and Mohammedans; for those who never had either peace, or love, or unity among themselves, do yet think meet to revile us with the want of them, because they know how highly we are obliged·unto them. But any men may be justly charged with the neglect of that duty which they profess, if they be found defective therein. Under the sad effects of the want of these things we may labour long enough, if we endeavour not to take away the causes of it. And yet in the entrance of our disquisition after them we are again entangled. Christians cannot come to an agreement about these causes; and so live under the severity of their effects, as not being able to conclude on a remedy. The multitude of them is here divided, and one crieth one thing, another another. Most place the cause of all our differences in a dissent from themselves and their judgments; yea, they do so apparently who yet disavow their so doing. And it may be here expected that we should give some account of our thoughts as to the causes of these differences, whereof we also have now complained, so far as they are contrary to the nature or obstructive of the ends of the gospel. We shall therefore briefly endeavour the satisfaction of such as may have those expectations. Particular evils, which contribute much unto our divisions, we shall not insist upon; much less shall we reflect upon and aggravate the failings of others, whether persons or societies. Some of the principal and more general reasons and causes of them, especially amongst Protestants, it shall suffice us to enumerate.

1. The principal cause of our divisions and schisms is no other than the *ignorance or misapprehension that is among Christians of the true nature of that evangelical unity* which they ought to follow after, with the ways and means whereby it may be attained and preserved. Hence it is come to pass, that, in the greatest pleas for unity and endeavours after it, most men have pursued a shadow, and fought uncertainly, as those that beat the air; for having lost every notion of gospel unity, and not loving the thing itself, under what terms soever proposed unto them, they consigned the name of it unto, and clothed with its ornaments and privileges, a vain figment of their own, which the Lord Christ never required, nor ever blessed any in their endeavours to attain. And when they had changed the end, it was needful for them also to change the means of attaining it, and to substitute those in their room which were suited to the new mark and aim they had erected. Farther to evidence these

things, we shall give some account of the nature of evangelical unity, the means of attaining it, with the false notion of it that some have embraced, and the corrupt means which they have used for the compassing of the same.

First, That unity which is recommended unto us in the gospel is *spiritual;* and in that which is purely so lies the foundation of the whole. Hence it is called " The unity of the Spirit," which is to be kept " in the bond of peace;" because " there is one body, and one Spirit," whereby that body is animated, Eph. iv. 3, 4. Thus, all true believers become one in the Father and the Son, or perfect in one, John xvii. 21, 22. It is their participation of, and quickening by, the same Spirit that is in Christ Jesus, whereby they become his body, or members of it, " even of his flesh and of his bones," Eph. v. 30; that is, no less really partakers of the same divine spiritual nature with him, 2 Pet. i. 4, than Eve was of the nature of Adam, when she was made of his flesh and his bones, Gen. ii. 23. The real union of all true believers unto the Lord Christ as their head, wrought by his Spirit, which dwelleth in them, and communicates of his grace unto them, is that which we intend; for as hereby they become one with and in him, so they come to be one among themselves, as his body; and all the members of the body, being many, are yet but one body, wherein their oneness among themselves doth consist. The members of the body have divers forms or shapes, divers uses and operations, much more may be diversely clothed and adorned; yet are they one body still, wherein their unity doth consist. And it were a ridiculous thing to attempt the appearance of a dead, useless unity among the members of the body, by clothing of them all in the same kind of garments or covering. But granting them their unity by their relation unto the Head, and thence to one another, unto the constitution of the whole, and their different forms, shapes, uses, operations, ornaments, all tend to make them serviceable in their unity unto their proper ends. And saith the apostle, "As the body is one, and hath many members, and all the members of that one body, being many, are one body; so also is Christ. For by one Spirit are we all baptized into one body, whether we be Jews or Gentiles, whether we be bond or free; and have been all made to drink into one Spirit," 1 Cor. xii. 12, 13. And he doth elsewhere so describe this fundamental unity of believers in one body, under and in dependence on the same Head, as to make it the only means of the usefulness and preservation of the whole. They " grow up into him in all things, which is the head, even Christ: from whom the whole body fitly joined together and compacted by that which every joint supplieth, according to the effectual working in the measure of every part, maketh increase of the body unto the edifying of itself in love,"

Eph. iv. 15, 16. The conjunctions of all the members into one body, their mutual usefulness unto one another, the edification of the whole, with its increase, the due exercise of love (which things contain the whole nature and the utmost ends of all church-communion), do depend merely and solely upon, and flow from, the relation that the members have to the Head, and their union with him. He speaketh again to the same purpose in the reproof of them who "hold not the Head, from which all the body by joints and bands having nourishment ministered, and knit together, increaseth with the increase of God," Col. ii. 19. This is the foundation of all gospel unity among believers, whereunto all other things which are required unto the completing of it are but accessory; nor are they, without this, of any value or acceptation in the sight of God. Whatever order, peace, concord, union in the church, any one may hold or keep who is not interested herein, he is but like a stone in a building, laid it may be in a comely order, but not cemented and fixed unto the whole; which renders its station useless to the building and unsafe unto itself: or like a dead, mortified part of the body, which neither receives any vital influence from the head, nor administers nourishment unto any other part. Now, it cannot be denied but that, in the contests that are in the world about church union and divisions, with what is pleaded about their nature and causes, there is little or no consideration had thereof. Yea, those things are principally insisted on, for the constituting of the one and the avoiding of the other, which casts a neglect, yea, a contempt upon it. It is the Romanists who make the greatest outcries about church-union, and who make the greatest advantage by what they pretend so to be. But hereunto they contend expressly, on the one side, that it is indispensably necessary that all Christians should be subject to the pope of Rome and united unto him; and, on the other, that it is not necessary at all that any of them be spiritually and savingly united unto Christ. Others, also, place it in various instances of conformity unto and compliance with the commands of men; which, if they are observed, they are wondrous cold in their inquiries after this relation unto the Head. But the truth is, that where any one is interested in this foundation of all gospel unity, he may demand communion with any church in the world, and ought not to be refused, unless in case of some present offence or scandal. And those by whom such persons are rejected from communion, to be held on gospel terms, on the account of some differences not intrenching on this foundation, do exercise a kind of church tyranny, and are guilty of the schism which may ensue thereon. So, on the other side, where this is wanting, men's compliance with any other terms or conditions that may be proposed unto them, and their obtaining of church-communion thereon, will be of little advantage unto their souls.

Secondly, Unto this foundation of gospel unity among believers, for and unto the due improvement of it, there is required *a unity of faith*, or of the belief and profession of the same divine truth; for as there is one Lord, so also [there is] one faith and one baptism unto believers. And this ariseth from and followeth the other; for those who are so united unto Christ are all taught of God to believe the truths which are necessarily required thereunto. And however, by the power of temptation, they may fall in it or from it for a season, as did Peter, yet, through the love and care of Jesus Christ, they are again recovered. Now, unto this unity of faith two things are required:—*First*, A precise and express profession of the *fundamental articles* of Christian religion; for we outwardly hold the Head by a consent unto the form of wholesome words wherein the doctrine of it is contained. Of the number and nature of such fundamental truths, whose express acknowledgment belongs unto the unity.of faith, so much has been discoursed by others as that we need not add any thing thereunto. The sum is, that they are but few, plainly delivered in the Scripture, evidencing their own necessity, all conducing to the begetting and increase of that spiritual life whereby we live unto God. *Secondly,* It is required hereunto, that in other things and duties " every man be *fully persuaded in his own mind,*" and, walking according to what he hath attained, do follow peace and love with those who are otherwise persuaded than he is, Rom. xiv. 5; Phil. iii. 16;—for the unity of faith did never consist in the same precise conceptions of all revealed objects; neither the nature of man nor the means of revelation will allow such a unity to be morally possible. And the figment of supplying this variety by an implicit faith is ridiculous; for herein faith is considered as professed, and no man can make profession of what he knoweth not. It is, therefore, condescension and mutual forbearance whereby the unity of faith, consisting in the joint belief of necessary truths, is to be preserved with respect unto other things about which differences may arise.

Yet is not this so to be understood as though Christians, especially ministers of the gospel, should content themselves with the knowledge of such fundamentals, or confine their Scripture inquiries unto them. Whatever is written in the Scripture is " written for our admonition," 1 Cor. x. 11; and it is our duty to search diligently into the whole counsel of God, therein revealed; yea, to inquire with " all diligence," 1 Tim. iv. 13–16, 2 Tim. iii. 15–17, 1 Pet. i. 10, 11, in the use of all means and the improvement of all advantages, with fervent supplications for light and aid from above, into the whole mystery of the will of God, as revealed in the Scripture, and all the parts of it, is the principal duty that is incumbent on us in this world. And those who take upon them to be ministers and instructers of others, by whom this is neglected, who take up with a superficiary knowledge of general principles, and those such, for the most part, as have a coincidence with the light of nature, do but betray the souls of those over whom they usurp a charge, and are unworthy of the title and office which they bear. Neither is there any thing implied in the means of preserving the unity of faith that should hinder us from explaining, confirming, and vindicating any truth that we have received, wherein others differ from us, provided that what we do be done with a spirit of meekness and love; yea, our so doing is one principal means of ministering nourishment unto the body, whereby the whole is increased as " with the increase of God."

But in the room of all this, what contendings, fightings, destructions of men, body and soul, upon variety of judgments about sacred things, have been introduced, by the craft of Satan and the carnal interest of men of corrupt minds, is known to all the world.

Thirdly, There is a *unity of love* that belongs unto the evangelical unity which we are in the description of; for love is the bond of perfection, that whereby all the members of the body of Christ are knit together among themselves, and which renders all the other ingredients of this unity useful unto them. And as we have discoursed of the nature of this love before, so the exercise of it, as it hath an actual influence into gospel unity among Christians, may be reduced unto two heads. For, *first*, It worketh effectually, according to the measure of them in whom it is, in the *contribution of supplies of grace, and light*, and helps of obedience, unto other members of the body. Every one in whom this love dwelleth, according to his ability, call, and opportunities, which make up his measure, will communicate the spiritual supplies which he receiveth from the head, Christ Jesus, unto others, by instructions, exhortations, consolations, and example, unto their edification. This he will do in love, and unto the ends of love,—namely, to testify a joint relation unto Christ, the head of all, and the increase of the whole by supplies of life from him. Instead hereof, some have invented bonds of ecclesiastical unity, which may bind men together in some appearance of order, whilst in the meantime they live in envy, wrath, and malice, biting and devouring one another; or if there be any thing of love among them, it is that which is merely natural, or carnal and sensual, working by a joint consent in delights and pleasure, or at best in civil things, belonging unto their conversation in this world. The love that is among such persons in this world is of the world, and will perish with the world. But it is a far easier thing to satisfy conscience with a pretence of preserving church-unity, by an acqui-escency in some outward rules and constitutions, wherein men's minds are little concerned, than to attend diligently unto the due exercise of this grace of love against all oppositions and temptations unto the contrary; for indeed the exercise of this love requires a sedulous and painful "labour," Heb. vi. 10. But yet this is that alone which is the bond of perfection unto the disciples of Christ, and without which all other pretences or appearances of unity are of no value with him. *Secondly*, This love acts itself by *forbearance and condescension* towards the infirmities, mistakes, and faults of others; wherein of what singular use it is for the preservation of church peace and order, the apostle at large declares, 1 Cor. xiii.

Fourthly, The Lord Christ, by his kingly authority, hath instituted *orders for rule*, and *ordinances for worship*, Matt. xxviii. 19, 20, Eph. iv. 8–13, to be observed in all his churches. That they be attended unto, and celebrated in a due manner, belongs unto the unity which he requires among his disciples. To this end he com-municates supplies of spiritual ability and wisdom, or the gifts of his Spirit, unto the guides and rulers of his churches, for their admini-stration unto edification. And hereon, if a submission unto his authority be accompanied with a due attendance unto the rule of the word, no such variety or difference will ensue as shall impeach that unity which is the duty of them all to attend unto.

In these things doth consist that evangelical church-unity which the gospel recommends unto us, and which the Lord Christ prayed for, with respect unto all that should believe on his name, John xvii. 20–23. One Spirit, one faith, one love, one Lord, there ought to be in and unto them all. In the possession of this unity, and no other, were the first churches left by the apostles; and had they in succeeding generations continued, according to their duty, in the pre-servation and liberty of it, all those scandalous divisions which after-ward fell out among them, on account of pre-eminences, jurisdictions, liturgies, rites, ceremonies, violently or fraudulently obtruded on their communion, had been prevented, 2 Cor. x. 4, 5.

The ways and means whereby this unity may be obtained and preserved amongst Christians are evident from the nature of it: for whereas it is spiritual, none other are suited thereunto, nor hath the Lord Christ appointed any other but his Spirit and his word; for to this end doth he promise the presence of his Spirit among them that believe unto the consummation of all things, Matt. xxviii. 20, John xiv. 16. And this he doth, both as to lead and "guide them into all truth" necessary unto the ends mentioned, so to assist and help them in the orderly performance of their duties in and about them. His word, also, as the rule which they are to attend unto, he hath committed unto them. And other ways and means for the compassing of this end, besides the due improvement of spiritual assistances in a compliance with the holy rule, he hath not designed or appointed.

This is that gospel unity which we are to labour after, and these are the means whereby we may do so. But now, through the mistake of the minds of men, with the strong influence which carnal and corrupt interests have upon them, we know how it hath been despised, and what hath been set up in the room thereof, and what have been the means whereby it hath been pursued and promoted. We may take an instance in those of the church of Rome. No sort of Christians in the world (as we have already observed) do at this day more pretend unto unity, or more press the necessity of it, or more fiercely judge, oppose, and destroy others for the breach of it, which they charge upon them, nor more prevail or advantage themselves by the pretence of it, than do they; but yet, notwithstanding all their pretences, it will not be denied but that the unity which they so make their boast of, and press upon others, is a thing utterly foreign to the gospel, and destructive of that peace, union, and concord among Christians which it doth require. They know how highly unity is commended in the Scripture, how much it is to be prized and valued by all true believers, how acceptable it is to Jesus Christ, and how severely they are condemned who break it or despise it: these things they press, and plead, and make their advantage by. But when we come to inquire what it is that they intend by church-unity, they tell us long stories of subjection unto the pope,— to the church in its dictates and resolutions, without farther examination, merely because they are theirs. Now, these things are not only of another nature and kind than the unity and concord commended unto us by Jesus Christ, but perfectly inconsistent with them, and destructive of them. And as they would impose upon us a corrupt confederacy, for their own secular advantage, in the room of the spiritual unity of the gospel; so it was necessary that they should find out means suitable unto its accomplishment and preservation, as distant from the means appointed by Christ for the attaining of gospel union as their carnal confederacy is from the thing itself. And they have done accordingly; for the enforcing men, by all ways of deceit and outward violence, unto a compliance with and submission unto their orders, is the great expedient for the establishment and preservation of their perverse union that they have fixed on. Now, that this fictitious unity and corrupt carnal pursuit of it have been the greatest occasion and cause of begetting, fomenting, and continuing the divisions that are among Christians in the world, hath been undeniably proved by learned men of all sorts. And so it will fall out, wherever any reject the union of Christ's institution, and

substitute in the room thereof an agreement of their own invention;
as his will be utterly lost, so they will not be able to retain their own.

Thus, others also, not content with those bounds and measures
which the gospel hath fixed unto the unity of Christians and churches,
will have it to consist almost wholly in an outward conformity unto
certain rites, orders, ceremonies, and modes of sacred administrations,
which themselves have either invented and found out or do observe
and approve. Whoever dissents from them in these things must
immediately be branded as a schismatic, a divider of the church's
unity, and an enemy unto the peace and order of it. Howbeit, of
conformity unto such institutions and orders of men, of uniformity in
the observation of such external rites in the worship of the church,
there is not one word spoken, nor any thing of that nature intimated,
in all the commands for unity which are given unto us, nor in the
directions that are sanctified unto the due preservation of it. Yet
such a uniformity being set up in the room of evangelical unity and
order, means suited unto the preservation of it, but really destructive
of that whose name it beareth and whose place it possesseth, have
not been wanting. And it is not unworthy of consideration how men
endeavour to deceive others, and are deceived themselves, by manifold
equivocations in their arguings about this matter. For, first, they
lay down the necessity of unity among Christians, with the evil that
is in breaches, divisions, and schisms; which they prove from the
commands of the one and the reproofs of the other that abound in
the Scripture. Then, with an easy deduction, they prove that it is
a duty incumbent on all Christians, in their several capacities, to observe, keep, further, and promote this unity; and to prevent, oppose,
resist, and avoid all divisions that are contrary thereunto. If so, the
magistrate must do the same in his place and capacity. Now, seeing
it is his office, and unto him of God it is committed, to exercise his
power in laws and penalties for the promoting of what is good, and
the punishing of what is contrary thereunto, it is his duty to coerce,
restrain, and punish, all those who oppose, despise, or any way break
or disturb, the unity of the church. And this ratiocination would
seem reasonable were it not doubly defective. For, first, the unity
intended in the first proposition, whose necessity is confirmed by
Scripture testimonies, is utterly lost before we come to the conclusion,
and the outward uniformity mentioned is substituted in the room
thereof. And hereby, in the second place, are they deceived to believe that external force and penalties are a means to be used by any
for the attaining or preserving of gospel unity. It is not improbable,
indeed, but that it may be suited to give countenance unto that external uniformity which is intended; but that it should be so unto
the promotion of gospel union among believers is a weak imagina-

tion. Let such persons keep themselves and their argument unto that union which the Scripture commends amongst the disciples of Christ and his churches, with the means fitted and appointed unto the preservation of it, and they shall have our compliance with any conclusion that will thence ensue.

Herein, therefore, lies *the fundamental cause of our divisions;* which will not be healed until it be removed and taken out of the way. Leave believers or professors of the gospel unto their duty in seeking after evangelical unity in the use of other means instituted and blessed unto that end,—impose nothing on their consciences or practice under that name, which indeed belongs not thereunto; and although, upon the reasons and causes afterward to be mentioned, there may for a season remain some divisions among them, yet there will be a way of healing continually ready for them, and agreed upon by them as such. Where, indeed, men propose unto themselves different ends, though under the same name, the use of the same means for the compassing of them will but increase their variance: as where some aim at evangelical union, and others at an external uniformity, both under the name of unity and peace, in the use of the same means for these ends, they will be more divided among themselves. But where the same end is aimed at, even the debate of the means for the attaining of it will insensibly bring the parties into a coalition, and work out in the issue a complete reconciliation. In the meantime, were Christians duly instructed how many lesser differences, in mind, and judgment, and practice, are really consistent with the nature, ends, and genuine fruit, of the unity that Christ requires among them, it would undoubtedly prevail with them so to manage themselves in their differences, by mutual forbearance and condescension in love, as not to contract the guilt of being disturbers or breakers of it; for suppose the minds of any of them to be invincibly prepossessed with the principles wherein they differ from others, yet all who are sincere in their profession cannot but rejoice to be directed unto such a managery of them as to be preserved from the guilt of dissolving the unity appointed by Christ to be observed. And, to speak plainly, among all the churches in the world which are free from idolatry and persecution, it is not different opinions, or a difference in judgment about revealed truths, nor a different practice in sacred administrations, but pride, self-interest, love of honour, reputation, and dominion, with the influence of civil or political intrigues and considerations, that are the true cause of that defect of evangelical unity that is at this day amongst them; for set them aside, and the real differences which would remain may be so managed, in love, gentleness, and meekness, as not to interfere with that unity which Christ requireth them to preserve. Nothing will from thence follow which shall impeach their common interest in one Lord, one faith, one love, one Spirit, and the administration of the same ordinances according to their light and ability. But if we shall cast away this evangelical union among the disciples and churches of Christ,—if we shall break up the bounds and limits fixed unto it, and set up in its place a compliance with, or an agreement in, the commands and appointments of men, making their observations the rule and measure of our ecclesiastical concord,—it cannot be but that innumerable and endless divisions will ensue thereon. If we will not be contented with the union that Christ hath appointed, it is certain that we shall have none in this world; for concerning that which is of men's finding out, there have been, and will be, contentions and divisions, whilst there are any on the one side who will endeavour its imposition, and on the other who desire to preserve their consciences entire unto the authority of Christ in his laws and appointments.

There is none who can be such a stranger in our Israel as not to know that these things have been the great occasion and cause of the divisions and contentions that have been among us near a hundred years, and which at this day make our breaches wide like the sea, that they cannot be healed. Let, therefore, those who have power and ability be instrumental to restore to the minds of men the true notion and knowledge of the unity which the Lord Christ requireth among his churches and disciples; and let them be left unto that liberty which he hath purchased for them, in the pursuit of that unity which he hath prescribed unto them; and let us all labour to stir up those gracious principles of love and peace which ought to guide us in the use of our liberty, and will enable us to preserve gospel unity; —and there will be a greater progress made towards peace, reconciliation, and concord, amongst all sorts of Christians, than the spoiling of the goods or imprisoning the persons of dissenters will ever effect. But, it may be, such things are required hereunto as the world is yet scarce able to comply withal; for whilst men do hardly believe that there is an efficacy and power accompanying the institutions of Christ, for the compassing of that whole end which he aimeth at and intendeth,—whilst they are unwilling to be brought unto the constant exercise of that spiritual diligence, patience, meekness, condescension, self-denial, renunciation of the world and conformity thereunto, which are indispensably necessary in church guides and church members, according to their measure, unto the attaining and preservation of gospel unity, but do satisfy themselves in the disposal of an ecclesiastical union into a subordination unto their own secular interests, by external force and power,—we have very small expectation of success in the way proposed. In the meantime, we are herewith satisfied: Take the churches of Christ in the world that are not infected with idolatry or persecution, and restore their unity unto the terms and conditions left unto them by Christ and his apostles, and if in any thing we are found uncompliant therewithal, we shall without repining bear the reproach of it, and hasten an amendment.

2. Another cause of the evil effects and consequences mentioned is, the *great neglect that hath been in churches and church rulers in the pursuance of the open, direct ends of the gospel*, both as to the doctrine and discipline of it.   This hath been such and so evident in the world that it is altogether in vain for any to deny it, or to attempt an excuse of it.   And men have no reason to flatter themselves that, whilst they live in an open neglect of their own duty, others will always, according to their wills or desires, attend with diligence unto what they prescribe unto them.   If churches or their rulers could excuse or justify their members in all the evils that may befall them through their miscarriages and maladministrations, it might justly be expected that they should go along with them under their conduct, whither ever they should lead them: but if it can never be obliterated out of the minds and consciences of men that *they must every one live by his own faith, and every one give an account of himself unto God;* and that every one, notwithstanding the interposition of the help of churches and their rulers, is obliged immediately, in his own person, to take care of his whole duty towards God; it cannot be but that in such cases they will judge for themselves, and what is meet for them to do.   In case, therefore, that they find the churches whereunto they do relate under the guilt of the neglect mentioned, it is probable that they will provide for themselves and their own safety.   In this state of things it is morally impossible but that differences and divisions will fall out, which might all of them have been prevented had there been a due attention unto the work, doctrine, order, and discipline of the gospel in the churches that were in possession of the care and administration of them; for it is hard for men to believe that, by the will and command of Christ, they are inevitably shut up under spiritual disadvantages, seeing it is certain that he hath ordered all things in the church for their edification.   But the consideration of some particular instances will render this cause of our divisions more evident and manifest.

The first end of preaching the gospel is, *the conversion of the souls of men unto God*, Acts xxvi. 17, 18.   This, we suppose, will not be questioned or denied.   That the work hereof, in all churches, ought to be attended and pursued with zeal, diligence, labour, and care, all accompanied with constant and fervent prayers for success, in and by the ministers and rulers of them, is a truth also that will not admit of any controversy among them that believe the gospel, 1 Tim. v. 17,

2 Tim. iv. 1, 2.   Herein principally do men in office in the church exercise and manifest their zeal for the glory of God, their compassion towards the souls of men, and acquit themselves faithfully in the trust committed unto them by the "great Shepherd of the sheep," Christ Jesus.   If, now, in any assembly or other societies professing themselves to be churches of Christ, and claiming the right and power of churches towards all persons living within the bounds or limits which they have prescribed unto themselves, this work be either totally neglected, or carelessly and perfunctorily attended unto; if those on whom it is immediately incumbent do either suppose themselves free from any obligation thereunto, upon the pretence of other engagements, or do so dispose of themselves, in their relation unto many charges or employments, as that it is impossible they should duly attend unto it, or are unable and insufficient for it; so that, indeed, there is not in such churches a due representation of the love, care, and kindness of the Lord Jesus Christ towards the souls of men, which he hath ordained the administration of his gospel to testify,— it cannot be but that great thoughts of heart, and no small disorder of mind, will be occasioned in them who understand aright how much the principal end of constituting churches in this world is neglected among them.   And although it is their duty for a season patiently to bear with, and quietly seek the reformation of, this evil in the churches whereunto they do belong, yet when they find themselves excluded,—it may be by the very constitution of the church itself, it may be by the iniquity of them that prevail therein,—from the performance of any thing that tends thereunto, it will increase their disquietment.   And whereas men do not join themselves, nor are by any other ways joined, unto churches, for any civil or secular ends or purposes, but merely for the promotion of God's glory, and the edification of their own souls in faith and gospel obedience, it is altogether vain for any to endeavour a satisfaction of their consciences that it is sin to withdraw from such churches, wherein these ends are not pursued nor attainable; and yet a confidence hereof is that which hath countenanced sundry church-guides into that neglect of duty which many complain of and groan under at this day.

The second end of the dispensation of the gospel, in the assemblies of the churches of Christ, by the ministers of them, is *the edification of them that are converted unto God and do believe.*   Herein consists that feeding of his sheep and lambs that the Lord Christ hath committed unto them; and it is mentioned as the principal end for which the ministry was ordained, or for which pastors and teachers are granted unto the church, Eph. iv. 8–13.   And the Scripture abounds in the declaration of what skill and knowledge in the mystery of the gospel, what attendance unto the word and prayer, what care, watchfulness, and diligent labour in the word and doctrine, are required unto a due discharge of the ministerial duty. Where it is omitted or neglected; where it is carelessly attended unto; where those on whom it is incumbent do act more like hirelings than true shepherds; where they want skill to divide the word aright, or wisdom and knowledge to declare from it "the whole counsel of God," or diligence to be urgent continually in the application of it,— there the principal end of all church-communion is ruined and utterly lost. And where it so falls out, let any man judge what thoughts they are like to be exercised withal who make conscience of the performance of their own duty, and understand the necessity of enjoying the means that Christ hath appointed for their edification. And it is certain that such churches will in vain, or at least unjustly, expect that professors of the gospel should abide in their particular communion, when they cannot or do not provide food for their souls, whereby they may live to God. Unless all the members of such churches are equally asleep in security, divisions among them will in this case ensue. Will any disciple of Christ esteem himself obliged to starve his own soul for the sake of communion with them who have sinfully destroyed the principal end of all church-communion? Is there any law of Christ, or any rule of the gospel, or any duty of love, that requires them so to do? The sole immediate end of men's joining in churches being their own edification and usefulness unto others, can they be bound in conscience always to abide there, or in the communion of those churches where it is not to be attained, where the means of it are utterly cast aside? This may become such as know not their duty, nor care to be instructed in it, and are willing to perish in and for the company of others; but for them which in such cases shall provide, according to the rules of the gospel, for themselves and their own safety, they may be censured, judged, and severely treated, by them whose interest and advantage it is so to do,—they may be despised by riotous persons, who sport themselves with their own deceivings,—but with the Lord Christ, the judge of all, they will be accepted. And they do but increase the dread of their own account, who, under pretence of church power and order, would forcibly shut up Christians in such a condition as wherein they are kept short of all the true ends of the institution of churches. To suppose, therefore, that every voluntary departure from the constant communion of such churches, made with a design of joining unto those where the word is dispensed with more diligence and efficacy, is a schism from the church of Christ, is to suppose that which neither the Scripture nor reason will give the least countenance unto. And it would better become such churches to return industriously unto a faithful discharge of their duty, whereby this occasion of divisions may be removed out of the way, than to attempt their own justification by the severe prosecution of such as depart from them.

Thirdly, In pursuit of the doctrine of the gospel so improved and applied, it is the known and open duty of churches, in their guides or ministers, by all means to countenance and *promote the growth of light, knowledge, godliness, strictness, and fruitfulness of conversation,* in those members of them in whom they may be found, or do appear in an especial manner. Such are they to own, encourage, and make their companions, and endeavour that others may become like unto them. For unless men, in their ordinary and common conversation, in their affections, and the interest which they have in the administration of discipline, do uniformly answer the doctrine of truth which they preach, it cannot be avoided but that it will be matter of offence unto others, and of reproach to themselves. Much more will it be so, if, instead of these things, those who preside in the churches shall beat their fellow-servants, and eat and drink with the drunken. But by all ways it is their duty to separate the precious from the vile, if they intend to be as the mouth of the Lord, even in their judgments, affections, and conversations. And herein what wisdom, patience, diligence, love, condescension, and forbearance are required, they alone know, and they full well know, who for any season have in their places conscientiously endeavoured the discharge of their duty. But whatever be the labour which is to be undergone therein, and the trouble wherewith it is attended, it is that which, by the appointment of Christ, all ministers of the gospel are obliged to attend unto. They are not, by contrary actings, to make sad the hearts of them whom God would not have made sad, nor to strengthen the hands of them whom God would not have encouraged, as they will answer it at their peril. The hearts of church guides, and of those who in an especial manner fear God, thriving in knowledge and grace under the dispensation of the word, ought to be knit together in all holy affections, that they may together grow up into him who is the Head; for where there is the greatest evidence and manifestation of the power and presence of Christ in any, there ought their affections to be most intense. For as such persons are the crown, the joy and rejoicing of their guides, and will appear to be so in the day of the Lord; so they do know, or may easily do so, what obligations are on them to honour and pay all due respects unto their teachers, how much on all accounts they owe unto them; whereby their mutual love may be confirmed. And where there is this uniformity between the doctrine of the gospel as preached, and the duties of it as practised, then are they both beautiful in the eyes of all believers, and effectual unto their proper ends. But where things in churches, through their negligence or corruption, or that of their guides, are quite otherwise, it is easy to conjecture what will ensue thereon. If those who are forwardest in profession, who give the greatest evidence that they have received the power of that religion which is taught and owned among them, who have apparently attained a growth in spiritual light and knowledge above others, shall be so far from being peculiarly cherished and regarded, from being loved, liked, or associated withal, as that on the other side they shall be marked, observed, reproached, and it may be on every slight provocation put even to outward trouble; whilst men of worldly and profane conversation, ignorant, perhaps riotous and debauched, shall be the delight and companions of church guides and rulers;—it cannot be that such churches should long continue in peace, nor is that peace wherein they continue much to be valued. An agreement in such ways and practices is rather to be esteemed a conspiracy against Christ and holiness than church order or concord; and when men once find themselves hated, and it may be persecuted, for no other cause, as they believe, but because they labour in their lives and professions to express the power of that truth wherein they have been instructed, they can hardly avoid the entertainment of severe thoughts concerning them from whom they had just reason to expect other usage, and also to provide for their own more peaceable encouragement and edification.

Fourthly, Hereunto also belongeth *the due exercise of gospel discipline*, according to the mind of Christ. It is, indeed, by some called into question whether there be any rule or discipline appointed by Christ to be exercised in his churches. But this doubt must respect such outward forms and modes of the administration of these things as are supposed, but not proved necessary: for whether the Lord Christ hath appointed some to *rule* and some to be *ruled;* whether he hath prescribed laws or rules, whereby the one should govern and the other obey; whether he hath determined the matter, manner, and end of this rule and government,—cannot well be called into controversy by such as profess to believe the gospel. Of what *nature* or kind these governors or rulers are to be, what is their *office,* how they are to be invested therewith, and by what authority, how they are to behave themselves in the administration of the laws of the church, are things determined by him in the word. And for the *matters* about which they are to be conversant, it is evidently declared of what nature they are, how they are to be managed, and to what end. The *qualifications* and *duties* of those who are to be admitted into the church, their deportment in it, their removal from it, are all expressed in the laws and directions given unto the same end. In particular, it is ordained that those who are unruly or disorderly, who walk contrary unto the rules and ways of holiness prescribed unto the church, shall be rebuked, admonished, instructed; and if, after all means used for their amendment, they abide in impenitency, that they be ejected out of communion. For the church, as visible, is a society gathered and erected to express and declare the holiness of Christ, and the power of his grace in his person and doctrine; and where this is not done, no church is of any advantage unto the interests of his glory in this world. The preservation, therefore, of holiness in them, whereof the discipline mentioned is an effectual means, is as necessary and of the same importance with the preservation of their being. The Lord Christ hath also expressly ordained, that in case offences should arise in and among his churches, that in and by them they should be composed, according to the rules of the word and his own laws; and, in particular, that in sinful miscarriages causing offence or scandal, there be a regular proceeding, according unto an especial law and constitution of his, for the removal of the offence and recovery of the offender; as also, that those who in other cases have fallen by the power of temptation should be restored by a spirit of meekness; and, not to instance in more particulars, that the whole flock be continually watched over, exhorted, warned, instructed, comforted, as the necessities or occasions of the whole, or the several members of it, do require. Now, supposing these and the like laws, rules, and directions, to be given and enjoined by the authority of Christ (which gives warranty for their execution unto men prudent for the ordering of affairs according to their necessary circumstances, and believers of the gospel, doing all things in obedience unto him), we judge that a complete rule or government is erected thereby in the church. However, we know that the exercise of discipline in every church, so far as the laws and rules of it are expressed in the Scripture, and the ends of it directed unto, is as necessary as any duty enjoined unto us in the whole course of our gospel obedience. And where this is neglected, it is in vain for any churches to expect peace and unity in their communion, seeing itself neglecteth the principal means of them. It is pleaded, that the mixture of those that are wicked and ungodly in the sacred administrations of the church doth neither defile the administrations themselves, nor render them unuseful unto those who are rightly interested in them and duly prepared for the participation of them. Hence, that no church ought to be forsaken, nor its communion withdrawn from, merely on that account, many of old and of late have pleaded. Nor do we say that this solely of itself is sufficient to justify a separation from any church. But when a church shall tolerate in its communion not only evil men, but their evils, and absolutely refuse to use the discipline of

Christ for the reformation of the one and the taking away of the other, there is great danger lest the " whole lump be leavened," and the edification of particular persons be obstructed beyond what the Lord Christ requires of them to submit unto and to acquiesce in.

Neither will things have any better success where the *discipline degenerates into an outward forcible jurisdiction and power.* The things of Christ are to be administered with the spirit of Christ. Such a frame of heart and mind as was in him is required of all that act under him and in his name. Wherefore, charity, pity, compassion, condescension, meekness, and forbearance, with those other graces which were so glorious and conspicuous in him and in all that he did, are to bear sway in the minds of them who exercise this care and duty for him in the church. To set up such a form of the administration of discipline, or to commit the exercise of it unto such persons, as whereby or by whom the Lord Christ, in his rule of the church, would be represented as furious, captious, proud, covetous, oppressive, is not the way to honour him in the world, nor to preserve the peace of the churches. And indeed some, while they boast of the imitation of Christ and his example, in opposition to his grace, do in their lives and practices make unto the world a representation of the devil. But an account of this degeneracy is given so distinctly by Pietro Soave,[1] the author of the History of the Council of Trent, lib. iv. ad ann. 1551, that we think it not unmeet to express it in his own words. He saith, therefore, that " Christ having commanded his apostles to preach the gospel and administer the sacraments, he left also unto them, in the person of all the faithful, this principal precept, to love one another, charging them to make peace between those that dissented; and, for the last remedy, giving the care thereof to the body of the church, promising it should be bound and loosed in heaven, whatever they did bind and loose on earth, and that whatever they did ask with a common consent should be granted by the Father. In this charitable office, to give satisfaction to the offended and pardon to the offender, the primitive church was always exercised. And in conformity to this, St Paul ordained that brethren having civil suits one against another should not go to the tribunals of infidels, but that wise men should be appointed to judge the differences. And this was a kind of civil judgment, as the other had the similitude of a criminal; but were both so different from the judgments of the world, that as these are executed by the power of the judge, who enforceth submission, so those only by the will of the guilty to receive them, who refusing of them, the ecclesiastical judge remaineth without execution, and hath no power but

---

[1] Now better known by his real name, Paul Sarpi.—Ed.

to foreshow the judgment of God, which, according to his omnipotent good pleasure, will follow in this life or the next. And, indeed, the ecclesiastical judgment did deserve the name of charity, in regard that it did only induce the guilty to submit, and the church to judge with such sincerity, that neither in the one any bad effect could have place, nor just complaint in the other; and the excess of charity in correcting did make the corrector to feel greater pain than the corrected, so that in the church no punishment was imposed without lamentation in the multitude, and greater of the better sort. And this was the cause why to correct was called to 'lament.' So St Paul, rebuking of the Corinthians for not chastising the incestuous, said, ' Ye have not lamented to separate such a transgressor from you.' And in another epistle, ' I fear that when I come unto you, I shall not find you such as I desire, but in contentions and tumults, and that at my coming I shall lament many of those who have sinned before.' The judgment of the church (as it is necessary in every multitude) was fit that it should be conducted by one, who should preside and guide the action, propose the matters, and collect the points to be consulted on. This care, due to the most principal and worthy person, was always committed to the bishop; and when the churches were many, the propositions and deliberations were made by the bishop first in the college of the priests and deacons, which they called the presbytery, and there were ripened, to receive afterward the last resolution in the general congregation of the church. This form was still on foot in the year 250, and is plainly seen by the epistles of Cyprian; who, in the matter concerning those who did eat of meats offered to idols, and subscribe to the religion of the Gentiles, writeth to the presbytery that he doth not think to do any thing without their counsel and consent of the people; and writeth to the people, that at his return he will examine the causes and merits thereof in their presence and under their judgment; and he wrote to those priests who of their own brain had reconciled some, that they should give an account to the people.

" The goodness and charity of the bishops made their opinion for the most part to be followed, and by little and little was cause that the church, charity waxing cold, not regarding the charge laid upon them by Christ, did lean the ear to the bishop; and ambition, a witty passion, which doth insinuate itself in the show of virtue, did cause it to be readily embraced. But the principal cause of the change was the ceasing of the persecutions; for then the bishops did erect, as it were, a tribunal, which was much frequented; because, as temporal commodities, so suits did increase. This judgment, though it were not as the former in regard of the form, to determine all by the opinion of the church, yet it was of the same sincerity. Whereupon

Constantine, seeing how profitable it was to determine causes, and that by the authority of religion captious actions were discovered which the judges could not penetrate, made a law that there should be no appeal from the sentences of bishops, which should be executed by the secular judge. And if, in a cause depending before a secular tribunal, in any state thereof, either of the parties, though the other contradict, shall demand the episcopal judgment, the cause shall be immediately remitted to him. Here the tribunal of the bishop began to be a common pleading-place, having execution by the ministry of the magistrate, and to gain the name of episcopal jurisdiction, episcopal audience, and such like. The emperor Valens did enlarge it, who in the year 365 gave the bishops the care over all the prices of vendible things. This judicial negotiation pleased not the good bishops. Possidonius doth recount that Austin being employed herein, sometimes until dinner-time, sometimes longer, was wont to say that it was a trouble, and did divert him from doing things proper unto him; and himself writeth, that it was to leave things profitable and to attend things tumultuous and perplexed. And St Paul did not take it unto himself, as being not fit for a preacher, but would have it given to others. Afterward, some bishops beginning to abuse the authority given them by the law of Constantine, that was seventy years after revoked by Arcadius and Honorius, and an ordinance made that they should judge causes of religion, and not civil, except both parties did consent, and declared that they should not be thought to have a court; which law being not much observed in Rome, in regard of the great power of the bishops, Valentinian being in the city in the year 452, did renew it, and made it to be put in execution. But a little after, some part of the power taken away was restored by the princes that followed, so that Justinian did establish unto them a court and audience, and assigned unto them the causes of religion, the ecclesiastical faults of the clergy, and divers voluntary jurisdictions also over the laity. By these degrees the charitable correction of Christ did degenerate into domination, and made Christians lose their ancient reverence and obedience. It is denied in words that ecclesiastical jurisdiction is dominion as is the secular, yet one knoweth not how to put a difference between them. But St Paul did put it when he wrote to Timothy, and repeated it to Titus, that a bishop should not be greedy of gain, nor a striker. Now, on the contrary, they made men pay for processes, and imprisoned the parties, as is done in the secular court," etc.

This degeneracy of discipline was long since esteemed burdensome, and looked on as the cause of innumerable troubles and grievances unto all sorts of people; yea, it hath had no better esteem among them who had little or no acquaintance with what is taught concerning these things in the Scripture, only they found an inconsistency in it with those laws and privileges of their several countries whereby their civil liberties and advantages were confirmed unto them.   And if at any time it take place or prevail amongst persons of more light and knowledge, who are able to compare it or the practice of it with the institutions of Christ in the gospel, and the manner of the administration therein also directed, it greatly alienates the minds of men from the communion of such churches.   Especially it doth so if set up unto an exclusion of that benign, kind, spiritual, and every way useful discipline that Christ hath appointed to be exercised in his church.   When corruptions and abuses were come to the height in the Papacy in this matter, we know what ensued thereon.   Divines, indeed, and sundry other persons learned and godly, did principally insist on the errors and heresies which prevailed in the church of Rome, with the defilements and abominations of their worship.   But that which alienated the minds of princes, magistrates, and whole nations from them, was the ecclesiastical domination which they had craftily erected and cunningly managed unto the ends of their own ambition, power, and avarice, under the name of church rule and discipline.   And wherever any thing of the same kind is continued,—that a rule under the same pretence is erected and exercised in any church after the nature of secular courts, by force and power, put forth in legal citations, penalties, pecuniary mulcts, without an open evidence of men being acted in what they do herein by love, charity, compassion towards the souls of men, zeal for the glory of God and honour of Christ, with a design for the purity, holiness, and reformation of the members of it,—that church may not expect unity and peace any longer than the terror of its proceedings doth overbalance other thoughts and desires proceeding from a sense of duty in all that belong unto it.   Yea, whatever is or is to be the manner of the administration of discipline in the church, about which there may be doubtful disputations, which men of an ordinary capacity may not be able clearly to determine, yet if the avowed end of it be not the purity and holiness of the church, and if the effects of it in a tendency unto that end be not manifest, it is hard to find out whence our obligation to a compliance with it should arise. And where an outward conformity unto some church-order is aimed at alone, in the room of all other things, it will quickly prove itself to be nothing or of no value in the sight of Christ.   And these things do alienate the minds of many from an acquiescence in their stations or relations to such churches; for the principal enforcements of men's obedience and reverence unto the rulers of the church are because they " watch diligently for the good of their souls, as those that must give an account," Heb. xiii. 17.   And if they see such set over them as give no evidence of any such watchful care acting itself according to those Scripture directions which are continually read unto them, but rather rule them with force and rigour, *seeking theirs, not them*, they grow weary of the yoke, and sometimes regularly, sometimes irregularly, contrive their own freedom and deliverance.

It may not here be amiss to inquire into the reasons and occasions that have seduced churches and their rulers into the miscarriages insisted on. Now, these are chiefly some principles with their application that they have trusted unto, but which indeed have really deceived them, and will yet continue so to do.

1. And the first of these is, that *whereas they are true churches, and thereon intrusted with all church power and privileges*, they need not farther concern themselves to seek for grounds or warranty to keep up all their members unto their communion; for be they otherwise what they will, so long as they are true churches, it is their duty to abide in their peace and order. If any call their church-state into question, they take no consideration of them but how they may be punished, it may be destroyed, as perverse schismatics. And they are ready to suppose, that upon an acknowledgment that they are true churches, every dissent from them in any thing must needs be criminal,—as if it were all one to be a true church, and to be in the truth and right in all things,—a supposition whereof includes a nullity in the state of those churches which in the least differ from them, than which there is no more uncharitable nor schismatical principle in the world. But in the common definition of schism, that it is a causeless separation from a true church, that term of *causeless* is very little considered or weighed by them whose interest it is to lay the charge of it on others. And hence it is come to pass, that wherever there have been complaints of faults, miscarriages, errors, defections of churches, in late ages, their counsels have only been how to destroy the complainers, not in the least how they should reform themselves; as though, in church affairs, truth, right and equity, were entailed on power and possession. How the complaints concerning the church of Rome, quickened by the outcries of so many provinces of Europe, and evidence and matter of fact, were eluded and frustrated in the council of Trent, leaving all things to be tried out by interest and force, is full well known. For they know that no reformation can be attempted and accomplished, but it will be a business of great labour, care, and trouble, things not delightful unto the minds of men at ease. Besides, as it may possibly ruffle or discompose some of the chiefs in their present ways or enjoyments, so it will, as they fear, tend to their disreputation, as though they had formerly been out of the way or neglective of their duty: and this, as they suppose, would draw after it another inconvenience, by reflecting on them and their

practices as the occasions of former disorders and divisions. They choose, therefore, generally to flatter themselves under the name and authority of the church, and lay up their defence and security against an humble, painful reformation, in a plea that they need it not. So was it with the church of Laodicea of old, who, in the height of her decaying condition, flattered herself " that she was rich, and increased with goods, and had need of nothing; and knew not," or would not acknowledge, " that she was wretched, and miserable, and poor, and blind, and naked," Rev. iii. 17. Now, it cannot but seem exceeding strange, unto men who wisely consider these things, that, whereas the churches which were planted and watered by the apostles themselves, and enjoyed for some good season the presence and advantage of their infallible guidance to preserve them in their original purity and order, did within a few years, many of them, so degenerate and stand in need of reformation, that our Lord Jesus Christ threatened from heaven to cast them off and destroy them, unless they did speedily reform themselves according to his mind, those now in the world, ordered at first by persons fallible, and who in many things were actually deceived, should so continue in their purity and holiness from age to age as to stand in need of no reformation or amendment. Well will it be if it prove so at the great day of visitation. In the meantime, it becomes the guides of all the churches in the world to take care that there do not such decays of truth, holiness, and purity in worship, fall out under their hand in the churches wherein they preside, as that for them they should be rejected by our Lord Jesus Christ, as he threatens to deal with those who are guilty of such defections; for the state of the generality of churches is such at this day in the world, as he who thinks them not to stand in need of any reformation may justly be looked on as a part of their sinful degeneracy. We are not ignorant what is usually pleaded in bar unto all endeavours after church reformation; for they say, " If, upon the clamours of a few humorous, discontented persons, whom nothing will please, and who, perhaps, are not agreed among themselves, a reformation must instantly be made or attempted, there will be nothing stable, firm, or sacred left in the church,—things once well established are not to be called into question upon every one's exceptions." And these things are vehemently pleaded and urged, to the exclusion of all thoughts of changing any thing, though evidently for the better. But long-continued complaints and petitions of multitudes, whose sincerity hath received as great an attestation as human nature or Christian religion can give, it may be, deserve not to be so despised. However, the jealousy which churches and their rulers ought to have over themselves, their state and condition, and the presence of the glory of Christ among them, or its departure from them, especially considering the fearful example of the defection and apostasy of many churches, which is continually before their eyes, seems to require a readiness in them, on every intimation or remembrance, to search into their state and condition, and to redress what they find amiss: for suppose they should be in the right, and blameless as to those orders and constitutions wherein others dissent from them, yet there may be such defects and declensions in doctrine, holiness, and the fruits of them in the world, as the most strict observation of outward order will neither countenance nor compensate. For to think to preserve a church by outward order, when its internal principles of faith and holiness are decayed, is but to do like him who, endeavouring to set a dead body upright, but failing in his attempt, concluded that there was somewhat wanting within.

2. Another principle of the same importance, and applied unto the same purpose, is, that *the people are neither able nor fit to judge for themselves*, but ought in all things to give themselves up unto the conduct of their guides, and to rest satisfied in what they purpose and prescribe unto them. The imbibing of this apprehension, which is exceedingly well suited to be made a covering to the pride and ignorance of those unto whose interests it is accommodated, makes them impatient of hearing any thing concerning the liberty of Christians in common to judge of what is their duty, what they are to do, and what they are not to do, in things sacred and religious. Only, it is acknowledged there is so much ingenuity in the management of this principle and its application, that it is seldom extended by any beyond their own concernments: For whereas the church of Rome hath no way to maintain itself, in its doctrine and essential parts of its constitution, but by an implicit faith and obedience in its subjects, seeing the animating principles of its profession will endure no kind of impartial test or trial, they extend it unto all things, as well in matters of faith as of worship and discipline : but those who are secure that the faith which they profess will endure an examination by the Scripture, as being founded therein and thence educed, they will allow unto the people at least a judgment of discerning truth from falsehood, to be exercised about the doctrines which they teach; but as for the things which concern the worship of God and rule of the church, wherein they have an especial interest and concern, there they betake themselves for relief unto this principle. Now, as there is more honesty and safety in this latter way than in the former, so it cannot be denied but that there is less of ingenuity and self-consistency; for if you will allow the people to make a judgment in and about any thing that is sacred or religious, you will never know how to hit a joint aright to make a separation among such things, so as

to say, with any pretence of reason, " About these things they may
judge for themselves, but not about those." And it is a little too open
to say that they may exercise a judgment about what God hath appointed, but none about what we appoint ourselves. But, without
offence be it spoken, this apprehension, in its whole latitude, and
under its restrictions, is so weak and ridiculous, that it must be
thought to proceed from an excess of prejudice, if any man of learning should undertake to patronize it. Those who speak in these
things out of custom and interest, without a due examination of the
grounds and reasons of what they affirm or deny, as many do, are of
no consideration; and it is not amiss for them to keep their distance
and stand upon their guard, lest many of those whom they exclude
from judging for themselves should be found more competent
judges in those matters than themselves. And let churches and
church rulers do what they please, every man at last will be determined in what is meet for him to do by his own reason and judgment. Churches may *inform* the minds of men; they cannot *enforce*
them. And if those that adhere unto any church do not do so, because they judge that it is their duty, and best for them so to do,
they therein differ not much from a herd of creatures that are called
by another name. And yet a secret apprehension in some, that the
disposal of the concernments of the worship of God is so left and
confined unto themselves as that nothing is left unto the people but
the glory of obedience, without any sedulous inquiry after what is
their own duty with respect unto that account which every one must
give of himself unto God, doth greatly influence them into the neglect insisted on. And when any of the people come to know their
own liberty and duty in these things, as they cannot but know it if
at all they apply their minds unto the consideration of them, they
are ready to be alienated from those who will neither permit them
to judge for themselves nor are able to answer for them if they should
be misled; for " if the blind lead the blind," as well he that is led
as he that leads " will fall into the ditch."

3. Add hereunto the thoughts of some, that *secular grandeur* and
outward pomp, with a distance and reservedness from the conversation of ordinary men, are necessary in ecclesiastics, to raise and preserve that popular veneration which they suppose to be their due.
Without this, it is thought, government will not be carried on, nor the
minds of men awed unto obedience. Certain it is that this was not
the judgment of the apostles of old, nor of the bishops or pastors of
the primitive churches. It is certain, also, that no direction is given
for it in any of the sacred or ancient ecclesiastical writings; and
yet they all of them abound with instructions how the guides of the
church should preserve that respect which is their due. The sum of

what they teach us to this purpose is, that in humility, patience, self-denial, readiness to take up the cross, in labours, kindness, compassion, and zeal in the exercise of all the gifts and graces of the Holy Spirit, they should excel and go before the flock as their example, 1 Pet. v. 1–3; Acts xx. 18–21, 28, 31. This way of procuring veneration unto church guides, by worldly state, greatness, seeming domination or power, was, as far as we can find, an utter stranger unto the primitive times; yea, not only so, but it seems to be expressly prohibited in that direction of our Saviour unto them for avoiding conformity in these things unto the rulers of the world, Luke xxii. 24–26. " But those times," they say, " are past and gone; there remains not that piety and devotion in Christians, as to reverence their pastors for their humility, graces, labours, and gifts. The good things of this world are now given them to be used; and it is but a popular levelling spirit that envies the dignities and exaltation of the clergy." Be it so, therefore, that in any place they are justly and usefully, at least as unto themselves, possessed of dignities and revenues, and far be it from us or any of us to envy them their enjoyments, or to endeavour their deprivation of them; but we must crave leave to say, that the use of them to the end mentioned is vain and wholly frustrate. And if it be so, indeed, that Christians, or professors of the gospel, will not pay the respect and duty which they owe unto their pastors and guides, upon the account of their office, with their work and labour therein, it is an open evidence how great a necessity there is for all men to endeavour the reduction of primitive light, truth, holiness, and obedience into churches; for this is that which hath endangered their ruin, and will effect it if continued,—namely, an accommodation of church order and discipline, with the state and deportment of rulers, unto the decays and irreligion of the people, which should have been corrected and removed by their reformation. But we hope better things of many Christians; whose faith and obedience are rather to be imitated than the corrupt degeneracy of others to be complied with or provided for. However, it is evident that this corrupt persuasion hath in most ages, since the days of Paulus Samosatenus, let out and given countenance unto the pride, covetousness, ambition, and vain-glory of several ecclesiastics; for how can it be otherwise with them, who, being possessed of the secular advantages which some churches have obtained in the world, are otherwise utterly destitute of those qualifications which the names of the places they possess do require? And yet all this while it will be impossible to give one single instance where that respect and estimation which the Scripture requires in the people towards their spiritual guides were ingenerated or improved by that worldly grandeur, pomp, and domination, which some pretend to be so useful unto that end and purpose; for that awe which is put thereby on the spirits of the common sort of men,—that terror which these things strike into the minds of any who may be obnoxious unto trouble and disadvantage from them,—that outward observance which is by some done unto persons vested with them, with the admission which they have thereby into an equality of society with great men in the world,—are things quite of another nature. And those who satisfy and please themselves herewith, instead of that regard which is due unto the officers or guides of the churches of Christ from the people that belong unto them, do but help on their defection from their duty incumbent on them. Neither were it difficult to manifest what innumerable scandalous offences,—proceeding from the pride and elation of mind that is found among many, who, being perhaps young and ignorant, it may be corrupt in their conversations, have nothing to bear up themselves withal but an interest in dignities and worldly riches,—have been occasioned by this corrupt persuasion. And it is not hard to judge how much is lost hereby from the true glory and beauty of the church. The people are quietly suffered to decay in that love and respect towards their pastors which is their grace and duty, whilst they will pay that outward veneration which worldly grandeur doth acquire; and pastors, satisfying themselves therewith, grow neglective of that exemplary humility and holiness, of that laborious diligence in the dispensation of the word and care for the souls of the flock, which should procure them that holy respect which is due unto their office by the appointment of Jesus Christ. But these things are here mentioned only on the occasion of what was before discoursed of.

Another great occasion of schisms and divisions among Christians ariseth from the remainders of that confusion which was brought upon the churches of Europe, by *that general apostasy* from gospel truth, purity, and order, wherein they were for sundry ages involved. Few churches in the world have yet totally freed themselves from being influenced by the relics of its disorders. That such an apostasy did befall these churches we shall not need to prove. A supposition of it is the foundation of the church-state of England. That things should so fall out among them was of old foretold by the Holy Ghost, 2 Thess. ii. That many churches have received a signal deliverance from the principal evils of that apostasy, in the Reformation, we all acknowledge; for therein, by several ways, and in several degrees of success, a return unto their pristine faith and order was sincerely endeavoured. And so far was there a blessing accompanying of their endeavours, as that they were all of them delivered from things in themselves pernicious and destructive to the souls of men. Nevertheless, it cannot be denied but that there do yet continue among them sundry remainders of those disorders, which under their fatal declension they were cast into. Nor doth there need any farther proof hereof than the incurable differences and divisions that are found among them; for had they attained their primitive condition, such divisions with all their causes had been prevented. And the Papists, upbraiding Protestants with their intestine differences and schisms, do but reproach them that they have not been able in a hundred years to rectify all those abuses and remove all those disorders which they were inventing and did introduce in a thousand. There is one thing only of this nature, or that owes itself unto this original, which we shall instance in, as an occasion of much disorder in the present churches, and of great divisions that ensue thereon. It is known none were admitted unto the fellowship of the church in the days of the apostles but upon their repentance, faith, and turning unto God. The plain story of their preaching, the success which they had therein, and their proceedings to gather and plant churches thereon, put this out of the reach of all sober contradiction. None will say that they gathered churches of Jews and Gentiles,— that is, while they continued such; nor of open sinners continuing to live in their sins. An evidence, therefore, and confession of conversion to God, were unavoidably necessary to the admission of members in the first churches; neither will we ever contend with such importune prejudices as, under any pretences capable of a wrangling countenance, shall set up against this evidence. Hence, in the judgment of charity, all the members of those churches were looked on as persons really justified and sanctified,—as effectually converted unto God; and as such were they saluted and treated by the apostles. As such, we say, they were looked on and owned; and as such, upon their confession, it was the duty of all men, even the apostles themselves, to look on them and own them, though absolutely in the sight of God, who alone is "searcher of the hearts of men," some among them were hypocrites, and some proved apostates. But this profession of conversion unto God by the ministry of the word, and the mutual acknowledgment of each other as so converted unto God, in a way of duty, was the foundation of holy, spiritual love and unity among them. And although this did not, nor could, preserve all the first churches absolutely free from schisms and divisions, yet was it the most sovereign antidote against that infection, and the most effectual means for the reduction of unity, after that, by the violent interposition of men's corruptions and temptations, it had been lost for a season. Afterward, in the primitive times, when many more took on them the profession of Christian religion, who had not such eminent and visible conversions unto God as most of those had who were changed by the ministry of the apostles, that persons unfit and unqualified for that state and condition, of being members of churches, might not be admitted into them, unto the disturbance of their order and disreputation of their holy conversation, they were for some good season kept in the condition of expectants, and called catechumens, or persons that attended the church for instruction. In this state they were taught the mysteries of religion, and trial was made of their faith, holiness, and constancy before their admission; and by this means was the preservation of the churches in purity, peace, and order, provided for. Especially were they so in conjunction with that severe discipline which was then exercised towards all the members of them. But after that the multitudes of the Gentile world, in the times of the first Christian emperors, pressed into the church, and were admitted on much easier terms than those before mentioned, whole nations came to claim successively the privilege of church-membership, without any personal duty performed or profession made unto the purpose on their part. And so do they continue to do in many places to this day. Men generally trouble themselves no farther about a title to church membership and privileges, but rest in the prepossession of their ancestors, and their own nativity in such or such places; for whatever may be owned or acknowledged concerning the necessity of a visible profession of faith and repentance, and that credible as to the sincerity of it, in the judgment of charity, it is certain for the most part no such thing is required of any, nor performed by them. And they do but ill consult for the edification of the church, or the good of the souls of men, who would teach them to rest in an outward, formal representation of things, instead of the reality of duties and the power of internal grace. And no small part of the present ruin of Christian religion owes itself unto this corrupt principle; for whereas the things of it,—which consist in powers internal and effectual operations of grace,—have outward representations of them, which, from their relation unto what they represent, are called by the same names with them, many take up with and rest in these external things, as though Christianity consisted in them, although they are but a dead carcase, where the quickening life and soul of internal grace is wanting. Thus it is in this matter, where there is a shadow and appearance of church-order, when the truth and substance of it is far away. Men come together unto all the ends of the church assemblies whereunto they are admitted, but on no other grounds, with no other hearts nor designs, but on and with what they partake in any civil society, or jointly engage in any other worldly concern. And this fundamental error in the constitution of many churches is the occasion, as of other evils, so in particular of divisions among professed Christians. Hence, originally, was the discipline of the church accommodated, by various degrees, to the rule and government of such persons as understood little, or were little sensible, of the nature, power, and efficacy of that spiritual discipline which is instituted in the gospel; which thereby at last degenerated into the outward way of force and power before described: for the churches began to be composed of such as could no otherwise be ruled, and instead of reducing them to their primitive temper and condition, whereunto the evangelical rule was suited, there was invented a way of government accommodate unto that state whereinto they were lapsed; which those concerned found to be the far easier work of the two. Hence did sincere mutual love, with all the fruits of it, begin to decay among church members, seeing they could not have that tolerable persuasion of that truth or profession in each other which is necessary to preserve it without dissimulation, and to provoke it unto a due exercise. Hence did *private spiritual communion* fail amongst them, the most being strangers unto all the ways and means of it, yea, despising and contemning it in all the instances of its exercise; which will yet be found to be as the life and soul of all useful church-communion. And where the public communion is only attended unto, with neglect hereof, it will quickly wither and come to nothing; for on this occasion do all duties of watchfulness, exhortations, and admonitions, proceeding from mutual love and care of each other's condition, so frequently recommended unto us in the Scripture, utterly cease and become disused. Hence members of the same church began to converse together as men only, or at the best, civil neighbours; and if at all as Christians, yet not with respect unto that especial relation unto a particular church wherein their usefulness as members of the same organical body is required, 1 Cor. xii. 14–21. Hence some persons, looking on these things as intolerable, and not only obstructive of their edification, but destructive unto all really useful church-communion, we ought not to wonder if they have thought meet to provide otherwise for themselves. Not that we approve of every departure or withdrawing from the communion of churches where things continue under such disorders, but only show what it is that occasioneth many so to do; for as there may sometimes be just cause hereof, and persons in so doing may manage what they do according unto Scripture rule, so we doubt not but that some may rashly and precipitately, without due attendance unto all the duties which in such undertakings are required of them, without that charity and forbearance which no circumstances can absolve them from, make themselves guilty of a blamable separation. And these are some of those things which we look upon as the general causes or occasions of all the schisms and divisions that are at this day found among professors of the gospel. Whether the guilt of them will not much cleave unto them by whom they are kept on foot and maintained is worth their inquiry; for so doth it befall our human nature, apt to be deceived and imposed on by various pretences and prejudices, that those are oftentimes highly guilty themselves of those miscarriages, whose chiefest satisfaction and glory consist in charging them on others. However, if these things do not absolutely justify any in a secession from the churches whereunto they did relate, yet they render the matter so highly questionable, and the things themselves are so burdensome upon the minds of many, as that divisions will thereon undoubtedly ensue. And when it is so fallen out, to design and contrive the reduction of all unto outward unity and concord, by forcing them who on such occasions have dissented and withdrawn themselves from the communion of any church, without endeavouring the removal of those occasions of their so doing and the reformation of those abuses which have given cause thereunto, is severe, if not unjust. But when the Lord Jesus Christ, in his care towards his churches, and watchfulness over them, shall be pleased to remove these and the like stumbling-blocks out of the way, there will, we hope, be a full return unto gospel unity and peace among them that serve and worship him on the earth.

In this state of things, wherever it be found, it is no wonder if the *weaknesses, ignorance, prejudices,* and *temptations* of men do interpose themselves unto the increase and heightening of those divisions whose springs and occasions lie elsewhere. When none of these provocations were given them, yet we know there was enough in professors themselves to bring forth the bitter fruit of differences and schisms, even in the days of the apostles, 1 Cor. i. 11, iii. 3. How much more may we fear the like fruits and effects from the like principles and corrupt affections! Now the occasions of drawing them forth are more, temptations unto them greater, directions against them less evident and powerful, and all sense of ecclesiastical authority, through its abuse and maladministration, is, if not lost and ruined, yet much weakened and impaired. But from the darkness of the minds of men and their unmortified affections (as the best know but in part, nor are they perfectly sanctified) it is that they are apt to take offence one at another, and thereon to judge and censure each other temerariously; and, which is worst of all, every one to make his own understanding and persuasion thereon the rule of truth and worship unto others. All such ways and courses are against us in the matter of love and union, all tending to make and increase divisions among us: and the evil that is in them we might here declare, but that it falls frequently under the chastisement of other hands; neither, indeed, can it well meet with too much severity of reproof. Only, it were desirable that those by whom such reproofs are managed would take care not to give advantages of retortion or self-justification unto them that are reproved by them; but this they do unavoidably, whilst they seem to make their own judgments and practices the sole rule and measure of what they approve or disallow. In what complies with them there is nothing perverse; and in what differs from them there is nothing sincere! And on this foundation, whilst they reprove censuring, rash-judging, and reproaching of others, with pride, self-conceitedness, false opinions, irregular practices in church-worship, or any other concerns of religion, backbiting, easiness in taking up false reports, with the like evils, as they deserve severely to be rebuked, those reproved by them are apt to think that they see the guilt of many of the crimes charged on themselves in them by whom they are reproved. So on all hands things gender unto farther strife; whilst every party, being conscious unto their own sincerity, according unto the rule of their present light, which is the only measure they can take of it, are ready to impeach the sincerity of them by whom they suppose themselves causelessly traduced and condemned. This evil, therefore, is to be diligently watched against by all that love unity, truth, holiness, or peace; and seeing there are rules and precepts given us in the Scriptures to this purpose, it may not be unmeet to call over some of them.

[First,] One rule of this nature and import is, that we should all of us "study to be quiet, and to do our own business," in things civil and sacred, 1 Thess. iv. 11. Who will harm men, who will be offended with them, whilst they are no otherwise busied in the world? And if any attempt to do them evil, what need have they to be troubled thereat? Duty and innocency will give peace to a worthy soul in the midst of all storms, and whatever may befall it. Now, will any one deny, or can they, but that it is the duty and ought to be the business of every man to seek his own edification and the saving of his soul? Deny this unto any man, and you put yourself in the place of God to him, and make him more miserable than a beast. And this, which no man can forbid, no man can otherwise do than according to that light and knowledge of the will of God which he hath received. If this, therefore, be so attended to as that we do not thereby break in upon the concerns of others, nor disturb them in what is theirs, but be carried on quietly and peaceably, with an evidence in what we do that it is merely our own personal duty that we are in the pursuance of, all cause of offence will be taken away; for if any will yet be offended with men because they peaceably seek the salvation of their own souls, or do that in order thereunto which they cannot but do, unless they will cast off all sense of God's authority over them, it is to seek occasions of offence against them where none are given. But when any persons are acted by a pragmatical curiosity to interpose themselves in the ways, affairs, and concerns of other men, beyond what the laws of love, usefulness, and mutual Christian aid do require, tumults, disorders, vexations, strife, emulations, with a world of evils, will ensue thereon;—especially will they do so when men are prone to dwell on the real or supposed faults of others, which, on various pretences of pity for their persons, or a detestation of their evils, or public reproof of them, they will aggravate, and so on all occasions expose them to public censure, perhaps, as they think, out of zeal to God's glory and a desire for the church's good; for the passions and interests of such persons are ready to swell over the bounds of modesty, sobriety, and peace, though, through the blindness which all self-love is accompanied withal, they seldom see clearly what they do. Would we, therefore, labour to see a beauty, desirableness, and honour in the greatest confinement of our thoughts, words, and actions, unto ourselves and our own occasions, that express duty will admit of, it might tend very much to the preservation of love and peace among professors, for unto this end it is prescribed unto us.

Secondly, It is strictly commanded us that we should " not judge, that we be not judged," Matt. vii. 1, 2. There is no rule for mutual conversation and communion in the Scripture that is oftener repeated or more earnestly inculcated, Luke vi. 37; nor is there any of more use, nor whose grounds and reasons are more evident or more cogent, Rom. xiv. 3, 4, 10. Judging and determining in ourselves, or divulging censures concerning others, their persons, states, and conditions towards God, their principles as to truth and sincerity, their ways as to righteousness and holiness, whether past or present, any otherwise than by the "perfect law of liberty," and that only when we are called thereunto in a way of duty, is the poison of common love and peace, and the ruin of all communion and society, be it of what nature it will. For us to judge and determine whether these or those churches are true churches or no, whether such persons are godly or no, whether such of their principles and actions are regular or no, and so condemn them in our minds (unless where open wickedness will justify the severest reflections), is to speak evil of the law, and to make ourselves judges of it as well as of them who, together with ourselves, are to be judged by it, James iv. 11, 12. Nor is a judgment of that nature necessary unto our advantage in the discharge of any duty required at our hands. We may order all our concernments towards churches and persons without making any such judgment concerning them. But so strong is the inclination of some persons unto an excess in this kind, that no consideration can prevail with them to cast it out, according to its desert. Whether they do it as approving and justifying themselves in what they condemn in others, or as a thing conducing unto their interests, or out of faction and an especial love to some one party of men, or some secret animosities and hatred against others, it is a matter they seldom will quit themselves of whilst they are in this world. Yea, so far do some suffer themselves to be transported, as that they cannot restrain from charging of others with the guilt of such things as they know to be charged on themselves by them who pretend to be the only competent judges in such cases; and so will they also reflect upon and complain of other men for miscarriages by severities, in instances exceedingly inferior, as by themselves represented, unto what it is known they were engaged in. But men are apt to think well of all they do themselves or those whom they peculiarly regard, and to aggravate whatever they conceive amiss in such as they dislike. Were it not better by love to cover a multitude of faults, and to leave the judgment of persons and things, wherein we are not concerned, unto "Him who judgeth righteously, and will render unto every man according to his works?" However, certain it is that until this evil fountain of bitter waters be stopped, until we cease to bless God, even the Father, and at the same time to curse men made after the similitude of God, the wounds that have been given to the love and peace of professors will not be healed.

Thirdly, Unto the same end are all men forbidden to think that they have a *dominion* over the faith of others, or that the ordering and disposal of it is committed unto them. It is Christ alone who is the Lord of the consciences of his disciples; and therefore the best and greatest of the sons of men who have been appointed by him to deal with others in his name, have constantly disclaimed all thoughts of power or rule over the consciences or faith of the meanest of his subjects, 2 Cor. i. 24; 1 Pet. v. 3. How many ways this may be done we are filled with experiences; for no way whereby it may be so hath been left unattempted. And the evil of it hath invaded both churches and particular persons; some whereof, who have been active in casting off the dominion of others, seemed to have designed a possession of it in themselves. And it is well if, where one pope is rejected, many do not rise in his place, who want nothing but his power and interest to do his work. The indignation of some, that others do not in all things comply with their sentiments and subject themselves unto their apprehensions and dictates, ariseth from this presumption; and the persecutions wherein others engage do all grow out of the same bitter root: for men can no otherwise satisfy their consciences herein but by a supposition that they are warranted to give measures unto the minds and practices of others,—that is, their faith and consciences,—in sacred things. And whilst this presumptuous supposition, under any pretence or colour, possesseth the minds of men, it will variously act itself unto the destruction of that gospel unity which it is our duty to preserve; for when they are persuaded that others ought to give up themselves absolutely to their guidance in the things of religion, either because of their office and dignity, or because they are wiser than they, or it may be are only able to dispute more than they, if they do not immediately so do, especially seeing they cannot but judge themselves in the right in all things, they are ready to charge their refusal on all the corrupt affections, principles, and practices which they can surmise, or their supposed just indignation suggest unto them. That they are proud, ignorant, self-conceited, wilful, factious, is immediately concluded; and a semblance unto such charges shall be diligently sought out and improved. Nothing but a deceiving apprehension that they are some way or other meet to have a dominion over the faith of their brethren and fellow-servants would prevail with men otherwise sober and learned so to deal with all that dissent from them as they are pleased to do.

Fourthly, All these evils mentioned are much increased in the minds of men when *they are puffed up with a conceit of their own knowledge and wisdom,* Rom. xii. 3; 1 Cor. viii. 1. This, therefore, we are warned to avoid, that the edification of the church may be promoted and love preserved; for hence are very many apt to take false measures of things, especially of themselves, and thereon to cast themselves into many mischievous mistakes, 2 Cor. x. 12. And this is apt to befall them who, for ends best known unto themselves, have with any ordinary diligence attended to the study of learning; for on a supposal of some competent furniture, with natural abilities, they cannot but attain some skill and knowledge that the common sort of unstudied persons are unacquainted withal;—ofttimes, indeed, their pre-eminence in this kind consists in matters of very small consequence or importance. But whatever it be, it is ready to make them think strange of the apostle's advice: "If any man among you seemeth to be wise in this world, let him become a fool, that he may be wise," 1 Cor. iii. 18. Apt it is to puff them up, to influence their minds with a good conceit of themselves, and a contempt of others. Hence may we see some, when they have got a little skill in languages, and through custom, advantaged by the reading of some books, are able readily to express some thoughts, perhaps not originally their own, presently conceit themselves to be so much wiser than the multitude of unlettered persons, that they are altogether impatient that in any thing they should dissent from them; and this is a common frame with them whose learning and wit being their all, do yet but reach half way towards the useful ends of such things. Others also there are, and of them not a few, who having been in the ways wherein the skill and knowledge mentioned are usually attained, yet through their incapacity or negligence, or some depraved habit of mind or course of life, have not really at all improved in them; and yet these also, having once attained the countenance of ecclesiastical offices or preferments, are as forward as any to declaim against and pretend a contempt of that ignorance in others which they are not so stupid as not to know that the guilt of it may be reflected on themselves. However, these things at best, and in their highest improvement, are far enough from solid wisdom, especially that which is from above, and which alone will promote the peace and edification of the church. Some have no advantage by them but that they can declare and speak out their own weakness; others, that they can rail, and lie, and falsely accuse, in words and language wherewith they hope to please the vilest of men. And certain it is that science,—which whatever it be, without the grace of God, is but falsely so called, and oftentimes falsely pretended unto, for this evil end of it alone,—is apt to lift up the minds of men above others, who perhaps come not behind them in any useful understanding. Yea, suppose men to have really attained a singular degree in useful knowledge and wisdom, and that either in things spiritual and divine, or in learning and sciences, or in political prudence, yet experience shows us that a hurtful elation of mind is apt to arise from them, if the souls of men be not well balanced with humility, and this evil particularly watched against. Hence ariseth that impatience of contradiction, that jealousy and tenderness of men's own names and reputations, those sharp revenges they are ready to take of any supposed inroads upon them or disrespects towards them, that contempt and undervaluation of other men's judgments, those magisterial impositions and censures, which proceed from men under a reputation of these endowments. The cautions given us in the Scripture against this frame of spirit, the examples that are proposed unto us to the contrary (even that of Christ himself), the commands that are multiplied for lowliness of mind, jealousy over ourselves, the sovereignty of God in choosing whom he pleaseth to reveal his mind and truth unto and by, may, in the consideration of them, be useful to prevent such surprisals with pride, self-conceit, and contempt of others, as supposed or abused knowledge is apt to cast men into, whereby divisions are greatly fomented and increased among us. But it may be these things will not much prevail with them who, pretending a zeal and principle above others in preaching and urging the example of Christ, do in most of their ways and actings, and in some of their writings, give us an unparalleled representation of the devil.

Lastly, It is confessed by all, that *false teachers*, seducers, broachers of novel, corrupt, and heretical doctrines, have caused many breaches and divisions among such as once agreed in the profession of the same truths and points of faith.   By means of such persons, whether within the present church-state or without, there is scarce any sacred truth, which had formerly secured its station and possession in the minds of the generality of Christians in this nation, but what hath been solicited or opposed.   Some make their errors the principal foundation, rule, and measure in communion; whoever complies with them therein is of them, and whoso doth not they avoid: so at once they shut up themselves from having any thing to do with them that love truth and peace.   And where these consequents do not ensue, men's zeal for their errors being overbalanced by their love of and concern in their secular interest, and their minds influenced by the novel prevailing opinion of a great indifference in all things appertaining unto outward worship, yet the advancing and fomenting of opinions contrary unto that sound doctrine which hath been generally owned and taught by the learned and godly pastors, and received by the people themselves, cannot but occasion strife, contentions, and divisions among professors.   And it may be there are very few of those articles or heads of religion which in the beginning of the Reformation, and a long time after, were looked on as the most useful, important, and necessary parts of our profession, that have not been among us variously opposed and corrupted.   And in these differences about doctrine lie the hidden causes of the animosities whereby those about worship and discipline are managed; for those who have the advantage of law and power on their side in these lesser things are not so unwise as to deal openly with their adversaries about those things wherein the reputation of established and commonly-received doctrines lie against them; but under the pretence and shelter of contending for legal appointments, not a few do exercise an enmity against those who profess the truth, which they think it not meet as yet openly to oppose.

Such are the causes and such are the occasions of the differences and divisions in and about religious concerns that are among us, by which means they have been fomented and increased: heightened they have been by the personal faults and miscarriages of many of all sorts and parties.   And as the reproof of their sinful failings is in its proper season a necessary duty, so no reformation or amendment of persons will give a full relief, nor free us from the evil of our divisions, until the principles and ways which occasion them be taken out of the way.

CHAPTER V.

Grounds and reasons of nonconformity.

HAVING briefly declared our sense concerning the general causes and occasions of our differences, and that present want of Christian love which is complained of by many, we shall now return to give some more particular account concerning our inconformity unto and non-compliance with the observances and constitutions of the church of England. It is acknowledged, that we do in sundry things dissent from them; that we do not, that we cannot, come up unto a joint practice with others in them. It is also confessed, that hereon there doth ensue an appearance of schism between them and us, according as the common notion of it is received in the world. And because in this distance and difference the dissent unto compliance is on our parts, there is a semblance of a voluntary relinquishment of their communion; and this we know exposeth us, in vulgar judgments and apprehensions, unto the charge of schism, and necessitateth us unto self-defence, as though the only matter in question were, whether we are guilty of this evil or no. For that advantage have all churches which have had an opportunity to fix terms of communion, right or wrong, just or unequal,—the differences which ensue thereon, they will try out on no other terms, but only whether those that dissent from them are schismatics or not. Thus they make themselves actors ofttimes in this cause who ought in the first place to be charged with injury; and a trial is made merely at the hazard of the reputation of those who are causelessly put upon their purgation and defence. Yea, with many, a kind of possession and multitude do render dissenters unquestionably schismatical; so that it is esteemed an unreasonable confidence in them to deny themselves so to be. So deals the church of Rome with those that are reformed. An open schism there is between them; and if they cannot sufficiently fix the guilt of it on the reformed by confidence and clamours, with the advantage of prepossession, yet, as if they were perfectly innocent themselves, they will allow of no other inquiry in this matter but what consists in calling the truth and reputation of the other party into question. It being our present condition to lie under this charge from many, whose interest it is to have us thought guilty thereof, we do deny that there is any culpable secession made by us from the communion of any that profess the gospel in these nations, or that the blame of the appearing schism that is among us can duly or justly be reflected on us; which, in the remainder of our discourse, we shall make to appear.

What are our thoughts and judgments concerning the church state and interest of the professors of the gospel in this nation, we have before declared; and we hope they are such that, in the judgment of persons sober and impartial, we shall be relieved from those clamorous accusations which are without number or measure by some cast upon us. Our prayers are also continually unto the God of love and peace, for the taking away of all divisions and their causes from among us. Nor is the satisfaction which ariseth from our sincerity herein in the least taken off or rent from us by the uncharitable endeavours of some to rake up pretences to the contrary. And should those in whose power it is think meet to imitate the pastors and guides of the churches of old, and to follow them in any of the ways which they used for the restoration of unity and agreement unto Christians, when lost or endangered, we should not decline the contribution of any assistance, by counsel or fraternal compliance, which God should be pleased to supply us withal. But whilst some, whose advantages render them considerable in these matters, seem to entertain no other thoughts concerning us but what issue in violence and oppression, the principal duty incumbent on us is quietly to approve our consciences unto God, that in sincerity of heart we desire in all things to please him, and to conform our lives, principles, and practices to his will, so far as he is graciously pleased to make it known unto us. And as for men, we hope so to discharge the duty required of us as that none may justly charge us with any disorders, unpeaceableness, or other evils; for we do not apprehend that we are either the cause or culpable occasion of those inconveniences and troubles which some have put themselves unto by their endeavours for our disturbance, impoverishing, and ruin. Let none imagine but that we have considered the evils and evil consequents of the schisms and divisions that are among us; and those who do so, do it upon the forfeiture of their charity. We know how much the great work of preaching the gospel, unto the conversion of the souls of men, is impeded thereby; as also what prejudice ariseth thence against the truth wherein we are all agreed, with what temptations and mutual exasperations, to the loss of love, and the occasioning of many sinful miscarriages in persons of all sorts, do hereon ensue: but we deny that it is in our power to remove them, or take them out of the way; —nor are we conscious unto ourselves of any sin or evil, in what we do, or in what we do not do, by our not doing of it in the worship of God. It is duty alone unto Jesus Christ whereunto in these things we attend, and wherein we ought so to do. And where matters of this nature are so circumstanced as that duty will contribute nothing towards unity, we are at a loss for any progress towards it. The sum of what is objected unto us (as hath been observed) is our nonconformity, or our forbearance of actual personal communion with the present church constitutions, in the modes, rites, and ceremonies of its worship: hence the schism complained of doth ensue. Unless the communion be total, constant, without endeavour of any alteration or reformation, we cannot, in the judgment of some, be freed from the guilt hereof. This we deny, and are persuaded that it is to be charged elsewhere; for,—

First, All the conditions of absolute and complete communion with the church of England, which are proposed unto us, and indispensably required of us, especially as we are ministers, are *unscriptural*,—such as the word of God doth neither warrant, mention, nor intimate, especially not under any such consideration as necessary conditions of communion in or among the churches of Christ. We dispute not now about the lawfulness or unlawfulness of things in themselves, nor whether they may be observed or no by such as have no conviction of any sin or evil in them; neither do we judge or censure them by whom they are observed. Our inquiry is solely about our own liberty and duty. And what concerneth them is resolved into this one question, as to the argument in hand: Whether such things or observances in the worship of God as are wholly unscriptural may be so made the indispensable condition of communion with any particular church, as that they by whom they are so made and imposed on others should be justified in their so doing; and that if any differences, divisions, or schisms do ensue thereon, the guilt and blame of them must necessarily fall on those who refuse submission to them or to admit of them as such? That the conditions proposed unto us, and imposed on us indispensably, if we intend to enjoy the communion of this church, are of this nature, we shall afterward prove by an induction of instances. Nor is it of any concernment, in this matter, what place the things inquired after do hold, or are supposed to hold, in the worship of God; our present inquiry is about their warranty to be made conditions of church communion. Now, we are persuaded that the Lord Christ hath set his disciples at liberty from accepting of such terms of communion from any churches in the world. And on the same grounds we deny that he hath given or granted unto them authority to constitute such terms and conditions of their communion, and indispensably to impose them upon all that enjoy it, according to their several capacities and concerns therein; for,—

1. The *rule of communion* among the disciples of Christ in all his churches is invariably established and fixed by himself. His commission, direction, and command, given out unto the first planters and founders of them, containing an obliging rule unto all that should succeed them throughout all generations, hath so established

the bounds, limits, and conditions of church-communion, as that it is not lawful for any to attempt their removal or alteration. "Go ye," saith he to them, "and teach all nations, baptizing them in the name of the Father, and of the Son, and of the Holy Ghost; teaching them to observe all things whatsoever I have commanded you: and, lo, I am with you alway, even unto the end of the world," Matt. xxviii. 19, 20. All the benefits and blessings, all the comfort and use of church assemblies and communion, depend alone on the promise of the presence of Christ with them. Thence doth all the authority that may be exercised in them proceed, and thence doth the efficacy of what they do unto the edification of the souls of men arise and flow. Now, that any one may thus enjoy the presence of Christ in any church, with the fruits and benefits of it, no more can be required of him but that, through the preaching of the gospel and baptism, being made a professed disciple, he do or be ready to do and observe all whatsoever Christ hath commanded. This hath he established as the rule of communion among his disciples and churches in all generations. In all other things which do relate unto the worship of God, he hath set them and left them at liberty, Gal. v. 1; which, so far as it is a grant and privilege purchased for them, they are obliged to make good and maintain. We know it will be here replied, that among the commands of Christ it is that we should "hear the church," and obey the guides and rulers thereof; whatever, therefore, is appointed by them, we are to submit unto and observe, even by virtue of the command of Christ. And, indeed, it is certainly true that it is the will and command of the Lord Jesus that we should both hear the church and obey the guides of it;—but, by virtue of this rule, neither the church nor its guides can make any thing necessary to the disciples of Christ, as a condition of communion with them, but only what he hath commanded; for the rule here laid down is given unto those guides or rulers, who are thereby bound up, in the appointments of what the disciples are to observe, unto the commands of Christ. And were a command included herein of obeying the commands or appointments of church guides, and the promise of the presence of Christ annexed thereunto, as he had given them all his own power and placed them in his throne, so we had been all obliged to follow them whither ever they had carried or led us, although it were to hell itself, as some of the canonists, on this principle, have spoken concerning the pope. Here, therefore, is a rule of communion fixed, both unto them that are to rule in the church and them that are to obey. And whereas, perhaps, it may be said, that if the rulers of the church may appoint nothing in and unto the communion of the church but what Christ hath himself commanded, then, indeed, is their authority little worth, yea, upon the matter none at all, for the commands of Christ are sufficiently confirmed and fixed by his own authority; and to what end, then, serves that of the rulers of the church?—we must say that their whole authority is limited in the text unto teaching of men to observe what Christ hath commanded; and this they are to do with authority, but under him and in his name, and according to the rules that he hath given them.   And those who think not this power sufficient for them must seek it elsewhere, for the Lord Christ will allow no more in his churches.

To make this yet more evident, we may consider that particular instance wherein the primitive Christians had a trial in the case as now stated before us; and this was in the matter of Mosaical ceremonies and institutions, which some would have imposed on them as a condition of their communion in the profession of the gospel.   In the determination hereof was their liberty asserted by the apostles, and their duty declared, to abide therein.   And this was the most specious pretence of imposing on the liberty of Christians that ever they were exercised withal; for the observation of these things had countenance given unto it from their divine original, and the condescending practice of the apostles for a good season.   That other instances of the like nature should be condemned in the Scripture is impossible, seeing none had then endeavoured the introduction of any of that nature.   But a general rule may be established in the determination of one case as well as in that of many, provided it be not extended beyond what is eminently included in that case.   Herein, therefore, was there a direction given for the duty and practice of churches in following ages, and that in pursuit of the law and constitution of the Lord Christ before mentioned.   Neither is there any force in the exception, that these things were imposed under a pretence of being commanded by God himself: for they say, to require any thing under that notion, which indeed he hath not commanded, is an adding to his command, which ought not to be admitted; but to require things indifferent without that pretence may be allowed. But as in the former way men add unto the commands of God formally, so in this latter they do it materially, which also is prohibited; for in his worship we are forbidden to add to the things that he hath appointed no less than to pretend commands from him which he hath not given.   He, therefore, who professeth and pleadeth his willingness to observe and do in church-communion whatever Christ hath instituted and commanded cannot regularly be refused the communion of any church, under any pretence of his refusal to do other things which confessedly are not so required.

It is pleaded, indeed, that no other things, as to the *substance* of the worship of God, can or ought to be appointed besides what is instituted by Jesus Christ; but as to the *manner* or modes of the performance of what he doth command, with other rites and ceremonies to be observed for order and decency, they may lawfully be instituted by the rulers of the church. Let it therefore at present be granted that so they may be, by them who are persuaded of the lawfulness of those modes, and of the things wherein they consist, seeing that is not the question at present under agitation;—neither will this concession help us in our present inquiry, unless it be also granted that whatever may be lawfully practised in the worship of God may be lawfully made a necessary condition of communion in that worship; but this will not be granted, nor can it ever be proved. Besides, in our present difference, this is only the judgment of one party, that the things mentioned may be lawfully observed in and among sacred administrations; and thereon the conclusion must be, that whatever some think may be lawfully practised in divine worship may lawfully be made an indispensable condition of communion unto the whole. Nor will it give force unto this inference, that those who judge them lawful are the rulers and guides of the church, unto whose determination the judgment of private persons is not to be opposed; for we have showed before that a judgment concerning what any one is to do or practise in the worship of God belongs unto every man who is to do or practise aught therein, and he who makes it not is brutish. And the judgment which the rulers of the church are to make for the whole, or to go before it, is in what is commanded, or not so, by Jesus Christ, not in what is fit to be added thereunto by themselves. Besides, if it must be allowed that such things may be made the conditions of church-communion, then any who are in places of authority may multiply such conditions according unto the utmost extent of their judgments, until they become burdensome and intolerable unto all, or really ridiculous in themselves; as it is fallen out in the church of Rome. But this would prove expressly destructive unto that certain and unvariable rule of church-communion which the Lord Christ hath fixed and established, whereof we shall speak again afterward.

Neither will that plea which is by some insisted on in this case yield any solid or universal relief. It is said that *some may warrantably and duly observe in the worship of God what is unduly and unwarrantably imposed on them by others.* And, indeed, all controversies about church constitution, discipline, and external worship, are by some reduced unto these two heads: That the magistrate may appoint what he pleaseth, and the people may observe whatever he appoints ; for as there is no government of the church determined in the Scripture, it is meet it should be erected and disposed by the supreme magistrate, who, no doubt, upon that supposition, is only fit and qualified so to do. And for outward worship, and the rites thereof, both it and they are so far indifferent as that we may comply with whatever is imposed on us; whether they be good and useful, or evil, lies at the doors of others to answer about. But this seems to rise up in express contradiction unto those commands which are given us to "stand fast in the liberty wherewith Christ hath made us free," and in these things not to be "the servants of men;" for what do we do less than renounce the privilege of our liberty, purchased for us at a high rate and price, or what are we less than "servants of men," whilst we bring ourselves in bondage unto the observation of such things in the worship of God as we judge neither commanded by him nor tending unto our own edification, but merely because by them ordained? Moreover, suppose it be the judgment of some, as it is of many, that the things mentioned, though in their own nature indifferent, do become unlawful unto them to observe when imposed as necessary conditions of all church-communion, contrary to the command and appointment of Christ. We know this is exceedingly declaimed against, as that which is perverse and froward: "For what," say many, "can be more unreasonable than that things in their own nature indifferent should become unlawful because they are commanded?" But it is at least no less unreasonable that things confessedly indifferent should not be left so, but be rendered necessary unto practice, though useless in it, by arbitrary commands. But the opinion traduced is also much mistaken; for although it be granted that the things themselves are indifferent in their own nature,—not capable, but as determined by circumstances, of either moral good or evil, yet it is not granted that the observation of them, even as uncommanded, is indifferent in the worship of God. And although the command doth not alter the nature, and make that which was indifferent become evil, yet that command of itself being contrary to many divine commands and instructions given us in the Scripture, a compliance with the things commanded therein may become unlawful to us. And what shall they do whose judgment this is? Shall they admit of them as lawful, upon the consideration of that change about them which renders them unlawful? This they will not easily be induced to give their assent unto.

Let, therefore, the rule of church-communion be observed which our Lord Jesus Christ hath fixed, and no small occasion of our strifes and divisions will be removed out of the way. But whilst there is this contest amongst us, if one pleads his readiness "to do and observe whatever the Lord Christ hath commanded," and cannot be convinced of insincerity in his profession, or of want of understanding in any known institution of his, and thereon requires the communion of any church; but others say, "Nay, you shall observe and do sundry other things that we ourselves have appointed, or you shall have no communion with us;"—as it cannot be but that divisions and schisms will ensue thereon, so it will not be difficult for an indifferent bystander to judge on whether side the occasion and guilt of them doth remain.

2. We have *the practice of the apostles*, in the pursuance of the direction and command of their Lord and ours, for our guide in this case. And it might be well and safely thought that this should give a certain rule unto the proceedings and actings of all church guides in future ages. Now, they did never make any thing unscriptural, or what they had not received by divine revelation, to be a condition of communion in religious worship and church-order among Christians: for as they testified themselves that "they would give themselves continually to prayer, and to the ministry of the word," Acts vi. 4, so it was of old observed concerning them, "that their constant labour was for the good of the souls of men in their conversion unto God, and edification in faith and holiness;"[1] but as for the institution of festivals or fasts, of rites or ceremonies, to be observed in the worship of the churches, they intermeddled with no such things. And thence it came to pass, that in the first entrance and admission of observances about such things, there was a great and endless variety in them, both as to the things themselves observed and as to the manner of their observation; and this was gradually increased unto such a height and excess, as that the burden of them became intolerable unto Christendom. Nor, indeed, could any better success be expected in a relinquishment and departure from the pattern of church-order given us in their example and practice. Neither is the plea from hence built merely on this consideration, that no man alive, either from their writings or the approved records of those times, can manifest that they ever prescribed unto the churches or imposed on them the observance of any uninstituted rite, to be observed as a measure and rule of their communion, but also it so fell out, in the good providence of God, that the case under debate was proposed unto them, and jointly determined by them; for, being called unto advice and counsel in the difference that was between the Jewish and Gentile converts and professors, wherein the former laboured to impose on the latter the observation of Moses' institutions as the condition of their joint communion, as was mentioned even now, they not only determine against any such imposition, but also expressly declare that nothing but "necessary things" (that is, such as are so from other reasons antecedently unto their prescriptions and appointments) ought to be required of any Christians in the communion or worship of the church, Acts xv. And as they neither did nor would, on that great

[1] Socrat. Hist., lib. v.

occasion, in that solemn assembly, appoint any one thing to be observed by the disciples and churches which the Lord Christ had not commanded, so in their direction given unto the Gentile believers for a temporary abstinence from the use of their liberty in one or two instances whereunto it did extend, they plainly intimate that it was the avoidance of a present scandal, which might have greatly retarded the progress of the gospel, that was the reason of that direction.   And in such cases it is granted that we may in many things for a season forego the use of our liberty.   This was their way and practice, this the example which they left unto all that should follow them in the rule and guidance of the church.   Whence it is come to pass in after ages that men should think themselves wiser than they, or more careful to provide for the peace and unity of the church, we know not.   But let the bounds and measures of church-communion fixed in and by their example stand unmoved, and many causes of our present divisions will be taken away.   But, it may be, it will be offered, that the present state of things in the world requires some alteration in or variation from the precise example of the apostles in this matter.   The due observation of the institutions of Christ, in such manner as the nature of them required, was then sufficient unto the peace and unity of the churches; but primitive simplicity is now decayed among the most, so that a multiplication of rules and observances is needful for the same ends.   But we have showed before, that the accommodation of church rule and communion to the degeneracy of Christians or churches, or their secular engagements, is no way advantageous unto religion.   Let them whose duty it is endeavour to reduce professors and profession to the *primitive standard* of light, humility, and holiness, and they may be ordered in all church concerns according to the apostolical pattern.   Wherefore, when Christians unto the former plea of their readiness to observe and do whatsoever Christ hath commanded them, do also add their willingness to comply with whatever the apostles of Christ have either by precept or example in their own practice commended unto them, or did do or require in the first churches, and cannot be convinced of failing to make good their profession, we do not know whence any can derive a warranty enabling them to impose any other conditions of communion on them.   The institution, therefore, of the Lord Christ, and the practice of the apostles, lie directly against the imposing of the conditions inquired about.   And first to invent them, then to impose them, making them necessary to be observed, and then to judge and censure them as schismatics, as enemies to love and peace, who do not submit unto them, looks not unlike the exercise of an unwarrantable dominion over the faith and consciences of the disciples of Christ.

3. Not only by their example and practice, but they have also *doctrinally* declared what is the duty of churches, and what is the liberty of Christians in this matter. The apostle Paul discourseth at large hereon, Rom. xiv., xv. The attentive reading of these two chapters is sufficient to determine this cause among all uninterested and unprejudiced persons. He supposeth in them,—and it is the case which he exemplifies in sundry instances,—that there were among Christians and churches at that time different apprehensions and observances about some things appertaining unto the worship of God; and these things were such as had some seeming countenance of a sacred and divine authority, for such was their original institution. Some, on the consideration hereof, judged that they were still to be observed, and their consciences had been long exercised in a holy subjection unto the authority of God in the observance of them. Nor was there yet any express and positive law enacted for their abrogation; but the ceasing of any obligation unto their observance from their primitive institution was to be gathered from the nature of God's economy towards his church. Many, therefore, continued to observe them, esteeming it their duty so to do. Others were persuaded and satisfied that they were freed from any obligation unto the owning and observance of them; and whereas this liberty was given them by Jesus Christ in the gospel, they were resolved to make use of it, and not to comply with the other sort, who pressed conformity upon them in their ceremonies and modes of divine worship. So it may fall out in other instances. Some may be persuaded that such or such things may be lawful for them to observe in the worship of God,—they may be so unto them, and, as is supposed, in their own nature; on the consideration of some circumstances, they may judge that it is convenient or expedient to attend unto their observance; lastly, all coincidences weighed, that it is necessary that so they should do, and that others also that walk with them in the profession of the gospel should conform themselves unto their order and practice. On the other hand, some there are who, because the things of the joint practice required are not appointed by Jesus Christ, nor doth it appear unto them that he hath given power unto any others to appoint them, do not judge it expedient, nor yet, all circumstances considered, lawful to observe them. Now, whereas this case answers unto that before proposed, the determination thereof given by the apostle may safely be applied unto this also. What rule, therefore, doth he give therein, which he would have attended unto as the means for the preservation of love, peace, and unity among them? Is it that the former sort of persons, provided they be the most or have the most power, ought to impose the practice of those things which they esteem lawful and convenient on those who judge them

not so, when it is out of question that they are not appointed by Christ, only it is pretended that they are not forbidden by him? Where, indeed, the question was about the institutions of Christ, he binds up the churches precisely unto what he had received from him, 1 Cor. xi. 23; but in cases of this nature, wherein a direct command of Christ cannot be pleaded nor is pretended, he absolutely rejects and condemns all thoughts of such a procedure.   But supposing that differences in judgment and practice were and would be among Christians, the sum of his advice is, that all offences and scandals ought to be diligently avoided; that censuring, judging, and despisings, on the account of such differences, be cast out; that tenderness be used towards them that are weak, and nothing severely pressed on them that doubt; and for their different apprehensions and ways, they should all walk in peace, condescending unto and bearing with one another.   Nothing can more evidently determine the unlawfulness of imposing on Christians unscriptural conditions of communion than do the discourses of that great apostle to this purpose.   Yea, better it is, and more agreeable unto the mind of Christ, that persons and particular churches should be left unto different observations in sundry things relating unto sacred worship, wherein they cannot join with each other nor communicate together, endeavouring in the meantime to "keep the unity of the Spirit in the bond of peace," than that they should be enforced unto a uniformity in the practice of things that have not the immediate authority of Christ enstamped on them.   Accordingly it so fell out among them unto whom the apostle gave these directions, and that suitably unto his intention in them; for the dissenting parties agreeing in the common faith and profession of the gospel, did yet constantly meet in distinct assemblies or churches for the celebration of holy worship, because of the different rites wherein they did not agree. And in this posture were peace and love continued among them, until in process of time, their differences through mutual forbearance being extinguished, they coalesced into one church state and order. And the former peace which they had in their distances was deemed sufficient, whilst things were not measured nor regulated by secular interest or advantages.   But it is a part of our present unhappiness, that such a peace among Christians and particular churches is mistaken to have an ill aspect upon the concerns of some belonging unto the church in power, honour, and revenue.   But as we apprehend there is, as things are now stated among us, a plain mistake in this surmise, so, if the glory of God and the honour of the gospel were chief in our consultations about church affairs, it would be with us of no such consideration as to hinder us from committing quietly the success and events of duty unto the providence of God.

4. There was also a signal vindication of the truth pleaded for, in an *instance of fact* among the primitive churches. There was an opinion which prevailed very early among them about the necessary observation of Easter, in the room of the Jewish passover, for the solemn commemoration of the death and resurrection of our Saviour. And it was taken for granted by most of them, that the observance hereof was countenanced, if not rendered necessary unto them, by the example of the apostles; for they generally believed that by them it was observed, and that it was their duty to accommodate themselves unto their practice; only there was a difference about the precise time or day which they were to solemnize as the head and rule of their festival, as every undue presumption hath one lameness or other accompanying it,—it is truth alone which is square and steady. Some, therefore, pleaded the example of John the apostle and evangelist, who, as it is strongly asserted and testified by multitudes, kept his Easter at such a time and by such a rule; whom they thought meet to follow and imitate. Others, not inferior unto them in number or authority, opposed unto their time the example of Peter, whom they affirmed (on what grounds and reasons they knew best, for they are now lost) to have observed his Easter at another time, and according unto a different rule. And it is scarcely imaginable how the contests hereabouts troubled the churches both of Europe and Asia, who certainly had things more material to have exercised themselves about. The church of Rome embraced that opinion which at length prevailed over the other, and obtained a kind of catholicism against that which was countenanced only by the authority of St John; as that church was always wondrous happy in reducing other churches unto an acquiescency in its sentiments, as seldom wanting desire or skill dexterously to improve its manifold advantages. Now, this was that Easter was to be celebrated on the Lord's day only, and not by the rule of the Jewish passover, on the fourteenth day of the first month, what day of the week soever it fell out upon. Hereon Victor, the bishop of that church, being confident that the truth was on his side,—namely, that Easter was to be observed on the Lord's day,—resolved to make it a condition of communion unto all the churches, for otherwise he saw not how there could be either union, peace, or uniformity among them. He did not question but that he had a good foundation to build upon; for that Easter was to be observed by virtue of apostolical tradition was generally granted by all. And he took it as unquestionable, upon a current and prevalent rumour, that the observation of it was confined to the Lord's day by the example of St Peter. Hereupon he refused the communion of all that would not conform unto his resolution for the observation of Easter on the Lord's day, and cast out of commu-

nion all those persons and churches who would observe any other day; which proved to be the condition of the principal churches of Asia, amongst whom the apostle John did longest converse. Here was our present case directly exemplified or represented so long beforehand. The success only of this fact of his remaineth to be inquired into. Now, it is known unto all what entertainment this his new rule of communion found among the churches of Christ. The reproof of his precipitancy and irregular fixing new bounds unto church-communion was famous in those days; especially the rebuke given unto him and his practice by one[1] of the most holy and learned persons then living is eminently celebrated, as consonant to truth and peace, by those who have transmitted unto us the reports of those times. He who himself first condemned others rashly was for his so doing generally condemned by all. Suppose, now, that any persons living at Rome, and there called into communion with the church, should have had the condition thereof proposed unto them,—namely, that they should assent and declare that the observation of Easter, by apostolical tradition, was to be on the Lord's day only,—and upon their refusal so to do should be excluded from communion, or on their own accords should refrain from it, where should the guilt of this disorder and schism be charged? And thus it fell out, not only with those who came out of Asia to Rome, who were not received by that Diotrephes, but also with sundry in that church itself, as Blastus and others; as what great divisions were occasioned hereby between the Saxons and Britons hath been by many declared. But, in the judgment of the primitive churches, the guilt of these schisms was to be charged on them that coined and imposed these new rules and conditions of communion; and had they not been judged by any, the pernicious consequences of this temerarious attempt are sufficient to reflect no inconsiderable guilt upon it. Neither could the whole observance itself, from first to last, ever compensate that loss of love and peace among Christians and churches which was occasioned thereby; nor hath the introduction of such things ever obtained any better success in the church of God. How free the churches were until that time, after they were once delivered from the attempt of the circumcised professors to impose upon them the ceremonies of Moses, from any appearance of unwritten conditions of communion, is manifest unto all who have looked into the monuments which remain of those times. It is very true that sundry Christians took upon them very early the observation of sundry rites and usages in religion whereunto they had no guidance or direction by the word of God; for as the corrupted nature of man is prone to the invention and use of sensible present things in religion, especially

---

[1] The allusion is to Irenæus; see Eus. v. 24.—Ed.

where persons are not able to find satisfaction in those that are purely spiritual, requiring great intension of mind and affections in their exercise, so were they many of them easily infected by that tincture which remained in them from the Judaism or Gentilism from which they were converted.   But these observances were free, and taken up by men of their own accord, not only every church, but every person in the most of them, as far as it appears, being left unto their own liberty.   Some ages it was before such things were turned into laws and canons, and that perhaps first by heretics, or at least under such a degeneracy as our minds and consciences cannot be regulated by. The judgment, therefore, and practice of the first churches are manifest against such impositions.

5. Upon a supposition that it should be lawful for any persons or churches to assign unscriptural conditions of their communion, it will follow that *there is no certain rule of communion* amongst Christians fixed and determined by Christ.   That this is otherwise we have before declared, and shall now only manifest the evil consequences of such a supposition: for if it be so, no man can claim an admission into the society or communion of any church, or a participation in the ordinances of the gospel with them, by virtue of the authority of Jesus Christ; for notwithstanding all his pleas of submission to his institutions, and the observation of his commands, every church may propose something, yea, many things, unto him that he hath not appointed, without an admission whereof and subjection thereunto he may be justly excluded from all church privileges among them.   Now, this seems not consonant unto the authority that Christ hath over the church, nor that honour which ought to be given unto him therein.   Nor, on the same supposition, are his laws sufficient to rule and quiet the consciences, or to provide for the edification of his disciples.   Now, if Diotrephes is blamed for not receiving the brethren who were recommended unto the church by the apostle, 3 John 9, 10, probably because they would not submit to that pre-eminence which he had obtained among them, they will scarcely escape without reproof who refuse those whom the Lord Christ commends unto them by the rules of the gospel, because they will not submit unto such new impositions as, by virtue of their pre-eminence, they would put upon them.   And what endless perplexities they must be cast into who have learned in these things to call him only Lord and Master is apparent unto all.   Baptism, with a voluntary credible profession of faith, repentance, and obedience unto the Lord Christ, in his commands and institutions, is all the warranty which he hath given unto any of his disciples to claim their admission into his churches, which are instituted and appointed to receive them, and to build them up in their faith.   And if any person who pro-

duceth this warranty, and thereon desireth, according to order, the communion of any church,—if he may be excluded from it or forbidden an entrance into it, unless it be on grounds sufficient, in the judgment of charity, to evince the falseness and hypocrisy of his profession, little regard is had to the authority of Christ, and too much unto men's own. Churches, indeed, may more or less insist upon the explicitness of this profession and the evidences of its sincerity, as they find it tend to their peace and edification, with a due attendance unto the rule and example left unto them in this matter in the gospel. And that the exercise of this power in any churches may not turn to the prejudice of any, every professor is allowed, with reference unto particular assemblies, to make his choice of the measure he will comply withal, at least if he will make the choice of his habitation subservient unto his edification. Hereby the peace and duty both of churches and private persons are secured. And this rule of church admission and communion furnished Christians with peace, love, and unity for many ages, setting aside the ruffle given them in the rashness of Victor before mentioned. It was also rendered practicable and easy by virtue of their communion as churches among themselves; for from thence commendatory letters supplied the room of actual profession in them who, having been admitted into one church, did desire the same privilege in any other. And on this rule were persons to be "received," though "weak in the faith," though it may be in some things " otherwise minded" than the generality of the church, though " babes" and " unskilful" as to degrees in the word of truth, Rom. xiv. 1; Phil. iii. 15; Heb. v. 12–14. But this rule was always attended with a proviso, that men did not contradict or destroy their own profession by any unholy conversation; for such persons never were, nor never are to be, admitted unto the especial ordinances of the church; and a neglect of due attendance hereunto is that which principally hath cast us into all our confusions, and rendered the institutions of Christ ineffectual. And if this warranty, which the Lord Christ hath given unto his disciples, of claiming a participation in all the privileges of his churches, an admission unto a joint performance of all the duties required in them, may, upon the supposition of a power left to impose other conditions of communion on them, be rejected and rendered useless, all church-communion is absolutely resolved into the variable wills of men. The church, no doubt, may judge and determine upon the laws of Christ, and their due application unto particular occasions,—as whether such persons may according to them be admitted into their fellowship; to deprive churches of this liberty is to take away their principal use and service: but to make laws of their own, the subject-matter whereof shall be things not commanded by Christ, and to make them the rule of admitting professed Christians unto their communion, is an assumption that cannot be justified. And it is certain that the assuming of an authority by some churches for such like impositions is that which hath principally occasioned many to deny them so to be; so at once to overthrow the foundation of all that authority which in so many instances they find to be abused. And although the church of Rome may prevail on weak and credulous persons, by proposing unto them an absolute acquiescency in their dictates and determinations, as the best, readiest, and most facile means of satisfaction, yet there is nothing that doth more alienate wise and conscientious persons from them than doth that unreasonable proposal. Moreover, it is highly probable that endless disputes will arise on this supposition about what is meet and convenient, and what not, to be added unto the Scripture rules of communion. They have done so in the ages past, and continue yet to do. Nor can any man on this principle know, or probably conjecture, when he hath a firm station in the church, or an indefeasible interest in the privileges thereof; for supposing that he hath concocted the impositions of one church, on the first removal of his habitation he may have new conditions of communion prescribed unto him. And from this perplexity nothing can relieve him but a resolution to do in every place whereunto he may come according to the manner of the place, be it good or bad, right or wrong. But neither hath the Lord Christ left his disciples in this uncertainty which the case supposeth, nor will accept of that indifferency which is in the remedy suggested. They, therefore, who regulate their communion with any churches by the firm stated law of their right and privilege, if they are not received thereon, do not by their abstinence from it contract the guilt of schism or any blamable divisions.

Moreover, upon a supposition of such a liberty and power to prescribe and impose unwritten conditions of church-communion on Christians, who or what law doth or shall prescribe bounds unto men, that they do not proceed in their prescriptions beyond what is useful unto edification, or unto what will be really burdensome and intolerable unto churches? To say that those who claim this power may be securely trusted with it, for they will be sure not to fall into any such excesses, will scarcely give satisfaction; for besides that such a kind of power is exceedingly apt to swell and extend itself unmeasurably, the common experience of Christendom lies against this suggestion. Was not an excess of this kind complained of by Austin of old, when yet the observation of ecclesiastical customs was much more voluntary than in after ages, neither were they made absolutely conditions of communion, unless among a very few? Do not all Protestants grant and plead that the papal church hath exceeded all bounds of moderation and sobriety herein, so that from thence they take the principal warranty of their secession from it? Do not other churches mutually charge one another on the same account? Hath not a charge of this excess been the ball of contention in this nation ever since the Reformation? If, then, there be such a power in any, either the exercise of it is confined unto certain instances by some power superior unto them, or it is left absolutely, as unto all particulars whereunto it may be extended, unto their own prudence and discretion. The first will not be asserted, nor can be so, unless the instances intended can be recounted, and the confirming power be declared. If the latter be affirmed, then let them run into what excesses they please, unless they judge themselves that so they do, which is morally impossible that they should, none ought ever to complain of what they do; for there is no failure in them who attend unto their rule, which in this case is supposed to be men's own prudence and discretion. And this was directly the state of things in the church of Rome; whence they thought it always exceedingly unequal that any of their ecclesiastical laws should be called in question, since they made them according to their own judgment, the sole rule of exercising their authority in such things. Where is the certainty and stability of this rule? Is it probable that the communion and peace of all churches and all Christians are left to be regulated by it? And who will give assurance that no one condition directly unlawful in itself shall be prescribed and imposed by persons enjoying this pretended power? or who can undertake that the number of such conditions as may be countenanced by a plea of being things in their own nature indifferent, shall not be increased until they come to be such a burden and yoke as are too heavy for the disciples of Christ to bear, and unlawful for them to submit themselves unto? May any make a judgment but themselves who impose them, when the number of such things grows to a blamable excess? If others may judge, at least for themselves and their own practice, and so of what is lawful or not, it is all that is desired. If themselves are the only judges, the case seems very hard, and our secession from the church of Rome scarcely warrantable. And who sees not what endless contests and differences will ensue on these suppositions, if the whole liberty of men's judgments and all apprehensions of duty in professors be not swallowed up in the gulf of atheistical indifferency as to all the concerns of outward worship?

The whole of what hath been pleaded on this head might be confirmed with the testimony of many of the learned writers of the church of England, in the defence of our secession from that of Rome; but we shall not here produce them in particular. The sum of what is pleaded by them is, *That the being of the catholic church lies in essentials; that for a particular church to disagree from all other particular churches in some extrinsical and accidental things is not to separate from the catholic church, so as to cease to be a church.* But still, whatever church makes such extrinsical things *the necessary conditions of communion, so as to cast men out of the church who yield not to them, is schismatical in its so doing, and the separation from it is so far from being schism, that being cast out of that church on these terms only returns them unto the communion of the catholic church; and nothing can be more unreasonable than that the society imposing such conditions of communion should be judge whether those conditions be just and equitable or no.* To this purpose do they generally plead our common cause. Wherefore, from what hath been discoursed, we doubt not but to affirm that where unscriptural conditions of communion, indispensably to be submitted unto and observed, are by any church imposed on those whom they expect or require to join in their fellowship, communion, and order, if they on whom they are so imposed do thereon withhold or withdraw themselves from the communion of that church, especially in the acts, duties, and parts of worship wherein a submission unto these conditions is expressed either verbally or virtually, they are not thereon to be esteemed guilty of schism; but the whole fault of the divisions which ensue thereon is to be charged on them who insist on the necessity of their imposition.

That this is the condition of things with us at present, especially such as are ministers of the gospel, with reference unto the church of England, as it is known in itself, so it may be evidenced unto all by an enumeration of the particulars that are required of us, if we will be comprehended in the communion and fellowship thereof. For,—

1. It is indispensably enjoined that we give *a solemn attestation unto the liturgy and all contained in it, by the subscription or declaration of our assent and consent thereunto;* which must be accompanied with the constant use of it in the whole worship of God. As was before observed, we dispute not now about the lawfulness of the use of liturgies in the public service of the church, nor of that in particular which is established among us by the laws of the land. Were it only proposed or recommended unto ministers for the use of it in whole or in part, according as it should be found needful unto the edification of their people, there would be a great alteration in the case under consideration. And if it be pretended that such a liberty would produce greater diversity, yea, and confusion in the worship of God, we can only say that it did not so of old, when the pastors of churches were left wholly to the exercise of their own gifts and abilities in all sacred administrations. But it is the making of an assent and consent unto it, with the constant use of it or attend-

ance unto it, a necessary condition of all communion with the church which at present is called into question. It will not, we suppose, be denied but that it is so made unto us all, both ministers and people, and that by such laws, both civil and ecclesiastical, as are sufficiently severe in their penalties; for we have rules and measures of church-communion assigned unto us by laws merely civil. Were there any colour or pretence of denying this to be so, we should proceed no farther in this instance; but things are evidently and openly with us as here laid down. Now, this condition of communion is unscriptural; and the making of it to be such a condition is without warranty or countenance from the word of God, or the practice of the apostolical and primitive churches. That there are no footsteps of any liturgy, or prescribed forms for the administration of all church ordinances, to be imposed on the disciples of Christ in their assemblies, to be found in the Scripture, no intimation of any such thing, no direction about it, no command for it, will, we suppose, be acknowledged. Commanded, indeed, we are to make "supplications and prayers" for all sorts of men in our assemblies; to instruct, lead, guide, and "feed the flock of God," 1 Tim. ii. 1; Acts xx. 28; 1 Pet. v. 2; to administer the holy ordinances instituted by him; and to do all these things "decently and in order." The apostles also, describing the work of the ministry in their own attendance unto it, affirm that they would "give themselves continually unto prayer, and to the ministry of the word," Acts vi. 4. But that all these things should be done (the preaching of the word only excepted) in and by the use or reading of a liturgy and the prescribed forms of it, without variation or receding from the words and syllables of it in any thing, that the Scripture is utterly silent of. If any one be otherwise minded, it is incumbent on him to produce instances unto his purpose. But withal he must remember, that in this case it is required not only to produce a warranty from the Scripture for the use of such forms or liturgies, but also that rules are given therein enabling churches to make the constant attendance unto them to be a necessary condition of their communion. If this be not done, nothing is offered unto the case as at present stated. And whatever confidence may be made use of herein, we know that nothing unto this purpose can be thence produced. It is pleaded, indeed, that our Saviour himself composed a form of prayer, and prescribed it unto his disciples: but it is not proved that he enjoined them the constant use of it in their assemblies, nor that they did so use it, nor that the repetition of it should be a condition of communion in them, though the owning of it as by him proposed, and for the ends by him designed, may justly be made so; least of all is it, or can it be proved, that any rule or just encouragement can hence be taken for other men who are neither Jesus

Christ nor his apostles, but weak and fallible as ourselves, to compose entire liturgies, and impose the necessary use of them in all the worship of the church. Neither is there the least countenance to be obtained unto such impositions from the practice or example of the *first churches*. Liturgies themselves were an invention of after ages, and the use of them now inquired after of a much later date: for those which pretend unto apostolical antiquity have long since been convicted to be spurious and feigned, nor is there scarce any learned man who hath the confidence to assert them to be genuine; and on a supposition that so they are, no tolerable reason can be given why the use of them should be neglected, and such others taken up as are of a most uncertain original. The first condition, therefore, of communion proposed unto us is not only unscriptural (which is sufficient unto our present argument), but also destitute of any ancient example or usage among the churches of Christ to give countenance unto it. This if we admit not of, if we attend not unto, we are not only refused communion in other things, but also excommunicated, or cast out of the whole communion of the church, as many are at this day; yet some are so, not only for refusing compliance with the whole of it in general, but for not observing every particular direction belonging unto it (as might be manifested in instances) of no great importance. If, therefore, any divisions or schisms do ensue among us on this account, that some indispensably require an assent and consent unto the liturgy and all things contained in it as the condition of complete church-communion, or a necessary attendance on the whole religious worship thereby performed and therein prescribed, which others refuse to admit of as such, and thereon forbear the communion proposed unto them, it is evident, from the rules laid down, where the guilt of them is to be charged. And we do not discourse of what any may do among themselves, judging it meet for their edification, nor of what a civil law may constitute with respect unto public places, employments, and preferments; but only where lies the sin and evil that attends divisions arising on these impositions, and which by their removal would be taken away. And there seems to be an aggravation of this disorder, in that not only all men are refused communion who will not submit unto these terms of it, but also they are sought out and exposed unto severe penalties if they will not admit of them, though expressly contrary to their consciences and persuasions.

2. *Canonical submission* unto the present ecclesiastical government of the church, and the administration of the discipline thereof, in their hands by whom the power of it is possessed, with an acquiescency therein, are to the same purpose required of us and expected from us. Who these are, and what are the ways and means of their

administrations, we shall not repeat, as unwilling to give offence unto any. We cannot but know how and in what sense these things are proposed unto us, and what is expected from us thereon. Neither dare we give another sense of them in our minds than what we judge to be the sense and intention of them who require our submission and obedience unto them. It is not, certainly, their design nor mind that we should look on the offices of the church as unwarrantable, and on their rule as inconvenient, so as to endeavour a reformation in the one and of the other. It is such a conformity they intend as whereby we do, virtually at least, declare our approbation of all these things in the church, and our acquiescency in them. Neither can we be admitted to put in any exception, nor discharge our consciences by a plain declaration of what we dislike or dissent from, or in what sense we can submit unto any of these things. We take it, therefore, for granted, that in the conformity required of us we must cordially and sincerely approve the present ecclesiastical government, and the administration of church discipline thereby, for it is the profession of our acceptance of it as proposed unto us; and if we acquiesce not therein, but express an uneasiness under it, we do it at the hazard of the reputation of our sincerity and honesty in conforming. Now, this condition of communion with the church of England is also unscriptural, and consequently unlawful to be made so. This is by many now plainly acknowledged; for they say there is no government determined in the Scripture. But this now in force amongst us is erected by the authority of the magistrate, who hath supreme power in things ecclesiastical; and on that ground a lawful government they plead it to be, and lawful to be exercised, and so also by others to be submitted to. But we have now sundry times declared that this is not our present question. We inquire not whether it be lawful or no, or on what account it may be so esteemed, or how far it may be submitted unto, or wherein; but we say, the professed acknowledging of it, with submission unto it, as the government of the church, is required of us as a necessary condition of our communion. If they are not so, give us liberty to declare our sense concerning it without prejudice; and if it be so, then may we refuse this condition as unscriptural. For in the case of conformity, there is not only a submission to the government required, but expressly (as was said) an approbation of it, that it is such as it ought to be; for in religious things our practice declares a cordial approbation, as being a part of our profession, wherein we ought to be sincere. Some again make some pleas, that bishops, and some government by them, are appointed by the apostles, and therefore a submission unto them may be justly required as a condition of communion. For we will not now dispute but that whatever is so appointed may be so required, although we believe that every particular instance of this nature is not rigidly to be insisted on, if it belong not unto the essentials of the church, and it be dubious to some whether it be so appointed or no; but yet neither doth an admittance of this plea give us any relief in this matter: for suppose it should or might be proved that there ought to be, according to the mind of Christ, in all churches, bishops, with a pre-eminence above presbyters in order or degree, and that the rule of the church doth principally belong unto them that are so, yet will not this concession bear an application to the present question, so as to afford us any relief; for the granting of things so dubious and questionable can never give them such an evidence of truth and firmitude in the church as to warrant the making of them necessary conditions of communion unto all Christians. Neither doth it follow, from any thing that pretendeth to fall under Scripture proof, that such bishops should be diocesan; that they should depend on archbishops over them; that they should assume the whole power of church rule and discipline into their hands; that they should administer it by chancellors, archdeacons, commissaries, and the like; that this should be done by presentments, or indictments, citations, processes, litigious pleadings, after the manner of secular or civil courts, to the exclusion of that rule and discipline which the gospel directs unto, with the management of it in love and brotherly compassion, in the name and by the Spirit of our Lord Jesus Christ. But these things we shall not in particular insist upon, for the reason before given. This we must say, that take the whole of the government and the administration thereof together,—which by the conformity required of us we must testify our approbation of and acquiescence in, or we deal hypocritically with them that require it of us,—and we know it to be so far unscriptural as that an acknowledgment of it and submission unto it cannot duly and justly be made a necessary condition of communion unto us. It may be it will be said that submission unto the government of the church is not so much a condition of communion with it as it is that wherein our communion itself with it doth consist, and it is but a fancy to think of communion with a church without it. But this is otherwise; as appears in those churches where all rule and government being left in the hand of the civil magistrate, there communion is merely spiritual in the administration of evangelical ordinances. And might but that be admitted which nature, reason, the law of the Christian faith and gospel obedience, do require,—namely, that church-fellowship and communion be built upon men's own judgment and choice, —this would go a great way towards the pacification of our differences. But if this be so, and that all church-communion consists in submission to the government of it, or at least that it doth so prin-

cipally, it becomes them by whom it is owned and avowed so to do
to take care that that government be derived from the authority of
Christ, and administered according to his mind, or all church-communion, properly so called, will be overthrown.

3. We are required to use and observe the *ceremonies* in worship
which the present church hath appointed, or doth use and observe.
This also is made a necessary condition of communion unto us; for
many are at this day actually cast out of all communion for not observing of them. Some are so proceeded against for not observing
of holy-days, some for not kneeling at the sacrament of the Lord's
supper, some for not using the sign of the cross in baptism; and
what would become of ministers that should neglect or omit to
wear the surplice in sacred administrations is easy to conjecture.
But these things are all of them unwritten and unscriptural. Great
and many, indeed, have been the disputes of learned men to prove
that although they have no divine institution, nor yet example of
apostolical or primitive practice, yet that they may be lawfully used,
for decency and order in the worship of God. Whether they have
evinced what they aimed at is as yet undetermined. But supposing
in this case all to be as they would pretend and plead that it should
be, yet because they are all granted to be arbitrary inventions of
men, and very few of those who make use of them are agreed what
is their proper use and signification, or whether they have any or no,
they are altogether unmeet to be made a necessary condition of communion; for inquiry may be made, on what warranty or by what
rule they may be appointed so to be? Those who preside in and
over the churches of Christ do so in his name and by his authority;
and therefore they can impose nothing on them, as a condition of
their communion together, but what his name is upon or what they
have his authority for, and it will be dangerous to set his seal unto
our own appointments. For what men think meet to do themselves
in the matters of the house of God and his worship, it may be measured and accepted with him according to their light and design;
but for what they impose on others, and that under no less penalty
than the deprivation of the outward administration of all the privileges procured for them by Jesus Christ, they ought to have his
warrant and authority for. And their zeal is to be bewailed who
not only cast men out of all church-communion, so far as in them
lieth, for a refusal to observe those voluntarily-imposed ceremonies
in sacred worship, but also prosecute them with outward force, to the
ruin of them and their families; and we cannot but wonder that any
should as yet think meet to make use of prisons, and the destruction
of men thereby, as an appendix of their ecclesiastical discipline, exercised in the highest severity, on no greater occasions than the

omission of the observance of these ceremonies. Whether such proceedings are measured by present interest, or the due consideration of what will be pleasing to the Lord Jesus Christ at the last day, is not difficult to determine.

4. As we are *ministers,* there is in some cases required of us, under the same penalty, *an oath of canonical obedience.* We need not labour to prove this to be unscriptural; nor, to avoid provocations, shall we at present declare the rise, nature, and use of it, with the fierce digladiations that have formerly been about it. We can look upon it no otherwise but as that which is contrary to the liberty and unworthy of the office of a minister of the gospel.

We know not any thing else which is required of us unto the end mentioned, unless it be of some *a subscription unto the articles of religion.* And this, because the Scripture enjoins unto all a consent unto sound doctrine and a form of wholesome words, may be admitted so far as those articles concern only points of faith; but whereas there is annexed unto them and enjoined, with other things, an approbation of all those instances of conditions of communion before insisted on, a subscription unto the whole becomes of the same nature with things themselves therein approved of.

These are the conditions of communion with the church of England which are proposed unto us, and which we are indispensably to submit unto if we intend to be partakers thereof; and these are all that we know of that nature. That any of these are in particular prescribed in the word of God, much less that they can derive any warranty from thence to be made necessary conditions of church-communion, will not, we suppose, be pretended by any. If, therefore, any divisions do ensue on the refusal of some to admit of these conditions, the guilt of them cannot, by any rule of Scripture, or from any example of the first churches, be charged on them who make that refusal. Other groundless accusations and charges we value not, for this is but man's day, the judgment whereof we neither stand nor fall unto; yea, we esteem ourselves obliged, in all peaceableness and sobriety, to bear witness against such impositions, and unto that liberty wherewith the Lord Christ hath made his churches and disciples free. And if once things were come unto that state that men would assign no other terms of church-communion than what Christ hath appointed, it would quickly appear where the guilt of our divisions would yet remain, if any such divisions would yet remain; but so long as there is a desire to make the wills and wisdoms of some men, fallible even as others, the rule and measure of obedience in spiritual things, an end of strife and contention among Christians will be expected in vain. And this we say with hearts in some measure sensible and pained to see the body of Christ torn in pieces by the lusts, passions, and carnal interests of men. Could we contribute any thing to the healing of the wounds and ruptures that are amongst Christians, provided it may have a consistency with the mind of Christ and the duty we owe unto him (as, indeed, nothing else will really contribute any thing thereunto), we should with all readiness and faithfulness give up our best endeavours therein; and where we can do nothing else, we hope we shall bear with patience those disdainful reproaches which the pride of men, blown up by a confluence of secular, perishing advantages, prompts them to pour out upon us for our non-compliance with their impositions.

Secondly, By the conformity required of us, we must consent unto *the omission of sundry duties*, which are made so unto us by the command and appointment of Jesus Christ. If we are at any time hindered in the discharge of any necessary duty by others, we have somewhat to plead in our own excuse, but if we ourselves voluntarily consent to the neglect or omission of them, we cannot avoid the guilt of sin; and the worst way whereby such a consent may be expressed is by compact and agreement with others, as though it were in our power to bargain with other men what duties we will observe and what we will omit in the worship of God. Now, in the conformity required of us we are to give this consent, and that as it were by compact and agreement, which deprives us of all pretence of excuse in our omissions. It is no time afterward to plead that we would discharge such duties were we not hindered or forbidden,—we have ourselves antecedently and voluntarily renounced a concern in such forbidden duties; for no man can honestly conform but it is with a declared resolution to accept of all the terms and consequents of it, with an approbation of them. Under this notion it is that we look on conformity; and what others apprehend thereby or understand therein, who seem to press men to conform unto what they do not approve, we know not. If, then, there be any omission of known duties inseparably accompanying our conformity, that thereby we solemnly consent unto.

This, therefore, we are obliged to refuse, because without sin, in the voluntary neglect and omission of duty, we cannot comply with it; which, therefore, can be no schism in us, nor what might in any way render us blamable. The Lord Christ hath prescribed no such law of unity and peace unto his churches as that his disciples should be bound constantly to neglect any known duty which they owe to himself for their sakes; nor do his institutions interfere, that the observance of any one should exclude a due attendance unto another. Neither doth he by his commands bring any one into a necessity of doing that which is evil, or of omitting any thing that is required of him in the way of duty. However, therefore, we value church peace and union, we dare not purchase it by an abrenunciation of any duty we owe to Jesus Christ; nor would an agreement procured on such terms be of any use unto us, or of advantage to the church itself. Wherefore, that compliance in church-communion which would be obstructive of any necessary duties is not by the Lord Christ enjoined us; and therefore its omission cannot be culpable in us: but it would itself be our sin; especially would it be thus where the duties so to be omitted are such as are incumbent on us by virtue of especial office, wherein we are peculiarly required to be faithful. It remaineth, therefore, only that we declare wherein we should by conformity engage unto the omission of such duties as are indispensably required of us; and this we shall do in some few instances:—

1. Every minister of the gospel hath, by the appointment of Jesus Christ, *the whole immediate care of the flock* whereof he is overseer committed unto him. That no part hereof which belongs unto their edification is exempted from him, the charge that is given unto him and the account which will be expected from him do sufficiently evidence. For as ministers are called overseers, rulers, guides, pastors, and the like, so are they commanded to feed the flock, to take the oversight of it, and to rule the house of God, Acts xx. 17, 28; 1 Tim. iii. 5; 1 Pet. v. 1–4; Heb. xiii. 17;—a discharge of all which must come into their account. Nor is there any word spoken in the whole Scripture, relating to the rule and government of the church, which is not spoken principally with respect unto them. Nor is there the least intimation of an exemption of any part of the discipline of the gospel from their office or care. If it be pretended that there is, let the places be produced wherein such an exemption is made, or any instances of it among the first churches, and they shall be considered; for hitherto no such thing has been attempted that we know of. Nor is it at all concluded from the plea that some are appointed unto a superior degree above others in the rule of the church; for a man may have the whole rule of his flock committed unto him, although he should be obliged to give an account unto others of his discharge thereof. It is, therefore, the duty of all ministers of the gospel, not only to teach, instruct, and preach to their flocks, but to go before them also in rule and government, and in the exercise of the spiritual discipline appointed in the gospel, in the order wherein it is appointed, for their edification. The keys of the kingdom of heaven are committed unto them, or they are not: if they are not, by what authority do they take upon them to open and shut in the house of God, in ministerial teaching and authoritative administration of sacred ordinances? for these things belong unto the authority which is given by Christ under that metaphorical expression of "the keys of the kingdom of heaven," the reason of the allusion and its application being obvious.

And if these are not received by any, they are usurpers if they undertake to administer unto the church authoritatively in the name of Jesus Christ. If they are given or granted unto them, how may it be made to appear that they are so for the ends mentioned only, but not for the rule and government of the church, which also belongs unto them? where is the exemption in the grant made to them? where are the limits assigned unto their power, that they shall exercise it in some concerns of the kingdom of heaven, but not in others? And whereas the greatest and most necessary parts of this power, such as are ministerial teaching and the administration of the sacraments, are confessedly committed unto them, how comes it to pass that the less should be reserved from them; for whereas the former are necessary to the very being of the church, the latter are esteemed by some scarcely to belong unto it. To say that bishops only receive these keys, and commit or lend the use of them to others, for such ends and purposes as they are pleased to limit, is both foreign to the Scripture and destructive of all ministerial power. And if ministers are not the ministers of Christ, but of men; if they have not their authority from him, but from others; if that may be parcelled out unto them which they have from him, at the pleasure of any over them,—there needs not much contending about them or their office.

Besides, the relation of these things one to another is such, as that if they were absolutely separated, their efficacy unto edification will be exceedingly impaired, if not destroyed. If those who have the dispensation of the word committed unto them have not liberty and authority; if it be not part of their office-duty to watch over them unto whom it is dispensed, and that accompanied with spiritual weapons, "mighty through God" towards the fulfilling of the obedience of some and the "revenging of disobedience" in others; if they have no power to judge, admonish, or censure them that walk unanswerably to the doctrine of the gospel preached unto them, and whose profession they have taken upon them,—they will be discouraged in the pursuit of their work, and the word itself be deprived of a helpful means appointed by Christ himself to further its efficacy. And those who shall content themselves with the preaching of the word only, without an inquiry after its success in the minds and lives of them that are committed to their charge, by virtue of that care and authoritative inspection which indeed belongs to their office, will find that as they do discharge but one part of their duty, so they will grow cold and languid therein also. And when there hath been better success,—as there hath where some against their wills have been hindered by power from the exercise of the charge laid on them by Christ in this matter, making up as they were able, by private solicitude and persuasion, what they were excluded from attending unto in public ministerial acts,—it hath been an effect of especial favour from God, not to be ordinarily expected on the account of any rule. And thence it is that, for the most part, things openly and visibly do fall out otherwise, the people being little reformed in their lives, and preachers waxing cold and formal in their work. And if the censures of the church are administered by them who preach not the word unto the people, they will be weak and enervous as unto any influence on the consciences of men. Their minds, indeed, may be affected by them so far as they are attended with outward penalties; but how little this tends unto the promotion of holiness or the reformation of men's lives experience doth abundantly testify. Church discipline and censures are appointed merely and solely to second, confirm, and establish the word, and to vindicate it from abuse and contempt, as expressing the sense that Jesus Christ hath of them by whom it is received, and of them by whom it is despised. And it is the word alone which gives authority unto discipline and censures. Where, therefore, they are so separated, as that those by whom the word is administered are excluded from an interest in the exercise of discipline, and those unto whom the administration of discipline is committed are such as neither do nor for the most part ought to preach the word, it cannot be but that the efficacy and success of them both will be impeded.

2. It is so, also, as to the administration of the sacraments, especially that of the supper of the Lord. These are the principal mysteries of our religion, as to its external form and administration,—the sacred rites whereby all the grace, mercy, and privileges of the gospel are sealed and confirmed unto them who are in a due manner made partakers of them. About them, therefore, and their orderly administration, did the primitive churches always use their utmost care and diligence; and these in an especial manner did they make use of with respect unto them to whom they were to be communicated: for they feared, partly lest men should be made partakers of them to their disadvantage, being not so qualified as to receive them to their benefit, as knowing that where persons through their own defaults obtain not spiritual profit by them, they are in no small danger of having them turned into a snare; and partly that these holy and sacred institutions themselves might neither be profaned, contaminated, nor exposed unto contempt. Hence, of those who gave up their names unto the church, and took upon them the profession of the gospel, the greatest part were continued for a long season under their care and inspection, but were not admitted into the society of the church in those ordinances until upon good trial they were approved. And if any one after his admittance was found to walk unanswerably unto his profession, or to fall into any known sin,

whence offence did ensue among the faithful, he was immediately
dealt withal in the discipline of the church, and, in case of impenitency, separated from the congregation. Nor did the guides or
pastors of the church think they had any greater trust committed
unto them than in this, that they should use their utmost care and
diligence that persons unmeet and unworthy might not be admitted
into that church relation wherein they should have a right to approach unto the table of the Lord, and to remove from thence such
as had demeaned themselves unworthy of that communion. This
they looked on as belonging unto their ministerial office, and as a
duty required of them in the discharge thereof by Jesus Christ.
And herein they had sufficient direction, both in the rule of the
word, as also in the nature of the office committed unto them, and
of the work wherewith they were intrusted; for all ministers are
stewards of the mysteries of Christ, of whom it is required that they
should be faithful. Now, as it belongs unto a faithful steward to dis-
tribute unto the household of his lord the provisions which he hath
made for them and allows unto them in due season; so also to keep
off those from partaking in them, who without his master's order
and warrant, would intrude themselves into his family, and unjustly
possess themselves of the privileges of it. In these things doth the
faithfulness of a steward consist. And the same is required in ministers of the gospel with respect unto the household of their Lord
and Master, and the provision that he hath made for it. These,
therefore, being undeniably parts of the duty of faithful pastors or
ministers, it is evident how many of them we must solemnly renounce
a concernment in, upon a compliance with the conformity in matter
and manner required of us. Neither are these duties such as are of
light importance, or such as may be omitted without any detriment
unto the souls of men. The glory of Christ, the honour of the gospel, the purity of the church and its edification, are greatly concerned in them. And they in whose minds a neglect of these things
is countenanced, by their attendance unto some outward forms and
appearances of order, have scarcely considered Him aright with whom
they have to do. Some, therefore, of these duties we shall instance
in:—First, it is the duty of all faithful ministers of the gospel *to
consider aright who are so admitted* into the church as to obtain a
right thereby unto a participation of all its holy ordinances. Take
care they must that none who have that right granted them by the
law of Christ be discouraged or excluded, nor any altogether un-
worthily admitted. And hereunto, as it is generally acknowledged,
a credible profession of repentance, faith, and obedience (that is, of
those which are sincere and saving) is required. To neglect an inquiry after these things in those that are to be admitted unto the

table of the Lord is to prostitute the holy ordinances of the gospel unto contempt and abuse, and to run cross to the constant practice of the church in all ages, even under its greatest degeneracy. And the right discharge of this duty,—if we may be allowed to be in earnest in spiritual things, if it be believed that it is internal grace and holiness for the sake whereof all outward administrations are instituted and celebrated,—is of great weight and importance to the souls of men; for on the part of persons to be admitted, if they are openly and visibly unworthy, what do we thereby but what lies in us to destroy their souls? It cannot be but that their hardening and impenitency in sin will be hazarded thereby; for whereas they have granted unto them the most solemn pledge of the Lord Christ's acceptance of them, and of his approbation of their state towards God, that the church is authorized to give, what reason have they to think that their condition is not secure, or to attend unto the doctrine of the church pressing them to look after a change and relinquishment of it? For although the administration of the sealing ordinances doth not absolutely set the approbation of Christ unto every individual person made partaker of them, yet it doth absolutely do so to the profession which they make. They witness in the name of Christ his approbation of it, and therewithal of all persons, according to their real interest in it and answering of it. But those who in no considerable instances do answer this profession can obtain nothing unto themselves but an occasion of hardening, and rendering them secure in a state of impenitency; for tell men whilst you please of the necessity of conversion to God, of reformation, and a holy life, yet if, in the course of their unholiness, you confirm unto them the love of Christ, and give them pledges of their salvation by him, they will not much regard your other exhortations. And thence it is come to pass in the world that the conformity (worth that we contend about ten thousand times over) which ought to be between the preaching of the word, the administration of the sacraments, and the lives of them who are partakers of them, is for the most part lost. The word still declares that without regeneration, without saving faith, repentance, and obedience, none can enter into the kingdom of God. In the administration of the other ordinances there is an abatement made of this rigorous determination, and men have their salvation assured unto them without a credible profession, yea, or a pretence of these qualifications; and the lives of the most who live in the enjoyment of these things seem to declare that they neither believe the one nor much regard the other.

In the meantime, the church itself, as to its purity and the holiness of its communion, is damaged by the neglect of a careful inspection into this duty; for it cannot be but that ignorance, worldliness, and profaneness, will spread themselves as a leprosy over such a church, whence their communion will be of very little use and advantage unto believers. And hereby do churches, which should be the glory of Christ, by their expression of the purity, the holiness, and excellency of his person and doctrine, become the principal means and occasions of his dishonour in the world ; and he that shall read that "Christ loved his church, and gave himself for it, that he might sanctify and cleanse it with the washing of water by the word, that he might present it unto himself a glorious church, not having spot, or wrinkle, or any such thing, but that it should be holy and without blemish," Eph. v. 25–27, will be much to seek after the effects of this design of Christ in his love and death, if he measure them by what appears in churches under the power and influence of this neglect. Nor do those who plead for the continuance of things in such a state, without reformation, sufficiently consider the representation that the Lord Christ made of himself when he was about to deal with his churches, some of which were overtaken with carelessness and negligence in this matter; and yet hath he therein laid down a rule as to what kind of proceedings particular churches are to expect from him in all generations. And it is a matter of no small amazement that any churches dare approve and applaud themselves in such a state of impurity and defection as is evidently condemned by him in those primitive patterns. Do men think he is changed, or that he will approve in them what he judged and condemned in others? or do they suppose he minds these things no more, and because he is unseen, that he seeth not? But we shall all find at length that he is " the same yesterday, to-day, and for ever," and that as the judge of all he stands at the door.

Now this duty, by conformity, we renounce a concernment in, so as to attend unto it, by virtue of ministerial authority; whence the guilt of all the evil consequents thereof before mentioned must fall on us: for it is known that a mere shadow of the work of this duty, and not so much as a shadow of authority for it, would be left unto us. For what is allowed in case of a sudden emergency, upon an offence taken by the whole congregation at the wickedness of any (which is instructed beforehand that this ought to be no matter of offence unto them), as it may be it cannot be proved ever to have been observed in any one instance, so the allowed exercise of it would yield no relief in this case. And if any should extend the rule beyond the interpretation that is put upon it by the present current administration of church-discipline, there is no great question to be made what entertainment he would meet withal for his so doing. And it is to no purpose to come into the church as it were on purpose to go out again. And if, instead of dealing with the souls and consciences of men in the name and authority of Christ, as stewards of his mysteries, any can content themselves to be informers of crimes unto others, we desire their pardon if we cannot comply with them therein.   And this is the sum of what at present we are pleading about: It is the duty of ministers of particular churches to judge and take care concerning the fitness of them, according unto the rule of the gospel and the nature of the duty required of them, who are to be admitted into the fellowship of the church, and thereby into a participation of all the holy ordinances thereof.   This charge the Lord Christ hath committed unto them, and hereof will require an account from them.   Upon the neglect or right discharge of this duty consequents of great moment do depend; yea, the due attendance unto it hath a great influence into the preservation of the being of the church, and is the hinge whereon the well-being of it doth turn.   But the power of exercising ministerial authority, in a just attendance unto this duty, we must renounce in our conformity, if we should submit thereunto; for we have showed before, that after we have conformed, we can pretend no excuse from what is enjoined of us or forbidden unto us by virtue thereof, all being founded in our own voluntary act and consent.   Hence, the guilt of this omission must wholly fall on us; which we are not willing to undergo.

There are, we know, many objections raised against the committing of this power and trust unto the ministers of particular congregations. Great inconveniences are pretended as the consequences of it.   The ignorance and unfitness of most ministers for the discharge of such a trust, if it should be committed unto them, the arbitrariness and partiality which probably others will exercise therein, the yoke that will be brought on the people thereby, and disorder in the whole, are usually pleaded to this purpose and insisted on.   But,—

1. This trust is committed unto some or other by Christ himself; and it is necessary that so it should be.   Never did he appoint, nor is it meet, nor was it ever practised in the primitive church, that every one should at his pleasure, on his own presumption, intrude himself into a participation of the holy things of the house of God. The consideration of men's habitations, with their age, and the like, are of no consideration with respect unto any rule of the gospel. Either, therefore, it must be left unto the pleasure and will of every man, be he never so ignorant, wicked, or profligate, to impose himself on the communion of any church of Christ, or there must be a judgment in the church concerning them who are to be admitted unto their communion.

2. From the first planting of the Christian religion, those who preached the gospel unto the conversion of the souls of men were principally intrusted with this power; and it was their duty to gather

them who were so converted into that church order and fellowship wherein they might partake of the sacred mysteries or solemn ordinances of the Christian worship. And this course of proceeding continued uninterrupted, with some little variation in the manner of the exercise of this power and duty, until corruption had spread itself over the face of the whole professing church in the world. But still a shadow and resemblance of it was retained; and in the papal church itself to this day, particular confessors are esteemed competent judges of the meetness of their penitents for an admission unto the sacraments of their church. And who shall now be esteemed more meet for the discharge of this duty than those who succeed in the office and work of preaching the word, whereby men are prepared for church-society? And as it is a thing utterly unheard-of in antiquity, that those who dispensed the word unto the illumination and conversion of men should not have the power of their disposal, as to their being added to the church or suspended for a time, as there was occasion; so it is as uncouth that those who now sustain the same place and office unto several congregations attending on their ministry should be deprived of it.

3. If there be that ignorance and disability in ministers as is pretended, the blame of it reflects on them by whom they are made; and we are not obliged to accommodate any of the ways or truths of Christ unto the sins and ignorance of men. And if they are insufficient for this work, how come they to be so sufficient for that which is greater,—namely, to divide the word aright unto all their hearers? But we speak of such ministers as are competently qualified, according to the rule of the gospel, for the discharge of their office, and no other ought there to be; and such there are, blessed be God, through the watchful care of our Lord Jesus Christ over his church, and his supplies of the gifts of his Spirit unto them. And such as these know it is their duty to study, meditate, pray, ask counsel and advice of others, perhaps of more wisdom and experience than themselves, that they may know how in all things to behave themselves in the house of God. Nor will God be wanting unto them who in sincerity seek direction from him for the discharge of any duty which he calls them unto. Other security of regular, orderly, and useful proceedings in this matter, Christ hath not given us, nor do we need; for the due observance of his appointments will not fail the attaining of his ends, which ought to be ours also.

4. The judgment and acting of the church-officers, in the admission of persons into the complete society of the faithful, is not arbitrary, as is pretended. They have the rule of the Scripture, which they are diligently to attend unto. This is the entire rule which the Lord Christ hath left unto his church, both for their doctrine and

discipline; whatever is beyond this or beside it is not his, nor owned by him. What is not done according to this rule is of no force in the consciences of men, though it may stand, until lawfully recalled, for the preservation of outward order. And whatever arbitrariness may be supposed in making a judgment upon the rule of the word, or in the application of its rule unto the present case, it must abide in some or other. And who shall be thought more meet or able to make a right determination thereon than those whose duty it is, and who have the advantage to be acquainted with all the circumstances belonging to the case proposed? Besides, there is the judgment of the church, or the congregation itself; which is greatly to be regarded. Even in the church of England, a suspension of any from the Lord's supper is allowed unto the curate, upon the offence of the congregation: which is a sufficient evidence that a judgment in this case is owned to be their due; for none can take offence but upon a judgment of the matter at which he is offended, nor, in this case, without a right to determine that some offences ought to debar persons from a participation of the holy ordinances, as also what those offences are. This, therefore, is to be considered as an aid and assistance unto ministers in the discharge of their duty. It is the church into whose communion persons are to be admitted. And although it be no way necessary that determinations in this case should be always made by suffrage or a plurality of votes in the body of the church, yet, if the sense or mind of the congregation may be known, or is so (upon the inquiry that ought to be made unto that purpose), that any persons are unmeet for their communion, it is not convenient they should be received; nor will their admission, in this case, be of any advantage to themselves or the church. The light of reason, and the fundamental, constitutive principles of all free societies, such as the church is, ascribe this liberty unto it; and the primitive church practised accordingly, Acts ix. 26–28; Rom. xiv. 1. So, also, is the judgment and desire of the congregation to be considered in the admission of any, if they are made known to the guides of it; for it is expected from them they should confirm their love unto them without dissimulation, as members of the same body: and, therefore, in their approbation of what is done, their rulers have light and encouragement in their own duty. Besides, there is appointed, and ought to be preserved, a communion among churches themselves. By virtue hereof, they are not only to make use of mutual aid, advice, and counsel, antecedently unto actings of importance, but each particular church is, upon just demand, to give an account unto other churches of what they do in the administration of the ordinances of the gospel among them; and if in any thing it hath mistaken or miscarried, to rectify them upon their advice and judgment. And it were easy to manifest how, through these means and advantages, the edification of the church and the liberty of Christians is sufficiently secured in that discharge of duty which is required in the pastors of the churches about the admission of persons unto a participation of holy ordinances in them.

5. This duty, therefore, must either be wholly neglected,—which will unavoidably tend to the corrupting and debauching of all churches, and in the end unto their ruin,—or it must be attended unto by each particular church under the conduct of their guides and rulers, or some others must take it upon themselves. What hath been the issue of a supposal that it may be discharged in the latter way is too well known to be insisted on: for whilst those who undertake the exercise of church-power are such as do not dispense the word or preach it unto them towards whom it is to be exercised, but are strangers unto their spiritual state, and all the circumstances of it; whilst they have no way to act or exercise their presumed authority but by citations, processes, informations, and penalties, according to the manner of secular courts of judicature in causes civil and criminal; whilst the administration of it is committed unto men utterly unacquainted with and unconcerned in the discipline of the gospel, or the preservation of the church of Christ in purity and order; and whilst herein many, the most, or all of them who are so employed, have thereby outward emoluments and advantages, which they do principally regard,—the due and proper care of the right order of the churches, unto the glory of Christ and their own edification, is utterly omitted and lost. It is true, many think this the only decent, useful, and expedient way for the government of the church; and think it wondrous unreasonable that others will not submit thereunto and acquiesce therein. But what would they have us do? or what is it that they would persuade us unto? Is it that this kind of rule in and over the church hath institution given it in the Scripture, or countenance from apostolical practice? Both they and we know that no pretence of any such plea can be made. Is it that the first churches after the apostles, or the primitive church, did find such a kind of rule to be necessary, and therefore erected it among themselves? There is nothing more remote from truth. Would they persuade us that as ministers of the gospel, and such as have or may have the care of particular churches committed unto us, we have no such concernment in these things but what we may solemnly renounce, and leave them wholly to the management of others? We are not able to believe them. The charge that is given unto us, the account that will be required of us, the nature of the office we are called unto, continually testify other things unto us. Wherefore, we dare not voluntarily engage into the neglect or omission of this duty,

which Christ requireth at our hands, and of whose neglect we see so many sad consequents and effects. The Lord Christ, we know, hath the same thoughts, and makes the same judgment of his churches, as he did of old, when he made a solemn revelation and declaration of them; and then we find that he charged the failings, neglects, and miscarriages of the churches principally upon the angels or ministers of them. And we would not willingly, by our neglect, render ourselves obnoxious unto his displeasure, nor betray the churches whereunto we do relate unto his just indignation, for their declension from the purity of his institutions, and the vigour of that faith and love which they had professed. We should, moreover, by the conformity required of us, and according to the terms on which it is proposed, engage ourselves against the exercise of our ministerial office and power, with respect unto them who are already members of particular churches; for this we carry along with us, that by conforming we voluntarily consent unto the whole state of conformity, and unto all that we are to do or not to do by the law thereof. Now, it is not to be expected that all who are duly initiated or joined unto any church shall always walk blameless, according unto the evangelical rule of obedience, without giving offence unto others. The state of the church is not like to be so blessed in this world, that all who belong unto it should be constantly and perpetually inoffensive. This, indeed, is the duty of all, but it will fall out otherwise. It did so amongst the primitive churches of old; and is not, therefore, otherwise to be expected amongst us, on whom the ends of the world are come, and who are even pressed with the decays and ruins of it. Many hypocrites may obtain an admission into church societies, by the strictest rules that they can proceed upon therein; and these, after they have known and professed the ways of righteousness, may, and often do, turn aside from the holy commandment delivered unto them, and fall again into the pollutions of the world. Many good men, and really sincere believers, may, through the power of temptations, be surprised into faults and sins scandalous to the gospel, and offensive to the whole congregation whereof they are members. Hath the Lord Christ appointed no relief in and for his churches in such cases; no way whereby they may clear themselves from a participation in such impieties, or deliver themselves from being looked on as those who give countenance unto them, as they who continue in this communion may and ought to be; no power whereby they may put forth from among them the old leaven, which would otherwise infect the whole; no way to discharge themselves and their societies of such persons as are impenitent in their sins; no means for the awakening, conviction, humiliation, and recovery of them that have offended; no way to declare his mind and judgment in such cases, with the sentence that he denounceth in heaven against them that are impenitent? 1 Cor. v. 1, 2, 6, 7; 2 Cor. ii. 6, vii. 11; Matt. xvi. 19, xviii. 15–20; Rev. ii. 1, 2. If he hath done none of these things, it is evident that no churches in this world can possibly be preserved from disorder and confusion. Nor can they, by love, and the fruits of a holy communion, be kept in such a condition as wherein he can be pleased with them, or continue to walk amongst them; for let men please themselves whilst they will with the name of the church, it is no otherwise with them where persons obstinately and impenitently wicked, and whose lives are wholly discrepant from the rule of the gospel, are suffered to abide without control. But if he hath made the provision inquired after in this case, as it is evident that he hath, both the authority he hath granted unto his church for these ends, his commands to exercise it with care and watchfulness, with the rules given them to proceed by, with the known end of all instituted churches for the promotion of holiness, being all open and plain in the Scripture, it must then be inquired unto whom this trust is firstly committed, and of whom these duties are principally required.

For private members of the church, what is their duty, and the way how they may regularly attend unto the discharge of it, according to the mind of Christ, in case of scandalous sins and offences among them, they are so plainly and particularly laid down and directed, as that, setting aside the difficulties that are cast on the rule herein by the extremely forced and unprovable exceptions of some interested persons, none can be ignorant of what is required of them, Matt. xviii. 15–20. And a liberty to discharge their duty herein, they are bound by the law of Christ in due order to provide for. If they are abridged hereof, and deprived thereby of so great a means of their own edification, as also of the usefulness required in them towards the church whereof they are members, it is a spiritual oppression that they suffer under. And where it is voluntarily neglected by them, not only the guilt of their own, but of other men's sins also lies upon them. Neither is their own guilt small herein; for suffering sin to abide on a brother without reproof is a fruit of hatred in the interpretation of the law, Lev. xix. 17; and this hatred is a sin of a heinous nature in the sense of the gospel, 1 John ii. 9, 11, iii. 15. The duty, also, of the whole church in such cases is no less evidently declared: for from such persons as walk disorderly, and refuse to reform on due admonition, they are to withdraw, and to put from amongst them such obstinate offenders; as also, previously thereunto, to "watch diligently lest any root of bitterness spring up among them, whereby they might be defiled." And hereunto, also, are subservient all the commands that are given them to exhort and admonish one another, that the whole church may be preserved in purity, order, holiness, and faithfulness. But the chief inquiry is, With whom rests the principal care and power, according to the mind of Christ, to see the discipline of the church in particular congregations exercised, and to exercise it accordingly? If this should be found to be in the ministers, and, through their neglect in the administration of it, offenders be left in their sins and impenitency, without a due application of the means for their healing and recovery; if the church itself come to be corrupted thereby, and to fall under the displeasure of Jesus Christ,—as these things, in one degree or other, more or less, will ensue on that neglect,—it will not turn unto their comfortable account at the great day. That this is their duty, that this authority and inspection is committed unto them, the reasons before insisted on in the case of admission do undeniably evince. And if those ministers who do conscientiously attend unto the discharge of their ministerial office towards particular flocks would but examine their own hearts by the light of open and plain Scripture testimonies, with the nature of their office, and of the work they are engaged in, there would need little arguing to convince them of what trust is committed unto them, or what is required from them. If the consciences of others are not concerned in these things, if they have no light into the duty which seems to be incumbent on them, their principles and practices, or as we think mistakes and neglects, can be no rule unto us. What we may be forbidden, what we may be hindered in, is of another consideration. But for us voluntarily to engage unto the omission of that duty, which we cannot but believe that it will be required of us, is an evil which we are every way obliged to avoid.

There are also sundry particular duties, relating unto these that are more general, which in like manner, on the terms of communion proposed unto us, must be foregone and omitted. And where, by these means or neglects, some of the principal ways of exercising church-communion are cast out of the church, some of the means of the edification of its members are wholly lost, and sundry duties incumbent on them are virtually prohibited unto them, until they are utterly grown into disuse, it is no wonder if, in such churches where these evils are inveterate and remediless, particular persons do peaceably provide for their own edification by joining themselves unto such societies as wherein the rule of the gospel is more practically attended unto. It is taken for granted that the church is not corrupted by the wicked persons that are of its communion, nor its administrations defiled by their presence and communication in them, nor the edification of others prejudiced thereby, because it hath been so said by some of the ancients, though whether suitably unto the doctrine of the apostles or no is very questionable, 1 Cor. v. 6, 9–11; 2 Thess.

iii. 6.   But suppose this should be so, yet where wicked persons are admitted, without distinction or discrimination, unto the communion of the church, where they are tolerated therein, without any procedure with them or against them, contrary to express rules of the Scripture given to that purpose, so that those who are really pious among them can by no means prevail for the reformation of the whole, they may, not only without breach of charity, impairing of faith or love, or without the least suspicion of the guilt of schism, forsake the communion of such a congregation to join unto another, where there is more care of piety, purity, and holiness, but if they have any care of their own edification, and a due care of their salvation, they will understand it to be their duty so to do.

And we may a little touch hereon once for all.   The general end of the institution of churches, as such, is the visible management of the enmity on the part of the seed of the woman, Christ the head, and the members of his body mystical, against the serpent and his seed.   In the pursuit of this end, God ever had a church in the world, separate from persons openly profane doing the work of the devil, their father; and there is nothing in any church-constitution which tends unto or is compliant with the mixing and reconciling these distinct seeds, whilst they are such, and visibly appear so to be. And therefore, as the types, prophecies, and promises of the Old Testament did declare that when all things were actually brought unto a head in Christ Jesus, the church and all things that belong unto it should be holy,—that is, visibly so,—so the description generally and uniformly given us of the churches of the New Testament when actually called and erected is, that they consisted of persons called, sanctified, justified, ingrafted into Christ, Isa. xxvi. 2; Ezek. xliii. 12, xliv. 9; or saints, believers, faithful ones, purified and separate unto God, Lev. xi. 44; Rom. i. 6; 1 Cor. i. 1, 2, xii. 13; Phil. i. 1; Col. ii. 11.   Such they professed themselves to be, such they were judged to be by them that were concerned in their communion; and as such they engage themselves to walk in their conversation. By what authority so great a change should be now wrought in the nature and constitution of churches, that it should be altogether indifferent of what sort of persons they do consist, we know not.   Yea, to speak plainly, we greatly fear that both the worship and worshippers are defiled, 2 Tim. ii. 22, where open impenitent sinners are freely admitted unto all sacred administrations without control.   And we are sure that as God complaineth that his sanctuary is polluted, when there are brought into it "strangers, uncircumcised in heart, and uncircumcised in flesh," Ezek. xliv. 7; so the true members of the church are warned of the evil and dangers of such defiling mixtures, and charged to watch against them, 1 Cor. v. 6; Heb. xii. 15, 16.

We might yet farther insist on the great evil it would be in us, if we should give a seeming, outward approbation unto those things and their use which we cannot but condemn and desire to have removed out of the worship of God; and, moreover, there is, as we believe, an obligation upon us to give a testimony unto the truth about the worship of God in his church, and not absolutely to hide the light we have received therein under a bushel.   Nor would we render the reformation of the church absolutely hopeless, by our professed compliance with the things that ought to be reformed.   But what hath been pleaded already is sufficient to manifest that there neither is nor can be a guilt of schism charged either on ministers or people who withhold themselves from the communion of that church or those churches whereof the things mentioned are made conditions necessary and indispensable, and that wherein they must be denied the liberty of performing many duties made necessary unto them by the command of Jesus Christ.   And as the rigid imposition of unscriptural conditions of communion is the principal cause of all the schisms and divisions that are among us, so let them be removed and taken out of the way, and we doubt not but that among all that sincerely profess the gospel there may be that peace and such an agreement obtained, as in observance whereof they may all exercise those duties of love which the strictest union doth require.   These we profess ourselves ready for so far as God shall be pleased to help us in the discharge of our duty; as also to renounce every principle or opinion whereof we may be convinced that they are in the least opposite unto or inconsistent with the royal law of love and the due exercise thereof.   If men will continue to charge, accuse, or revile us, either out of a causeless distaste against our persons, or misunderstanding of our principles and ways, or upon certain reports, or merely prompted thereunto through a vain elation of mind, arising from the distance wherein, through their secular advantages, they look upon us to stand from them; as we cannot help it, so we shall endeavour not to be greatly moved at it, for it is known that this hath been the lot and portion of those who have gone before us in the profession of the gospel, and sincere endeavours to vindicate the worship of God from the disorders and abuses that have been introduced into it, and probably will be theirs who shall come after us.   But the whole of our care is, that "in godly simplicity and sincerity we may have our conversation in the world, not corrupting the word of God, nor using our liberty as a cloak of maliciousness, but as becomes the servants of God."

But perhaps it will yet be pleaded that this is not the whole which we are charged withal: for it is said that *we do not only withdraw ourselves from the communion of the church of England, but also that we assemble in separate congregations for the celebration of the whole worship of God; whereby we evidently make a division in the church, and contract unto ourselves the guilt of schism,* for what can there be more required thereunto?   But what would those who make use of this objection have us to do?   Would they have us starve our souls by a wilful neglect of the means appointed for their nourishment?   or would they have us live in a constant omission of all the commands of Christ?   By them, or those whose cause they plead, we are cast out and excluded from church-communion with them, by the unscriptural conditions of it which they would force upon us.   The distance between us that ensues hereon they are the causes of, not we; for we are ready to join with them or any others upon the terms of Christ and the gospel.   And do they think it meet that we should revenge their faults upon ourselves by a voluntary abstinence from all the ways and means of our edification?   Doth any man think that Jesus Christ leaves any of his disciples unto such a condition as wherein it is impossible they should observe his commands and institutions without sin?   That we should join in some societies, that in them we should assemble together for the worship of God in him, and that we should in him do and observe whatever he hath appointed, we look upon as our indispensable duty, made so unto us by his commands.   " These things," say some, " you shall not do with us, if you will do no more ; and if you do them among yourselves, you are schismatics."   But this is a severity which we know we shall not meet with at the last day.   *We stand at the judgment-seat of Jesus Christ.*

It will, it may be, be demanded by what warrant or authority we do assemble ourselves in church societies, for the administration of gospel ordinances? and who gave us this authority?   We answer, that it is acknowledged there is a difference between them and us, so that with them we cannot enjoy the worship of God; but of this difference we are not the cause, nor do give occasion to any blamable divisions by our principles or practices.   Where the cause is found, there the guilt remains.   This being the state of things with us, it is fond to imagine that any professors of the gospel do absolutely want a warranty or authority to obey Jesus Christ, to observe his commands, and to serve him according to his revealed will.   His command in his word, his promise of the acceptance of them, and of his presence among them in all the acts of their holy obedience, the assistance and guidance of his Holy Spirit, which he affords graciously unto them, are a sufficient warranty and authority for what they do in express compliance with his commands; and more they will not plead a power for.   Where the Spirit and word of Christ are, there is his authority; and this is no otherwise committed unto men but to enable them to act *obedientially* towards him and *ministerially* towards others.   And were church actings considered more with respect unto the obedience that in them is performed unto Christ, which is their first and principal consideration, it would quickly be evident whence men might have authority for their performance.   And by the same means are we directed in their order and manner.   Besides, the ministers, who go before the people in their assemblies, are all of them (so far as we know) solemnly set apart unto their office and work according unto what Christ hath appointed; and their duty it is to teach unto all men the good ways of Christ, and to go before them who are convinced and persuaded by them in their practice.   These things hath their Lord and Master required of them; and an account concerning them will he call them unto at the last day.   A dispensation is committed unto them, and a necessity is thence incumbent on them to preach the gospel; and who shall excuse them if they neglect so to do? for that all those who are ministers of the gospel are called to preach the gospel, and that diligently, every one according as he hath received the gift of the grace of God, is out of question with them that do believe the gospel. And of the stewardship which is committed unto them herein are they to give an account; and we do know that " it is a fearful thing" for sinners, that is, wilful neglecters of his commands, " to fall into the hands of the living God."   Our Lord Jesus Christ also hath testified beforehand that " he who setteth his hand to this plough, and looketh back again, is not fit for the kingdom of God."   He alone who calls them to this work can discharge them of it, and that either by the rule of his word or his providence; and when men are invincibly hindered, as many are at this day, it is their suffering, but not their sin.   Otherwise none can absolve them from the duty they owe to Jesus Christ in this matter, and that debt which they owe to the souls of men in undertaking the work of the ministry.   Some, indeed, suppose, or pretend to suppose, that a prohibition given them by superiors, forbidding them to preach, though not by nor according unto any rule of the gospel, doth discharge them from any obligation so to do, that it shall be no more their duty.   It would do so, no doubt, had they received no other command to preach the gospel, nor from any other authority, than that of and from those superiors by whom they are forbidden; but being persuaded that they have so from Him who is higher than the highest, they cannot acquiesce in this discharge, nor, being " bought with a price," can they now be servants of men.   But by whom are they thus forbidden to preach?   It will be supposed that the church which differs from them, and which originally makes itself a party in these differences, by the conditions of communion which it would impose upon them, is no competent judge in this case; nor will their prohibitions, who apparently thereby revenge their own quarrel, influence the consciences of them that dissent from them: for we speak not of what will or may take place, but what the consciences of men will or may be concerned in. By the civil magistrate they are not forbidden to preach, that we know of. It is true they are prohibited to preach in the legal public meeting-places or churches; and these places being in the power and care of the magistrate, it is meet his terms and conditions of their use should be accepted of, or his prohibition observed, or his penalty quietly undergone, where a peaceable occasion is made use of contrary unto it. As to other places, ministers are not absolutely forbid to preach in them,—no such power is as yet assumed or exercised; only, the manner of assemblies for sacred worship, and the number of them that may assemble, are regulated by laws for secular ends or civil security, and that under express penalties incurred on a contrary practice. But the consciences of ministers cannot be concerned in such laws, so far as to be exempted by them from the obligation that lies upon them from the command of Christ to preach the gospel. This they are commanded by him to do, and others know the penalties from men, under the danger whereof they must attend unto them. Besides, the reasons of these legal prohibitions, so far as they do extend, are taken from civil considerations alone, —namely, of the peace and quiet of the nation,—and not from any Scripture or religious rules. And were these prohibitions only temporary or occasional, suited unto such emergencies as may give countenance unto their necessity, there might be a proportionable compliance with them. But whereas they respect all times alike, it is no doubt incumbent on them who act any thing contrary unto such prohibitions to secure their own consciences that they no way interfere with the intention and end of the law, by giving the least countenance or occasion unto civil disturbances; and others, also, by their peaceable deportment in all they do. But whereas they have received a talent from the Lord Christ to trade withal, have accepted of his terms, and engaged into his service, without any condition of exception in case of such prohibitions, it is not possible they should satisfy their consciences in desisting from their work on such occurrences, any farther than in what they must yield unto outward force and necessity. It is pretended by some that if such a legal prohibition were given unto all the ministers of the gospel, it would not be obligatory unto them; for if it should be so esteemed, it were in the power of any supreme magistrate lawfully to forbid the whole work of preaching the gospel unto his subjects, which is contrary to the grant made by God the Father unto Jesus Christ, that "all nations shall be his inheritance," and the commission he gave thereon unto his apostles, to

" teach all nations," and to " preach the gospel to every creature" under heaven : but it being some only that are concerned in this prohibition, it is their duty, for peace' sake, to acquiesce in the will of their superiors therein, whilst there are others sufficient to carry on the same work.   That peace is or may be secured on other terms hath been already declared; but that one man's liberty to attend unto his duty, and his doing it accordingly, should excuse another from that which is personally incumbent on himself, is a matter not easily apprehended, nor can be readily digested.   Besides, what is pretended of the sufficient number of preachers, without any contribution of aid from the Nonconformists, is indeed but pretended; for if all that are found in the faith, gifted and called to the work of the ministry, in these nations, were equally encouraged unto and in their work, yet would they not be able to answer the necessities of the souls of men requiring an attendance unto it in a due measure and manner : and those who have exercised themselves unto compassionate thoughts towards the multitudes of poor sinners in these nations will not be otherwise minded.   Wherefore, these things being premised, we shall shut up these discourses with a brief answer unto the foregoing objection, which was the occasion of them; and we say,—

1. That schism being the name of a sin, or somewhat that is evil, it can in no circumstances be any man's duty.   But we have manifested, as satisfactorily unto our own consciences, so we hope unto the minds of unprejudiced persons, that in our present condition our assemblies for the worship of God are our express duty; and so can have no affinity with any sin or evil.   And those who intend to charge us with schism in or for our assemblies must first prove them not to be our duty.

2. Notwithstanding them, or any thing by us performed in them, we do preserve our communion entire with the church of England (that is, all the visible professors of the gospel in this nation), as it is a part of the catholic church, in the unity of the faith owned therein, provided it be not measured by the present opinions of some who have evidently departed from it.   Our non-admittance of the present government and discipline of the church, as apprehended national, and as it is in the hands of merely ecclesiastical persons, or such as are pretended so to be, we have accounted for before.   But we are one with the whole body of the professors of the protestant religion, in a public avowment of the same faith.

3. Into particular churches we neither are nor can be admitted, but on those terms and conditions which not only we may justly, but which we are bound in a way of duty to refuse; and this also hath been pleaded before.   Besides, no man is so obliged unto communion with any particular or parochial church in this nation, but

that it is in his own power at any time to relinquish it, and to secure himself also from all laws which may respect that communion, by the removal of his habitation. It is therefore evident that we never had any relation unto any parochial church but what is civil and arbitrary, a relinquishment whereof is practised at pleasure every day by all sorts of men. Continuing, therefore, in the constant profession of the same faith with all other Protestants in the nation, and the whole body thereof as united in the profession of it under one civil or political head; and having antecedently no evangelical obligation upon us unto local communion in the same ordinances of worship numerically with any particular or parochial church; and being prohibited from any such communion, by the terms, conditions, and customs indispensably annexed unto it by the laws of the land and the church, which are not lawful for us to observe, being Christ's freemen; it being, moreover, our duty to assemble ourselves in societies for the celebration of the worship of God in Christ, as that which is expressly commanded;—we are abundantly satisfied that, however we may be censured, judged, or condemned by men in and for what we do, yet that He doth both accept us here and will acquit us hereafter whom we serve and seek in all things to obey. Wherefore, we are not convinced that any principle or practice which we own or allow is in any thing contrary to that love, peace, and unity which the Lord Christ requireth to be kept and preserved among his disciples, or those that profess faith in him and obedience unto him according to the gospel. We know not any thing in them but what is consistent and compliant with that evangelical union which ought to be in and among the churches of Christ; the terms whereof we are ready to hold and observe even with them that in sundry things differ from us; as we shall endeavour, also, to exercise all duties of the same love, peaceableness, and gentleness towards them by whom we are hated and reviled.

AN INQUIRY

INTO

THE ORIGINAL, NATURE, INSTITUTION, POWER, ORDER, AND COMMUNION

OF

EVANGELICAL CHURCHES.

THE FIRST PART.

WITH

AN ANSWER TO THE DISCOURSE OF THE UNREASONABLENESS OF SEPARATION,

WRITTEN BY DR EDWARD STILLINGFLEET, DEAN OF PAUL'S;

AND IN DEFENCE OF THE VINDICATION OF THE NONCONFORMISTS FROM THE GUILT OF SCHISM.

———

"Stand ye in the ways, and see, and ask for the old paths, where is the good way, and walk therein, and ye shall find rest for your souls."—Jer. vi. 16.

PREFATORY NOTE.

A GENERAL account of the controversy occasioned by Stillingfleet's sermon "On the Mischief of Separation," will be found prefixed to Owen's pamphlet, entitled "A Brief Vindication of the Nonconformists," etc., vol. xiii. of his works. Stillingfleet in reply published a large work, with the title, "The Unreasonableness of Separation; or, an impartial account of the history, nature, and pleas of the present separation from the communion of the Church of England. To which several late letters are annexed of eminent protestant divines abroad, concerning the nature of our differences, and the way to compose them." The first part of this elaborate work consists of a long preface, in which the author first retorts upon the Nonconformists the charge of encouraging Popery from the schism and divisions they had fomented, from their opposition to episcopal polity, which was a main bulwark against Popery, and from certain curious facts, according to which the Jesuits, it would seem, had insinuated themselves among the early Puritans, in order to excite them against the Church of England. He next mentions that he had been led to preach the sermon which had given rise to the controversy by a perusal of two works of Mr Baxter, in which the Church of England was assailed, and to which he had a right to offer a reply. He alludes, finally, to the five antagonists, Owen, Baxter, Howe, Alsop, and Barret, whom his present work was intended to answer. Of Owen, whom he mentions first, he says, "He treated me with that civility and decent language, that I cannot but return him thanks for it." The work itself is divided into three parts,—an historical account of the rise and progress of separation, the nature of the present separation, and an examination of the pleas for separation. The praise of great tact and ability must be accorded to this production of Stillingfleet. He takes up the weapons of the Presbyterians against the Independents, during the discussions of the Westminster Assembly, and wields them against the Presbyterians themselves in defence of his own church. With both, his main argument is simply, that separation from a church which they admitted to be a true church of Christ was of necessity schism, and that no grounds could justify separation where there was agreement "in regard to doctrine and the substantials of religion." In the appendix to the work there are three letters, expressing concurrence with his views, from foreign divines,—Le Moyne, De l'Angle, and Claude. It is affirmed by Robinson, in his Life of Claude, that these letters were procured by Compton, bishop of London, on an unfair representation of the case at issue between Stillingfleet and his opponents, and published as the judgment of these foreign divines against English Nonconformity; and that, on a true statement of the case, they complained of the duplicity with which they had been treated, and gave forth an opinion adverse to the cause of the bishop and Stillingfleet. It is certain that in the letter by Le Moyne, he argues as if the question related to the possibility of salvation within the pale of the Church of England, accounting it "a very strange thing" that the Nonconformists should have "come to that extreme as to believe that a man cannot be saved in the Church of England." He might well have felt such surprise if there had been the least ground for imputing this uncharitable sentiment to Owen and his compeers in the defence of Nonconformity. Perhaps Stillingfleet himself had most reason to complain of the mistake, by whatever means it was occasioned, for it really deprived his chief argument against them of all its strength and relevancy.

In its first aspect, the following work of Owen, in reply to the Dean of St Paul's, seems irregular and confused. The dean is assailed, however, in a way most effective, and extremely characteristic of our author, who commonly refutes an antagonist not so much by exposing the weakness of his reasoning, as by establishing on solid grounds the positive truth to be embraced. He had been preparing a work on the nature of evangelical churches before "The Unreasonableness of Separation" appeared. He felt that the substance of his views on the main points involved in the controversy was contained in it, and, like another Scipio, he transfers the war to Africa, by putting the Church of England on its defence for innovations in its ecclesiastical polity, which had no sanction in Scripture or apostolic antiquity, the guilt of schism lying with the church that departed from the apostolic model, not with the church that adhered to it. Opinions, of course, will vary as to the perfect success of the argument. Few will question the ability with which it is conducted; and his sagacity in selecting this point of attack may be gathered from the fact, that in the view which he presents of the constitution and working of the primitive churches, he has but anticipated the judgment of the learned Neander.

In a preliminary note to the reader, he disposes of the calumny that the Dissenters were abettors of the papal interest in Britain, classing it with stories still more ridiculous, as that they had been receiving large bribes to pursue this unprincipled course. Then follows a preface of some length, in which he meets the argument contained in the first part of Stillingfleet's work, and founded on the history of separation. He appends to the treatise on evangelical churches a long answer to the remaining parts of his opponent's work, in which the Nonconformists are charged with schism, and their pleas in vindication of themselves are met and considered. The main treatise—the Inquiry into Evangelical Churches—is but the first part of a work which was completed by the publication in 1689 of "The True Nature of a Gospel Church." See vol. xvi. of his works.—ED.

TO THE READER.

I THOUGHT to have wholly omitted the consideration of that part of the discourse of Dr Stillingfleet, in his preface, which concerneth *the furtherance and promotion of the designs of the Papists and interest of Popery by Nonconformists,* and accordingly I passed it by in the ensuing discourses; for I supposed that all unprejudiced persons would assign it unto the provocation which he seems to have received from those who answered his sermon, or otherwise, and so have passed it by among such other excursions as divines are incident unto in their controversial writings, for that no countenance was given unto it, either from truth or any useful end as unto the present state of the protestant religion amongst us, is evident unto all. But things are fallen out more according unto the humour of the times, or rather the supposed interest of some, than any just, rational projections. For what other success this book hath had I know not, nor am solicitous. Certain it is that many of the same mind and persuasion with himself have been encouraged and emboldened by it confidently to report that "the Nonconformists are great promoters of the papal interest," yea, and do the work of the Papists to facilitate its introduction; for it is now made so evident in the preface of that book (I will not say on what topics, which seem not wakeful thoughts in such an important cause, and such a season as this is) that no man need doubt of the truth of it. Some, indeed, think that it were better at this time to consider how to get out Popery from amongst us than to contend about the ways whereby it came in, as unto our present danger of it. But if nothing will prevail against the resolutions of others, influenced by interest and the sweetness of present advantages, to desist from this inquiry, it will be necessary that such an account be given of the true reasons and means of the advance of Popery in this nation as shall give them occasion to consider themselves and their own ways; for we are to look for the causes of such effects in things and means that are suited and fitted to be productive of them, so as that they cannot but follow on their being and operation, and not in old stories, surmises, and far-fetched or feigned inferences. And if we do reckon that the real advancement of religion depends only on the secular advancement of some that do profess it, we may be mistaken in our measures, as others have been before us.

But, at present, the insinuations of that preface do seem to prevail much with those of the same party with its author, who want nothing at any time but the countenance of such a pen and story to vent their ill-will against Nonconformists. "Report," say they, "and we will report it." But also as he said, "Mendacium mendacio tegendum ne perpluat." First, evil inventions always tend unto, and stand in need of, new additions, to render them useful unto their end; without which they quickly evaporate. Wherefore, lest the insinuations of this worthy person should not be sufficiently subservient unto the uniting of all Protestants in one common interest against Popery, which was the original design of the Doctor's sermon, some have added unto it that which is homogeneal, as unto truth, and so easily mixing with the other discourse, that "the Nonconformists, some of them at least, do receive, or have received, money from the Papists, to act their affairs and promote their interest." And although this be such a putid calumny, such a malicious false-hood, such a frontless lie, as impudence itself would blush at being made an instru-ment to vent it, and withal extremely ridiculous, yet because it seems useful unto the good end of uniting Protestants and opposing Popery, it hath not only been reported by sundry of the clergy, but embraced and divulged also by some of their weak and credulous followers, who seem to believe that other men's advantage is their religion. But when the utmost bounds of modesty are passed, nothing but an outrage in lying and calumny, out of hopes that something will stick at last, can give countenance to men in such false accusations. And those by whom they are first whispered probably understand better than the Nonconformists what influence money, or the things which they know how to turn into it, hath into their profes-sion and actings in religion. It seems to me that some such men are afraid lest the present opposition unto Popery should issue in such an establishment of the protestant religion as that hereafter it should not be in the disposal of any, nor in their power to make a bargain of it, either for their advantage or in their necessity. For unless we should suppose such a defect in common prudence as is not charge-able on men of understanding in other affairs, it is hard to judge that these things can proceed from any other ground but a design to increase distrusts and jealousies amongst Protestants, to heighten their differences, to exasperate and provoke them to animosities, to weaken the hands of each party by a disbelief of the sincerity of each other in the same common cause; whence, whether it be designed or no, it will follow that we shall be all made a prey unto our restless adversaries. For what else but a strong inclination thereto can give the least credit or reputation to such vile insinuations, false surmises, and fables (I do not say in the preface, but in the reports that have been occasioned thereby), wherein folly and malice rival one another against that plain, open, uncontrollable evidence, which the Nonconformists always gave, and yet continue to give, of their faithful, cordial adherence unto the protestant religion and interest in the nation? And what now if, in way of re-taliation, a charge should be laid and managed against those of the episcopal way, that they should contribute their assistance (whether knowingly or being deluded it is all one) to the introduction of Popery, would not all things be cast into an admirable posture amongst us for an opposition thereunto? But let none mistake nor deceive themselves; neither the past sufferings of the Nonconformists, nor their present hopes of liberty, nor the reproaches cast upon them, shall shake them in their resolutions for a conjunction with all sincere Protestants in the preservation of their religion, and opposition unto all popish designs whatever. And (to speak with modesty enough) as they have hitherto, in all instances of zeal and duty for the preservation of the protestant religion, been as ready and forward as any other sort of men, so whatever may befall them, however they may be traduced or falsely accused, they do and will continue in giving the highest security that conscience, profession, principles, interest, and actions can give, of their stability in the same cause. Only, they desire to be excused if they make not use of this notable engine for opposing of Popery,—namely, the stirring up at this present time of jealousies, fears, and animosities amongst Protestants,—which others judge serviceable unto that end. But that which animates all these insinuations, charges, and reports, is our thankful acceptance of the indulgence granted by his majesty by a public declaration some years ago; whereby it should seem the Papists thought to make some advantage, though they were deceived in their expectation. I must needs say, that whatever be the true case in reference thereto in point of law, in my judgment it scarcely answereth that loyalty and regard unto his majesty's honour which some men profess, when all his actions are suited to their interests, to con-tinue such outcries about that which was his own sole act, by the advice of his council. We did, indeed, thankfully accept and make use of this royal favour; and after that, for so many years, we had been exposed to all manner of sufferings and penalties, whereby multitudes were ruined in their estates, and some lost their lives, and that without hopes of any remission of severity from the parliament that then sat, by their mistake of the true interest of the kingdom, wherein alone they did not miss it, we were glad to take a little breathing space from our troubles under his majesty's royal protection, designed only as an expedient (as was usual in former times) for the peace and prosperity of the kingdom, until the whole matter might be settled in parliament. And if this were a crime, " habetis confitentem reum" as to my part. But because I know myself herein peculiarly reflected on, I do avow that never any one person in authority, dignity, or power in the nation, nor any one that had any relation unto public affairs, nor any from them, Papist or Protestant, did once speak one word to me or advise with me about any indulgence or toleration to be granted unto Papists. I challenge all the world who are otherwise minded to intermit their service for a season unto the great false accuser, and prove the contrary if they can. The persons are sufficiently known of whom they may make their inquiry.

But I can cast this also into the same heap or bundle of other false surmises and reports concerning me, almost without number; which it would be a wonder that some men should pretend to believe and divulge, as they have done, if we were bound to judge that their charity and prudence were proportionable unto their dignities and promotions. These things must be, whilst interest, with hopes and fears, vain love, and hatred thence arising, do steer the minds of men.

But what if we have not designed the prevalence or introduction of Popery, yet, being a company of silly fellows, we have suffered ourselves to be wheedled by the Jesuits to be active for the cutting of our own throats? for we are full well satisfied that we should be the very first who should drink of the cup of their fury, could they ruin the protestant interest in England. And into such an unhappy posture of affairs are we fallen, that whereas it is evident we do nothing for the promotion of Popery, but only pray against it, preach against it, write against it, instruct the people in principles of truth whereon to avoid it, and cordially join with all true Protestants in the opposition of it, wherein we are charged with an excess that is like to spoil all, yet these crafty blades know how to turn it all unto their advantage. As it should seem, therefore, there remains nothing for Nonconformists to do in this matter, but to bind themselves hand and foot and give themselves up unto the power of the Papists; for all they do against them doth but promote their interest. But this, I am persuaded, they will be greatly unwilling unto, unless they are well assured that their episcopal friends will be more ready to expose themselves to hazard for their preservation and deliverance than yet they have reason to expect that they will. But, for my part, I was a long time since taught an expedient by an eminent personage for the freeing myself from any inclination to a compliance with Popery, and that in the instance of himself; for being in Ireland when there was, in former days, a great noise about reconciliation, a person of his own order and degree in the court of England wrote unto him, to inform him of a report that he was inclined to a reconciliation with Popery, or a compliance on good terms with the church of Rome, and withal desired him, that if it were so he would communicate unto him the reason of his judgment. But that great and wise personage, understanding full well whereunto these things tended, returned no answer but this only, that he knew no reason for any such report; for he was sure that he believed the pope to be antichrist, which put an absolute period unto the intercourse. And I can insist on the same defensative against forty such arguments as are used to prove us compliant with the papal interest; and so I believe can all the Nonconformists. And if this be not enough, I can, for my part, subscribe unto the conclusion which that most eminent champion of the protestant religion in

England, namely, Whitaker, gives unto his learned disputation about antichrist: "Igitur," saith he, "sequamur praeeuntem Spiritum Sanctum, et libere dicamus, defendamus, clamemus, et per eum qui vivit in aeternum juremus, pontificem Romanum esse antichristum."

If this will not suffice, we know better how to spend our remaining hours of life in peace than in contending about impertinent stories and surmises, exhaled by wit and invention out of the bog of secular interest; and shall, therefore, only assure those by whom we are charged, in the pulpit, or coffee-houses, or from the press, to countenance the promotion of the papal interest in the nation, that as they deal unjustly with us herein, and weaken the protestant interest what lies in them, so let them and others do and say what they please, nothing shall ever shake us in our resolution, by the help of God, to abide in a firm conjunction with all sincere Protestants for the preservation of our religion, and in opposition to the Papists; yea, that we would do so with our lives at the stake, if there were none left to abide in the same testimony but ourselves. But if they think that there is no way for us to be serviceable against Popery but by debauching our consciences with that conformity which they prescribe unto us, we beg their pardon, we are of another mind.

THE PREFACE.

THE differences and contests among professed Christians about the nature, power, order, rule, and residence of the gospel church-state, with the interest of each dissenting party therein, have not only been great and of long continuance, but have also so despised [defied?] all ways and means of allaying or abatement, that they seem to be more and more inflamed every day, and to threaten more pernicious consequents than any they have already produced; which yet have been of the worst of evils that the world for some ages hath groaned under: for the communion so much talked of amongst churches is almost come only unto an agreement and oneness in design for the mutual and forcible extermination of one another; at least, this is the professed principle of them who lay the loudest claim to the name and title, with all the rights and privileges, of the church. Nor are others far remote from the same design, who adjudge all who dissent from themselves into such a condition as wherein they are much inclined to think it meet they should be destroyed. That which animates this contest, which gives it life and fierceness, is a supposed enclosure of certain privileges and advantages, spiritual and temporal, real or pretended, unto the church-state contended about. Hence, most men seem to think that the principal, if not their only concernment in religion, is of what church they are; so as that a dissent from them is so evil as that there is almost nothing else that hath any very considerable evil in it. When this is once well rivetted in their minds by them whose secular advantages lie in the enclosure, they are in a readiness to bear a share in all the evils that unavoidably ensue on such divisions. By this means, among others, is the state or condition of Christian religion, as unto its public profession, become at this day so deplorable as cannot well be expressed. What with the bloody and desolating wars of princes and potentates, and what with the degeneracy of the community of the people from the rule of the gospel, in love, meekness, self-denial, holiness, zeal, the universal mortification of sin, and fruitfulness in good works, the profession of Christianity is become but a sad representation of the virtues of Him who calls out of darkness into his marvellous light. Neither doth there seem at present to be any design or expectation in the most for the ending of controversies about the church but force and the sword; which God forbid.

It is, therefore, high time that a sober inquiry be made, *whether there be any such church-state of divine institution as those contended about;* for if it should appear upon trial that indeed there is not, but that all the fierce digladiations of the parties at variance, with the doleful effects that attend them, have proceeded on a false supposition, in an adherence whereunto they are confirmed by their interests, some advances may be made towards their abatement. However, if this may not be attained, yet directions may be taken from the discovery of the truth, for the use of them who are willing to be delivered from all concernment in these fruitless, endless contests, and to reduce their whole practice in religion unto the institutions, rules, and commands of our Lord Jesus Christ. And where all hopes of a general reformation seem to fail, it savours somewhat of an unwarrantable severity to forbid them to reform themselves who are willing so to do; provided they admit of no other rule in what they so do but the declaration of the mind of Christ in the gospel, carrying it peaceably towards all men, and firmly adhering unto the faith once delivered unto the saints.

To make an entrance into this inquiry the ensuing discourse is designed. And there can be no way of the management of it but by a diligent, impartial search into the nature, order, power, and rule of the gospel church-state, as instituted, determined, and limited by our Lord Jesus Christ and his apostles. When we depart from this rule, so as not to be regulated by it in all instances of fact or pleas of right that afterward fall out, we fall into the confusion of various presumptions, suited unto the apprehensions and interests of men, imposed on them from the circumstances of the ages wherein they lived. Yet is it not to be denied but that much light into the nature of apostolical institutions may be received from the declared principles and practices of the first churches, for the space of two hundred years or thereabouts. But that, after this, the churches did insensibly depart in various degrees from the state, rule, and order of the apostolical churches, must, I suppose, be acknowledged by all those who groan under the final issue of that gradual degeneracy in the papal antichristian tyranny; for Rome was not built in a day, nor was this change introduced at once or in one age. Nor were the lesser alterations which began this declension so prejudicial unto the being, order, and purity of the churches, as they proved afterward, through a continual additional increase in succeeding ages.

Having affirmed something of this nature in my brief "Vindication of the Nonconformists from the Guilt of Schism," the Rev. Dr Stillingfleet, in his late treatise, entitled "The Unreasonableness of Separation," doth not only deny it, but reflects with some severity upon the mention of it, part ii. sect. 3, pp. 225, 226, etc. I shall, therefore, on this occasion, resume the consideration of it, although it will be spoken unto also afterwards.

The words he opposeth are these:—" It is possible that an impartial account may, ere long, be given of the state and ways of the first churches after the decease of the apostles; wherein it will be made to appear how they did insensibly deviate in many things from the rule of their first institution; so as that though their mistakes were of small moment, and not prejudicial unto their faith and order, yet occasion was administered unto succeeding ages to increase those deviations until they issued in a fatal apostasy." I yet suppose these words inoffensive, and agreeable unto the sentiments of the generality of Protestants; for,—

1. Unto *the first churches* after the apostles I ascribe nothing but such *small mistakes* as did no way prejudice their faith or order; and that they did preserve the latter as well as the former, as unto all the substantial parts of it, shall be afterwards declared. Nor do I reflect any more upon them than did Hegesippus in Eusebius, who confines the virgin purity of the church unto the days of the apostles, lib. iii. cap. 29. The greater deviations, which I intend, began not until after the end of the second century. But,—

2. To evince the improbability of any alteration in church rule and order upon my own principles, he intimates, both here and afterward, that "my judgment is that the government of the church was democratical, and the power of it in the people, in distinction from its officers:" which is a great mistake; I never thought, I never wrote any such thing. I do believe that the authoritative rule or government of the church was, is, and ought to be, in the elders and rulers of it, being an act of the office-power committed unto them by Christ himself. Howbeit, my

judgment is, that they ought not to rule the church with force, tyranny, and corporal penalties, or without their own consent; whereof we shall treat afterward. There are also other mistakes in the same discourse, which I shall not insist upon.

3. This, therefore, is that which he opposeth,—namely, that *there was a deviation in various degrees, and falling off from the original institution, order, and rule of the church, until it issued in a fatal apostasy.* This is that which, on the present occasion, must be farther spoken unto; for if this be not true, I confess there is an end of this contest, and we must all acquiesce in the state, rule, and order that was in the church of Rome before the Reformation. But we may observe something yet farther in the vindication and confirmation of this truth, which I acknowledge to be the foundation of all that we plead for in point of church reformation; as,—

(1.) That the reasons and arguings of the Doctor in this matter,—the necessity of his cause compelling him thereunto,—are the same with those of the Papists about the apostasy of their church, in faith, order, and worship, wherewith they are charged, namely, when, where, how was this alteration made? who made opposition unto it? and the like. When these inquiries are multiplied by the Papists, as unto the whole causes between them and us, he knows well enough how to give satisfactory answers unto them, and so might do in this particular unto himself also; but I shall endeavour to ease him of that trouble at present. Only, I must say that it is fallen out somewhat unexpectedly that the ruins of the principal bulwark of the Papacy, which hath been effectually demolished by the writings of Protestants of all sorts, should be endeavoured to be repaired by a person justly made eminent by his defence of the protestant religion against those of the church of Rome.

(2.) But it may be pleaded, that although the churches following the first ages did insensibly degenerate from the purity and simplicity of gospel faith and worship, yet they neither did nor could do so from an adherence unto and abiding in their original constitution, or from the due observation of church order, rule, and discipline, least of all could this happen in the case of diocesan episcopacy. I answer,—

[1.] That as unto the *original* of any thing that looks like diocesan episcopacy, or the pastoral relation of one person of a distinct order from presbyters unto many particular complete churches with officers of their own, with power and jurisdiction in them and over them, unto the abridgment of the exercise of that right and power unto their own edification which every true church is intrusted withal by Jesus Christ, it is very uncertain, and was introduced by insensible degrees, according unto the effectual working of the mystery of iniquity. Some say that there were two distinct orders,—namely, those of bishops and presbyters,—instituted at first in all churches planted by the apostles; but as the contrary may be evidently proved, so a supposition of it would no way promote the cause of diocesan episcopacy, until those who plead for it have demonstrated the state of the churches wherein they were placed to be of the same nature with those now called diocesan. Wherefore, this hypothesis begins generally to be deserted, as it seems to be by this author. Others suppose that immediately upon, or at, or after the decease of the apostles, this new order of bishops was appointed, to succeed the apostles in the government of the churches that were then gathered or planted; but how, when, or by whom,—by what authority, apostolical and divine, or ecclesiastical only and human,—none can declare, seeing there is not the least footstep of any such thing either in the Scripture or in the records that remain of the primitive churches. Others think this new order of officers took its occasional rise from the practice of the presbyters of the church at Alexandria, who chose out one among themselves constantly to preside in the rule of the church and in all matters of order, unto

whom they ascribed some kind of pre-eminence and dignity, peculiarly appropri-
ating unto him the name of bishop.   And if this be true as unto matter of fact,
I reckon it unto the beginnings of those less harmful deviations from their original
constitution which I assigned unto primitive churches; but many additions must
be made hereunto before it will help the cause of diocesan episcopacy.   What
other occasions hereof were given or taken, what advantages were made use of to
promote this alteration, shall be touched upon afterwards.

[2.] Why may not the churches be supposed to have departed from their original constitution, order, and rule, as well as from their first faith and worship?
which they did gradually, in many successive ages, until both were utterly corrupted.   The causes, occasions, and temptations leading unto the former, are to
the full as pregnant as those leading unto the latter; for,—

1st. There was no vicious, corrupt disposition of mind that began more early to
work in church-officers, nor did more grow and thrive in the minds of many, than
ambition, with desire of pre-eminence, dignity, and rule.   It is not to be supposed
that Diotrephes was alone in his desire of pre-eminence, nor in the irregular actings of his unduly assumed authority.   However, we have one signal instance in
him of the deviation that was in the church with him, from the rule of its original
constitution; for he prevailed so far therein as, by his own single episcopal power, to
reject the authority of the apostles, and to cast them out of the church who complied not with his humour.   How effectually the same ambition wrought afterward, in many others possessing the same place in their churches with Diotrephes,
is sufficiently evident in all ecclesiastical histories.   It is far from being the only
instance of the corruption of church order and rule by the influence of this ambition, yet it is one that is pregnant, which is given us by Ambrose; for, saith he,
"Ecclesia ut synagoga, seniores habuit, quorum sine consilio nihil agebatur in
ecclesia; quod quâ negligentiâ obsoleverit nescio, nisi forte doctorum desidiâ, aut
magis superbiâ, dum soli volunt aliquid videri," in 1 ad Timoth. cap. v.   It seems
there was some alteration in church rule and order in his time, whose beginning
and progress he could not well discover and trace, but knew well enough that so
it was then come to pass.   And if he, who lived so near the times wherein such
alterations were made, could not yet discover their first insinuation nor their
subtle progress, it is unreasonable to exact a strict account of us in things of the
same nature, who live so many ages after their first introduction.   But this he
judgeth, that it was the pride or ambition of the doctors of the church which introduced that alteration in its order.   Whereas, therefore, we see in the event that
all deviations from the original constitution of churches, all alterations in their rule
and order, did issue in a compliance with the ambition of church-rulers, as it did
in the papal church,—and this ambition was signally noted as one of the first depraved inclinations of mind that wrought in ecclesiastical rulers, and which, in the
fourth and fifth centuries, openly proclaimed itself, unto the scandal of Christian
religion,—there was a greater disposition in them unto a deviation from the original
institution, rule, and order of the church, no way suited unto the satisfaction of
that ambition, than unto a defection from the purity of faith and worship; which
yet also followed.

2dly. As the inclination of many lay towards such a deviation, so their interests
led them unto it, and their temptations cast them upon it.   For, to acknowledge
the truth unto our author and others, the rule and conduct of the church, the preservation of its order and discipline according unto its first institution, and the directions given in the Scripture about it, are, according unto our apprehension of
these things, a matter so weighty in itself, so dangerous as unto its issue, attended
with so many difficulties, trials, and temptations, laid under such severe interdictions of lordly power, or seeking either of wealth or dignity, that no wise man will

ever undertake it, but merely out of a sense of a call from Christ unto it, and in compliance with that duty which he owes unto him. It is no pleasant thing unto flesh and blood to be engaged in the conduct and oversight of Christ's volunteers; —to bear with their manners; to exercise all patience towards them in their infirmities and temptations; to watch continually over their walkings and conversation, and thereon personally to exhort and admonish them all; to search diligently and scrupulously into the rule of the Scripture for their warranty in every act of their power and duty; under all their weaknesses and miscarriages, continuing a high valuation of them, as of the flock of God, " which he hath purchased with his own blood;" with sundry other things of the like kind; all under an abiding sense of the near approach of that great account which they must give of the whole trust and charge committed unto them before the judgment-seat of Christ: for the most part peculiarly exposed unto all manner of dangers, troubles, and persecutions, without the least encouragement from wealth, power, or honour. It is no wonder, therefore, if many in the primitive times were willing gradually to extricate themselves out of this uneasy condition, and to embrace all occasions and opportunities of introducing insensibly another rule and order into the churches, that might tend more unto the exaltation of their own power, authority, and dignity, and free them in some measure from the weight of that important charge, and continual care with labour, which a diligent and strict adherence unto the first institution of churches, and rules given for their order and government in the Scripture, would have obliged them unto. And this was done accordingly, until, in the fourth and fifth centuries, and so onward, the bishops, under various titles, began by their arbitrary rules and canons to dispose of the flock of Christ, to part and divide them among themselves, without their own knowledge or consent, as if they had conquered them by the sword. " This bishop shall have such a share and number of them under his power, and that other so many; so far shall the jurisdiction of one extend, and so far that of another," was the subject of many of their decrees and laws for the rule of the church. But yet neither did they long keep within those bounds and limits which their more modest ambition had at first prescribed unto them, but took occasion from these beginnings to contend among themselves about pre-eminence, dignity, and power; in which the bishop of Rome at length remained master of the field, thereby obtaining a second conquest of the world.

3*dly.* That there was such a gradual deviation from the original institution of churches, their order and rule, is manifest in the *event;* for the change became at length as great as the distance is between the gospel and the rule of Christ over his church on the one hand, and the canon law with the pope or antichrist set over the church on the other. This change was not wrought at once, not in one age, but by an insensible progress, even from the days of the apostles unto those dark and evil times wherein the popes of Rome were exalted into an absolute tyranny over all churches, unto the satiety of their ambition; for,—

4*thly.* This mystery of iniquity began to work in the days of the apostles themselves, in the suggestions of Satan and the lusts of men, though in a manner latent and imperceptible unto the wisest and best of men; for that this mystery of iniquity consisted in the effectual workings of the pride, ambition, and other vices of the minds of men, excited, enticed, and guided by the craft of Satan, until it issued in the idolatrous, persecuting state of the church of Rome, wherein all church rule, order, and worship of divine institution was utterly destroyed or corrupted, we shall believe, until we see an answer given unto the learned writings of all sorts of Protestants, whereby it hath been proved.

These things are sufficient to vindicate the truth of the assertion which the Doctor opposeth, and to free it from his exceptions; but because, as was observed before, the supposition hereof is the foundation of all our present contests about church order and rule, I shall yet proceed a little farther in the declaration of the way and manner whereby the apostasy asserted was begun and carried on. And I shall not herein insist on particular instances, nor make a transcription of stories out of ancient writers giving evidence unto the truth, because it hath been abundantly done by others, especially those of Magdeburg in the sixth and seventh chapters of their Centuries, unto whose observations many other learned men have made considerable additions; but I shall only treat in general of the causes, ways, and manner of the beginning and progress of the apostasy or declension of churches from their first institution, which fell out in the successive ages after the apostles, especially after the end of the second century, until when divine institutions, as unto the substance of them, were preserved entire.

Decays in any kind, even in things natural and political, are hardly discernible but in and by their effects. When an hectic distemper befalls the body of any man, it is ofttimes not to be discerned until it is impossible to be cured. The Roman historian gives this advice unto his readers, after he hath considered the ways and means whereby the empire came to its greatness: "Labente deinde disciplinâ velut dissidentes primo mores sequatur animo; deinde ut magis magisque lapsi sint, tum ire cæperint præcipites, donec ad hæc tempora, quibus nec vitia nostra, nec remedia pati possumus, periculum est," Liv. Præfat. His words do not give us a more graphical description of the rise and decay, as unto virtue and vice, of the Roman empire, than of the Roman church, as unto its rise by holiness and devotion, and its ruin by sensuality, ambition, the utter neglect of the discipline of Christ, and superstition. But yet let any man peruse that historian, who wrote with this express design, he shall hardly fix upon many of those instances whereby the empire came into that deplorable condition wherein it was not able to bear its distempers nor its cure, such as was the state of the church before the Reformation. But besides the common difficulty of discovering the beginnings and gradual progression of decays, declensions, and apostasy, those which we treat of were begun and carried on in a mysterious manner; that is, by the effectual working of "the mystery of iniquity." As this almost hid totally the work of it from the ages wherein it was wrought, so it renders the discovery of it now accomplished the more difficult. Passengers in a ship setting out to sea ofttimes discern not the progressive motion of the ship, yea, for a while the land rather seems to move from them than the vessel wherein they are from it; but after a season, the consideration of what distance they are at from their port gives them sufficient assurance of the progress that hath been made: so this declension of the churches from their primitive order and institution is discoverable rather by measuring the distance between what it left and what it arrived unto, than by express instances of it. But yet is it not altogether like unto that of a ship at sea, but rather unto "the way of a serpent on a rock," which leaves some slime in all its turnings and windings, whereby it may be traced. Such marks are left on record of the serpentine works of this mystery of iniquity as whereby it may be traced, with more or less evidence, from its original interests unto its accomplishment.

The principal promoting causes of this defection on the part of men were those assigned by St Ambrose, in one instance of it,—namely, the negligence of the people, and the ambition of the clergy. I speak as unto the state, rule, discipline, and order of the church; for as unto the doctrine and worship of it, there were many other causes and means of their corruption, which belong not unto our present purpose. But as unto the alterations that were begun and carried on in the state, order, and rule of the church, they arose from those springs of negligence on the one hand, and ambition on the other, with want of skill and wisdom to manage outward occurrences and incidences, or what alteration fell out in the outward state and condition of the church in this world. For hence it came to pass, that in the accession of the nations in general unto the profession of the gospel, church-order was suited and framed unto their secular state, when they ought to have been brought into the spiritual state and order of the church, leaving their political state entire unto themselves. Herein, I say, did the guides of the church certainly miss their rule and depart from it, in the days of Constantine the emperor, and afterward under other Christian emperors, when whole towns, cities, yea, and nations, offered at once to join themselves unto it. Evident it is that they were not wrought hereunto by the same power, nor induced unto it on the same motives, or led by the same means, with those who formerly under persecution were converted unto the faith of our Lord Jesus Christ. And this quickly manifested itself in the lives and conversations of many, yea, of the most of them. Hence those which were wise quickly understood that what the church had got in multitude and number it had lost in the beauty and glory of its holy profession. Chrysostom in particular complains of it frequently, and in many places cries out, " What have I to do with this multitude? A few serious believers are more worth than them all." However, the guides of the church thought meet to receive them, with all their multitudes, into their communion, at least so far as to place them under the jurisdiction of such and such episcopal sees; for hereby their own power, authority, dignity, revenues, were enlarged and mightily increased. On this occasion, the ancient, primitive way of admitting members into the church being relinquished, the consideration of their personal qualifications and real conversion unto God omitted, such multitudes being received as could not partake in all acts and duties of communion with those particular churches whereunto they were disposed, and being the most of them unfit to be ruled by the power and influence of the commands of Christ on their minds and consciences, it was impossible but that a great alteration must ensue in the state, order, and rule of the churches, and a great deviation from their original institution. Men may say that this alteration was necessary, that it was good and useful, that it was but the accommodation of general rules unto especial occasions and circumstances; but that there was an alteration hereon in all these things none can with modesty deny. And this is enough unto my present design, being only to prove that such alterations and deviations did of old fall out. Neither ought we to cover the provoking degeneracy of the generality of Christians in the fourth and fifth centuries, with those that followed. The consideration of it is necessary unto the vindication of the holy providence of God in the government of the world, and of the faithfulness of Christ in his dealing with his church; for there hath been no nation in the world which publicly received Christian religion, but it hath been wasted and destroyed by the sword of pagan idolaters, or such as are no better than they. At first, all the provinces of the western empire were, one after another, made desolate by the pagan nations of the northern countries; who themselves did afterward so turn Christians as to lay among them the foundation of Antichristianism, Rev. xvii. 12, 13. The eastern empire, comprehending the residue of the provinces that had embraced the Christian religion, was first desolated in the chief branches of it by the Saracens, and at length utterly destroyed by the Turks. And I pray God that the like fate doth not at this day hang over the *reformed* nations, as from their profession they are called. Do we think that all this was without cause? Did God give up his inheritance to the spoil of barbarous infidels without such provocations as the passing by whereof was inconsistent with the holiness and righteousness of his rule? It was not the wisdom, nor the courage, nor the multitude of their enemies, but their own sins, wickedness, superstition, and apostasy from the rule of gospel order, worship, and obedience, which ruined all Christian nations.

But to give farther evidence hereunto, I shall consider the causes afore-mention-

ed distinctly and apart. And the first of them is *the negligence of the people them-*
selves. But in this negligence I comprise both the ignorance, sloth, worldliness,
decay in gifts and graces, with superstition in sundry instances, that in many of
them were the causes of it. Dr Stillingfleet pleads that "it is very unlikely that
the people would forego their interest in the government of the churches, if ever
they had any such thing, without great noise and trouble. For," saith he, "government is so nice and tender a thing, and every one is so much concerned for
his share in it, that men are not easily induced to part with it. Let us suppose
the judgment of the church to have been democratical at first, as Dr Owen seems
to do; is it probable that the people would have been wheedled out of the sweetness of government so soon and made no noise about it?" p. 226. His mistake
about my judgment herein hath been marked before. No other interest or share
in the government is ascribed by us unto the people, but that they may be ruled by
their own consent, and that they may be allowed to yield obedience in the church
unto the commands of Christ and his apostles, given unto them for that end.
This interest they neither did nor could forego without their own sin and guilt,
in neglecting the exercise of the gifts and graces which they ought to have had, and
the performance of the duties whereunto they were obliged. But for any engagement on their minds from the " sweetness of government," wherein their concern
principally consists, in an understanding, voluntary obedience unto the commands
of Christ, they had nothing of it. Take also, in general, government to be, as the
government of the church is, merely a duty, labour, and service, without those advantages of power, ease, dignity, and wealth, which have been annexed unto it,
and it will be hard to discover such "a nicety" or "sweetness" in it as to oblige
unto pertinacy in an adherence unto it. If the government of the church were
apprehended to consist in men's giving themselves wholly to the word and prayer;
in watching continually over the flock; in accurate carefulness to do and act nothing in the church but in the name and authority of Christ, by the warranty of
his commands; with a constant exercise of all gifts and graces of the Holy Spirit,
which they have received, in these and all other duties of their office; and that
without the least appearance of domination, or the procuring of dignity, secular
honours, and revenues thereby,—it may be, a share and interest in it would not be
so earnestly coveted and sought after as at present it is. Nor is there any more
pertinency in his ensuing supposal of a "change in the government of the congregational churches in London, in setting up one man to rule over them all and to
appoint their several teachers," etc., p. 227, "which could not be done without
noise." It is in vain to fear it,

> —— " Non isto vivimus illic
> Quo tu rere, modo,"

and impertinent in this case to suppose it; for it speaks of a sudden total alteration in the state, order, and rule of churches, to be made at once, whereas our
discourse is of that which was gradual in many ages, by degrees almost imperceptible. But yet I can give no security that the churches of our way shall not, in
process of time, decline from their primitive constitution and order, either in their
power and spirit, in faith and love, or in the outward practice of them, unless they
continually watch against all beginnings and occasions of such declensions, and
frequently renew their reformation; or if it be otherwise, they will have better
success than any churches in the world ever yet had, even those that were of
the planting of the apostles themselves, as is manifested in the judgment that
our Lord Jesus Christ passed on them, Rev. ii. iii. The negligence of the people,
which issued in their unfitness to be disposed of and ruled according to the
principles of the first constitution of church-order, may be considered either as it
gave occasion unto those lesser deviations from the rule, which did not much pre-

judice the faith and order of the churches, or as it occasioned greater alterations in the ensuing ages. And,—

1. The great, and perhaps in some things excessive, veneration which they had of their bishops or pastors, did probably occasion in them some neglect of their own duty; for they were easily induced hereon, not only implicitly to leave the management of all church affairs unto them, but also zealously to comply with their mistakes. The church of Smyrna, giving an account of the martyrdom of holy Polycarpus, tells us that when he ascended the pile wherein he was to be burned, "he pulled off his own clothes, and endeavoured to pull off his shoes, which he had not done before, because the faithful strove among themselves who should soonest touch his body," Euseb. lib. iv. cap. 15. I think there can be no veneration due to a man which was not so unto that great and holy person. But those who did so express it might easily be induced to place too much of their religion in an implicit compliance with them unto whom they were so devoted. Hence a negligence in themselves as unto their particular duties did ensue. They were quickly far from esteeming it their duty to say unto their pastor or bishop that he should "take heed to the ministry which he had received in the Lord, to fulfil it," as the apostle enjoins the Colossians to say to Archippus their pastor, chap. iv. 17, but began to think that the glory of obsequious obedience was all that was left unto them. And hence did some of the clergy begin to assume to themselves, and to ascribe unto one another, great swelling titles of honour and names of dignity (amongst which the blasphemous title of "His Holiness" was at length appropriated unto the bishop of Rome); wherein they openly departed from the apostolical simplicity and gravity. But these things fell out after the writing of the epistle of Clemens, and of those of the churches of Vienne and Smyrna, wherein no such titles do appear.

2. Many of the particular churches of the first plantations increasing greatly in the number of their members, it was neither convenient nor safe that the whole multitude should on all occasions come together, as they did at first, to consult about their common concerns, and discharge the duties of their communion; for by reason of danger from their numerous conventions, they met in several parcels as they had opportunity. Herewith they were contented, unless it were upon the greater occasions of choosing their officers and the like, whereon the whole church met together. This made them leave the ordinary administration of all things in the church unto the elders of it, not concerning themselves farther therein; but still continuing members of the same particular church. It is altogether improbable what Platina from Damasus affirms, in the Life of Euarestus, about the end of the first century, that he distributed the faithful at Rome into distinct titles or parishes, with distinct presbyters of their own; for it is apparent that in those days, wherein persecution was at its height, the meetings of believers were occasional, with respect unto their security, ofttimes by night, sometimes in caves under the earth, or in deserted burial-places, at best in private houses. And they had for what they did the example of the apostolical churches, Acts i. 13, 14, ii. 46; iv. 23–31, xii. 12, xviii. 7, xx. 8, xxi. 8. Instances of such meetings may be multiplied, especially in the church of Rome. And to manifest that they took this course upon necessity, when peace began to be restored at any time unto them, they designed temples that might receive the whole multitude of the church together. The distribution mentioned into titles and parishes began a long time after, and in very few places within three hundred years. In this state it is easy to conceive what alterations might fall out in some churches from their primitive order, especially how the people might desert their diligence and duty in attending unto all the concerns of the church. And if those things which the apostles wrote unto them in their epistles, the instructions, directions, and com-

mands how in all things they should act and deport themselves in the church, be esteemed to be obligatory in all ages, I cannot see how, after the second century, they were much complied withal, unless it were in the single instance of *choosing their own officers* or rulers.

But, secondly, After these there ensued greater occasions of greater variations from the primitive institution and order of the churches on the part of the people; for,—

1. Such *numbers* of them were received into a relation unto particular churches as was inconsistent with the ends of their institution and the observance of the communion required in them; as will afterward appear. And the reliefs that were invented for this inconveniency in distinct conventions, supplied with the administration of the word and sacraments from the first church, or by stated titles, did alter the state of the church.

Among those multitudes which were added unto the churches, especially in the fourth century, many, if not the most, did come short inexpressibly in knowledge, gifts, grace, holiness, and uprightness of conversation of the primitive Christians, as the writers of that age complain. And being hereby incapable of walking according unto the order, rule, and discipline of the apostolical churches, there seemed to be a necessity of another rule, of other ways and means for their government, without their own concurrence or consent, than what was at first appointed, which were gradually introduced; whence the original of a multitude of those canons, which were arbitrarily invented afterward for their rule and government, is to be derived. And it may be made to appear that the accommodation of the rule, yea, and of the worship of the church, in the several ages of it, unto the ignorance, manners, and inclinations of the people, who were then easily won unto the outward profession of Christian religion, was one means of the ruin of them both, until they issued in downright tyranny and idolatry.

But much more of the cause of the deviation of the churches from their primitive rule and order is to be ascribed unto the ambition and love of pre-eminence in many of the clergy, or rulers of the churches; but this is no place nor season to manifest this by instances, besides it hath been done by others. I shall therefore inquire only into one or two things in particular, which are of principal consideration in the declension of the churches from their primitive institution, order, and rule; and,—

(1.) It is evident that there was an *alteration* made in the state of the church as to its *officers*; for it issued at last in popes, patriarchs, cardinals, metropolitan and diocesan bishops, who were utterly foreign unto the state and order of the primitive churches, and that for some ages. Nor were these officers introduced into the church at once, or in one age, nor with the powers which they afterward claimed and assumed unto themselves. It was done gradually, in many succeeding ages, working by design to accommodate the state of the church unto the political state of the empire in the distribution of its government.

(2.) The *beginnings* of this great alteration were *small*, nor at all perceived in the days wherein they were first acted. Nor is it agreed, nor, as far as I see, will it ever be agreed among learned men, when first a disparity among the ordinary officers of the church, in order, degree, or power, did first begin, nor by what means it was brought about. The apostles were all equal among themselves; no one had either office or office-power above others. So were all the ordinary bishops and presbyters mentioned in the Scripture, as shall be proved afterward. No intimation is given of any pre-eminence or superiority amongst them of one over others. Yet afterward, in the third and fourth centuries, much of that nature appears. It begins to be granted that the bishops and elders mentioned in the Scripture were the same, and that there was no difference in name, office, or power, during the apostles' times; which was the judgment of Jerome, and our author seems to me to be of the same mind, p. 267   But they say that after the decease of the apostles, there were some appointed to succeed them in that part of their office which concerned the rule of many churches.   And this, they say, was done for the prevention of schism, but with ill success; for as Clemens affirms that the apostles foresaw that there would be strife and contention about episcopacy, even when it was confined unto its original order, because of the ambition of Diotrephes and others like him, so it became much more the cause of all sorts of disorders, in schisms and heresies, when it began to exalt itself in dignity and reputation. The first express attempt to corrupt and divide a church, made from within itself, was that in the church of Jerusalem, made by Thebuthis, because Simon Cleophas was chosen bishop, and he was refused, Euseb., lib. iv. cap. 22.   The same rise had the schisms of the Novatians and Donatists, the heresies of Arius, and others.   Neither is there any thing certain in this pretended succession of some persons unto the apostles in that part of their office which concerns the rule of many churches by one overseer.   No intimation of any such appointment by the apostles, or any of them,—no record of the concurrence of the churches themselves in and unto this alteration,—can be produced.   Nor is there any analogy between the extraordinary power of every apostle over all churches and care for them, and the ordinary power of a bishop over a small number, which lot or accident disposeth unto him.   Besides, it cannot be proved, no instance can be given, or hath been, for the space of two hundred years, or until the end of the second century, of any one person who had the care of more churches than one committed unto him, or did take the charge of them on himself.   But whereas this change did fall out, and appears evidently so to have done, in the fourth century, we may briefly inquire into the causes and occasions of it.

Churches were originally planted in cities and towns for the most part; not absolutely, for the word was preached and churches gathered by the apostles κατὰ πόλεις καὶ χώρας, as Clemens testifieth.   In such cities there was but one church, whereunto all believers did belong.   I mention this the rather because our present author, who is pleased frequently to mistake my words and principles, affirms " that the thing which I should have proved is, that there were more churches at first planted in one city than one."   I know not why I should be obliged to do so, because I never said so.   I do believe, indeed, that there may be more particular churches than one in one city; and that sometimes it is better that it should be so than that all believers in the same city should be kept up unto one congregation, to the obstruction of their edification.   But that there were originally, or in the days of the apostles, more churches than one, in any one city or town, I do wholly deny; though I grant, at the same time, there were churches in villages also, as will appear afterward.   But though there was one church only in one town or city, yet all the believers that belonged unto that church did not live in that city, but sundry of them in the fields and villages about.   So Justin Martyr tells us, that on the first day of the week, when the church had its solemn assemblies, all the members of it, in the city and out of the country, the fields and villages about, met together in the same place.   In process of time these believers in the country did greatly increase, by the means of the ministry of the city church, which diligently attended unto the conversion of all sorts of men, with some extraordinary helps besides.   But hereon the example of the apostles was overseen; for on this account of the conversion of many unto the faith in the towns and villages of any province, they erected and planted new churches among them, not obliging them all unto that first church from whence the word went forth for their conversion.   But those who succeeded them, being hindered by many reasons, which may be easily recounted, from thoughts of the multiplication of churches, chose rather to give the believers scattered up and down in the country occasional assistance by presbyters of their own, than to dispose them into a church-state and order. But after a while, their number greatly increasing, they were necessitated to supply them with a constant ministry, in several parcels or divisions. The ministers or elders thus disposed amongst them for their edification, in the administration of the ordinances of the gospel, did still relate unto and depend upon that *city first church* from whence they came. But the numbers of believers daily increasing, and a succession of presbyters in their distinct assemblies being found necessary, they came to be called churches, though continuing in dependence, both for a supply of officers and for rule, on the first or city church, whereunto they esteemed themselves to belong. This was the way and manner of the multiplication of Christian assemblies throughout the Roman empire; and hereby all the bishops of the first churches became, by common consent, to have a distinction from and pre-eminence above the presbyters that were fixed in the country, and a rule over those assemblies or churches themselves. And, therefore, when they met together in the council of Nice, among the first things they decreed, one was to confirm unto the bishops of the great cities that power over the neighbouring churches which they had enjoyed from this occasional rise and constitution of them. Hereby was a difference and distinction between bishops and presbyters, between mother and dependent churches, introduced, equally almost in all places, without taking any notice of the departure which was therein from the primitive pattern and institution. But these things fell out long after the days of the apostles,—namely, in the third and fourth centuries, there being no mention of them before.

2. But, secondly, There was another occasion of this alteration, which took place before that insisted on; for in many of those city churches, especially when the number of believers much increased, there were *many bishops or elders, who had the rule of them in common.* This is plain in the Scripture, and in the ensuing records of church affairs; and they had all the same office, the same power, and were of the same order. But after a while, to preserve order and decency among themselves and in all their proceedings, they chose one from among them who should preside in all church affairs for order's sake, unto whom, after a season, the name of bishop began to be appropriated. Whether the rule they proceeded by herein was to choose them unto this dignity who had been first converted unto the faith, or first called and ordained to be presbyters, or had respect unto the gifts and graces of those whom they chose, is not certain; but this way began in those churches wherein some extraordinary officer, apostle or evangelist, had long resided. It cannot, therefore, be doubted but they had some design to represent hereby somewhat of the dignity of such an officer, and a resemblance of the continuance of his presence among them; and this, I suppose, fell out early in the churches, though without ground or warrant. And the principal pastors of other churches, which had not any great number of elders in them, yet quickly assumed unto themselves the dignity which the others had attained.

Justin Martyr, in the account he gives of the church, its order, rule, worship, and discipline in his days, mentions one singular person in one church, whom he calls Προεστώς, who presided in all the affairs of the church, and himself administered all the sacred ordinances, every Lord's day, unto the whole body of the church gathered and met out of the city and the villages about. This was the bishop; and if any one desired this office, he desired a " good work," as the apostle speaks. Whatever accessions were made unto the church, these προεστῶτες,—which were either the first converted to the faith, or the first ordained presbyters, or obtained their pre-eminence, " non pretio, sed testimonio," as Tertullian speaks, upon the account of their eminency in gifts and holiness,—were yet quickly sensible of their own dignity and prelation, and by all means sought the enlargement of it; supposing that it belonged unto the honour and order of the church itself.

Under this state of things, the churches increasing every day in number and wealth, growing insensibly more and more ("indies magis magisque decrescente disciplina") into a form and state exceeding the bounds of their original institution, and becoming unwieldy as unto the pursuit of their ends, unto mutual edification, it is not hard to conjecture how a stated distinction between bishops and presbyters did afterward ensue; for as the first elder, bishop, or pastor, had obtained this small pre-eminence in the church wherein he did preside and the assemblies of the villages about, so the management of those affairs of the church which they had in communion with others was committed unto him, or assumed by him. This gave them the advantage of meeting in synods and councils afterward; wherein they did their own business unto the purpose. Hereon, in a short time, the people were deprived of all their interest in the state of the church, so as to be governed by their own consent; which, indeed, they also had rendered themselves unmeet to enjoy and exercise;—other elders were deprived of that power and authority which is committed unto them by Christ, and thrust down into an order or degree inferior unto that wherein they were originally placed;—new officers in the rule of the church, utterly unknown to the Scripture and primitive antiquity, were introduced;—all charitable donations unto the church, for the maintenance of the ministry, the poor, and the redemption of captives, were for the most part abused, to advance the revenues of the bishops;—such secular advantages, in honour, dignity, and wealth, were annexed unto episcopal sees, as that ambitious men shamefully contested for the attaining of them; which, in the instance of the bloody conflict between the parties of Damasus and Ursacius at Rome, Ammianus Marcellinus, a heathen, doth greatly and wisely reflect upon. But yet all these evils were as nothing in comparison of that dead sea of the Roman tyranny and idolatry whereinto at last these bitter waters ran, and were therein totally corrupted.

I thought, also, to have proceeded with an account of the declension of the churches from their first institution, in their matter, form, and rule; but because this would draw forth my discourse beyond my present intention, I shall forbear, having sufficiently vindicated my assertion in this one instance.

It is no part of my design to give an answer at large unto the great volume that Dr Stillingfleet hath written on this occasion, much less to contend about particular sayings, opinions, the practices of this or that man, which it is filled withal. But whereas his treatise, so far as the merit of the cause is concerned in it, doth consist of two parts, the first whereof contains such stories, things, and sayings as may load the cause and persons whom he opposeth with prejudices in the minds of others,—in which endeavour he exceeds all expectation,—and [the second] what doth more directly concern the argument in hand; I shall, at the end of the ensuing discourse, speak distinctly unto all that is material of the second sort, especially so far as is needful unto the defence of my former "Vindication of the Nonconformists from the Guilt of Schism."

For the things of the first sort,—wherein the Doctor doth so abound, both in his preface and in the first part of his book, as to manifest himself, I fear, to be a little too sensible of provocation (for the actings of interest in wise men are usually more sedate),—I shall only oppose some general considerations unto them, without arguing or contending about particulars; which would be endless and useless. And whereas he hath gathered up almost every thing that hath been done, written, or spoken to the prejudice of the cause and persons whom he opposeth (though frequently charged before), adding the advantage of his style and method unto their reinforcement, I shall reduce the whole unto a few heads, which seem to be of the greatest importance.

I shall leave him without disturbance unto the satisfaction he hath in his own love, moderation, and condescension, expressed in his preface. Others may possibly call some things in it unto a farther account. But the first part of his book is cast under two heads:—1. A *commendation of the first reformers and their reformation*, with some reflections upon all that acquiesce not therein, as though they esteemed themselves wiser and better than they. From this topic proceed many severe reflections and some reproaches. 2. The other consists in a story of the rise and progress of separation from the church of England, with the great miscarriages among them who first attempted it, and the opposition made unto them by those who were themselves Nonconformists. The whole is closed with the difference and debate between the divines of the assembly of the presbyterian way, and the " dissenting brethren," as they were then called. Concerning these things the discourse is so prolix, and so swelled with long quotations, that I scarce believe any man would have the patience to read over a particular examination of it; especially considering how little the cause in hand is concerned in the whole story, whether it be told right or wrong, candidly or with a design to make an advantage unto the prejudice of others. I shall, therefore, only mark something with respect unto both these heads of the first part of the book, which, if I mistake not, will lay it aside from being of any use to our present cause:—

1. As unto the first reformers and reformation in the days of King Edward, the plea from them and it, which we have been long accustomed unto, is, that they were persons great, wise, learned, holy; that some of them died martyrs; that the work of the reformation was greatly owned and blessed of God: and, therefore, our non-acquiescency therein, but desiring a farther reformation of the church than what they saw and judged necessary, is unreasonable; and that what we endeavour therein, though never so peaceably, is schismatical. But,—

(1.) None do more bless God for the first reformers, and the work they did, than we do; none have a higher esteem of their persons, abilities, graces, and sufferings, than we have; none cleave more firmly to their doctrine, which was the life and soul of the reformation, than we, nor desire more to follow them in their godly design. They are not of us who have declared that the death of King Edward was a happiness or no unhappiness to the church of England, nor who have reflected on the Reformation as needless, and given assurance that if it had not been undertaken, salvation might have been obtained safely enough in the church of Rome. Nor were they of us who have questioned the zeal and prudence of the martyrs in those days of suffering. We have other thoughts concerning them,—another kind of remembrance of them.

(2.) The titles assigned unto them, of wise, learned, holy, zealous, are fully answered by that reformation of the church in its doctrine and worship which God wrought by their ministry; so that none without the highest ingratitude can derogate any thing from them in these things. But it is no disparagement unto any of the sons of men, any officers of the church since the days of the apostles, the first reformers, or those that followed them, to judge that they were not infallible, that their work was not absolutely perfect, like the work of God, whereunto nothing can be added nor aught taken away. Wherefore,—

(3.) We are not obliged to make what they did, and what they attained unto, and what they judged meet as unto the government and worship of the church, to be our absolute rule, from which it should be our sin to dissent or depart. They never desired or designed that it should be so; for to do so would have been to have cast out one Papacy and to have brought in another. And the arguments of the Papists for their absolute adherence unto the men of their veneration, those who have been formerly of great reputation in their church, for learning, holiness, and devotion, are as forcible unto them as any can be unto us for an adherence unto the first reformers in all things; but yet are they not excused in their errors thereby. Had we received a command from heaven to hear them in all things, it had altered the case: but this we have received only with respect unto Jesus Christ; and shall, therefore, in these things, ultimately attend only unto what he speaks. And we have sundry considerations which confirm us in the use and exercise of that liberty wherewith Christ hath made us free, to inquire ourselves into our duty in these things, and to regulate our duty in them by his word, notwithstanding what was done by our first reformers; for,—

[1.] They did not think themselves obliged, they did not think meet, to abide within the bounds and limits of that reformation of the church which had been attempted before them, by men wise, learned, and holy, even in this nation. Such was that which was endeavoured by Wickliffe and his followers; in giving testimony whereunto many suffered martyrdom, and prepared the way unto those that were to come after. They approved of what was then done, or attempted to be done, for the substance of it, yet esteemed themselves at liberty to make a farther progress in the same work; which they did accordingly. Surely such persons never designed their own judgment and practice to give boundaries unto all reformation for evermore, or pretended that they had made so perfect a discovery of the mind of Christ, in all things belonging unto the rule and worship of the church, as that it should not only be vain but sinful to make any farther inquiries about it. Some thought they were come unto the utmost limits of navigation and discovery of the parts of the world before the West Indies were found out; and some men, when in any kind they know as much as they can, are apt to think there is no more to be known. It was not so with our reformers.

[2.] They did not at once make what they had done themselves to be a *fixed rule* in these things, for themselves made many alterations in the service-book which they first composed; and if they judged not their first endeavour to be satisfactory to themselves they had no reason to expect their second should be a standing rule unto all future ages. Nor did they so, but frequently acknowledged the imperfection of what they had done.

[3.] The first reformers, both bishops and others, both those who underwent martyrdom at home and those who lived in exile abroad, *differed* among themselves in their judgments and apprehensions about those things which are now under contest, whereas they perfectly agreed in all doctrines of faith and gospel obedience. The public records of these differences do so remain as that they cannot modestly be denied nor handsomely covered. And this must needs weaken the influence of their authority in the settlement of the church, which was an act only of the prevalent party among them.

[4.] They *differed in these things from all other reformed churches*, with whom they did absolutely agree in doctrine, and had the strictest communion in faith and love; for it is known that their doctrine, which they owned and established, was the same with that of the churches abroad called particularly Reformed, in distinction from the Lutherans. But as unto the state, rule, and order of the church, they differed from them all. I press not this consideration unto the disadvantage of what they attained unto and established in the way of reformation, or in a way of preferring other churches above them, but only to evidence that we have reason enough not to esteem ourselves absolutely obliged unto what they did and determined as unto all endeavours after any farther reformation.

[5.] In their reformation they avowedly proposed *a rule and measure* unto themselves which was both uncertain and in many things apparently various from the original rule of these things given by Christ and his apostles, with the practice of the first churches; and this was the state and example of the church under the first Christian emperors, as our author confesseth. This rule is uncertain; for no man living is able to give a just and full account of what was the state and rule of all the churches in the world in the reign of any one emperor, much less during the succession of many of them, continual alterations in the state or order of the church following one upon another. And that in those days there was a prevalent deviation from the original rule of church-order hath been before declared. We dare not, therefore, make them and what they did to be our rule absolutely, who missed it so much in the choice of their own.

[6.] We may add hereunto the consideration of *the horrid darkness* which they newly were delivered from; the close adherence of some traditional prejudices unto the best of men in such a condition; the difficulties and oppositions they met withal as unto their whole work; their prudence, as they judged it, in an endeavour to accommodate all things unto the inclinations and desires of the body of the people (extremely immersed in their old traditions), which might not be destructive unto their salvation, in heresy or idolatry;—all which could not but leave some marks of imperfection on their whole work of reformation.

Upon these and the like considerations it is that we are enforced to assert the use of our own liberty, light, and understanding, in the inquiring after and compliance with the true original state and order of the evangelical churches, with our duty in reference thereunto, and not to be absolutely confined unto what was judged meet and practised in these things by the first reformers. And the truth is, if present interest and advantage did not prevail with men to fix the bounds of all church-reformation in what was by them attained and established, they would think it themselves a papal bondage, to be bound up absolutely unto their apprehensions; from a confinement whereunto in sundry other things they declare themselves to be at an absolute liberty. Wherefore, neither we nor our cause are at all concerned in the rhetorical discourse of Dr Stillingfleet concerning the first reformers and their reformation; neither do we at all delight in reflecting on any of the defects of it, desiring only the liberty avowed on protestant principles, in the discharge of our own duty.

2. Nor, secondly, are we any more concerned in the long story that ensues about *the rise and progress of separation from the church of England*, with the mistakes of some in principles, and miscarriages in practice, who judged it their duty to be separate; for as, in our refraining from total communion with the parochial assemblies of the church of England, we proceed not on the same principles, so we hope that we are free from the same miscarriages with them, or any of an alike nature. But it is also certain, that after the great confusion that was brought on the whole state and order of the church under the Roman apostasy, many of those who attempted a reformation fell into different opinions and practices in sundry things; which the Papists have made many a long story about. We undertake the defence only of our own principles and practices according unto them; nor do we esteem ourselves obliged to justify or reflect on others.

And it were no difficult task to compose a story of the proceedings of some in the church of England, with reference unto these differences, that would have as ill an aspect as that which is here reported. Should an account be given of their unaccountable rigour and severity, in that through so many years, yea ages, they would never think of the least abatement of their impositions, in any one instance, though acknowledged by themselves indifferent and esteemed by others unlawful, although they saw what woful detriment arose to the churches thereby; yea, how, instead thereof, they did to the last of their power make a progress in the same course, by attempting new canons, to inflame the difference, and increased in severities towards all dissenters;—should an account be given of the silencings, deprivings, imprisonings, by the High Commission Court, and in most of the dioceses of the kingdom, of so great numbers of godly, learned, faithful, painful ministers, to the unspeakable disadvantage of the church and nation, with the ruin of the most of them and their families;—the representation of their names, qualifications, evident usefulness in the ministry, with the causes of their sufferings, wherein the observance of some ceremonies was openly preferred before the edification of the church and a great means of the conversion of souls, would give as ill a demonstration of Christian wisdom, love, moderation, condescension, zeal for the propagation of the gospel, as any thing doth, on the other hand, in the history before us. It would not be omitted, on such an occasion, to declare what multitudes of pious, peaceable Protestants were driven by their severities to leave their native country, to seek a refuge for their lives and liberties, with freedom for the worship of God, in a wilderness in the ends of the earth; and if it be said that what some did herein they did in the discharge of the duties of their office, I must say I shall hardly acknowledge that office to be of the institution of Christ, whereunto it belongs, in a way of duty, to ruin and destroy so many of his disciples, for no other cause but a desire and endeavour to serve and worship him according unto what they apprehend to be his mind revealed in the gospel. Should there be added hereunto an account of the administration of ecclesiastical discipline in the courts of chancellors, commissaries, officials, and the like, as unto the authority and causes, with the way and manner of their proceedings in the exercise of their jurisdiction, with the woful scandals that have been given thereby, with an addition of sundry other things which I will not so much as mention, I suppose it would as much conduce unto peace and reconciliation among Protestants as the story here given us by our author.

But setting aside the aggravations of things gathered out of controversial writings (wherein few men do observe the due rules of moderation, but indulge unto themselves the liberty of severe censures and sharp reflections on them they do oppose), the sum and truth of the story concerning these things may be reduced into a narrow compass; for,—

(1.) It is certain that, from the first dawning of the Reformation in this nation, there were different apprehensions, among them that jointly forsook the Papacy, as unto its doctrine and worship, about the state, rule, order, and discipline of the church, with sundry things belonging unto its worship also. I suppose this will not be denied.

(2.) There doth not remain any record of a due attempt and endeavour for the composing these differences before one certain way was established by those in power. And whereas, [from] the state and condition wherein they were at that time, from the confusions about religion that were then abroad, and the pertinaciousness of the generality of the people in an adherence unto their old ways and observances in religion, with a great scarcity in able ministers, the greatest part of the bishops and clergy disliking the whole Reformation, they found themselves, as they judged, necessitated to make as little alteration in the present state of things as was possible, so as to keep up an appearance of the same things in the church which had been in former use,—on these grounds the state and rule of the church was continued in the same form and posture that it was before under the Papacy, the authority of the pope only being excluded, and the power of disposal of ecclesiastical affairs, usurped by him, declared to be in the king; so also, in imitation of that book of worship and service which the people had been accustomed unto, another was established, with the ceremonies most obvious unto popular observation.

(3.) This order was unsatisfactory unto great numbers of ministers and others; who yet, considering what the necessity of the times did call for, did outwardly acquiesce in it in several degrees, in hopes of a farther reformation in a more convenient season. Nor did they cease to plead and press for it by all quiet and peaceable means, abstaining, in the meantime, from the use of the ceremonies, and full compliance with episcopal jurisdiction.

(4.) Hereon those who were for the establishment, having secured their interests therein and obtained power, began after a while to oppress, excommunicate, silence, deprive, and imprison those who dissented from them, and could not come up unto a full practical compliance with their institutions and rules. Yet the generality of those so silenced and deprived abode in privacy under their sufferings, hoping for a reformation at one time or another, without betaking themselves unto any other course for the edification of themselves or their people.

(5.) After sundry years, some men, partly silenced and deprived as unto their ministry, and partly pursued with other censures and penalties, began to give place unto severe thoughts of the church of England and its communion, and, withdrawing themselves into foreign parts, openly avowed a separation from it. And if the extremities which many had been put unto for their mere dissent and nonconformity unto the established rule,—which, with a good conscience, they could not comply with,—were represented, it might, if not excuse, yet alleviate the evil of that severity in separation which they fell into.

(6.) But hereon a double inconvenience, yea, evil, did ensue, whence all the advantages made use of in this story to load the present cause of the Nonconformists did arise. For,—

[1.] Many of those who refused to conform unto the church in all its constitutions yet thought it their duty to wait quietly for a *national reformation*, thinking no other possible, began to oppose and write against them who utterly separated from the church, condemning its assemblies as unlawful. And herein, as the manner of men is on such occasions, they fell into sharp invectives against them, with severe censures and sentences concerning them and their practice. And,—

[2.] Those who did so separate, being not agreed among themselves as unto all principles of church-order, nor as unto the measure of their separation from the church of England, there fell out differences and disorders among them, accompanied with personal imprudences and miscarriages in not a few. Neither was it scarcely ever otherwise among them who first attempted any reformation; unless, like the apostles, they were infallibly guided. These mutual contests which they had among themselves, and with the Nonconformists who abode in their private stations in England, with their miscarriages also, were published unto the world, in their own writings and those of their enemies

"Hinc omnis pendet Lucilius." These were the things that gave advantage unto, and are the substance of, the history of our author concerning separation; wherein all I can find unto our present instruction is, that

"Iliacos intra muros peccatur et extra."

There are and ever were sins, faults, follies, and miscarriages among all sorts of men; which might be farther evidenced by recounting, on the other hand, what were the ways, acts, and deeds, at the same time, of those by whom the others were cast out and rejected. And whereas it was the design of the reverend author to load the cause and persons of the present Nonconformists with prejudice and contempt, it is well fallen out, in the merciful disposal of things towards and amongst us, by the providence and grace of God, that he is forced to derive the principal matter of his charge from what was done by a few private persons, three or four score years ago and more, in whose principles and practices we are not concerned. And as for the difference that fell out more lately among the divines in the assembly at Westminster, about the ways, means, and measures of reformation and mutual forbearance, which he gives us a large account of in a long transcription out of their writings, I must have more health, and strength, and leisure than now I have (which I look not for in this world), before I esteem myself concerned to engage in that contest, or to apologize for the one side or other. The things in agitation between them had no relation unto our present dissent from the church of England, being here insisted on merely to fill up the story, with reference unto the general end designed.

Neither, to my knowledge, did I ever read a book wherein there was a greater appearance of diligence in the collection of things, words, sayings, expressions, discourses unto other ends, which might only cast odium on the cause opposed, or give advantage for arguings unto a seeming success, very little or no way at all belonging unto the cause in hand, than there is in this of our reverend author; though much in the same way and kind hath been before attempted.

But separation it is and schism which we are all charged withal; and the evil thereof is aggravated in the words of the author himself, and in large transcriptions out of the writings of others. Schism, indeed, we acknowledge to be an evil, a great evil, but are sorry that with some a pretended, unproved schism is become almost all that is evil in the churches or their members; so that let men be what they will, drenched, yea, overwhelmed in ignorance, vice, and sin, so they do not separate (which, to be sure, in that state they will not do, for why should he who hath plague-sores upon him depart from the society of them that are infected?) they seem to be esteemed, as unto all the concerns of the church, very unblamable.

The truth is, considering the present state and condition of the inhabitants of this nation, who are generally members of the church of England,—how " the land is filled with sin against the Holy One of Israel," God giving us every day renewed tokens and indications of his displeasure, no compliance with his calls, no public reformation being yet attempted,—it seems a more necessary duty, and of more importance unto them upon whom the care of such things is incumbent, to endeavour in themselves, and to engage a faithful ministry throughout the nation, both to give a due example in their conversations, and to preach the word with all diligence, for the turning of the people from the evil of their ways, than to spend their time and strength in the management of such charges against those who would willingly comply with them as unto all the great ends of religion amongst men.

But this must be farther spoken unto. I say, therefore, first, in general, that whereas the whole design of this book is to charge all sorts of Nonconformists with schism, and to denounce them schismatics, yet the author of it doth not once endeavour to state the true notion and nature of schism, wherein the consciences of men may be concerned. He satisfies himself in the invectives of some of the ancients against schism, applicable unto those which were in their days, wherein we are not concerned. Only, he seems to proceed on the general notion of it, that it is a causeless separation from a true church; which departs from that of the Romanists, who will allow no separation from the church but what is causeless. To make application hereof unto us, it is supposed,—

(1.) That *the church of England* is a true church in its *national constitution*, and so are all the parochial churches in it; which can be no way justified but by a large, extensive interpretation of the word "true," for there is but one sort of churches instituted by Christ and his apostles, but national and parochial churches differ in their whole kind, and therefore cannot both of them be of a divine original.

(2.) That we are members of this church *by our own consent*. How we should come to be so otherwise, I know not. If we are so by being born and baptized in

England, then those who are born beyond sea and baptized there are made members of this church by an act of Parliament for their naturalization, and no otherwise.

(3.) That we *separate* from this church in things wherein we are obliged by the *authority of Christ* to hold communion with it; which neither is nor will ever be proved, nor is it endeavoured so to be by any instances in this treatise.

(4.) That to withhold communion from *parochial assemblies* in the worship of God, as unto things confessedly not of divine institution, is schism,—that kind of schism which is condemned by the ancient writers of the church. Upon these and the like suppositions it is no uneasy thing to make vehement declamations against us and severe reflections on us; all is schism and schismatic, and all of the same kind with what was written against by Cyprian, and Austin, and others a great many.

But the true state of the controversy between him and us is this, and no other, —namely, *Whether a dissent in, and forbearance from, the communion of churches, in their state and kind not of divine institution, or so far as they are not of divine institution, and from things in other churches that have no such divine institution, nor any scriptural authority to oblige us unto their observance, be to be esteemed schism in them who maintain and professedly avow communion in faith and love with all the true churches of Christ in the world?* This is the whole of what we are concerned in; which, where it is spoken unto, it shall be considered. But because there were in the primitive churches certain persons who, on arbitrary principles of their own, consisting for the most part in gross and palpable errors, which they would have imposed on all others, did separate from the catholic church,—that is, all other Christians in the world, and all the churches of Christ, condemning them as no churches, allowing not the administration of sacraments unto them nor salvation unto their members,—whom the ancient church condemned with great severity, and that justly, as guilty of schism, their judgment, their words and expressions, are applied unto us, who are no way concerned in what they speak of or unto. We are not, therefore, in the least terrified with what is alleged out of the ancients about schism; no more than he is when the same instances, the same authorities, the same quotations, are made use of by the Papists against the church of England, as they are continually: for, as was said, we know that we are no way concerned in them. And suppose that all that the Doctor allegeth against us be true, and that we are in the wrong in all that is charged on us, yet I dare refer it to the Doctor himself to determine whether it be of the same nature with what was charged on them who made schisms in the church of old. I suppose I guess well enough what he will say to secure his charge; and it shall be considered when it is spoken.

But, as was said, the great and only design of the author of this book is to prove all Nonconformists to be schismatics, or guilty of the sin of schism. How he hath succeeded in this attempt shall be afterward considered. And something I have spoken in the ensuing discourse concerning the nature of schism, which will manifest how little we are concerned in this charge. But yet it may not be amiss in this place to mind both him and others of some of those principles whereon we ground our justification in this matter, that it may be known what they must farther overthrow, and what they must establish, who shall persist in the management of this charge; that is, indeed, through want of love, in a design to heighten and perpetuate our divisions. And,—

The first of these principles is, That *there is a rule prescribed by our Lord Jesus Christ unto all churches and believers, in a due attendance whereunto all the unity and peace which he requireth amongst his disciples do consist.*

We acknowledge this to be our fundamental principle. Nor can the rhetoric or arguments of any man affect our consciences with a sense of the guilt of schism until one of these things be proved; namely, either, first, That the Lord Christ hath *given no such rule* as in the observance whereof peace and unity may be preserved in his church; or, secondly, That we *refuse a compliance* with that rule in some one instance or other of what therein he hath himself appointed. Unless one or the other be proved, and that strictly and directly, not pretended so to be by perpetual diversions from the things in question, no vehement assertions of any of us to be schismatics nor aggravations of the guilt of schism will signify any thing in this cause.

But that our principle herein is according unto truth we are fully persuaded. There is a rule of Christ's given, which whosoever walk according unto, "peace shall be on them, and mercy, and upon the whole Israel of God," Gal. vi. 16. And we desire no more, no more is needful unto the peace and unity of the church; and this rule, whatever it be, is of his giving and appointment. No rule of men's invention or imposition can, by its observance, secure us of an interest in that peace and mercy which is peculiar unto the Israel of God. God forbid we should entertain any such imagination! We know well enough men may be thorough conformists to such rules, unto whom, as unto their present state and condition, neither peace nor mercy do belong; for "there is no peace to the wicked." He who hath directed and commanded the end of church unity and peace hath also appointed the means and measures of them. Nothing is more disagreeable unto, nothing more inconsistent with, the wisdom, care and love of Christ unto his church, than an imagination that whereas he strictly enjoins peace and unity in his church, he hath not himself appointed the rules, bounds, and measures of them, but left it unto the will and discretion of men. As if his command unto his disciples had been, "Keep peace and unity in the church, by doing and observing whatever some men, under a pretence of being the guides of the church, shall make necessary unto that end;" whereas it is plainly otherwise,—namely, that we should so keep the peace and unity of the church by doing and observing all whatever that he commands us. And, besides, we strictly require that some one instance be given us of a defect in the rule given by Christ himself, which must be supplied by human additions, to render it complete for the end of church peace and unity. In vain have we desired, in vain may we for ever expect, any instance of that kind.

This principle we shall not be easily dispossessed of; and whilst we are under the protection of it, we have a safe retreat and shelter from the most vehement accusations of schism for a non-compliance with a rule, none of his, different from his, and in some things contrary unto his, for the preservation of church peace and unity. All the dispute is, whether we keep unto this rule of Christ or no; wherein we are ready at any time to put ourselves upon the trial, being willing to teach or learn, as God shall help us.

Secondly, we say, That *this rule in general is the rule of faith, love, and obedience contained and revealed in the Scripture; and in particular, the commands that the Lord Christ hath given for the order and worship that he requires in his churches.* It may seem strange to some that we should suppose the due observance of the rule of faith, love, and obedience,—that is, of faith real and unfeigned, love fervent and without dissimulation, and of universal, gracious, evangelical obedience,—to be necessary unto the preservation of church peace and unity; but we do affirm, with some confidence, that the only real foundation of them doth lie herein, nor do we value that ecclesiastical peace which may be without it or is neglective of it. Let all the Christian world, or those therein who concern themselves in us, know that this is our principle and our judgment,—that no church peace or unity is valued by or accepted with Jesus Christ that is not founded in, that doth not arise from, and is the effect of, a diligent attendance unto and observance of the entire gospel rule of faith and obedience. In the neglect hereof, peace is but carnal security, and unity is nothing but a conspiracy against the rule of Christ. Add hereunto the particular, the due observation of what the Lord Christ hath appointed to be done and observed in his churches, as unto their order, rule, and worship; and they who walk according unto this rule need not fear the charge of schism from the fiercest of their adversaries. Wherefore we say,—

Thirdly, *Those who recede from this rule, in any material branch of it, are guilty of the breach of church-unity, according to the measure of their exorbitancy;* —as suppose that any preach, teach, or profess doctrines that are contrary to the form of wholesome words, especially with reference unto the person, offices, and grace of Christ, which are the subject of doctrines purely evangelical, they break the peace of the church, and we are bound to separate or withdraw communion from them; which is a means of preserving the true peace and unity of the church. " Speciosum quidem est nomen pacis, et pulchra opinio unitatis, sed quis ambigat eam solam, unicam, ecclesiæ pacem esse, quæ Christi est," saith Hilary. Suppose that men retain a form of godliness in the profession of the truth, but deny the power of it, acting their habitual lusts and corruptions in a vicious conversation; they overthrow the foundation of the church's unity, and we are obliged from such to turn away. The like may be said of those who live in a constant neglect of any of the commands of Christ with respect unto the order, rule, and worship of the church, with a contempt of the means appointed by him for their edification. All these, according unto the measures of their deviations from the rule of Christ, do disturb the foundation of all church peace and unity. And therefore we say,—

Fourthly, That *conscience is immediately and directly concerned in no other church unity, as such, but what is an effect of the rule of Christ given unto that end.* We know what is spoken concerning obedience unto the guides and rulers of the church; which is a part of the rule of Christ. But we know withal, that this obedience is required of us only as they teach us to observe and do all that he hath commanded; for other commission from him they have none. When this rule is forsaken, and another substituted in the room of it, as it quickly diverts the minds of men from a conscientious attendance unto that rule of Christ as the only means of church-unity, so that other doth either proceed from men's secular interests or may easily be accommodated thereunto. And whereas the lines of it must be drawn in the fields of *pretended indifferences* and *real arbitrariness*, it will be the cause of endless contentions, whilst whatever some think themselves to have power to appoint, others will judge themselves to have liberty to refuse.

Fifthly, *It is unity of Christ's appointment that schism respects as a sin against it, and not uniformity in things of men's appointment.* And,—

Lastly, Those who charge schism on others for a dissent from themselves, or the refraining of total communion with them, must,—

1. *Discharge themselves* of the charge of it, in a consistence with their charge on them; for we find as yet no arrows shot against us but such as are gathered up in the fields, shot at them that use them out of the Roman quiver. Neither will it avail them to say that they have other manner of reason for their separation from the church of Rome than any we have for our withdrawing communion from them; for the question is not, what reasons they have for what they do? but, what right and power they have to do it?—namely, to separate from the church whereof they were, constituting a new church-state of their own, without the consent of that church, and against the order and authority of the same.

2. *Require no communion* but by virtue of the rule before declared. In no other are we concerned, with respect unto the peace and unity of the church.

3. Give a farther confirmation than what we have yet seen unto the principles or presumptions they proceed upon in the management of the charge of schism; as that,—(1.) *Diocesan bishops*, with their *metropolitans*, are of divine institution; (2.) That the *power of rule* in and over all churches is committed unto them alone; (3.) That the church hath power to *ordain* religious rites and ceremonies nowhere prescribed in the Scripture, and impose the observation of them on all members of the church; (4.) That *this church* they are; (5.) That no man's *voluntary consent* is required to constitute him a member of any church, but that every one is surprised into that state whether he will or no; (6.) That there is *nothing of force* in the arguments pleaded for non-compliance with arbitrary, unnecessary impositions; (7.) That the church standeth in no need of *reformation*, neither in doctrine, discipline, nor conversation; with sundry other things of an alike nature that they need unto their justification.

But yet, when all is done, it will appear that mutual forbearance, first removing animosities, then administering occasion of inoffensive converse, unto the revival of decayed affections, leading unto sedate conferences and considerations of a more entire conjunction in the things whereunto we have attained, will more conduce unto universal peace and gospel unity than the most fierce contentions about things in difference, or the most vehement charges of schism against dissenters.

But I must return to the argument, and shall add something giving light into the nature of schism, from an instance in the primitive churches.

That which is first in any kind gives the measure of what follows in the same kind, and light into the nature of them. Whereas, therefore, the schism that was among the churches about the observation of Easter was the first that fell out unto the disturbance of their communion, I shall give a brief account of it, as far as the question in hand is concerned in it.

It is evident that the apostles did with care and diligence teach the doctrine of Christian liberty, warning the disciples to " stand fast" in it, and not submit their necks unto any " yoke of bondage" in the things of the worship of God; especially the apostle Paul had frequent occasions to treat of this subject. And what they taught in doctrine, they established and confirmed in their practice; for they enjoined nothing to be observed in the church but what was necessary, and what they had the command of Christ for, leaving the observation of things indifferent unto their original indifference. But whereas they had decreed, by the direction of the Holy Ghost, some necessary condescensions in the Gentile believers towards the Jews, in case of offence or scandal, they did themselves make use of their liberty to comply with the same Jews in some of their observances not yet unlawful. Hereon there ensued in several churches different observations of some rites and customs, which they apprehended were countenanced by the practice of the apostles, at least as it had been reported unto them: for, immediately after the decease of the apostles, very many mistakes and untruths were reported concerning what they said, did, and practised; which some diligently collected from old men (it may be almost delirant), as Eusebius gives an instance in Papias, lib. iii. cap 36; and even the great Irenæus himself was imposed upon, in a matter directly contrary to the Scripture, under a pretence of apostolical tradition. Among those reports was that of the observation of Easter. And for a while the churches continued in these different observances, without the least disturbance of their communion, each one following that which it thought the most probable tradition; for rule of Scripture they pretended not unto. But after a while they began to fall into a contest about these things, which began at Laodicea; which church was as likely to strive about such things as any other: for Eusebius tells us that Melito, the bishop of Sardis, wrote two books about Easter, beginning the first with an

account that he wrote them when Servilius Paulus was proconsul, there being
then a great stir about it at Laodicea, Euseb., lib. iv. cap. 26. But, as it falls out
on such occasions, much talk and disputing ensuing thereon, the differences were
increased, until one side or party at variance would make their opinion and practice the rule and terms of communion unto all other churches. But this was
quickly condemned by those who were wise and sober; for, as Sozomen affirms,
they accounted it " a frivolous or foolish thing to differ about a custom, whereas
they agreed in all the principal heads of religion." And thereon he gives a large
account of different rites and observances in many churches, without any breach
of communion among them; adding, that besides those enumerated by him, there
were many others in cities and villages which they did in a different manner adhere unto, Hist., lib. vii. cap. 19.

At length this matter fell into the handling of Victor, bishop of Rome; and his
judgment was, that the observation of Easter on the Lord's day, and not on the
fourteenth day of the first month precisely, according to the computation of the
Jews in the observation of the passover, was to be imposed on all the churches of
Christ everywhere. It had all along, until his time, been judged a thing indifferent, wherein the churches and all believers were left unto the use of their own
liberty. He had no pretence of any divine institution making it necessary, the
writers of those days constantly affirming that the apostles made no canons, rules,
or laws about such things. He had persons of as great worth as any in the
world, as Melito, Polycrates, Polycarpus, that opposed him, not only as unto the
imposition of his practice on others, but as unto his error, as they judged, in the
matter of fact and right; yet all this could not hinder but that he would needs
have the reputation of the father of schisms among the churches of Christ by his
impositions, and he cut off all the Asian churches from communion, declaring them
and their members excommunicate, Euseb., lib. v. cap. 23.

The noise hereof coming abroad unto other churches, great offence was taken
at it by many of them, and Victor was roundly dealt withal by sundry of them
who agreed with him in practice, but abhorred his imposition of it, and making it
a condition of church-communion.

Among those who so opposed and rebuked him, Irenæus was the most eminent.
And I shall observe some few things out of the fragment of his epistle, as it is recorded by Eusebius, lib. v. cap. 23.

And,—(1.) He tells us that " he wrote unto Victor in the name of those
brethren in France whom he did preside amongst." The custom of considering
things of this nature with all the brethren of the church, and writing their determination in their name, was not yet grown out of use, though the practice of it
now would be esteemed novel and schismatical.

(2.) He tells Victor that " there were great varieties in this thing, as also in
the times and seasons of fasting; which did not," saith he, " begin or arise in our
days, but long before was introduced by such who, being in places of rule, rejected
and changed the common and simple customs which the church had before."
The Doctor, therefore, need not think it so strange that an alteration in church
order and rule should fall out in after ages, when long before Irenæus' time such
changes were begun.

(3.) He gives hereon that excellent rule: 'Η διαφωνία τῆς νηστείας τὴν ὁμόνοιαν τῆς
πίστεως συνίστησιν—" The difference of fastings" (and consequently things of an
alike nature) " commends the concord or agreement of faith."

This was the first effect of a departure from the only rule of unity and communion among the churches which was given by Christ himself and his apostles.
As hereby great confusion and disorder was brought upon the churches, so it was
the first public inroad that was made on the doctrine of the Scripture concerning

Christian liberty. And as it was also the first instance of rejecting men otherwise
sound in the faith from communion for nonconformity, or the non-observance of
human institutions or traditions,—which had therein an unhappy consecration unto
the use of future ages,—so it was the first notorious entrance into that usurpation
of power in the Roman bishops, which they carried on by degrees unto an absolute tyranny. Neither was there ever a more pernicious maxim broached in the
primitive times, nor which had a more effectual influence into the ruin of the first
institution and liberty of the churches of Christ; for although the fact of Victor
was condemned by many, yet the principle he proceeded on was afterward espoused
and put in practice.

Our reverend author will hardly find an instance before this of schism among
any churches that retained the substance of the doctrine of faith, unless it be in
those divisions which fell out in some particular churches, among the members of
them. And this we affirm to be in general the case of the Nonconformists at this
day: for admitting such variations as time and other circumstances must necessarily infer, and they are rejected from communion on the same grounds that
Victor proceeded on in the excommunication of the churches of Asia; neither will
there be any end of differences whilst the same principle is retained. Before this,
schism was only esteemed a defect in love and breach of the rule of Christ's appointment for the communion and walking together of believers in the same
church.

But this notion of schism is, in the judgment of Dr Stillingfleet, preface, p. 46,
" so mean, so jejune, so narrow a notion of it, that I cannot," saith he, " but wonder that men of understanding should be satisfied with it." But, in my judgment,
the author of it was a man of good understanding. Indeed, I have heard him
spoken of as one of abstruse speculations, that did not advantage Christian religion;
and one hath published in print that " he is one of the obscurest writers that ever
he read;" but I never heard him before charged with mean and jejune notions.
Now, this was St Paul, who expressly chargeth schism on the church of Corinth
because of the divisions that were among them,—namely, the members of the same
particular church,—so as they could not " come together in one place" in a due
manner; nor, in all his writings, doth he anywhere give us any other notion of
schism. " But," saith he, " this is short of that care of the church's peace which
Christ hath made so great a duty of his followers." But if there be no other rule,
no other duty for the preservation of the church's peace, but only that no separation be made from it, which is called schism, we might have been all quiet in the
church of Rome. Let no man think to persuade us but that, for the preservation
of the church's peace, it is required of us that we do and observe all things that
Christ requireth of us, and that we enjoin not the observation of what he hath
not commanded on Victor's penalty, of being excluded from communion: that
faith, and love, and holiness be kept and promoted in the church, by all the ways
of his appointment; and when these things are attended unto, St Paul's mean and
jejune notion of schism will be of good use also.

Nor was there the least appearance of any other kind of schism among the
churches of Christ until that which was occasioned by Victor; of which we have
spoken. The schisms that followed afterward were, six to one, from the contentions of bishops, or those who had an ambition so to be: which the apostle foresaw,
as Clemens witnesseth, and made provision against it; but that no banks are strong
enough to confine the overflowing ambition of some sort of persons. But saith
the Doctor, preface, p. 47, " The obligation to preserve the peace of the church
extends to all lawful constitutions in order to it: therefore, to break the peace
of the church we live in, for the sake of any lawful orders and constitutions made
to preserve it, is directly the sin of schism."

1. Now, schism, he tell us, is "as great and dangerous a sin as murder," p. 45; and we know that " no murderer hath eternal life abiding in him," 1 John iii. 15. So that all men here seem to be adjudged unto hell who comply not with, who submit not unto, our ecclesiastical constitutions or canons. God forbid that ever such doctrine should be looked on as to have the least affinity unto the gospel, or such censures to have any savour of the Spirit of Christ in them! The Lord Jesus Christ hath not cast the eternal condition of those whom he purchased with his own most precious blood into the arbitrary disposal of any that shall take upon them to make ecclesiastical constitutions and orders, for conformity in rites and ceremonies, etc. Shall we think that he who, upon the best use of means for his instruction which he is capable of, with fervent prayers to God for light and direction, cannot comply with and submit unto some ecclesiastical constitutions and orders, however pretended to be made for the preservation of peace and unity in the church, on this ground principally, because they are not of the appointment nor have the approbation of Jesus Christ, though he should mistake herein, and miss of his duty, is guilty of no less sin than that of murder,—suppose of Cain in killing his brother? for all murder is from hatred and malice. This is that which inflames the differences amongst us; for it is a scandal of the highest nature, when men do see that persons who in any thing dissent from our ecclesiastical constitutions, though otherwise sober, honest, pious, and peaceable, are looked on as bad, if not worse than thieves and murderers, and are dealt withal accordingly. Nor can any thing be more effectual to harden others in their immoralities than to find themselves approved by the guides of the church, in comparison with such dissenters.

2. But who is it that shall make these orders and constitutions, that must be observed for the preservation of the unity and peace of the church? It can be none but those who have power so to do by being uppermost in any place or time. Who shall judge them to be lawful? No doubt they that make them. And what shall these constitutions be about, what shall they extend unto? Any thing in the world, so there be no mention of it in the Scripture, one way or other. What if any one should now dissent from these constitutions, and not submit unto them? Why, then, he is guilty of schism!—as great and dangerous a sin as that of murder!! But when all is done, what if these constitutions and orders should be no ways needful or useful unto the preservation of the peace of the church? what if a supposition that they are so reflects dishonour on the wisdom and love of Christ? what if they are unlawful and unwarrantable, the Lord Christ not having given power and authority unto any sort of men to make any such constitutions? what if they are the great ways and means of breaking the unity and peace of the church? These, and other inquiries of the like nature, must be clearly resolved, not by the dictates of men's own minds and spirits, but from the word of truth, before this intimation can be complied withal.

But that which is fallen out most beyond expectation in this whole discourse is, that the reverend author, seeking, by all ways and means countenanced with the least resemblance or appearance of truth, to load the Nonconformists and their cause with the imputation of things invidious and burdensome, should fix upon their prayers, by virtue of the grace and gift of prayer which they have received, ascribing the original of its use unto the artifice and insinuation of the Jesuits, as he doth, preface, pp. 14, 15. But because I look on this as a thing of the greatest importance of all the differences between them and us,—as that wherein the life of religion, the exercise of faith, and the labour of divine love do much consist,—the nature and necessity of that kind of prayer which is here reflected on and opposed shall, God willing, be declared and vindicated in a peculiar discourse unto that purpose; for the differences that are between us cannot possibly have any more pernicious consequence than if we should be influenced by them to oppose or condemn any principles or exercise of the duties of practical holiness, as thinking them to yield matter of advantage to one party or another.

The great pains he hath taken, in this preface, to prove the Nonconformists to have been the means of furthering and promoting Popery in this nation might, as I suppose, have been omitted without any disadvantage unto himself or his cause; for the thing itself is not true. As it is utterly impossible to affect the minds or consciences of the Nonconformists with a sense of it, because they have a thousand witnesses in themselves against the truth of the charge, so it is impossible it should be believed by any who are in the least acquainted with their principles, or have their eyes open to see any thing that is doing at this day in religion. But as there are many palpable mistakes in the account he gives of things among ourselves to this purpose, so if, on the other hand, any should, out of reports, surmises, Jesuits' letters and politics, particularly those of Contzen; books written to that purpose against them; agreement of principles; notorious compliance of some bishops and others of the same way with the Papists, some dying avowedly such; stories of what hath been said at Rome and elsewhere, which are not few nor unprovable, concerning the inclinations of many unto a fair composition of things with the church of Rome; the deportment of some before and since the discovery of the plot; with such other topics as the discourse of our author with respect unto the Nonconformists will furnish them withal; as also from the woful neglect there hath been of instructing the people in the principles of religion, so as to implant a sense of the life and power of it on their souls; with all things that may be spoken on that head with reference unto the clergy under their various distributions, with the casting out of so great a number of ministers, whom they knew in their own conscience to be firmly fixed against Popery and its interest in this nation, and could not deny but they might be useful to instruct the people in the knowledge of the truth, and encourage them by their example unto the practice of it;—if any, I say, should, on these and the like grounds, not in a way of recrimination, nor as a requital of the Doctor's story, but merely as a necessary part of the defence of their own innocency, charge the same guilt, of giving occasion unto the growth, increase, and danger of Popery in this nation, on the episcopal party, I know not now how they could be well blamed for it, nor what will be done of that kind; for they who will take liberty to speak what they please must be content sometimes to hear what will displease. For my part, I had rather, if it were possible, that these things at present might be omitted, and that all those who are really united in opposition unto Popery,—as I am assured in particular that this reverend author and I are,—would rather consider how we might come out of the danger of it wherein we are, than at present contest how we came into it. This I speak seriously, and that under the consideration of this discourse; which, upon the account of sundry mistakes in matter of fact, of great defects in point of charity, with a design to expose others unto reproach for their *great crime* of being willing to be a little freed from being beaten, fined, punished, and imprisoned, by their means and on their account, is as apt to excite new exasperations, and to provoke the spirits of them concerned, as any I have read of late. However, the defence of our own innocency must not be forsaken. But,—

" Cumque superba foret Babylon spolianda trophæis,"

it is not praiseworthy to abide in these contests beyond necessity.

This discourse, indeed, of the reverend author is increased into so large a volume as might justly discourage any from undertaking the examination of it who hath any other necessary duties to attend unto. But if there be separated from it the consideration of stories of things and persons long since past, wherein we are not concerned, with the undue application of what was written by some of the ancients against the schisms in their days unto our present differences; as also the repetition of a charge that we do not refrain communion from the parochial churches on the grounds and reasons which we know to the contrary that we do; with the report and quotation of the words and sayings of men by whose judgment we are not determined; with frequent diversions from the question, by attempting advantages from this or that passage or expression in one or another; and the rhetorical aggravations of things that might be plainly expressed and quickly issued,—the controversy may be reduced into a narrower compass.

It is acknowledged that the differences which are amongst Protestants in this nation are to be bewailed, because of the advantages which the common enemy of the protestant interest doth endeavour to make thereby. Howbeit the evil consequences of them do not arise from the nature of the things themselves, but from the interest, prejudices, and biassed affections of them amongst whom they are. Nor shall any man ever be able to prove but that, on the doctrinal agreement which we all profess (provided it be real), we may, notwithstanding the differences that remain, enjoy all that peace and union which are prescribed unto the churches and disciples of Christ, provided that we live in the exercise of that love which he enjoineth us; which whilst it continues, in the profession of the same faith, it is impossible there should be any schism among us. Wherefore, whereas some are very desirous to state the controversy on this supposition, that there is a schism among us, and issue it in an inquiry on which side the blame of it is to be laid, —wherein they suppose they need no farther justification but the possession of that church-state which is established by law,—I shall willingly forego the charging of them with the whole occasion of the schism pretended, until they can prove tnere is such a schism, which I utterly deny; for the refraining of communion with parochial assemblies, on the grounds whereon we do refrain, hath nothing of the nature of schism in it, neither as it is stated in the Scripture nor as it was esteemed of in the primitive churches, amongst whom there were differences of as great importance, without any mutual charges of schism. Wherefore, although we cannot forego utterly the defence of our own innocency against such charges as import no less than a heinous guilt of sin against God, and imminent danger of ruin from men, yet we shall constantly unite ourselves with and unto all who sincerely endeavour the promotion of the great ends of Christian religion, and the preservation of the interest of protestant religion in this nation.

Something I judge necessary to add concerning my engagement, or rather surprisal, into this controversy, against my inclination and resolution.

The Doctor tells us, preface, p. 51, " That when his sermon came first out, it went down quietly enough, and many of the people began to read and consider it, being pleased to find so weighty and necessary a point debated with so much calmness and freedom from passion; which being discovered by the leaders and managers of the party, it was soon resolved that the sermon must be cried down, and the people dissuaded from reading of it. If any of them were talked withal about it, they shrunk up their shoulders, and looked sternly, and shook their heads, and hardly forbore some bitter words, both of the author and the sermon," (which it seems he knows, though they did forbear to do so!) and much more to the same purpose. And, p. 53, " As if they had been the Papists' instruments to execute the fury of their wrath and displeasure against me, they summon in the power of their party, and resolve with their force and might to fall upon me;" with more to the same purpose. And p. 59, " After a while they thought fit to draw their strength into the open field; and the first who appeared was," etc.

I confess I was somewhat surprised, that, coming into this coast, all things should appear so new and strange unto me as that I could fix on no one mark to discover that I had ever been there before; for I am as utter a stranger unto all these things as unto the counsels of the Pope or Turk. The Doctor seems to apprehend that, at the coming forth of his sermon, at least after its worth and weight were observed, there was a consternation and disorder among the Nonconformists, as if Hannibal had been at the gates; for hereby he supposeth they were cast into those ugly postures of shrinking, and staring, and shaking, and swelling with what they could hardly forbear to utter. But these things, with those that follow, seem to me to be romantic, and somewhat tragically expressed, sufficiently evidencing that other stories told by the same author in this case stand in need of some grains of allowance to reduce them to the royal standard; for whereas I am the first person instanced in that should have a hand in the management of these contrivances, I know nothing at all of them, nor, upon the utmost inquiry I have made, can I hear of any such things among the parties, or the "managers" of them, as they are called. It is true, the preaching and publishing of the Doctor's sermon at that time was by many judged unseasonable, and they were somewhat troubled at it; more upon the account that it was done by him than that it was done. But otherwise, as to the charge of schism managed therein against them, they were neither surprised with it nor discomposed at it. And, so far as I know, it was the season alone, and the present posture of affairs in the nation, calling for an agreement among all Protestants, that occasioned any answer unto it.

It is, therefore, no small mistake, that we " dissuaded" any from reading his sermon; which hath been commonly objected by some other writers of the same way. But if we were enemies unto these worthy persons, we could not desire they should have more false intelligence from our tents than they seem to have. This is not our way. Those who are joined with us are so upon their own free choice and judgment; nor do we dissuade them from reading the discourses of any on the subject of our differences. The rule holds herein, " Prove all things, and hold fast that which is good."

Nor do I know any thing in the least of advices or agreements to cry down and oppose, confute or answer, the Doctor's sermon; nor do I believe that there were ever any such among those who are charged with them. And what shall be said unto those military expressions of "summoning in the power of the party, resolved to fall on, think fit to draw their strength into the field?" etc. I say, what shall we say to these things? I am not a little troubled that I am forced to have any concernment in the debate of these differences, wherein men's sense of their interest, or of provocations they have received, cast them on such irregular ways of defence and retaliation; for all these things are but fruits of imagination, that have nothing of truth or substance to give countenance unto them.

The way whereby I became to be at all engaged in this contest, and the reasons whereon I undertook a harmless defence of our innocency, as to the charge of schism at this time, I shall give a brief account of:—

Some days after the Doctor's sermon was printed and published, one of those whom he supposeth we persuaded not to read it brought it unto me, and gave it me, with such a character of it as I shall not repeat. Upon the perusal of it (which I did on his desire, being uncertain to this day whether, without that occasion, I had ever read it at all), I confess I was both surprised and troubled, and quickly found that many others were so also; for as there was then a great hope and expectation that all Protestants would cement and unite in one common cause and interest for the defence and preservation of religion against the endeavours of the Papists for its subversion, so it was thought by wise men of all sorts that the only medium and expedient for this end was the deposing of the consideration of the lesser differences among ourselves, and burying all animosities that had arisen from them. And I yet suppose myself at least excusable, that I judged the tendency of that discourse to lie utterly another way. Nor is it in my power to be-

lieve that a peremptory charge of schism upon any dissenters,—considering what is
the apprehension and judgment of those who make that charge concerning it with
respect unto God and men,—is a means to unite us in one common religious interest.
And on this account, not knowing in the least that any other person had undertaken, or would undertake, the consideration of the Doctor's sermon, I thought
that my endeavour for the removal of the obstacle cast in the way unto a sincere
coalition in the unity of faith among all sorts of Protestants, might not be unac-
ceptable.   Neither did I see any other way whereby this might be done but only
by a vindication of the dissenters from the guilt of that state, which, if it be truly
charged on them, must render our divisions irreconcilable.   And continuing still of
the same mind, I have once more renewed the same defensative, with no other design
but to maintain hopes that peace and love may yet be preserved among us during
the continuation of these differences.   And whereas it is a work of almighty power
to reduce Christian religion unto its first purity and simplicity, which will not be
effected but by various providential dispensations in the world, and renewed effu-
sions of the Holy Spirit from above, which are to be waited for; and seeing that
all endeavours for national reformation are attended with insuperable difficulties,
few churches being either able or willing to extricate themselves from the dust of
traditions and time, with the rust of secular interests; I would hope that they
shall not be always the object of public severities who, keeping the unity of the
Spirit in the bond of truth and peace, with all sincere disciples of Christ everywhere, do design nothing but a reformation of themselves and their ways, by a
universal compliance with the will and word of Christ alone, whom God hath
commanded them in all things to hear and obey.

   The reduction, I say, of the profession of Christianity in general unto its primitive purity, simplicity, separation from the world, and all implication with secular interests, so as that it should comprise nothing but the guidance of the souls
of men in the life of God towards the enjoyment of him, is a work more to be
prayed for to come in its proper season than to be expected in this age.   Nor do
any yet appear fitted in the least measure for the undertaking or attempting such
a work, any farther than by their own personal profession and example.   And
whilst things continue amongst protestant churches in the state wherein they are,
—under the influence of divided secular interests, and advantageous mixtures with
them, with the relics of the old general apostasy, by differences in points of doctrine
in rules of discipline, in orders of divine worship,—it is in vain to look for any union
or communion among them, in a compliance with any certain rule of uniformity,
either in the profession of faith or in the practice of worship and discipline.   Nor
would such an agreement among them, could it be attained, be of any great advantage unto the important ends of religion, unless a revival of the power of it in
the souls of men do accompany it.   In the meantime, the glory of our Christian
profession, in righteousness, holiness, and a visible dedication of its professors unto
God, is much lost in the world, innumerable souls perishing through the want of
effectual means for their conversion and edification.   To attempt public national
reformation whilst things ecclesiastic and civil are so involved as they are, the one
being rivetted into the legal constitution of the other, is neither the duty nor work
of private men: nor will, as I suppose, wise men be over forward in attempting any
such thing, unless they had better evidence of means to make it effectual than any
that do as yet appear; for the religion of a nation, in every form, will answer the
ministry of it.   What is the present duty, in this state of things, of those private
Christians or ministers who cannot satisfy their consciences, as unto their duty
towards God, without endeavouring a conformity unto the will of Christ, in the
observance of all his institutions and commands, confining all their concerns in
religion unto things spiritual and heavenly? is the inquiry before us.

AN INQUIRY

THE ORIGINAL, NATURE, INSTITUTION, POWER, ORDER, AND COMMUNION OF EVANGELICAL CHURCHES.

CHAPTER I.

Of the original of churches.

WHEN any tning which is pleaded to belong unto religion or the worship of God is proposed unto us, our first consideration of it ought to be in that inquiry which our Lord Jesus Christ made of the Pharisees concerning the baptism of John, " Whence is it? from heaven, or of men?" He distributes all things which come under that plea or pretence into two heads, as unto their original and efficient cause, —namely, "heaven" and "men." And these are not only different and distinct, but so contradictory one unto another, that, as unto any thing wherein religion or the worship of God is concerned, they cannot concur as partial causes of the same effect. What is of men is not from heaven; and what is from heaven is not of men. And hence is his determination concerning both sorts of these things: " Every plant, which my heavenly Father hath not planted, shall be rooted up," Matt. xv. 13.

Designing, therefore, to treat of churches, their *original, nature, use,* and *end,* my first inquiry must be whether they are from heaven or of men,—that is, whether they are of a divine original, having a divine institution, or whether they are an ordinance or creation of men; for their pedigree must be derived from one of these singly. They never concurred in the constitution of any part of divine worship, or any thing that belongs thereunto.

This would seem a case and inquiry of an exceeding easy determination; for the Scripture everywhere makes mention of the church or churches as the ordinances and institutions of God. But such things have fallen out in the world in latter ages as may make men justly question whether we understand the mind of God aright or no in what is spoken of them; at least, if they should allow that the churches so mentioned in the Scripture were of divine appointment, yet it might be highly questionable whether those which have since been in the world be not a mere product of the invention and power of men.

1. For many ages, such things alone were proposed unto the world, and imposed on it for *the only church*, as were from hell rather than from heaven; at least from men, and those none of the best: for all men in these western parts of the world were obliged to believe and profess, on the penalties of eternal and temporal destruction, that the pope of Rome and those depending on him were the only church in the world. If this should be granted,—as it was almost universally in some ages, and in this is earnestly contended for,—there would be a thousand evidences to prove that the institution of churches is not from heaven, but from men. Whether the inventions of men in the mystery of iniquity be to be received again or no, men of secular wisdom and interest may do well to consider; but he must be blind and mad, and accursed in his mind and understanding, who can think of receiving it as from heaven, as a divine institution. But I have treated of this subject in other discourses.

2. The name, pretence, and *presumed power of the church* or churches, have been made and used as the greatest engine for the promoting and satisfying the avarice, sensuality, ambition, and cruelty of men that ever was in the world. Never any thing was found out by men, or Satan himself, so fitted, suited, and framed to fill and satisfy the lusts of multitudes of men, as this of the church hath been, and yet continues to be: for it is so ordered, is of that make, constitution, and use, that corrupt men need desire no more for the attainment of wealth, honour, grandeur, pleasure, all the ends of their lusts, spiritual or carnal, but a share in the government and power of the church; nor hath an interest therein been generally used unto any other ends. All the pride and ambition, all the flagitious lives, in luxury, sensuality, uncleanness, incests, etc., of popes, cardinals, prelates, and their companions, with their hatred unto and oppression of good men, arose from the advantage of their being reputed "the church." To this very day, "the church" here and there, as it is esteemed, is the greatest means of keeping Christian religion in its power and purity out of the world, and a temptation to multitudes of men to prefer the church before religion, and to be obstinate in their oppositions unto it. These things being plain and evident unto wise men who had no share in the conspiracy nor the benefit of it, how could they think that this church-state was from heaven, and not of men?

3. By "the church" (so esteemed), and in pursuit of its interests, by

its authority and power, innumerable multitudes of Christians have been slain or murdered, and the earth soaked with their blood. Two emperors of Germany alone fought above *eighty battles* for and against the pretended power and authority of the church. It hath laid whole countries desolate with fire and sword, turning cities into ashes and villages into a wilderness, by the destruction of their inhabitants. It was the church which killed, murdered, and burnt innumerable holy persons, for no other reason in the world but because they would not submit their souls, consciences, and practices unto her commands, and be subject unto her in all things. Nor was there any other church conspicuously visible in all these parts of the world; nor was it esteemed lawful once to think that this was not the true church, or that there was or could be any other. For men to believe that this church-state was from heaven, is for them to believe that cruelty, bloodshed, murder, the destruction of mankind, especially of the best, the wisest, and the most holy among them, is the only way to heaven.

4. The *secular, worldly interest* of multitudes lying in this presumptive church and the state of it, they preferred and exalted it above all that is called God, and made the greatest idol of it that ever was in the world; for it was the faith and profession of it, that its authority over the souls and consciences of men is above the authority of the Scriptures, so that they have no authority towards us unless it be given unto them by this church, and that we neither can nor need believe them to be the word of God unless they inform us and command us so to do. This usurpation of divine honour, in putting itself and its authority above that of the Scripture or word of God, discovers full well whence it was. In like manner, those who assumed it unto themselves to be the church, without any other right, title, or pretence unto it, have exalted one amongst them, and with him themselves in their several capacities, above all emperors, kings, and princes, nations and people, trampling on them at their pleasure. Is this church-state from heaven? Is it of divine institution? Is it the heart and centre of Christian religion? Is it that which all men must be subject to on pain of eternal damnation? Who that knows any thing of Christ or the gospel can entertain such a thought without detestation and abhorrency?

5. This *pretence of the church* is at this day one of the greatest causes of the atheism that the world is filled withal. Men find themselves, they know not how, to belong unto this or that church; they suppose that all the religion that is required of them is no more but what this church suggests unto them; and abhorring, through innumerable prejudices, to inquire whether there be any other ministerial church-state or no, understanding at length the church to be a political combination, for the wealth, power, and dignity of some

persons, they cast away all regard of religion, and become professed atheists.

6. Unto this very day, the woful *divisions*, distractions, and endless controversies that are among Christians, with the dangerous consequences and effects of them, do all spring and arise from the churches that are in the world. Some are for the church of Rome, some for the church of England, some for the Greek church, and so of the rest; which, upon an acknowledgment of such a state of them as is usually allowed, cannot but produce wars and tumults among nations, with the oppression of particular persons in all sorts of calamities. In one place men are killed for not owning of one church, and in another for approving of it. Amongst ourselves prisons are filled, and men's goods spoiled, divisions multiplied, and the whole nation endangered, in a severe attempt to cause all Christians to acknowledge that church-state which is set up among us. In brief, these churches, in the great instance of that of Rome, have been, and are, the scandal of Christian religion, and the greatest cause of most of the evils and villanies which the world hath been replenished withal. And. is it any wonder if men question whether they are from heaven or of men?

For my part, I look upon it as one of the greatest mercies that God hath bestowed on any professed Christians in these latter ages, that he hath, by the light and knowledge of his word, disentangled the souls and consciences of any that do believe from all respect and trust unto such churches, discovering the vanity of their pretences and wickedness of their practices; whereby they openly proclaim themselves to be of men, and not from heaven. Not that he hath led them off from a church-state thereby; but by the same word revealed that to them which is pure, simple, humble, holy, and so far from giving occasion unto any of the evils mentioned as that the admittance of it will put an immediate end unto them all. Such shall we find the true and gospel church-state to be in the following description of it. He that comes out of the confusion and disorder of these human (and, as unto some of them, hellish) churches, who is delivered from this "mystery of iniquity," in darkness and confusion, policies and secular contrivances, coming thereon to obtain a view of the true native beauty, glory, and use of evangelical churches, will be thankful for the greatness of his deliverance.

Whereas, therefore, for many ages, the church of Rome, with those claiming under it and depending on it, was esteemed to be the only true church in the world, and nothing was esteemed so highly criminal,—not murder, treason, nor incest,—as to think of or to assert any other church-state, it was impossible that any wise man not utterly infatuated could apprehend a church, any church whatever, to be of divine institution or appointment; for all the evils mentioned, and others innumerable, were not only occasioned by it, but they were effects of it, and inseparable from its state and being. And if any other churches also, which, although the people whereof they consist are of another faith than those of the Roman church, are like unto it in their make and constitution, exercising the right, power, and authority which they claim unto themselves by such ways and means as are plainly of this world and of their own invention, they do leave it highly questionable from whence they are, as such; for it may be made to appear that such churches, so far as they are such, are obstructive of the sole end of all churches,—which is the edification of them that do believe,—however any that are of them or belong unto them may promote that end by their personal endeavours.

But, notwithstanding all these things, it is most certain that churches are of a divine original,—that they are the ordinance and institution of Christ. I am not yet arrived, in the order of this discourse, to a convenient season of declaring what is the especial nature, use, and end of such churches as are so the institution of God, and so to give a definition of them, which shall be done afterward; but treat only as unto the general notion of a church, and what is signified thereby. These are of God. And in those churches before described, under a corrupt, degenerate estate, three things may be considered:—1. *What is of man*, without the least pretence unto the appointment or command of God. Such is the very form, fabric, and constitution of the church of Rome, and those that depend thereon or are conformed thereunto. That which it is, that whereby it is what it is, in its kind, government, rule, and end, is all of man, without the least countenance given unto it from any thing of God's institution. This is that which, through a long effectual working of men and Satan, in a mystery of iniquity, it arrived unto. Herewith the saints of God ought to have no compliance, but bear witness against it with their lives, if called thereunto. This in due time the Lord Christ will utterly destroy. 2. Such things as pretend unto a countenance to be given them by *divine institution*, but horribly corrupted. Such are the name of a church and its power, a worship pretended to be religious and divine, an order as to officers and rulers different from the people, with sundry things of the like nature. These things are good in themselves, but as engrossed into a false church-state and worship, corrupt in themselves, they are of men, and to be abhorred of all that seek after the true church of Christ. 3. There is that which is the essence of a true church,—namely, that it be a society of men united for the celebration of divine worship. This, so far as it may be found among them, is to be approved.

But churches, as was said, are of a divine original, and have the warrant of divine authority. The whole Scripture is an account of God's institution of churches, and of his dealing with them.

God laid the foundation of church societies and the necessity of them in the law of nature, by the creation and constitution of it. I speak of churches in general, as they are societies of the human race, one way or other joined and united together for the worship of God. Now, the sole end of the creation of the nature of man was the glory of God, in that worship and obedience which it was fitted and enabled to perform. For that end, and no other, was our nature created, in all its capacities, abilities, and perfections. Neither was man so made merely that every individual should singly and by himself perform this worship, though that also every individual person is obliged unto. Every man alone, and by himself, will not only find himself indigent and wanting supplies of sundry kinds, but also that he is utterly disabled to act sundry faculties and powers of his soul, which by nature he is endued withal. Hence the Lord God said, "It is not good that man should be alone," Gen. ii. 18.

These things, therefore, are evident in themselves:—1. That God created our nature, or made man, for his *own worship* and service, and fitted the powers and faculties of his soul thereunto. 2. That this nature is so fitted for *society*, so framed for it as its next end, that without it it cannot act itself according unto what it is empowered unto; and this is the foundation of all order and government in the world among mankind. 3. That by the light of nature this *acting in society* is principally designed unto the worship of God. The power, I say, and necessity of acting in society is given unto our nature for this end principally, that we may thus glorify God in and by the worship which he requires of us. 4. That without the *worship of God in societies* there would be an absolute failure of one principal end of the creation of man; nor would any glory arise unto God from the constitution of his nature, so fitted for society as that it cannot act its own powers without it. 5. All societies are to be regulated, in the light of nature, by such circumstances as whereby they are suited unto their end, for which they may be either too large or too much restrained.

Hence have we the original of churches in the light of nature. Men associating themselves together, or uniting in such societies for the worship of God, which he requires of them, as may enable them unto an orderly performance of it, are a church. And hereunto it is required,—1. That the persons so uniting are sensible of their duty, and have not lost the knowledge of the end of their creation and being. 2. That they are acquainted with that divine religious worship which God requires of them. The former light and persuasion being lost issues in atheism; and by the loss of this, instead of churches, the generality of mankind have coalesced into idolatrous combinations. 3. That they do retain such innate principles of the light of nature as will guide them in the discharge of their duties in these societies. As,—(1.) That the societies themselves be such as are meet for their end, fit to exercise and express the worship of God in them, not such as whose constitution makes them unfit for any such end; and this gives the natural bounds of churches in all ages, which it is in vain for any man to endeavour an alteration of, as we shall see afterward. (2.) That all things be done decently and in order, in and by these societies. This is a prime dictate of the law of nature, arising from the knowledge of God and ourselves, which hath been wrested into I know not what religious ceremonies of men's invention. (3.) That they be ready to receive all divine revelations with faith and obedience, which shall either appoint the ways of God's worship and prescribe the duties of it, or guide and direct them in its performance, and to regulate their obedience therein. This also is a clear, unquestionable dictate of the light and law of nature, nor can be denied but on the principles of downright atheism.

Farther we need not seek for the divine original of churches, or societies of men fearing God, for the discharge of his public worship, unto his glory and their own eternal benefit, according unto the light and knowledge of his mind and will which he is pleased to communicate unto them.

What concerns the framing and fashioning of churches by arbitrary and artificial combinations, in provinces, nations, and the like, we shall afterward inquire into. This is the assured foundation and general warranty of particular societies and churches, whilst men are continued on the earth; the especial regulation of them by divine revelation will in the next place be considered. And he who is not united with others in some such society, lives in open contradiction unto the law of nature and its light, in the principal instances of it.

1. Whereas the directions given by the light of nature in and unto things concerning the outward worship of God are general only, so as that by them alone it would be very difficult to erect a church-state in good and holy order, God did always from the beginning, by especial revelations and institution, ordain such things as might perfect the conduct of that light unto such a complete order as was accepted with himself. So, first, he appointed a *church-state* for man in innocency, and completed its order by the *sacramental* addition of the two trees,—the one of life, the other of the knowledge of good and evil.

2. That before the coming of Christ,—who was to perfect and com-

plete all divine revelations, and state all things belonging unto the house and worship of God, so as never to admit of the least change or alteration,—this church-state, as unto outward order, rites of worship, ways and manner of the administration of things sacred, with its bounds and limits, was changeable, and variously changed. The most eminent change it received was in the giving of the law, which fixed its state unalterably unto the coming of Christ, Mal. iv. 4–6.

3. That it was *God himself alone* who made all these alterations and changes; nor would he, nor did he, ever allow that the wills, wisdom, or authority of men should prescribe rules or measures unto his worship in any thing, Heb. iii. 1–6.

4. That the foundation of every church-state that is accepted with God is in an express covenant with him, that they receive and enter into who are to be admitted into that state. A church not founded in a covenant with God is not from heaven, but of men. Hereof we shall treat more at large, as I suppose, afterward. See it exemplified, Exod. xxiv.

5. There is no good in, there is no benefit to be obtained by, any church-state whatever, unless we enter into it and observe it by *an act of obedience*, with immediate respect unto the authority of Christ, by whom it is appointed and the observation of it prescribed unto us, Matt. xxviii. 18–20. Hence,—

6. Unless men, by their voluntary choice and consent, out of a sense of their duty unto the authority of Christ in his institutions, do enter into a church-state, they cannot, by any other ways or means, be so framed into it as to find acceptance with God therein, 2 Cor. viii. 5. And the interpositions that are made by custom, tradition, the institutions and ordinances of men, between the consciences of them who belong or would belong unto such a state, and the immediate authority of God, are highly obstructive of this divine order and all the benefits of it;[1] for hence it is come to pass that most men know neither how nor whereby they come to be members of this or that church, but only on this ground, that they were born where it did prevail and was accepted.

CHAPTER II.

The especial original of the evangelical church-state.

OUR principal concernment at present is in the evangelical church-state, or the state of churches under the New Testament; for this is

---

[1] See "Discourse concerning Evangelical Love," p. 88 of this volume.

that about which there are many great and fierce contests among
Christians, and those attended with pernicious consequents and effects.
What is the original, what is the nature, what is the use and power,
what is the end of the churches, or any church, what is the duty of
men in it and towards it, is the subject of various contests, and the
principal occasion of all the distractions that are at this day in the
Christian world; for the greatest part of those who judge themselves
obliged to take care and order about these things having interwoven
their own secular interests and advantages into such a church-state
as is meet and suited to preserve and promote them, supposing
πορισμὸν εἶναι τὴν εὐσέζειαν, or that religion may be made a trade for
outward advantage, they do openly seek the destruction of all those
who will not comply with that church form and order that they have
framed unto themselves. Moreover, from men's various conceptions
and suitable practices about this church-state is advantage and occasion taken to charge each other with schism, and all sorts of evils
which are supposed to ensue thereon. Wherefore, although I design
all possible brevity, and only to declare those principles of truth
wherein we may safely repose our faith and practice, avoiding as
much as possibly I can, and the subject will allow, the handling of
those things in a way of controversy with others, yet somewhat more
than ordinary diligence is required unto the true stating of this important concernment of our religion. And that which we shall first
inquire into is the special original and authoritative constitution of
this church-state. Wherefore,—

1. The church-state of the New Testament doth not less relate
unto, and receive force from, *the light or law of nature,* than any other
state of the church whatever. Herein, as unto its general nature,
its foundation is laid. What that directs unto may receive new enforcements by revelation, but changed, or altered, or abolished, it
cannot be. Wherefore, there is no need of any new express institution of what is required by that light and law in all churches and
societies for the worship of God, but only an application of it unto
present occasions and the present state of the church, which hath
been various. And it is merely from a spirit of contention that
some call on us or others to produce express testimony or institution
for every circumstance in the practice of religious duties in the church,
and on a supposed failure herein, do conclude that they have power
themselves to institute and ordain such ceremonies as they think
meet, under a pretence of their being circumstances of worship; for
as the directive light of nature is sufficient to guide us in these things,
so the obligation of the church unto it makes all stated additions to
be useless, as on other accounts they are noxious. Such things as
these are:—the times and seasons of church assemblies; the order and

decency wherein all things are to be transacted in them; the bounding of them as unto the number of their members, and places of habitation, so as to answer the ends of their institution; the multiplication of churches when the number of believers exceeds the proportion capable of edification in such societies; what especial advantages are to be made use of in the order and worship of the church, such as are methods in preaching, translations and tunes of psalms in singing, continuance in public duties, and the like. The things themselves being divinely instituted, are capable of such general directions in and by the light of nature as may, with ordinary Christian prudence, be on all occasions applied unto the use and practice of the church. To forsake these directions, and instead of them to invent ways, modes, forms, and ceremonies of our own, which the things whereunto they are applied and made use of in do no way call for, require, or own (as it is with all humanly-invented stated ceremonies); and thereon, by laws and canons, to determine their precise observation at all times and seasons to be one and the same, which is contrary to the very nature of the circumstances of such acts and duties as they are applied unto,—their use, in the meantime, unto the general end of edification, being as indemonstrable as their necessity unto the duties whereunto they are annexed is also, —is that which hath no warranty either from divine authority or Christian prudence.

This respect of the gospel church-state unto the light of nature the apostle demonstrates, in his frequent appeals unto it in things that belong unto church-order, 1 Cor. vii. 29, 33, 37, ix. 7, xi. 14–16, xiv. 8–11, 32, 33, 40; and the like is done in sundry other places. And the reasons of it are evident.

2. But such is the especial nature and condition of the evangelical church-state; such the relation of it unto the person and mediation of Jesus Christ, with all things thereon depending; such the nature of that especial honour and glory which God designs unto himself therein (things that the light of nature can give no guidance unto nor direction about); and, moreover, so different and distant from all that was before ordained in any other church-state are the ways, means, and duties of divine worship prescribed in it,—that it must have a *peculiar, divine institution* of its own, to evidence that it is from heaven, and not from men. The present state of the church under the New Testament the apostle calls τελείωσις, Heb. vii. 11,— its perfection, its consummation, that perfect state which God designed unto it in this world. And he denies that it could be brought into that state by the law, or any of the divine institutions that belonged thereunto, chap. vii. 19, ix. 9, x. 1. And we need go no farther, we need no other argument to prove that the gospel church-

state, as unto its especial nature, is founded in a peculiar divine institution; for it hath a τελείωσις, a perfect consummate state, which the law could not bring it unto, though itself, its ordinances of worship, its rule and policy, were all of divine institution. And herein doth its excellency and preference above the legal church-state consist, as the apostle proves at large. To suppose that this should be given unto it any other way but by divine authority in its institution, is to advance the wisdom and authority of men above those of God, and to render the gospel church-state a machine to be moved up and down at pleasure, to be new moulded or shaped according unto occasions, or to be turned unto any interest, like the wings of a mill unto the wind.

All the dignity, honour, and perfection of the state of the church under the Old Testament depended solely hereon, that it was, in the whole and all the particulars of it, of divine institution. Hence it was "glorious," that is, very excellent, as the apostle declares, 2 Cor. iii. And if the church-state of the New Testament have not the same original, it must be esteemed to have a greater glory given unto it by the hand of men than the other had, in that it was instituted by God himself; for a greater glory it hath, as the apostle testifieth. Neither can any man, nor dareth any man alive, to give any instance in particular wherein there is the least defect in the being, constitution, rule, and government of the gospel church-state, for want of divine institution, so as that it should be necessary to make a supply thereof by the wisdom and authority of men. But these things will be more fully spoken unto, after we have declared who it is who hath divinely instituted this church-state.

3. The *name* of the church under the New Testament is capable of a threefold application, or it is taken in a threefold notion; as,— (1.) For the *catholic invisible church*, or society of elect believers in the whole world, really related by faith in him unto the Lord Jesus Christ as their mystical head; (2.) For the whole *number of visible professors* in the whole world, who, by baptism, and the outward profession of the gospel, and obedience unto Christ, are distinguished from the rest of the world; and,—(3.) For such a state as wherein *the worship of God is to be celebrated* in the way and manner by him appointed, and which is to be ruled by the power which he gives it, and according to the discipline which he hath ordained. Of the nature of the church under these distinct notions, with our relation unto either or all of them, and the duties required of us thereon, I have treated fully in my discourse of Evangelical Love, Church Peace, and Unity; and thither I must remit the reader. It is the church in the latter sense alone whose original we now inquire after; and I say,—

4. The original of this church-state is directly, immediately, and solely from *Jesus Christ;* he alone is the author, contriver, and institutor of it.   When I say it is immediately and solely from him, I do not intend that in and by his own person, or in his personal ministry here in the earth, he did absolutely and completely finish this state, exclusively unto the ministry of any others that he was pleased to make use of therein; for as he took it on himself as his own work to build his church, and that upon himself as its foundation, so he employed his apostles to act under him and from him, in the carrying on that work unto perfection.   But what was done by them is esteemed to be done all by himself.   For,—

(1.) It was immediately from him that they received *revelations* of what did belong unto this church-state, and what was to be prescribed therein.   They never did, neither jointly nor severally, once endeavour, in their own wisdom, or from their own invention, or by their own authority, to add or put into this church-state, as of perpetual use, and belonging unto it as such, either less or more, any one thing greater or less whatever.   It is true, they gave their advice in sundry cases of present emergencies, in and about church-affairs; they gave direction for the due and orderly practice of what was revealed unto them, and exercised authority both as unto the ordination of officers, and the rejection of obstinate sinners from the society of all the churches;—but to invent, contrive, institute, or appoint any thing in the church and its state, which they had not by immediate revelation from Christ, they never attempted it nor went about it. And unto this rule of proceeding they were precisely obliged by the express words of their commission, Matt. xxviii. 19, 20.   This, I say, is so plainly included in the tenor of their commission, and so evident from all that is divinely recorded of their practice, that it will admit of no sober contradiction.   In what others think it meet to do in this kind, we are not concerned.

(2.) The *authority* whereby they acted in the institution of the church in its order, whereon the consciences of all believers were obliged to submit thereunto, and to comply with it in a way of obedience, was the authority of Christ himself, acted in them and by them, 2 Cor. i. 24, iv. 5.   They everywhere disclaim any such power and authority in themselves.   They pleaded that they were only stewards and ministers; not lords of the faith or obedience of the church, but helpers of its joy; yea, the servants of all the churches for Christ's sake.   And hereon it follows, that what is recorded of their practice, in their institution, ordering, or disposing of any thing in the church that was to be of an abiding continuance, hath in it the obliging power of the authority of Christ himself.   Wherefore, if the distinction that some make concerning the apostles,—namely,

that they are to be considered as apostles, or as church-governors,—
should be allowed, as it is liable to just exceptions, yet would no advantage accrue thereby unto what is pretended from it; for as what
they did, appointed, and ordered in the church for its constant observation, as apostles, they did it by immediate revelation from Christ,
and in his name and authority, so what, in distinction from hence, as
church-governors, they did or ordered, they did it only by a due application unto present occasions of what they had received by revelation.   But as they were apostles, Christ sent them, as his Father
sent him; and he was so sent of the Father as that he did "stand and
feed in the strength of the LORD, in the majesty of the name of the
LORD his God," Mic. v. 4.   So did they feed the sheep of Christ in
his strength, and in the authority or majesty of his name.

5. Christ, therefore, alone is *the author of the gospel church-state.*
And because this is the only foundation of our faith and obedience,
as unto all that we are to believe, do, and practise, by virtue of that
church-state, or in order thereunto, the Scripture doth not only
plainly affirm it, but also declares the grounds of it, why it must be
so, and whence it is so, as also wherein his doing of it doth consist.

Three things, amongst others, are eminently necessary in and unto
him who is to constitute this church-state, with all that belongs thereunto; and as the Scripture doth eminently and expressly ascribe
them all unto Christ, so no man, nor all the men of the world, can
have any such interest in them as to render them meet for this work,
or any part of it:—

(1.) The first of these is *right* and *title.*   He who institutes this
church-state must have a right and title to dispose of all men, in all
their spiritual and eternal concernments, as seemeth good unto him;
for unto this church-state, namely, as it is purely evangelical, no man
is obliged by the law of nature, nor hath any creature power to dispose of him into a condition whereon all his concernments, spiritual
and eternal, shall depend.   This right and title to the sovereign disposal of mankind, or of his church, Christ hath alone, and that upon
a treble account:—[1.] Of *donation* from the Father: he appointed
him the "heir of all things," Heb. i. 2, 3.   He gave him "power
over all flesh," John xvii. 2.   Especially he hath given unto him and
put into his absolute disposal all those who are to be his church,
verse 6.   [2.] By virtue of *purchase:* he hath by the price of his
most precious blood purchased them unto his own power and disposal.   He "purchased his church with his own blood," Acts xx. 28;
which the apostle makes the ground of that care which ought to
be had of it.   And this is pleaded as a sufficient reason why we
should be wholly at his disposal only, and be free from any imposition of men in things spiritual: 1 Cor. vii. 23, "Ye are bought with

a price; be ye not the servants of men." The purchase of this right
and title was one great end of the principal mediatory acts of Christ:
Rom. xiv. 9, 10, " For to this end," etc. [3.] Of *conquest:* for all
those who were thus to be disposed by him were both under the
power of his enemies, and were themselves enemies unto him in their
minds. He could not, therefore, have a sovereign right unto their
disposal but by a double conquest;—namely, first of their enemies,
by his power; and then of themselves by his word, his Spirit, and
his grace. And this twofold conquest of his is fully described in the
Scripture.

Whereas, therefore, there is a disposal of the persons that are to
belong unto this church-state, as unto their souls, consciences, and
all the eternal concernments of them, by an indispensable moral
obligation to a compliance therewithal, until men can manifest that
they have such a right and title over others, and that either by the
especial grant and donation of God the Father, or a purchase that
they have made of them unto themselves, or conquest, they are
not to be esteemed to have either right or title to institute any thing
that belongs unto this church-state. And it is in vain pretended (as
we shall see more afterward) that Christ, indeed, hath appointed this
church-state in general, but that he hath appointed no particular
form of churches or their rule, but left that unto the discretion and
authority of men as they think meet, when they have outward power
for their warranty. But if by these particular appointments and
framings of churches with their order, men are disposed of, as unto
their spiritual concernments, beyond the obligation of the light of
nature or the moral law, we must yet inquire who gave them this
right and title to make this disposal of them.

(2.) *Authority.* As right and title respect the persons of men to be
reduced into a new form of government so authority respects the
rules, laws, orders, and statutes to be made, prescribed, and established, whereby the privileges of this new society are conveyed, and
the duties of it enjoined, unto all that are taken into it. Earthly
potentates, who will dispose of men into a state and government absolutely new unto them, as unto all their temporal concernments of
life, liberty, inheritances, and possessions, so as that they shall hold
all of them in dependence on and according unto the rules and laws
of their new government and kingdom, must have these two things;
—namely, right and title unto the persons of men, which they have
by conquest, or an absolute resignation of all their interests and concerns into their disposal; and authority, thereon to constitute what
order, what kind of state, rule, and government, they please. Without
these they will quickly find their endeavours and undertakings frustrate. The gospel church-state in the nature of it, and in all the

laws and constitution of it, is absolutely new, whereunto all the world
are naturally foreigners and strangers. As they have no right unto
it as it containeth privileges, so they have no obligation unto it as
it prescribes duties; wherefore, there is need of both these;—right, as
unto the persons of men; and authority, as unto the laws and constitution of the church, unto the framing of it. And until men can
pretend unto these things, both unto this right and authority with
respect unto all the spiritual and eternal concernments of the souls
of others, they may do well to consider how dangerous it is to invade
the right and inheritance of Christ, and leave hunting after an interest of power in the framing or forming evangelical churches, or
making of laws for their rule and government.

This authority is not only ascribed unto Jesus Christ in the Scripture, but it is *enclosed* unto him, so as that no other can have any
interest in it. See Matt. xxviii. 18; Rev. iii. 7; Isa. ix. 6, 7. By
virtue hereof he is the only "lawgiver" of the church, James iv. 12;
Isa. xxxiii. 22. There is, indeed, a derivation of power and authority
from him unto others, but it extends itself no farther, save only that
they shall direct, teach, and command those whom he sends them
unto to do and observe what he hath commanded, Matt. xxviii. 20.
"He builds his own house," and he is "over his own house," Heb.
iii. 3–6. He both constitutes its state, and gives laws for its rule.

The disorder, the confusion, the turning of the kingdom of Christ
upside down, which have ensued upon the usurpation of men, taking
upon them a legislative power in and over the church, cannot easily
be declared; for upon a slight pretence, no way suited or serviceable
unto their ends,—of the advice given and determination made by the
apostles with the elders and brethren of the church of Jerusalem, in a
temporary constitution about the use of Christian liberty,—the bishops
of the fourth and fifth centuries took upon themselves power to make
laws, canons, and constitutions for the ordering of the government
and the rule of the church, bringing in many new institutions on a
pretence of the same authority. Neither did others who followed
them cease to build on their sandy foundation, until the whole frame
of the church-state was altered, a new law made for its government,
and a new Christ or antichrist assumed in the head of its rule by
that law; for all this pretended authority of making laws and constitutions for the government of the church issued in that sink of
abominations which they call the canon-law. Let any man but of a
tolerable understanding, and freed from infatuating prejudices, but
read the representation that is made of the gospel church-state, its
order, rule, and government, in the Scripture on the one hand, and
what representation is made on the other of a church-state, its order,
rule, and government, in the canon-law,—the only effect of men's

assuming to themselves a legislative power with respect unto the church of Christ,—if he doth not pronounce them to be contrary as light and darkness, and that by the latter the former is utterly destroyed and taken away, I shall never trust to the use of men's reason or their honesty any more.

This authority was first usurped by *synods*, or *councils* of *bishops*. Of what use they were at any time to declare and give testimony unto any article of the faith which in their days was opposed by heretics, I shall not now inquire; but as unto the exercise of the authority claimed by them to make laws and canons for the rule and government of the church, it is to be bewailed there should be such a monument left of their weakness, ambition, self-interest, and folly, as there is in what remaineth of their Constitutions. Their whole endeavour in this kind was at best but the building of wood, hay, and stubble on the foundation, in whose consumption they shall suffer loss, although they be saved themselves. But in making of laws to bind the whole church,—in and about things useless and trivial, no way belonging to the religion taught us by Jesus Christ; in and for the establishment or increase of their own power, jurisdiction, authority, and rule, with the extent and bounds of their several dominions; in and for the constitution of new frames and states of churches, and new ways of the government of them; in the appointment of new modes, rites, and ceremonies of divine worship; with the confusions that ensued thereon, in mutual animosities, fightings, divisions, schisms, and anathematisms, to the horrible scandal of Christian religion,—they ceased not until they had utterly destroyed all the order, rule, and government of the church of Christ, yea, the very nature of it, and introduced into its room a carnal, worldly church-state and rule, suited unto the interests of covetous, ambitious, and tyrannical prelates. The most of them, indeed, knew not for whom they wrought in providing materials for that Babel, which, by a hidden skill in a mystery of iniquity, was raised out of their provisions; for after they were hewed and carved, shaped, formed, and gilded, the pope appeared in the head of it, as it were, with those words of his mouth: " Is not this great Babylon, that I have built for the house of the kingdom by the might of my power, and for the honour of my majesty?" This was the fatal event of men's invading the right of Christ, and claiming an interest in authority to give laws to the church. This, therefore, is absolutely denied by us,—namely, that any men, under what pretence or name soever, have any right or authority to constitute any new frame or order of the church, to make any laws of their own for its rule or government that should oblige the disciples of Christ in point of conscience unto their observation. That there is nothing in this assertion that should in the least impeach the power of magistrates, with reference unto the outward, civil, and political concerns of the church, or the public profession of religion within their territories, —nothing that should take off from the just authority of the lawful guides of the church, in ordering, appointing, and commanding the observation of all things in them, according to the mind of Christ, shall be afterward declared. In these things "the LORD is our judge, the LORD is our statute-maker, the LORD is our king; he will save us."

It is, then, but weakly pleaded, " That seeing the magistrate can appoint or command nothing in religion that God hath forbidden, nor is there any need that he should appoint or command what God hath already appointed and commanded; if so be he may not by law command such things in the church as before were neither commanded nor forbidden, but indifferent, which are the proper field of his ecclesiastical legislative power, then hath he no power nor authority about religion at all;"—that is, if he hath not the same and a co-ordinate power with God or Christ, he hath none at all! One of the best arguments that can be used for the power of the magistrate in things ecclesiastical is taken from the approved example of the good kings under the Old Testament. But they thought it honour enough unto them, and their duty, to see and take care that the things which God had appointed and ordained should be diligently observed by all those concerned therein, both priests and people, and to destroy what God had forbidden. To appoint any thing of themselves, to make that necessary in the church and the worship thereof which God had not made so, they never esteemed it to be in their power, or to belong unto their duty. When they did any thing of that nature, and thereby made any additions unto the outward worship of God not before commanded, they did it by immediate revelation from God, and so by divine authority, 1 Chron. xxviii. 19. And it is left as a brand on those that were wicked, not only that they commanded and made "statutes" for the observation of what God had forbidden, Mic. vi. 16, but also that they commanded and appointed *what God had not appointed,* 1 Kings xii. 32, 33. And it will be found at last to be honour enough to the greatest potentate under heaven to take care that what Christ hath appointed in his church and worship be observed, without claiming a power like unto that of the Most High, to give laws unto the church for the observation of things found out and invented by themselves or other men.

Of the same nature is the other part of their plea against this denial of a legislative power in men with respect unto the constitution of the evangelical church-state, or the ordaining of any thing to be observed in it that Christ hath not appointed: for it is said, "That if this be allowed, as all the dignity, power, and honour of the governors of the church will be rejected or despised, so all manner of confusion and disorder will be brought into the church itself; for how can it otherwise be, when all power of law-making, in the preservation of the dignity of the rulers and order of the church, is taken away? And therefore we see it was the wisdom of the church in former ages that all the principal laws and canons that they made, in their councils or otherwise, were designed unto the exaltation and preservation of the dignity of church-rulers; wherefore, take this power away, and you will bring in all confusion into the church."

Ans. 1. They do not, in my judgment, sufficiently think of whom and of what they speak who plead after this manner; for the substance of the plea is, that if the church have its whole frame, constitution, order, rule, and government from Christ alone, though men should faithfully discharge their duty in doing and observing all what he hath commanded, there would be nothing in it but disorder and confusion. Whether this becomes that reverence which we ought to have of him, or be suited unto that faithfulness and wisdom which is particularly ascribed unto him in the constitution and ordering of his church, is not hard to determine, and the truth of it shall be afterward demonstrated.

Ans. 2. As unto the dignity and honour of the rulers of the church, the subject of so many ecclesiastical laws, they are, in the first place, to be desired themselves to remember the example of Christ himself in his personal ministry here on earth: Matt. xx. 28, "Even as the Son of man came not to be ministered unto, but to minister, and to give his life a ransom for many;"—with the rule prescribed by him thereon, verses 25–27, "But Jesus called them unto him, and said, Ye know that the princes of the Gentiles exercise dominion over them, and they that are great exercise authority upon them. But it shall not be so among you: but whosoever shall be great among you, let him be your minister; and whosoever will be chief among you, let him be your servant;"—with the occasion of the instruction given therein unto his apostles, verse 24, "And when the ten heard it, they were moved with indignation against the two brethren;"—as also the injunction given them by the apostle Peter, on whom, for their own advantage, some would fasten a monarchy over the whole church, 1 Epist. v. 2, 3, "Feed the flock of God which is among you, taking the oversight thereof, not by constraint, but willingly; not for filthy lucre, but of a ready mind; neither as being lords over God's heritage, but being ensamples to the flock;"—and the blessed expressions of the apostolical state by Paul, 1 Cor. iv. 1, "Let a man so account of us, as of the ministers of Christ, and stewards of the mysteries of God;" 2 Cor. i. 24, "Not for that we have dominion over your faith, but are helpers of your joy;" chap. iv. 5, " For we preach not ourselves, but Christ Jesus the Lord, and ourselves your servants for Jesus' sake." It may prepare their minds for the right management of that honour which is their due. For, secondly, there is, in and by the constitution of Christ and his express laws, an honour and respect due unto those church-guides which he hath appointed, abiding in the duties which he requireth. If men had not been weary of apostolical simplicity and humility, if they could have contented themselves with the honour and dignity annexed unto their office and work by Christ himself, they had never entertained pleasing dreams of thrones, pre-eminencies, chief sees, secular grandeur and power, nor framed so many laws and canons about these things, turning the whole rule of the church into a worldly empire. For such it was, that as of all the popes which ever dwelt at Rome, there was never any pretended or acted a greater zeal for the rule and government of the church, by the laws and canons that it had made for that end, than Gregory VII., so if ever there were any antichrist in the world (as there are many antichrists) he was one. His Luciferian pride; his trampling on all Christian kings and potentates; his horrible tyranny over the consciences of all Christians; his abominable dictates asserting of his own god-like sovereignty; his requiring all men, on the pain of damnation, to be sinful subjects to God and Peter (that is, himself), which his own acts and epistles are filled withal,—do manifest both who and what he was. Unto that issue did this power of law or canon making, for the honour and dignity of church rulers, at length arrive.

Ans. 3. Let the constitution of the church by Jesus Christ abide and remain,—let the laws for its rule, government, and worship, which he hath recorded in the Scripture, be diligently observed by them whose duty it is to take care about them, both to observe them themselves and to teach others so to do,—and we know full well there will be no occasion given or left unto the least confusion or disorder in the church. But if men will be froward, and, because they may not make laws themselves or keep the statutes made by others, will neglect the due observation and execution of what Christ hath ordained; or will deny that we may and ought, in and for the due observation of his laws, to make use of the inbred light of nature and rules of common prudence (the use and exercise of both which are included and enjoined in the commands of Christ, in that he requires a compliance with them in the way of obedience, which we cannot perform without them),—I know of no relief against the perpetuity of our differences about these things. But after so much scorn and contempt hath been cast upon that principle, that it is not lawful to observe any thing in the rule of the church or divine worship, in a constant way, by virtue of any human canons or laws, that is not prescribed in the Scripture, if we could prevail with men to give us one single instance, which they would abide by, wherein the rules and institutions of Christ are so defective as that, without their canonical additions, order cannot be observed in the church, nor the worship of God be duly performed, it shall be diligently attended unto. Allow the general rules given us in Scripture for church order and worship to be applied unto all proper occasions and circumstances, with particular, positive, divine precepts; allow, also, that the apostles, in what they did and acted in the constitution and ordering of the churches and their worship, did and acted it in the name and by the authority of Christ; as also that there needs no other means of affecting and obliging our consciences in these things, but only that the mind and will of Christ be intimated and made known unto us, though not in the form of a law given and promulgated, which, I suppose, no men of sober minds or principles can disallow; and then give an instance of such a deficiency as that mentioned in the institutions of Christ, and the whole difference in this matter will be rightly stated, and not else.   But to return from this digression.

The Scripture doth not only ascribe this authority unto Christ alone, but it giveth instances of his use and exercise thereof; which comprise all that is necessary unto the constitution and ordering of his churches and the worship of them.   (1.) He *buildeth his own house*, Heb. iii. 3.   (2.) He *appointeth offices* for rule in his churches, and officers, 1 Cor. xii. 5; Rom. xii. 6–8.   (3.) He gives *gifts* for the administrations of the church, Eph. iv. 8, 11–13; 1 Cor. xi. 12.   (4.) He gives *power and authority* unto them that are to minister and rule in the church, etc.; which things must be afterward spoken unto.

(3.) As unto this constitution of the gospel church-state, the Scripture assigneth, in an especial manner, *faithfulness* unto the Lord Christ, Heb. iii. 2–6.   This power is originally in God himself; it belongs unto him alone, as the great sovereign of all his creatures. Unto Christ, as mediator, it was given by the Father, and the whole of it intrusted with him.   Hence it follows, that in the execution of it he hath respect unto the mind and will of God, as unto what he would have done and ordered, with respect whereunto this power was committed unto him.   And here his faithfulness takes place, exerted in the revelation of the whole mind of God in this matter, instituting, appointing, and commanding all that God would have so ordained, and nothing else.   And what can *any man do that cometh after the King?*

Hereunto there is added, on the same account, the consideration of his wisdom, his love, and care for the good of his church; which in him were ineffable and inimitable. By all these things was he fitted for his office and the work that was reserved for him, so as that he might in all things have the pre-eminence. And this was to make the last and only full, perfect, complete revelation of the mind and will of God, as unto the state, order, faith, obedience, and worship of the church. There was no perfection in any of these things until he took this work in hand; wherefore, it may justly be supposed that he hath so perfectly stated and established all things concerning his churches and worship therein, being the last divine hand that was to be put to this work, and this his hand, Heb. i. 2, 3, that whatever is capable of a law or a constitution for the use of the church at all times, or is needful for his disciples to observe, is revealed, declared, and established by him. And in this persuasion I shall abide, until I see better fruits and effects of the interposition of the wisdom and authority of men, unto the same ends which he designed, than as yet I have been able, in any age, to observe.

The substance of the things pleaded may, for the greater evidence of their truth, be reduced unto the ensuing heads or propositions:—

First. *Every church-state that hath an especial institution of its own, giving [it] its especial kind*, supposeth and hath respect unto the law and light of nature, requiring and directing in general those things which belong unto the being, order, and preservation of such societies as that is. That there ought to be societies wherein men voluntarily join together for the solemn performance of divine worship and joint walking in obedience before God; that these societies ought to use such means for their own peace and order as the light of nature directs unto; that where many have a common interest they ought to consult in common for the due management of it, with other things of the like importance, are evident dictates of this light and law. Now, whatever church-state may be superinduced by divine institution, yet this light and law, in all their evident dictates, continue their obliging power in and over the minds of men, and must do so eternally. Wherefore, things that belong hereunto need no new institution in any church-state whatever. But yet,—

Secondly. Whatever is required by the *light of nature* in such societies as churches, as useful unto their order, and conducing unto their end, is *a divine institution*. The Lord Christ, in the institution of gospel churches, their state, order, rule, and worship, doth not require of his disciples that in their observance of his appointments they should cease to be men, or forego the use and exercise of their rational abilities, according to the rule of that exercise, which is the light of nature. Yea, because the rules and directions are in this case to be applied unto things spiritual and of mere revelation, he giveth wisdom, prudence, and understanding, to make that application in a due manner, unto those to whom the guidance and rule of the church is committed. Wherefore, as unto all things which the light of nature directs us unto, with respect unto the observation of the duties prescribed by Christ in and unto the church, we need no other institution but that of the use of the especial spiritual wisdom and prudence which the Lord Christ gives unto his church for that end.

Thirdly. There are in the Scripture *general rules* directing us, in the application of natural light, unto such a determination of all circumstances, in the acts of church rule and worship, as are sufficient for their performance " decently and in order." Wherefore, as was said before, it is utterly in vain and useless to demand express institution of all the circumstances belonging unto the government, order, rule, and worship of the church, or for the due improvement of things in themselves indifferent unto its edification, as occasion shall require; nor are they capable to be any otherwise stated, but as they lie in the light of nature and spiritual prudence, directed by general rules of Scripture.

These things being premised, our principal assertion is,—*That Christ alone is the author, institutor, and appointer, in a way of authority and legislation, of the gospel church-state, its order, rule, and worship, with all things constantly and perpetually belonging thereunto, or necessary to be observed therein.* What is not so is of men, and not from heaven. This is that which we have proved in general, and shall farther particularly confirm in our progress. Hence,—

6. There is no spiritual use nor benefit of any church-state, nor of any thing therein performed, but what, on the part of men, consists in *acts of obedience unto the authority of Christ.* If, in any thing we do of this nature, we cannot answer that inquiry which God directs in this case to be made, namely, " Why we do this or that thing," Exod. xii. 25–27, with this, " That it is because Christ hath required it of us," we do not acknowledge him the Lord over his own house, nor hear him as the Son. Nor is there any act of power to be put forth in the rule of the church, but in them by whom it is exerted it is an act of obedience unto Christ, or it is a mere usurpation. All church-power is nothing but a faculty or ability to obey the commands of Christ in such a way and manner as he hath appointed; for it is his constitution that the administration of his solemn worship in the church, and the rule of it, as unto the observance of his commands, should be committed unto some persons set apart unto that end, according unto his appointment. This is all their authority, all that they have of order or jurisdiction, or by any other ways whereby they are pleased to express it. And where there is any gospel

administration, any act of rule or government in the church, which those that perform do not give an evidence that they do it in obedience unto Christ, it is null, as unto any obligation on the consciences of his disciples. The neglect hereof in the world,—wherein many, in the exercise of church-discipline or any acts that belong unto the rule of it, think of nothing but their own offices, whereunto such powers are annexed, by human laws and canons, as enable them to act in their own names, without designing obedience unto Christ in all that they do, or to make a just representation of his authority, wisdom, and love thereby,—is ruinous unto church order and rule.

7. There is no *legislative power* in and over the church, as unto its form, order, and worship, left unto any of the sons of men, under any qualification whatever; for,—

(1.) There are none of them who have an interest in those *rights*, qualifications, and endowments, which are necessary unto an investiture into such a legislative power; for what was given and granted unto Christ himself unto this end, that he might be the lawgiver of the church, must be found also in them who pretend unto any interest therein. Have they, any of them, a right and title unto a disposal of the persons of believers in what way they please, as unto their spiritual and eternal concernments? Have they sovereign authority over all things, to change their moral nature, to give them new uses and significations, to make things necessary that in themselves are indifferent, and to order all those things by sovereign authority in laws obliging the consciences of men? And the like may be said of his personal qualifications, of faithfulness, wisdom, love, and care, which are ascribed unto him in this work of giving laws unto his churches, as he was the Lord over his own house.

(2.) The *event* of the assumption of this legislative power, under the best pretence that can be given unto it,—namely, in councils or great assemblies of bishops and prelates,—sufficiently demonstrates how dangerous a thing it is for any man to be engaged in; for it issued at length in such a constitution of churches, and such laws for the government of them, as exalted the canon law into the room of the Scripture, and utterly destroyed the true nature of the church of Christ, and all the discipline required therein.

(3.) Such an *assumption* is derogatory unto the glory of Christ, especially as unto his faithfulness in and over the house of God, wherein he is compared unto and preferred above Moses, Heb. iii. 3–6. Now, the faithfulness of Moses consisted in this, that he did and appointed all things according to the pattern showed him in the mount; that is, all whatever it was the will of God to be revealed and appointed for the constitution, order, rule, and worship of his church, and nothing else. But it was the will of God that there should be all those things in the gospel church-state also, or else why do men contend about them? And if this were the will of God, if they were not all revealed, appointed, prescribed, legalized by Christ, where is his faithfulness in answer to that of Moses? But no instance can be given of any defect in his institutions, that needs any supplement to be made by the best of men, as unto the end of constituting a church-state, order, and rule, with rites of worship in particular.

(4.) How it is derogatory unto the glory of the Scripture, as unto its *perfection*, shall be elsewhere declared.

8. There is no more required to give authority, obliging the consciences of all that do believe, unto any institution, or observation of duty, or acts of rule in the church, but only that it is made evident in the Scripture to be *the mind and will of Christ*. It is not necessary that every thing of this nature should be given out unto us in form of a law or precise command, in express words. It is the mind and will of Christ that immediately affects the consciences of believers unto obedience, by what way or means soever the knowledge of it be communicated unto them in the Scripture, either by express words, or by just consequence from what is so expressed. Wherefore,—

9. The example and practice of the apostles in the erection of churches, in the appointment of officers and rulers in them, in directions given for their walking, order, administration of censures, and all other holy things, are *a sufficient indication* of the mind and will of Christ about them. We do not say that in themselves they are institutions and appointments, but they infallibly declare what is so, or the mind of Christ concerning those things. Nor can this be questioned without a denial of their infallibility, faithfulness, and divine authority.

10. The assertion of some, that *the apostles took their pattern for the state and rule of the churches, and as unto divers rites of worship, from the synagogues of the Jews, their institutions, orders, and rules,* not those appointed by Moses, but such as themselves had found out and ordained, is both temerarious and untrue. In the pursuit of such bold conjectures, one[1] of late hath affirmed that Moses took most of his laws and ceremonies from the Egyptians, whereas it is much more likely that many of them were given on purpose to alienate the people by prohibitions from any compliance with the Egyptians, or any other nation; whereof Maimonides, in his " Moreh

[1] It was not till five years after the publication of this work that Dr Spencer's celebrated work, " De Legibus Hebræorum Ritualibus," appeared, in which he contends that the Hebrew ritual had been borrowed from the religious ceremonies of the Egyptians, and accommodated by Moses to the purposes of divine revelation. It is impossible, therefore, that Owen can allude to this work, although, from the wide-spread influence it exerted on theological literature in this country and abroad, it has been named as one of the causes that gave birth and impulse to neological speculation. Mr Orme (" Biblioth. Biblic.") affirms that the hypothesis had been already borrowed from

Nevochim," gives us sundry instances. This assertion, I say, is rash and false; for,—(1.) As unto the instances given for its confirmation, who shall assure us that they were then in use and practice in the synagogues when the apostles gave rules unto the churches of the New Testament? We have no record of theirs, not one word in all the world, of what was their way and practice, but what is at least two hundred and fifty years younger and later than the writings of the New Testament; and in the first of their writings, as in them that follow, we have innumerable things asserted to have been the traditions and practices of their forefathers from the days of Moses, which we know to be utterly false. At that time when they undertook to compose a new religion out of their pretended traditions, partly by the revolt of many apostates from Christianity unto them, especially of the Ebionites and Nazarenes, and partly by their own study and observation, coming to the knowledge of sundry things in the gospel churches, their order and worship, they took them in as their own. Undeniable instances may be given hereof. (2.) Wherein there is a real coincidence between what was ordained by the apostles and what was practised by the Jews, it is in things which the light of nature and the general rules of the Scripture do direct unto. And it is dishonourable unto the apostles, and the Spirit of Christ in them, to think or say that in such things they took their pattern from the Jews, or made them their example. Surely the apostles took not the pattern and example for the institution of excommunication from the Druids, among whom there was some things that did greatly resemble it, so far as it hath its foundation in the light of nature.

CHAPTER III.

The continuation of a church-state and of churches unto the end of the world—
What are the causes of it, and whereon it depends.

THAT there was a peculiar church-state instituted and appointed by Christ, and his apostles acting in his name and authority, with the infallible guidance of his Spirit, hath been declared; but it may be yet farther inquired, whether this church-state be still continued

Maimonides, and warmly urged by Sir John Marsham in his "Canon Chronicus Ægyptiacus," published in 1672; and perhaps Dr Owen refers to this author. In a learned treatise, however, on the "Urim and Thummim," published by Spencer in 1669, the same opinion is maintained, and the allusion of our author may after all be to Spencer. The views of the latter as to the Egyptian origin of the Urim and Thummim had been already propounded by Le Clerc; and Grotius had long before committed himself to the notion of Maimonides, that the Hebrew rites had been copied from Egypt. Witsius and Shuckford have distinguished themselves in the refutation of this hypothesis.—ED.

by *divine authority*, or whether it ceased not together with the apostles by whom it was erected.

There was a church-state under the Old Testament solemnly erected by God himself; and although it was not to be absolutely perpetual or everlasting, but was to continue only unto the time of reformation, yet unto that time its continuation was secured in the causes and means of it.

1. The *causes* of the continuation of this church-state unto its appointed period were two:—(1.) The *promise of God* unto Abraham that he would keep and preserve his seed in covenant with him, until he should be the heir of the world and the father of many nations in the coming of Christ, whereunto this church-state was subservient. (2.) The *law of God itself*, and the institutions thereof, which God appointed to be observed in all their generations, calling the covenant, the statutes and laws of it, "perpetual" and "everlasting;" that is, never to cease, to be abrogated or disannulled, until by his own sovereign authority he would utterly change and take away that whole church-state, with all that belonged unto its constitution and preservation.

2. The *means* of its continuance were three:—(1.) *Carnal generation*, and that on a twofold account; for there were two constituent parts of that church, the priests and the people. The continuation of each of them depended on the privilege of carnal generation; for the priests were to be all of the family of Aaron, and the people of the seed of Abraham by the other heads of tribes, which gave them both their foundation in and right unto this church-state. And hereunto were annexed all the laws concerning the integrity, purity, and legitimacy of the priests, with the certainty of their pedigree. (2.) *Circumcision*, the want whereof was a bar against any advantage by the former privilege of generation from those two springs; and hereby others also might be added unto the church, though never with a capacity of the priesthood. (3.) The *separation* of the people from the rest of the world, by innumerable divine ordinances, making their coalition with them impossible.

From these causes and by these means it was that the church-state under the Old Testament was preserved unto its appointed season. Neither the outward calamities that befell the nation, nor the sins of the generality of the people, could destroy this church-state; but it continued its right and exercise unto the time of reformation. And if it be not so, if there be not causes and means of the infallible continuance of the gospel church-state unto the consummation of all things, the time expressly allotted unto their continuance, then was the work of Moses more honourable, more powerful and effectual, in the constitution of the church-state under the Old Testament, than that of Christ in the constitution of the New; for that work and those institutions which had an efficacy in them for their own infallible continuation, and of the church thereby, throughout all generations, must be more noble and honourable than those which cannot secure their own continuance, nor the being and state of the church thereon depending. Nothing can be more derogatory unto the glory of the wisdom and power of Christ, nor of his truth and faithfulness, than such an imagination. We shall, therefore, inquire into the causes and means of the continuation of this church-state, and therein show the certainty of it; as also disprove that which by some is pretended as the only means thereof, when, indeed, it is the principal argument against their perpetual continuation that can be made use of.

The *essence* and *nature* of the church instituted by the authority of Jesus Christ was always the same from the beginning that it continues still to be. But as unto its outward form and order it had a double state; and it was necessary that so it should have, from the nature of the thing itself. For,— 1. The church may be considered in its relation unto those *extraordinary officers* or rulers whose office and power was antecedent unto the church, as that by virtue whereof it was to be called and erected. 2. With respect unto *ordinary officers*, unto whose office and power the church essentially considered was antecedent; for their whole work and duty, as such, is conversant about the church, and the object is antecedent unto all acts about it.

The first state has ceased, nor can it be continued; for these officers were constituted,—1. By an *immediate call* from Christ, as was Paul, Gal. i. 1, which none now are, nor have been since the decease of them who were so called at first; 2. By *extraordinary gifts* and power, which Christ doth not continue to communicate; 3. By *divine inspiration* and infallible guidance, both in preaching the word and appointing things necessary in the churches, which none now pretend unto; 4. By *extensive commission*, giving them power towards all the world for their conversion, and over all churches for their edification. Of these officers, in their distinction into apostles and evangelists, with their call, gifts, power, and work, I have treated at large in my "Discourse of Spiritual Gifts."[1] The state and condition of the church with respect unto them has utterly ceased; and nothing can be more vain than to pretend any succession unto them, in the whole or any part of their office, unless men

---

[1] These words are printed in the original edition as if they were the title of a particular treatise by our author. His treatise under that title will be found in vol. iv. of his doctrinal works; but it seems to have been published in 1693, twelve years after the present work appeared. Such a discourse is promised in his preface to his treatise on "the Work of the Holy Spirit in Prayer," which was published in 1682, a year after the publication of the present work. There is some discussion on the subject

can justify their claim unto it by any or all of those things which concurred unto it in the apostles, which they cannot do.

But it doth not hence follow that the church-state instituted by Christ did fail thereon, or doth now so fail, because it is impossible that these apostles should have any successors in their office or the discharge of it; for by the authority of the Lord Christ, the church was to be continued under ordinary officers, without the call, gifts, or power of the others that were to cease.   Under these the church-state was no less divine than under the former; for there were two things in it:—1. That the offices themselves were of the appointment of Christ; and if they were not so, we confess the *divine right* of the church-state would have ceased.   The office of the apostles and evangelists was to cease, as hath been declared; and it did cease actually, in that Christ after them did call no more unto that office, nor provided any way or means whereby any one should be made partaker of it.   And for any to pretend a succession in office, or any part of their office, without any of those things which did constitute it, is extreme presumption.   It is therefore granted, that if there were not other offices appointed by the authority of Christ, it had not been in the power of man to make or appoint any unto that purpose, and the church-state itself must have ceased.   But this he hath done, Eph. iv. 11, 12; 1 Cor. xii. 28.   2. That persons were to be interested in these offices according unto the way and means by him prescribed; which were not such as depended on his own immediate extraordinary actings, as it was with the former sort, but such as consisted in the church's acting according to his law and in obedience unto his commands.

This church-state was appointed by the *authority of Christ*.   The direction which he gave in his own person for addresses unto the church in case of scandal, which is an obliging institution for all ages, Matt. xviii. 17–20, proves that he had appointed a church-state that should abide through them all.   And when there was a church planted at Jerusalem, there were not only apostles in it, according to its first state, but elders also, which respected its second state that was approaching, Acts xv. 23; the apostles being in office *before* that church-state, the elders [being] ordained *in* it: so chap. xi. 30.   And the apostles " ordained them elders in every church," Acts xiv. 23, Tit. i. 5, 1 Tim. v. 17; whom they affirmed to be made so by the Holy Ghost, Acts xx. 28.   The churches to whom the apostle Paul wrote his epistles were such, all of them under the rule of ordinary officers,

---

of spiritual gifts in the first chapter of his great work on the Holy Spirit; but a special and separate treatise seems alluded to in the text above.   To the " Discourse of Spiritual Gifts," as published in 1693, there is a preface by Nathaniel Mather; from which the reader is led to infer that it was then published for the first time.   Perhaps the difficulty may be obviated by the supposition that Owen intended to publish it immediately, and refers to it in this work by anticipation.—ED.

Phil. i. 1. Rules and laws are given for their ordination in all ages, Tit. i., 1 Tim. iii.; and the Lord Christ treateth from heaven with his churches in this state and order, Rev. i. ii. iii. He hath promised his presence with them unto the consummation of all things, Matt. xviii. 20, xxviii. 20, and assigned them their duty until his second coming, 1 Cor. xi. 26; with other evidences of the same truth innumerable.

Our inquiry, therefore, is, whereon the continuation of this church-state unto the end of the world doth depend; what are the causes, what are the means of it; whence it becomes infallible and necessary. I must only premise that our present consideration is not so much " de facto," as unto what hath fallen out in the world unto our knowledge and observation, but " de jure," or of a right unto this continuation; and this is such as makes it not only lawful for such a church-state to be, but requires also from all the disciples of Christ, in a way of duty, that it be always in actual existence. Hereby there is a warrant given unto all believers, at all times, to gather themselves into such a church-state, and a duty imposed on them so to do.

The reasons and causes appointing and securing this continuation are of various sorts, the principal whereof are these that follow:—

1. The supreme cause hereof is, the Father's grant of a *perpetual kingdom* in this world unto Jesus Christ, the mediator and head of the church, Ps. lxxii. 5, 7, 15–17; Isa. ix. 7; Zech. vi. 13. This grant of the Father our Lord Jesus Christ pleaded as his warranty for the foundation and continuation of the church, Matt. xxviii. 18–20. This everlasting kingdom of Jesus Christ, given him by the irrevocable grant of the Father, may be considered three ways:—

(1.) As unto the *real subjects* of it,—true believers; which are the object of the internal spiritual power and rule of Christ. Of these it is necessary, by virtue of this grant and divine constitution of the kingdom of Christ, that in every age there should be some in the world, and those perhaps no small multitude, but such as the internal rule over them may be rightly and honourably termed a kingdom. For as that which formally makes them such subjects of Christ gives them no outward appearance or visibility, so if, in a time of the universal prevalency of idolatry, there were seven thousand of these in the small kingdom of Israel, undiscerned and invisible unto the most eagle-eyed prophet who lived in their days, what number may we justly suppose to have been within the limits of Christ's dominions, which is the whole world, in the worst, darkest, most profligate, and idolatrous times, that have passed over the earth since the first erection of this kingdom? This, therefore, is a fundamental article of our faith,—that by virtue of this grant of the Father, Christ ever had, hath, and will have, in all ages, some, yea, a multitude, that are the true, real, spiritual subjects of his kingdom. Neither the power of

Satan, nor the rage or fury of the world, nor the accursed apostasy of many or of all visible churches from the purity and holiness of his laws, can hinder but that the church of Christ in this sense must have a perpetual continuation in this world, Matt. xvi. 18.

(2.) It may be considered with respect unto the *outward visible profession* of subjection and obedience unto him, and the observation of his laws. This also belongs unto the kingdom granted him of his Father. He was to have a kingdom *in* this world, though it be not *of* this world. He was to have it not only as unto its being, but as unto its glory. The world and the worst of men therein were to see and know that he hath still a kingdom and multitude of subjects depending on his rule. See the constitution of it, Dan. vii. 13, 14. Wherefore it is from hence indispensably and absolutely necessary that there should, at all times and in all ages, be ever an innumerable multitude of them who openly profess faith in Christ Jesus, and subjection of conscience unto his laws and commands. So it hath always been, so it is, and shall for ever be in this world. And those who would, on the one hand, confine the church of Christ, in this notion of it, unto any one church falling under a particular denomination, as the church of Rome, which may utterly fail; or are ready, on the other hand, upon the supposed or real errors or miscarriages of them or any of them who make this profession, to cast them out of their thoughts and affections, as those that belong not unto the kingdom or the church of Christ, are not only injurious unto them, but enemies unto the glory and honour of Christ.

(3.) This grant of the Father may be considered with respect unto *particular churches* or congregations; and the end of these churches may be twofold:—[1.] That believers, as they are internal, spiritual, real subjects of Christ's kingdom, may together act that faith and those graces whereby they are so, unto his glory. I say, it is that true believers may together and in society act all those graces of the Spirit of Christ wherein, both as unto faculty and exercise, their internal spiritual subjection unto Christ doth consist. And as this is that whereby the glory of Christ in this world doth most eminently consist,—namely, in the joint exercise of the faith and love of true believers,—so it is a principal means of the increase and augmentation of those graces in themselves, or their spiritual edification. And from this especial end of these churches it follows, that those who are members of them, or belong to them, ought to be saints by calling, or such as are endued with those spiritual principles and graces in whose exercise Christ is to be glorified; and where they are not so, the principal end of their constitution is lost. So are those churches to be made up, fundamentally and materially, of those who in their single capacity are members of the church catholic invisible. [2.] Their second end is, that those who belong unto the church and kingdom of Christ under the second consideration, as visibly professing subjection unto the rule of Christ and faith in him, may express that subjection in acts and duties of his worship, in the observance of his laws and commands, according unto his mind and will; for this alone can be done in particular churches, *be they of what sort they will;* whereof we shall speak afterward. Hence it follows, that it belongs unto the foundation of these particular churches that those who join in them do it on a public profession of faith in Christ and obedience unto him; without which this end of them also is lost. Those, I say, who make a visible profession of the name of Christ and their subjection unto him, have no way to express it regularly and according to his mind but in these particular churches wherein alone those commandments of his, in whose observance our profession consisteth, do take place, being such societies as wherein the solemn duties of his worship are performed, and his rule or discipline is exercised.

Wherefore, this state of the church also, without which both the others are imperfect, belongs unto the grant of the Father, whereby a perpetual continuation of it is secured. Nor is it of any weight to object that such hath been the alterations of the state of all churches in the world, such the visible apostasy of many of them unto false worship and idolatry, and of others into a worldly, carnal conversation, with vain traditions innumerable, that it cannot be apprehended where there were any true churches of this kind preserved and continued, but that there were an actual intercision of them all; for I answer,—First, No individual man, nay, no company of men that come together, can give a certain account of what is done in all the world, and every place of it where the name of Christ is professed; so as that what is affirmed of the state of all churches universally is mere conjecture and surmise. Secondly, There is so great a readiness in most to judge the church-state of others, because in some things they agree not in judgment or practice with what they conceive to belong thereunto, as obstructs a right judgment herein; and it hath risen of late unto such a degree of frenzy, that some deny peremptorily the church-state, and consequently the salvation, of all that have not diocesan bishops. Alas! that poor men, who are known to others, whether they are unto themselves or no, what is their office, and what is their discharge of it, should once think that the being and salvation of all churches should depend on them and such as they are; yea, some of the men of this persuasion, that Christians cannot be saved unless they comply with diocesan bishops, do yet grant that heathens may be saved without the knowledge of Christ! Thirdly, Whatever defect there hath been " de facto" in the constitution of these churches and the celebration of divine worship, in any places or ages whatever, it will not prove that there was a total failure of them, much less a discontinuation of the right of believers to reform and erect them according unto the mind of Christ.

It is hence evident that the perpetual continuation of the church-state instituted by Christ under the gospel depends originally on the grant of the kingdom unto him by his Father, with his faithfulness in that grant, and his almighty power to make it good. And they do but deceive themselves and trouble others who think of suspending this continuation on mean and low conditions of their own framing.

2. The continuation of this church-state depends *on the promise of Christ himself* to preserve and continue it. He hath assured us that he will so build his church on the rock, that "the gates of hell shall not prevail against it," Matt. xvi. 18. Under what consideration soever the church is here firstly intended, the whole state of it, as before described, is included in the promise. If the gates of hell do prevail either against the faith of sincere believers, or the catholic profession of that faith, or the expression of that profession in the duties and ordinances to be observed in particular churches, the promise fails and is of no effect.

3. It depends *on the word or law of Christ*, which gives right and title unto all believers to congregate themselves in such a church-state, with rules and commands for their so doing. Suppose,—(1.) That there are a number of believers, or the disciples of Christ, in any such place as wherein they can assemble and unite themselves or join together in a society for the worship of God; (2.) That they are as yet in no church-state, nor do know or own any power of men that can put them into that state;—I say, the institution of this church-state by the authority of Christ, his commands unto his disciples to observe therein whatever he hath commanded, and the rules he hath given whereby such a church-state is to be erected, what officers are to preside therein, and what other duties belong thereunto, are warranty sufficient for them to join themselves in such a state. Who shall make it unlawful for the disciples of Christ to obey the commands of their Lord and Master? Who shall make it lawful for them to neglect what he requires at any time? Wherever, therefore, men have the word of the Scripture to teach them their duty, it is lawful for them to comply with all the commands of Christ contained therein. And whereas there are many privileges and powers accompanying this church-state, and those who are interested therein are, as such, the especial object of many divine promises, this word and law of Christ doth make a conveyance of them all unto those who, in obedience unto his institutions and commands, do enter into that state by the way and means that he hath appointed. Whilst we hear him, according to the reiterated direction given us from heaven, whilst we do and observe all that he hath commanded us, we need not fear that promised presence of his with

us, which brings along with it all church power and privileges also. Wherefore, this state can have no intercision but on a supposition that there are none in the world who are willing to obey the commands of Christ; which utterly overthrows the very being of the church catholic.

4. It depends on *the communication of spiritual gifts* for the work of the ministry in this church-state, as is expressly declared, Eph. iv. 8, 11–15. The continuation of the church, as unto the essence of it, depends on the communication of saving grace. If Christ should no more give of his grace and Spirit unto men, there would be no more a church in the world, as unto its internal form and essence. But the continuation of the church as it is organical,—that is, a society incorporated according unto the mind of Christ, with rulers and officers for the authoritative administration of all its concerns, especially for the preaching of the word and administration of the sacraments,—depends on the communication of spiritual gifts and abilities; and if the Lord Jesus Christ should withhold the communication of spiritual gifts, this church-state must cease. An image of it may be erected, but the true church-state will fail; for that will hold no longer, but whilst the "whole body fitly joined together and compacted by that which every joint supplieth, according to the effectual working in the measure of every part, maketh increase of the body unto the edifying of itself in love," Eph. iv. 16; whilst it "holds the Head," etc., Col. ii. 19. Such dead, lifeless images are many churches in the world. But this communication of spiritual gifts unto the use of his disciples, to the end of the world, the Lord Christ hath taken the charge of on himself, as he is faithful in the administration of his kingly power, Eph. iv. 8, 11–15.

Whereas, therefore, the Lord Christ, in the exercise of his right and power, on the grant of the Father of a perpetual visible kingdom in this world, and the discharge of his own promise, hath,—(1.) Appointed the ordinary offices, which he will have continue in his church by an unalterable institution; (2.) Ordained that persons shall be called and set apart unto those offices, and for the discharge of that work and those duties which he hath declared to belong thereunto; (3.) Furnished them with gifts and abilities for this work, and declared what their spiritual qualifications and moral endowments ought to be; (4.) Made it the duty of believers to observe all his institutions and commands, whereof those which concern the erection and continuance of this church-state are the principal; and, (5.) Hath, in their so doing, or their observance of all his commands, promised his presence with them, by which, as by a charter of right, he hath conveyed unto them an interest in all the power, privileges, and promises that belong unto this state;—it is evident that its perpetual continuation depends hereon and is secured hereby. He hath not left this great concernment of his glory unto the wills of men, or any order they shall think meet to appoint.

Lastly: As a means of it, it depends on three things in believers themselves:—(1.) *A due sense of their duty,* to be found in obedience unto all the commands of Christ. Hereby they find themselves indispensably obliged unto all those things which are necessary unto the continuation of this state; and that all believers should absolutely at any time live in a total neglect of their duty, though they may greatly mistake in the manner of its performance, is not to be supposed. (2.) *The instinct of the new creature* and those in whom it is to associate themselves in holy communion, for the joint and mutual exercise of those graces of the Spirit, which are the same, as unto the essence of them, in them all. The laws of Christ in and unto his church, as unto all outward obedience, are suited unto those inward principles and inclinations which, by his Spirit and grace, he hath implanted in the hearts of them that believe. Hence his yoke is easy, and his commandments are not grievous. And therefore none of his true disciples, since he had a church upon the earth, did or could satisfy themselves in their own faith and obedience, singularly and personally; but would venture their lives and all that was dear unto them for communion with others, and the associating themselves with them of the same spirit and way, for the observance of the commands of Christ. The martyrs of the primitive churches of old lost more of their blood and lives for their meetings and assemblies than for personal profession of the faith; and so also have others done under the Roman apostasy. It is a usual plea among them who engage in the persecution or punishment of such as differ from them, that if they please they may keep their opinions, their consciences, and faith unto themselves, without meetings for communion or public worship; and herein they suppose they deal friendly and gently with them. And this is our present case. It is true, indeed, as Tertullian observed of old, that men in these things have no power over us but what they have from our own wills: we willingly choose to be, and to continue, what they take advantage to give us trouble for. And it is naturally in our power to free ourselves from them and their laws every day. But we like it not; we cannot purchase outward peace and quietness at any such rate. But, as was said, the inward instinct of believers, from the same principles of faith, love, and all the graces of the Spirit in them all, doth efficaciously lead and incline them unto their joint exercise in societies, unto the glory of Christ, and their own edification, or increase of the same graces in them. When this appears to be under the guidance of the commands of Christ, as unto the ways of communion led unto, and to consist in a compliance therewithal, they find themselves under an indispensable obligation unto it. Nor hath the Lord Christ left them liberty to make a composition for their outward peace, and to purchase quietness with foregoing any part of their duty herein.

This, therefore, I say, is a means and cause on the part of believers themselves of the continuation of this church-state: for this instinct of believers, leading them unto communion, which is an article of our faith, in conjunction with the law and commands of Christ giving direction how and in what ways it is to be attained and exercised, binds and obliges them unto the continuation of this state; and the decay of this inward principle in them that profess Christian religion hath been the great and almost only ground of its neglect. (3.) The open evidence there is that sundry duties required of us in the gospel can never be performed in a due manner but where believers are brought into this state; which that they should enter into is, therefore, in the first place required of them. What these duties are will afterward appear.

On these sure grounds is founded the continuation of the gospel church-state, under ordinary officers, after the decease of the apostles; and so far secured as that nothing needs be added unto them for that end. Do but suppose that the Lord Christ yet liveth in heaven in the discharge of his mediatory office; that he hath given his word for a perpetual law unto all his disciples, and a charter to convey spiritual privileges unto them; that he abides to communicate gifts for the ministry unto men; and that there are any believers in the world who know it to be their duty to yield obedience unto all the commands of Christ, and have any internal principle inclining them to that which they profess to believe as a fundamental article of their faith, namely, the communion of saints;—and no man is desired to prove the certainty and necessity of the continuance of this state.

But there are some who maintain that the continuation and preservation of this church-state depends solely on a successive ordination of church-officers from the apostles, and so down throughout all ages unto the end of the world; for this, they say, is the only means of conveying church-power from one time to another, so as that if it fail, all church-state, order, and power must fail, never in this world to be recovered. There is, they say, a flux of power through the hands of the ordainers unto the ordained, by virtue of their outward ordination, whereon the being of the church doth depend. Howbeit those who use this plea are not at all agreed about those things which are essential in and unto this successive ordination. Some think that the Lord Christ committed the keys of the kingdom of heaven unto Peter only, and he to the *bishop of Rome* alone; from whose person, therefore, all their ordination must be derived. Some think, and those on various grounds, that it is committed unto all and only *diocesan bishops;* whose being and beginning are very uncertain.   Others require no more unto it but that *presbyters* be ordained by presbyters, who are rejected in their plea by both the former sorts. And other differences almost innumerable among them who are thus minded might be reckoned up.

But whereas this whole argument about personal successive ordination hath been fully handled, and the pretences of it disproved, by the chiefest protestant writers against the Papists, and because I design not an opposition unto what others think and do, but the declaration and confirmation of the truth in what we have proposed to insist upon, I shall very briefly discover the falseness of this pretence, and pass on unto what is principally intended in this discourse.

1. The church is before all its ordinary officers; and therefore its continuation cannot depend on their successive ordination.   It is so as essentially considered, though its being organical is simultaneous with their ordination.   Extraordinary officers were before the church, for their work was to call, gather, and erect it out of the world; but no ordinary officers can be or ever were ordained, but to a church in being. Some say they are ordained unto the universal visible church of professors, some unto the particular church wherein their work doth lie; but all grant that the church-state whereunto they are ordained is antecedent unto their ordination.   The Lord Christ could and did ordain apostles and evangelists when there was yet no gospel church; for they were to be the instruments of its calling and erection.   But the apostles neither did nor could ordain any ordinary officers until there was a church or churches, with respect whereunto they should be ordained.   It is, therefore, highly absurd to ascribe the continuation of the church unto the successive ordination of officers, if any such thing there were, seeing this successive ordination of officers depends solely on the continuation of the church.   If that were not secured on other foundations, this successive ordination would quickly tumble into dust.   (Yea, this successive ordination, were there any such thing appointed, must be an act of the church itself, and so cannot be the means of communicating church-power unto others.   A successive ordination in some sense may be granted, —namely, that when those who were ordained officers in any church do die, others be ordained in their steads; but this is by an act of power in the church itself, as we shall manifest afterward.)

2. Not to treat of papal succession, the limiting of this successive ordination, as the only way and means of communicating church-power, and so of the preservation of the church-state, unto diocesan prelates or bishops, is built on so many inevident presumptions and

false principles as will leave it altogether uncertain whether there be any church-state in the world or no; as,—(1) That such bishops were ordained by the *apostles;* which can never be proved. (2.) That they received power from the apostles to ordain others, and communicate *their whole power* unto them, by an authority inherent in themselves alone, yet still reserving their whole power unto themselves also, giving all and retaining all at the same time; which hath no more of truth than the former, and may be easily disproved. (3.) That they never did nor could, any of them, *forfeit* this power by any crime or error, so as to render their ordination invalid, and interrupt the succession pretended. (4.) That they all ordained others in such *manner* and way as to render their ordination valid, whereas multitudes were never agreed what is required thereunto. (5.) That whatever heresy, idolatry, flagitiousness of life, persecution of the true churches of Christ, these prelatical ordainers might fall into; by whatever arts, simoniacal practices, or false pretences unto what was not, they came themselves into their offices; yet nothing could deprive them of their right of *communicating all church-power* unto others by ordination. (6.) That persons so ordained, whether they have any call from the church or no; whether they have any of the qualifications required by the law of Christ in the Scripture to make them capable of any office in the church, or have received any *spiritual gifts* from Christ for the exercise of their office and discharge of their duty; whether they have any design or no to pursue the ends of that office which they take upon them;—yet all is one, being any way prelatically-ordained bishops, they may ordain others, and so the successive ordination is preserved. And what is this but to take the rule of the church out of the hand of Christ, to give law unto him, to follow with his approbation the actings of men besides and contrary to his law and institution, and to make application of his promises unto the vilest of men, whether he will or no? (7.) That it is not lawful for believers, or the disciples of Christ, to yield obedience unto his commands without this episcopal ordination; which many churches cannot have, and more will not, as judging it against the mind and will of Christ. (8.) That one worldly, ignorant, proud, sensual beast, such as some of the heads of this successive ordination, as the popes of Rome, have been, should have more power and authority from Christ to preserve and continue a church state by ordination, than any the most holy church in the world that is or can be gathered according to his mind; with other unwarrantable presumptions innumerable.

3. The pernicious consequences that may ensue on this principle do manifest its inconsistency with what our Lord Jesus Christ hath ordained unto this end, of the continuation of his church. I need

not reckon them up on the surest probabilities. There is no room left for fears of what may follow hereon, by what hath already done so. If we consider whither this successive ordination hath already led a great part of the church, we may easily judge what it is meet for. It hath, I say, led men, for instance in the church of Rome, into a presumption of a good church-state, in the loss of holiness and truth, in the practice of false worship and idolatry, in the persecution and slaughter of the faithful servants of Christ,—unto a state plainly antichristian. To think there should be a flux and communication of heavenly and spiritual power from Jesus Christ and his apostles, in and by the hands and actings of persons ignorant, simoniacal, adulterous, incestuous, proud, ambitious, sensual, presiding in a church-state never appointed by him, immersed in false and idolatrous worship, persecuting the true church of Christ, wherein was the true succession of apostolical doctrine and holiness, is an imagination for men who embrace the shadows and appearances of things, never once seriously thinking of the true nature of them. In brief, it is in vain to derive a succession, whereon the being of the church should depend, through the presence of Christ with the bishops of Rome, who for a hundred years together, from the year 900 to 1000, were monsters for ignorance, lust, pride, and luxury, as Baronius acknowledgeth, A. D. 912. 5, 8; or by the church of Antioch, by Samosatenus, Eudoxius, Gnapheus, Severus, and the like heretics; or in Constantinople, by Macedonius, Eusebius, Demophilus, Anthorinus, and their companions; or at Alexandria, by Lucius, Dioscorus, Ælurus, Sergius, and the rest of the same sort.

4. The principal argument whereby this conceit is fully discarded must be spoken unto afterward. And this is the due consideration of the proper subject of all church-power, unto whom it is originally, formally, and radically given and granted by Jesus Christ; for none can communicate this power unto others but those who have received it themselves from Christ, by virtue of his law and institution. Now, this is the whole church, and not any person in it or prelate over it. Look, whatever constitutes it a church, that gives it all the power and privilege of a church; for a church is nothing but a society of professed believers, enjoying all church-power and privileges, by virtue of the law of Christ. Unto this church, which is his spouse, doth the Lord Christ commit the keys of his house; by whom they are delivered into the hands of his stewards, so far as their office requires that trust. Now, this (which we shall afterward more fully confirm) is utterly inconsistent with the committing of all church-power unto one person by virtue of his ordination by another.

Nothing that hath been spoken doth at all hinder or deny but that, where churches are rightly constituted, they ought, in their offices, officers, and order, to be preserved by a successive ordination of pastors and rulers, wherein those who actually preside in them have a particular interest in the orderly communication of church-power unto them.

CHAPTER IV.

The especial nature of the gospel church-state appointed by Christ.

THE principal inquiry, which we have thus far prepared the way unto, and whereon all that ensues unto it doth depend, is concerning the especial nature of that church-state, rule, and order, which the Lord Christ hath instituted under the gospel, of what sort and kind it is; and hereunto some things must be premised:—

1. I design not here to oppose, nor any way to consider, such *additions* as men may have judged necessary to be added unto that church-state which Christ hath appointed, to render it, in their apprehension, more useful unto its ends than otherwise it would be. Of this sort there are many things in the world, and of a long season have been so. But our present business is to prove the truth, and not to disprove the conceits of other men. And so far as our cause is concerned herein, it shall be done by itself, so as not to interrupt us in the declaration of the truth.

2. Whereas there are great contests about communion with churches, or separation from them, and mutual charges of impositions and schisms thereon, they must be all regulated by this inquiry,—namely, What is that church-state which Christ hath prescribed? Herein alone is conscience concerned as unto all duties of ecclesiastical communion. Neither can a charge of schism be managed against any but on a supposition of sin with respect unto that church-state and order which Christ hath appointed. A dissent from any thing else, however pretended to be useful, yea, advantageous unto church ends, must come under other prudential considerations. All which shall be fully proved, and vindicated from the exceptions of Dr Stillingfleet.

3. There have been and are in the world several sorts of churches of great power and reputation, of several forms and kinds, yet contributing aid to each other in their respective stations; as,—(1.) The *papal* church, which pretends itself to be catholic or universal, comprehensive of all true believers or disciples of Christ, united in their subjection unto the bishop of Rome. (2.) There were of old, and the shadow of them is still remaining, churches called *patriarchal*, first three, then four, then five of them, whereinto all other churches

and professed Christians in the Roman world were distributed, as unto a dependence on the authority, and subjection to the jurisdiction and order, of the bishops of five principal cities of the empire; who were thereon called patriarchs. (3.) Various divisions under them of *archiepiscopal* or metropolitical churches; and under them of those that are now called diocesan, whose bounds and limits were fixed and altered according to the variety of occasions and occurrences of things in the nations of the world. What hath been the original of all these sorts of churches, how from parochial assemblies they grew up, by the degrees of their descent now mentioned, into the height and centre of papal omnipotency, hath been declared elsewhere sufficiently.*

4. Some there are who plead for a *national* church-state, arising from an association of the officers of particular churches, in several degrees, which they call *classical* and *provincial,* until it extend itself unto the limits of a whole nation; that is, one civil body, depending as such on its own supreme ruler and law. I shall neither examine nor oppose this opinion; there hath been enough, if not too much, already disputed about it. But,—

5. The visible church-state which Christ hath instituted under the New Testament consists in *an especial society or congregation of professed believers, joined together according unto his mind, with their officers, guides, or rulers, whom he hath appointed, which do or may meet together for the celebration of all the ordinances of divine worship, the professing and authoritatively proposing the doctrine of the gospel, with the exercise of the discipline prescribed by himself, unto their own mutual edification, with the glory of Christ, in the preservation and propagation of his kingdom in the world.*

The things observable in this description, and for the farther declaration of it, are,—(1.) The *material cause* of this church, or the matter whereof it is composed, which are *visible believers.* (2.) The *formal cause* of it, which is their voluntary coalescency into such a society or congregation, according to the mind of Christ. (3.) The *end of it* is, presential local communion, in all the ordinances and institutions of Christ, in obedience unto him and [for] their own edification. (4.) In particular these ends are,—[1.] The *preaching of the word,* unto the edification of the church itself and the conversion of others; [2.] *Administration* of the sacraments, or all the mystical appointments of Christ in the church; [3.] The preservation and exercise of *evangelical discipline,* [4.] Visibly to profess their *subjection* unto Christ in the world by the observation of his commands. (5.) The *bounds* and limits of this church are taken from the number of the members; which ought not to be so small as that they cannot observe and do all that Christ hath commanded in due order, nor yet so great as not to meet together for the ends of the institution of the church before mentioned.   (6.) That this church, in its complete state, consists of *pastors*, or *a pastor and elders*, who are its guides and rulers; and the community of the faithful under their rule.   (7.) That unto such a church, and every one of them, belong of right all the privileges, promises, and power that Christ doth give and grant unto the church in this world.

These, and sundry other things of the like nature, shall be afterward spoken unto in their order, according unto the method intended in the present discourse.

Two things I shall now proceed unto:—First, To prove that Christ hath appointed this church-state under the gospel,—namely, of a particular or single congregation.   Secondly, That he hath appointed no other church-state that is inconsistent with this, much less that is destructive of it:—

First, Christ appointed that church-state which is meet and accommodated unto all the ends which he designed in his institution of a church.   But such alone is that church form and order that we have proposed.   In Christ's institution of the church, it was none of his ends that some men might be thereby advanced to rule, honour, riches, or secular grandeur, but the direct contrary, Matt. xx. 25–28. Nor did he do it that his disciples might be ruled and governed by force or the laws of men, or that they should be obstructed in the exercise of any graces, gifts, or privileges that he had purchased for them or would bestow on them.   And to speak plainly (let it be despised by them that please), this cannot greatly value that church-state which is not suited to guide, excite, and direct the exercise of all evangelical graces unto the glory of Christ in a due manner; for to propose peculiar and proper objects for them, to give peculiar motives unto them, to limit the seasons and circumstances of their exercise, and regulate the manner of the performance of the duties that arise from them, is one principal end of its institution.

It would be too long to make a particular inquiry into all the ends for which the Lord Christ appointed this church-state; which, indeed, are all the duties of the gospel, either in themselves or in the manner of their performance.   We may reduce them unto these three general heads:—

1. The *professed subjection* of the souls and consciences of believers unto his authority, in their observance of his commandments. He requireth that all who are baptized into his name be taught to do and observe "all things whatsoever he hath commanded," Matt. xxviii. 18–20.   And God is to be glorified, not only in their subjection, but in their " professed subjection unto the gospel of Christ," 2 Cor. ix. 13.

Having given an express charge unto his disciples to make public profession of his name, and not to be deterred from it by shame or fear of any thing that may befall them on the account thereof, and that on the penalty of his disowning them before his heavenly Father, Mark viii. 34–38, Matt. x. 33, he hath appointed this church-state as the way and means whereby they may jointly and visibly make profession of this their subjection to him, dependence on him, and freedom in the observation of all his commands. He will not have this done singly and personally only, but in society and conjunction. Now, this cannot be done, in any church-state imaginable wherein the members of the church cannot meet together for this end; which they can only do in such a church as is congregational.

2. The *joint celebration* of all gospel ordinances and worship is the great and principal end of the evangèlical church-state. How far this is directed unto by the law of nature was before declared. Man was made for society in things natural and civil, but especially in things spiritual, or such as concern the worship of God. Hereon depends the necessity of particular churches, or societies for divine worship. And this is declared to be the end of the churches instituted by Christ, Acts ii. 42; 1 Cor. v. 4, xi. 20; 2 Tim. ii. 1, 2; as also of the institution of officers in the church, for the solemn administration of the ordinances of his worship. And the reasons of this appointment are intimated in the Scripture; as,—(1.) That it might be a way for *the joint exercise* of the graces and gifts of the Spirit, as was in general before mentioned. The Lord Christ gives both his grace and his gifts in great variety of measures, Eph. iv. 7, but "the manifestation of the Spirit is given unto every man to profit withal," 1 Cor. xii. 7–10. He gives neither of them unto any merely for themselves. Saving grace is firstly given for the good of him that receives it, but respect is had in it unto the good of others; and the Lord Christ expects such an exercise of it as may be to others' advantage. And the first end of gifts is the edification of others; and all that do receive them are thereby and so far "stewards of the manifold grace of God," 1 Pet. iv. 10. Wherefore, for the due exercise of these gifts and graces unto his glory and their proper ends, he hath appointed particular congregations, in whose assemblies alone they can be duly exercised. (2.) Hereby all his disciples are *mutually edified;* that is, increased in light, knowledge, faith, love, fruitfulness in obedience, and conformity unto himself. This the apostle affirms to be the especial end of all churches, their offices, officers, gifts, and order, Eph. iv. 12–16, and again, chap. ii. 19–22. No church-state that is not immediately suited unto this end is of his institution; and though others may in general pretend unto it, besides that of particular congregations, it were to be wished that they were

not obstructive of it, or were any way fitted or useful unto it. (3.) That he might hereby express and testify his *promised presence* with his disciples unto the end of the world, Matt. xxviii. 20, xviii. 20; Rev. i. 13. It is in their church assemblies, and in the performance of his holy worship, that he is present with his disciples according unto his promise. (4.) In these churches, thus exercised in the holy worship of God, he gives us *a resemblance* and representation of the great assembly above, who worship God continually before his throne; which is too large a subject here to insist upon.

And to manifest that assemblies of the whole church, at once and in one place, for the celebration of divine worship, is of the essence of a church, without which it hath no real being; when God had instituted such a church-form as wherein all the members of it could not ordinarily come together every week for this end, yet he ordained that, for the preservation of their church-state, three times in the year the males (which was the circumcised church) should appear together in one place to celebrate the most solemn ordinances of his worship, Exod. xxiii. 14, xxxiv. 23; Deut. xvi. 16. All those difficulties which arose from the extent of the limits of that church unto the whole nation being removed, these meetings of the whole church for the worship of God become a continual duty; and when they cannot be observed in any church, the state or kind of it is not instituted by Christ.

3. The third end of the institution of the gospel church-state is the exercise and *preservation of the discipline* appointed by Christ to be observed by his disciples. The ancients do commonly call the whole religion of Christianity by the name of the "discipline of Christ," —that is, the faith and obedience which he hath prescribed unto them, in contradistinction and opposition unto the rules and prescriptions of all philosophical societies; and it is that without which the glory of Christian religion can in no due manner be preserved. The especial nature of it shall be afterward fully spoken unto. For the use of the present argument I shall only speak unto the ends of it, or what it is that the Lord Christ designeth in the institution of it; and these things may be referred unto four heads:—

(1.) *The preservation of the doctrine of the gospel in its purity,* and obedience unto the commands of Christ in its integrity. For the first, the Scripture is full of predictions, all confirmed in the event, that after the days of the apostles there should be various attempts to wrest, corrupt, and pervert the doctrine of the gospel, and to bring in pernicious errors and heresies. To prevent, or reprove and remove them, is no small part of the duty of the ministerial office, in the dispensation of the word. But whereas those who taught such perverse things did for the most part arise at first in the churches

themselves, Acts xx 30, 2 Pet. ii. 1, 1 John ii. 19, as the preaching
of the word was appointed for the rebuke of the doctrines themselves, so this discipline was ordained in the church with respect
unto the persons of them by whom they were taught, Rev. ii. 2,
14, 20; 3 John 8, 9; Gal. v. 12. And so also it was with respect
unto schisms and divisions that might fall out in the church. The
way of suppressing things of this nature by external force, by the
sword of magistrates, in prisons, fines, banishments, and death, was
not then thought of, nor directed unto by the Lord Jesus Christ,
but is highly dishonourable unto him; as though the ways of his
own appointment were not sufficient for the preservation of his own
truth, but that his disciples must betake themselves unto the secular powers of this world, who for the most part are wicked, profane,
and ignorant of the truth, for that end.

And hereunto belongeth the preservation of his *commands* in the
integrity of obedience; for he appointed that hereby care should be
taken of the ways, walkings, and conversations of his disciples, that
in all things it should be such as became the gospel. Hence, the
exercise of this discipline he ordained to consist in exhortations,
admonitions, reproofs, of any that should offend in things moral or
of his especial institution, with the total rejection of them that
were obstinate in their offences; as we shall see afterward.

(2.) The second end of it was to *preserve love entire* among his
disciples. This was that which he gave in especial charge unto all
that should believe in his name, taking the command of it to be his
own in a peculiar manner, and declaring our observance of it to be
the principal pledge and evidence of our being his disciples; for although mutual love be an "old commandment," belonging both unto
the moral law and sundry injunctions under the Old Testament, yet
the degrees and measure of it, the ways and duties of its exercise, the
motives unto it and reasons for it, were wholly his own, whereby it
becomes a "new commandment" also. For the preservation and continuance of this love, which he lays so great weight upon, was this
discipline appointed, which it is several ways effectual towards; as,—
[1.] In the prevention or removal of offences that might arise among
believers, to the impeachment of it, Matt. xviii. 15–17; [2.] In that
watch over each other, with mutual exhortations and admonitions,
without which this love, let men pretend what they please, will not
be preserved. That which keepeth either life or soul in Christian
love consists in the exercise of those graces mutually, and the discharge of those duties whereby they may be partakers of the fruits
of love in one another. And, for the most part, those who pretend
highly unto the preservation of love, by their coming to the same
church who dwell in the same parish, have not so much as the carcase,

nay, not a shadow of it. In the discipline of the Lord Christ it is appointed that this love, so strictly by him enjoined unto us, so expressive of his own wisdom and love, should be preserved, continued, and increased by the due and constant discharge of the duties of mutual exhortation, admonition, prayer, and watchful care over one another, Rom. xv. 14; 1 Thess. v. 11, 12; 2 Thess. iii. 15; Heb. iii. 12, 13, xii. 15, 16.

(3.) A third end of it is, that it might be *a due representation of his own love*, care, tenderness, patience, meekness, in the acting of his authority in the church. Where this is not observed and designed in the exercise of church-discipline, I will not say it is antichristian, but will say it is highly injurious, and dishonourable unto him; for all church-power is in him and derived from him. Nor is there any thing of that nature which belongs unto it, but it must be acted in his name, and esteemed, both for the manner and matter of it, to be his act and deed. For men, therefore, to pretend unto the exercise of this discipline in a worldly frame of spirit, with pride and passion, by tricks of laws and canons, in courts foreign to the churches themselves which are pretended to be under this discipline, it is a woful and scandalous representation of Christ, his wisdom, care, and love towards his church. But as for his discipline, he hath ordained that it shall be exercised in and with meekness, patience, gentleness, evidence of zeal for the good and compassion of the souls of men, with gravity and authority; so as that therein all the holy affections of his mind towards his church or any in it, in their mistakes, failings, and miscarriages, may be duly represented, as well as his authority acted among them, Isa. xl. 11; 2 Cor. x. 1; Gal. v. 22, 23; 1 Thess. ii. 7; 2 Tim. ii. 24–26; James iii. 17; 1 Cor. xiii.

(4.) It is in part appointed to be an evidence and pledge of *the future judgment*, wherein the whole church shall be judged before the throne of Christ Jesus; for in the exercise of this discipline Christ is on his own judgment-seat in the church: nor may any man pronounce any sentence but what he believeth that Christ himself would pronounce were he visibly present, and what is according to his mind as declared in his word. Hence Tertullian calls the sentence of excommunication in the church, "Futuri judicii præjudicium," —a representation of the future judgment.

In all that degeneracy which the Christian professing church hath fallen into, in faith, worship, and manners, there is no instance can exceed the corruption of this *divine institution:* for that which was the honour of Christ and the gospel, and an effectual means to represent him in the glory of his wisdom and love, and for the exercise of all graces in the church, unto the blessed ends now declared, was turned into a domination, earthly and secular, exercised in a profane, litigious, unintelligible process, according unto the arts, ways, and terms of the worst of law courts, by persons for the most part remote from any just pretence of the least interest in church-power, on causes and for ends foreign unto the discipline of the gospel, by a tyranny over the consciences and over the persons of the disciples of Christ, unto the intolerable scandal of the gospel and rule of Christ in his church; as is evident in the state and rule of the church of Rome. As these are the general ends of the institution of a church-state under the gospel, and in order unto them, it is a great divine ordinance for the glory of Christ, with the edification and salvation of them that do believe. Wherefore, that church-state which is suited unto these ends is that which is appointed by Christ; and whatever kind of church or churches is not so, primarily and as such, are not of his appointment. But it is in congregational churches alone that these things can be done and observed; for unto all of them there are required assemblies of the whole church, which, wherever they are, that church is congregational. No such churches as those mentioned before,—papal, patriarchical, metropolitical, diocesan, or in any way national,—are capable of the discharge of these duties or attaining of these ends. If it be said, that what they cannot do in themselves, as that they cannot together in one place profess and express their subjection unto the commands of Christ, they cannot have personal communion in the celebration of gospel ordinances of worship, nor exercise discipline in one body and society, they can yet do the same things otherwise, partly in single congregations appointed by themselves, and partly in such ways, for the administration of discipline, as are suited unto their state and rule,— that is, by ecclesiastical courts, with jurisdiction over all persons or congregations belonging unto them,—it will not help their cause; for,—(1.) Those particular congregations wherein these things are to be observed are churches, or they are not. If they are churches, they are of Christ's appointment, and we obtain what we aim at; nor is it in the power of any man to deprive them of any thing that belongs unto them as such. If they are not, but inventions and appointments of their own, then that which they say is this, that " what is absolutely necessary unto the due observation of the worship of God, and unto all the ends of churches, being not appointed by Christ, is by them provided for, appointed, and ordained;" which is to exalt themselves in wisdom and care above him, and to place themselves in a nearer relation to the church than he. To grant that many of those things which are the ends for which any church-state under the gospel is appointed, cannot be performed or attained but in and by particular congregations, and yet to deny that those particular congregations are of Christ's institution, is to speak contradictions, and at the same time to affirm that they are churches and are not churches.   (2.) A church is such a body or society as hath spiritual power, privileges, and promises annexed unto it and accompanying of it.   That which hath not so, as such, is no church.   The particular congregations mentioned have this power, with privileges and promises belonging to them, or they have not.   If they have not, they are no churches, at least no complete churches; and there are no churches in the earth wherein those things can be done for which the being of churches was ordained,—as, namely, the joint celebration of divine worship by all the members of them.   If they have such power, I desire to know from whence or whom they have it; if from Christ, then are they of his institution, and who can divest them of that power, or any part of it?   That they have it from men, I suppose will not be pretended.   (3.) As unto that way of the exercise of discipline suited unto any other church-state but that which is con-- gregational, we shall consider it afterward.   (4.) What is done in particular congregations is not the act of any greater church, as a diocesan, or the like; for whatever acts any thing, acts according unto what it is.   But this of joint worship and discipline in assemblies is not the act of such a church according unto what it is; for so it is impossible for it to do any thing of that nature.   But thus it is fallen out.   Some men, under the power of a tradition that particular congregations were originally of a divine institution, and finding the absolute necessity of them unto the joint celebration of divine worship, yet finding what an inconsistency with their interest, and some other opinions which they have imbibed, should they still be acknowledged to be of the institution of Christ, seeing thereon the whole ordinary power given by Christ unto his church must reside in them, they would now have them to be only conveniences for some ends of worship of their own finding out.   Something they would have like Christ's institution, but his it shall not be; which is an image.

Secondly, The very *notation of the word* doth determine the sense of it unto a particular congregation.   Other things may in churches, as we shall see afterward, both in the rule and administration of the duties of holy worship, be ordered and disposed in great variety; but whilst a church is such as that ordinarily the whole body, in its rulers and those that are ruled, do assemble together in one place for the administration of gospel ordinances and the exercise of discipline, it is still one single congregation, and can be neither diocesan, provincial, nor national: so that although the essence of the church doth not consist in actual assemblies, yet are they absolutely necessary unto its constitution in exercise.

Hence is the name of a church. קָהַל, the verb in the Old Testament, is to congregate, to assemble, to call and meet together, and

nothing else.   The LXX. render it mostly by ἐκκλησιάζω, to congregate in a church-assembly; and sometimes by other words of the
same importance, as συνίστημι, συνάγω, ἐπισυνάγω.   So they do the noun
קָהָל by συναγωγή, ἐκκλησία, seldom by any other word; but where they
do so it is always of the same signification.   Wherefore, this word
signifies nothing but a congregation which assembles for the ends
and uses of it, and acts its duties and powers; so doth ἐκκλησία also
in the New Testament.   It may be sometimes applied unto that
whose essence is not denoted thereby, as the church catholic invisible, which is only a mystical society or congregation.   But where-
ever it is used to denote an outward visible society, it doth connote
their assembling together in one.   It is frequently used for an actual
assembly, Acts xix. 32, 39, 40, which was the signification of it in
all Greek writers, 1 Cor. xiv. 4, 5; and sometimes it is expressly
affirmed that it "met together in the same place," chap. xiv. 23.
Wherefore, no society that doth not congregate, the whole body
whereof doth not meet together, to act its powers and duties, is a
church, or may be so called, whatever sort of body or corporation it
may be.

In this sense is the word used when the first intimation is given of
an evangelical church-state with order and discipline: Matt. xviii.
17, "If he shall neglect to hear them, tell the church," etc.   There
have been so many contests about the sense of these words and the
interpretation of them, so many various and opposite opinions about
them, and those debated in such long and operose discourses, that
some would take an argument from thence that nothing can be
directly proved from them, nor any certain account of the state and
duty of the church be thence collected.   But nothing can be insinuated more false and absurd, nor which more directly tendeth to the
overthrow of the whole authority of the Scripture; for if when men
are seduced, by their interests or otherwise, to multiply false exposi-
tions of any place of Scripture, and to contend earnestly about them,
thereon, as unto us, they lose their instructive power and certain
determination of the truth, we should quickly have no bottom or
foundation for our faith in the most important articles of religion, nor
could have so at this day.   But all the various pretences of men,—
some whereof would have the pope, others a general council, some
the civil magistrate, some the Jewish synagogue, some a company
of arbitrators,—are nothing but so many instances of what interest,
prejudice, corrupt lusts, ambitious designs, with a dislike of the
truth, will bring forth.   To me it seems strange that any impartial
man, reading the context, can take " the church" in this place in any
other sense but for such a society as whereunto an offending and
offended brother or disciple of Christ might and ought to belong, to

the body whereof they might address themselves for relief and remedy, or the removal of offences, by virtue of the authority and appointment of Jesus Christ.

It were an endless task, and unsuited unto our present design, to examine the various pretensions unto the church in this place: enough, also, if not too much, hath been written already about them. I shall, therefore, observe only some few things from the context, which will sufficiently evidence what sort of church it is that is here intended:—

1. The rule and direction given by our Saviour in this place unto his disciples doth not concern *civil injuries* as such, but such sins as have *scandal* and offence in them, either causing other men to sin, or giving them grief and offence for sin; whereby the exercise of love in mutual communion may be impeded. Private injuries may be respected herein, but not as injuries, but so far as they are scandalous, and matter of offence unto them unto whom they are known. And this appears,—

(1.) From the proper signification of the phrase here used: 'Εὰν ἁμαρτήσῃ εἰς σέ—" If thy brother sin against thee." Doing of an injury is expressed by ἀδικέω, and to be injured by ἀποστερέομαι, 1 Cor. vi. 7, 8,—that is, to be wronged, to be dealt unjustly withal, and to be defrauded or deprived of our right; but ἁμαρτάνω εἰς is not used but only for so to sin as to give scandal unto them against whom that sin is said to be, 1 Cor. viii. 11, 12. To be guilty of "sin against Christ," in the light of their consciences, is to " sin against them."

(2.) It is evident in the context. Our Saviour is treating directly about all sorts of scandals and offences, or sins, as occasions of falling, stumbling, and sinning, and so of perishing unto others, giving rules and directions about them from the eighth verse unto these words wherein direction is given about their cure and removal. And two things he ascribes unto these scandals,—first, That weak Christians are *despised* in them, verse 10; secondly, That they are in danger to be *destroyed* or lost for ever by them, verse 14; which gives us a true account of the nature of scandalous offences. Wherefore ἁμαρτάνω, to sin, is used here in the same sense with σκανδαλίζω before, to give offence by a scandalous miscarriage.

(3.) Where the same rule is again recorded, the words used enforce this application of them, Luke xvii. 1–3. The Lord Christ foretells his disciples that scandals and offences would arise, with the nature and danger of them, verse 1. And because that they obtain their pernicious effects mostly on them that are weak, he gives caution against them with especial respect to such among his disciples: "Better any one were cast into the sea," ἢ ἵνα σκανδαλίσῃ ἕνα τῶν μικρῶν τούτων,—" than that he should give scandal or offence unto one of these little ones," verse 2. And what he expresseth by σκανδαλίση, verse 2, he expresseth by ἀμάρτη εἰς σέ, verse 3, " sin against thee;" and this is plain from the direction which he gives hereon, ἐπιτίμησον αὐτῷ, " rebuke him." The word is never used with respect unto private injuries, but as they are sins or faults; so is it joined with ἔλεγξον, 2 Tim. iv. 2. And ἐπιτιμία is the only word used for the rebuke given, or to be given, unto a scandalous offender, 2 Cor. ii. 6.

(4.) Another rule is given in case of private injuries that are only such; and that is, that we immediately forgive them.

(5.) It doth not seem a direction suited unto that *intense love* which the Lord Christ requireth in all his disciples one towards another, nor the nature of that love in its exercise, as it is described, 1 Cor. xiii., that for a private injury done unto any man, without respect unto sin against God therein, which is the scandal, he should follow his brother so far as to have him cast out of the communion of all churches and believers; which yet, in case of sin unrepented of, is a necessary duty.

2. The rule here prescribed, and the direction given, were so prescribed and given for the use of all the disciples of Christ in all ages, and are not to be confined unto any present case or the present season.   For,—(1.) There was no such case at present, no mutual offence among any of his disciples, that should require this determination of it; only respect is had unto what might afterward fall out in the church.   (2.) There was no need of any such direction at that time, because Christ himself was then constantly present with them, in whom all church-power did reside both eminently and formally Accordingly, when any of them did offend unto scandal, he did himself rebuke them, Matt. xvi. 22, 23; and when any thing of mutual offence fell out among them, he instructed them and directed them into the way of love, doing what any church could do, and much more also, chap. xx. 24–28.   (3.) This was a case which our Saviour foreknew and foretold that it would fall out in the church in future generations, even unto the end of the world.   It doth so every day, and will do so whilst men are in an imperfect state here below.   Nor is there any thing wherein the church, as unto its order, purity, and edification, is more concerned; nor can any of them be preserved without a certain rule for the cure and healing of offences, nor are so in any church where such a rule is not, or is neglected.   It is therefore fond to suppose that our Saviour should prescribe this rule for that season wherein there was no need of it, and not for those times wherein the church could not subsist in order without it.

3. The church here directed unto is a Christian church; for,—(1.) Whereas it hath been proved it concerned the times to come afterward, there was in those times nothing that could pretend unto the

name of the church but a Christian church only.   The Jewish synagogues had an utter end put unto them, so as that an address unto any of them in this case was not only useless but unlawful.   And as unto magistrates or arbitrators, to have them called the church, and that in such a sense as that after the interposition of their authority or advice a man should be freed from the discharge of all Christian duties, such as are mutually required among the disciples of Christ, towards his brother, is a fond imagination: for,—(2.) It is such a church as can exercise *authority in the name of Christ* over his disciples, and such as in conscience they should be bound to submit themselves unto; for the reason given of the contempt of the voice, judgment, and sentence of the church in case of offence, is their power of spiritual binding and loosing, which is committed by Christ thereunto, and so he adds immediately, Matt. xviii. 18, "Whatsoever ye shall bind on earth shall be bound in heaven, and whatsoever ye shall loose on earth shall be loosed in heaven;" [which] is the privilege of a Christian church only.

4. It is a visible *particular congregation* alone that is intended; for,—(1.) As unto "the church" in other acceptations of that name, either for the catholic invisible church, or for the whole body of professed believers throughout the world, it is utterly impossible that this duty should be observed towards it, as is manifest unto all.   (2.) We have proved that the first and most proper signification of the word is of a *single* congregation, assembling together for its duties and enjoyments.   Wherever, therefore, the church in general is mentioned, without the addition of any thing or circumstance that may lead unto another signification, it must be interpreted of such a particular church or congregation.   (3.) The persons intended, offending and offended, must belong unto the *same society* unto whom the address is to be made, or else the one party may justly decline the judicatory applied unto, and so frustrate the process; and it must be such a church as unto whom they are known in their circumstances, without which it is impossible that a right judgment in sundry cases can be made in point of offence.   (4.) It is a church of an easy address: " Go, tell the church;" which supposeth that free and immediate access which all the members of a church have unto that whole church whereof they are members.   Wherefore,—(5.) It is said, Εἶπε τῇ ἐκκλησίᾳ, "Tell the church;" not *a* church, but *the* church,—namely, whereunto thou and thy brother do belong.   (6.) One end of this direction is, that the offending and the offended parties may continue together in the communion of the same church, in love without dissimulation; which thing belongs unto a particular congregation.   (7.) The meaning is not, "Tell the *diocesan bishop*," for whatever church he may have under his rule, yet is not he himself

a church.   Nor is it (8.) the chancellor's court that our Saviour intended.   Be it what it will, it is a disparagement unto all churches
to have that name applied thereunto.   Nor, lastly, is it a presbytery,
or association of the elders of many particular congregations, that is
intended; for the power proclaimed in such associated presbyteries
is with respect unto what is already in or before particular congregations, which they have not either wisdom or authority, as is supposed,
finally to order and determine.   But this supposeth that the address
in the first place be made unto a particular congregation; which,
therefore, is firstly and properly here intended.

All things are plain, familiar, and exposed to the common understandings of all believers whose minds are any way exercised about
these things, as, indeed, are all things that belong unto the discipline
of Christ.   Arguments pretendedly deep and learned, really obscure
and perplexed, with logical notions and distinctions applied unto
things thus plain and evident in themselves, do serve only to involve
and darken the truth.   It is plain in the place,—(1.) That there was
a church-state for Christians then designed by Christ, which afterward he would institute and settle; (2.) That all true disciples were
to join and unite themselves in some such church as might be helpful
unto their love, order, peace, and edification; (3.) That among the
members of these churches offences would or might arise, which in
themselves tend unto pernicious events; (4.) That if these offences
could not be cured and taken away, so as that love without dissimulation might be continued among all the members of the churches,
an account of them at last was to be given unto that church or society whereunto the parties concerned do belong as members of it;
(5.) That this church should hear, determine, and give judgment,
with advice, in the cases so brought unto it, for the taking away and
removal of all offences; (6.) That this determination of the church
is to be rested in, on the penalty of a deprivation of all the privileges
of the church; (7.) That these things are the institution and appointment of Christ himself, whose authority in them all is to be
submitted unto, and which alone can cast one that is a professed
Christian into the condition of a heathen or a publican.

These things, in the notion and practice of them, are plain, easy,
and exposed to the understanding of the meanest of the disciples of
Christ, as it is meet that all things should be wherein their daily
practice is concerned; but it is not easily to be expressed into what
horrible perplexities and confusions they have been wrested in the
church of Rome, nor how those who depart from the plain, obvious
sense of the words, and love not the practice they direct unto, do
lead themselves and others into ways and paths that have neither
use nor end.   From the corrupt abuse of the holy institution of our

Lord Jesus Christ, here intended, so many powers, faculties, courts, jurisdictions, legal processes, with litigious, vexatious, oppressive courses of actions and trials,—whose very names are uncouth, horrid, foreign unto religion, and unintelligible without cunning in an artificial, barbarous science of the canon law,—have proceeded, as are enough to fill a sober, rational man with astonishment how it could ever enter into the minds of men to suppose that they can possibly have any relation unto this divine institution. Those who are not utterly blinded with interest and prejudice, wholly ignorant of the gospel and the mind of Christ therein, as also strangers from the practice of the duties which it requires, will hardly believe that in this context our Lord Jesus Christ designed to set up and erect an earthly domination in and over his churches, to be administered by the rules of the canon law and the Rota[1] at Rome. They must be spiritually mad and ridiculous who can give the least entertainment unto such an imagination.

Nor can the discipline of any diocesan churches, administered in and by courts and officers foreign to the Scripture, both name and thing, be brought within the view of this rule, nor can all the art of the world make any application of it thereunto; for what some plead concerning magistrates or arbitrators, they are things which men would never betake themselves unto, but only to evade the force of that truth which they love not. All this is fallen out by men's departing from the simplicity of the gospel, and a contempt of that sense of the words of the Lord Jesus which is plain and obvious unto all who desire not only to hear his words but also to observe his commands.

Thirdly, Our third argument is taken from the nature of the churches instituted by the apostles and their order, as it is expressed in the Scripture; for they were all of them congregational, and of no other sort. This the ensuing considerations will make evident:—

1. There were *many churches* planted by the apostles in very small provinces. Not to insist on the churches of Galatia, Gal. i. 2, concerning which it is nowhere intimated that they had any one head or mother church, metropolitical or diocesan; nor of those of Macedonia, distinct from that of Philippi, whereof we have spoken before; upon the first coming of Paul after his conversion unto Jerusalem, which was three years, chap. i. 18, in the fourth year after the ascension of Christ, there were churches planted in all Judea, and Galilee, and Samaria, Acts ix. 31. Neither of the two latter provinces was equal unto one ordinary diocese; yet were there churches in both of them, and that

---

[1] The Rota is an important ecclesiastical court at Rome, before which all suits in the territory of the church may be carried by appeal, and which takes cognizance of all beneficiary and patrimonial interests. Twelve prelates are the judges; of whom one must be a German, another a Frenchman, two Spaniards, and the rest Italians.—ED.

in so short a time after the first preaching of the gospel as that it is impossible they should be conceived to be any other but single congregations. What is excepted or opposed hereunto by the Rev. Dr Stillingfleet shall be examined and disproved afterward by itself, that the progress of our discourse be not here interrupted.

2. These churches were such as that the apostles appointed in them *ordinary elders and deacons,* that might administer all ordinances unto the whole church, and take care of all the poor, Acts xiv. 23, xx. 17, 28. Now, the care, inspection, and labour of ordinary officers can extend itself no farther than unto a particular congregation. No man can administer all ordinances unto a diocesan church. And this "ordaining elders in every church" is the same with "ordaining them in every city," Tit. i. 5,—that is, in every town wherein there was a number converted unto the faith; as is evident from Acts xiv. 23. And it was in towns and cities ordinarily that the gospel was first preached and first received. Such believers being congregated and united in the profession of the same faith and subjection unto the authority of Christ, did constitute such a church-state as it was the will of Christ they should have bishops or elders and deacons ordained amongst them; and were, therefore, as unto their state, such churches as he owned.

3. It is said of most of these churches expressly that they respectively *met together in one place,* or had their assemblies of the whole church for the discharge of the duties required of them; which is peculiar unto congregational churches only: so did the church at Jerusalem on all occasions, Acts xv. 12, 22, xxi. 22; see chap. v. 11, vi. 2. It is of no force which is objected from the multitude of them that are said to believe, and so, consequently, were of that church, so as that they could not assemble together; for whereas the Scripture says expressly that the "multitude" of the church did "come together," it is scarce fair for us to say they were such a multitude as that they could not come together. And it is evident that the great numbers of believers that are said to be at Jerusalem were there only occasionally, and were not fixed in that church; for many years after, a small village beyond Jordan could receive all that were so fixed in it. The church at Antioch gathered together in one assembly, chap. xiv. 27, to hear Paul and Silas. This church, thus called together, is called "The multitude," chap. xv. 30; that is, the whole brotherhood, at least, of that church. The whole church of Corinth did assemble together in one place, both for solemn worship and the exercise of discipline, 1 Cor. v. 4, 5, xi. 17, 18, 20, xiv. 23–26.

It is no way necessary to plead any thing in the illustration or for the confirmation of these testimonies. They all of them speak positively in a matter of fact, which will admit of no debate, unless we will put in exceptions unto the veracity of their authors. And they are of themselves sufficient to establish our assertion; for whatever may be the state of any church as unto its officers or rule, into what order soever it be disposed ordinarily or occasionally for its edification, so long as it is its duty to assemble in and with all its members in one place, either for the exercise of its power, the performance of its duty, or enjoyment of its privileges, it is a single congregation, and no more.

4. The duties prescribed unto all church-members in the writings of the apostles, to be diligently attended unto by them, are such as, either in their nature or the manner of their performance, cannot be attended unto and duly accomplished but in a *particular congregation only.* This I shall immediately speak distinctly unto, and therefore only mention it in this place.

These things being so plainly, positively, and frequently asserted in the Scripture, it cannot be questionable unto any impartial mind but that particular churches or congregations are of divine institution, and consequently that unto them the whole power and privilege of the church doth belong; for if they do not so, whatever they are, churches they are not. If, therefore, any other church-state be supposed, we may well require that its name, nature, use, power, and bounds be some or all of them declared in the Scripture. Reasonings drawn from the superiority of the apostles above the evangelists, of bishops above presbyters, or from church-rule in the hands of the officers of the church only, from the power of the Christian magistrate in things ecclesiastical, from the meetness of union among all churches, are of no use in this case; for they are all consistent with the sole institution of particular congregations, nor do in the least intimate that there is or needs to be any other church-state of divine appointment.

CHAPTER V.

The state of the first churches after the apostles, to the end of the second century.

In confirmation of the foregoing argument, we urge the precedent and example of the primitive churches that succeeded unto those which were planted by the apostles themselves, and so may well be judged to have walked in the same way and order with them. And that which we allege is,—

That in no approved writers for the space of two hundred years after Christ is there any mention made of any other organical, visibly-professing church, but that only which is parochial or congregational.

A church of any other form, state, or order,—papal or œcumenical, patriarchal, metropolitical, diocesan, or classical,—they knew not, neither name nor thing, nor any of them appear in any of their writings.

Before I proceed unto the confirmation of this assertion by particular testimonies, I shall premise some things which are needful unto the right understanding of what it is that I intend to prove by them; as,—

1. All the churches at first planted by the apostles, whether in the greatest cities, as Jerusalem, Antioch, Corinth, Rome, etc., or those in the meanest villages of Judea, Galilee, or Samaria, were, as unto their church-state, in order, power, privilege, and duty, every way equal,— not superior or inferior, not ruling over or subject unto one another. No *institution* of any inequality between them, no instance of any *practice* supposing it, no *direction* for any compliance with it, no one word of intimation of it, can be produced from the Scripture; nor is it consistent with the nature of the gospel church-state.

2. In and among all these churches there was " one and the same Spirit, one hope of their calling, one Lord, one faith, one baptism; " whence they were all obliged mutually to seek and endeavour the good and edification of each other, to be helpful to one another in all things, according unto that which any of them had received in the Lord. This they did by prayer, by advice and counsel, by messengers sent with salutations, exhortations, consolations, supplies for the poor, and on all the like occasions. By these means, and by the exercise of that mutual love and care which they were obliged unto, they kept and preserved unity and communion among themselves, and gave a common testimony against any thing that in doctrine or practice deviated from the rule and discipline of Christ. This order, with peace and love thereon, continued among them until pride, ambition, desire of rule and pre-eminence, in Diotrephes, and a multitude of the same spirit with him, began to open a door unto the entrance of "the mystery of iniquity," under pretence of a better order than this, which was of the appointment of Christ.

3. It must be acknowledged, that notwithstanding this equality among all churches, as unto their state and power, there were great differences between them, some real and some in reputation; which, not being rightly managed, proved an occasion of evil in and unto them all. For instance:—

(1.) Some were more eminent in *spiritual gifts* than others. As this was a privilege that might have been greatly improved unto the honour of Christ and the gospel, yet we know how it was abused in the church of Corinth, and what disorders followed thereon. So weak and frail are the best of men, so liable unto temptation, that all pre-eminence is dangerous for them, and often abused by them; which, I confess, makes me not a little admire to see men so earnestly pleading for it, so fearlessly assuming it unto themselves, so fiercely contending that all power and rule in the church belongs unto them alone.   But,—

(2.) Reputation was given unto some by the long abode of some of the apostles in them.   Of this advantage we find nothing in the Scripture; but certain it is it was much pleaded and contended about among the primitive churches, yea, so far, until by degrees disputes arose about the *places* where this or that apostle *fixed his seat;* which was looked on as a pre-eminence for the present and a security for the future.   But yet we know how soon some of them degenerated from the church order and discipline wherein they were instructed by the apostles.   See Rev. ii. iii.

(3.) The greatness, power, fame, or civil authority of the *place or city* where any church was planted, gave it an advantage and privilege in reputation above others; and the churches planted in such cities were quickly more numerous in their members than others were. Unless men strictly kept themselves unto the force of primitive institutions, it was very hard for them to think and judge that a church, it may be in a small village or town in Galilee, should be equal with that at Jerusalem or at Antioch, or afterward at Rome itself.   The generality of men easily suffered themselves to be persuaded that those churches were advanced in state and order far above the other obscure, poor congregations.   That there should be a church at Rome, the head city of the world, was a matter of great joy and triumph unto many; and the advancement of it in reputation they thought belonged unto the honour of our religion.   Howbeit there is not in the Scripture the least regard expressed unto any of these things, of place, number, or possibility of outward splendour, either in the promises of the presence of Christ in and with his churches, or in the communication of power and privileges unto them.   Yet such an improvement did this foolish imagination find, that after those who presided in the churches called in the principal cities had tasted of the sweetness of the bait which lay in the ascription of a pre-eminence unto them, they began openly to claim it unto themselves, and to usurp authority over other churches, confirming their own usurpations by canons and rules, until a few of them in the council of Nice began to divide the Christian world among themselves, as if it had been conquered by them.   Hence proceeded those shameful contests that were among the greater prelates about their pre-eminency: and hence arose that pretence of the bishops of Rome unto no less a right of rule and dominion over all Christian churches than the city had over all the nations and cities of the empire; which being carried on by all sorts of evil artifices, as by downright forgeries, shameless intrusions of themselves, impudent laying hold of all advantages unto their own exaltation, prevailed at length unto the utter ruin of all church order and worship.   There is no sober history of the rise and growth by several degrees of any city, commonwealth, or empire, that is filled with so many instances of ambitious seeking of pre-eminence as our church stories are.

By this imagination were the generality of the prelates in those days induced to introduce and settle a government in and among the churches of Christ answering unto the civil government of the Roman empire.   As the civil government was cast into national, or diocesan, or provincial, in less or greater divisions, each of which had its capital city, the place of the residence of the chief civil governor; so they designed to frame an image of it in the church, ascribing an alike dignity and power unto the prelates of those cities, and a jurisdiction extending itself unto nations, dioceses, and provinces.   Hereby the lesser congregations, or parochial churches, being weakened in process of time in their gifts and interest, were swallowed up in the power of the others, and became only inconsiderable appendices unto them, to be ruled at their pleasure.   But these things fell out long after the times which we inquire into; only, their occasion began to present itself unto men of corrupt minds from the beginning.   But we have before at large discoursed of them.

(4.) Some churches had a great advantage, in that the gospel, as the apostle speaks, "went forth from them" unto others.   They in their ministry were the means, first, of the conversion of others unto the faith, and then of their gathering into a church-state, affording them assistance in all things they stood in need of.   Hence these newly-formed churches, in lesser towns and villages, had always a great reverence for the church by whose means they were converted unto God and stated in church-order; and it was meet that so they should have.   But in process of time, as these lesser churches decreased in spiritual gifts, and fell under a scarcity of able guides, this reverence was turned into obedience and dependence; and they thought it well enough to be under the rule of others, being unable well to rule themselves.

On these and the like accounts there was quickly introduced an inequality among churches; which, by virtue of their first institution, were equal as unto state and power.

4. Churches may admit of many *variations* as unto their outward form and order, which yet change not their state, nor cause them to cease from being congregational; as,—

(1.) Supposing that any of them might have many elders or presbyters in them, as it is apparent that most of them had, yea, all that are mentioned in the Scripture had so, Acts xi. 30, xiv. 23, xv. 6, 22, 23, xvi. 4, xx. 17, 18, 28, xxi. 18; Phil. i. 1; 1 Tim. v. 17; Tit. i. 5,

—they might, and some of them did, choose out some one endued with especial gifts, that might in some sort preside amongst them, and who had quickly the name of bishop appropriated unto him.   This practice is thought to have had its original at Alexandria, and began generally to be received in the third century.   But this changed not the state of the church, though it had no divine warrant to authorize it; for this order may be agreed unto among the elders of a particular congregation, and sundry things may fall out inclining unto the reception of it.   But from a distinct mention (if any such there be), in the writings of the second century, of bishops and presbyters, to fancy metropolitical and diocesan churches is but a pleasant dream.

(2.) The members of those churches that were great and numerous, being under the care and inspection of their *elders in common*, might, for the ordinary duty of divine worship, meet in parts or several actual assemblies; and they did so, especially in time of persecution. Nothing occurs more frequently in ecclesiastical story than the meetings of Christians in secret places, in private houses, yea, in caves and dens of the earth, when in some places it was impossible that the whole body of the church should so assemble together.   How this disposition of the members of the church into several parts, in each of which some elder or elders of it did officiate, gave occasion unto the distinction of greater churches into particular titles or parishes, is not here to be declared; it may be so elsewhere.   But neither yet did this alter the state of the churches from their original institution; for,—

(3.) Upon all extraordinary occasions, all such as concerned the whole church,—as the choice of elders or the deposition of them, the admission or exclusion of members, and the like,—the whole church continued to meet together; which practice was plainly continued in the days of Cyprian, as we shall see afterward.   Neither doth it appear but that, during the first two hundred years of the church, the whole body of the church did ordinarily meet together in one place for the solemn administration of the holy ordinances of worship, and the exercise of discipline.

Wherefore, notwithstanding these and other the like variations from the original institution of churches, which came in partly by inadvertency unto the rule, and partly were received from the advantages and accommodations which they pretended unto, the state of the churches continued congregational only for two hundred years, so far as can be gathered from the remaining monuments of those times.   Only, we must yet add, that we are no way concerned in testimonies or sayings taken from the writings of those in following ages, as unto the state, way, and manner of the churches in this season, but do appeal unto their own writings only.   This is the great artifice whereby Baronius, in his Annals, would impose upon the credulity of men an apprehension of the antiquity of any of their Roman inventions;—he affixeth them unto some of the first ages, and giving some countenance unto them, it may be from some spurious writings, lays the weight of confirmation on testimonies and sayings of writers many years, yea, for the most part, ages afterward; for it was and is of the latter ages of the church, wherein use and custom have wrested ecclesiastical words to other significations than at first they were applied unto, to impose the present state of things among them on those who went before, who knew nothing of them.

I shall, therefore, briefly inquire into what representation is made of the state of the churches by the writers themselves who lived in the season inquired after, or in the age next unto it, which was acquainted with their practice.

That which first offereth itself unto us, and which is an invaluable testimony of the state of the first churches immediately after the decease of the apostles, is the epistle of Clemens Romanus unto the brethren of the church of Corinth. This epistle, according to the title of it, Irenæus ascribes unto the whole church at Rome, and calls it "potentissimas literas:"—" Sub hoc Clemente dissensione non modica inter eos qui Corinthi erant fratres facta, scripsit quæ est Romæ ecclesia, potentissimas literas," lib. iii. cap. 3. By Eusebius it is termed μεγάλη καὶ θαυμασία,—" great and admirable;" who also affirms that it was publicly read in some churches, Eccles. Hist., lib. iii. cap. 16. And again he calls it ἰκανωτάτην γραφήν,—a " most powerful writing," lib. v. cap. 7.

There is no doubt but some things in the writing of it did befall him " humanitus," that the work of such a companion of some of the apostles as he was might not be received as of divine institution,— such was the credit which he gives unto the vulgar fable of the phœnix;—but for the substance of it, it is such as every way becomes a person of an apostolical spirit, consonant unto the style and writings of the apostles themselves, a precious jewel and just representation of the state and order of the church in those days. And sundry things we may observe from it:—

1. There is nothing in it that gives the least intimation of any other church-state but that which was *congregational*, although there were the highest causes and reasons for him so to do had there been any such churches then in being. The case he had in hand was that of ecclesiastical sedition or schism in the church of Corinth, the church or body of the brethren having unjustly deposed their elders, as it should seem, all of them. Giving advice herein unto the whole church, using all sorts of arguments to convince them of their sin, directing all probable means for their cure, he never once sends

them to the bishop or church of Rome, as the head of unity unto all churches; makes no mention of any metropolitical or diocesan church and its rule, or of any single bishop and his authority.   No one of any such order doth he either commend, or condemn, or once address himself unto, with either admonitions, exhortations, encouragements, or directions.   He only handles the cause by the rule of the Scripture, as it was stated between the church itself and its elders.   I take it for granted that if there were any church at Corinth consisting of many congregations, in the city and about it, or comprehensive, as some say, of the whole region of Achaia, that there was a single officer or bishop over that whole church; but none such is here mentioned.   If there were any such, he was either deposed by the people or he was not.   If he were deposed, he was only one of the presbyters; for they were only presbyters that were deposed.   If he were not, why is he not once called on to discharge his duty in curing of that schism, or blamed for his neglect?   Certainly there was never greater prevarication used by any man in any cause than is by Clemens in this, if the state of the church, its rule and order, were such as some now pretend; for he neither lets the people know wherein their sin and schism did lie,—namely, in a separation from their bishop,—nor doth once mention the only proper cure and remedy of all their evils.   But he knew their state and order too well to insist on things that were not then " in rerum natura," and wherein they were not concerned.

2.   This epistle is written, as unto *the whole church* at Corinth, so in the name of *the whole church of Rome:* Ἐκκλησία τοῦ Θεοῦ ἡ παροικοῦσα Ῥώμην, τῇ ἐκκλησίᾳ τοῦ Θεοῦ παροικούσῃ Κόρινθον—" The church of God which dwelleth" (or sojourneth, as a stranger) " at Rome " (in the city of Rome) " to the church of God that dwelleth" (or sojourneth) " at Corinth."   For although that church was then in disorder, under no certain rule, having cast off all their elders, etc., yet the church of Rome not only allows it to be a sister church, but salutes the brethren of it in the following words: Κλητοῖς ἡγιασμένοις ἐν θελήματι Θεοῦ, διὰ τοῦ Κυρίου ἡμῶν Ἰησοῦ Χριστοῦ—" Called and sanctified through the will of God by our Lord Jesus Christ."   The churches of Christ were not so ready in those days to condemn the persons, nor to judge the church-state and condition of others, on every miscarriage, real or supposed, as some have been and are in these latter ages.

3.   This address being from the body of the church at Rome unto that at Corinth, without the least mention of the officers of them in particular, it is evident that the churches themselves,—that is, the whole entire community of them,—had communion with one another, as they were sister churches, and that they had themselves the trans-

action of all affairs wherein they were concerned, as they had in the days of the apostles, Acts xv. 1–3. It was the brethren of the church at Antioch who determined that Paul and Barnabas, and certain others, should go up to Jerusalem to consult the apostles and elders: see also chap. xxi. 22. This they did not, nor ought to do, without the presence, guidance, conduct, and consent of their elders or rulers, when they had any; but this they were now excluded from. And that church, the whole body or fraternity whereof doth advise and consult in those things wherein they are concerned, on the account of their communion with other churches, is a congregational church, and no other. It was the church who sent this epistle unto the Corinthians. Claudius Ephebus, Valerius, Bito, Fortunatus, are named[1] as their messengers: Τοὺς ἀπεσταλμένους ἀφ᾿ ἡμῶν,—" That are sent by us," our messengers, our apostles in these matters; such as the churches made use of on all such occasions in the apostles' days, 2 Cor. viii. 23. And the persons whom they sent were only members of the church, and not officers; nor do we anywhere hear of them under that character. Now, they could not be sent in the name of the church but by its consent; nor could the church consent without its assembling together.

This was the state and order of the first churches. In that communion which was amongst them, according to the mind of Christ, they had a singular concern in the welfare and prosperity of each other, and were solicitous about them in their trials. Hence, those who were planted at a greater distance than would allow frequent personal converse with their respective members, did on all occasions send messengers unto one another; sometimes merely to visit them in love, and sometimes to give or take advice. But these things, as indeed almost all others that belong unto the communion of churches, either in themselves or with one another, are either utterly lost and buried, or kept above ground in a pretence of episcopal authority, churches themselves being wholly excluded from any concernment in them. But as the advice of the church of Rome was desired in this case by the whole church of Corinth (περὶ τῶν ἐπιζητουμένων παρ᾿ ὑμῖν πραγμάτων), so it was given by the body of the church itself, and sent by messengers of their own.[2]

4. The description given of the state, ways, and walking of the church of Corinth,[3]—that is, that whole fraternity of the church, which fell afterward into that disorder which is reproved,—before their fall, is such as that it bespeaks their walking together in one and the same society, and is sufficient to make any good man desire that he might see churches yet in the world unto whom, or the generality of whose members, that description might be honestly and justly ac-

commodated. One character which is given of them I shall mention only: Πλήρης πνεύματος ἁγίου ἔκχυσις ἐπὶ πάντας ἐγίνετο· μεστοίτε ὁσίας βουλῆς, ἐν ἀγαθῇ προθυμίᾳ μετ᾽ εὐσεβοῦς πεποιθήσεως ἐξετείνατε τὰς χεῖρας ὑμῶν πρὸς τὸν παντοκράτορα Θεὸν, ἱκετεύοντες αὐτὸν ἵλεως γενέσθαι, εἴτι ἄκοντες ἡμάρτετε. Ἀγὼν ἦν ὑμῖν ἡμέρας τε καὶ νυκτὸς ὑπὲρ πασῆς τῆς ἀδελφότητος, εἰς τὸ σώζεσθαι μετ᾽ ἐλέους καὶ συνειδήσεως, τὸν ἀριθμὸν τῶν ἐκλεκτῶν αὐτοῦ·—"There was a full" (or plentiful) "effusion of the Holy Ghost upon you all; so that, being full" (or filled) "with a holy will" (holiness of will) "and a good readiness of mind, with a pious devout confidence, you stretched out your hands in prayers to almighty God, supplicating his clemency" (or mercy) "for the pardon of your involuntary sins" (sins fallen into by infirmity, or the surprisals of temptations not consented to, nor delighted or continued in). "Your labour" (or contention of spirit,—Ἀγὼν ἦν ὑμῖν, as the apostle speaks, ἡλίκον ἀγῶνα ἔχω, Col. ii. 1) "was night and day" (in your prayers) "for the whole brotherhood" (that is, especially of their own church itself), "that the number of God's elect might be saved in mercy, through a good conscience towards him."

This was their state, this was their liturgy, this their practice:—
(1.) There was on all the members of the church a plentiful effusion of the Holy Spirit in his gifts and graces; wherein, it may be, respect is had unto what was affirmed by the apostle before of the same church, 1 Cor. i. 4–7, the same grace being yet continued unto them. (2.) By virtue of this effusion of the Spirit on all of them, their wills and affections being sanctified, their minds were enabled to pour forth fervent prayers unto God. (3.) They were not such as lived in any open sin, or any secret sin, known to be so, but were only subject unto involuntary surprisals, whose pardon they continually prayed for. (4.) Their love and sense of duty stirred them up to labour mightily in their prayers, with fervency and constancy, for the salvation of the whole fraternity of elect believers, whether throughout the world, or more especially those in and of their own church.

He that should ascribe these things unto any of those churches which now in the world claim to be so only, would quickly find himself at a loss for the proof of what he asserts. Did we all sedulously endeavour to reduce and restore churches unto their primitive state and frame, it would bring more glory to God than all our contentions about rule and domination.

4. It is certain that the church of Corinth was fallen into a sinful excess, in the deposition and rejection of their elders,[1] whom the church at Rome judged to have presided among them laudably and unblamably, as unto their whole walk and work amongst them. And this they did by the suggestion of two or three envious, discontented

[1] Pages 57, 58, 62.

persons, and, as is probable from some digressions in the epistle, tainted with those errors which had formerly infested that church, as the denial of the resurrection of the flesh; which is therefore here reflected on. But in the whole epistle, the church is nowhere reproved for assuming an authority unto themselves which did not belong unto them. It seems what Cyprian afterward affirmed was then acknowledged,—namely, that the right of choosing the worthy, and of rejecting the unworthy, was in the body of the people. But they are severely reproved for the abuse of their liberty and power; for they had exercised them on ill grounds, by ill means, for ill ends, and in a most unjust cause. He therefore exhorts the body of the church to return unto their duty, in the restoration of their elders; and then prescribes unto them who were the first occasion of schism that every one would subject themselves unto the restored presbyters, and say, Ποιῶ τὰ προστασσόμενα ὑπὸ τοῦ πλήθους[1]—" I will do the things appointed or commanded by the multitude," the church in the generality of its members. The " plebs," the multitude, the body of the fraternity in the church,—τὸ πλῆθος, as they are often called in the Scripture, Acts iv. 32, vi. 2, 5, xv. 12, 30,—had then right and power to appoint things that were to be done in the church, for order and peace. I do not say they had it without, or in distinction from, their officers, rulers, and guides, but in a concurrence with them, and subordination to them; whence the acts concluded on may be esteemed, and are, the acts of the whole church. This order can be observed, or this can fall out, only in a congregational church, all whose members do meet together for the discharge of their duties and exercise of their discipline. And if no more may be considered in it but the miscarriage of the people, without any respect to their right and power, yet such churches as wherein it is impossible that that should fall out in them as did so fall out in that church, are not of the same kind or order with it.

But, for the sake of them who may endeavour to reduce any church-state into its primitive constitution, that they may be cautioned against that great evil which this church, in the exercise of their supposed liberty, fell into, I cannot but transcribe a few of those excellent words which are used plentifully with cogent reasons in this epistle[2] against it: Ἀισχρὰ, ἀγαπητοὶ, καὶ λίαν αἰσχρὰ, καὶ ἀνάξια τῆς ἐν Χριστῷ ἀγωγῆς ἀκούεται, τὴν βεβαιοτάτην καὶ ἀρχαίαν Κορινθίων ἐκκλησίαν, δι' ἓν ἢ δύο πρόσωπα στασιάζειν πρὸς τοὺς πρεσβυτέρους—" It is shameful, beloved, exceeding shameful, which is reported of you, that the most firm and ancient church of the Corinthians should, for the sake of one or two persons, seditiously tumultuate against their elders." And hereon he proceeds to declare the dreadful scandal that ensued thereon, both among believers and infidels. The instruction, also, which he adds hereunto is worthy the remembrance of all church-members: Ἥτω τὶς πιστὸς, ἤτω δυνατὸς γνῶσιν ἐξειπεῖν, ἤτω σοφὸς ἐν δικαία κρίσει λόγων, ἤτω ἁγνὸς ἐν ἔργοις· τοσούτῳ μᾶλλον ταπεινοφρεῖν ὀφείλει, ὅσῳ δοκεῖ μᾶλλον μείζων εἶναι.   It is blessed advice for all church-members that he gives: " Let a man be faithful; let him be powerful in knowledge" (or the declaration of it); " let him be wise to judge the words or doctrines; let him be chaste or pure in his works: the greater he seems to be, the more humble he ought to be, that so the church may have no trouble by him nor his gifts." But to return.

5. Having occasion to mention the officers of the church, he nameth only the two ranks of bishops and deacons,[1] as the apostle also doth, Phil. i. 1.   Speaking of the apostles he says, Κατὰ χώρας καὶ πόλεις κηρύσσοντες, καθίστανον τὰς ἀπαρχὰς αὐτῶν, δοκιμάσαντες τῷ πνεύματι εἰς ἐπισκόπους καὶ διακόνους τῶν μελλόντων πιστεύειν·—" Preaching the word through regions and cities, they appointed the first-fruits"— as the house of Stephanas was the "first-fruits of Achaia," who therefore "addicted themselves to the ministry of the saints," 1 Cor. xvi. 15, —(or the first converts to the faith), "after a spiritual trial of them" (as unto their fitness for their work), " to be bishops and deacons of them that should afterward believe."   Where there were as yet but a few converted, the apostles gathered them into church-order; and so soon as they found any fit among them, appointed and ordained them to be bishops and deacons; so that provision might be made for the guidance and conduct of them that should be converted and added unto them after they were left by the apostles. These bishops he affirms to be, and to have been, the presbyters or elders of the church,[2] even the same with those deposed by the Corinthians, in the same manner as the apostle doth, Acts xx. 28: Ἁμαρτία γὰρ οὐ μικρὰ ἡμῖν ἔσται, ἐὰν τοὺς ἀμέμπτως καὶ ὁσίως προσενέγκοντας τὰ δῶρα τῆς ἐπισκοπῆς ἀποβάλωμεν· μακάριοι δὲ προοδοιπορήσαντες πρεσβύτεροι, etc.;—" It is no small sin in us to reject or cast off them who have offered the gifts" (or discharged the duties) " of episcopacy holily and without blame. Blessed are the elders who went before!"—namely, as he expresseth it, because they are freed from that amotion from their office which those elders now amongst them had undergone, after they had duly discharged the office of episcopacy. Other distinction and difference of ordinary officers, besides that of bishops or elders and deacons, the church at Rome in those days knew not.   Such ought to be in every particular church. Of any one single person to preside over many churches, which is necessary unto the constitution of a church-state distinct from that which is congregational,

[1] Pages 54, 55.   [2] Pages 57, 58.

Clemens knew nothing in his days, but gives us such a description of the church and its order as is inconsistent with such a pretence.

6. I shall add no more from this excellent epistle, but only the account given in it of the first constitution of officers in the churches: Καὶ οἱ ἀπόστολοι ἡμῶν ἔγνωσαν διὰ τοῦ Κυρίου ἡμῶν Ἰησοῦ Χριστοῦ, ὅτι ἔρις ἔσται ἐπὶ τοῦ ὀνόματος τῆς ἐπισκοπῆς, διὰ ταύτην οὖν τὴν αἰτίαν πρόγνωσιν εἰληφότες τελείαν, κατέστησαν τοὺς προειρημένους, καὶ μεταξὺ ἐπινομὴν δεδώκασιν, ὅπως ἐὰν κοιμηθῶσιν, διαδέξωνται ἕτεροι, δεδοκιμασμένοι ἄνδρες, τὴν λειτουργίαν αὐτῶν, τοὺς οὖν κατασταθέντας ὑπ᾽ ἐκείνων, ἢ μεταξὺ ὑφ᾽ ἑτέρων ἐλλογίμων ἀνδρῶν, συνευδοκησάσης τῆς ἐκκλησίας πάσης, κ. τ. λ.—"Our apostles, therefore, knowing by our Lord Jesus Christ that there would contention arise about the name of episcopacy" (that is, episcopacy itself); "for this cause, being endued with a perfect foresight of things, they appointed those fore-mentioned" (their first converts, unto the office of the ministry), "for the future describing or giving order about the course of the ministry, that other approved men might succeed them in their ministry. These" (elders), "therefore, who were so appointed by them, and afterward by other famous men, with the consent of the whole church," etc.

Sundry things we may observe in this discourse:—1. The apostles foresaw there would be strife and contention about *the name of episcopacy;* that is, the office itself, and those who should possess it. This episcopacy was that office which the deposed elders had well discharged in the church of Corinth. This they might foresee from the nature of the thing itself, the inclination of men unto pre-eminence, and the instance they had seen in their own days, in such as Diotrephes, with the former division that had been in this very church about their teachers, 1 Cor. i. 12. But, moreover, they were instructed in the knowledge of it by our Lord Jesus Christ, through his divine Spirit abiding with them and teaching them all things. This, therefore, they sought by all means to prevent, and that two ways:—(1.) In that, for the first time, themselves appointed approved persons unto the office of the ministry; not that they did it of themselves, without the consent and choice of the church whereunto any of them were appointed (for this was directly contrary unto their practice, Acts i. 15–26, vi. 1–6, xiv. 23), but that the peace and edification of the churches might be provided for, they themselves spiritually tried and approved of fit persons, so to lead the church in their choice. Wherefore, that which is added afterward, of "the consent of the whole church," is to be referred unto those who were ordained by the apostles themselves. (2.) They gave rules and orders, namely, in their writings, concerning the offices and officers that were to be in the church, with the way whereby they should be substituted in the place and room of them that were de-

ceased, as we know they have done in their writings.   (3.) After this
was done by the apostles, other excellent persons, as the evangelists,
did the same.   These assisted the churches in the ordination and
choice of their officers, according unto the rules prescribed by the
apostles.   And I know not but that the eminent pastors of other
churches, who usually gave their assistance in the setting apart and
ordination of others unto the ministry, be intended.

I have insisted long on this testimony, being led on by the excellency of the writing itself.   Nothing remains written so near the
times of the apostles, nor doth any that is extant which was written
afterward give such an evidence of apostolical wisdom, gravity, and
humility.   Neither is there in all antiquity, after the writings of the
apostles, such a representation of the state, order, and rule of the first
evangelical churches.   And it is no small prejudice unto the pretensions of future ages that this apostolical person, handling a most
weighty ecclesiastical cause, makes not the least mention of such
offices, power, and proceedings, as wherein some would have all
church rule and order to consist.

The epistle of Polycarpus, and the elders of the church of Smyrna
with him, unto the church of the Philippians, is the next on the roll
of antiquity.   Nothing appears in the whole to intimate any other
church-state or order than that described by Clemens.   The epistle
is directed unto the whole church at Philippi, not unto any particular
bishop: Πολύκαρπος, καὶ οἱ σὺν αὐτῷ πρεσβύτεροι τῇ ἐκκλησίᾳ τοῦ Θεοῦ
τῇ παροικούσῃ Φιλίππους.   This was the usual style of those days.   So
was it used, as we have seen, by Clemens: Ἐκκλησία ἡ παροικοῦσα
Ῥώμην.   So it was used presently after the death of Polycarpus
by the church at Smyrna, in the account they gave unto other
churches of his death and martyrdom: Ἡ ἐκκλησία τοῦ Θεοῦ ἡ παροικοῦσα Σμύρναν τῇ ἐκκλησίᾳ παροικούσῃ ἐν Φιλομελίῳ.   And the same
was the inscription of the epistle of the churches at Vienne and
Lyons in France, unto the churches in Phrygia, as we shall see immediately.   And these are plain testimonies of that communion
among the churches in those days which was held in and by the
body of each church, or the community of the brotherhood; which is
a clear demonstration of their state and order.   And those whom the
apostle, writing to the Philippians, calls their bishops and deacons,
Polycarpus calls their presbyters and deacons.   "It behoves you,"
saith he unto the church there, " to abstain from these things,"
ὑποτασσομένοις τοῖς πρεσβυτέροις καὶ διακόνοις,—"being subject unto the
elders and deacons."   Nor doth he mention any other bishop among
the Philippians.   And it may be observed, that in all these primitive
writings there is still a distinction made, after the example of Scripture, between the church and the guides, rulers, bishops, or elders of

it; and the name of *the church* is constantly assigned unto the body of the people as distinct from the elders, nowhere to the bishops or elders as distinct from the people, though the church, in its complete state, comprehendeth both sorts.

Unto this time,—that is, about the year 107 or 108,—do belong the epistles ascribed unto Ignatius, if so be they were written by him; for Polycarpus wrote his epistle to the Philippians after Ignatius was carried to Rome, having wrote his epistle before in Asia. Many are the contests of learned men about those epistles which remain, whether they are genuine, or the same that were written by him; for that he did write epistles unto sundry churches is acknowledged by all. And whereas there have in this age been two copies found and published of those epistles, wherein very many things that were obnoxious unto just exception in those before published do not at all appear, yet men are not agreed which of them ought to be preferred; and many yet deny that any of them were those written by Ignatius. I shall not interpose in this contest; only, I must say, that if any of his genuine writings do yet remain, yet the corruption and interpolation of them for many ages must needs much impair the authority of what is represented in them as his; nor am I delivered from these thoughts by the late either more sound or more maimed editions of them. And the truth is, the corruption and fiction of epistolical writings in the first ages was so intolerable, as that very little in that kind is preserved sincere and unquestionable. Hence Dionysius, the bishop of Corinth, complained that in his own time his own epistles were so corrupted, by additions and detractions, as that it seems he would have them no more esteemed as his, Euseb. Ecclesiast. Hist., lib. iv. cap. 23.

But yet, because these epistles are so earnestly contended for by many learned men as the genuine writings of Ignatius, I shall not pass by the consideration of them as unto the argument in hand. I do therefore affirm, that in these epistles (in any edition of them) there is no mention made or description given of any church or church-state but only of that which is congregational; that is, such a church as all the members whereof did meet, and were obliged to meet, for divine worship and discipline in the same place. What was the distinction they observed among their officers, of what sort they were, and what number, belongs not unto our present inquiry. Our concernment is only this, that they did preside in the same particular church, and were none of them bishops of more churches than one, or of any church that should consist of a collection or association of such particular churches as had no bishops, properly so called, of their own.

All these epistles,—that is, the seven most esteemed,—were written, as that of Clemens, unto the bodies or whole fraternity of the churches, unto whom they are directed, in distinction from their bishops, elders, and deacons, excepting that only unto Polycarpus, which is unto a single person. Under that consideration,—namely, of the entire fraternity in distinction from their officers,—doth he address unto them, and therein doth he ascribe and assign such duties unto them as could not be attended unto nor performed but in the assembly of them all. Such is the direction he gives unto the church of the Philadelphians, how and in what manner they should receive penitents returning unto the church, that they might be encouraged unto that duty by their benignity and patience; and many things of the like nature doth he deal with them about. And this assembling together in the same place,—namely, of the whole church,—he doth frequently intimate and express. Some instances hereof we may repeat:—

Πάντες ἐπὶ τὸ αὐτὸ ἐν τῇ προσευχῇ ἅμα συνέρχεσθε· μία δέησις ἔστω κοινή· —" Meet all of you together in the same place; let there be one prayer in common of all," Epist. ad Magnes. [cap. vii.] This direction can be given unto no other but a particular church. And again to the Philadelphians [cap. ii.]: ῞Οπου ὁ ποιμήν ἐστιν, ἐκεῖ ὡς πρόβατα ἀκολουθεῖτε·—" Where your pastor is, there follow you as sheep." And how they may do so is declared immediately afterward [cap. iv.]: Θαῤῥῶν γράφω τῇ ἀξιοθέῳ ἀγάπῃ ὑμῶν, παρακαλῶν ὑμᾶς μιᾷ πίστει, καὶ ἑνὶ κηρύγματι καὶ μιᾷ εὐχαριστίᾳ χρῆσθαι· μία γάρ ἐστιν ἡ σὰρξ τοῦ Κυρίου Ἰησοῦ, καὶ ἓν αὐτοῦ τὸ αἷμα τὸ ὑπὲρ ἡμῶν ἐκχυθέν, εἷς καὶ ἄρτος τοῖς πᾶσιν ἐθρύφθη, καὶ ἓν ποτήριον τοῖς ὅλοις διενεμήθη, ἓν θυσιαστήριον πάσῃ τῇ ἐκκλησίᾳ, καὶ εἷς ἐπίσκοπος ἅμα τῷ πρεσβυτερίῳ, καὶ τοῖς διακόνοις τοῖς συνδούλοις μου·—" I write with confidence unto your godly love, and persuade you to use one faith" (or the confession of it), " one preaching of the word, and one eucharist" (or administration of the holy sacrament). " For the flesh of Christ is one, and the blood of Christ that was shed for us is one: one bread is broken to all, and one cup distributed among all; there is one altar to the whole church, and one bishop, with the presbytery, and the deacons my fellow-servants." Nothing can be more evident than that it is a particular church, in its order and assembly for worship *in one place*, that he describes; nor can these things be accommodated unto a church of any other form. And towards the end of the epistle, treating about the churches sending their bishops or others on their occasions, he tells them in particular [cap. x.]: Πρέπον ἐστὶν ὑμῖν ὡς ἐκκλησίᾳ Θεοῦ χειροτονῆσαι ἐπίσκοπον, εἰς τὸ πρεσβεῦσαι ἐκεῖ Θεοῦ πρεσβείαν εἰς τὸ συγχωρηθῆναι αὐτοῖς ἐπὶ τὸ αὐτὸ γενομένοις, καὶ δοξάσαι τὸ ὄνομα τοῦ Θεοῦ·—" It becometh you as a church of God to choose or appoint a bishop, who may perform the embassy of God, that it may be granted unto them to glorify the

name of God, being gathered together in one place." It is somewhat
difficult [to conceive] how the church of Philadelphia should choose
or ordain a bishop at this time, for they had one of their own, whom
Ignatius greatly extols in the beginning of the epistle. Nor was it
in their power or duty to choose or ordain a bishop for the church
of Antioch, which was their own right and duty alone; nor had the
church of Antioch any the least dependence on that at Philadelphia.
It may be he intends only their assistance therein, as immediately
before he ascribes the peace and tranquillity of the Antiochians unto
the prayers of the Philadelphians. For my part, I judge he intends
not the proper bishop of either place, but some elder, which they
were to choose as a messenger to send to Antioch, to assist them in
their present condition; for in those days there were persons chosen
by the churches to be sent abroad to assist other churches on the like
occasions. These were called ἀπόστολοι ἐκκλησιῶν, 2 Cor. viii. 23,—the
especial "apostles of the churches;" as verse 19, it is said of Luke
that he was χειροτονηθεὶς ὑπὸ τῶν ἐκκλησιῶν,—" chosen" and appointed
" by the churches" for the service there mentioned. Such was this
bishop, who was sent on God's errand to assist the church by his
advice and counsel as unto the continuance of their assemblies, unto
the glory of God, though at present their bishop was taken from
them. In that epistle unto the Ephesians, he lets them know that
he rejoiced at their πολυπλήθεια, their " numerous multitude;" whom
he persuades and urgeth unto a common concurrence in prayer with
their bishop [cap. v.]: Εἰ γὰρ ἑνὸς καὶ δευτέρου προσευχὴ τοσαύτην ἰσχὺν
ἔχει ὥστε τὸν Χριστὸν ἐν αὐτοῖς ἑστάναι, πόσῳ μᾶλλον ἤ τε τοῦ ἐπισκόπου καὶ
πάσης τῆς ἐκκλησίας προσευχὴ σύμφωνος;—" And if the prayers of one or
two be so effectual that they bring Christ among them, how much
more will the consenting prayer of the bishop and the whole church
together?" So he again explains his mind towards the end of the
epistle [cap. xiii.]: Σπουδάζετε οὖν πυκνότερον συνέρχεσθαι· ὅταν γὰρ συνε-
χῶς ἐπὶ τὸ αὐτὸ γένησθε, καθαιροῦνται αἱ δυνάμεις τοῦ Σατανᾶ·—" Do your
diligence to meet together frequently; for when you frequently meet
together in the same place, the powers of Satan are destroyed." And
many other expressions of the like nature occur in those epistles. We
are no way, at present, concerned in the controversy about that distinction of bishops and presbyters which the writer of those epistles
doth assert; this only I say, that he doth in none of them take the
least notice, or give the least intimation, of any church-state but such
alone wherein the members of the whole church did constantly meet
together in the same place, for the worship of God and communion
among themselves. And not only so, but he everywhere, in all his
epistles to them, ascribes such duties and rights unto the churches as
cannot be observed and preserved but in particular churches only.

Nor doth he leave any room for any other church-state whatever. Although, therefore, there might have been, and probably there were, some alterations in the order of the churches from what was of primitive institution, yet was there as yet no such change in their state as to make way for those greater alterations which not long after ensued; for they were not introduced until, through a defect in the multiplication of churches in an equality of power and order,— which ought to have been done,—they were increased into that multitude for number of members, and were so diffused as unto their habitations, as made an appearance of a necessity of another constitution of churches and another kind of rule than what was of original appointment.

Justin Martyr wrote his Second Apology for the Christians unto the Roman emperors about the year 150. It is marvellous to consider how ignorant not only the common sort of the Pagans, but the philosophers also, and governors of the nations, were of the nature of Christian churches, and of the worship celebrated in them. But who are so blind as those who will not see? Even unto this day not a few are willingly, or rather wilfully, ignorant of the nature of such assemblies, or what is performed in them, as were among the primitive Christians, that they may be at liberty to speak all manner of evil of them falsely. Hence were all the reports and stories among the heathen concerning what was done in the Christian conventicles; which they would have to be the most abominable villanies that were ever acted by mankind. Even those who made the most candid inquiry into what they were and did, attained unto very little knowledge or certainty concerning them and their mysteries; as is evident in the epistles of Trajan and Pliny, with the rescript of Adrian unto Minutius Fundanus about them.

In this state of things, this our great and learned philosopher, who afterward suffered martyrdom about the year 160, undertook to give an account unto Antoninus Pius and Lucius, who then ruled the Roman empire, of the nature, order, and worship of the Christian churches; and that in such an excellent manner, as that I know nothing material that can be added unto it, were an account of the same things to be given unto alike persons at this day. We may touch a little upon some heads of it:—

1. He declares *the conversion of men unto the faith* as the foundation of all their church order and worship: "Ὅσοι ἂν πεισθῶσι καὶ πιστεύωσιν ἀληθῆ ταῦτα τὰ ὑφ᾽ ἡμῶν διδασκόμενα καὶ λεγόμενα εἶναι, καὶ βιοῦν οὕτως δύνασθαι ὑπισχνῶνται, εὔχεσθαί τε καὶ αἰτεῖν νηστεύοντας παρὰ τοῦ Θεοῦ τῶν προημαρτημένων ἄφεσιν διδάσκονται ἡμῶν συνευχομένων καὶ συννηστευόντων αὐτοῖς·—" As many as are persuaded and do believe the things to be true which are taught and spoken by us, and take upon them-

selves that they are able to live according to that doctrine, they are taught to seek of God, by fasting and prayer, the pardon of their foregoing sins; and we also do join together with them in fasting and prayer for that end." And herein,—(1.) The only means of conversion which he insists upon is the preaching of the word, or truth of the gospel, wherein they especially insisted on the doctrine of the person and offices of Christ, as appears throughout his whole Apology. (2.) This preaching of the word, or declaration of the truth of the gospel, unto the conversion of the hearers, he doth not confine unto any especial sort of persons, as he doth afterward the administration of the holy things in the church; but speaks of it in general as the work of all Christians that were able for it, as doth the apostle, 1 Cor. xiv. 24, 25. (3.) Those who were converted did two things: —[1.] They *professed their faith* or assent unto the truth of the doctrine of the gospel; [2.] They took it on themselves to *live according to the rule of it*,—to do and observe the things commanded by Jesus Christ, as he appointed they should, Matt. xxviii. 18–20. (4.) To lay a sure and comfortable foundation of their future profession, they were taught to confess their former sins, and by earnest prayer, with fastings, to seek of God the pardon and forgiveness of them. And,—(5.) Herein (such was their love and zeal) those who had been the means of their conversion joined with them, for their comfort and edification. It is well known how this whole process is lost, and on what account it is discontinued; but whether it be done so unto the advantage of Christian religion, and the good of the souls of men, is well worth a strict inquiry.

2. In the next place he declares how those who were so converted were conducted unto *baptism*, and how they were initiated into the mysteries of the gospel thereby.

3. When any was so baptized, they brought him unto the church which he was to be joined unto: 'Ημεῖς δὲ μετὰ τὸ οὕτως λοῦσαι τὸν πεπεισμένον καὶ συγκατατεθειμένον ἐπὶ τοὺς λεγομένους ἀδελφοὺς ἄγομεν, ἔνθα συνηγμένοι εἰσί, κοινὰς εὐχὰς ποιησόμενοι ὑπέρ τε ἑαυτῶν, καὶ τοῦ φωτισθέντος καὶ ἄλλων πανταχοῦ πάντων εὐτόνως, κ. τ. λ.—" Him who is thus baptized, who believeth, and is received" (by consent) " among us" (or to be of our number), " we bring him unto those called the brethren, when they are met" (or gathered together) " for joint prayers and supplications for themselves, and for him who is now illuminated, and all others, with intension of mind," etc. We have here another illustrious instance of the care and diligence of the primitive church about the instating professed believers in the communion of the church. That hereon those who were to be admitted made their public confession we shall afterward declare. And the brethren here mentioned are the whole fraternity of the church, who were concerned in these

things. And Justin is not ashamed to declare by what name they called one another among themselves, even to the heathen, though it be now a scorn and reproach among them that are called Christians.

4. He proceeds to declare the nature of their *church meetings* or assemblies, with the duties and worship of them. And he tells us, first, that they had frequent meetings among themselves: "They that have any wealth," saith he, "do help the poor," καὶ συνεσμὲν ἀλλήλοις αἰεί, "and we are continually together;" that is, in the lesser occasional assemblies of the brethren, for so, in the next place, he adds immediately, Τῇ τοῦ ἡλίου λεγομένῃ ἡμέρᾳ, πάντων κατὰ πόλεις καὶ ἀγροὺς μενόντων ἐπὶ τὸ αὐτὸ συνέλευσις γίνεται·—"On the day called Sunday there is a meeting of all that dwell in the towns and fields or villages about." This was the state, the order, the proceeding of the church in the days of Justin; whence it is undeniably evident that he knew no other church-state or order but that of a particular congregation, whose members, living in any town or city, or fields adjacent, did constantly, all of them, meet together in one place on the first day of the week, for the celebration of divine worship.

5. In this church he mentions only two sorts of officers, προεστῶτες and διάκονοι, "presidents and deacons." Of the first sort, in the duty of one of their assemblies, he mentions but one, ὁ προεστώς, "the president," the ruler, the bishop; to whom belonged the administration of all the holy mysteries. And that we may not think that he is called the προεστώς with respect unto any pre-eminence over other ministers or elders, like a diocesan bishop, he terms him προεστὼς τῶν ἀδελφῶν, he that "presided over the brethren" of that church. Now, certainly that church wherein one president, elder, presbyter, or bishop, did administer the holy ordinances in one place unto all the members of it, was a particular congregation.

6. The things that he ascribeth unto this *leader*, to be done at this general meeting of the church every Lord's day, were,—(1.) That he *prayed;* (2.) That after the reading of the Scripture he *preached;* (3.) That he *consecrated the eucharist*, the elements of the bread and wine being distributed by the deacons unto the congregation; (4.) That he closed the whole worship of the day in prayer.

7. In the consecration of the sacramental elements, he observes that the president prayed at large, giving thanks to God: Εὐχαριστίαν ἐπὶ πολὺ ποιεῖται. So vain is the pretence of some, that in the primitive times they consecrated the elements by the repetition of the Lord's prayer only. After the participation of the eucharist there was a collection made for the poor, as he describeth it at large; what was so gathered being committed to the pastor, who took care for

the distribution of it unto all sorts of poor belonging unto the church. Hereunto was added, as Tertullian observes, the exercise of discipline in their assemblies; whereof we shall speak afterward. The close of the administration of the sacrament Justin gives us in these words: Καὶ ὁ προεστὼς εὐχὰς ὁμοίως καὶ εὐχαριστίας ὅση δύναμις αὐτῷ ἀναπέμπει· —" The pastor again, according to his ability" (or power), " poureth forth" (or sends up) " prayers, the people all joyfully crying, Amen," etc. ʿΟση δύναμις,—that is, as Origen expounds the phrase often used by himself, Κατὰ τὴν παροῦσαν καὶ δοθεῖσαν δύναμιν, lib. viii. ad Cels.;— "According unto the present ability given unto him."

This was the state, the order, and the worship of the church, with its method, in the days of Justin Martyr. This and no other is that which we plead for.

Unto these times belongs the most excellent epistle of the churches of Vienne and Lyons in France, unto the brethren in Asia and Phrygia, recorded at large by Eusebius, Hist., lib. v. cap. 1. Their design in it is to give an account of the holy martyrs who suffered in the persecution under Marcus Antoninus. I am no way concerned in what state Irenæus was in the church at Lyons, whereon, after the writing of this epistle, he was sent to Eleutherius, the bishop of Rome, which he gives an account of, cap. iv. He is, indeed, in that epistle called a presbyter of the church, although, as some suppose, it was sundry years after the death of Pothinus, whom they call bishop of Lyons, into whose room he immediately succeeded; and Eusebius himself, cap. viii., affirming that he would give an account of the writings of the ancient ecclesiastical presbyters, in the first place produceth those of Irenæus. But these things belong not unto our present contest. The epistle we intend was written by the brethren of those churches, and it was written to the brethren of the churches in Asia and Phrygia, after the manner of the Scripture; wherein the *fraternity or body of the church* was designed or intended in all such epistles. From them was this epistle, and unto those of the same sort was it written,—not from one bishop unto another. And as this manifests the concern of the brotherhood in all ecclesiastical affairs, so, with all other circumstances, it evidenceth that those churches were particular or congregational only. Nor is there any thing in the whole epistle that should give the least intimation of any other church-state known unto them. This epistle, as recorded by Eusebius, gives us a noble representation of the spirit and communion that was then among the churches of Christ; being written with apostolical simplicity and gravity, and remote from those titles of honour and affected swelling words, which the feigned writings of that age, and some that are genuine in those that followed, are stuffed withal.

Tertullian, who lived about the end of the second century, gives us the same account of the state, order, and worship of the churches, as was given before by Justin Martyr, Apol. ad Gen. cap. xxxix. The description of a church he first lays down in these words: " Corpus sumus de conscientia religionis, et disciplinæ unitate, et spei fœdere;"—" We are a body" (united) " in the conscience of religion" (or a conscientious observation of the duties of religion), " by an agreement in discipline" (whereby it was usual with the ancients to express universal obedience unto the doctrine and commands of Christ), " and in a covenant of hope." For whereas such a body or religious society could not be united but by a covenant, he calls it " a covenant of hope," because the principal respect was had therein unto the things hoped for. They covenanted together so to live and walk in the discipline of Christ, or obedience unto his commands, as that they might come together unto the enjoyment of eternal blessedness.

This religious body or society, thus united by covenant, did meet together in the same assembly or congregation: " Corpus sumus, coimus in cœtum et congregationem, ut ad Deum quasi manu factâ precationibus ambiamus orantes;" and, " Cogimur ad divinarum literarum commemorationem," etc. Designing to declare, as he doth in particular, " Negotia Christianæ factionis," as he calls them, or the duties of Christian religion, which in their churches they did attend unto, he lays the foundation in their meetings in the same assembly or congregation.

In these assemblies there presided the elders, that, upon a testimony of their meetness unto that office, were chosen thereunto: " President probati quique seniores, honorem istum non pretio sed testimonio adepti." And in the church thus met together in the same place, assembly, or congregation, under the rule and conduct of their elders, among other things they *exercised discipline;* that is, in the presence and by the consent of the whole: " Ibidem etiam, exhortationes, castigationes, et censura divina. Nam et judicatur magno cum pondere, ut apud certos de Dei conspectu; summumque futuri judicii præjudicium est, si quis ita deliquerit, ut a communicatione orationis et conventus, et omnis sancti commercii relegetur." The loss of this discipline and the manner of its administration hath been one of the principal means of the apostasy of churches from their primitive institution.

To the same purpose doth Origen give us an account of the way of the gathering and establishing churches under elders of their own choosing, in the close of his last book against Celsus. And although in the days of Cyprian, in the third century, the distinction between the bishop in any church, eminently so called, and those who are only presbyters, with their imparity, and not only the precedency but superiority of one over others, began generally to be admitted, yet it is sufficiently manifest from his epistles that the church wherein he did preside was so far a *particular church* as that the whole body or fraternity of it was admitted unto all advice in things of common concernment unto the whole church, and allowed the exercise of their power and liberty in choosing or refusing the officers that were to be set over them.

Some few things we may observe from the testimonies insisted on; as,—

1. There is in them a true and *full representation* of the state, order, rule, and discipline of the churches in the first ages. It is a sufficient demonstration that all those things wherein at the present the state and order of the church are supposed to consist are indeed later inventions; not merely because they are not mentioned by them, but because they are not so when they avowedly profess to give an account of that state and order of the church which was then in use and practice. Had there been then among Christians metropolitan archbishops, or bishops diocesan, churches national or provincial, an enclosure of church power or ecclesiastical jurisdiction, in and for the whole rule of the church, unto bishops and officers utterly foreign unto any pretence of apostolical institution or countenance; had many churches, or many hundreds of churches, been without rule in or among themselves, subject to the rule of any one man standing in no especial relation unto any of them; with other things of the like nature been then invented, known, and in use,—how could they possibly be excused in passing them over without the least taking notice of them, or giving them the honour of being once mentioned by them? How easy had it been for their pagan rulers, unto whom they presented their accounts (some of them) of the state of their churches, to have replied that they knew well enough there were other dignities, orders, and practices than what they did acknowledge, which they were either afraid or ashamed to own! But besides this silence, on the other hand, they assert such things of the officers appointed in the church,—of the way of their appointment, of the duty of officers in the church, of the power and liberty of the people, of the nature and exercise of discipline,—as are utterly inconsistent with that state of these things which is by some pleaded for. Yea, as we have showed, whatever they write or speak about churches or their order can have no being or exercise in any other form of churches but of particular congregations.

2. That account which they give, that representation which they make, of the kind, state, and order of the churches among them, doth absolutely agree with and answer unto what we are taught in the

divine writings about the same things. There were, indeed, before the end of the second century, some practices in and about some lesser things (such as sending the consecrated elements from the assembly unto such as were sick) that they had no warrant for from any thing written or done by the apostles; but as unto the substance of what concerns the state, order, rule, discipline, and worship of evangelical churches, there is not any instance to be given wherein they departed from the apostolical traditions or institution, either by adding any thing of their own unto them, or omitting any thing that was by them ordained.

3. From this state the churches did by degrees and insensibly degenerate, so as that another form and order of them did appear towards the end of the third century; for some in the first churches not applying their minds unto the apostolical rule and practice, who " ordained elders in every church," and that not only in cities and towns, but, as Clemens affirms, κατὰ χώρας, in the country villages, many disorders ensued with respect unto such collections of Christians and congregations as were gathered at some distance from the first or city church. Until the time of Origen, the example of the apostles in this case was followed, and their directions observed; for so he writes: Ἡμεῖς ἐν ἑκάστῃ πόλει ἄλλο σύστημα πατρίδος, κτισθὲν λόγῳ Θεοῦ ἐπιστάμενοι, τοὺς δυνατοὺς λόγῳ καὶ βίῳ ὑγιεῖ χρωμένους ἄρχειν ἐπὶ τὸ ἄρχειν ἐκκλησιῶν παρακαλοῦμεν.—Καὶ εἰ ἄρχουσιν οἱ καλῶς ἄρχοντες ἐν τῇ ἐκκλησίᾳ, ὑπὸ τῆς κατὰ Θεὸν πατρίδος, λέγω δὲ τῆς ἐκκλησίας, ἐκλεγόμενοι· ἄρχουσι κατὰ τὰ ὑπὸ τοῦ Θεοῦ προτεταγμένα·—" And we, knowing that there are other congregations gathered in the towns up and down, by the preaching of the word of God" (or, that there is another heavenly city in any town, built by the word of God), " we persuade some that are sound in doctrine and of good conversation, and meet for their rule, to take on them the conduct or rule of those churches ; and these, whilst they rule within the churches those societies of divine institution by whom they are chosen, they govern them according to the prescriptions" (or commands) " and rules given by God himself," Adver. Cels., lib. viii.

Those of whom he speaks, ἡμεῖς, were the pastors or principal members of the churches that were established. When they understood that, in any place distant from them, a number of believers were called and gathered into church-order by the preaching of the word, they presently, according unto their duty, took care of them,—inquired into their state and condition, assisting them, in particular, in finding out, trying, and recommending unto them persons meet to be their officers and rulers. These he acknowledgeth to be churches and cities of God, upon their collection by the preaching of the word, antecedently unto the constitution of any officers among them; as the apostles also did, Acts xiv. 22, 23. Wherefore, the church is essentially before its ordinary officers, and cannot, as unto its continuance, depend on any succession of theirs; which they have none but what it gives unto them. These officers thus recommended were *chosen*, as he tells us, by the churches wherein they were to preside, and thereon did govern them by the rule of God's word alone.

Hereby was the original constitution and state of the first churches for a good season preserved. Nor was there the least abridgment of the power either of these churches or of their officers, because, it may be, they were some of them planted in poor country villages; for as no man in the world can hinder but that every true church hath "de jure" all the rights and powers that any other church in the world hath or ought to have, or that every true officer, bishop, elder, or pastor hath all the power that Christ hath annexed unto that office (be they at Rome or Eugubium,[1]) so there was no abridgment of this power in the meanest of them as yet attempted.

But this course and duty in many places, not long after, became to be much omitted. Whether out of ignorance, or negligence, or unwillingness of men to undertake the pastoral charge in poor country churches, I know not, but so it was, that believers in the regions round about any city, ἐν χώραις, were looked on as those which belonged unto the city churches, and were not settled in particular congregations for their edification, which they ought to have been; and the councils that afterward ensued made laws and canons that they should be under the government of the bishops of those city churches. But when the number of such believers was greatly increased, so as that it was needful to have some always attending the ministry among them, they came, I know not how, to have "chorepiscopi" among them and over them. The first mention of them is in the synod of Ancyra in Galatia, about the year 314, can. 13; and mention is again made of them in a synod of Antioch, an. 341, and somewhat before at the council of Neocæsarea, can. 13, and frequently afterward, as any one may see in the late collections of the ancient canons. I verily believe, nor can the contrary be proved, but that these "chorepiscopi" at first were as absolute and complete in the office of episcopacy as any of the bishops of the greater cities, having their name or denomination from the places of their residence (ἐπίσκοποι κατὰ χώρας), and not for an intimation of any inferiority in them unto other city bishops; but so it came to pass, that through their poverty and want of interest, their ministry being confined unto a small country parish, and perhaps through a comparative meanness of their gifts or abilities, the city bishop claimed a superiority over them, and made canons about their power, the bounding

---

[1] A small town about eighty miles from Rome. The expression is borrowed from Jerome ad Evang.: "Ubicunque fuerit episcopus, sive Romæ, sive Eugubii, etc."—ED.

and exercising of it, in dependence on themselves. For a while they were esteemed a degree above mere presbyters, who accompanied or attended the bishop of the city church in his administrations, and a degree beneath the bishop himself,—in a posture never designed by Christ nor his apostles. Wherefore, in process of time, the name and thing were utterly lost, and all the country churches were brought into an absolute subjection unto the city churches, something being allowed unto them for worship, nothing for rule and discipline; whereby the first state of churches in their original institution, sacredly preserved in the first centuries, was utterly lost and demolished.

I shall add but one argument more to evince the true state and nature of evangelical churches herein,—namely, that they were only particular congregations; and that is taken from the duties and powers ascribed in the Scripture unto churches, and the members or entire brotherhood of them. It was observed before that the epistles of the apostles were written all of them unto the body of the churches, in contradistinction unto their elders, bishops, or pastors, unless it were those that were written unto particular persons by name. And as this is plain in all the epistles of Paul, wherein sometimes distinct mention is made of the officers of the church, sometimes none at all, so the apostle John affirms that he wrote unto the church, but that Diotrephes (who seems to have been their bishop) received him not, at once rejecting the authority of the apostle and overthrowing the liberty of the church; which example was diligently followed in the succeeding ages, 3 John 9. And the apostle Peter, writing unto the churches on an especial occasion, speaks distinctly of the elders, 1 Pet. v. 1, 2. See also Heb. xiii. 24, the body of the epistle being directed to the body of the churches. Wherefore, all the instructions, directions, and injunctions given in those epistles as unto the exercise of power or the performance of duty, they are given unto *the churches themselves.* Now, these are such, many of them, as cannot be acted or performed in any church by the body of the people, but that which is congregational only. It were too long here to insist on particulars,—it shall be done elsewhere; and it will thence appear that this argument alone is sufficient to bear the weight of this whole cause. The reader may, if he please, consider what representation hereof is made in these places compared together, Matt. xviii. 15–18; Acts i. 12, 23, ii. 1, 42, 44, 46, v. 11–13, xi. 21, 22, 25, 26, 28–30, xii. 5, 12, xiv. 26, 27, xv. 1–4, 6, 12, 13, 22, 23, 27, 28, 30, xx. 28; Rom. xv. 5, 6, 14, 25, 26, xvi. 1, 17, 18; 1 Cor. i. 4, 5, chap. v. throughout, xii. 4, 7–9, 11, 15, 18, 28–31, chap. xiv. throughout, xvi. 10, 11; 2 Cor. iii. 1–3, vii. 14, 15, viii. 22–24, ii. 6–11, viii. 5; Eph. ii. 19–22, v. 11, 12; Gal. vi. 1; Phil. ii. 25–28; Col. i. 1, 2, ii. 2, iii. 16, iv. 9, 12, 16, 17; 1 Thess. v. 11–14; 2 Thess.

iii. 6, 7, 14, 15; Heb. x. 24, 25, xii. 15, 16. In these, I say, and other places innumerable, there are those things affirmed of and ascribed unto the apostolical churches, as unto their state, order, assemblies, duties, powers, and privileges, as evince them to have been only *particular congregations.*

CHAPTER VI.

Congregational churches alone suited unto the ends of Christ in the institution of his church.

HAVING given an account of that state and order of the gospel churches which are of divine institution, it is necessary that we declare also their *suitableness* and *sufficiency* unto all the ends for which the Lord Christ appointed such churches; for if there be any true proper end of that nature which cannot be attained in or by any church-state in this or that form, it must be granted that no such form is of divine appointment. Yea, it is necessary not only that such a state as pretends unto a divine original be not only not contradictory unto or inconsistent with such an end, but that it is effectually conducing thereunto, and in its place necessary unto that purpose. This, therefore, is that which we shall now inquire into,— namely, whether this state and form of gospel churches in single congregations be suited unto all those ends for which any such churches were appointed; which they must be on the account of the wisdom of Jesus Christ, the author and founder of them, or be utterly discarded from their pretence. Nor is there any more forcible argument against any pretended church-state, rule, or order, than that it is obstructive unto the souls of men in attaining the proper ends of their whole institution. What these ends are was in general before declared; I shall not here repeat them, or go over them again, but only single out the consideration of those which are usually pleaded as not attainable by this way of churches in single congregations only, or that at least they are not suited unto their attainment.

1. The first of these is *mutual love* among all Christians, all the disciples of Christ. By the disciples of Christ I intend them, and them only, who profess faith in his person and doctrine, and to hear him, or to be guided by him alone, in all things that appertain unto the worship of God, and their living unto him. If there are any called Christians who in these things choose other guides, call other ministers, hear them in their appointments, we must sever them from our present consideration; though there are important duties required of us towards them also. But what is alleged is necessary unto the con-

stitution of a true disciple of Christ. Unto all those his great command is, mutual love among themselves. This he calls in an especial manner " his commandment," and " a new commandment;" as for other reasons, so because he had given the first absolute great example of it in himself, as also discovered motives unto it and reasons for it which mankind before was in the dark unto. And such weight doth he lay on this command, that he declares the manifestation of the glory of God, his own honour, and the evidence to be given unto the world that we are his disciples, do depend on our obedience thereunto.

To express and exercise this love, in all the acts and duties of it, among his disciples, was one end of his appointing them to walk in church-relation one unto another, wherein this love is the bond of perfectness. And the loss of this love, as unto its due exercise, is no less a pernicious part of the fatal apostasy of the churches than is the loss of faith and worship: for hereon is Christendom, as it is usually called, become the greatest stage of hatred, rage, wrath, bloodshed, and mutual desolations that is in the whole world; so as that we have no way to answer the objection of the Jews arguing against us from the divine promises of love and peace in the kingdom of the Messiah, but by granting that all these things arise from a rebellion against his rule and kingdom. Now, this love in its exercise is eminently preserved in this order of particular churches; for,—

(1.) The principle of their collection into such societies, next unto that of faith in Christ Jesus, is *love unto all the saints;* for their conjunction being with some of them as such only, they must have a love unto all that are so. And none of them would join in such societies if their so doing did in any thing impair their love unto all the disciples of Christ, or impede it in any of its operations. And the communion of these churches among themselves is, and ought to be, such as that all of them do constitute as it were one body and common church; as we shall see afterward. And it is one principal duty of them to stir up themselves, in all their members, unto a continual exercise of love towards all the saints of Christ, as occasion doth require; and if they are defective in this catholic love, it is their fault, contrary to the rule and end of their institution.

(2.) Unto the constant expression and exercise of this love there are required,—[1.] *Present suitable objects* unto all the acts and duties of it; [2.] A *description and prescription* of those acts and duties; [3.] *Rules* for the right performance and exercise of them; [4.] An *end* to be attained in their discharge. All these things hath the Lord Christ provided for his disciples in the constitution and rule of these churches. And a due attendance unto them hath he appointed as the instance, trial, and experiment of their love unto all his disciples; for whereas they might pretend such a love, yet plead that they know not how nor wherein to express and exercise it, especially as unto sundry duties mentioned in the Scripture as belonging thereunto, he hath provided this way, wherein they cannot be ignorant of the duties of love required of them, nor of suitable objects, rules, and ends for their practice. It were too long to go over these things in particular. I shall only add (what is easily defensible) that gospel love will never be recovered and restored unto its pristine glory until particular churches or congregations are reformed and reduced to that exercise of love without dissimulation which is required in all their members among themselves; for whilst men live in envy and malice, be hateful and hating one another, or whilst they live in an open neglect of all those duties which the Lord Christ hath appointed to be observed towards the members of that society whereunto they do belong, as a pledge and evidence of their love unto all his disciples, no such thing can be attained. And thus is it in most parochial assemblies, who, in the midst of their complaints of the breach of love and union, by some men's withholding communion in some parts of divine worship with them, yet, besides the common duties of civility and neighbourhood, neither know nor practise any thing of that spiritual love, delight, and communion that ought to be amongst them as members of the same church.

We boast not ourselves of any attainments in this kind,—we know how short we come of that fervent love that flourished in the first churches; but this we say, that there is no way to recover it but by that state and order of particular churches which we propose, and, κατὰ τὴν δοθεῖσαν δύναμιν, do adhere unto.

But pretences unto the contrary are vehemently urged, and the clamours unto that end are loud and many: for this way, it is said, *of setting up particular congregations* is that which hath caused endless divisions, and lost all love and Christian affection among us, being attended with other mischievous consequents, such as the most rhetorical adversaries of it are scarce able to declare, nor could Tertullus himself do it if he were yet alive; for by this means, men not meeting as they used to do at the administration of the sacrament and common-prayer, *all love is lost among them.* I answer,—

[1.] This objection, so far as I am able to observe, is mostly managed by them who seem to know very little of the nature and duties of that love which our Lord Jesus Christ enjoins in the gospel, nor do give any considerable evidence of their living, walking, and acting in the power of it. And as unto what they fancy unto themselves under that name, whereas it is evident from common practice that it extends no farther but to peaceableness in things civil and indifferent, with some expressions of kindness in their mirth and feastings, and other jovial societies, we are not concerned in it.

[2.] This objection lies not at all against the thing itself,—namely, that all churches of divine institution are congregational, which alone at present is pleaded for,—but against the gathering of such societies or congregations in that state of things which now prevails amongst us. But whereas this depends on principles not yet declared and confirmed, the consideration of this part of the objection must be referred unto another place. I shall only say at present, that it is the greatest and most powerful engine in the hand of Satan, and men of corrupt secular interest, to keep all church reformation out of the world.

But if the way itself be changed (which alone, as absolutely considered, we at present defend), that change must be managed with respect unto some *principles* contrary unto love and its *due exercise*, which it doth assert and maintain, or some *practices* that it puts men upon of the same nature and tendency. But this hitherto hath not been attempted, at least not effected.

[3.] We do not find that a *joint participation of the same ordinances at the same time*, within the same walls, is in itself either an effect, or evidence, or duty of gospel love, or any means for the preservation or promotion of it; for it was diligently observed in the Papacy, when all true evangelical love, faith, and worship were lost. Yea, this kind of communion and conjunction, added unto an implicit dependence on the authority of the church, was substituted in their room; and multitudes were contented with them, as those which did bestead them in their neglect of all other graces and their exercise. And I wish it were not so among others, who suppose they have all the love that is required of them, if they are freed from such scandalous variances with their neighbours as should make them unfit for the communion.

[4.] If this be the only means of love, how do men maintain it towards any not of their own parish, seeing they never meet with them at the sacrament of the Lord's supper? And if they can live in love with those of other parishes, why can they not do so with those who, having the same faith and sacraments with them, do meet apart, for the exercise of divine worship, in such congregations as we have described? Wherefore,—

[5.] The *variance* that is pretended to be caused by the setting up of these particular congregations is a part of that variance which Christ came to send into the world: Matt. x. 34–36, " Think not that I am come to send peace on earth: I came not to send peace, but a sword. For I am come to set a man at variance against his father, and the daughter against her mother, and the daughter-in-law against her mother-in-law. And a man's foes shall be they of his own household." He was the Prince of Peace; he came to make peace between God and men, between men themselves, Jews and Gentiles; he taught nothing, enjoined nothing that in its own nature should have the least inconsistency with peace, or give countenance unto variance: but he declares what would ensue and fall out, through the sin, the darkness, unbelief, and enmity unto the truth that would continue on some under the preaching of the gospel, whilst others of their nearest relations should embrace the truth and profession of it. What occasion for this variance is taken from the gathering of these congregations, which the way itself doth neither cause nor give the least countenance unto, we are not accountable for. Whereas, therefore, there is with those among whom these variances, and loss of love thereby, are pretended, " one Lord, one faith, one baptism, one hope of their calling,"—the same truth of the gospel preached, the same sacraments administered; and whereas both the principles of the way and the persons of those who assemble in distinct corporations for the celebration of divine worship, do lead unto love and the practice of it in all its known duties,—all the evils that ensue on this way must be charged on the enmity, hatred, pride, and secular interest of men; which it is not in our power to cure.

2. Another end of the institution of this state is, that the church might be the "pillar and ground of the truth," 1 Tim. iii. 15,—that is, that it might be the principal outward means to support, preserve, publish, declare, and propagate the doctrine or truth of the gospel, especially that concerning the person and offices of Christ; which the apostle subjoins unto this assertion in the next words. That church-state which doth not answer this end is not of divine institution; but this the ministry of these churches is eminently suited unto. There are three things required in this duty, or required unto this end, that the church be the pillar and ground of truth:—(1.) That it *preserve the truth in itself*, and in the profession of all its members, against all seducers, false teachers, and errors. This the apostle gives in special charge unto the elders of the church of Ephesus, adding the reasons of it, Acts xx. 28–31. This is in an especial manner committed unto the officers of the church, 1 Tim. v. 20; 2 Tim. i. 13, 14. This the ministry of these churches is meet and suited unto. The continual inspection which they may and ought to have into all the members of the church, added unto that circumspection about and trial of the doctrines preached by themselves, in the whole body of the church, fits them for this work. This is the fundamental means (on the matter the only outward means) that the Lord Christ hath appointed for the preservation of the truth of the gospel in this world, whereby the church is the pillar and ground of

truth. How this can be done where churches are of that make and constitution that the officers of them can have no immediate inspection into or cognizance of either the knowledge, opinions, or practices of the members of their church, nor the body of the church know on any evident ground what it is that their principal officer believes and teaches, I know not. By this means was the truth preserved in the churches of the first two centuries, wherein they had no officers but what were placed in particular churches, so as that no considerable error made any entrance among them. (2.) That each church take care that the same truth be preserved entire, as unto the profession of it, in all other churches. Their communion among themselves (whereof afterward) is built upon their common ὁμολογία, or profession of the same faith. This, therefore, it is their duty, and was always their practice, to look after, that it was preserved entire; for a change in the faith of any of them they knew would be the dissolution of their communion. Wherefore, when any thing of that nature fell out, as it did in the church of Antioch upon the preaching of the necessity of circumcision and keeping of the law, whereby the souls of many of the disciples were subverted, the church at Jerusalem, on the notice and knowledge of it, helped them with their advice and counsel. And Eusebius tells us, that upon the first promulgation of the heresies and frenzies of Montanus, the faithful, or churches in Asia, met frequently in sundry places to examine his pretences and condemn his errors; whereby the churches in Phrygia were preserved, Hist. Eccl., lib. v. cap. 14. So the same was done afterward in the case of Samosatenus at Antioch, whereby that church was delivered from the infection of his pernicious heresy, lib. vii. cap. 27, 28, 29. And this care is still incumbent on every particular church, if it would approve itself to be the pillar and ground of truth. And in like manner Epiphanius, giving an account of the original of the heresy of Noetus, a Patropassian, affirms that the holy presbyters of the church called him, and inquired of his opinion several times; whereon, being convicted before the presbytery of enormous errors, he was cast out of the church: Ἀλλὰ μεταξὺ τούτων (when he began to disperse his errors) ἀπὸ τῆς περὶ αὐτὸν ἐνηχήσεως οἱ μακάριοι πρεσβύτεροι τῆς ἐκκλησίας προσκαλεσάμενοι αὐτὸν ἐξήταζον περὶ τούτων ἁπάντων—ὁ δὲ τὰ πρῶτα ἠρνεῖτο ἐπὶ τοῦ πρεσβυτερίου ἀγόμενος, Epiphanius, Hæres. cont. Noet., Hær. xxxviii. sec. 57.

Hence it was that the doctrine of the church, as unto the substance of it, was preserved entire during the first two centuries, and somewhat after. Indeed, as when the Israelites came out of Egypt, there came along with them a "mixed multitude" of other people, Exod. xii. 38, which fell to "lusting" for meat when they came into the wilderness, Numb. xi. 4, to the danger of the whole congregation: so when

Christianity was first preached and received in the world, besides
those who embraced it sincerely, and were added unto the church,
there was a great mixture of stubborn Jews, as the Ebionites; of
philosophical Greeks, as the Valentinians and the Marcionites; of
plain impostors, such as Simon Magus and Menander; who all of
them pretended to be Christians, but they fell a lusting, and exceedingly troubled and perplexed the churches with an endeavour to
seduce them unto their imaginations. Yet none of their abominations could force an entrance into the churches themselves; which, by
the means insisted on, were preserved. But when this church-state
and order was changed, and another gradually introduced in the
room of it, errors and heresies got new advantages, and entered into
the churches themselves, which before did only assault and perplex
them; for,—

[1.] When prerogative and pre-eminence of any *single person* in
the church began to be in esteem, not a few who failed in their
attempts of attaining it, to revenge themselves on the church made
it their business to invent and propagate pernicious heresies. So
did Thebuthis at Jerusalem, Euseb., lib. iv. cap. 22; and Valen-
tinus, Tertul. ad Valentin., cap. iv.; and Marcion at Rome, Epiphan.
Hæres. xlii. Montanus fell into his dotage on the same account; so
did Novatianus at Rome, Euseb., lib. vi. cap. 43, and Arius at Alexandria. Hence is that censure of them by Lactantius, lib. iv. cap. 30:
" Ii quorum fides fuit lubrica, cum Deum nosse se et colere simula-
rent, augendis opibus et honori studentes, affectabant maximum
sacerdotium, et a potioribus victi, secedere cum suffragatoribus malu-
erunt, quam eos ferre præpositos quibus concupierant ipsi ante præ-
poni."

[2.] When any of their bishops of the new constitution, whether
patriarchal or diocesan, fell into heresies, which they did frequently,
and that numbers of them, they had so many advantages to diffuse
their poison into the whole body of their churches, and such political
interests for their promotion, as that the churches themselves were
thoroughly infected with them. It is true, the body of the people in
many places did oppose them, withdraw and separate from them;
but it cannot be denied but that this was the first way and means
whereby the churches ceased to be the ground and pillar of truth,
many destructive errors being received into them, which did only
outwardly assault them whilst they abode in their first institution.
And had not the churches, in process of time, utterly lost their
primitive state and order, by coalescing into one papal, pretended
universal church, the faith itself could never have been so utterly
corrupted, depraved, and lost among them, as in the issue it was.

(3.) To *propagate the gospel* is in like manner required hereunto.

This, I acknowledge, doth more immediately concern the duty of persons in any church-order than the order itself; for it must be the work of some particular persons dedicating themselves unto their ministry, as it was in the first churches, 3 John 5–8.

The like may be said of any other public acknowledged end of the institution of churches. If the way pleaded for be not consistent with them all, and the proper means of attaining them, if it be not suited unto their accomplishment, let it be discarded. I shall insist on one more only.

3. Our Lord Jesus Christ hath given that state unto his churches, hath instated them in that order, as that *his interest*, kingdom, and religion might be carried on in the world without prejudice or disadvantage *unto any of the lawful interests of men*, especially without any opposition unto or interfering with the civil authority or magistracy, which is the ordinance of God; and no church-way that doth so is of his institution. Wherefore, I shall briefly declare what are the principles of those of this way in these things, which are the principles of the way itself which they do profess:—

(1.) Our first general assertion unto this purpose is this: *The Lord Jesus Christ taught no doctrine, appointed no order in his church, gave it no power, that is opposite unto or inconsistent with any righteous government in this world, of what sort soever it be, of those whereinto government is distributed in reason and practice.* His doctrine, indeed, is opposed unto all unrighteousness in and of all men, magistrates and others; but not to *the legal rule of magistrates* that are unrighteous men. And this opposition is doctrinal only, confirmed with promises and threatenings of eternal things, refusing and despising all outward aids of force and restraint. This rule we allow for the trial of all churches and their state, whether they be according unto the mind of Christ.

But whereas the Lord Jesus Christ hath taught, commanded, appointed nothing that is contrary unto or inconsistent with righteous government of any sort, if rulers or magistrates shall forbid the observance of what he hath commanded, appointed, and ordered, and then charge it on him or his way that his disciples cannot, dare not, will not comply with that prohibition, and accuse them thereon of sedition and opposition unto government, they deal injuriously with him, whereof they must give an account; for, whereas " all power is given unto him in heaven and earth," all nations are his inheritance, all people in his absolute disposal, and it is his pleasure to set up his kingdom in the earth, without which the earth itself would not be continued, he could not deal more gently with the righteous rulers of this world (and he did it because righteous rule is the ordinance of God), than to order all things so, that whether they receive his law and doctrine or no, nothing should be done in opposition unto them or their rule. And if any of them are not contented with this measure, but will forbid the observance of what he commands, wherein he alone is concerned, and not they, this is left to be determined between him and them. In the meantime, when rulers are not able to fancy, much less give a real instance of, any one principle, doctrine, or practice, in any of the churches of Christ, or any belonging unto them, that is contrary unto, or inconsistent with, the rights or exercise of their rule and government, and yet shall not only prohibit the doing of those things which he hath commanded merely with respect unto the spiritual and eternal ends of his kingdom, but shall also punish and destroy those who will not disown his authority and comply with their prohibition, it doth scarce answer their interest and prudence; for to what purpose is it for any to provoke him who is mightier than they, when they have no appearance of necessity for their so doing, nor advantage thereby?

(2.) In particular, the Lord Christ hath ordained *no power or order in his church, no office or duty, that should stand in need of the civil authority,* sanction, or force to preserve it, or make it effectual unto its proper ends. It is sufficient to discharge any thing of a pretence to be an appointment of Christ in his church, if it be not sufficient unto its own proper end, without the help of the civil magistrate. That church-state which is either constituted by human authority, or cannot consist without it, is not from him. That ordinance which is in its own nature divine, or is pretended so to be, so far as it is not effectual unto its end without the aid of human authority is not of him; he needs it not. He will not borrow the assistance of civil authority to rule in and over the consciences of men, with respect unto their living to God and coming unto the enjoyment of himself.

The way of requiring the sanction of civil authority unto ecclesiastical orders and determinations began with the use of general councils in the days of Constantine; and when once it was engaged in and approved, so far as that what was determined in the synods, either as to doctrine or as unto the rule of the church, should be confirmed by the imperial authority, with penalties on all that should gainsay such determinations, it is deplorable to consider what mutual havoc was made among Christians upon the various sentiments of synods and emperors. Yet this way pleased the rulers of the church so well, and, as they thought, eased them of so much trouble, that it was so far improved amongst them, that at last they left no power in or about religion or religious persons unto the civil magistrate, but what was to be exercised in the execution of the decrees and determinations of the church.

It is necessary, from this institution of particular churches, that they have their subsistence, continuation, order, and the efficacy of all that they act and do as churches, from Christ himself; for whereas all that they are and do is heavenly, spiritual, and not of this world, so that it reacheth nothing of all those things which are under the power of the magistrate (that is, the lives and bodies of men, and all civil interests appertaining to them), and affects nothing but what no power of all the magistrates under heaven can reach unto (that is, the souls and consciences of men),—no trouble can hence arise unto any rulers of the world, no contests about what they ought and what they ought not to confirm; which have caused great disorders among many.

(3.) In particular, also, *there neither is nor can be in this church-state the least pretence of power or authority to be acted towards or over the persons of kings or rulers, which should either impeach their right or impede the exercise of their just authority;* for as Christ hath granted no such power unto the church, so it is impossible that any pretence of it should be seated in a particular congregation, especially being gathered on this principle, that there is no church-power properly so called but what is so seated, and that no concurrence, agreement, or association of many churches can add a new, greater, or other power or authority unto them than what they had singly before. And what power can such churches act towards kings, potentates, or rulers of nations? Have they not the highest security that it is utterly impossible that ever their authority, or their persons in the exercise of it, should be impeached, hindered, or receive any detriment from any thing that belongs to this church-state?

These principles, I say, are sufficient to secure Christian religion, and the state, order, and power of churches instituted therein, from all reflections of inconsistency with civil government, or of influencing men unto attempts of its change or ruin. The sum is:—Let the outward frame and order of righteous government be of what sort it will, nothing inconsistent with it, nothing intrenching on it, nothing making opposition unto it, is appointed by Jesus Christ, or doth belong unto that church-state which he hath ordained and established.

Two things only must be added unto these principles, that we may not seem so to distinguish the civil state and the church as to make them unconcerned in each other; for,—

First, It is the unquestionable duty of the rulers and governors of the world, upon the preaching of the gospel, *to receive its truth,* and to yield obedience unto its commands. And whereas all power and offices are to be discharged for God, whose ministers all rulers be, they are bound, in the discharge of their office, to countenance, supply, and protect the profession and professors of the truth,—that is, the church,—according unto the degrees and measures which they shall judge necessary.

Secondly, It is the duty of the church, *materially* considered,—that is, of all those who are members of it,—in any kingdom or common-wealth, to be usefully subservient, even as Christians, unto that rule which is over them as men, in all those ways, and by all those means, which the laws, usages, and customs of the countries whereof they are do direct and prescribe. But these things are frequently spoken unto.

There are sundry other considerations whereby it may be evinced that this order and state of gospel churches is not only consistent with every righteous government in the world (I mean, that is so in its constitution, though, as all other forms, it be capable of maladministration), but the most useful and subservient unto its righteous administration, being utterly incapable of immixing itself, as such, in any of those occasions of the world or state affairs as may create the least difficulty or trouble unto rulers. With others it is not so. It is known that the very constitution of the papal church, as it is stated in the canons of it, is inconsistent with the just rights of kings and rulers, and ofttimes, in the exercise of its power, destructive unto their persons and dominions. And herein concurred the prelatical church-state of England, whilst it continued in their communion, and held its dependence on the Roman church; for although they had all their power originally from the kings of this realm,—as the records and laws of it do expressly affirm, " That the church of England was founded in episcopacy by the king and his nobles,"—yet they claimed such an addition of power and authority, by virtue of their office from the papal omnipotency, as that they were ringleaders in perplexing the government of this nation, under the pretence of maintaining what they called the " rights of the church." And hereunto they were enabled by the very constitution of their church-order, which gave them that power, grandeur, with political interest, that were needful to effectuate their design. And since they have been taken off from this foundation of contesting kings and princes on their own ecclesiastical authority, and deprived of their dependence on the power and interest of the papal see, having no bottom for or supportment of their church state and order but regal favour and mutable laws, there have, on such causes and reasons which I shall not mention, ensued such emulations of the nobility and gentry, and such contempts of the common people, as leave it questionable whether their adherence unto the government be not more burdensome and dangerous unto it than were their ancient contests and oppositions.

CHAPTER VII.

No other church-state of divine institution.

It may be it will be generally granted, I am sure it cannot be modestly denied, that particular churches or congregations are of a divine original institution; as also, that the primitive churches continued long in that form or order. But it will be farther pleaded, that granting or supposing this divine institution of particular churches, yet there may be churches of another form and order also, as diocesan or national, that we are obliged to submit unto: for although the apostles appointed that there should be bishops or elders ordained κατὰ πόλιν,—that is, in every city and town where Christian religion was received; and Clemens affirmeth that they did themselves constitute bishops and deacons κατὰ χώρας καὶ πόλεις,—in the regions, or villages and cities; yet there was another form afterward introduced. Theodoret, bishop of Cyprus, affirms that there were eight hundred churches committed to his care, Epist. cxiii. whereof many were in towns and cities having no bishop of their own. The whole country of Scythia, though there were in it many cities, villages, and fortresses, yet had but one bishop, whose residence was at Tomis, all other churches being under him; as Sozomen declares, lib. vi. cap. 20. So it is at this day in divers provinces belonging of old unto the Greek church; as in Moldavia and Wallachia, where they have one whom they call the ἡγούμενος,—the leader or ruler, that presides over all the churches in the nation. And this order of things, that there should not be a bishop in smaller churches, was first confirmed in the sixth canon of the council of Sardis, in the year 347.

In answer hereunto I shall do these two things:—First, I shall show that there is no church order, state, or church form of divine institution, that doth any way impede, take away, or overthrow the liberty, power, and order of particular congregations, such as we have described. Secondly, I shall inquire into the causes of churches of another state or order, as the power of magistrates and rulers, or their own choice and consent:—

1. *There is no form, order, or church-state, divinely instituted, that should annul the institution of particular congregations, or abridge them of their liberties, or deprive them of the power committed unto them.*

It is such a church-state alone that we are now concerned to inquire after. Whatever of that kind either is or may be imagined that intrenches not on the state, liberty, and power of particular congregations, is not of our present consideration. Men may frame and order what they please; and what advantage they make thereby shall not be envied unto them, whilst they injure not any of the institutions of Christ. But,—

(1.) These churches, *as they are churches*, are meet and able to attain the ends of churches. To say they are churches, and yet have not in themselves power to attain the ends of churches, is to speak contradictions, or to grant and deny the same thing in the same breath; for a church is nothing but such a society as hath power, ability, and fitness to attain those ends for which Christ hath ordained churches: that which hath so is a church, and that which hath not so is none. Men may, if they please, deny them to be churches, but then I know not where they will find any that are so. For instance, suppose men should deny all the parochial churches in England to be such churches as are intrusted with church-power and administrations, what church, in the first instance, could they require our communion withal? Will they say, it is with the national or diocesan churches? Neither of these do or can, as such, administer sacred ordinances. A man cannot preach nor hear the word but in a particular assembly; the Lord's supper cannot be administered but in a particular congregation; nor any presential, local communion of believers among themselves, like that described by the apostle, 1 Cor. xii. and xiv., be otherwise attained. No communion is firstly and immediately required, or can be required, with diocesan churches, as such. Wherefore, it is parochial, particular churches that we are required to hold communion with. We say, therefore, these parochial churches are either really and truly so endued with church power and liberty, or they are not. If they are, or are acknowledged so to be, we have herein obtained what we plead for;—if they are not, then are we required to join in church-communion with those societies that are not churches; and if we refrain so doing, we are charged with schism, which is to turn religion into ridicule: for,—

(2.) It is utterly foreign to the Scripture, and a monster unto antiquity (I mean that which is pure and regardable in this cause), that there should be churches with a *part, half, more* or *less*, of church-power, and not the whole, neither in right nor exercise; or that there should be church-officers, elders, presbyters, or bishops, that should have a partiary power, half or a third part, or less, of that which entirely belongeth unto the office they hold. Let *one testimony* be given out of the Scripture, or that antiquity which we appeal unto, unto this purpose, and we shall cease our plea. But this is that which our understandings are set on rack withal every day;—there is a national church, that is intrusted with supreme church-power in the nation whereof it is. Here, at the entrance, we fall into a double disquietment.

For,—[1.] We know not as yet what this national church is, here (or in France), nor of what persons it doth consist. [2.] We know not whether this national church have all the power that Christ hath given unto the church, or that there is a reserve for some addition from beyond sea, if things were well accommodated. Then, that there are diocesan churches, whose original, with the causes and occasions of their bounds, limits, power, and manner of administration, I think God alone knows perfectly, we do but guess; for there is not one word mentioned of any of their concernments in the Scripture. And we know that these churches cannot be said to have all the power that Christ hath intrusted his church withal, because there is another church unto which they are in subjection, and on which they do depend; but it seems they have the next degree of power unto that which is uppermost. But whatever their power be, it is so administered by chancellors, commissaries, officials, in such ways and for such ends, that I shall believe a dissent from them and it to be schism when I believe it is midnight whilst the sun shines in his full strength and glory. And then we are told of parochial churches, who have this power only, that if we do not in them whatever is required of us, not by them but those that are put over them, they can inform against us, that we may be mulcted and punished.

(3.) It will be said that these churches, as such, were indeed originally intrusted and invested with all church rights, power, and authority, but for many weighty reasons are abridged in sundry things of the exercise of them; for who can think it meet that every single parish should be intrusted with the exercise of all church rule and power among themselves?

Ans. 1. Whose fault is it that these churches are not meet for the exercise of that power which Christ hath granted unto such churches? If it be from themselves, their negligence, or ignorance, or wickedness, it is high time they were reformed, and brought into that state and condition wherein they may be fit and able to answer the ends of their institution. 2. They are indeed sorry churches that are not as meet to exercise all church-power, according to the mind of Christ, as the chancellor's court. 3. There is no power pleaded for in congregational churches but what is granted unto them by the word and constitution of Christ. And who is he that shall take this from them, or deprive them of its exercise or right thereunto? (1.) It is not done, nor ever was by Jesus Christ himself. He doth not pull down what himself hath built; nor doth any one institution of his in the least interfere with any other. It is true, the Lord Christ by his law deprives all churches of their power, yea, of their state, who walk, act, and exercise a power not derived from him, but set up against him, and used unto such ends as are opposite unto and destructive of the ends of church-order by him appointed; but to imagine that whilst a church claims no power but what it receives from him, useth it only for him and in obedience unto his commands, he hath, by any act, order, or constitution, taken away that power or any part of it from such a church, is a vain supposition. (2.) *Such churches cannot by any act of their own deprive themselves of this right and power;* for,—[1.] It is committed unto them in a way of trust, which they falsify if by their own consent they part with it; [2.] Without it they cannot discharge many duties required of them. To part with this power is to renounce their duty; which is the only way whereby they may lose it. And if it be neither taken from them by any law, rule, or constitution of Christ, nor can be renounced or fore-gone by themselves, what other power under heaven can justly de-prive them of it or hinder them in its execution? The truth is, the principal means which hath rendered the generality of parochial churches unmeet for the exercise of any church-power is, that their interest in it and right unto it hath been so long unjustly detained from them, as that they know not at all what belongs thereunto, being hidden from them by those who should instruct them in it. And might they be admitted, under the conduct of pious and prudent officers, unto any part of the practice of this duty in their assemblies, their understanding in it would quickly be increased.

That right, power, or authority which we thus assign unto all par-ticular churches gathered according unto the mind of Christ, is that, and that only, which is necessary to their own preservation in their state and purity, and unto the discharge of all those duties which Christ requireth of the church.

2. Now, although they may not justly by any be deprived hereof, yet it may be inquired whether there may not an addition of eccle-siastical power be made unto that which is of original institution, for the good of the whole number of churches that are of the same com-munion. And this may be done, either by the power and authority of the supreme magistrate, with respect unto all the churches in his dominion; or it may be so by the churches themselves erecting a new power, in a combination of some, many, or all of them, which they had not in them singly and distinctly before.

For the power of the magistrate in and about religion, it hath been much debated and disputed in some latter ages. For three hundred years there was no mention of it in the church, because no supreme powers did then own the Christian religion. For the next three hundred years there were great ascriptions unto supreme ma-gistrates, to the exaltation of their power; and much use was made thereof among the churches by such as had the best interest in them. The next three hundred years was, as unto this case, much taken up with disputes about this power between the emperors and the popes of Rome; sometimes one side gaining the advantage in some especial instances, sometimes the other.   But from that period of time, or thereabouts, the contest came to blows, and the blood of some hundred thousands was shed in the controversy,—namely, about the power of emperors and kings on the one side, and the popes of Rome on the other.   In the issue, the popes abode masters of the field, and continued in actual possession of all ecclesiastical power, though sometimes mixed with the rebellion of one stubborn prince or other, as here frequently in England, who controlled them in some of their new acquisitions.   Upon the public reformation of religion, many princes threw off the yoke of the papal rule, and, according to the doctrine of the reformers, assumed unto themselves the power which, as they judged, the godly kings of Judah of old and the first Chris tian emperors did exercise about ecclesiastical affairs.   From that time there have been great and vehement disputes about the ecclesiastical power of sovereign princes and states.   I shall not here undertake to treat concerning it, although it is a matter of no great difficulty to demonstrate the extremes that many have run into, some by granting too much, and some too little unto them.   And I shall grant, for my part, that too much cannot well be assigned unto them whilst these two principles are preserved:—1. That no supreme magistrate hath power to deprive or abridge the churches of Christ of any right, authority, or liberty granted unto them by Jesus Christ; 2. Nor hath any to coerce, punish, or kill any persons (being civilly peaceable and morally honest) because they are otherwise minded in things concerning gospel faith and worship than he is.

It hath not yet been disputed whether the supreme magistrate hath power to ordain, institute, and appoint any new form or state of churches, supposedly suited unto the civil interest, which were never ordained or appointed by Christ.   It hath not, I say, been disputed under these terms expressly, though really the substance of the controversy lies therein.   To assert this expressly would be to exalt him above Jesus Christ, at least to give him power equal unto his; though really unto the institution of the gospel church-state, and the communication of graces, offices, and gifts to make it useful unto its end, no less than all power in heaven and earth be required.

Some plead that there is no certain form of church-government appointed in the Scripture,—that there was none ordained by Christ, nor exemplified by the apostles; and therefore it is in the power of the magistrate to appoint any such form thereof as is suited unto the public interest.   It would seem to follow more evidently that no form at all should by any be appointed; for what shall he do that cometh after the King?—what shall any one ordain in the church which the Lord Christ thought not meet to ordain? And this is the proper inference from this consideration: Such a church-government as men imagine, Christ hath not appointed; therefore, neither may men do so. But suppose that the Lord Christ hath appointed a church-state, or that there should be churches of his disciples on the earth; let them therein but yield obedience unto all that he hath commanded, and in their so doing make use of the light of nature and rules of common prudence, so as to do it unto their own edifica-tion (which to deny to be their duty is to destroy their nature as created of God), trusting in all things unto the conduct of the pro-mised divine assistance of the Holy Spirit;—if any instance can be given of what is wanting unto the complete state and rule of the church, we shall willingly allow that it be added by the civil magis-trate, or whomsoever men can agree upon, as was before declared. If it be said there is yet something wanting to accommodate these churches and their rule unto the state of the public interest and political government under which they are placed, whereon they may be framed into churches diocesan and metropolitical, with such a rule as they are capable of, I say,—1. That in their original constitution they are more accommodated unto the interest of all righteous secular government than any arbitrary moulding them unto a pretended meetness to comply therewithal can attain unto. This we have proved before, and shall farther enlarge upon it if it be required. And we find it by experience, that those additions, changes, and alterations in the state, order, and rule of the churches, pretended for the end mentioned, have proved the cause of endless contentions; which have no good aspect on the public peace, and will assuredly continue for ever so to be. 2. It is granted that the magistrate may dispose of many outward concerns of these churches; may im-part of his favour to them, or any of them, as he sees cause; may take care that nothing falls out among them that may occasion any public disturbance in and by itself; may prohibit the public exercise of worship idolatrous or superstitious; may remove and take away all instruments and monuments of idolatry; may coerce, restrain, and punish, as there is occasion, persons who, under pretence of reli-gion, do advance principles of sedition, or promote any foreign interest opposite and destructive to his government, the welfare of the nation, and the truth of religion; with sundry things of the like nature. And herein lies an ample field, wherein the magistrate may exercise his power and discharge his duty.

It cannot well be denied but that the present pretences and pleas of some to reduce all things in the practice of religion into the power and disposal of the civil magistrate are full of offence and scandal.

It seems to be only a design and contrivance to secure men's secular interests under every way of the profession of Christian religion, true or false, which may have the advantage of the magistrate's approbation. By this device conscience is set at liberty from concerning itself in an humble, diligent inquiry into the mind of God as unto what is its duty in his worship; and when it is so with the conscience of any, it will not be much concerned in what it doth attend unto or observe. What is, in divine things, done or practised solely on the authority of the magistrate is immediately and directly obedience unto him, and not unto God.

Whatever, therefore, the supreme power in any place may do, or will be pleased to do, for the accommodation of the outward state of the church and the exercise of its rule unto the political government of a people or nation, yet these two things are certain:—

1. That he can form, erect, or institute *no new church-state* which is not ordained and appointed by Christ, and his apostles by virtue of his authority; and what he doth of that nature appoint is called a church only equivocally, or by reason of some resemblance unto that which is properly so called.

2. To dissent from what is so appointed by the supreme power, in and about the state, form, rule, and worship of churches, whatever other evil it may be charged with or supposed liable unto, can have nothing in it of that which the Scripture condemns under *the name of schism*, which hath respect only unto what is stated by Christ himself.

That which in this place we should next inquire into is, what these particular churches themselves may do, by their own voluntary consent and act, in a way of association or otherwise, for the accumulation and exercise of a power not formally inherent in them as particular churches; but I shall refer it unto the head of the communion of churches, which must be afterward spoken unto.

CHAPTER VIII.

The duty of believers to join themselves in church-order.

Unto some one or other of those particular congregations which we have described, continuing to be the pillar and ground of truth, it is the duty of every believer, of every disciple of Christ, to *join himself*, for the due and orderly observation and performance of the commands of Christ, unto the glory of God and their own edification, Matt. xxviii. 18–20.

This, in general, is granted by all sorts and parties of men; the grant of it is the ground whereon they stand in the management of their mutual feuds in religion, pleading that men ought to be of, or join themselves unto, this or that church,—still supposing that it is their duty to be of one or another.

Yea, it is granted, also, that persons ought to choose what churches they will join themselves unto, wherein they may have the best advantage unto their edification and salvation. They are to choose, to join themselves unto, that church which is in all things most according to the mind of God.

This, it is supposed, is the liberty and duty of every man; for if it be not so, it is the foolishest thing in the world for any to attempt to get others from one church unto another; which is almost the whole business of religion that some think themselves concerned to attend unto.

But yet, notwithstanding these concessions, when things come to the trial in particular, there is very little granted in compliance with the assertion laid down; for besides that it is not a church of divine institution that is intended in these concessions, when it comes unto the issue where a man is born, and in what church he is baptized in his infancy, then *all choice is prevented,* and in the communion of that church he is to abide, on the penalties of being esteemed and dealt withal as a schismatic. In what national church any person is baptized, in that national church he is to continue, or answer the contrary at his peril; and in the precincts of what parish his habitation falls to be, in that particular parish church is he bound to communicate in all ordinances of worship. I say, in the judgment of many, whatever is pretended of men's joining themselves unto the truest and purest churches, there is no liberty of judgment or practice in either of these things left unto any of the disciples of Christ.

Wherefore, the liberty and duty proposed being the foundation of all orderly evangelical profession, and that wherein the consciences of believers are greatly concerned, I shall lay down one proposition wherein it is asserted in the sense I intend, and then fully confirm it.

The proposition itself is this:—

It is the duty of every one who professeth faith in Christ Jesus, and takes due care of his own eternal salvation, voluntarily and by his own choice to join himself unto some particular congregation of Christ's institution, for his own spiritual edification, and the right discharge of his commands.

1. This duty is prescribed unto them only who *profess faith in Christ Jesus,* who own themselves to be his disciples, that call Jesus Lord; for this is the method of the gospel, that first men by the preaching of it be made disciples, or be brought unto faith in Christ

Jesus, and then be taught to do and observe whatever he commands, Matt. xxviii. 18–20,—first to " believe," and then to be " added unto the church,"Acts ii. 41, 42, 44, 46, 47. Men must first *join themselves unto the Lord,* or give up themselves unto him, before they can give up themselves unto the church, according to the mind of Christ, 2 Cor. viii. 5. We are not, therefore, concerned at present as unto them who either do not at all profess faith in Christ Jesus, or else, through ignorance of the fundamental principles of religion and wickedness of life, do destroy or utterly render useless that profession. We do not say it is the duty of such persons,—that is, their immediate duty,—in the state wherein they are, to join themselves unto any church. Nay, it is the duty of every church to refuse them their communion whilst they abide in that state. There are other duties to be in the first place pressed on them, whereby they may be made meet for this. So in the primitive times, although in the extraordinary conversions unto Christianity that were made among the Jews, who before belonged unto God's covenant, they were all immediately added unto the church, yet afterward, in the ordinary way of the conversion of men, the churches did not immediately admit them into complete communion, but kept them as catechumeners, for the increase of their knowledge and trial of their profession, until they were judged meet to be joined unto the church. And they are not to blame who receive not such into complete communion with them, unto whom it is not a present duty to desire that communion. Yea, the admission of such persons into church-societies, much more the compelling of them to be members of this or that church, almost whether they will or no, is contrary to the rule of the word, the example of the primitive churches, and a great expedient to harden men in their sins.

We do therefore avow, that we cannot admit any into our church-societies, as to complete membership and actual interest in the privileges of the church, who do not, by a profession of faith in and obedience unto Jesus Christ, no way contradicted by sins of life, manifest themselves to be such as whose duty it is to join themselves unto any church. Neither do we injure any baptized persons hereby, or oppose any of their right unto and interest in the church; but only, as they did universally in the primitive churches, after the death of the apostles, we direct them into that way and method wherein they may be received, unto the glory of Christ and their own edification. And we do therefore affirm, that we will never deny that communion unto any person, high or low, rich or poor, old or young, male or female, whose duty it is to desire it.

2. It is added, in the description of the subject, that it is *such a one who takes due care of his own salvation.* Many there are who

profess themselves to be Christians, who, it may be, hear the word willingly, and do many things gladly, yet do not esteem themselves obliged unto a diligent inquiry into and a precise observation of all the commands of Christ. But it is such whom we intend who constantly fix their minds on the enjoyment of God as their chiefest good and utmost end; who thereon duly consider the means of attaining it, and apply themselves thereunto. And it is to be feared that the number of such persons will not be found to be very great in the world; which is sufficient to take off the reproach from some particular congregations of the smallness of their number. Such they ever were; and such is it foretold that they should be. Number was never yet esteemed a note of the true church by any, but those whose worldly interest it is that it should so be; yet at present, absolutely in these nations, the number of such persons is not small.

3. Of these persons it is said that *it is their duty so to dispose of themselves.* It is not that which they may do as a convenience or an advantage, not that which others may do for them, but which they must do for themselves in a way of duty. It is an obediential act unto the commands of Christ; whereunto is required subjection of conscience unto his authority, faith in his promises, as also a respect unto an appearance before his judgment-throne at the last day. The way of the church of Rome, to compel men into their communion, and keep them in it, by fire and fagot, or any other means of external force, derives more from the Alcora than the Gospel. Neither doth it answer the mind of Christ, in the institution, end, and order of church-societies, that men should become members of them partly by that which is no way in their own power, and partly by what their wills are regulated in by the laws of men; for it is, as was said, commonly esteemed that men being born and baptized in such a nation are thereby made members of the church of that nation, and by living within such parochial precincts as the law of the land hath arbitrarily established are members of this or that particular congregation. At least, they are accounted so far to belong unto these churches, as to render them liable unto all outward punishments that shall be thought meet to be inflicted on them who comply not with them. So far as these persuasions and actings according unto them do prevail, so far are they destructive of the principal foundation of the external being and order of the church. But that men's joining themselves in or unto any church-society is, or ought to be, a voluntary act, or an act of free choice, in mere obedience unto the authority and commands of Christ, is so sacred a truth, so evident in the Scripture, so necessary from its subject-matter, so testified unto by the practice of all the first churches, as that it despiseth all opposition. And I know not how any can reconcile the

common practice of giving men the reputation or reality of being members of or belonging unto this or that church, as unto total communion, who desire or choose no such thing, unto this acknowledged principle.

4. There is *a double joining unto the church:*—(1.) That which is as unto *total communion* in all the duties and privileges of the church; which is that whereof we treat. (2.) An *adherence unto the church* as unto the means of instruction and edification to be attained thereby. So persons may adhere unto any church who yet are not meet or free, on some present consideration, to confederate with it as unto total communion; see Acts v. 13, 14. And of this sort, in a peculiar manner, are the baptized children of the members of the church; for although they are not capable of performing church-duties or enjoying church-privileges in their tender years, nor can have a right unto total communion before *the testification of their own voluntary consent* thereunto and choice thereof, yet are they in a peculiar manner under the care and inspection of the church, so far as the outward administration of the covenant, in all the means of it, is committed thereunto; and their duty it is, according to their capacity, to attend unto the ministry of that church whereunto they do belong.

5. The proposition respects a *visible professing church*. And I intend such a church in general as avoweth authority from Christ,—(1.) For the *ministerial preaching* of the word; (2.) *Administration of the sacraments;* (3.) For the *exercise of evangelical discipline;* and, (4.) To *give a public testimony* against the devil and the world, not contradicting their profession with any corrupt principles or practices inconsistent with it. What is required in particular, that any of them may be meet to be joined unto such a church we shall afterward inquire.

6. It is generally said that "*out of the church there is no salvation;*" and the truth hereof is testified unto in the Scriptures, Acts ii. 47; 1 Pet. iii. 20, 21; Matt. xvi. 18; Eph. v. 25–27; John x. 16.

7. This is true both positively and negatively of the *catholic church* invisible, of the elect; all that are of it shall be saved, and none shall be saved but those that belong unto it, Eph. v. 25–27; —of the catholic visible professing church negatively; that no adult person can be saved that doth not belong unto this church, Rom. x. 10.

8. This *position of truth* is abused by interest and pride, an enclosure of it being made by them who, of all Christians in the world, can lay the least and weakest claim unto it,—namely, the church of Rome; for they are so far from being that catholic church out of which there is no salvation, and wherein none can perish, like the ark of Noah, that it requires the highest charity to reckon them unto

that visible professing church whereof the greatest part may perish, and do so undoubtedly.

9. Our inquiry is, what truth there is in this assertion with respect unto these particular churches or societies for the celebration of gospel worship and discipline whereof we treat; and I say,—

(1.) No church, of what *denomination soever*, can lay a claim unto this privilege as belonging unto itself alone. This was the ancient *Donatism;* they confined salvation unto the churches of their way alone. And after many false charges of it on others, it begins really to be renewed in our days; for some dispute that salvation is confined unto that church alone *wherein there is a succession of diocesan bishops;* which is the height of Donatism. The judgments and determinations made concerning the eternal salvation or damnation of men, by the measures of some differences among Christians about churches, their state and order, are absurd, foolish, and impious; and for the most part used by them who sufficiently proclaim that they know neither what it is to be saved, nor do use any diligence about the necessary means of it. Salvation depends absolutely on no particular church-state in the world; he knows not the gospel who can really think it doth. Persons of believers are not for the church, but the church is for them. If the ministry of angels be for them who are heirs of salvation, much more is the ministry of the church so. If a man be an adulterer, an idolater, a railer, a hater and scoffer of godliness; if he choose to live in any known sin, without repentance, or in the neglect of any known duty; if he be ignorant and profane; in a word, if he be not born again from above, be he of what church he will, and whatsoever place he possesses therein, he cannot be saved. And on the other side, if a man believe in Christ Jesus,— that is, know him in his person, offices, doctrine, and grace; trust unto him for all the ends of the wisdom and love of God towards mankind in him; if he endeavour to yield sincere and universal obedience unto all his commands, and to be conformed unto him, in all things following his example, having for these ends received of his Spirit,—though all the churches in the world should reject him, yet he shall undoubtedly be saved. If any shall hence infer that then it is all one of what church any one is, I answer,—[1.] That although the being of this or that or any particular church in the world will not secure the salvation of any men, yet the adherence unto some churches, or such as are so called, in their constitution and worship, may prejudice, yea, ruin the salvation of any that shall so do. [2.] The choice of what church we will join unto belongs unto the choice and use of the means for our edification; and he that makes no conscience hereof, but merely with respect unto the event of being saved at last, will probably come short thereof.

(2.) On this supposition, that there be no insuperable difficulties lying in the way of the discharge of this duty,—as that a person be cast by the providence of God into such a place or season as wherein there is no church that he can possibly join himself unto, or that he be unjustly refused communion, by unwarrantable conditions of it, as it was with many during the prevalency of the Papacy in all the western empire,—it is the indispensable duty of every disciple of Christ, in order unto his edification and salvation, voluntarily, and of his own choice, to join himself in and unto some particular congregation, for the celebration of divine worship, and the due observation of all the institutions and commands of Christ: which we shall now farther confirm:—

[1.] The foundation of this duty, as was before declared, doth lie in *the law and light of nature.* Man cannot exercise the principal powers and faculties of his soul, with which he was created, and whereby he is enabled to glorify God, which is the end of him and them, without a consent and conjunction in the worship of God in communion and society; as hath been proved before.

[2.] The way whereby this is to be done God hath declared and revealed from the beginning, by the constitution of a church-state, through the addition of arbitrary institutions of worship unto what was required by the law of nature: for this gives the true state, and is the formal reason of a church,—namely, a divine addition of arbitrary institutions of worship unto the necessary dictates of the law of nature unto that end; and the especial nature of any church-state doth depend on the especial nature of those institutions, which is constitutive of the difference between the church-state of the Old Testament and that of the New.

[3.] Such a church-state was constituted and appointed under the Old Testament, founded in and on an especial covenant between God and the people, Exod. xxiv. Unto this church every one that would please God and walk before him was bound to join himself, by the ways and means that he had appointed for that end,—namely, by circumcision, and their " laying hold on the covenant of God," Exod. xii. 48; Isa. lvi. 4. And this joining unto the church is called " joining unto the Lord," Isa. lvi. 6, Jer. l. 5; as being the means thereof, without which it could not be done. Herein was the tabernacle of God with men, and he dwelt among them.

[4.] As a new church-state is prophesied of under the New Testament, Ezek. xxxiv. 25–29, Isa. lxvi. 18–22, and other places innumerable, so it was actually erected by Jesus Christ; as we have declared. And whereas it is introduced and established in the place and room of the church-state under the Old Testament, which was to be removed at the time of reformation, as the apostle demonstrates at large in his Epistle to the Hebrews, all the commands, promises, and threatenings given or annexed unto that church-state, concerning the conjunction of men unto it and walking in it, are transferred unto this of the new erection of Christ. Wherefore, although the state of the church itself be reduced from that which was nationally congregational unto that which is simply and absolutely so, and all the ordinances of its instituted worship are changed, with new rules for the observation of what we are directed unto by the light of nature, yet the commands, promises, and threatenings made and given unto it as a church are all in full force with respect unto this new church-state; and we need no new commands to render it our duty to join in evangelical churches for the ends of a church in general.

[5.] The Lord Christ hath *disposed all the ways and means of edification* unto these churches; so that ordinarily, and under an expectation of his presence in them and concurrence unto their efficacy, they are not otherwise to be enjoyed. Such are the ordinary dispensation of the word, and administration of the sacraments. For any disciple of Christ to live in a neglect of these things and the enjoyment of them according to his mind, is to despise his care and wisdom in providing for his eternal welfare.

[6.] He hath *prescribed sundry duties* unto us, both as necessary and as evidences of our being his disciples, such as cannot be orderly performed but as we are members of some particular congregation. This also hath been before declared.

[7.] The *institution of these churches* is the way which Christ hath ordained to render his kingdom visible or conspicuous, in distinction from and opposition unto the kingdom of Satan and the world. And he doth not, in a due manner, declare himself a subject in or unto the kingdom of Christ who doth not solemnly engage in this way. It is not enough to constitute a legal subject of the kingdom of England that he is born in the nation, and lives in some outward observance of the laws of it, if he refuse solemnly to express his allegiance in the way appointed by the law for that end. Nor will it constitute a regular subject of the kingdom of Christ that he is born in a place where the gospel is professed, and so professeth a general compliance therewith, if he refuse to testify his subjection by the way that Christ hath appointed for that end. It is true, the whole nation, in their civil relation and subordination according to law, is the kingdom of England; but the representation of the kingly power and rule in it is in the courts of all sorts, wherein the kingly power is acted openly and visibly. And he that lives in the nation, yet denies his homage unto these courts, is not to be esteemed a subject. So doth the whole visible professing church, in one or more nations or lesser precincts of people and places, constitute the visible kingdom of Christ; yet is no particular person to be esteemed a legal, true subject of Christ that doth not appear in these his courts with a solemn expression of his homage unto him.

[8.] The *whole administration of the rule and discipline appointed by Christ* is confined unto these churches, nor can they be approved by whom that rule is despised. I shall not argue farther in a case whose truth is of so uncontrollable evidence. In all the writings of the New Testament, recording things after the ascension of Christ, there is no mention of any of his disciples with approbation, unless they were extraordinary officers, but such as were entire members of these assemblies.

CHAPTER IX.

The continuation of a church-state and of the administration of evangelical ordinances of worship briefly vindicated.

THE controversy about *the continuation* of a church-state and the administration of gospel ordinances of worship is not *new* in this age, though some pride themselves as though the invention of the error whereby they are denied were their own. In former ages, both in the Papacy and among some of them that forsook it, there were divers who, on a pretence of a peculiar spirituality and imaginary attainments in religion, wherein these things are unnecessary, rejected their observation. I suppose it necessary briefly to confirm the truth, and vindicate it from this exception; because, though it be sufficiently weak in itself, yet what it is lies against the foundation of all that we are pleading about. But to reduce things into the lesser compass, I shall first confirm the truth by those arguments or considerations which will defeat all the pleas and pretences of them by whom it is opposed, and then confirm it by positive testimonies and arguments, with all brevity possible.

First, therefore, I shall argue from the removal of all causes whereon such a cessation of churches and ordinances is pretended; for it is granted on all hands that they had a divine original and institution, and were observed by all the disciples of Christ as things by him commanded. If now, therefore, they cease as unto their force, efficacy, and use, it must be on some of these reasons:—

1. *Because a limited time and season was fixed unto them,* which is now expired. So was it with the church-state and ordinances of old; they were appointed unto the "time of reformation," Heb. ix. 10. They had a certain time prefixed unto their duration; according to

the degrees of whose approach they waxed old, and at length utterly disappeared, Heb. viii. 13; until that time they were all punctually to be observed, Mal. iv. 4. But there were many antecedent indications of the will of God concerning their cessation and abolition; whereof the apostle disputes at large in his Epistle unto the Hebrews. And from a pretended supposition that such was the state of evangelical ordinances,—namely, that they had a time prefixed unto their duration,—did the first opposition against them arise; for Montanus, with his followers, imagined that the appointments of Christ and his apostles in the gospel were to continue in force only unto the coming of the Paraclete, or the Comforter, promised by him. And adding a new frenzy hereunto, that that Paraclete was then first come in Montanus, they rejected the institutions of the gospel, and made new laws and rules for themselves. And this continues to be the principal pretence of them by whom the use of gospel ordinances is at present rejected, as that which is of no force or efficacy. Either they have received or do speedily look for such a dispensation of the Spirit or his gifts as wherein they are to cease and disappear. But nothing can be more vain than this pretence:—

(1.) It is so as unto the limitation of any time as unto their duration and continuance; for,—[1.] There is no intimation given of any such thing, either in the divine word, promise, declaration about them, or the nature of the institutions themselves. But whereas those of the Old Testament were in time to be removed, that the church might not be offended thereby, seeing originally they were all of immediate divine institution, God did by all manner of ways, as by promises, express declarations, and by the nature of the institutions themselves, fore-signify their removal; as the apostle proves at large in his Epistle to the Hebrews. But nothing of this nature can be pretended concerning the gospel church-state or worship. [2.] There is no *prediction* or intimation of any other way of worship, or serving God in this world, that should be introduced in the room of that established at first; so that upon a cessation thereof the church must be left unto all uncertainties and utter ruin. [3.] The principal reason why a church-state was erected of old, and ordinances of worship appointed therein, that were all to be removed and taken away, was that the Son, the Lord over his own house, might have the pre-eminence in all things. His glory it was to put an end unto the law, as given by the disposition of angels and the ministry of Moses, by the institution of a church-state and ordinances of his own appointment. And if his revelation of the will of God therein be not complete, perfect, ultimate, unalterable, if it be to expire, it must be that honour may be given above him unto one greater than he.

(2.) It is so as *unto their decay, or the loss of their primitive force and efficacy;* for their efficacy unto their proper ends depends on,—[1.] The *institution of Christ.* This is the foundation of all spiritual efficacy unto edification in the church, or whatever belongs thereunto. And, therefore, whatever church-state may be framed, or duties, ways, or means of worship appointed by men that have not his institution, how specious soever they may appear to be, have no spiritual force or efficacy as unto the edification of the church. But whilst this institution of Christ continues irrevocable, and is not abrogated by a greater power than what it was enacted by, whatever defect there may be as unto faith and obedience in men, rendering them useless and ineffectual unto themselves, however they may be corrupted by additions unto them or detractions from them, changing their nature and use, in themselves they continue to be of the same use and efficacy as they were at the beginning. [2.] On *the promise of Christ* that he will be present with his disciples, in the observation of his commands, unto the consummation of all things, Matt. xxviii. 20. To deny the continued accomplishment of this promise, and that on any pretence whatever, is the venom of infidelity. If, therefore, they have an irrevocable divine institution, if Christ be present in their administrations, as he was of old, Rev. ii. 1, there can be no abatement of their efficacy unto their proper ends, in the nature of instrumental causes. [3.] On *the covenant of God,* which gives an infallible, inseparable conjunction between the word, or the church and its institution by the word, and the Spirit, Isa. lix. 21. God's covenant with his people is the foundation of every church-state, of all offices, powers, privileges, and duties thereunto belonging. They have no other end, they are of no other use, but to communicate, express, declare, and exemplify, on the one hand, the grace of God in his covenant unto his people, and, on the other, the duties of his people according unto the tenor of the same covenant unto him. They are the way, means, and instruments appointed of God for this end, and other end they have none; and hereon it follows, that if it be not in the power of men to appoint any thing that shall be a means of communication between God and his people, as unto the grace of the covenant on the one hand, or the duties of obedience which it requires on the other, they have no power to erect any new church-state, or enact any thing in divine worship not of his institution. This being the state of churches and their ordinances, they cannot be altered, they cannot be liable unto any decay, unless the covenant whereunto they are annexed be altered or decayed; and therefore the apostle, to put finally and absolutely his argument unto an issue to prove that the Mosaical church-state and ordinances were changed, because useless and ineffectual, doth it on this ground, that the covenant whereunto they were annexed was changed and become useless. This, I suppose, at present, will not be said concerning the new covenant, whereunto all ordinances of divine worship are inseparably annexed.

Men might at a cheaper rate, as unto the eternal interest of their own souls, provide another covering for their sloth, negligence, unbelief, and indulgence unto proud, foolish imaginations, whereby they render the churches and ordinances of the gospel useless and ineffectual unto themselves; thereby charging them with a decay and uselessness, and so reflecting on the honour and faithfulness of Christ himself.

2. They do not cease because there is at present, or at least there is shortly to be expected, *such an effusion of the gifts and graces of the Spirit as to render all these external institutions needless, and consequently useless.* This, also, is falsely pretended. For,—(1.) The greatest and most plentiful effusion of the Holy Spirit in his gifts and graces was in the days of the apostles, and of the first churches planted by them; nor is any thing beyond it, or indeed equal unto it, any more to be expected in this world;—but yet then was the gospel church-state erected, and the use of all its ordinances of worship enjoined. (2.) The ministry of the gospel, which compriseth all the ordinances of church-worship as its object and end, is *the ministration of the Spirit;* and therefore no supplies or communication of him can render it useless. (3.) One of the principal ends for which the communication of the Spirit is promised unto the church is to make and render all the institutions of Christ effectual unto its edification. (4.) 1 John ii. 20, 27, is usually pleaded as giving countenance unto this fond pretence. But,—[1.] The *unction* mentioned by the apostle was then upon all believers. Yet,—[2.] It is known that then they all walked in *church-order,* and in the sacred observation of all the institutions of Christ. [3.] If it takes away any thing, it is *the preaching of the word,* or all manner of teaching and instruction; which is to overthrow the whole Scripture, and to reduce religion into barbarism. [4.] Nothing is intended in these words but the different way of teaching and degrees of success between that under the law and that now established in the gospel, by the plentiful effusion of the Spirit; as hath been evidenced at large elsewhere. Nor,—

3. Do they cease in their administration for *want either of authority or ability to dispense them,* which is pleaded unto the same end? But neither is this pretence of any force; it only begs the thing in question. (1.) The authority of office for the administration of all other ordinances is an institution; and to say that all institutions cease because none have authority to administer them is to say they must all cease because they are ceased. (2.) The office of the mini-

stry, for the continuation of the church-state, and administration of all ordinances of worship, unto the end of the world, is sufficiently secured,—[1.] By the *law*, constitution, and appointment of our Lord Jesus Christ erecting that office, and giving warranty for its continuance to the consummation of all things, Matt. xxviii. 20; Eph. iv. 13. [2.] By his continuance, according unto his promise, to communicate *spiritual gifts* unto men, for the ministerial edification of the church. That this he doth so continue to do that it is the principal external evidence of his abiding in the discharge of his mediatory office, and of what nature these gifts are, I have declared at large in a peculiar discourse on that subject. [3.] On the duty of believers or of the *church*, which is to choose, call, and solemnly set apart unto the office of the ministry such as the Lord Christ by his Spirit hath made meet for it, according unto the rule of his word.

If all these, or any of them, do fail, I acknowledge that all ministerial authority and ability for the dispensation of gospel ordinances must fail also, and consequently the state of the church. And those who plead for the continuation of a successive ministry without respect unto these things, without resolving both the authority and office of it into them, do but erect a dead image, or embrace a dead carcase, instead of the living and life-giving institutions of Christ. They take away the living creature, and set up a skin stuffed with straw. But if these things do unalterably continue; if the law of Christ can neither be changed, abrogated, nor disannulled; if his dispensation of spiritual gifts according unto his promise cannot be impeded; if believers, through his grace, will continue in obedience unto his commands,—it is not possible there should be an utter failure in this office and office-power of this ministry. It may fail in this or that place, in this or that church, when the Lord Christ will remove his candlestick; but it hath a living root, whence it will spring again in other places and churches, whilst this world doth endure. Neither,—

4. Do they cease because they have been all of them *corrupted*, *abused*, and *defiled*, in the apostasy which fell out among all the churches in the latter ages, as it was fully foretold in the Scripture. For,—(1.) This supposition would make the whole kingdom of Christ in the world to depend on the corrupt lusts and wills of men, which have got by any means the outward possession of the administration of his laws and ordinances. This is all one as if we should say, that if a pack of wicked judges should for a season pervert justice, righteousness, and judgment, the being of the kingdom is so overthrown thereby as that it can never be restored. (2.) It would make all the duties and all the privileges of all true believers to depend on the wills of wicked apostates; for if they may not make use of what they

have abused, they can never yield obedience to the commands of Christ, nor enjoy the privileges which he hath annexed unto his church and worship. (3.) On this supposition all reformation of an apostatized church is utterly impossible. But it is our duty to heal even Babylon itself, by a reduction of all things unto their first institution, if it would be healed, Jer. li. 9; and if not, we are to forsake her and reform ourselves, Rev. xviii. 4.

There is nothing, therefore, in all these pretences, that should in the least impeach the infallible continuation of the evangelical churches and worship, as to their right, unto the end of the world. And the heads of those arguments whereby the truth is invincibly confirmed may be briefly touched on:—

1. There are express testimonies of the will of Christ, and his promise for its accomplishment, that *the church and all its ordinances of worship should be continued always, unto the end of the world.* So as to the church itself, Matt. xvi. 18, Rev. xxi. 3; the ministry, Matt. xxviii. 20, Eph. iv. 13; baptism, Matt. xxviii. 19, 20; the Lord's supper, 1 Cor. xi. 26. As for other institutions, public prayer, preaching the word, the Lord's day, singing of God's praises, the exercise of discipline, with what belongs thereunto, they have their foundation in the law and light of nature, being only directed and applied unto the gospel church-state and worship by rules of especial institution; and they can no more cease than the original obligation of that law can so do.

If it be said, that notwithstanding what may be thus pleaded, yet, "de facto," the true state of gospel churches and their whole worship, as unto its original institution, did fail under the papal apostasy, and therefore may do so again, I answer,—(1.) We do not plead that this state of things must be always *visible* and conspicuous; wherein all protestant writers do agree. It is acknowledged, that as unto public view, observation, and notoriety, all these things were lost under the Papacy, and may be so again under a renewed apostasy. (2.) I do not plead it to be necessary, " de facto," that there should be really at all times a true visible church, as the seat of all ordinances and administrations in the world; but all such churches may fail, not only as unto visibility, but as unto their existence. But this supposition of a failure of all instituted churches and worship I grant only with these limitations:—[1.] That it is of necessity, from innumerable divine promises and the nature of Christ's kingly office, that there be always in the world *a number, greater or lesser, of sincere believers,* that openly profess subjection and obedience unto him; [2.] That in these persons there resides an *indefeasible right* always to gather themselves into a church-state, and to administer all gospel ordinances, which all the world cannot deprive them of:

which is the whole of what I now plead for. And let it be observed, that all the ensuing arguments depend on this right, and not on any matter of fact. [3.] I do not know how far God may accept of churches in a very corrupt state, and of worship much depraved, until they have new means for their reformation; nor will I make any judgment of persons, as unto their eternal condition, who walk in churches so corrupted, and in the performance of worship so depraved: but as unto them who know them to be so corrupted and depraved, it is a damnable sin to join with them or not to separate from them, Rev. xviii. 4.

2. The nature and use of the gospel church-state require and prove *the uninterrupted continuance* of the right of its existence, and the observance of all ordinances of divine worship therein, with a power in them in whom that right doth indefeasibly reside,—that is, all true believers,—to bring it forth into exercise and practice, notwithstanding the external impediments which in some places at some times may interrupt its exercise. In the observation of Christ's institutions and celebration of the ordinances of divine worship doth the church-state of the gospel, as professing, consist. It doth so in opposition,—(1.) Unto the *world* and the kingdom of Satan; for hereby do men call Jesus " Lord," as 1 Cor. xii. 3, and avow their subjection unto his kingly power. (2.) Unto *the church-state of the Old Testament*, as the apostle disputes at large in his Epistle unto the Hebrews. And this state of the professing church in this world is unalterable, because it is the best state that the believing church is capable of; for so the apostle plainly proves, that hereby the believing church is brought εἰς τελείωσιν, which it was not under the law,—that is, unto its consummation, in the most complete perfection that God hath designed unto it on this side glory, Heb. vii. 11, 19. For Christ in all his offices is the immediate head of it; its constitution, and the revelation of the ways of its worship, are an effect of his wisdom; and from thence is it eminently suited unto all the ends of the covenant, both on the part of God and man, and is therefore liable to no intercision or alteration.

3. *The visible administration of the kingdom of Christ* in this world consists in this church-state, with the administration of his institutions and laws therein. A kingdom the Lord Jesus Christ hath in this world; and though it be not of the world, yet in the world it must be until the world shall be no more. The truth of all God's promises in the Scripture depends on this one assertion. We need not here concern ourselves what notions some men have about the exercise of this kingdom in the world, with respect unto the outward affairs and concerns of it; but this is certain, that this kingdom of Christ in the world, so far as it is external and visible, consists in

the laws he hath given, the institutions he hath appointed, the rule or polity he hath prescribed, with the due observance of them. Now, all these things do make, constitute, and are the church-state and worship inquired after. Wherefore, as Christ always hath, and ever will have, an invisible kingdom in this world, in the souls of elect believers, led, guided, ruled by his Spirit, so he will have a visible kingdom also, consisting in a professed, avowed subjection unto the laws of his word, Rom. x. 10. And although this kingdom, or his kingdom in this sense, may, as unto the essence of it, be preserved in the external profession of individual persons, and it may be so exist in the world for a season, yet the honour of it and its complete establishment consist in the visible profession of churches; which he will therefore maintain unto the end. But by *visible* in this discourse, I understand not that which is conspicuous and eminent unto all, though the church hath been so, and shall yet be so again; nor yet that which is actually seen or known by others; but only that which may be so, or is capable of being so known. Nor do I assert a necessity hereof, as unto a constant preservation of purity and regularity in order and ordinances, according to the original institution of them in any place; but only of *an unalterable right and power in believers to render them visible:* which it becomes their indispensable duty to do when outward impediments are not absolutely insuperable. But of these things thus far, ὡς ἐν παρόδῳ.

CHAPTER X.

What sort of churches the disciples of Christ may and ought to join themselves
unto as unto entire communion.

WE have proved before that it is the duty of all individual Christians to give themselves up unto the conduct, fellowship, and communion of some particular church or congregation. Our present inquiry hereon is, whereas there is a great diversity among professing societies in the world, concerning each whereof it is said, " Lo, here is Christ," and " Lo, there is Christ," what church, of what constitution and order, any one that takes care of his own edification and salvation ought to join himself unto. This I shall speak unto first *in general,* and then in the examination of *one particular case* or instance, wherein many at this day are concerned. And some things must be premised unto the right stating of the subject of our inquiry:—

1. The diversities and divisions among churches, which respect is

to be had unto in the choice of any which we will or ought to join unto, are of two sorts:—

(1.) Such as are *occasioned* by the remaining weaknesses, infirmities, and ignorance of the best of men, whereby they know but in part, and prophesy only in part; wherein our edification is concerned, but our salvation not endangered.

(2.) Such as are in and about things *fundamental* in faith, worship, and obedience. We shall speak to both of them.

2. All Christians were *originally of one mind* in all things needful unto joint communion, so as that there might be among them all love without dissimulation. Howbeit there was great variety, not only in the measure of their apprehensions of the doctrines of truth, but in some doctrines themselves,—as about the continuance of the observations of the law, or at least of some of them; as also oppositions from without unto the truth by heretics and apostates: neither of which hindered the church-communion of true believers. But the diversity, difference, and divisions that are now among churches in the world is the effect of the great apostasy which befell them all in the latter ages, as unto the spirit, rule, and practice of those which were planted by the apostles; and will not be healed until that apostasy be abolished.

3. Satan having possessed himself of the *advantage of these divisions*, whereof he was the author, he makes use of them to act his malice and rage, in stirring up and instigating one party to persecute, oppress, and devour another, until the life, power, and glory of Christian religion is almost lost in the world. It requires, therefore, great wisdom to deport ourselves aright among these divisions, so as to contribute nothing unto the ends of malice designed by Satan in them.

4. In this state of things, until it may be cured,—which it will never be by any of the ways yet proposed and insisted on,—the inquiry is concerning the duty of any one who takes care of his own soul as unto a conjunction with some church or other. And on the negative part, I say,—

(1.) Such a one is bound *not to join* with any church or society where any *fundamental* article of faith is rejected or corrupted. There may be a fundamental error in a true church for a season, when the church erreth not fundamentally, 1 Cor. xv. 12; 2 Tim. ii. 18. But I suppose the error in or against the foundation is part of the profession of the church or society to be joined unto; for thereby the nature of the church is destroyed,—it doth not hold the Head, nor abide on the foundation, nor is the pillar and ground of truth. Wherefore, although the Socinians, under a pretence of love, forbearance, and mutual toleration, do offer us the communion of their churches, wherein there is somewhat of order and discipline commendable, yet it is unlawful to join in church fellowship or communion with them: for their errors about the Trinity, the incarnation of Christ, and his satisfaction, are destructive of the foundation of the prophets and apostles; and idolatry, in the divine worship of a mere creature, is introduced by them.

(2.) Where there is in any church taught or allowed *a mixture of doctrines or opinions that are prejudicial unto gospel holiness and obedience*, no man that takes due care of his salvation can join himself unto it; for the original rule and measure of all church-communion is agreement in the doctrine of truth. Where, therefore, there is either not a stable profession of the same doctrine in all substantial truths of the gospel, but an uncertain sound is given, some saying one thing, some another, or that opposition is made unto any truths of the importance before mentioned, none can be bound or obliged to hold communion with it, nor can incur any blame by refraining from it: for it is the duty of a Christian in all things προτιμᾶν τὴν ἀλήθειαν, and to join with such a church would,—[1.] Stain their profession; [2.] Hinder their edification; [3.] Establish a new rule of communion, unknown to the Scriptures,—namely, besides truth; as might easily be manifested.

(3.) Where *the fundamentals of religious worship* are corrupted or overthrown, it is absolutely unlawful to join unto or abide in any church. So is it with the church of Rome. The various ways whereby the foundations of divine religious worship are overthrown in that church, by superstition and idolatry, have been sufficiently declared. These render the communion of that church pernicious.

(4.) Nor can any man be obliged to join himself with any church, nor can it be his duty so to do, where the eternally fixed rule and measure of religious worship,—namely, that it be of divine institution,—is varied or changed by any additions unto it or subtractions from it; for whereas one principal end of all churches is the joint celebration of divine worship, if there be not a certain stable rule thereof in any church of divine prescription, no man can be obliged unto communion therewith.

(5.) Where the fundamentals of church order, practice, and discipline are destroyed, it is not lawful for any man to join in church communion. These fundamentals are of two sorts,—[1.] Such as concern the *ministry of the church;* [2.] Such as concern the *church itself.*

[1.] There are four things that are *necessary fundamentals* unto the order of the church on the part of the ministry:—

1st. That all the ministers or officers of it be *duly chosen* by the church itself, and solemnly set apart in the church unto their office, according unto the rule and law of Christ. This is fundamental unto church-order, the root of it, from whence all other parts of it do spring. And it is that which is ῥητῶς, or expressly provided for in the Scripture, as we shall see. If there be a neglect herein, and no other relation required between ministers, elders, rulers, bishops, and the church, but what is raised and created by ways and rules of men's appointment; or if there be a temporary disposal of persons into a discharge of that office, without a solemn call, choice, ordination, and separation unto the office itself and its work,—the law of Christ is violated, and the order of the church disturbed in its foundation.

2*dly.* That those who are called unto the office of the ministry be *duly qualified,* by their endowment with spiritual gifts, for the discharge of their duty, is fundamental unto the ministry. That the Lord Jesus Christ doth still continue his dispensation of spiritual gifts unto men, to fit and enable them unto the office and work of the ministry; that if he doth not do so, or should at any time cease so to do, the whole office of the ministry must cease, and the being of the church with it; that it is altogether useless for any churches or persons to erect an image of the gospel ministry by outward rites and ceremonies, without the enlivening force of these spiritual gifts,—I have proved sufficiently in my "Discourse of Spiritual Gifts, and their Continuance in the Church."[1] Wherefore, a communication of spiritual gifts, peculiarly enabling men unto the work of the ministry, antecedent unto their solemn separation unto the office, in some good measure, is absolutely necessary unto the due continuance of the office and its work. See Eph. iv. 7, 11–15. To suppose that the Lord Christ doth call and appoint men unto a certain office and work in his church, secluding all others from any interest in the one or other, and yet not endow them with peculiar gifts and abilities for the discharge of that office and work, is to ascribe that unto him which is every way unbecoming his wisdom and grace, with his love unto the church. But when men look on all church-order as a lifeless machine, to be acted, moved, and disposed by external rules, laws, canons, and orders, without respect unto the actings of the Spirit of Christ going before in the rule of his word, to enliven every part of it, the true disciples of Christ will receive no advantage thereby.

3*dly.* It is of the same importance that persons so called do *take heed unto their ministry that they fulfil it,*—that they give themselves unto the word and prayer, that they labour continually in the word and doctrine, and all those other duties which in the Scripture are prescribed unto them; and this, not only as unto the matter of them, but as unto the manner of their performance,—with zeal, love,

[1] See note on page 249.

compassion, and diligence. Where there is a great defect in any of these things, on what pretence soever it be; where men esteem themselves exempted from this work, or not obliged unto it; when they suppose that they may discharge their office at a cheaper rate, and with less trouble as unto their present interest, by such ways as I shall not here express,—no man is, no man can be, obliged to confine his church-communion unto such a ministry.

4thly. It is required that they be *examples* unto the flock, in the expression of the nature and power of the doctrine which they preach, in their conversation, especially in zeal, humility, self-denial, and readiness for the cross.

Where these things are not, there is such a defect in the fundamentals of church-practice, as unto the ministry of it, that no man who takes care of his own edification can join himself unto a church labouring under it; for ministers and churches are nothing but instituted means of the conversion of sinners and the edification of believers. And when any of them, through their own default, cease so to be, there is no obligation unto any man to join or continue in their communion, nor do they contract any guilt in a peaceable departure from them, but discharge their duty. That this be done peaceably, without strife or contention, without judging of others, as unto their interest in Christ and eternal salvation, the law of moral obedience doth require; that it be done with love, and compassion, and prayer towards and for them who are left, is the peculiar direction of that moral duty by the gospel. Such a practice at present would fall under severe charges and accusations, as also brutish penalties, in some places. But when all church-craft shall be defeated, and the uses that are made of its imaginary authority be discarded, there will be little occasion of this practice, and none at all of offence.

[2.] Again; there are things fundamental unto church practice and order in the church itself, which, where they are neglected, no man ought of choice to join himself unto that church, seeing he cannot do it without the prejudice of his edification, the furtherance whereof he ought to design in that duty. And these are,—

1st. That the *discipline of Christ* be duly exercised in it according unto his mind, and by the rules of his prescription. There never was any sect, order, or society of men in the world, designed for the preservation and promotion of virtue and things praiseworthy, but they had rules of discipline proper unto the ends of their design, to be observed in and by all that belong unto them. Where the erection of such societies is continued in the world, as it is much in the Papacy, both their constitution and their conversation depend on the especial rules of discipline which they have framed unto themselves.

And this is done by them in great variety; for being ignorant of the discipline of the gospel, and so esteeming it insufficient unto their design, they have made no end of coining rules unto themselves. To suppose that our Lord Jesus Christ, who in his church-state, according to his infinite wisdom, hath erected the most perfect society for the most perfect ends of religion, of obedience towards God, of love and usefulness among ourselves, hath not appointed a discipline, and given rules concerning its administration, for the preservation of that society and the attaining of those ends, is highly injurious unto his honour and glory.

Where, therefore, there is a church, or any society that pretends so to be, wherein there is an utter neglect of this discipline of Christ, or the establishment of another not administered by the laws and rules that he hath prescribed, no disciple of Christ can be obliged to join unto or to continue in the total, sole communion of such a church. And whereas there are two parts of this discipline of Christ, —that which is private, among the members of the church, for the exercise and preservation of love; and that which is public, in and by the authority of the rulers of the church, for the preservation of purity and order,—a neglect in either of them doth much impeach the fundamental constitution of a church as unto its practice.

2*dly.* There are sundry other things which belong unto this *discipline* in general, which are of great consideration in the discharge of the duty we inquire into. Among them are,—(1*st.*) That *constant difference* be put between the good and the bad in all church administrations; (2*dly.*) That persons *openly or flagitiously wicked* be not admitted into the society of the church, or a participation of its privileges; (3*dly.*) That *holiness*, love, and usefulness be openly avowed as the design and interest of the church. But they are all so comprised in the general head of discipline as that I shall not in particular insist upon them.

From what hath been thus declared, it will appear, on the other hand, what church it is that a disciple of Christ, who takes due care of his own edification and salvation, ought in duty to join himself unto in complete communion. To answer this inquiry is the end of all those discourses and controversies which have been about the notes of the true church. I shall briefly determine concerning it, according to the principles before evinced:—

(1.) It must be such a church as wherein all *the fundamental truths* of the gospel are believed, owned, and professed, without controversy, and those not borne withal by whom they are denied or opposed. Without this a church is not the pillar and ground of truth, it doth not hold the Head, it is not built on the foundation of the prophets and apostles. Neither is it sufficient that those things are generally professed, or not denied. A church that is filled with wranglings and contentions about fundamental or important truths of the gospel is not of choice to be joined unto; for these things subvert the souls of men, and greatly impede their edification. And although, both among distinct churches and among the members of the same church, mutual forbearance be to be exercised, with respect unto a variety in apprehensions in some doctrines of lesser moment, yet the incursion that hath been made into sundry protestant churches, in the last and present age, of novel doctrines and opinions, with differences, divisions, and endless disputes which have ensued thereon, have rendered it very difficult to determine how to engage in complete communion with them; for I do not judge that any man is or can be obliged unto constant, total communion with any church, or to give up himself absolutely unto the conduct thereof, wherein there are incurable dissensions about important doctrines of the gospel. And if any church shall publicly avow, countenance, or approve of doctrines contrary unto those which were the foundation of its first communion, the members of it are at liberty to refrain the communion of it, and to provide otherwise for their own edification.

(2.) It must be such a church as wherein *the divine worship instituted* or approved by Christ himself is diligently observed, without any addition made thereunto. In the observance of this worship, as unto all external, occasional incidences and circumstances of the acts wherein it doth consist, it is left unto the prudence of the church itself, according to the light of nature and general rules of Scripture; and it must be so, unless we shall suppose that the Lord Jesus Christ, by making men his disciples, doth unmake them from being rational creatures, or refuseth the exercise of the rational faculties of our souls in his service. But this is so remote from truth, that, on the contrary, he gives them an improvement for this very end, that we may know how to deport ourselves aright in the observance of his commands, as unto the outward discharge of them in his worship and the circumstances of it; and this he doth by that gift of spiritual wisdom whereof we shall treat afterward.

But if men, if churches, will make *additions* in or unto the rites of religious worship, unto what is appointed by Christ himself, and require their observance in their communion, on the force and efficacy of their being so by them appointed, no disciple of Christ is or can be obliged, by virtue of any divine institution or command, to join in total, absolute communion with any such church. He may be induced, on various considerations, to judge that something of that nature at some season may not be evil and sinful unto him, which, therefore, he will bear with or comply withal; yet he is not, he cannot be obliged, by virtue of any divine rule or command, to join himself with or continue in the communion of such a church.   If any shall suppose that hereby *too much liberty* is granted unto believers in the choice of their communion, and shall thereon make severe declamations about the inconveniencies and evils which will ensue, I desire they would remember the principle I proceed upon; which is, that churches are not such *sacred machines* as some suppose, erected and acted for the outward interest and advantage of any sort of men, but only means of the edification of believers, which they are bound to make use of, in obedience unto the commands of Christ, and no otherwise.   Whereas, therefore, the disciples of Christ have not only a divine warranty justifying them in the doing of it, but an express command, making it their indispensable duty to join in the celebration of all that religious worship which the Lord Christ, the only lawgiver of the church, and who was faithful both in and over the house of God as the Son, hath instituted and commanded, but have no such warranty or command for any thing else, it is their duty to stand fast in the liberty wherewith Christ has made them free.   And if by the same breath, in the same rule, law, or canon, they are commanded and obliged to observe in the worship of God what the Lord Christ hath appointed and what he hath not ap- pointed, both on the same grounds,—namely, the authority of the church,—and on the same penalties for their omission, no man can be divinely obliged to embrace the communion of any church on such terms.

(3.) It is required that *the ministry of a church* so to be joined with is not defective in any of those things which, according to the rule of the gospel, are *fundamental* thereunto.   What these are hath been declared.   And because edification, which is the end of church- communion, doth so eminently depend on the ministry of the church, there is not any thing which we ought to have a more diligent con- sideration of in the joining of ourselves unto any such communion. And where the ministry of any church, be the church of what sort or size it will, is incurably ignorant or negligent, or, through a defect in gifts, grace, or conscientious attendance unto their duty, is insufficient unto the due edification of the souls of them that believe, no man can account himself obliged unto the communion of the church but he that can be satisfied with a shadow and the names of things for the substance and reality of them.

If, therefore, it be granted, as I think it is, that edification is the principal end of all church-communion, it is not intelligible how a man should be obliged unto that communion, and that alone, wherein due edification cannot be obtained.   Wherefore, a ministry enabled by spiritual gifts, and engaged by sense of duty, to labour constantly in the use of all means appointed by Christ for the edification of the church, or increase of his mystical body, is required in such a church as a believer may conscientiously join himself unto ; and where it is otherwise, let men cry out " schism" and "faction" whilst they please, Jesus Christ will acquit his disciples in the exercise of their liberty, and accept them in the discharge of their duty.

If it be said, that if all men be thus allowed to judge of what is best for their own edification, and to act according unto the judgment which they make, they will be continually parting from one church unto another, until all things are filled with disturbance and confusion, I say,—

[1.] That the contrary assertion,—namely, that *men are not allowed to judge* what is meet and best for their own edification, or not to act according to the judgment they make herein,—may possibly *keep up some churches*, but is the ready way *to destroy all religion*.

[2.] That many of those by whom this liberty is denied unto professing Christians yet do indeed take it for granted that *they have such a liberty*, and that it is their duty to make use of it. For what are all the contests between the church of Rome and the church of England, so far as Christians that are not churchmen are concerned in them? Is it not, in whether of the churches edification may be best obtained? If this be not the ball between us, I know not what is. Now, herein do not all the writers and preachers of both parties give their reasons and arguments unto the people why edification is better to be had in the one church than in the other? And do they not require of them to form a judgment upon those reasons and arguments, and to act accordingly? If they do not, they do but make a flourish, and act a part, like players on a stage, without any determinate design.

[3.] All Christians *actually do so*. They do judge for themselves unless they are brutish; they do act according unto that judgment, unless they are hardened in sin; and therefore who do not so are not to be esteemed disciples of Christ. To suppose that in all things of spiritual and eternal concernment men are not determined and acted every one by his own judgment, is an imagination of men who think but little of what they are, or do, or say, or write. Even those who shut their eyes against the light and follow in the herd, resolving not to inquire into any of these things, do it because they *judge it is best for them so to do*.

[4.] It is commonly acknowledged by Protestants that private Christians have *a judgment of discretion* in things of religion. The term was invented to grant them some liberty of judgment, in opposition unto the blind obedience required by the church of Rome; but withal to put a restraint upon it, and a distinction of some superior judgment, it may be in the church or others. But if by *discretion* they mean the best of men's understanding, knowledge, wisdom, and prudence, in and about the things wherein it is exercised, I should be glad to be informed what other judgment than this of discretion, in and about the things of religion, this, or that, or any church in the world, can have or exercise. But to allow men a judgment of discretion, and not to grant it their duty to act according unto that judgment, is to oblige them to be fools, and to act not *discreetly*, at least not according unto their *own discretion*.

(4.) The same is to be spoken of *gospel discipline*, without which neither can the duties of church-societies be observed nor the ends of them attained.   The neglect, the loss, the abuse hereof, is that which hath ruined the glory of Christian religion in the world, and brought the whole profession of it into confusion.   Hereon have the fervency and sincerity of true, evangelical, mutual love been abated, yea, utterly lost; for that love which Jesus Christ requireth among his disciples is such as never was in the world before amongst men, nor can be in the world but on the principles of the gospel, and faith therein.   Therefore it is called his " new commandment." The continuation of it amongst the generality of Christians is but vainly pretended; little or nothing of the reality of it in its due exercise is found.   And this hath ensued on the neglect of evangelical discipline in churches, or the turning of it into a worldly domination; for one principal end of it is the preservation, guidance, and acting of this love.   That mutual watch over one another that ought to be in all the members of the church, the principal evidence and fruit of love without dissimulation, is also lost hereby.   Most men are rather ready to say, in the spirit and words of Cain, " Am I my brother's keeper?" than to attend unto the command of the apostle, " Exhort one another daily, lest any of you be hardened through the deceitfulness of sin;" or comply with the command of our Saviour, "If thy brother offend thee, tell him of it between him and thee." By this means likewise is the purity of communion lost, and those received as principal members of churches who, by all the rules of primitive discipline, ought to be cast out of them.   Wherefore this also is to be considered in the choice we are to make of what churches we will join ourselves unto, as unto constant, complete communion, and in whose communion we will abide; for these things are matters of choice, and consist in voluntary, free acts of obedience.   With those unto whom they are not so, who would on the one hand have them to be things that men may be compelled unto, and ought so to be, or, on the other, that follow no other guidance in them but outward circumstances, from the times and places where they are born and inhabit, I will have no contest.   It follows from hence, also, that where there are many churches wherein these things are found, whereon we may lawfully, and ought in duty, to join with some of them in particular, every one is obliged to join himself unto such a church as whose principles and practices are most suited unto his edification.

CHAPTER XI.

Of conformity and communion in parochial assemblies.

FROM what we have insisted on we may borrow some light into the determination of that case wherein multitudes are at this day concerned. And the case itself may be briefly stated in this inquiry, —namely, *Whether all Protestants, ministers and people, are bound to join themselves unto the church of England, as now by law established in its parochial assemblies, as unto complete, constant communion, without the use of any other church means for their own edification, so as if they do not so do they are guilty of schism?* This is that which is called "conformity unto the church of England;" which, as unto private persons, can be expressed only in constant, complete communion in parochial assemblies, according to their present constitution, without the use or exercise of any other church worship or discipline but what is by law established in them. Refraining from an absolute compliance herein is called *schism*. But whereas ecclesiastical schism, whatever it be in particular, in its general nature hath respect only unto divine institutions, this, which respecteth only the laws, rules, and determinations of men, can have no alliance thereunto. Yet it is not only charged as such, without the least countenance from Scripture or antiquity, so far as it may be allowed of authority with us, but the supposition of it is accumulated with another evil,—namely, that those who are so guilty (of it), in the judgment of them who are intrusted with secular power, though peaceable and orthodox, ought to be punished with various penalties, gradually coming unto the loss of goods, liberty, and in some cases of life itself;—an opinion *ignominious unto Christian religion*, however vapoured withal by young men, whose wit flies above all serious consideration of things and their circumstances, and countenanced by others, from an influence of interest, who otherwise would not be imposed on by such an anti-evangelical presumption. I shall, therefore, at the utmost distance from interest or passion, briefly consider the case proposed, and give an account of my thoughts concerning it.

1. One or two things are usually premised unto the consideration of this case; as, namely,—

(1.) That those who refrain from that communion with the church of England which we insist upon do yet agree therewith in all important doctrines of faith; which is the foundation, the life and soul of church union and communion. This I freely grant, but with this limitation, that this agreement respects the doctrine as declared at the first reformation, and explained in the age next ensuing thereon. If there be a change made in or of these doctrines, or any of them, by any in or of the church of England, we profess our disagreement from them, and do declare that thereby the foundation of our communion with them is weakened, and the principal bond of it loosened.

(2.) That not only as Christians, but as reformed Protestants, we do agree in the renunciation of the doctrines and worship of the church of Rome; which are opposed by the common consent of all those who are usually so called. Yet this must be added thereunto, that if any in or of the church of England should make an accession unto any parts of the doctrine and worship of the Roman church, not avowed or warranted by the consent of the church in its first reformation, we are not, we cannot be, obliged unto communion with them therein; and by their so doing, the original bond of our communion is weakened, if not dissolved.

2. These things being premised, we shall inquire, in the first place, what is the rule of that communion with the church of England in its parochial assemblies which is required of us. If this be pleaded to be a rule of divine prescription, we acknowledge that great diligence and humility are required unto the consideration of it, that we be not mistaken. And if it prove to be according to the mind of Christ,—that is, of his institution,—if we fail of a compliance with it, we are guilty of schism. But if the rule prescribing, limiting, and exacting this communion, be not so much as pleaded to be of divine institution, whatever fault there may be in our dissent from it, schism it is not: for ecclesiastical schism neither hath nor can have respect unto any thing but divine institutions; for if it hath, it is in the power of any sort of men to make schismatics of whom they please, as, practically and in pretence, it is come to pass at this day in the world. Now, the rule of the communion required is, the *law of the land, the Book of Canons*, with the *rubric of the Common Prayer*. If, according to the prescriptions, directions, and commands given in them, we do join ourselves in communion with parochial assemblies, then are we judged conformable to the church of England, and not else. By and according unto these are all inquiries made concerning communion with the church; and if they are observed, the return is, " omnia bene." Now, this rule hath no divine warrant for its institution, no example in the primitive churches, especially considering

what are the things which it obliges us unto, nor can be made consistent with the liberty wherewith Christ hath made his disciples free. A dissent from this rule is as far from schism as any man need desire it; for nothing is so but what respects some command or institution of Christ, which immediately affects the conscience. It is true, the Lord Christ hath commanded that love, union, peace, and order, whereof schism is a disturbance, and whereunto it is opposite; but they are that love, union, and order which he hath appointed. To suppose that he hath left it unto men to invent and appoint a new kind of union and order,—which is done in the rule we treat of, —which he never required, and then to oblige his disciples unto the observation of it, be it what it will, so as that their dissent from it should be criminal, and that for this reason, that it is so appointed of men, is no small mistake. And if all that love, union, peace, and order, which the Lord Jesus hath enjoined his disciples, may be punctually observed without any respect unto this rule as a rule of church-communion, to dissent from it, whatever fault of another kind it may be, is no more schism than it is adultery. And if, on some men's arbitrary constitution of this rule, and the dissent of others from it, such differences and divisions ensue as seem to have the general nature of schism, the evil of them belongs unto those alone by whom the rule is framed. If, indeed, some should frame such a rule of church-communion because they suppose they see cause for it, and would then leave it unto others to observe as they see cause, if it be not of use, it would not be liable unto much abuse. But whereas our Lord Jesus Christ hath given one and the same rule equally unto all his disciples in these things,—namely, that they should observe and do all that he hath commanded them,—for some of them, on any pretence or plea whatever, as of their being the church, or the like, arbitrarily to frame a rule of their own, as an addition unto his, obliging all others unto a strict observance of it because they have so framed it, is that which neither the Scripture nor primitive antiquity knows any thing of.

I will not inquire what is that power and authority whereby this rule is constituted and confirmed, nor in whom it doth reside. The name of the church is usually pretended and pleaded. But before any can be concerned herein, all that hath been pleaded for the true state and nature of evangelical churches must be overthrown; which will not be done speedily. Railings, revilings, and reproaches will not do it. But until this is done, it will be believed that every particular congregation is indispensably obliged in itself to observe and do all the commands of Christ, and is left at liberty so to regulate the outward circumstances of its worship and order as is best for its own edification, whereof itself is the most competent judge. But as for a church of another sort, invested with authority to make a rule, not only as unto the outward circumstances of those actions wherein church order and worship do consist, but as unto sundry religious rites and observances, which thereby are added unto it, and impose the observance of it on a great multitude of other congregations, without their consent, whether they judge the things enjoined to be for their edification or otherwise, it is apparently not from heaven, but of men. Wherefore, leave Christians and churches at that liberty which Christ hath purchased for them, wherewith he hath made them free, and then let those who first break union and order bear the charge of schism; which they cannot avoid.

3. The church-communion required by virtue of this rule is *constant and complete*, exclusive unto any other church-order or means of public edification. It doth not command or appoint that men should communicate in parochial assemblies when there is occasion, when it is for their edification, when scandal would arise if they should refuse it; but absolutely and completely. And whereas there are many things relating unto church-order and divine worship enjoined in that rule, there is no distinction made between them,—some things that are always necessary (that is, in the seasons of them), and some things wherein men may forbear a compliance,—but they are all equally required in their places and seasons, though perhaps on different penalties. And whoever fails in the observation of any ceremony, time, or place, appointed therein, is in the power of them who are intrusted with the administration of church power or jurisdiction; for the discipline of the church it cannot be called. Suppose a man would comply with all other things, only he esteems the use of one rite or ceremony, as the cross in baptism, or the like, to be unlawful; if he forbear the use of it, or to tender his child unto baptism where it is used, he is to be cut off as a schismatic from the communion of the church, no less than if he had absolutely refused a compliance with the whole rule. And, therefore, whatever condescension and forbearance in some things is pretended, he that doth not in all things observe the whole rule is in "misericordia cancellarii;" which oft proves an uneasy posture. If any men think that the Lord Christ hath given them such a power and authority over the souls and consciences of his disciples, as that they can bind them unto the religious observance of every rite and ceremony that they are pleased to appoint, on the penalty of excision from all church-communion and the guilt of schism, I shall only say that I am not of their mind, nor ever shall be so.

4. This communion contains a virtual *approbation* of all that is contained in the rule of it, as good for the edification of the church. It is certain that nothing is to be appointed in the church but what

is so; even order itself, which these things it is said are framed for, is good only with respect thereunto. Now, it is to be judged that whatever a man practiseth in religion, that he approveth of; for if he do not, he is a vile hypocrite. Nor is he worthy the name of a Christian who will practise any thing in religion but what he approveth. The disputes that have been amongst us about doing things with a doubting conscience, upon the command of superiors, and consenting unto the use of things which we approve not of in themselves, tend all to atheism and the eternal dishonour of Christian religion, begetting a frame of mind which an honest heathen would scorn. Wherefore, unless men be allowed to declare what it is they approve and what they do not, their practice is their profession of what they approve, which is the whole rule of communion prescribed unto them.

These things being premised, I shall propose some of those reasons on the account whereof many cannot conform unto the church of England, by joining in constant, complete communion with parochial assemblies, so as by their practice to approve the rule of that communion obliging themselves to use no other public means for their own edification:—

I. The church of England in its parochial assemblies stands in need of reformation; for it is apparent that either they fail in their original institution or else have degenerated from it. What hath already been discoursed concerning the original institution of churches, with men's voluntary coalescency into such sacred societies, with what shall be afterward treated concerning their essential parts in matter and form, will sufficiently evidence their present deviation from the rule of their first institution. Neither, so far as I know, is it pleaded that they are distinct churches of divine institution, but secular appointments, as for other ends, so for an accommodation of men in the performance of some parts of divine worship. And if they are found no more, they can have no concernment into the inquiry about schism; for withholding church-communion from such societies as are not churches is a new kind of schism, unknown to all antiquity. And for that which takes itself to be a church by a divine warranty, suppose it be so, to command constant, complete communion, exclusive unto all other church-communion, with that or them which are no churches, determining a refusal thereof to be schism, is to undertake a cause which needs not only great parts but great power also to defend it.

But let these parochial assemblies be esteemed churches (without a supposition whereof I know not what ecclesiastical concernment we can have in them), three things will be said thereon:—1. That the church of England, as in other things so in these *parochial assemblies*, stands in need of reformation.   2. That they neither do, nor will, nor can *reform themselves*.   3. On this supposition, it is lawful for any of the disciples of Christ to yield obedience unto him by joining in such societies for their edification as he hath appointed; which is the whole of the cause in hand.   Nor doth any necessity from hence ensue of a departure from communion with the church of England in faith and love, or the profession of the same faith, and the due exercise of all the acts and duties of Christian love.

1. Unto the proof of the first assertion some things are to be premised; as,—

(1.) Churches instituted, planted, ruled according to the mind of Christ in all things, *may degenerate* into a corrupt state, such as shall stand in need of reformation; in a neglect whereof they must perish as unto their church-state and privileges.   This needs no confirmation; for besides that it is possible, from all the causes of such an apostasy and defection, that so it should be, and it is frequently foretold in the Scripture that so it would be, the event in and among all churches that had originally a divine institution doth make uncontrollably evident.   The seven churches of Asia, most of them within few years of their first plantation, were so degenerated that our Lord Jesus Christ threatened them with casting off unless they reformed themselves.   What a woful apostasy all other churches, both of the east and west, were involved in, is known unto and confessed by all Protestants.   But yet the case of none of them was deplorable or desperate, until, through pride and carnal interest, they fell some of them into a persuasion that they needed no reformation, nor could be reformed; which is become a principal article of faith in the Roman church.   There was a reformation attempted, and attained in some measure, by some nations or churches in the last ages, from the corruption and impositions of the church of Rome.   However, none of them ever pretended that it was complete or perfect, according to the pattern of the Scripture, as unto the institution and discipline of the churches; no, nor yet to the example of the primitive church of after ages, as is acknowledged by the church of England in the beginning of the "commination against sinners."   But suppose it to be complete, to conclude that because an outward rule of it was established, so long as that outward rule is observed there can be no need of reformation, is a way to lead churches into a presumptuous security unto their ruin; for whereas men, being secured in their interests by that rule, are prejudiced against any progress in reformation beyond what they have attained,—which that it should be a duty is contrary unto the whole nature of Christian religion, which is the conduct of a spiritual life, in the growth and increase of light and a suitable obedience,—so they are apt to think that whilst they adhere unto that rule they can stand in no need of reformation, which is but a new name for trouble and sedition, though it be the foundation on which they stand. But generally churches think that others stand in need of reformation, but they need none themselves. If they would but give them leave to reform themselves who judge that it is needful for them, without the least prejudice unto their church profession or secular interest, it is all that is desired of them.

(2.) Where churches do so stand in need of reformation, and will not reform themselves, being warned of their duty, the Lord Christ threatens to leave them, and assuredly will do so in the time that he hath limited unto his patience. This is the subject of five of his epistles or messages unto the churches of Asia, Rev. ii. iii. And where the Lord Christ doth, on any cause or provocation, withdraw his presence, in any kind or degree, from any church, it is the duty of any of the members of that church to remove from themselves the guilt of that provocation, though it cannot be done without a separation from that church. It is safer leaving of any church whatever than of Jesus Christ. I suppose most men think that if they had a warning from Christ charging their defection and calling for reformation, as those churches of Asia had, they would repent and reform themselves. But whereas it doth not appear that some of them did so,—whereon they were, not long after, deserted and destroyed,—it is like that there are others who would follow their steps though one should rise from the dead to warn them of their danger. But this instruction, that churches who lose their first faith, love, and works, who are negligent in discipline, and tolerate offensive evils in doctrines and manners among them, who are lukewarm as unto zeal, and dead, for the greatest part of their members, as unto the life of holiness, are disapproved by Christ, and in danger of being utterly deserted by him, is given unto all churches, no less divinely than if they had an immediate message from heaven about these things. Those, therefore, who, being under the guilt of them, do not reform themselves, cannot claim the necessity of a continuance in their communion from any disciples of Christ, as we shall see afterward.

(3.) Reformation respects either doctrine and worship, or obedience becoming the gospel. The debates about such a reformation as concerns the retaining or removing of certain ceremonies, we concern not ourselves in at present; nor shall we in this place insist on what concerns doctrine and worship, which may afterward be spoken unto. But we shall confine ourselves here unto the consideration of gospel obedience only. And we say,—

That the church of England, in the generality of its parochial assemblies, and in itself, stands in need of reformation, by reason of the woful degeneracy of the generality of its members,—that is, the inhabitants of the land,—from the rule of the gospel and commands of Christ, as unto spiritual light, faith, love, holiness, charity, and abounding in the fruits of righteousness unto the praise of God by Jesus Christ. These things are the immediate ends of church societies, the principal means whereby God is glorified in the world. Where they are neglected, where they are not attained, where they are not duly improved by the generality of the members of any church, that church, I think, stands in need of reformation.

This assertion may seem somewhat importune and severe; but when the sins of a church or nation are come to that height, in all ranks, sorts, and degrees of men, that all persons of sobriety do fear daily that desolating judgments from God will break in upon us, it cannot be unseasonable to make mention of them, when it is done with no other design but only to show the necessity of reformation, or how necessary it is for some, if all will not comply therewith; for if a city be on fire, it is surely lawful for any of the citizens to save and preserve, if they can, their own houses, though the mayor and aldermen should neglect the preservation of the whole city in general.

It might be easily demonstrated what great numbers [there are] amongst us,—[1.] Who have imbibed *atheistical opinions,* and either vent them or speak presumptuously, according unto their influence and tendency every day; [2.] Who are *profane scoffers* at all true Christian piety and the due expressions of the power of godliness,— an evil not confined unto the laity,—such things being uttered and published by them as should be astonishable unto all that know the fear of the Lord and his terror; [3.] Who are *profoundly ignorant* of the mysteries of the gospel, or those doctrines of Christian religion whose knowledge is of the highest importance and necessity; [4.] Who are openly *flagitious in their lives,* whence all sorts of gross immoralities do fill the land from one end unto the other; [5.] Who live in a *constant neglect* of all more private holy duties, whether in their families or in personal retirement; [6.] Who are evidently under *the power of pride,* vanity, covetousness, profaneness of speech in cursed oaths and swearing; [7.] Who *instruct the worst of men* unto an approbation of themselves in such ways as these, by petulant scoffing at the very name of the Spirit and grace of Christ, at all expectation of his spiritual aids and assistances, at all fervency in religious duties, or other acts of a holy converse. These, and such like things as these, do sufficiently evidence the necessity of reformation; for where they are continued, the use and end of church-societies is impaired or lost. And it

is in vain to pretend that this is the old plea of them who caused
schisms in the church,—namely, that bad men were mixed with the
good, for which cause they rejected those churches wherein that was
allowed as no true churches of Christ; for no such thing is included
in what we assert, nor doth follow thereon. We do own that wicked
hypocrites may be joined in true churches, and be made partakers of
all the privileges of them. Neither is this a cause of withdrawing
communion from any church, much less of condemning it as no
true church of Christ. But this we say, that if such hypocrites discover themselves in open scandalous sins,—which upon examination
will prove to be of a larger extent than some suppose, with respect
unto sins of omission as well as of commission,—if they are not dealt
withal according as the discipline of Christ doth require in such cases,
the church wherein they are allowed, especially if the number of
such persons be many, or the most, the generality of the people,
and their sins notorious, doth stand in need of reformation; as the
church of England doth acknowledge in the " commination against
sinners."

The substance of what is proposed under this consideration may
be expressed in the ensuing observations:—(1.) The generality of
the inhabitants of this nation are joined and do belong unto the
church of England, in its parochial assemblies. (2.) That many
walk and live without any visible compliance unto the rule of Christ
in gospel obedience: yea,—(3.) Great, notorious, provoking sins do
abound among them, for which it ought to be feared continually
that the judgments of God will speedily follow; as is acknowledged
in the " commination." (4.) That hereon they all stand in need of
reformation, without which the principal ends of church-communion
cannot be obtained among them. (5.) That this reformation is the
duty of these churches themselves; which if it be neglected, they live
in a contempt of the commands of Christ; for,—(6.) Unto them, in
the preaching of the word and exercise of discipline, are the means
of this reformation committed: for we treat not at present of the
power or duty of the supreme magistrate in these things. (7.) That
this state of churches cannot hinder, nor ought so to do, if continued
in, the true disciples of Christ from reforming themselves, by endeavouring the due observance of all his commands.

2. In this state the church of England doth not, and it is to be
feared *will not, nor can reform itself.* But although the weight of
the whole argument in hand depends very much on this assertion,
yet I shall not insist on its particular confirmation, for sundry reasons
not now to be mentioned. It is enough that no such work hath
been as yet attempted, nor is at this day publicly proposed, notwithstanding all the mercies that some have received, the losses which

the church for want of it hath sustained, the judgments for sins that are feared; which ought to be motives thereunto. Yea, the generality of ecclesiastical persons seem to judge that all things among them are as they ought to be, that there is no crime or disorder but only in complaining of their good estate, and calling upon them for re-formation.

3. This being the state of the parochial churches in England, the inquiry is, Whether *every believer in England be indispensably obliged, by virtue of any law, rule, or direction of a divine original, to continue in constant, complete communion with them, so as not to make use of any other ways and means of Christ's appointment for their own edification, on the penalty of the guilt of schism?* Now, although we do not (as we shall see immediately) lay the weight of refraining from their communion on this consideration, yet is there enough in it to warrant any man in his so doing; for a man in his conforming thereunto makes it a part of his religious profession, not only that the church wherein he is joined is a true church, but that there is in its state and actings a due representa-tion of the mind of Christ, as unto what he requireth of his churches, and what he would have them to be. The Lord Christ is the " apostle and high priest of our profession:" and in all things that belong there-unto we declare that we do it in compliance with his will; and we do so, or we are hypocrites. This no man can do in such a church-state who is convinced of its defects, without reflecting the greatest dishonour on Christ and the gospel.

More weight will be added unto this consideration when we shall treat of the matter of gospel churches, or of what sort of persons they ought to consist. In the meantime, those who pretend a reverence unto antiquity in those things wherein they suppose countenance to be given unto their interest, may do well sometimes to consider what was *the discipline of the primitive churches,* and what were the manners, the lives, the heavenly conversations of their members. Because in the third and fourth centuries there is mention made of bishops distinct from presbyters, with some ecclesiastical practices and ceremonies in worship not mentioned in the Scripture nor known unto the apostolical churches, shall we judge ourselves obliged to conform thereunto as our rule and pattern, so as that in the judg-ment of some they are to be esteemed no churches who conform not their outward state and practice unto the same rule? and shall we judge ourselves at liberty to reject all that they did in the exercise of discipline, and in the preservation of purity of life and holiness in the churches, and that according to the command of Christ and rule of the Scripture? Who knows not upon what diligent trial, and experience first obtained of their knowledge, faith, and godliness, they admitted members into their churches? Yea, such was their care and severity herein that they would not admit a Roman emperor unto communion with them, unless he first confessed his sins, and joined amongst other penitents before his admission, Euseb., lib. vi. cap. 33. Who knows not with what diligence they watched over the walkings and conversations of all that were admitted among them, and with what severity they animadverted on all that fell into scandalous sins? What was hereon their conversation, in all holiness, righteousness, temperance, usefulness unto the world, in works of charity and benevolence, as in all other Christian virtues, we have sufficient testimony. The heathen who were morally sober and virtuous, desired no more than that they might find out among them an indulgence unto any sort of sin, crime, or wickedness; which because they could not charge any of them withal, they invented those brutish and foolish lies about their nightly meetings. But when a sober inquiry was made concerning them, their enemies were forced to confess that they were guilty of no open sin, no adulteries, no swearings or perjuries; as is evident in the epistles of Pliny and Trajan the emperor. In particular, they utterly rejected from their communion all that resorted unto public stage-plays or other spectacles; a solemn renunciation whereof was required of them who were admitted unto baptism when they were adult. See Clem. Pedag., lib. iii. cap. 12. If the reader would have an account of the lives and manners of the first churches in their members, he may find it in Clem. Epist. ad Cor. pp. 2–4; Justin Mart. Apol. ii.; Tertullian in his Apol. and lib. ii. ad Uxor. et de cultu fœminarum ; Cyprian, Epist. ii. et xii.; Euseb. Hist. lib. ix. cap. 8; Athanas. Epist. ad Solit., et Epiphan. lib. iii. t. 2, sect. 24; and the multiplied complaints of Chrysostom concerning the beginning of degeneracy in this matter, with others. If the example of the primitive churches had been esteemed of any value or authority in these things, much of our present differences had been prevented.

II. The constitution of these parochial assemblies is not from heaven, but of men. There is almost nothing which is required unto the constitution of evangelical churches found in them; nor are they looked on by any as complete churches, but only as conveniencies for the observance of some parts of the worship of God. What some have in their wisdom found out for conveniency, others are engaged unto a compliance therewithal by necessity; for being born within the precincts of the parish makes them to belong unto the assemblies of it, whether they will or no. To refrain from the communion of such churches, whose bond of relation consists only in cohabitation within the precincts of a political constitution, is a new kind of schism, which may be cured by a removal out of those precincts. If it be said that these parochial assemblies have their foundation in the light of nature, and are directed unto in the institution of particular churches in the Scripture,—that they are not men's inventions for convenience, but have somewhat divine in them,—I say, let them be left unto the warranty which they have from these causes and principles, let nothing be mixed in their constitution which is contrary unto them, nor let them be abridged of what they direct unto, and there will be no more contending about them, as unto their constitution. For instance, whatever there is of warranty in the light of nature, or direction in evangelical institutions for such assemblies, they absolutely suppose these three things:—

1. That a conjunction in them is a *voluntary act* of free choice in them that so join together in them. Other kind of assemblies for the worship of God neither the one nor the other doth give the least countenance unto.

2. That they have in themselves sufficient *right, power, and authority* unto the attaining all the ends of such assemblies in holy worship and rule. Other kind of churches they know nothing of.

3. That they are enabled to *preserve their own purity* and continue their own being.

But all these things are denied unto our parochial assemblies by law; and therefore they can claim no warranty from either of those principles. Wherefore, there can be no obligation upon any believer to join himself with such churches in constant communion as are judged none by them that appoint them, or only partially and improperly so, or are of such a constitution as hath in its essentially constituent parts no warranty either from the light of nature or Scripture direction, so as that his dissent from them should be esteemed schism. How far communion with them for some duties of worship,—which is, indeed, all that they can pretend unto,—may be admitted, we do not now inquire.

III. There is not in them (and therefore not in the church of England, as unto its present profession) a *fixed standard of truth*, or rule of faith to be professed, which every believer may own, and have his part or interest therein. This I grant is not from the original constitution of the church, nor from what is established by any law therein, but from persons who at present have the declaration of its profession committed unto them. But from what cause soever it be, it is sufficient to warrant any man who takes care of his own edification and salvation to use his own liberty in the choice of the most effectual means unto those ends. Wherefore some things may be added in farther explanation of this consideration; as,—

1. It is the duty of every church *to be the pillar and ground of truth*, to hold fast the form of wholesome words, or to keep the truth

pure and uncorrupted from all mixture of false doctrines, errors, heresies, or the speaking of perverse things in it, unto the hurt of the disciples of Christ, 1 Tim. iii. 15; 2 Tim. ii. 2; Acts xx. 28–30, etc. When any church ceaseth so to be, the obligation unto communion with it is dissolved.

2. This is the *principal end* of the ministry of the church in particular, Eph. iv. 11–13; 1 Tim. vi. 20. And where those who possess and exercise it do eminently fail herein, it is the duty of others to withdraw from them; for,—

3. Every private man's confession is included in the public profession of the church or assembly whereunto he belongs. And,—

4. Oneness or agreement in the truth, whereby we come to have "one Lord, one faith, one baptism," is the foundation of all church-communion; which if it be taken away, the whole fabric of it falls to the ground. If the trumpet in any church, as unto these things, gives an uncertain sound, no man knows how to prepare himself for the battle, or to "fight the good fight of faith."

It will be said that this cannot be justly charged on the church of England, yea, not without open wrong and injustice; for she hath a fixed, invariable standard of truth in the Thirty-nine Articles, which contain its public profession of faith and the rule of its communion. Wherefore I say, that it is not the *primitive constitution* of the church nor its *legal establishment* that are reflected on, but only the present practice of so many as makes it necessary for men to take the care of their own edification on themselves. But here also some things are to be observed:—

1. These articles at present are exceeding defective, in their being a fixed standard of the profession of truth, with respect unto those errors and heresies which have invaded and pestered the churches since their framing and establishment. We know it was the constant, invariable custom of the primitive churches, upon the emergency of any new errors or heresies, to add unto the rule and symbol of their confession a testimony against them, so as to preserve themselves from all communion in them or participation of them. And a usage it was both necessary and laudable, as countenanced by Scripture example, however afterward it was abused; for no writing, such as all church-confessions are, can obviate unforeseen heresies, or errors not broached at the time of its writing, but only that which is of divine institution, wherein infinite wisdom hath stored up provision of truth, for the destruction of all errors that the subtlety or folly of man can invent. When these articles of the church of England were composed, neither Socinianism nor Arminianism, which have now made such an inroad on some protestant churches, were in the world, either name or things. Wherefore, in their

confession no testimony could be expressly given against them, though I acknowledge it is evident, from what is contained in the articles of it, and the approved exposition they received for a long time in the writings of the most eminent persons of the church, that there is a virtual condemnation of all these errors included therein. But in that state whereunto things are come amongst us, some more express testimony against them is necessary to render any church the pillar and ground of truth.

2. Besides, a distinction is found out, and passeth current among us, that the articles of this confession are *not articles of faith*, but of outward agreement for peace' sake among ourselves: which is an invention to help on the ruin of religion; for articles of peace in religion, concerning matters of faith, which he that subscribes doth it not because they are true or articles of faith, are an engine to accommodate hypocrisy, and nothing else. But according unto this supposition they are used at men's pleasure, and turned which way they have a mind to. Wherefore,—

3. Notwithstanding this standard of truth, differences in important doctrines, wherein the edification of the souls of men is highly concerned, do abound among them who manage the public profession of the church. I shall not urge this any farther by instances; in general it cannot modestly be denied. Neither is this spoken to abridge ministers of churches of their due liberty in their management of the truths of the gospel; for such a liberty is to be granted as,—

(1.) Ariseth from the *distinct gifts* that men have received; for "unto every one is given grace according to the measure of the gift of Christ," Eph. iv. 7. "As every man hath received the gift, even so minister the same one to another, as good stewards of the manifold grace of God," 1 Pet. iv. 10.

(2.) As followeth on that *spiritual wisdom* which ministers receive in great variety, for the application of the truths of the gospel unto the souls and consciences of men. Hereon great variety in public church-administrations will ensue, but all unto edification.

(3.) Such as consists in a *different exposition* of particular places of Scripture, whilst the analogy of faith is kept and preserved, Rom. xii. 6.

(4.) Such as admits of *different stated apprehensions* in and about such doctrines as wherein the practice and comfort of Christians are not immediately nor greatly concerned.

Such a liberty, I say, as the dispensation of spiritual gifts, and the different manner of their exercise, as the unsearchable depths that are in the Scripture, not to be fathomed at once by any church or any sort of persons whatever, and our knowing the best of us but in part, with the difference of men's capacities and understandings in and about things not absolutely necessary unto edification, must be allowed in churches and their ministry. But I speak of that variety of doctrines, which is of greater importance. Such it is as will set men at liberty to make their own choice in the use of means for their edification. And if such novel opinions about the person, grace, satisfaction, and righteousness of Christ, about the work of the Holy Spirit of God in regeneration, or the renovation of our nature into the image of God, as abound in some churches, should at any time, by the suffrage of the major part of them who by law are intrusted with its conduct, be declared as the sense of the church, it is and would be sufficient to absolve any man from an obligation unto its communion by virtue of its first institution and establishment.

IV. *Evangelical discipline* is neither observed nor attainable in these parochial assemblies, nor is there any relief provided by any other means for that defect. This hath in general been spoken unto before; but because it belongs in an especial manner unto the argument now in hand, I shall yet farther speak unto it. For, to declare my mind freely, I do not judge that any man can incur the guilt of schism who refrains from the communion of the church wherein the discipline of the gospel is either wholly wanting or is perverted into rule and domination, which hath no countenance given unto it in the word of truth. And we may observe,—

1. The *discipline of the church* is that alone for which any rule or authority is given unto it or exercised in it. Authority is given unto the ministers of the church to dispense the word and administer the sacraments; which, I know not why, some call the " key of order." But the only end why the Lord Christ hath given authority, or rule, or power for it unto the church, or any in it, is for the exercise of discipline, and no other. Whatever power, rule, dignity, or pre-eminence is assumed in the churches, not merely for this end, is usurpation and tyranny.

2. The outward means appointed by Jesus Christ, for the preservation of his churches in order, peace, and purity, consists in this discipline. He doth by his word give directions and commands for this end; and it is by discipline alone that they are executed. Wherefore, without it the church cannot live in its health, purity, and vigour. The word and sacraments are its spiritual food, whereon its life doth depend; but without that exercise, and medicinal applications unto its distempers which are made by discipline, it cannot live a healthy, vigorous, faithful life in the things of God.

3. This discipline is either private or public:—

(1.) That which is *private* consists in the mutual watch that all the members of the church have over one another, with admonitions, exhortations, and reproofs, as their edification doth require. The loss of this part of the discipline of Christ in most churches hath lost us much of the glory of Christian profession.

(2.) That which is *public*, in the rulers of the church, with and by its own consent. The nature and acts of it will be afterward considered.

4. There are three things considerable in this discipline:—(1.) The *power* and authority whereby it is exercised; (2.) The *manner* of its administration; (3.) The especial *object* of it, both as it is susceptive of members and corrective; whereunto we may add its general end:—

(1.) The *authority* of it is only a power and liberty to act and ministerially exercise the authority of Christ himself. As unto those by whom it is exercised, it is in them an act of obedience unto the command of Christ; but with respect unto its object, the authority of Christ is exerted in it. That which is exercised on any other warranty or authority (as none can exert the authority of Christ but by virtue of his own institutions), whose acts are not acts of obedience unto Christ, whatever else it be, belongs not unto the discipline of evangelical churches.

(2.) As unto the *manner* of its administration, it is that which the Lord Christ hath appointed to express his love, care, and tenderness towards the church. Hence the acts of it which are corrective are called " lamenting" or " bewailing" of them towards whom they are exercised, 2 Cor. xii. 20. Whatever, therefore, is done in it that is not expressive of the love, care, patience, and holiness of Christ, is dishonourable unto him.

(3.) The *object* of it, as it is *susceptive of members*, is professed believers; and as it is *corrective*, it is those who stubbornly deviate from the rule of Christ, or live in disobedience of his commands. Wherefore, the general end of its institution is, to be a representation of the authority, wisdom, love, care, and patience of Christ towards his church, with a testimony unto the certainty, truth, and holiness of his future judgment. The especial nature of it shall be afterward considered.

Unto this discipline, either as unto its right or exercise, there is no pretence in parochial assemblies, yea, it is expressly forbidden unto them. Whereas, therefore, it is a matter of so great importance in itself, so subservient unto the glory of Christ, so useful and necessary unto the edification of his disciples, so weighty a part of our professed subjection unto him, without which no church can be continued in gospel purity, order, and peace, the total want or neglect of it is a sufficient cause for any man who takes care of his own salvation, or is concerned in the glory and honour of Christ, to refrain the communion of those churches wherein it is so wanting or neglected, or at least not to confine himself thereunto.

It will be said that this defect is supplied, in that the administration of church-discipline is committed unto others,—namely, the bishops and their officers, that are more meet and able for it than the ministers and people of parochial assemblies; what, therefore, is wanting in them is supplied fully another way, so that no pretence can be taken from hence for refraining communion in them. But it will be said,—

1. That this discipline is not to be placed where and in what hands men please, but to be left where Christ hath disposed it.

2. That one reason of the unmeetness of parochial churches for the exercise of this discipline is because they have been unjustly deprived of it for so many ages.

3. It is to be inquired, whether the pretended discipline doth in any thing answer that which Christ hath plainly and expressly ordained. For if a discipline should be erected whose right of exercise is derived from secular power, whose administration is committed unto persons who pretend not in the least unto any office of divine institution, as chancellors, commissaries, officials, etc., every way unknown unto antiquity, foreign unto the churches over which they rule, exercising their pretended power of discipline in a way of civil jurisdiction, without the least regard unto the rules or ends of evangelical discipline, managing its administration in brawlings, contentions, revilings, fees, pecuniary mulcts, etc., in open defiance of the spirit, example, rule, and commands of our Lord Jesus Christ,—it would be so far from supplying this defect, that it would exceedingly aggravate the evil of it. God forbid that any Christian should look on such a power of discipline, and such an administration of it, to be that which is appointed by Jesus Christ, or any way participant of the nature of it! Of what expediency it may be unto other ends I know not, but unto ecclesiastical discipline it hath no alliance; and therefore in its exercise, so far as it is corrective, it is usually applied unto the best and most sober Christians.

Wherefore, to deal plainly in this case, whereas there is neither the power nor exercise of discipline in parochial assemblies or their ministry, not so much by their own neglect as because their right thereunto is denied and its exercise wholly forbidden by them in whose power they are; and whereas, in the supply that is made of this defect, a secular power is erected, coercive by pecuniary and corporal penalties, administered by persons no way relating unto the churches over which they exercise this power, by rules of human laws and constitutions, in litigious and oppressive courts, in the room of that institution of Christ, whose power and exercise is spiritual, by spiritual means, according to the Scripture rules,—it is lawful for any man who takes care of his own salvation and of the means of it to withdraw from the communion of such churches, so far as it hinders or forbids him the use of the means appointed by Christ for his edification. Men may talk what they please of schism, but he that forsakes the conduct of his own soul, in things of so plain an evidence, must answer for it at his own peril.

V. This defect in parochial churches, that they are intrusted by law with no part of the rule of themselves, but are wholly governed and disposed of by others at their pleasure, in the ways before mentioned,—which shakes their very being as churches, though there be in them assemblies for divine worship, founded in common right and the light of nature, wherein men may be accepted with God,—is accompanied with such other wants and defects also as will weaken any obligation unto complete and constant communion with them. I shall give one only instance hereof : The *people's free choice of all their officers,* bishops, elders, pastors, etc., is, in our judgment, of divine institution, by virtue of apostolical example and directions. It is also so suitable unto the light of nature,—namely, that in a society absolutely founded in the *voluntary consent* of them who enter into it, and [which] doth actually exist thereby, without any necessity imposed on them from prescription, former usage, or the state of being born in and under such rules and laws, as it is with men in their political societies, the people should have the election of them who are to rule among them and over them, there being no provision of a right unto a successive imposition of any such rulers on them without their own consent,—that nothing can rationally be pleaded against it. And, therefore, whereas in all ordinarily settled governments in the world, setting aside the confusion of their originals, by war and conquests, the succession of rulers is either by *natural generation,* the rule being confined unto such a line, or by a *popular election,* or by a temperature of both; there hath been a new way invented for the communication of power and rule in churches, never exemplified in any political society,—namely, that it shall neither be successive, as it was under the Old Testament, nor elective, nor by any temperature of these two ways in one, but by a strange kind of flux of it through the hands of men who pretend to have so received it themselves from others. But whether hereon the people of the church can have that respect and devotion unto them as they would have unto hereditary rulers (long succession in rulers being the great cause of veneration in the people), especially such as had a succession one unto another by a natural descent through divine appointment, as the priests had under the law, or as unto those whom, on the account of their worth, ability, and fitness for the work of the ministry among them, they do choose themselves, they may do well to consider who are concerned. The necessity there is of maintaining a reputation and interest by secular grandeur, pomp, and power, of ruling the people of the church in church-matters by external force, with many other inconveniencies, do all proceed from this order of things, or rather disorder, in the call of men unto the ministry. And hence it is that the city of God and the people of Christ therein,— which is, indeed, the only true, free society in the world,—have rulers in and over them, neither by a natural right of their own, as in paternal government, nor by hereditary succession, nor by election, nor by any way or means wherein their own consent is included, but are under a yoke of an imposition of rulers on them above any society on the earth whatever. Besides, there is that relation between the church and its guides that no law, order, or constitution, can create without their mutual voluntary consent; and therefore, this right and liberty of the people, in every church, to choose their own spiritual officers, was for many ages preserved sacredly in the primitive times. But hereof there is no shadow remaining in our parochial churches; sundry persons, as patrons and ordinaries, have a concurring interest into the imposing of a minister, or such whom they esteem so, upon any such church, without the knowledge, consent, or approbation of the body of the church,—either desired or accepted. If there be any who cannot comply with this constitution of things relating unto the ministry, because it is a part of their profession of the gospel which they are to make in the world, which yet really consists only in an avowed subjection unto the commands of Christ, they can be no way obnoxious unto any charge of schism upon their refusal so to do; for a schism that consists in giving a testimony unto the institutions of Christ, and standing fast in the liberty wherewith he hath made his disciples free, is that whose guilt no man need to fear.

VI. What remaineth of those reasons whereon those who cannot comply with the conformity under consideration are cleared, in point of conscience, from any obligation thereunto, and so from all guilt of schism whatever, belongs unto the head of impositions on their consciences and practice, which they must submit unto. These being such as many whole books have been written about, the chief whereof have no way been answered,—unless railings and scoffings, with contempt and fierce reproaches, with false accusations, may pass for answers,—I shall not here again insist upon them. Some few things of that nature I shall only mention, and put an end unto this dispute:—

1. The *conformity* required of ministers consists in a public *assent and consent* unto the Book of Common Prayer, with the rubric, in it, which contains all the whole practice of the church of England, in its commands and prohibitions. Now, these being things that concern the worship of God in Christ, the whole entire state, order,

rule, and government of the gospel church, whoever gives solemnly this assent and consent, unless he be allowed to enter his protestation against those things which he dislikes, and of the sense wherein he doth so assent and consent,—which by law is allowed unto none, —the said assent and consent is his public profession that all these things, and all contained in them, are according to the mind of Christ, and that the ordering of them, as such, is part of their professed subjection unto his gospel. Blessed be God, most ministers are too wise and honest to delude their consciences with distinctions, equivocations, and reservations; and do thereon rather choose to suffer penury and penalty than to make the least intrenchment upon their own consciences, or the honour of the gospel in their profession! What they do and declare of this nature they must do it in sincerity, as in the sight of God, as approving what they do; not only as pardonable effects of necessity, but as that which is the best they have or can do in the worship of God, with a solemn renunciation of whatever is contrary unto what they do so approve. And whether this be a meet imposition on the consciences of ministers, with reference unto a great book or volume of a various composition, unto things almost without number, wherein exceptions have been given of old and lately, not answered nor answerable, with rules, laws, orders, not pretending to be scriptural prescriptions, is left unto the judgment of all who have due thoughts of their approaching account before the judgment-seat of Jesus Christ.

2. The conformity that is required of others being precise, and without power of dispensation in them by whom it is required, to answer the rule or law of it before declared, every man by his so conforming doth thereby take it on his conscience, and make it *part of his Christian profession*, that all which he so conforms unto is not only what he may do, but what he ought to do, both in matter and manner, so far as the law, or any part of it, doth determine or enjoin them. No man is allowed to make either distinction or protestation with respect unto any thing contained in the rules; and, therefore, whatever he doth in compliance therewith is interpretable, in the sight of God and man, as an approbation of the whole. Sincerity and openness in profession is indispensably required of us in order unto our salvation. And, therefore, to instruct men, as unto the worship of God, to do what they do not judge to be their duty to do, but only hope they may do without sin, or to join themselves in and unto that performance of it which either they approve not of as the best in the whole, or not lawful or approvable in some parts of it, is to instruct them unto the debauching of their consciences and ruin of their own souls. " Let every man be persuaded in his own mind;" for " what is not of faith is sin."

3. There is in this conformity required a *renunciation* of all other ways of public worship or means of edification that may be made use of; for they are all expressly forbidden in the rule of that conformity. No men, therefore, can comply with that rule, but that a renunciation of all other public ways of edification as unlawful is part of the visible profession which they make. " Video meliora proboque, Deteriora sequor," is no good plea in religion. It is uprightness and integrity that will preserve men, and nothing else. He that shall endeavour to cheat his conscience by distinctions and mental reservations, in any concernment of religious worship, I fear he hath little of it, if any at all, that is good for aught.

On these suppositions, I say, the imposition of the things so often contended about on the consciences and profession of Christians,—as, namely, the constant, sole use of the liturgy in all church administrations, in the matter and manner prescribed; the use and practice of all canonical ceremonies; the religious observation of stated holidays, with other things of the like nature,—is sufficient to warrant any sober, peaceable disciple of Christ, who takes care of his own edification and salvation, to refrain the communion required in this rule of conformity, unless he be fully satisfied in his own mind that all that it requires is according to the mind of Christ, and all that it forbids is disapproved by him. And whereas the whole entire matter of all these impositions are things whereof the Scripture and the primitive churches know nothing at all, nor is there any rumour of them to be imposed in or on any church of Christ for some centuries of years, I can but pity poor men who must bear the charge and penalties of schism for dissenting from them, as well as admire the fertility of their inventions who can find out arguments to manage such a charge on their account.

But whereas the dissent declared from that communion with parochial assemblies is that whereon we are so fiercely charged with the guilt of schism, and so frequently called schismatics, I shall divert a little to inquire into the nature and true notion of schism itself; and so much the rather, because I find the author of the " Unreasonableness of Separation" omit any inquiry thereinto, that he might not lose the advantage of any pretended description or aggravation of it.

CHAPTER XII.

Of schism.

ALTHOUGH it be no part of my present design to treat of the nature of schism, yet with respect unto what hath already been discoursed, and to manifest our unconcernment in the guilt of it, I shall, as was said, divert to give a plain and brief account of it. And in our inquiry I must declare myself wholly unconcerned in all the discords, divisions, and seditions, that have fallen out among Christians in the latter ages about things that were of their own invention. *Schism is a sin against Christian love*, with reference unto the deportment of men in and about the institutions of Christ, and their communion in them. As for contentions, divisions, or separations amongst men, about that order, agreement, unity, or uniformity which are of their own appointment, whatever moral evil they have had in them, they do not belong unto that church-schism which we inquire after. Such have been the horrid divisions and fightings that have prevailed at seasons in the church of Rome; a departure from whose self-constituted state, order, and rule, hath not the least affinity unto schism. It will not, therefore, be admitted that any thing can fall under the note and guilt of schism which hath not respect unto some church-state, order, rule, unity, or uniformity that is of Christ's institution.

There are three notions of schism that deserve our consideration:—

1. The first is that of *divisions among the members of the same church*, all of them abiding still in the same outward communion, without any separation into distinct parties. And unto schism in this notion of it three things do concur:—

(1.) Want of that *mutual love*, condescension, and forbearance, which are required in all the members of the same church; with the moral evils of whisperings, back-bitings, and evil surmises, that ensue thereon.

(2.) All *undue adherence* unto some church offices above others, causing disputes and janglings.

(3.) *Disorder* in the attendance unto the duties of church assemblies, and the worship of God performed in them. This is the only notion of schism that is exemplified in the Scripture, the only evil that is condemned under that name. This will appear unto any who shall with heedfulness read the Epistles of Paul the apostle unto the Corinthians; wherein alone the nature of this evil is stated and exemplified. But this consideration of schism hath been almost utterly lost for many ages. Whatever men do in churches, so that they depart not from the outward communion of them, it would be accounted ridiculous to esteem them schismatics. Yet this is that which, if not only, yet principally, the consciences of men are to regard, if they will avoid the guilt of schism. But this notion of it, as was said, being not suited unto the interest or advantages of any sort of men, in the charge of it on others, nor any way subservient to secure the inventions and impositions of the most, is on the matter lost in the world.

2. The second instance of ecclesiastical schism was given us in the same church of the Corinthians afterward; an account whereof we have in the epistle of Clemens, or of the church of Rome unto them about it; the most eminent monument of primitive antiquity, after the writings by divine inspiration. And that which he calls schism in that church, he calls also " strife, contention, sedition, tumult." And it may be observed concerning that schism, as all the ancients call it,—

(1.) That the church continued its state and outward communion. There is no mention of any that *separated from it*, that constituted a new church; only in the same church they agreed not, but were divided among themselves. Want of love and forbearance, attended with strife and contention among the members of the same church, abiding in the same outward communion, was the schism they were guilty of.

(2.) The effect of this schism was, that the body of the church, or *multitudes of the members*, by the instigation of *some few disorderly persons, had deposed their elders and rulers* from their offices, and probably had chosen others in their places; though that be not mentioned expressly in the epistle.

(3.) That the church itself is not blamed for assuming a power unto themselves to depose their elders, much less that they had done it without the consent, advice, or authority of any bishop or other church, but only that they had dealt unjustly with those whom they had deposed; who, in the judgment of the church of Rome, unto which they had written for advice, were esteemed not only innocent, but such as had *laudably and profitably discharged their office;* whereon the whole blame is cast on those who had instigated the church unto this procedure.

(4.) There was not yet, nor in a hundred and fifty years after, the least mention or intimation of any schism in a dissent from any humanly-invented rules or canons for order, government, or worship in any church, or religious ceremonies imposed on the practice of any in divine service,—that is, on any church or any of the members of it. There is not the least rumour of any such things in primitive antiquity, no instance to be given of any man charged with schism for a dissent from such a rule. Any such rule, and any ecclesiastical censure upon it, is apocryphal, not only unto the Scripture, but unto that which I call primitive antiquity. The first attempt of any thing in this kind was in reference unto *the time and day of the observation of Easter.* This was the first instance among Christians of an endeavour to impose the observation of human or church constitutions or groundless traditions on any churches or persons in them. And whereas that which was called a schism between the churches of Italy and Asia, or some of them, did ensue thereon, we have a most illustrious testimony from the best, the wisest, and the holiest of that age (for Irenæus in France and Polycrates in Asia were not alone herein), that the blame of all that division and schism was to be charged on them who attempted to deprive the churches of their liberty, and imposed on them a necessity of the observation of the time and season which they had determined on. After a rebuke was given unto the attempt of the Judaizing Christians to impose the observation of Mosaical ceremonies, from the pretence of their divine institution, on the churches of the Gentiles, by the apostles themselves, this was the original of all endeavours to impose human constitutions, for which there was no such pretence, upon the practice of any. And as it was an original not unmeet for the beginning and foundation of such impositions, being in a matter of no use unto the edification of the church, so it received such a solemn rebuke at its first entrance and attempt, that had it not been for the ignorance, pride, interest, and superstition of some in the following ages, it had perished without imitation. The account hereof is given in Eusebius, lib. v. cap. 21–23; as also of the rule which then prevailed, though afterward shamefully forsaken,—namely, that *an agreement in the faith was the only rule of communion*, which ought to be kept under any diversity in voluntary observations. And the discourse of Socrates on this occasion, lib. v. cap. 21, concerning the non-institution of any days of fastings or feastings, or other rites or ceremonies then in use, with the liberty which is therefore to be left in such things unto all Christians, is the plain truth, whatever some except against it, declared with much judgment and moderation.

This beginning, I say, had the imposition of unscriptural, uninstituted rites, ceremonies, and religious observations, among the churches of Christ, and this solemn rebuke was given unto it. Howbeit the ignorance, superstition, and interest of following ages, with the contempt of all modesty, brake through the boundaries of this holy rebuke, until their own impositions and observations became the substance of all their church-discipline, unto the total subversion of Christian liberty.

Wherefore, to allow church-rulers, or such as pretend so to be, a liberty and power to appoint a rule of communion,—comprising institutions and commands of sundry things to be constantly observed in the whole worship and discipline of the church, not warranted in themselves by divine authority,—and then to charge believers, abiding firm in the doctrines of the faith, with schism, for a non-compliance with such commands and appointments, is that which, neither in the Scripture nor in primitive antiquity, hath either instance, example, precedent, testimony, rumour, or report, to give countenance unto it. The pedigree of this practice cannot be derived one step higher than the fact of Victor, the bishop of Rome, in the excommunication of the churches and Christians of Asia; which was solemnly condemned as an intrenchment on Christian liberty.

3. After these things the notion of schism began to be managed variously, according unto the interest of them who seemed to have the most advantage in the application of it unto those who dissented from them. It were an endless thing to express the rise and declare the progress of these apprehensions; but after many loose and declamatory discourses about it, they are generally issued in two heads. The first is, that *any kind of dissent from the pope and church of Rome is schism*, all the schism that is or can be in the world; the other is, that a causeless separation from a true church is schism, and this only is so. But whereas, in this pretended definition, there is no mention of any of its internal causes nor of its formal reason, but a bare description of it by an outward effect, it serves only for a weapon in every man's hand to perpetuate digladiations about it; for every church esteems itself true, and every one that separates himself esteems himself to have just cause so to do.

In the following times, especially after the rise and prevalency of the Arian heresy, it was ordinary for those of the orthodox persuasion to forsake the communion of those churches wherein Arian bishops did preside, and to gather themselves into separate meetings or conventicles for divine worship; for which they were accused of schism, and in sundry places punished accordingly, yea, some of them unto the loss of their lives. Yet I suppose there are none now who judge them to have been *schismatics*.

The separation of Novatus and Donatus from the communion of the whole catholic visible church, on unwarrantable pretences, is that which makes the loudest noise about schism in antiquity. That there was in what was done by them and their followers the general nature and moral evil of causeless schisms and divisions, will be easily granted. But it is that wherein we are not concerned, be the especial nature of schism what it will. Nor did they make use of any one reason whereon the merit of the present cause doth depend. The Novatians[1] (the modester sect of the two) pretended only a defect in discipline, in granting church-communion unto such as they would not have received, though they were apparently in the wrong, proceeding on mistaken principles. The Donatists pleaded only

---

[1] Novatianus, or, as the name is given by Eusebius, Novatus, protested against the choice of Cornelius as bishop of Rome in A.D. 251, on the ground of his leniency towards those who, during the Decian persecution, had lapsed into a denial of Christ. He withdrew from communion with Cornelius, and procured his own ordination as bishop of Rome. At first, the Novatians, as those who joined him were called, held simply that

some personal crimes in some few bishops, fallen into in the time of persecution, which they could never prove, and thereon grew angry with all the world, who would not condemn them and renounce their communion as well as they. These slight pretences they made the occasion and reason of renouncing the communion of the whole visible catholic church, in all its distributions for communion,—that is, all particular churches,—and confined sacraments and salvation absolutely unto their own parties. And hereon they fell into many other woful miscarriages, especially those of the latter sort. It is indifferent by what name any are pleased to call this evil and folly. A sin and evil it was, schism, or what you please to term it, and justly condemned by all Christians not joining with them in those days. And that which was the animating principle of the tumult of the Donatists[1] was a supposition that the continuation of the true church-state depended on the successive ordination of bishops; which having, as they thought (unduly enough), failed in one or two instances, it became the destruction of a church-state, not only in the churches where such mistakes had happened, as they surmised, but unto all the churches in the world that would hold communion with them.

But in these things we have no concernment. Other notions of schism besides those insisted on we acknowledge not, nor is any other advanced with the least probability of truth. Nor are we to be moved with outcries about schism, wherein, without regard to truth or charity, men contend for their own interest. Of those notions of it which have been received by men sober and learned we decline a trial by none, that only excepted, that the refusal of obedience unto the pope and church of Rome is all that is schism in the world; which, indeed, is none at all.

That which is now so fiercely pleaded by some concerning different observations of external modes, rites, customs, some more, or none at all, to make men schismatics, is at once to judge all the primitive churches to be schismatical. Their differences, varieties, and diversities among them about these things cannot be enumerated; and so, without any disadvantage unto the faith or breach of love, they continued to be until all church order and power was swallowed up in

---

no man who had shrunk from avowing Christ under the terrors of martyrdom should be admitted again into the church, whatever evidence he gave that he had repented of the sin. Latterly, they adopted a principle of African origin, that all who had lapsed into gross sins after baptism should be subjected to perpetual exclusion from the communion of the church.—ED.

[1] When the archdeacon Cæcilian was elected bishop at Carthage in A.D. 311, a party rose up against him, who chose Majorinus, and latterly, in A.D. 313, Donatus, as their bishops, in preference to Cæcilian; against whom they objected that his ordination as bishop was not valid, as Felix, bishop of Aptunga, who had ordained, had been a traditor; in other words, during the time of persecution, had delivered up the Scriptures to the heathen magistrates to be burned.—ED.

the papal tyranny, ten thousand times more pernicious than ten thousand such disputes.

For a close unto this whole discourse concerning the original, nature, and state of gospel churches, I shall use that liberty which love of the truth puts into my possession. Churches mentioned in the Scripture, ordained and appointed by the authority of Jesus Christ, were nothing but a certain number of men and women converted to God by the preaching of the gospel, with their baptized seed, associating themselves, in obedience unto Christ's commands and by the direction of his apostles, for the common profession of the same faith, the observance and performance of all divine institutions of religious worship, unto the glory of God, their own edification, and the conversion of others. These believers, thus associated in societies, knowing the command and appointment of Jesus Christ by his apostles for that end, did choose from among themselves such as were to be their rulers, in the name and authority of Christ, according to the law and order of his institutions,—who in the Scripture are called, on various considerations, elders, bishops, pastors, and the like names of dignity, authority, and office,—who were to administer all the solemn ordinances of the church among them. Unto this office they were solemnly appointed, ordained, or set apart by the apostles themselves, with fasting, prayer, and imposition of hands, or by other ordinary officers after their decease.

This was the way and method of the call and setting apart of all *ordinary officers* in the church, both under the Old Testament and in the New. It is founded in the light of nature. In the first institution of ordinary church-rulers under the law, the people looked out and chose fit persons, whom Moses set apart to the office, Deut. i. 13–15. And in the call of deacons, the apostles use the same words, or words of the same importance, unto the church as Moses did to the people, Acts vi. 3, asserting the continuation of the same way and order in their call. And whereas he who was first to be called to office under the New Testament after the ascension of Christ fell under a double consideration,—namely, of an officer in general, and of an apostle, which office was extraordinary,—there was a threefold act in his call: The people chose two, one of which was to be an officer, Acts i. 23; God's immediate determination of one, as he was to be an apostle, verse 24, 25; and the obedient consent of the people in compliance with that determination, verse 26.

The foundation of these churches was generally in *a small number* of believers. But that church-state was not complete until they were supplied with all ordinary officers, as bishops and deacons. The former were of several sorts, as shall be proved hereafter; and of them there were many in every church, whose number was increased as the members of the church were multiplied. So God appointed in the church of the Jews, that every ten families should have a peculiar ruler of their own choice, Deut. i. 13–15. For there is no mention in the New Testament of any one single bishop or elder in any church, of any sort whatever, either absolutely or by way of preeminence. But as the elders of each church were many, at least more than one, so there was a parity among them, and an equality in order, power, and rule. Nor can any instance be given unto the contrary.

Of these churches one only was originally planted. in *one city*, town, or village. This way was taken from conveniency for edification, and not from any positive institution; and it may be otherwise where conveniency and opportunity do require it. The number in these churches multiplying daily, there was a necessity for the multiplication of bishops or elders among them. Hereon the advantage of some one person in priority of conversion, or of ordination, in age, gifts, and graces, especially in ability for preaching the gospel and administering the holy ordinances of the church, with the necessity of preserving order in the society of the elders themselves, gave him peculiar dignity, pre-eminence, and title. He was soon after *the bishop*, without any disadvantage to the church.

For in those churches, in some of them at least, evangelists continued for a long season, who had the administration of church-affairs in their hands. And some there were who were of note among the apostles, and eminently esteemed by them, who had eminent, yea, apostolical gifts as to preaching of the word and prayer, which was the peculiar work of the apostles. These were the ἄνδρες ἐλλόγιμοι mentioned by Clemens. Of the many other elders who were associated in the rule of the church, it may be not many had gifts for the constant preaching of the word, nor were called thereunto. Hence Justin Martyr seems to assign the constant public administration of sacred ordinances unto one president. And this also promoted the constant presidency of one, in whom the apostolical aid by evangelists might be supplied. These churches, thus fixed and settled in one place (each of them), city, town, or village, were each of them intrusted with all the power and privileges which the Lord Christ hath granted unto or endued his church withal. This power is called the "power of the keys," or of "binding and loosing;" which hath respect only unto the consciences of men as unto things spiritual and eternal, being merely ministerial.

Every one of these churches were bound by the command of Christ to live in peace and unity, through the exercise of peculiar, sincere, and fervent love among all their members; as also to walk in peace and useful communion with all other churches in the world, according as they had opportunity of converse with them. And when on any occasion any division or schism fell out among any of their members in this church-state, it was severely rebuked by the apostles.

All these churches, and all the members of them, were obliged, by virtue of divine institution, to *obey their guides*, to honour and reverence them; and by their voluntary contribution to provide for their *honourable subsistence* and maintenance, according to their ability. Other church-state neither the Scripture nor antiquity unto the end of the second century doth know any thing of; which I shall hereafter more fully manifest. Neither was there any thing known then to be schism or so esteemed, but a division falling out in some one of these churches: which happened for the most part, if not only, by some of their teachers falling into heresy and drawing away disciples after them, Acts xx. 30; or by various opinions about their guides, 1 Cor. i. 12; or the ambition of some in seeking the power and authority of office among them. To seek for any thing among those churches, wherein our present contest about schism is concerned, is altogether in vain. There was then no such subordination of churches, of many unto one, as is now pleaded; no such distinction of officers into those who have a plenary and those who have a partiary power only, in the rule of the church; no church with a single officer over it, comprehending, in a subjection unto its jurisdiction, a multitude of other churches. No invention, no imposition of any orders, forms of prayer, or ceremonies of worship not of divine institution, were once thought of; and when any thing of that nature was first attempted, it caused great troubles amongst them. In a word, the things on the account of a noncompliance wherewithal we are vehemently charged with schism were then neither laid nor hatched, neither thought of nor invented.

To erect new kinds of churches; to introduce into them new orders, new rules, rites and ceremonies; to impose their observation on all churches and all members of them; and to charge their dissent with the guilt of schism, that schism which is prohibited and condemned in the Scripture,—hath much of an assumed authority and severity in it, nothing of countenance from the Scripture or primitive antiquity.

But after that churches began to depart from this original constitution by the ways and means before declared, every alteration produced a new supposition of church unity and peace, whereto every church of a new constitution laid claim. New sorts of schism were also coined and framed; for there was a certain way found out and carried on, in a mystery of iniquity, whereby those meek, holy, humble churches or societies of Christ's institution, who, as such, had nothing to do with the things of the world, in power, authority, dignity, jurisdiction, or wealth, in some instances wherein they got the advantage one of another, became in all these things to equal kingdoms and principalities, yea, one of them to claim a monarchy over the whole world!

During the progression of this apostasy, church-unity and schism declined from their centre, and varied their state according unto the present interest of them that prevailed. Whoever had got possession of the name of the church in a prevailing reputation, though the state of it was never so corrupt, made it bite and devour all that disliked it, and would swear that submission unto them in all things was church-unity, and to dissent from them was schism. Unto that state all the world know that things were come in the church of Rome. Howbeit, what hath been disputed about or contended for, of power, privileges, authority, pre-eminence, jurisdiction, catholicism, ways of worship, rule, and discipline, which the world is filled with such a noise about, and in the dispute whereof so many various hypotheses are advanced that cannot be accommodated unto such Christian congregations as we have described, are but the effects of the prudence or imprudence of men; and what it will prove the event will show.

Things of this nature being once well understood will deliver the world from innumerable fruitless, endless contests, sovereign princes from all disturbance on the account of religion, and private persons from the fatal mistake of intrusting the eternal concernments of their souls unto their relation unto one church and not unto another. I am not so vain as at this time to expect the reduction of Christian religion unto its primitive power, purity, and simplicity; nor do I reflect blame on them who walk conscientiously in such a church state and order as they approve of, or suppose it the best they can attain unto; only I think it lawful for all Christ's disciples at all times to yield obedience unto all his commands, and to abstain from being servants of men in what he hath not enjoined.

AN ANSWER

DR STILLINGFLEET'S BOOK OF THE UNREASONABLENESS OF SEPARATION;

IN DEFENCE OF THE VINDICATION OF NONCONFORMISTS FROM THE GUILT OF SCHISM.

THE preceding discourse was written, for the most part, before the publishing of the treatise of the Rev. Dr Stillingfleet, entitled " The Unreasonableness of Separation;" yet was it not so without a prospect, at least a probable conjecture, that something of the same kind and tendency with the Doctor's book would be published in defence of the cause which he had undertaken. And I was not without hopes that the whole of it might have been both finished and communicated unto public view before any thing farther were attempted against our cause, whereby many mistakes might have been prevented; for as I was willing, yea, very desirous, if it were the will of God, that I might see, before my departure out of this world, the cause of conformity, as things are now stated between us and the church of England, pleaded with judgment, moderation, and learning, with the best of those arguments whereby our principles or practices are opposed, so, considering on what hand that work was now like to fall, I thought, " si Pergama dextra," etc.; and am of the same mind still. But my expectation being frustrate, of representing our whole cause truly stated, for the prevention of mistakes, by the coming out of this book against all sorts of Nonconformists, I thought it convenient to publish this first part of what I had designed, and to annex unto it the ensuing " Defence of the Vindication of Nonconformists from the Charge of Schism:" for although I do know that there is nothing material in the whole book of the " Unreasonableness of Separation" but what is obviated or answered beforehand in the preceding discourse, so as that the principles and demonstrations of them contained therein may easily be applied unto all the reasonings, exceptions, and pleas in and of that book, to render them useless unto the end designed, which is to reinforce a charge of schism against us; yet I think it necessary to show how unsuccessful, from the disadvantage of his cause, the Doctor hath been in his laborious endeavour to stigmatize all protestant dissenters from the church of England with the odious name of *schismatics.* I have, therefore, altered nothing of what I had projected, either as to matter or method, in this first part of the discourse designed on the whole subject of church affairs; for as I have not found either cause or reason from any thing in the Doctor's book to make the least change in what I had written, so my principal design being the instruction and confirmation of them who have no other interest in these things but only to know and perform their own duty, I was not willing to give them the trouble of perpetual diversions from the matter in hand, which all controversial writings are subject unto. Wherefore, having premised some general considerations of things insisted on by the Doctor, of no great influence into the cause in hand, and vindicated one principle, a supposition whereof we rely upon,—namely, the declension of the churches in the ages after the apostles, especially after the end of the second century, from the primitive institution of their state, rule, and order,—in the preface, I shall now proceed to consider and examine distinctly what is opposed unto the defence of our innocency as unto the guilt of schism. But some things must be premised hereunto; as,—

1. I shall not depart from the state of the question as laid down by ourselves on our part, as unto our judgment of parochial churches, and our refraining from communion with them. Great pains are taken to prove the several sorts of dissenters to be departed farther from the church of England than they will themselves allow, and on such principles as are disavowed by them; but no disputations can force our assent unto what we know to be contrary unto our principles and persuasions.

2. We do allow those parochial assemblies which have a settled, unblamable ministry among them to be true churches, so far as they can pretend themselves so to be;—churches whose original form is from occasional cohabitation within precincts limited by the law of the land;—churches without church-power to choose or ordain their officers, to provide for their own continuation, to admit or exclude members, or to reform at any time what is amiss among them;—churches which are in all things under the rule of those who are set over them by virtue of civil constitutions foreign unto them, not submitted willingly unto by them, and such, for the most part, as whose offices and power have not the least countenance given unto them from the Scripture or the practice of the primitive churches; such as are chancellors, commissaries, officials, and the like;—churches in which, for the most part, through a total neglect in evangelical dis-

cipline, there is a great degeneracy from the exercise of brotherly love and the holiness of Christian profession. Whatever can be ascribed unto such churches we willingly allow unto them.

3. We do and shall abide by this principle, that communion in faith and love, with the administration of the same sacraments, is sufficient to preserve all Christians from the guilt of schism, although they cannot communicate together in some rites and rules of worship and order. As we will not admit of any presumed notions of schism, and inferences from them, nor allow that any thing belongs thereunto which is not contrary to gospel love, rules, and precepts, in the observance of Christ's institutions; so we affirm, and shall maintain, that men abiding in the principles of communion mentioned, walking peaceably among themselves; refraining communion with others, peaceably, wherein they dissent from them; ready to join with other churches in the same confession of faith and in the defence of it, and to concur with them in promoting all the real ends of Christian religion; not judging the church-state of others so as to renounce all communion with them, as condemning them to be no churches, continuing in the occasional exercise of all duties of love towards them and their members,—are unduly charged with the guilt of schism, to the disadvantage of the common interest of the protestant religion amongst us.

4. Whereas there are two parts of the charge against us,—the one for refraining from total communion with parochial assemblies, which what it is, and wherein it doth consist, hath been before declared; the other for gathering ourselves into another church-order in particular congregations,—as the reasons and grounds of the things themselves are distinct, so must they have a distinct consideration, and be examined distinctly and apart.

These things being premised, I shall proceed to examine what the reverend Doctor hath farther offered against our former vindication of the Nonconformists from the charge of schism. And I desire the reader to take notice that we delight not in these contentions, that we desire nothing but mutual love and forbearance; but we are compelled, by all rules of Scripture and natural equity, to abide in this defence of ourselves. For whereas we are charged with a crime, and that aggravated as one of the most heinous that men can incur the guilt of in this world, and to justify men in severities against us; being not in the least convinced in our consciences of any accessions thereunto, or of any guilt on the account of it, I suppose the Doctor himself will not think it reasonable that we should altogether neglect the protection of our own innocency.

In the method whereinto he hath cast his discourse, he begins with the reinforcement of his charge against our refraining from total

communion with parochial assemblies. If the reader will be pleased
to take a review of what is said in the preceding discourse unto this
head of our charge, in several chapters, he will easily perceive that
either the reasonings of the Doctor reach not the cause in hand, or
are insufficient to justify his intention; which I must say, though I
am unwilling to repeat it, is by all ways and means to load us with
the guilt and disreputation of schism.

That which I first meet withal directly unto this purpose is part
ii. p. 157. The forbearance of communion with the church of England in its parochial assemblies (that is, in the way and manner
before described) he opposeth with two arguments. The first respects those who allow occasional communion with parochial churches,
but will not comply with them in that which is constant and absolute; for he says, " If the first be lawful, the latter is necessary,
from the commands we have to preserve the peace and unity of the
church.   And the not doing it," he says, " is one of the provoking
sins of the Nonconformists." But whether it be a sin or no is " sub
judice;" that it is provoking unto some is sufficiently evident. I shall
not make this any part of my contest. Those who have so expressed
their charity as to give countenance unto this pretended advantage
will easily free themselves from the force of this inference; for it
must be remembered that this constant, total communion doth not
only include a conscientious observance of all things appointed to be
done by the rules or canons in those assemblies, but a renunciation
also of all other ways and means of edification by joint communion
as unlawful and evil. And it will be hard to prove that, on a concession of the lawfulness of communion in some acts of divine worship, it will be necessary for men to oblige themselves unto total,
constant communion, with a renunciation and condemnation of all
other ways and means of joint edification. It may also be lawful to
do a thing, with some respects and limitations, at some times, which
it may not be lawful to do absolutely and always. It may be necessary, from outward circumstances, to do that sometimes which is lawful in itself, though not necessary from itself ; it can never be necessary to do that which is unlawful. Of the first sort they esteem
occasional communion, and the other of the latter.

Some time is spent in taking off an exception unto this inference
from the practice of our Saviour, who had *occasional communion*
with the Jews in the temple and synagogues; which he proves to
have been constant and perpetual, and not occasional only, and that
he prescribed the same practice unto his disciples. But I think this
labour might have been spared: for there is nothing more clear and
certain than that our Lord Jesus Christ did join with the Jews in the
observance of God's institutions among them on the one hand; and,

on the other, that he never joined with them in the observance of their own traditions and pharisaical impositions, but warned all his disciples to avoid them and refuse them; whose example we desire to follow: for concerning all such observances in the church he pronounced that sentence, " Every plant which my heavenly Father hath not planted shall be rooted up."

But the Doctor proceeds unto a second argument, p. 163, to the same purpose, from, as he calls it, " the particular force of that text," Phil. iii. 16, " Whereto we have already attained, let us walk by the same rule, let us mind the same thing." This is the text which gave the first occasion unto this whole dispute. The Doctor's intention is so indefensible from this place, that I thought, however he might persist in the defence of the cause he had undertaken, he would have forborne from seeking countenance unto it from these words of the apostle. But it is fallen out otherwise; and I am here, in the first place, called unto an account for the exceptions I put in unto his application of these words of the apostle in my "Vindication of the Nonconformists."

I will spare the reader as much as is possible in the repetition of things formerly spoken, and the transcription of his words or my own, without prejudice unto the cause itself.

After a reflection of some *obscurity and intricacy* in my discourse, he repeats my sense of the words according unto his apprehension, under four heads, about which I shall not contend, seeing whether he hath apprehended my mind aright or no, or expressed the whole of what I declared, belongs not unto the merit of the cause in hand. Nor, indeed, do I yet know directly what he judgeth this text doth prove, or what it is that he infers from it; though I know well enough what it is designed to give countenance unto, and what is the application that is made of it. And, therefore, he issues his whole dispute about it in this inquiry, *how far the apostle's rule hath an influence on this case.* But whosoever shall come unto a sedate consideration of this text and context, without prejudice, without preconceived opinions, without interest in parties or causes, will judge it to be a matter of art to apply them unto the present controversy, as unto the imposition of an arbitrary rule of walking in churches on all that are presumed to belong unto them.

But to clear these things, the Doctor proposeth three things to be debated:—" 1. Whether the apostle speaks of different opinions or different practices. 2. Whether the rule he gives be mutual forbearance. 3. How far the apostle's rule hath an influence into this case."

The first two of these belong not at all unto the present argument, and the last is but faintly proposed and pursued, though it be the foundation of his whole fabric. The reader, if he will put himself to so much trouble as to compare my former discourse with what is here offered in answer or opposition unto it, will easily see that nothing is pleaded that may abate the force of what was insisted on; for indeed the discourse of these things consists for the most part in diversions from the argument in hand, whereby an appearance is made of various arguings, and the proof of sundry things which belong not unto the case in hand.

Without any long deductions, artificial insinuations, or diverting reasonings, without wresting the text or context, these things are plain and evident in them:—

1. A *supposition of differences* among believers in and about opinions and practices relating unto religion and the worship of God. So is [it] at present between us and those of the church of England by whom we are opposed.

2. In this state, whilst these differences do continue, there is *one common rule*, according unto which those who so dissent among themselves are to walk in the things wherein they are agreed. Such is *the rule of faith and love;* which we all assent unto and are agreed in.

3. This rule cannot consist in a *precise determination* of the things in difference, with an authoritative prescription of *uniformity* in opinions and practice, because it is directed unto upon a supposition of the continuation of those differences between believers.

4. That during the continuation of these differences, or different apprehensions and practices, whilst on all hands they use the means of coming unto the knowledge of the truth in all things, *they should walk in love, mutually forbearing one another* in those things wherein they differed.

Until it be manifested that these things are not the design of the context, and to contain [not] the sense of the words, they are not only *useless* unto the Doctor's design, but *opposite* unto it, and destructive of it. But nothing is here attempted unto that purpose.

To draw any argument from these words applicable unto his design, it must be proved,—

1. That *besides the rule of faith, love, and worship* given by divine institution, and obligatory unto all the disciples of Christ or all churches, in all times and ages, the apostles gave a rule concerning outward rites, ceremonies, modes of worship, feasts, and fastings, ecclesiastical government, liturgies, and the like, unto which all believers ought to conform, on the penalty of being esteemed schismatics, and dealt withal accordingly; for this only is that wherein we are concerned.

2. That because the apostles made such a rule (which we know not what it is, or what is become of it), *the guides of the church* (and that in such a church-state as the apostles knew nothing of) *have power to frame such a rule* as that described, and to impose the observation of it on all believers, on the penalties before mentioned.

It is manifest that no advantage unto the cause of imposition and uniformity, as it is stated at present, can be taken from these words of the apostle unless these two things be contained in them; but that either of them is so our author doth not say, nor go about to prove, in his large discourse on this place. I might therefore forbear any farther examination of it without the least disadvantage unto our cause; but, that I may not seem to waive the consideration of any thing that is pretended material, I shall inquire into the particulars of it.

He proceeds, therefore, to answer *his own queries;* which he judged conducing unto his purpose. The first of them is, " *Whether the apostle speaks of different principles or of different practices.*" And I find nothing in the discourse ensuing that hath the least respect unto this inquiry, until towards the close of it, where he grants that different apprehensions are intended, such as were accompanied with different practices; but, in order hereunto, he gives us a large account of the scope of the place and the design of the apostle in it. The substance of it is: That the apostle treats concerning Judaical seducers; that the things in difference were the different apprehensions of men about the law, its ceremonies and worship, with the continuation of them, and the different practices that ensued thereon.

Be it so; what is our or his concernment herein? For it is most certain the apostle designed not the imposition of these things on the churches of the Gentiles, nor did urge them unto a uniformity in them, but declared their liberty from any obligation unto them, and advised them to " stand fast in that liberty," whatever others did practise themselves or endeavour to impose on them. What this conduceth unto his purpose I cannot understand.

But on the occasion of that expression, being " otherwise minded," he demands, " What sense can Dr Owen here put upon the being ' otherwise minded?' otherwise than what?—' As many as be perfect be thus minded,' to pursue your main end; but if any be ' otherwise minded.' Did any think they ought not to mind chiefly their great end?—that is incredible. Therefore the apostle must be understood of somewhat about which there were then very different apprehensions; and that, it is certain, there were about the law among Christian churches."

Neither do I well understand these things, or what is intended in them; for,—

1. I never gave occasion to him or any else to think that I would affix such a sense unto the apostle's words, as if they gave an allowance to men to be otherwise minded as unto the pursuit of their main end, of living to God in faith and love, with mutual peace among themselves.

2. What, then, do I intend by being otherwise minded? Even the same that he doth, and nothing else,—namely, different apprehensions about some things in religion, and particularly those concerning the law and its ceremonies; for,—

3. Let it be supposed that the apostle in particular intends dissensions about the law and the observance of its institutions, yet he doth not determine the case from the especial circumstances of that difference, so adjudging the truth unto one of the parties at variance, but from a general rule how the disciples of Christ ought to deport themselves towards one another during the continuation of such differences.   But,—

4. The truth is, the apostle hath dismissed the case proposed in the beginning of the chapter, verses 1–3, etc.; and upon the occasion of his expression of his own voluntary relinquishment and renunciation of all the privileges which the Jews boasted in, and of his attainments thereon in the mysteries of the gospel, verses 12–14, he gives a general direction for the walking of all Christians, in the several degrees and measures of their attainments in the same kind. And herein he supposeth two things: (1.) That there were things,— all the fundamental doctrines of the gospel, concerning the person, offices, and grace of Christ,—which they had all in common attained unto: "Whereto we have already attained,"—we, all of us in general. (2.) That in some things there were different apprehensions and practices amongst them, which hindered not their agreement in what they had attained: " If any one be ' otherwise minded,' "—one than another.   " We that are perfect and those which are weak, 'let us walk by the same rule.' "

Wherefore, although I cannot discern how any thing in this discourse hath the least influence into the case in hand, yet to give a little more light unto the context, and to evidence its unserviceableness unto the Doctor's intention, I shall give a brief account of the Judaical teachers of those days.

The Jews were by this time distributed into three sorts:—

1. Such as, being *obdurate* in their unbelief and rejection of the person of Christ, opposed, persecuted, and blasphemed the gospel in all places.   Thus was it with the generality of the nation.   And the teachers of this sort advanced the excellency, necessity, and usefulness of the law in contradiction unto Christ and the gospel.   These the apostle describes, 1 Thess. ii. 14, 15: "The Jews, who both

killed the Lord Jesus, and their own prophets, and have persecuted us; and they please not God, and are contrary to all men: forbidding us to speak to the Gentiles that they might be saved, to fill up their sins alway: for the wrath is come upon them to the uttermost."

2. Such as *professing faith in Christ Jesus* and obedience unto the gospel, yet were of the mind that the whole law of Moses was not only to be continued and observed among the Jews, but also that it was to be imposed on the Gentiles who were converted unto the faith. They thought the gospel did not erect a new church-state, with a new kind of worship, but only was a peculiar way of proselyting men into Judaism; against which the apostle disputes in his Epistle unto the Hebrews, especially in the seventh and eighth chapters. The teachers of this sort greatly troubled the churches, even after the declaration of the mind of the Holy Ghost in these things by the apostles, Acts xv. Those who continued obstinate in this persuasion became afterward to be Ebionites and Nazarenes, as they were called, wholly forsaking the Christian church of the Gentiles. These were generally of the sect of the Pharisees, and seem to be the least sort of the three; for,—

3. There were others who, acquiescing in the liberty of the Gentiles declared by the apostles, Acts xv., yet judged themselves and all other circumcised Jews obliged unto the observation of the law and its institutions. These legal observances were of two sorts:—

(1.) Such as were confined and limited unto the temple, and unto the land of Canaan; and,—

(2.) Such as might be observed anywhere among the nations.

They acted accordingly. Those who lived at Jerusalem adhered unto the temple worship; the whole church there did so. Their judgment in these things is declared, Acts xxi. 20, 21, "Thou seest, brother, how many thousands of Jews there are which believe; and they are all zealous of the law: and they are informed of thee, that thou teachest all the Jews which are among the Gentiles to forsake Moses, saying that they ought not to circumcise their children, neither to walk after the customs." They were not at all offended with Paul that he did not impose the law on the Gentiles, verse 25, but only that, as they had been informed, he taught the Jews to forsake the law, and to reject all the institutions of it. This they thought unlawful for them. And this they spoke principally with respect unto the temple-service, as appears by the advice given unto Paul on this occasion, verses 23, 24. Those who lived amongst the Gentiles knew that there was no obligation on them unto the sacrifices and especial duties of the temple, but continued only in the observance of such rites and institutions about meats, washings, days, new-moons, sabbaths, and the like, which the Gentiles were freed from.

Hence there were two sorts of churches in those days (if not three) in separation, more or less, from the apostate church of the unbelieving Jews, which yet was not finally taken away:—

1. The church of Jerusalem and those churches of Judea which were of the same mind and communion with them. These continued in the observance of all the law and of the services of the temple, being allowed them by the apostles.

2. Those of the Jews who lived in the *nations*, and observed all the rites of the law which were not confined unto the land of Canaan. And,—

3. The churches of the Gentiles, which observed none of these things, forbearing only their liberty in one or two instances, not to give the others offence. Some differences and disputes happened sometimes about these things and the practice of them; whereon Peter himself fell into a mistake, Gal. ii. 14. And there seems to have been great disputes about them at Rome, Rom. xiv. Yea, it is judged that, according unto their different apprehensions of these things, there were two churches at Rome, one of the Circumcision, the other of the Gentiles, walking in distinct communion each by themselves. However, the different rule of this kind that was between the churches of Jerusalem and Antioch is sufficiently declared, Acts xv.; the one church continued "zealous of the law," chap. xxi. 20, and the other "rejoiced for the consolation" of being delivered from it, chap. xv. 31. Yet was there no schism between these churches, but a constant communion in faith and love. Such differences in opinions and practices were not yet formed into an interest, obliging men to condemn them as schismatics who differ from them; for, not to speak of what orders and rules for decency particular churches may make by common consent among themselves, to make the observation of arbitrary institutions, not prescribed in the Scripture, upon many churches, to be the rule of communion in them and between them, which whosoever observe not are to be esteemed guilty of schism (which Victor, bishop of Rome, first attempted), is contrary to the rules of the Scripture, to the principles of Christian faith, love, and liberty, to the example of the apostles, hath no countenance given unto it in the primitive churches, and will certainly make our differences endless.

I judge that in the beginning of the chapter the apostle intends those of the first sort; and that as well because he calls them "dogs" and the "concision,"—which answers unto the account he gives of them, 1 Thess. ii. 14, 15,—as also because he speaks of them as those who advanced the pretended privileges of Judaism absolutely against Christ, the gospel, and the righteousness of God revealed therein.

Hereon, in opposition unto them, he declares that they had nothing to boast of but what he himself had a right unto as well as they, and which he had voluntarily relinquished and renounced for Christ and the gospel; whereon he testifies what he had attained. If any one do judge that he intends those of the second sort, I will not contend about it, because of the severity of expression which he useth concerning them, Gal. v. 12. But discharging the consideration of them, the direction in this place concerns those of the third sort only, answering unto that which was prescribed and followed by the apostles in all places,—namely, that there should be mutual forbearance, in some difference of practice, between them and the Gentile believers.

His second inquiry, p. 168, is, "Whether the rule which the apostle lays down be only a rule of mutual forbearance." I do not find that I said anywhere that it was only a rule of mutual forbearance, but that the words of the apostle do enjoin a mutual forbearance among those who are differently minded, p. 26. And I must here say (which I desire to do without offence), that there is no need of any farther answer unto that part of the Doctor's discourse, but a transcription of that which he pretends to oppose; for what is spoken unto that end consists in a perpetual diversion from the argument in hand.

I did not before precisely determine what was the rule which the apostle doth intend; I only proved sufficiently that it was not such a rule as is pleaded for by the Doctor. But the meaning of the phrase and expression is plain enough, Τῷ αὐτῷ στοιχεῖν κανόνι. It is directly used once more by the apostle, Gal. vi. 16, "Ὅσοι τῷ κανόνι τούτῳ στοιχήσουσιν—" As many as walk according to this rule." And what rule is that?—namely, what, as unto the substance of it, he lays down in the words foregoing: Verses 14–16, " God forbid that I should glory, save in the cross of our Lord Jesus Christ. For in Christ Jesus neither circumcision availeth any thing, nor uncircumcision, but a new creature. And as many as walk according to this rule;" that is, the rule of faith in Christ alone for justification and sanctification, without trusting unto or resting on any of those things which were in difference among them. The places, in scope, design, and manner of expression, are parallel; for this is plainly that which he pleads for in this context,—namely, that justification and sanctification are to be obtained alone through Christ, and faith in him, by the gospel, without the least aid and assistance from the things that were in difference among them. Wherefore, not farther to contend in so plain a matter, the rule here intended by the apostle is no Book of Canons, but the analogy of faith, or the rule of faith in Christ as declared in the gospel, in opposition unto all other ways and means of justification, sanctification, and salvation; which we ought to walk in a compliance withal, and that with love and forbearance towards them that in things not corruptive or destructive of this rule do differ from us.

But saith our author, "The sense, according to Dr Owen, is this, that those who are agreed in the substantials of religion should go on and do their duty, without regarding lesser differences." Abate that expression of, "Without regarding lesser differences," which is not mine, and supply in the room of it, "Mutually forbearing each other in lesser differences." And be it so that it is my sense; at first view it looks as like the sense of the apostle as any man need desire. But saith the Doctor, "This sense is uncertain; because it sets no bounds to differences, and supposeth the continuance of such differences among them, which he designed to prevent by persuading them so often in this epistle to be of 'one mind.' Besides, the differences then on foot were none of the smaller differences of opinions, but that which they differed about was urged on the one hand as necessary to salvation, and opposed on the other as pernicious and destructive unto it." And again, p. 169, "Let Dr Owen name any other smaller differences of opinions which might be an occasion of the apostle's giving such a rule of mutual forbearance."

I answer briefly,—1. The sense is very *certain;* because it gives the *due bounds* unto the differences supposed,—namely, such as concern not *the substantials of religion.*

2. It doth *suppose the continuance* of these differences, because the apostle doth suppose the same: "If in any thing ye be otherwise minded;" which hinders no kind of endeavours to compose or remove them.

3. The differences intended were not those between them who *imposed the observation of the law on the Gentiles as necessary unto salvation,* and those by whom they were opposed; for the apostle gives no such rule as this in that case.

4. I do expressly assign those *lesser differences,* which the direction here is applicable unto,—namely, those between the blind sort of Jews mentioned before and the Gentile believers; which the apostle states and applies the same rule unto, Rom. xiv. What remains in answer unto this second inquiry doth proceed on mistaken suppositions, and concerns not the case under consideration.

Page 170, he proceeds unto his last inquiry, which, indeed, is alone pertinent unto his purpose,—namely, "How this rule hath an influence on our case."

What *this rule is,* concerning which this inquiry is made, he doth not declare. Either the precise signification of the rule in this place, or the direction given with respect unto that rule, may be intended; that is, the general rule of our walking in our profession of the gospel, or the especial rule given by the apostle with respect thereunto in the case under consideration, may be so intended. If by the rule in the first sense, he understands a rule, canon, or command, establishing a church-state, with rites and modes of worship, with ceremonies, orders, and government, nowhere appointed in the Scripture or of divine revelation, it is openly evident that there was no such rule then, that no such is here intended but that only whereunto the grace of the gospel in mercy and peace is annexed, as Gal. vi. 16; which is not such a rule. If he intend by it a direction, that where there are different apprehensions in matters of less importance, not breaking in on the analogy of faith, accompanied with different practices, so far as they are necessary from those different apprehensions, the major part of those among whom the differences are should compel the minor to forbear their practice according unto their apprehensions, and comply with them in all things, on all sorts of penalties if they refuse so to do,—it will be hard to find such a direction in these words. Yet this must be the rule and this the direction that can give any countenance unto the Doctor's cause. But if by *this rule*, the analogy of faith as before described be intended, and the direction be to walk according to it, with mutual forbearance and love as unto things of lesser moment, then this rule hath little advantageous influence into it.

1. But then saith the Doctor, " So far as men agree they are bound to join together, as to opinion or communion." I grant it (though it be not proved from this place), where such a communion is required of them regularly and in a way of duty. And,—

2. Saith he, " That the best Christians are bound to unite with others, though of lower attainments, and to keep within the same rule." No doubt; howbeit the apostle speaks of no such things in this place, but only that we should all " walk by the same rule," in what we have " already attained." Yea, but, —

3. " This rule takes in all such orders which are lawful and judged necessary to hold the members of a Christian society together." What rule doth this? Who shall appoint the orders intended? Who shall judge of their necessity? Are they of the institution of Christ or his apostles? Are they determined to be necessary in the Scripture, the rule of faith? If so, we are agreed. But if by these " orders" he intends such as men do or may at any time, under pretence of church authority, invent and impose as necessary, making alterations in the original state and rule of the church, as also in its worship and discipline, it will be strange to me if he can find them out either in the rule here mentioned or the direction given with reference unto it, seeing such a practice seems to be plainly condemned in the words themselves. And it is known that this pretended power of rule or canon making for the unity of the church was that which

at length ruined all churches in their state, order, and worship, if such a ruin be acknowledged to have befallen them in the Roman apostasy.

He therefore objects out of my discourse, p. 171, "Let the apostle's rule be produced, with any probability of proof to be his, and we are all ready to subscribe and conform unto it." To which he replies, "This is the apostle's rule, to go as far as they can, and if they can go no farther, to sit down quietly and wait for farther instruction, and not to break the peace of the church upon present dissatisfaction, nor to gather new churches out of others, upon supposition of higher attainments."

Ans. 1. Upon a supposition that those who make and impose these new, *unscriptural orders* are *the church*, and that as the church they have authority so to make and impose them, if this be not the rule of the apostle, I believe some men judge it ought so to have been. But,—

2. The apostle's rule is not that *we should go as far as we can*, as though there were any thing of dispute and difficulty in the matter; but that "whereto we have already attained," we should "walk by the same rule."

3. He doth not intimate any thing about *breaking the peace of the church*, but only what would do so, by an imposition on one another in differences of lesser moment, whilst the general rule of faith and love is attended unto.

4. "To be quiet, and wait for farther instruction," is the direction given unto both parties, whilst the differences did continue between them, and that in opposition unto mutual impositions.

5. A church that is really so, or so esteemed, may break the peace with its own members and others as well as they with it; and where the fault is must be determined by the causes of what is done.

6. For what is added about "gathering of churches," it shall be considered in its proper place. But as unto the application of these things unto the present case, there lies in the bottom of them such an unproved presumption of their being *the church*,—that is, according unto divine institution, for in their being so in any other sense we are not concerned,—of their church power and authority by whom such orders and rules are made, as we can by no means admit of.

I can more warrantably give this as the apostle's rule than that of our author: "What you have attained unto in the knowledge of the doctrine and mysteries of the gospel, walk together in holy communion of faith and love; but take heed that you multiply not new causes of divisions and differences, by inventing and imposing new orders in divine worship or the rule of the church, casting them out who agree with you in all things of divine revelation and institution."

He adds from my words, "If the rule reach our case, it must be such as requires such things to be observed as were never divinely appointed, as national churches, ceremonies, and modes of worship." To which he replies, "And so this rule doth, in order unto peace, require the observation of such things; which, although they be not particularly commanded of God, yet are enjoined by lawful authority, provided that they be not unlawful in themselves, nor repugnant unto the word of God."

Ans. 1. Let the reader, if he please, consult the place whence these words are taken in my discourse, and he will find this evasion obviated.

2. What is intended by "*This rule?*" Is it the rule given by the apostle? Who that reads the words can possibly pretend unto any such conception of their meaning? If he understand a rule of his own, I know not what it may or may not include.

3. I deny, and shall for ever deny, that the rule here intended by the apostle doth give the least countenance unto the invention and imposition of things not divinely instituted, not prescribed, not commanded in the word, on the pretence that those who so invent and impose them judge them lawful, and that they have authority so to do.

He objects again unto himself out of my discourse, that "The apostles never gave any such rules themselves about outward modes of worship, with ceremonies, feasts, fasts, liturgies," etc. Whereunto he replies, "What then?" I say then,—

1. It had been happy for Christians and Christian religion if those who pretended to be their successors had followed their example, and made *no such rules* at all; that they would not have thought themselves wiser than they, or more careful for the good of the church, or better acquainted with the mind of Christ in these things than they were; for that multiplication of rules, laws, canons, about the things mentioned, and others of an alike nature, which the apostles never gave any example of or encouragement unto, which afterward ensued, hath been a principal means of altering the state of the church from its original institution, of corrupting its worship, and administering occasion unto scandal and endless strifes.

2. If the *apostles gave no such rules themselves*, it may be concluded safely that it was because in their judgment *no such rule was to be given.* Other reason hereof cannot be assigned; for if it might have been done according to the mind of Christ, and by virtue of the commission which they had from him, innumerable evils might have been prevented by the doing it. They foresaw what differences would arise in the church, what divisions the darkness and corrupt

lusts of men would cast them into, about such things as these, and probably knew much whereunto the mystery of iniquity tended; yet would they not appoint any arbitrary rules about things not ordained by our Lord Jesus Christ, which might have given some bounds unto the inclinations of men in making and multiplying rules of their own, unto the ruin of the church.

3. Then, I say, we beg the pardon of all who concern themselves herein, that we scruple the complying with such rules in religion and the worship of God as the apostles thought not meet to appoint or ordain.

But he adds, " It is sufficient that they gave this general rule, that all lawful things are to be done for the church's peace."

Ans. What is to be done for the church's peace we shall afterward consider. "To be done," is intended of acts of religion in the worship of God. I say, then, the apostles never gave any such rule as that pretended. The rule they gave was, that all things which Christ hath commanded were to be done and observed; and for the doing of any thing else they gave no rule. Especially, they gave not such a large rule as this, that might serve the turn and interest of the worst of men in imposing on the church whatever they esteemed lawful, as (not by virtue of any rule of the apostles, but in an open rejection of all they gave) it afterward fell out in the church. This is a rule which would do the work to the purpose of all that have the reputation of governors in the church, be it the pope or who it will: for they are themselves the sole judges of what is lawful; the people, as it is pretended, understand nothing of these things. Whatever, therefore, they have a mind to introduce into the worship of God, and to impose on the practice of men therein, is to be done by virtue of this apostolical rule for the " church's peace," provided they judge it "lawful;" and surely no pope was ever yet so stark mad as to impose things in religion which he himself judged unlawful. Besides, things may be lawful in themselves, that is, morally, which yet it is not lawful to introduce into the worship of God, because not expedient nor for edification; yea, things may be lawful to be done sometimes, on some occasions, in the worship of God, which yet it would be unlawful to impose by virtue of a general binding rule for all times and seasons. Instances may be multiplied in each kind. Therefore, I say, the apostles never gave this rule; they opened no such door unto arbitrary imposition; they laid no such yoke on the necks of the disciples, which might prove heavier, and did so, than that of the Jewish ceremonies which they had taken away,—namely, that they were to do and observe all that should by their rulers be imposed on them as lawful in their judgment. This sovereignty over their consciences was reserved by the apostles unto the authority of

Christ alone, and their obedience was required by them only unto his commands. This is that which, I see, some would be at:—To presume themselves to be the church, at least the only rulers and governors of it; to assume to themselves alone the judgment of what is lawful and what is unlawful to be observed in the worship of God; to avow a power to impose what they please on all churches, pretended to be under their command, so that they judge it lawful, be it never so useless or trifling, if it hath no other end but to be an instance of their authority; and then assert that all Christian people must, without farther examination, submit quietly unto this state of things and comply with it, unless they will be esteemed damned schismatics. But it is too late to advance such principles a second time.

He adds from my paper, or as my sense, "The apostles gave rules inconsistent with any determining rule,—namely, of mutual forbearance," Rom. xiv. "But then," saith he, "the meaning must be, that whatever differences happen among Christians, there must be no determination either way. But this is directly contrary to the decree of the apostles at Jerusalem, upon the difference that happened in the Christian churches." But they are not my words which he reports. I said not that "the apostles gave rules inconsistent with any determining rule," but with such a rule, and the imposition of the things contained in it on the practice of men, in things not determined (that is, whilst differences about them do continue), as he contends for. And,—

1. Notwithstanding this rule of forbearance given by the apostle expressly, Rom. xiv., yet as unto the right and truth in the things wherein men are at difference, *every private believer is to determine of them*, so far as he is able, in his own mind; "every man is to be fully persuaded in his own mind" in such things, so far as his own practice is concerned.

2. The church wherein such differences do fall out may *doctrinally determine* of the truth in them, as it is the pillar and ground of truth, supposing them to be of such weight as that the edification of the church is concerned in them; for otherwise there is no need of any such determination, but every one may be left unto his own liberty. There are differences at this day in the church of England in doctrine and practice, some of them, in my judgment, of more importance than those between the same church and us; yet it doth not think it necessary to make any determination of them, no, not doctrinally.

3. If the church wherein such differences fall out be not able in and of itself to make a doctrinal determination of such differences, they may and ought to crave the counsel and advice of other churches

with whom they walk in communion in faith and love. And so it was in the case whereof an account is given us, Acts xv. The determination or decree there made, concerning the necessary observance of the Jewish rites by the Gentiles converted unto the faith, by the apostles, elders, and brethren, under the guidance of the Holy Ghost, as his mind was revealed in the Scripture, gives not the least countenance unto the making and imposing such a rule on all churches and their members as is contended for.

For,—(1.) It was only a *doctrinal determination*, without imposition on the practice of any. (2.) It was a *determination against impositions* directly. And whereas it is said that it was a determination contrary to the judgment of the imposers, which shows that the rule of forbearance, where conscience is alleged both ways, is no standing rule,—I grant that it was contrary to the judgment of the imposers, but imposed nothing on them, nor was their practice concerned in that erroneous judgment. They were not required to do any thing contrary to their own judgment, and the not doing whereof did reflect on their own consciences. Wherefore, the whole rule given by the apostles, and the whole determination made, is, that no impositions be made on the consciences or practice of the disciples of Christ, in things relating to his worship, but what were necessary by virtue of divine institution. They added hereunto, that the Gentiles enjoying this liberty ought to use it without offence, and were at liberty, by virtue of it, to forbear such things as wherein they had, or thought they had, a natural liberty, in case they gave offence by the use of them. And the apostles, who knew the state of things in the minds of the Jews, and all other circumstances, give an instance in the things which at that season were to be so forborne. And whereas this determination was not absolute and obligatory on the whole case unto all churches,—namely, whether the Mosaical law were to be observed among Christians,—but some churches were left unto their own judgment and practice, who esteemed it to be still in force, as the churches of the Jews; and others left unto their own liberty and practice also, who judged it not to oblige them; both sides or parties being bound to continue communion among them in faith and love; there is herein a perpetual establishment of the rule of mutual forbearance in such cases, nothing being condemned but impositions on one another, nothing commended but an abstinence from the use of liberty in the case of scandal or offence. I had therefore reason to say that the false apostles were the only imposers,—that is, of things not necessary by virtue of any divine institution. And if the author insinuate that the true apostles were such imposers also, because of the determination they made of this difference, he will fail in his proof of it. It is true, they imposed on or charged the consciences of men with the observance of all the institutions and commands of Christ, but of other things none at all.

The last thing which he endeavours an answer unto on this occasion lies in these words: "The Jewish Christians were left unto their own liberty, provided they did not impose on others; and the dissenters at this day desire no more than the Gentile church did,— namely, not to be imposed on to observe those things which they are not satisfied it is the mind of Christ should be imposed on them." So is my sense, in the places referred unto, reported. Nor shall I contend about it, so as that the last clause be changed; for my words are not, "They are not satisfied it is the mind of Christ that they should be imposed on them," but, "They were not satisfied it is the mind of Christ they should observe." This respects the things themselves, the other only their imposition. And one reason against the imposition opposed is, that the things themselves imposed are such as the Lord Christ would not have us observe, because not appointed by himself.

But hereunto he answers two things:—

1. "That it was agreed by all the governors of the Christian church that the Jewish Christians should be left unto their own liberty, out of respect unto the law of Moses, and out of regard unto the peace of the Christian church, which otherwise might have been extremely hazarded." But,—

(1.) The *governors* of the Christian church which made the determination insisted on were the apostles themselves.

(2.) There was no such determination made, that *the Jews should be left unto their own liberty in this matter*, but there was only a connivance at their inclination to bear their old yoke for a season; the determination was only on the other hand, that no imposition of it should be made on the Gentiles.

(3.) The determination itself was no act of *church government or power*, but a *doctrinal declaration* of the mind of the Holy Ghost.

(4.) It is well that *church-governors* once judged that impositions in things not necessary were to be forborne, for the sake of the peace of the church; others, I hope, may in due time be of the same mind.

2. He says, "The false apostles imposing on the Gentile Christians had two circumstances in it, which extremely alter their case from that of our dissenters;" for,—

(1.) "They were none of their lawful governors, but went about as seducers, drawing away the disciples of the apostles from them." It seems, then,—

[1.] That those who are lawful governors, or pretend themselves so to be, may impose what they please without control, as they did in the Papacy and the councils of it. But,—

[2.] Their imposition was merely doctrinal, wherein there was no pretence of any act of government or governing power; which made it less grievous than that which the dissenters have suffered under. Were things no otherwise imposed on us, we should bear them more easily.

(2.) Saith he, " They imposed the Jewish rites as necessary to salvation, and not merely as indifferent things." And the truth is, so long as they judged them so to be, they are more to be excused in their doctrinal impositions of them than others are who by an act of government, fortified with I know not how many penalties, do impose things which themselves esteem indifferent, and those on whom they are imposed do judge to be unlawful.

Whereas he adds, " That he hath considered all things that are material in my discourse, which seem to take off the force of the argument drawn from this text," I am not of his mind; nor I believe will any indifferent person be so, who shall compare what I wrote therein with his exceptions against it; though I acknowledge it is no easy thing to discover wherein the force of the pretended argument doth lie. That we must walk according unto the same rule in what we have attained; that wherein we differ we must wait on God for teaching and instruction; that the apostles, elders, and brethren at Jerusalem determined from the Scriptures, or the mind of the Holy Ghost therein, that the Jewish ceremonies should not be imposed on the Gentile churches and believers; and that thereon those churches continued in communion with each other who did and did not observe those ceremonies,—are the only principles which, in truth, the Doctor hath to proceed upon. To infer from these principles and propositions that there is a national church of divine institution (for what is not so hath no church-power properly so called, the nature of its power being determined by the authority of its institution or erection); that this church hath power in its governors and rulers to invent new orders, ceremonies, and rites of worship, new canons for the observation of sundry things in the rule of the church and worship of God, which have no spring nor cause but their own invention and prescription, and is authorized to impose the observation of them on all particular churches and believers who never gave their consent unto their invention or prescription; and hereon to declare them all to be wicked schismatics who yield not full obedience unto them in these things,—it requires a great deal of art and skill in the managers of the argument.

SECTION II.

PART ii., sect. 21, p. 176, our author proceeds to renew his charge of schism, or sinful separation, against those " who though they agree with us," saith he, " in the substantials of religion, yet deny any communion with our church to be lawful." But apprehending that the state of the question here insinuated will not be admitted, and that it would be difficult to find them out who deny any communion with the church of England to be lawful, he adds, that he doth not speak of " any improper acts of communion, which Dr Owen calls communion in faith and love, which they allow to the church of England." But why the acts hereof are called " Improper acts of communion," I know not. Add unto faith and love the administration of the same sacraments, with common advice in things of common concernment, and it is *all the communion* that the true churches of Christ have among themselves in the whole world; yea, this church-communion is such as that,—

1. Where *it is not*, there is no evangelical communion at all. Whatever acts of worship or church-order men may agree in the practice of, if the foundation of that agreement be not laid in a joint communion in faith and love, they are neither accepted with God nor profitable unto the souls of men; for,—

2. These are the things,—namely, faith and love,—which enliven all joint duties of church order and worship, are the life and soul of it; and how they should be only improperly that which they alone make other things to be properly, I cannot understand.

3. Where there is no defect in these things,—namely, in faith and love,—the charge of schism on dissenting in things of lesser moment is altogether unreasonable. It is to be desired that an overweening of our differences make us not overlook the things wherein we are agreed. This is one of the greatest evils that attend this controversy. Men are forced by their interest to lay more weight on a few outward rites and ceremonies, which the world and the church might well have spared, had they not come into the minds of some men none know how, than upon the *most important graces and duties* of the gospel. Hence, communion in faith and love is scarce esteemed worth taking up in the streets, in comparison of uniformity in rites and ceremonies! Let men be as void of, and remote from, true gospel faith and love as is imaginable, yet if they comply quietly with, and have a little zeal for, those outward things, they are to be approved of as very orderly members of the church! And whatever evidences, on the other hand, any can or do give of their communion in faith and love with all that are of that communion, yet if they cannot in

conscience comply in the observance of those outward things mentioned, they are to be judged schismatics and breakers of the church's unity, whereas no part of the church's unity doth, or ever did, consist in them.

In his procedure hereon, our author seems to embrace occasions of contending, seeking for advantages therein in things not belonging unto the merit of the cause; which I thought was beneath him. From my concession, that some at least of our parochial churches are true churches, he asks, " In what sense ? Are they churches rightly constituted, with whom they may join in communion as members ?" I think it is somewhat too late now, after all this dispute about the reasons of refraining from their communion, and his severe charge of schism upon us for our so doing, to make this inquiry. Wherefore he answers himself. "No; but his meaning is, saith he, ' that they are not guilty of any such heinous errors in doctrine, or idolatrous practice in worship, as should utterly deprive them of the being and nature of churches;'"—which I suppose are my words. But then comes in the advantage. " Doth," saith he, " this kindness belong only unto some of our parochial churches ? I had thought that every parochial church was true or false according unto its frame or constitution; which, among us, supposeth the owning the doctrine and worship established in the church of England." I answer briefly, It is true, every church is true or false according unto its original frame and constitution. This frame and constitution of churches, if it proceed from, and depend upon, the institution of Christ, is true and approvable; if it depend only on a national establishment of doctrine and worship, I know not well what to say unto it. But let any of these parochial churches be so constituted as to answer the legal establishment in the land, yet if the generality of their members are openly wicked in their lives, and they have no lawful or sufficient ministry, we cannot acknowledge them for true churches. Some other things of the like nature do ensue, but I shall not insist on them.

He gathers up, in the next place, the titles of the causes alleged for our refraining communion with those parochial assemblies; which he calls our separation from them. And hereon he inquires, " Whether these reasons be a ground for a separation from a church wherein it is confessed there are no heinous errors in doctrine, or idolatrous practice in worship;" that is, as he before cited my words, " as should utterly deprive them of the being and nature of churches." And if they be not, then saith he, " Such a separation may be a formal schism, because they set up other churches of their own."

The rule before laid down, " That all things lawful are to be done for the church's peace," taking in the supposition on which it proceeds, is as sufficient to establish church tyranny as any principle made use of by the church of Rome, notwithstanding its plausible appearance. And that here insinuated of the unlawfulness of separation from any church in the world (for that which hath pernicious errors in doctrine and idolatry in worship, destroying its being, is no church at all), is as good security unto churches in an obstinate refusal of reformation, when the souls of the people are ruined amongst them for the want of it, as they need desire. And I confess I suspect such principles as are evidently suited unto the security of the corrupt interests of any sort of men.

I say, therefore,—1. That though a church, or that which pretends itself on any grounds so to be, do not profess any heinous error in doctrine, nor be guilty of idolatrous practice in worship, destroying its nature and being, yet there may be sufficient reasons to refrain from its communion in church order and worship, and to join in or with other churches for edification; that is, that where such a church is not capable of reformation, or is obstinate in a resolution not to reform itself, under the utmost necessity thereof, it is lawful for all or any of its members to reform themselves, according to the mind of Christ and commands of the gospel.

2. That where men are no otherwise members of any church but by an inevitable necessity and outward penal laws, preventing their own choice and any act of obedience unto Christ in their joining with such churches, the case is different from theirs whose relation unto any church is founded in their own voluntary choice, as submitting themselves unto the laws, institution, and rule of Christ in that church; which we shall make use of afterward.

3. The Doctor might have done well to have stated the true nature of schism, and the formal reason of it, before he had charged a formal schism on a supposition of some outward acts only.

4. What is our judgment concerning parochial assemblies, how far we separate from them or refrain communion with them, what are the reasons whereon we do so, hath been now fully declared, and thereunto we must appeal on all occasions; for we cannot acquiesce in what is unduly imposed on us, either as unto principles or practice.

"To show," as he saith, "the insufficiency of our cause of separation, he will take this way,—namely, to show the great absurdities that follow on the allowance of them;" and adds, "These five especially I shall insist upon:—1. That it weakens the cause of Reformation; 2. That it hinders all union between the protestant churches; 3. That it justifies the ancient schisms, which have been always condemned by the Christian church; 4. That it makes separation endless; 5. That it is contrary to the obligation that lies on all Christians to preserve the peace and unity of the church."

Now, as I shall consider what he offers on these several heads, and his application of it unto the case in hand, so I shall confirm the reasons already given of our separation (if it must be so called) from parochial assemblies, with these five considerations:—1. That they strengthen the cause of Reformation; 2. That they open a way to union between all protestant churches; 3. That they give the just grounds of condemning the ancient schisms that ever any Christian church did justly condemn; 4. That they give due bounds unto separation; 5. That they absolutely comply with all the commands of the Scripture for the preservation of the peace and unity of the church.

I shall begin with the consideration of the absurdities charged by him on our principles and practice.

The FIRST of them is, "That it weakens the cause of the Reformation." This he proves by long quotations out of some French divines. We are not to expect that they should speak unto our cause, or make any determination in it, seeing to the principal of them it was unknown. "But they say that which is contrary unto our principles." So they may do, and yet this not weaken the cause of the Reformation; for it is known that they say somewhat also that is contrary to the principles of our episcopal brethren, for which one of them is sufficiently reviled, but yet the cause of Reformation is not weakened thereby.

The first testimony produced is that of Calvin. A large discourse he hath, Institut., lib. iv. cap. 1, against causeless separations from a true church;—and by whom are they not condemned? No determination of the case in hand can be thence derived; nor are the grounds of our refraining communion with parochial assemblies the same with those which he condemns as insufficient for a total separation; nor is the separation he opposed in those days, which was absolute and total, with a condemnation of the churches from which it was made, of the same nature with that wherewith we are charged, at least not with what we own and allow. He gives the notes of a true church to be,—the pure preaching of the word, and the administration of the sacraments according unto Christ's institution. Where these are he allows a true church to be, not only without diocesan episcopacy, but in a form and under a rule opposite unto it and inconsistent with it. And if he did at all speak to our case, as he doth not, nor unto any of the grounds of it, why should we be pressed with his authority on the one hand more than others from whom he differed also on the other? Besides, there is a great deal more belongs unto the pure preaching of the word and the administration of the sacraments according unto Christ's institution than some seem to apprehend. They may, they ought to be so explained, as that, from the consideration of them, we may justify our whole cause. Both these may be wanting in a church which is not guilty of such heinous errors in doctrine or idolatry in worship as should overthrow its being; and their want may be a just cause of refraining communion from a church which yet we are not obliged to condemn as none at all.

Calvin expresseth his judgment, N. 12: " I would not give countenance unto errors, no, not to the least, so as to cherish them by flattery or connivance. But though I say that, the church is not to be forsaken for trifling differences, wherein the doctrine (of the gospel) is retained safe and sound, wherein the integrity of godliness doth abide, and the use of the sacraments appointed of the Lord is preserved;"—and we say the same.

And this very Calvin, who doth so severely condemn separation from a true church as by him stated, did himself quietly and peaceably withdraw and depart from the church of Geneva, when they refused to admit that discipline which he esteemed to be according to the mind of Christ. It is certain, therefore, that, by the separation which he condemns, he doth not intend the peaceable relinquishment of the communion of any church, as unto a constant participation of all ordinances in it, for want of due means of edification, much less that which hath so many other causes concurring therewith.

For the other learned men whom he quotes unto the same purpose, I see not any thing that gives the least countenance unto his assertion that our principles weaken the cause of the Reformation. It is true, they plead other causes of separation from the church of Rome than those insisted on by us with respect unto the church of England; and, indeed, they had been otherwise much to blame, having so many things as they had to plead of greater importance. Did we say that the reasons which we plead are all that can be pleaded to justify the separation of the Reformed churches from the church of Rome, it would weaken the cause of Reformation; for we should then deny that idolatry and fundamental errors in faith were any cause or ground of that separation. However, we know that the imposition of them on the faith and practice of all Christians is more pleaded in justification of a separation from them than the things themselves. But allowing those greater reasons to be pleaded against the Roman communion, as we do, it doth not in the least follow that our reasons for refraining communion with parochial assemblies do weaken the cause of the Reformation.

However, let me not be misinterpreted as unto that expression of " destroying our faith,"—which the communion required with the church of England, as unto all the important articles of it, doth not do,—and I can subscribe unto the words of Daillè, as quoted by our author out of his Apology: " If," saith he, " the church of Rome hath not required any thing of us which destroys our faith, offends our consciences, and overthrows the service which we believe due to God,—if the differences have been small, and such as we might safely have yielded unto,—then he will grant their separation was rash and unjust, and they guilty of the schism."

He closeth his transcription of the words of sundry learned men who have justified the separation of the Reformed churches from the church of Rome, wherein we are not in the least concerned, with an inquiry, " What triumph would the church of Rome make over us, had we no other reasons to justify our separation from them but only those which (as is pretended) we plead in our cause?" I say, whereas we do plead, confirm, and justify all the reasons and causes pleaded for the separation of the Reformed churches from them, not opposing, not weakening any of them by any principle or practice of ours, but farther press the force of the same reasonings and causes in all instances whereunto they will extend, I see neither what cause the Papists have of triumph nor any thing that weakens the cause of the Reformation. He adds farther, " How should we be hissed and laughed at, all over the Christian world, if we had nothing to allege for our separation from the Roman church but such things as these!" I answer, that as the case stands, if we did allege no other reasons but those which we insist on for our refraining communion with our own parochial assemblies, we should deserve to be derided for relinquishing the plea of those other important reasons which the heresies, and idolatries, and tyranny of that church do render just and equal: but if we had no other causes of separation from the church of Rome but what we have for our separation from our parochial assemblies at home, as weak as our allegations are pretended to be, we should not be afraid to defend them against all the Papists in the world; and let the world act like itself in hissing.

Whereas, therefore, the cause of Reformation is not in any thing weakened by our principles, no argument, no reason solidly pleaded to justify the separation from the church of Rome being deserted by us, neither testimony, proof, nor evidence being produced to evince that it is weakened by us, I shall, in the second place, as was before proposed, prove that the whole cause of the Protestants' separation from the church of Rome is strengthened and confirmed by us:—

There were some general principles on which the Protestants proceeded in their separation from the church of Rome, and which they constantly pleaded in justification thereof.

1. The first was, that *the Scripture, the word of God, is a perfect rule of faith and religious worship;* so as that nothing ought to be

admitted which is repugnant unto it in its general rule or especial prohibitions, nothing imposed that is not prescribed therein, but that every one is at liberty to refuse and reject any thing of that kind. This they all contended for, and confirmed their assertion by the express testimonies of the writers of the primitive churches. To prove this to have been their principle in their separation from the church of Rome were to light, as they say, a candle in the sun. It were easy to fill up a volume with testimonies of it. After a while this principle began to be weakened, when the interest of men made them except from this rule things of outward order, with some rites and ceremonies, the ordaining whereof they pleaded to be left unto churches as they saw good. Hereby this principle, I say, was greatly weakened; for no certain bounds could ever be assigned unto those things that are exempted from the regulation of the Scripture. And the same plea might be managed for many of the popish orders and ceremonies that were rejected, as forcibly as for them that were retained. And whereas all the Reformed churches agreed to abide by this principle in matters of faith, there fell out an admirable harmony in their confessions thereof. But leaving the necessity of attending unto this rule in the matter of order, ceremonies, rites, and modes of worship, with the state of churches in their rule and polity, those differences and divisions ensued amongst them which continue unto this day. But this persuasion in some places made a farther progress,—namely, that it was lawful to impose on the consciences and practices of men such things in religious worship, provided that they concerned outward order, rites, rule, and ceremonies, as are nowhere prescribed in the Scripture, and that on severe penalties, ecclesiastical and civil. This almost utterly destroyed the great fundamental principle of the Reformation, whereon the first reformers justified their separation from the church of Rome; for whereas it is supposed the right of them who are to be the imposers to determine what doth belong unto the heads mentioned, they might under that pretence impose what they pleased, and refuse those whom they imposed them on the protection of the aforesaid principle,—namely, that nothing ought to be so imposed that is not prescribed in the Scripture. This hath proved the rise of all endless differences and schisms amongst us; nor will they be healed until all Christians are restored unto their liberty of being obliged, in the things of God, only unto the authority of the Scripture.

The words of Mr Chillingworth unto this purpose are emphatical; which I shall therefore transcribe, though that be a thing which I am very averse from:—

"Require," saith he, "of Christians only to believe Christ, and to call no man master but him only; let those leave claiming of infallibility who have no right unto it, and let them that in their words disclaim it, disclaim it likewise in their actions; in a word, take away tyranny, which is the devil's instrument to support errors, and super-stitions, and impieties in the several parts of the world, which could not otherwise long withstand the power of truth,—I say, take away tyranny, and restore Christians to their just and full liberty of cap-tivating their understandings to the Scripture only, that universal liberty, thus moderated, may quickly reduce Christendom to truth and unity," part i., chap. 4, sect. 16.

This fundamental principle of the first Reformation we do not only firmly adhere unto, rejecting all those opinions and practices whereby its force is weakened and impaired, but also do willingly suffer the things that do befall us in giving our testimony thereunto. Neither will there ever be peace among the churches of Christ in this world until it be admitted in its whole latitude, especially in that part thereof wherein it excludes all impositions of things not prescribed in the Scripture; for there are but few persons who are capable of the subtlety of those reasonings, which are applied to weaken this principle in its whole extent. All men can easily see this, that *the sufficiency of the Scripture* in general, as unto all the ends of reli-gion, is the only foundation they have to rest and build upon. They do see, actually, that where men go about to prescribe things to be observed in divine worship not appointed in the Scripture, no two churches have agreed therein, but endless contentions have en-sued; that no man can give an instance in particular of any thing that is necessary unto the rule of the church, or the observance of the commands of Christ in the worship of God, that is not contained in the Scripture; and hereon are ready to resolve to call no man master but Christ, and to admit of nothing in religion but what is warranted by his word.

2. The second principle of the Reformation, whereon the reform-ers justified their separation from the church of Rome, was this: " That Christian people were not tied up unto blind obedience unto church-guides, but were not only at liberty, but also obliged to judge for themselves as unto all things that they were to believe and prac-tise in religion and the worship of God." They knew that the whole fabric of the Papacy did stand on this basis or dunghill, that the mystery of iniquity was cemented by this device,—namely, that *the people were ignorant*, and to be kept in ignorance, being obliged in all things unto an implicit obedience unto their pretended guides. And that they might not be capable of nor fit for any other condi-tion, they took from them the only means of their instruction unto their duty, and the knowledge of it; that is, the use of the holy Scripture. But the first reformers did not only vindicate their

right unto the use of the Scripture itself, but insisted on it as a principle of the Reformation (and without which they could never have carried on their work), that they were in all concernments of religion to judge for themselves. And multitudes of them quickly manifested how meet and worthy they were to have this right restored unto them, in laying down their lives for the truth,—suffering as martyrs under the power of their bishops.

This principle of the Reformation, in like manner, is in no small degree weakened by many, and so the cause of it. Dr Stillingfleet himself, pp. 127, 128, denies unto the people all liberty or ability to choose their own pastors, to judge what is meet for their own edification, what is heresy or a pernicious error, and what is not, or any thing of the like nature. This is almost the same with that of the Pharisees concerning them who admired and followed the doctrine of our Saviour, 'Ο ὄχλος οὗτος ὁ μὴ γινώσκων τὸν νόμον, John vii. 49; —"This rabble which knoweth not the law." Yet was it this people whom the apostles directed to choose out from among themselves persons meet for an ecclesiastical office, Acts vi.; the same people who joined with the apostles and elders in the consideration of the grand case concerning the continuation of the legal ceremonies, and were associated with them in the determination of it, Acts xv.; the same to whom all the apostolical epistles, excepting some to particular persons, were written, and unto whom such directions were given, and duties enjoined on them, as suppose not only a liberty and ability to judge for themselves in all matters of faith and obedience, but also an especial interest in the order and discipline of the church; those who were to say unto Archippus, their bishop, "Take heed to the ministry which thou hast received in the Lord, that thou fulfil it," Col. iv. 17; unto whom of all sorts it is commanded that they should examine and try antichrists, spirits, and false teachers,—that is, all sorts of heretics, and heresies, and errors, 1 John ii., iii., etc.; that people who, even in following ages, adhered unto the faith and the orthodox profession of it when almost all their bishops were become Arian heretics, and kept their private conventicles in opposition unto them, at Constantinople, Antioch, Alexandria, and other places, and who were so many of them burnt here in England by their own bishops, on the judgment they made of errors and heresies. And if the present people with whom the Doctor is acquainted be altogether unmeet for the discharge of any of these duties, it is the fault of somebody else besides their own.

This principle of the Reformation, in vindication of the rights, liberties, and privileges of the Christian people, to judge and choose for themselves in matters of religion, to join freely in those church-duties which are required of them, without which the work of it had never

been carried on, we do abide by and maintain. Yea, we meet with
no opposition more fierce than upon the account of our asserting the
liberties and rights of the people in reference unto church order and
worship. But I shall not be afraid to say, that as the Reformation
was begun and carried on on this principle, so when this people
shall, through an apprehension of their ignorance, weakness, and unmeetness to discern and judge in matters of religion for themselves
and their own duty, be kept and debarred from it; or when, through
their own sloth, negligence, and viciousness, they shall be really
incapable to manage their own interest in church-affairs, as being fit
only to be governed, if not as brute creatures, yet as mute persons,
and that these things are improved by the ambition of the clergy,
engrossing all things in the church unto themselves, as they did in
former ages,—if the old popedom do not return, a new one will be
erected as bad as the other.

3. Another principle of the Reformation is, "That there was not
any catholic, visible, organical, governing church, traduced by succession into that of Rome, whence all church power and order was to
be derived." I will not say that this principle was absolutely received by all the first reformers here in England, yet it was by the
generality of them in the other parts of the world; for as they constantly denied that there was any catholic church but that invisible of
elect believers, allowing the external denomination of "the church"
unto the diffused community of the baptized world, so believing and
professing that the pope is antichrist, that Rome is mystical Babylon, the seat of the apostatized church of the Gentiles, devoted to destruction, they could acknowledge no such church-state in the Roman
church, nor the derivation of any power and order from it. So far
as there is a declension from this principle, so far the cause of the
Reformation is weakened, and the principal reason of separation
from the Roman church is rejected; as shall be farther manifested if
occasion require it.

This principle we do firmly adhere unto; and not only so, but it
is known that our fixed judgment concerning the divine institution,
nature, and order of evangelical churches, is such as is utterly exclusive of the Roman church, as a body organized in and under the
pope and his hierarchy, from any pretence unto church state, order,
or power. And it may be hence judged who do most weaken the
cause of Reformation, we or some of them at least by whom we are
opposed.

A SECOND absurdity that he chargeth on our way is, "That it
would make union among the protestant churches impossible, supposing them to remain as they are," sect. xxiv., p. 186. To make
good this charge he insists on two things:—

" 1. That the Lutheran churches have the same and more ceremonies and unscriptural impositions than our church hath.

" 2. That notwithstanding these things, yet many learned protestant divines have pleaded for union and communion with them; which upon our principles and suppositions they could not have done." But whether they plead for union and communion with them, by admitting into their churches, and submitting unto those ceremonies and unscriptural impositions,—which is alone unto the Doctor's purpose,—or whether they judge their members obliged to communicate in local communion with them under those impositions, he doth not declare. But whereas neither we nor our cause are in the least concerned in what the Doctor here insists upon, yet because the charge is no less than that our principles give disturbance unto the peace and union of all protestant churches, I shall briefly manifest that they are not only conducive thereunto, but such as without which that peace and union will never be attained:—

1. It is known unto all, that from the first beginning of the Reformation there were *differences* among the churches which departed from the communion of the church of Rome. And as this was looked on as the greatest impediment unto the progress of the Reformation, so it was not morally possible that in a work of that nature, begun and carried on by persons of all sorts, in many nations, of divers tongues and languages, none of them being divinely inspired, it should otherwise fall out. God, also, in his holy, wise providence, suffered it so to be, for causes known then to himself; but since, sundry of them have been made manifest in the event. For whereas there was an agreement in all fundamental articles of faith among them, and all necessary means of salvation, a farther agreement, considering our sloth, negligence, and proneness of men to abuse security and power, might have produced as evil effects as the differences have done; for those which have been on the one hand, and those which have been on the other, have been, and would have been, from the corrupt affections of the minds of men and their secular interests.

2. These differences were principally in or about *some doctrines of faith*, whereon some fiery spirits among them took occasion, mutually and unjustly enough, to charge each other with heresy; especially was this done among the Lutherans, whose writings are stuffed with that charge, and miserable attempts to make it good. There were also other differences among them, with respect unto church order, rites, ceremonies, and modes of worship. The church of England, as unto the government of the church and sundry other things, took a way by itself; which at present we do not consider.

3. Considering the *agreement* in all fundamental articles of faith

between these churches thus at difference, and of what great use
their union might be unto the protestant religion, both as unto its
spiritual and political interest in this world, the effecting of such a
union among them hath been attempted by many.   Private persons,
princes, colloquies or synods of some of the parties at variance, have
sedulously engaged herein.   I wish they had never missed it, in
stating the nature of that union, which in this case is alone desirable
and alone attainable, nor in the causes of that disadvantageous difference that was between them; for hence it is come to pass, that although some verbal compositions have sometimes by some been consented unto, yet all things continue practically amongst them as
they were from the beginning.   And there are yet persons who are
managing proposals for such a union, with great projection in point
of method for the compassing of it and stating of the principles of
agreement; some whereof I have by me.   But the present state of
things in Europe, with the minds of potentates not concerned in
these things, leave little encouragement for any such attempt, or
expectation of any success.

4. After the trial and experience of a *hundred and fifty years*, it
is altogether in vain to be expected that any farther reconciliation or
union should be effected between these protestant churches by either
party's relinquishment of the doctrines they have so long taught,
professed, and contended for, or of their practice in divine worship,
which they have so long been accustomed unto.   We may as well
expect that a river should run backwards as expect any such things.

In this state of things, I say, the principles we proceed upon are
the most useful unto the procuring of peace and union among these
churches, in the state wherein they are, and without which it will
never be effected.   I shall, therefore, give an account of those of
them which are of this nature and tendency:—

1. And the first is, *the absolute necessity of a general reformation in life and manners of all sorts of persons belonging unto these
churches.*   It is sufficiently known what a woful condition the profession even of the protestant religion is fallen unto.   How little
evidence is there left of the power of evangelical grace working in
the hearts of men!   What little diligence in the duties of holiness
and righteousness!   What a deluge of all sorts of vices hath overwhelmed the nations!   And what indications there are of the displeasure of God against us on the account of these things!   Who
doth not almost tremble at them?   Calvin, unto whom I was newly
sent by our reverend author, in answer to them who pleaded for a
separation from a true church because of the wickedness of many of
its members, or any of them, adds unto it: " It is a most just offence,
and unto which there is too much occasion given in this miserable

age. Nor is it lawful to excuse our cursed sloth, which the Lord will
not let go unpunished, as he begins already to chastise us with grievous stripes. Woe, therefore, unto us, who by our dissolute licenti-
ousness in flagitious sins do cause that the weak consciences of men
should be wounded for us!" And if it were so then, the matter is
not much mended in the age wherein we live. The truth is, sin and
impiety are come to that height and impudence, sensuality and oppression are so diffused among all sorts of persons, conformity unto
the fashion of the world become so universal, and the evidences of
God's displeasure, with the beginnings and entrances of his judgments, are so displayed, as that if the reformation pleaded for be
not speedily endeavoured and vigorously pursued, it will be too late
to talk of differences and union; destruction will swallow up all.
Until this be agreed on, until it be attempted and effected in some
good measure, all endeavours for farther union, whatever their appearing success should be (as probably it will be very small), will be
of no use unto the honour of religion, the glory of Christ, nor good
of the souls of men. In the meantime, individual persons will do
well to take care of themselves.

2. That all these *differing churches*, and whilst these differences
do continue, be taught to prefer their *general interest*, in opposition
unto the kingdom of Satan and Antichrist in the world, before the
lesser things wherein they differ, and those occasional animosities
that will ensue upon them. It hath been observed in many places
that 'the nearer some men or churches come together in their profession, the more distant they are in their affections; as the Lutherans
in many places do more hate the Calvinists than the Papists. I hope
it is not so among us. This makes it evident that the want of necessary peace and union among churches doth not proceed from the
things themselves wherein they differ, but from the corrupt lusts and
interests of the persons that differ. This evil can no otherwise be
cured but by such a reformation as shall, in some measure, reduce
primitive simplicity, integrity, and love, such as were among the
churches of the converted Jews and Gentiles, when they walked according unto the same rule in what they had attained, forbearing
one another in love as unto the things wherein they differed. Until
this also be effected, all endeavours for farther union, whilst these
differences continue (as they are like to do, unless the whole frame
of things in Europe should be changed by some great revolution),
will be fruitless and useless.

Were this conscientiously insisted on, out of a pure love unto Jesus
Christ, with zeal for his glory, it would not only be of more use than
innumerable wrangling disputes about the points in difference, but
more than the exactest methods in contriving formularies of con-

sent, or colloquies, or synodical conferences of the parties at variance, with all their solemnities, orders, limitations, precautions, concessions, and orations. Let men say what they will, it must be the revival, flourishing, and exercise of evangelical light, faith, and love that shall heal the differences and breaches that are among the churches of Christ; nor shall any thing else be honoured with any great influence into that work.

3. That all *communion of churches*, as such, consists in the communion of faith and love, in the administration of the same sacraments, and common advice in things of common concernment. All these may be observed when, for sundry reasons, the members of them cannot have local, presential communion in some ordinances with each church distinctly. If this truth were well established and consented unto, men might be easily convinced that there is nothing wanting unto that evangelical union among churches which the gospel requires, but only their own humble, holy, peaceable, Christian walking in their several places and stations. But where men put their own interests and possession of present advantages, clothed under the pretence of things necessary thereunto, into *conditions of communion*, or divest it of that latitude wherein Christ hath left it, by new limitations of their own, it will never be attained on the true evangelical principles that it must proceed upon; for however any may be displeased with it, I must assert and maintain that there is nothing required by our Lord Jesus Christ unto this end of the communion of churches, nor to any other end of church order or worship whatever, but that only in whose observance and performance there is an actual exercise of evangelical grace in obedience unto him.

4. That all private members of these several churches which agree in the communion before mentioned be left unto their own *liberty* and consciences to communicate in any of these churches, either occasionally or in a fixed way and manner. Neither orders nor compulsory decrees will be useful in this matter, in comparison of their own declared liberty. And so it was among the primitive churches.

5. Where men are invincibly hindered from *total communion* with any church, by impositions which they cannot comply withal without sin; or, by continuing in it, are deprived of the due means of their edification, the churches whereunto they did belong refusing all reformation; it is lawful for them, in obedience unto the law of Christ, to reform themselves, and to make use of the means appointed by him for their edification, abiding constantly in the communion of all true churches before described. I confess this is that which we cannot digest,—namely, an imagination that the Lord Jesus Christ hath

obliged his disciples, those that believe in him, to abide always in such societies as wherein not only things are imposed on their obedience and observance which he hath not commanded, but they are also forced to live in the neglect of expressed duties which he requireth of them, and the want of that means of their own edification which, without the restraint at present upon them, they might enjoy according unto his mind and will. Believers were not made for churches, nor for the advantage of them that rule in them; but churches were made for believers and their edification, nor are of any use farther than they tend thereunto.

These are the premises whereon we proceed in all that we do; and they are so far from being obstructive of the peace and union of the protestant churches, as that without them they will never be promoted nor attained. And I do beg of this worthy person that he would not despise these things, but know assuredly that nothing would be so effectual to procure the union he desireth as a universal reformation of all sorts of persons, according unto the rule and law of Christ; which, it may be, no man hath greater ability and opportunity in conjunction for than himself: for woe be unto us, if, whilst we contend about outward peace in smaller things, we neglect to make peace with God, and so expose ourselves and the whole nation unto his desolating judgments, which seem already to be impendent over us!

The THIRD absurdity which he chargeth on our practice is, "That it will justify the ancient schisms, which have been always condemned in the Christian church;" and in the management of this charge he proceedeth, if I mistake not, with more than ordinary vehemency and severity, though it be a matter wherein we are least of all concerned.

To make effectual this charge, he first affirms in general, "That, setting aside a few things, they pleaded the same reasons for their separation as I do for ours;" which how great a mistake it is shall be manifested immediately. Secondly, He gives instances in several schisms that were so condemned by the Christian church, and whose practice is justified by us.

In answer hereunto, I shall first premise some things in general, showing the insufficiency of this argument to prove against us the charge of schism, and then consider the instances produced by him. I say,—

1. In times of *decay*, the declining times of churches or states, it cannot be but that some will be uneasy in their minds, although they know not how to remedy what is amiss, nor, it may be, fix on the particulars which are the right and true causes of the state which they find troublesome unto them; and whilst it is so with them, it is not

to be admired at that some persons do fall into irregular attempts for the redressing of what is amiss. The church, where the instances insisted on happened, was falling into a mysterious decay from its original institution, order, and rule; which afterward increased more and more continually. But all being equally involved in the same declension, the remedies which they proposed who were uneasy, either in themselves or in the manner of their application, were worse than the disease; which yet lying uncured and continually increasing, proved in the issue the ruin of them all. But here lay the original of the differences and schisms which fell out in the third, fourth, and fifth centuries, that having all in some measure departed from the original institution, rule, and order of evangelical churches in sundry things, and cast themselves into new forms and orders, their differences and quarrels related all unto them, and could have had no such occasion had they kept themselves unto their primitive constitution. Wherefore, those schisms which were said to be made by them that continued sound in the faith, as those of the Audians and Meletians, as by some is pretended, and Johannites[1] at Constantinople, with sundry others, seeing they deserted not any order of divine institution, but another which the churches were insensibly fallen into, no judgment can be made, upon a mere separation, whether of the parties at difference were to blame. I am sure enough that sometimes neither of them could be excused. Whether the causes, reasons, ends, designs, and ways of the management of those differences that were between them, on which schisms in their present order did ensue, were just, regular, according to the mind of Christ, proceeding from faith and love, is that whose determination must fix aright the guilt of the divisions that were among them. And whereas we judge most of those who so separated from the church of old, as is here alleged, to have failed in these things, and therein to have contracted guilt unto themselves, as occasioning unwarrantable divisions and missing wholly the only way of cure for what was really blameworthy in others; yet, whereas we allow nothing to be schism properly but what is contrary to Christian love, and destructive of some institution of Christ, we are not much concerned who was in the right or wrong in those contests which fell out among the orthodox themselves, but only as they were carried on unto a total renunciation of all communion whatever but only that which was enclosed unto their own party.

2. To evidence that we give the *least countenance* unto the ancient schisms, or do contract the guilt with the authors of them, the thing aimed at, there are three things incumbent on him to prove:—

(1.) That our *parochial churches*, from whom we do refrain actual

[1] An account of these schisms is given by Dr Owen afterwards. See page 413.—Ed.

presential communion in all ordinances where it is required by law, which cannot be many and but one at one time, do succeed into the room of that church in a separation from which those schisms did consist; for we pass no judgment on any other church but what concerns ourselves as unto present duty, though that in a nation may be extended unto many or all of the same sort. But these schisms consisted in a professed separation from the whole catholic church,—that is, all Christians in the world who joined not with them in their opinions and practices,—and from the whole church-state then passant and allowed. But our author knows full well that there are others, who, long before our parochial churches, do lay claim unto the absolute enclosure of this church-state unto themselves, and thereon condemn both him and us, and all the Protestants in the world, of the same schism that those of old were guilty of; especially they make a continual clamour about the Novatians and Donatists. I know that he is able to dispossess the church of Rome from that usurpation of the state and rights of the ancient catholic church from whence those separations were made; and it hath been sufficiently done by others. But so soon as we have cast that out of possession, to bring in our parochial assemblies into the room of it, and to press the guilt of separation from them with the same reasons and arguments as we were all of us but newly pressed withal by the Romanists,—namely, that hereby we give countenance unto them, yea, do the same things with them who made schisms in separating from the catholic church of old,—is somewhat severe and unequal.

Wherefore, unless the church from which they separated, which was the whole catholic church in the world not agreeing and acting with them, and those parochial assemblies from whose communion we refrain, are the same and of the same consideration, nothing can be argued from those ancient schisms against us, nor is any countenance given by us unto them; for if it be asked of us, whether it be free or lawful for believers to join in society and full communion with other churches besides those that are of our way and especial communion, we freely answer that we no way doubt of it, nor do judge them for their so doing.

(2.) It must be proved, unto the end proposed, that the *occasions and reasons* of their separation of old were the same, or of the same nature only, with those which we plead for our refraining communion from parochial assemblies. Now, though the Doctor here makes a flourish with some expressions about zeal, discipline, purity of the church, edification (which he will not find in any of their pretences), yet in truth there is not one thing alleged wherein there is a coincidence between the occasions and reasons pleaded by them and ours.

It is known that the principal thing in general which we insist upon is, *the unwarrantable imposition of unscriptural terms and conditions of communion upon us.* Was there any such thing pleaded by them that made the schisms of old? Indeed, they were all of them imposers, and separated from the church because they would not submit unto their impositions. Some bishops, or some that would have been bishops but could not, entertaining some new conceit of their own, which they would have imposed on all others, being not submitted unto therein, were the causes of all those schisms which were justly esteemed criminal. So was it with the Novatians and Donatists in an especial manner. Even the great Tertullian (though no bishop) left the communion of the church on this ground; for because they would not admit of the strict observance of some austere severities, in fasting, abstinence from sundry meats, and watching, with the like, which he esteemed necessary, though no way warranted by Scripture rule or example, he utterly renounced their communion, and countenanced himself by adhering unto the dotages of Montanus. It is true, some of them contended for a severity of discipline in the church; but they did it not upon any pretence of the neglect of it in them unto whom the administration of it was committed, but for the want of establishing a false principle, rule, or erroneous doctrine which they advanced,—namely, that the most sincere penitents were never more to be admitted into ecclesiastical communion: whereby they did not establish but overthrow one of the principal ends of church discipline. They did not, therefore, press for the power or the use of the keys, as is pretended, but advanced a false doctrine, in prejudice both unto the power and use of them. They pretended, indeed, unto the purity of the church; not that there were none impure, wicked, and hypocritical among them, but that none might be admitted who had once fallen, though really made pure by sincere repentance. This was their zeal for purity: If a man were overtaken, if they could catch him in such a fault as, by the rules of the passant discipline, he was to be cast out of the church, there they had him safe for ever. No evidence of the most sincere repentance could prevail for a re-admission into the church. And because other churches would admit them, they renounced all communion with them, as no churches of Christ. Are these our principles? are these our practices? do we give any countenance unto them by any thing we say or do? I somewhat wonder that the Doctor, from some general expressions, and casting their pretences under new appearances, should seem to think that there is the least coincidence between what they insisted on and what we plead in our own defence He may see now more fully what are the reasons of our practice, and I hope thereon will be of another mind;

not as unto our cause in general, which I am far enough from the expectation of, but as unto this invidious charge of giving countenance unto the schisms condemned of old in the church. And we shall see immediately what were the occasions of those schisms; which we are as remote from giving countenance unto as unto the principles and reasons which they pleaded in their own justification.

(3.) It ought, also, to be proved that the separation which is charged on us is of the same nature with that charged on them of old; for otherwise we cannot be said to give any countenance unto what they did: for it is known they so separated from all other churches in the world as to confine the church of Christ unto their own party, to condemn all others, and to deny salvation unto all that abode in their communion; which the Donatists did with the greatest fierceness. This was that which, if any thing, did truly and properly constitute them schismatics; as it doth those also who deny at this day church-state and salvation unto such churches as have not diocesan bishops. Now, there is no principle in the world that we do more abhor. We grant a church-state unto all, however it may be defective or corrupted, and a possibility of salvation unto all their members, which are not gathered in pernicious errors, overthrowing the foundation, nor idolatrous in their worship, and who have a lawful ministry, with sufficient means for their edification, though low in its measures and degrees. We judge none but with respect unto our own duty, as unto the impositions attempted to be laid on us, and the acts of communion required of us, which we cannot avoid; nor can any man else, let him pretend what he will to the contrary, avoid the making of a judgment for himself in these things, unless he be brutish. These things are sufficient to evidence that there is not the least countenance given unto the ancient schisms by any principles of ours; yet I shall add some farther considerations, on the instances he gives unto the same purpose.

The first is that of the Novatians, whose pretences were the discipline and purity of the churches; wherein he says, " There was a concurrence of Dr Owen's pleas; zeal for reformation of discipline, the greater edification of the people, and the asserting of their right in choosing such a pastor as was likely to promote their edification." I am sorry that interest and party should sway with learned men to seek advantages unto their cause so unduly. The story, in short, is this:—Novatus, or Novatianus rather, being disappointed in his ambitious design to have been chosen bishop of the church of Rome, Cornelius being chosen by much the major part of the church, betook himself to indirect means to weaken and invalidate the election of Cornelius; and this he did by raising a new principle of false doctrine, whereunto he as falsely accommodated the matter of fact. The error he broached and promoted was, that "there was no place for repentance" (such as whereon they should be admitted into the church) "unto them who had fallen into sin after baptism;" nor, as some add, "any salvation to be obtained by them who had fallen in the time of persecution." This the ancient church looked on as a pestilent heresy; and as such was it condemned in a considerable council at Rome with Cornelius, Euseb., lib. vi. cap. 43; where also is reported the decree which they made in the case, wherein they call his opinion "cruel" or inhuman, and "contrary to brotherly love." As such it is strenuously confuted by Cyprian, Epist. li., ad Antonianum. But because the church would not submit unto this novel, false opinion of his, contrary to the Scripture and the discipline of the church, he and all his followers separated from all the churches in the world, and rebaptized all that were baptized in the orthodox churches, they denying unto them the means of salvation, Cyprian ad Jubaianum, Epist. lxxi., Euseb., lib. vii. cap. 8. That which was most probably false also in matter of fact when this foolish opinion,— which Dionysius of Alexandria, in his epistle to Dionysius of Rome, calls " a most profane doctrine, reflecting unmerciful cruelty on our most gracious Lord Jesus Christ," Euseb. lib. vii. cap. 8,—was invented, to be subservient unto it, was, that many of those by whom Cornelius was chosen bishop were such as had denied the faith under the persecution of Decius the emperor. This also was false in matter of fact; for although that church continued in the ancient faith and practice of receiving penitents after their fall, yet there were no such number of them as to influence the election of Cornelius. So Cyprian testifieth : " Factus est Cornelius episcopus, de Dei et Christi ejus judicio, de clericorum pœne omnium testimonio, de plebis suffragio," etc., Epist. li. On that false opinion and this frivolous pretence they continued their schism. Hence, afterward, when Constantine the emperor spake with Acesius the bishop of the Novatians at Constantinople, finding him sound in the faith of the Trinity, which was impugned by Arius, he asked him why then he did not communicate with the church; whereon he began to tell him a story of what had happened in the time of Decius the emperor, pleading nothing else for himself; the emperor replying only, " O Acesius, set up a ladder, and climb alone by thyself into heaven," left him, Socrat., lib. i. cap. 7.

This error endeavoured to be imposed on all churches, this false pretence in matter of fact, with the following pride in the condemnation of all other churches, denying unto them the lawful use of the sacraments, and rebaptizing them who were baptized in them, do, if we may believe the Doctor herein, contain all my pleas for the for-

bearance of communion with parochial assemblies, and have countenance given unto them by our principles and practices!

Of the Meletians, whom he reckons up in the next place, no certain
account can be given.   Epiphanius reports Meletius himself to have
been a good, honest, orthodox bishop, and in the difference between
him and Peter, bishop of Alexandria, to have been more for truth, as
the other was more for love and charity; and according unto him, it
was Peter, and not Meletius, that began the schism, Hæres. lxviii.,
N. 2, 3. But others give quite another account of him.   Socrates affirms that in time of persecution he had sacrificed to idols; and was
for that reason deposed from his episcopacy by Peter of Alexandria, lib.
iii. cap. 6.   Hence he was enraged against him, and filled all Thebais
and Egypt with tumults against him, and the church of Alexandria,
with intolerable arrogance, because he was convicted of sundry wickednesses by Peter, Theod. Hist., lib. i. cap. 8; and his followers
quickly complied with the Arians for their advantage.   The error he
proceeded on, according to Epiphanius, was the same with that of
Novatus; which how it could be if he himself had fallen in persecution and sacrificed, as Socrates relates, I cannot understand.   This
schism of bishop Meletius also it is thought meet to be judged that
we should give countenance unto!

All things are in like manner uncertain concerning Audius and
his followers, whom he mentions in the next place.   The man is represented by Epiphanius to have been a good man, of a holy life,
sound in the faith, full of zeal and love to the truth; but finding
many things amiss in the church, among the clergy and people, he
freely reproved them for covetousness, luxury, and disorders in ecclesiastical affairs.   Hereon he stirred up the hatred of many against
himself, as Chrysostom did for the same cause afterward at Constantinople.   Hereupon he was vexed, persecuted, and greatly abused;
all which he bare patiently, and continued in the discharge of his
duty; as it fell out also with Chrysostom.   Nevertheless, he abode
firmly and tenaciously in the communion of the church, but was at
length cast out, as far as it appears by him, for the honest discharge
of his duty; whereon he gathered a great party unto himself.   But
Theodoret and others affirm him to have been the author of the
impious heresy of the Anthropomorphitæ, his principal followers
being those monks of Egypt who afterward made such tumults
in defence of that foolish imagination; and that this was the cause
why he was cast out of the church, and set up a party of the same
opinion with him, lib. iv. cap. 10.   Yea, he also ascribes unto him
some foolish opinions of the Manichees.   What is our concernment
in these things I cannot imagine.

Eustathius, the bishop of Sebaste in Armenia, and his followers,

are also instanced in as *orthodox schismatics;* and as such were condemned in a council at Gangræ in Paphlagonia. But, indeed, before that council, Eustathius had been condemned by his own father,
Eulanius, and other bishops, at Cæsarea in Cappadocia; and he
was so for sundry foolish opinions and evil practices, whereby he deserved to be so dealt withal. It doth not unto me appear certainly
whether he fell into those opinions before his rejection at Cæsarea,
where he was principally if not only charged with his indecent and
fantastical habit and garments. Wherefore, at the council of Gangræ he was not admitted to make any apology for himself, nor could
be heard, because he had innovated many things after his deposition
at Cæsarea; such as forbidding of marriage, shaving of women, denying the lawfulness of priests keeping their wives who were married
before their ordination, getting away servants from their masters,
and the like, Socrat. Hist., lib. ii. cap. 3. These were his pretences
of sanctity and purity, as the Doctor acknowledgeth; and I appeal
unto his ingenuity and candour whether any countenance be given
unto such opinions and practices thereon by any thing we say or do.

This instance, and some others of an alike nature, the Doctor
affirms that he produced in his sermon, but that "they were gently
passed over by myself and Mr. B." I confess I took no notice of
them, because I was satisfied that the cause under consideration was
no way concerned in them. And the Doctor might to as good purpose have instanced in forty other schisms, made for the most part
by the ambition of bishops, in the churches of Alexandria, Antioch,
Constantinople, Rome, and sundry other places; yea, in that made
by Epiphanius himself at Constantinople, upon as weighty a cause
as that of those who contended about and strove for and against the
driving of sheep over the bridge, when there were none present.

The story of the Luciferians is not worth repeating. In short, Lucifer, the bishop of Caralli in Sardinia, being angry that Paulinus,
whom he had ordained bishop at Antioch, was not received, fell into
great dissension with Eusebius, bishop of Vercelli in Italy, who had
been his companion in banishment, because he approved not what
he had done at Antioch. And continuing to contend for his own
bishop, it occasioned a great division among the people, whereon he
went home to his own place, leaving behind him a few followers,
who wrangled for a time about the ordination of bishops by Arians,
by whose means Lucifer had been banished, and so after a while disappeared.

I had almost missed the instance of the Donatists, but the story
of them is so well known that it will not bear the repetition; for
although there be no mention of them in Socrates or Sozomen, or
the History of Theodoret, yet all things that concerned them are

so fully declared in the writings of Austin and Optatus against them, as there needs no other account of them. And this instance of an heretical schism is that which the Papists vehemently urge against the church of England itself and all other Protestants. Here their weapon is borrowed for a little while to give a wound unto our cause, but in vain; yet I know full well that it is easier for some men, on their principles, to flourish with this weapon against us than to defend themselves against it in the hands of the Papists. In brief, these Donatists were upon the matter of the same opinion with the Novatians; and as these grounded their dissension on the receiving those into the church who had fallen and sacrificed under Decius, so did those on a pretence of severity against those who had been traditors under Maximinus. Upon this pretence, improved by many false allegations, Donatus, and those that followed him, rejected Cæcilianus, who was lawfully chosen and ordained bishop of Carthage, setting up one Majorinus in opposition unto him. Not succeeding herein on this foolish unproved pretence, that Cæcilianus had been ordained by a traditor, they rejected the communion of all the churches in the world, confined the whole church of Christ unto their own party, denied salvation unto any other, rebaptized all that came unto them from other churches, and, together with a great number of bishops that joined with them, fell into most extravagant exorbitances.

Upon the consideration of these schisms the Doctor concludes, "That, on these grounds, there hath scarce been any considerable schism in the Christian church but may be justified upon Dr Owen's reasons for separation from our church." Concerning which I must take the liberty to say, that I do not remember that ever I read, in any learned author, an inference made or conclusion asserted that had so little countenance given unto it by the premises whence it is inferred, as there is unto this by the instances before insisted on, whence it is pretended to be educed.

All that is of argument in this story is this: That there were of old some bishops, with one or two who would have been bishops and could not, who, to exalt and countenance themselves against those who were preferred to bishoprics before them and above them, invented and maintained false doctrinal principles, the confession whereof they would have imposed on other churches; and because they were not admitted, they separated at once from all other churches in the world but their own, condemning them as no churches, as not having the sacraments or means of salvation; for which they were condemned as schismatics: therefore, those who own not subjection to diocesan bishops by virtue of any institution or command of Christ, who refrain communion from parochial assemblies, because they cannot, without sin to themselves, comply with all things imposed on them in the worship of God and ecclesiastical rule, without judging their state, or the salvation of their members, are, in like manner as they, guilty of schism.

But we have fixed grounds whereon to try, examine, judge, and condemn all schisms that are justly so called,—all such as those before mentioned. If separations arise and proceed from principles of false doctrine and errors, like those of the Novatians and Donatists; if they are occasioned by ambition and desire of pre-eminence, like those that fell out among the bishops of those days, when their parishes and claims were not regulated by the civil power as now they are; if they do so from a desire to impose principles and practices not warranted in the Scripture on others, as it was with Tertullian; if for slight reasons they rend and destroy that church state and order which themselves approve of, as it was with all the ancient schismatics who were bishops, or would fain have been; if those that make them or follow in them deny salvation unto all that join not with them, and condemn all other churches as being without God's covenant and the sacraments, as did the Donatists and those do who deny these things unto all churches who have not diocesan bishops; if there be not a sufficient justifiable cause pleaded for it, that those who make such a separation cannot abide in the communion which they forsake without wounding their own consciences, and do give evidences of their abiding in the exercise of love towards all the true disciples of Christ,—we are satisfied that we have a rule infallibly directing us to make a judgment concerning it.

Our author adds, [in the FOURTH place,] sect. xxvi. p. 197, "Another argument against this course of separation is, that these grounds will make separation endless; which is to suppose all the exhortations of the Scripture to peace and unity among Christians useless." But why so? Is there nothing in the authority of Christ and the sense of the account which is to be given unto him, nothing in the rule of the word, nothing in the work of the ministry and exercise of gospel discipline, to keep professed disciples of Christ unto their duty, and within the bounds of order divinely prescribed unto them, unless they are fettered and staked down with human laws and constitutions? Herein I confess I differ, and shall do so whilst I am in this world, from our reverend author and others. To say, as he doth (upon a supposition of the taking away of human impositions, laws, and canons), that "there are no bounds set unto separation but what the fancies of men will dictate unto them," is dishonourable unto the gospel, and somewhat more. To suppose that the authority of Christ, the rule of the word, and the work of the ministry, are not sufficient to prescribe bounds unto separation, efficaciously affecting the consciences of believers, or that any other bounds can be assigned as obligatory unto their consciences, is what cannot be admitted. The Lord Christ hath commanded love and union among his disciples; he hath ordained order and communion in his churches; he hath given unto them and limited their power; he hath prescribed rules whereby they and all their members ought to walk; he hath forbidden all schisms and divisions; he hath appointed and limited all necessary separations, and hath truly given all the bounds unto it that the consciences of men are or can be affected withal. But then it is said, " If this be all, separation will be endless." If such a separation be intended as is an unlawful schism, I say, it may be it will; even as persecution and other evils, sins and wickednesses, will be, notwithstanding his severe prohibition of them. What he hath done is the only means to preserve his own disciples from all sinful separation, and is sufficient thereunto. Herein lieth the original mistake in this matter,— we have lost the apprehension that the authority of Christ, in the rule of his word and works of his Spirit, is every way sufficient for the guiding, governing, and preserving of his disciples, in the church-order by him prescribed, and the observance of the duties by him commanded. It hath been greatly lost in the world for many ages; and, therefore, instead of faithful ministerial endeavours to enforce a sense of it on the consciences of all Christians, they have been let loose from it, through a confidence in other devices to keep them unto their duty and order. And if these devices, be they ecclesiastical canons or civil penalties, be not enforced on them all, the world is made to believe that they are left unto the dictates of their own fancies and imaginations; as if they had no concern in Christ or his authority in this matter. But, for my part, I shall never desire nor endeavour to keep any from schism or separation, but by the ways and means of Christ's appointment, and by a sense of his authority on their own consciences.

The remainder of his discourse on this head consists in a lepid dramatical oration, framed and feigned for one of his opposers, wherein he makes him undertake the patronage of schism before Cyprian and Austin. The learned person intended is very well able to defend and vindicate himself; which I suppose also he will do. In the meantime, I cannot but say two things:—

1. That the *imposition* on him of extenuating the guilt of any real schism is that which none of his words do give the least countenance unto.

2. That the Doctor's attempt, in his feigned oration, to accommodate his principles or ours unto the case of the Donatists, for their justification (the weakness whereof is evident to every one who knows any thing of the case of the Donatists), is such an instance

of the power of interest, a design to maintain a cause causelessly
undertaken, by all manner of artifices and pretences, prevailing
in the minds of men otherwise wise and sober, as is to be lamented.

We come at length, in the FIFTH place, sect. xxviii., p. 209, unto that
which is indeed of more importance duly to be considered than all
that went before; for, as our author observes, it is that " wherein the
consciences of men are concerned." This argument, therefore, he
takes from the obligation which lies upon all Christians to preserve
the peace and unity of the church. For the confirmation of this
argument, and the application of it unto the case of them who refrain
from total communion with our parochial assemblies,—which alone is
the case in hand,—he lays down sundry suppositions, which I shall
consider in their order, although they may be all granted without any
disadvantage unto our cause. But they will be so the better when
they are rightly stated:—His first supposition is, " That Christians
are under the strictest obligations to preserve the peace and unity of
the church." This being the foundation of all that follows, it must
be rightly stated; and to that end three things may be inquired
into:—1 What is *that church* whose peace and unity we are obliged
to preserve; for there are those who lay the firmest claim unto the
name, power, and privileges of the church, with whom we are obliged
to have neither peace nor unity in the worship of God. 2. What is
that peace and unity which we are so obliged to preserve. 3. By
what means they are to be preserved.

1 (1.) We are obliged to " follow peace with all men," to " seek
peace and pursue it," and " if it be possible, to live peaceably with
all men."

(2.) There is a peculiar obligation upon us to seek the peace and
prosperity of the *whole visible church of Christ* on earth, and therein,
as we have opportunity, to do good unto the whole household of
faith. And, considering what differences, what divisions, what exasperations there are among professors of the name of Christ all the
world over, to abide steadfast in seeking the good of them all, and
doing good unto them as we have opportunity, is as evident an indication of gospel love as any thing else whatever can be.

(3.) As unto *particular churches*, there is an especial obligation
upon us to preserve their peace and unity, from our own voluntary
consent to walk in them, in obedience unto the commands of Christ.
Where this is not, we are left unto the general obligation of seeking
the peace of all men, and of the whole professing church in an especial manner, but have no other peculiar obligation thereunto: for
being cast into churches of this or that form, merely by human constitution and laws, or by inveterate traditions, lays no new obligation

upon any to seek their peace and unity; but whilst they abide in them, they are left unto the influence of other general commands, which are to be applied unto their present circumstances. For into what state or condition soever Christians are cast, they are obliged to live peaceably whilst they abide in it.

2. It may be inquired, what is that peace and unity of the church that we are bound to preserve. There may be an agreement, with some kind of peace and unity, in evil. They are highly pretended unto in the church of Rome; but they are so in idolatry, superstition, and heresy. There may be peace and unity in any false and heretical church,—the unity of Simeon and Levi, brethren in evil. But the peace and unity which we are obliged to observe in particular churches is the consent and agreement of the church in general, and all the members of it, walking under the conduct of this guide in a due observation of all the institutions and commands of Christ, performing towards the whole and each other the mutual duties required by him, from a principle of faith and love. This, and this alone, is that unity and peace which we are peculiarly obliged to preserve in particular churches; what is more than this relates unto the general commands of love, unity, and peace, before mentioned.

3. Wherefore this states the means whereby we are to preserve this peace and unity: for we are not to endeavour it,—(1.) By a *neglect* or omission of the observance of any of the commands of Christ; nor, (2.) By *doing or practising* any thing in divine worship which he hath not appointed; nor, (3.) By *partaking* in other men's sins, through a neglect of our own duty; nor, (4.) By *foregoing* the means of our own edification, which he commands us to make use of;—for these things have no tendency to the preservation of that peace. And his third supposition is, "That nothing can discharge a Christian from the obligation to communion with his fellow-members, but what is allowed by Christ or his apostles as a sufficient reason of it." It is fully agreed unto, where a man is a member of any church of divine institution by his own consent and virtual consideration, nothing can discharge him from communion with that church but what is allowed by Christ as a sufficient reason for it.

But a little farther inquiry may be made into these things. It was before asserted that all things lawful were to be done for the preservation of the peace of the church. Here it is pleaded that there are many obligations on us to preserve its peace and unity. I desire to know unto whom these rules are obligatory,—who they are that ought to yield obedience unto them. If it be said that these rules are not prescribed unto the rulers and guides of the church, but unto them only who are under their conduct, I desire a proof of it, for at the first view it is very absurd; for as the preservation of the peace and unity of the church is properly incumbent on them who are the rulers of it, and it is continually pleaded by them that so it doth, so all the rules given for that end do or should, principally and in the first place, affect them and their consciences. And these are the rules of their duty herein which are laid down by the Doctor. I desire therefore to know, that since there are such obligations on us to preserve the peace and unity of the church, that for that end we must do what we lawfully may, whether the same rule doth not oblige us to forbear the doing of what we may lawfully forbear, with respect unto the same end. Nay, this obligation of forbearing what we may do, and yet may forbear to do without sin, for the peace and unity of the church,—especially when any would be offended with our doing that which we may lawfully forbear to do,—is exemplified in the Scripture, confirmed by commands and instances, is more highly rational, and less exposed unto danger in practice, than the other of doing what we can.

Now, things that are not necessary in themselves, nor necessary to be observed by a just scandal and offence in case of their omission, are things that may be lawfully forborne. Suppose, now, the rules insisted on to be given principally and in the first place unto the rulers of the church, I desire to know whether they are not obliged by them, for the preservation of the peace and unity of the church, to forbear the imposition of such things on the practice of the whole church in the worship of God as, being no way necessary in themselves, nor such whose omission or the omission of whose imposition, can give scandal or offence unto any. If they are obliged by them so to do, it will be evident where the blame of the division amongst us must lie. To say they are not obliged hereunto by virtue of these rules, is to say that although the preservation of the peace and unity of the church be incumbent on them in a particular manner, —and the chief of them can assign no other end of the office they lay claim unto but only its expediency, or, as is pretended, its necessity unto the preservation of the peace and unity of the church,—yet they are not, by virtue of any divine rules, obliged thereunto. But it seems to me somewhat unequal, that in this contest about the preservation of the peace of the church, we should be bound by rules to do all that we can, whatever it be, and those who differ from us be left absolutely at their liberty, so as not to be obliged to forbear what they may lawfully so do. But to proceed.

Upon these suppositions, and in the confirmation of them, the Doctor produceth a passage out of Irenæus, whose impartial consideration he chargeth on us with great solemnity, "As we love our own souls." Now, although that passage in that great and holy person be not new unto me, having not only read it many a time in his book, but frequently met with it urged by Papists against all Protestants, yet, upon the Doctor's intimation, I have given it again the consideration required.   The words as they lie in the author are to this purpose:—

" We shall also judge them who make schisms, being vain, ' qui sunt immanes,' or ' inanes,' not having the love of God, rather considering their own profit than the unity of the church,—who, for small or any causes, rend and divide the glorious body of Christ, and as much as in them lies destroy it, speaking peace but designing war, straining at a gnat and swallowing a camel; for there can be no rebuke of things by them, to equal the mischief of schism," lib. iv. cap. 62.

I know not why he should give us such a severe charge for the impartial consideration of these words,—that as we love our souls, we should impartially and without prejudice consider them.   We hope that, out of love to the truth, the glory of Christ, and care of our own souls, we do so consider, and have long since so considered, whatever belongs unto the cause wherein we engaged, and the oppositions that are made unto it; nor will we be offended with any that shall yet call on us to persist and proceed in the same way: but why such a charge should be laid on us with respect unto these words of Irenæus, I know not; for although we greatly value the words and judgment of that holy person, that great defender of the mystery and truth of the gospel and of the liberty of the churches from unwarrantable impositions, yet it is the word of Christ and his apostles alone whereby we must be regulated and determined in these things, if we love our own souls.

Besides, what are we concerned in them?   Is every separation from a church a schism?   Our author shows the contrary immediately.   Is refraining communion in a church-state not of divine institution, and in things not prescribed by the Lord Christ in the worship of God, [yet] holding communion in faith and love with all the true churches of Christ in the world, a damnable schism, or any schism at all? Hath the reverend author in his whole book once attempted to prove it to be so, though this be the whole of the matter in difference between us?   Is our forbearance of communion in parochial assemblies, upon the reasons before pleaded, especially that of human impositions, of the same nature with the schism from the whole catholic church, without pretence of any such impositions?   Doth he judge us to be such as have no love unto God, such as prefer our own profit before the unity of the church?   I heartily wish and pray that he may never have a share in that profit and advantage which we have made unto ourselves by our principles and practice.   Poverty, distress, ruin to our families, dangers, imprisonments, revilings, with contemptuous reproaches, comprise the profit we have made unto ourselves. Is our refraining communion in some outward order, modes, and rites, of men's institution,—our want of conscientious submission unto the courts of chancellors, commissaries, officials, etc.,—a rending and destroying of the glorious body of Christ? Is it cemented, united, and compacted or "fitly framed together" by these things? They formerly pretended to be his coat; and must they now be esteemed to be his glorious body, when they no way belong unto the one or the other? Is the application of these things unto us an effect of that love, charity, and forbearance which are the only preventive means of schism, and whereof if men are void it is all one upon the matter whether they are schismatics or no, for they will be so when it is for their advantage? Wherefore, we are not concerned in these things. Let whosoever will declare and vehemently assert us to be guilty of schism, which they cannot prove, we can cheerfully subscribe unto these words of Irenæus.

It may not be impertinent on this occasion to desire of some others that, as they love their own souls, and have compassion for the souls of other men, they would seriously consider what state and condition things are come unto in the church of England;—how much ignorance, profaneness, sensuality, do spread themselves over the nation; what neglect of the most important duties of the gospel, yea, what scoffing at the power of religion, doth abound amongst us; what an utter decay and loss there is of all the primitive discipline of the church; what multitudes are in the way of eternal ruin, for want of due instruction and example from them who should lead them; how great a necessity there is of a universal reformation, and how securely negligent of it all sorts of persons are ; what have been the pernicious effects of imposing things unnecessary and unscriptural on the consciences and practices of men in the worship of God, whereby the church hath been deprived of the labour of so many faithful ministers, who might have at least assisted in preventing that decay of religion which every day increaseth among us; how easy a thing it were for them to restore evangelical peace and unity amongst all Protestants, without the loss of their ministry, without the diminution of their dignity, without deprivation of any part of their revenues, without the neglect of any duty, without doing any thing against their light and consciences, with respect unto any divine obligation;—and thereon set themselves seriously to endeavour the remedy of these and other evils of the like nature, under a sense of that great account which they must shortly give before the judgment-seat of Jesus Christ.

He proceeds to consider the cases wherein the Scripture allows of separation; which he affirms to be three:—

The first is, in case of *idolatrous worship.* This, none can question, they do not see, from whom yet we all separate as from idolaters.

The second is, in case of *false doctrine being imposed instead of true;* which he confirms with sundry instances. But there is a little difficulty in this case; for,—

1. It is uncertain when a doctrine may be said to be *imposed.* Is it when it is taught and preached by the guides and governors of the church, or any of them, without control? If so, then is such preaching a sufficient cause of separation, and will justify them who do at present separate from any church whose ministers preach false doctrine. How false doctrine can be otherwise imposed I know not, unless it be by exacting an express confession of it as truth.

2. What false doctrine it is, which is of this importance as to justify separation, is not easily determinable.

3. If the guides and governors of the church do teach this false doctrine, who shall judge of it, and determine it so to be, and that ultimately, so as to separate from a church thereon? Shall the people do it themselves? are they meet, are they competent for it? are they to make such a judgment on the doctrine of their guides? do they know what is heresy? have they read Epiphanius or Binius? How comes this allowance to be made unto them, which elsewhere is denied?

The third is, *in case men make things indifferent necessary to salvation, and divide the church on that account.* But,—

1. I know not which is to precede or go before, their division of the church or the just separation, nor how they are to be distinguished; but it was necessary to be so expressed.

2. There are two things in such an imposition,—first, The practice of things imposed; secondly, The judgment of them that impose them. The former alone belongs unto them who are imposed on; and they may submit unto it without a compliance with the doctrine, as many did in the apostles' days. For the judgment of the imposers, it was their own error and concernment only.

3. Why is not the imposing of things indifferent, so as to make the observation of them necessary unto men's temporal salvation in this world, so as that the refusal of it shall really affect the refusers with trouble and ruin, as just a cause of separation as the imposing of them as necessary unto eternal salvation, which shall never affect them?

4. This making things indifferent necessary unto salvation, and as such imposing of them on others, is a thing impossible, that never was nor ever can be; for it is the judgment of the imposers that is spoken of, and to judge things indifferent in themselves to be in

themselves necessary to salvation is a contradiction.   If only the
judgment of the imposers, that such things are not indifferent, but
necessary to salvation, be intended, and otherwise the things themselves may lawfully be imposed, I know not how this differs from
the imposition of indifferent things under any other pretence.

In his following discourse concerning miscarriages in churches,
where no separation is enjoined, we are not at all concerned, and
therefore shall not observe the mistakes in it, which are not a few.

But may there not be other causes of peaceable withdrawing from
the communion of a church besides those here enumerated?

1. Suppose a church should impose the observation of *Judaical
ceremonies*, and make their observation necessary, though not to salvation, yet unto the order and decency of divine worship, it may
declare them to be in themselves indifferent, but yet make them
necessary to be observed.   Or,—

2. Suppose a church should be so *degenerated* in the life and conversation of all its members, that, being immersed in various sins, they
should have only a form of godliness, but deny the power of it; the
rule of the apostle being to avoid and turn away from them.

3. Suppose a church be fallen *into such decays in faith*, love, and
fruits of charity, as that the Lord Jesus Christ by his word declares
his disapprobation of it; and in that state refuses to reform itself, and
persecutes them who would reform themselves.   Or,—

4. Suppose the ministry of any church be such as is insufficient
and unable to dispense the word and sacraments unto edification, so
as that the whole church may perish as unto any relief by or from
the administration of the ordinances of the gospel.   I say, in these
and such other cases, a peaceable withdrawing from the communion
of such churches is warrantable by the rule of the Scripture.

SECTION III.

THE third part of the Doctor's discourse he designs to examine the
pleas, as he speaks, for *separation*; and these he refers to four
heads, whereof the first respects the constitution of the church.
And those which relate hereunto are four also:—1. That parochial
churches are not of Christ's institution; 2. That diocesan churches
are unlawful; 3. That our national church hath no foundation;
4. That the people are deprived of their right in the choice of their
pastors.

The first of these,—namely, that our parochial churches are not of
Christ's institution,—he begins withal, and therein I am alone called

to an account. I wonder the Doctor should thus *state the question* between us. The meaning of this assertion, that our parochial churches are not of Christ's institution, must be either they are not so because they are parochial, or at least in that they are parochial. But is this my judgment? have I said any thing to this purpose? Yea, he knows full well that in my judgment there are no churches directly of divine institution but those that are parochial or particular churches. We are not, therefore, to expect much in the ensuing disputation, when the state of the question is so mistaken at the entrance.

If he say or intend that there are many things in their parochial churches observed, practised, and imposed on all their members, in and about the worship of God, which are not of divine institution, we grant it to be our judgment, and part of our plea in this case. But this is not at all spoken unto.

Wherefore, the greatest part of the ensuing discourse on this head is spent in perpetual diversions from the state of the case under consideration, with an attempt to take advantage for some reflections, or an appearance of success, from some passages and expressions belonging nothing at all unto the merit of the cause;—a course which I thought so learned a person would not have taken in a case wherein conscience is so nearly concerned.

Some mistakes occurring in it have been already rectified, as that wherein he supposeth that my judgment is for the democratical government of the church; as also what he allegeth in the denial of the gradual declension of the primitive churches from their first original institution, hath been examined.

I shall, therefore, plainly and directly propose the things which I assert and maintain in this part of the controversy, and then consider what occurs in opposition unto them, or otherwise seems to be of any force towards the end in general of charging us with schism; and they are these that follow:—

1. *Particular churches or congregations, with their order and rule,* are of divine institution, and are sufficient unto all the ends of evangelical churches. I take *churches* and *congregations* in the same sense and notion as the church of England doth, defining the church by *a congregation of believers;* otherwise there may be occasional congregations that are not stated churches.

2. Unto these churches there is committed by Christ himself all the ordinary power and privileges that belong unto any church under the gospel; and of them is required the observance of all church duties, which it is their sin to omit.

3. There is *no church of any other form, kind, nature, or constitution that is of divine institution.* Things may be variously ordered

in and amongst Christians, or their societies may be cast or disposed
of into such respective relations to and dependence on one another,
in compliance with the political state, and other circumstances of
times and places, as may be thought to tend unto their advantage.
That which we affirm is, that no alteration of their state from the
nature and kind of particular churches is of *divine institution.*

4. *Such churches whose frame, constitution, and power are de-*
structive of the order, liberty, power, privileges, and duties of par-
ticular churches, are so far contrary unto divine institution, and
not to be complied withal.

Hereon we affirm, that whereas we are excluded from total communion in our parochial assemblies, by the imposition of things unto us
unlawful and sinful as indispensable conditions of their communion,
and cannot comply with them in their rule and worship on the reasons before alleged, it is part of the duty we owe to Jesus Christ to
gather ourselves into particular churches or congregations for the
celebration of divine worship, and the observation, doing, or performance of all his commands. These are the things which in this case
we adhere unto, and which must all of them be overthrown before
any colour can be given unto any charge of schism against us; and
what is spoken unto this purpose in the Doctor's discourse we shall
now consider. Only, I desire the reader to remember that all these
principles or assertions are fully confirmed in the preceding discourse.

That which first occurs in the treatise under consideration unto
the point in hand is the exception put in unto a passage in my former discourse, which is as follows:—

" We do not say that because communion in ordinances should be
only in such churches as Christ hath instituted, that therefore it is
lawful and necessary to separate from parochial churches; but if it be
on other grounds necessary so to separate or withhold communion
from them, it is the duty of them that do so to join themselves in or
unto some other particular congregation."

I have not observed any occasion wherein the Doctor is more
vehement in his rhetoric than he is on that of this passage, which
yet appears to me to be good sense and innocent.

1. Hereunto he says, p. 221,—

" That this is either not to the business, or it is a plain giving up of
the cause of Independency." If he judge that it is " not to the business," I cannot help it, and he might, as I suppose, have done well
to have taken no notice of it, as I have dealt with many passages in
his discourse; but if it be " a giving up of the cause of Independency," I say, whatever that be, let whoso will take it, and dispose
of it as it seems good unto them. But in proof hereof he says,—

" Wherefore did the dissenting brethren so much insist upon their separate congregations, when not one of the things now particularly alleged against our church was required of them?"

I answer,—

(1.) If any did in those times plead for separate congregations, let them answer for themselves; I was none of them. They did, indeed, plead for distinct congregations, exempt in some few things from a penal rule then endeavoured by some to be imposed on all. But there was no such difference nor restraint of communion between any of them as is at present between us and parochial churches.

(2.) It is very possible that there may be other reasons of forbearing a conjunction in some acts of church-rule, which was all that was pleaded for by the dissenting brethren, than those which are alleged against total communion with parochial churches, in worship, order, and discipline.

2. He adds, secondly, "But if he insists on those things common to our church with other reformed churches, then they are such things as he supposes contrary to the first institution of churches," etc.

I fear I do not well understand what this means, nor what it tends unto; but according as I apprehend the sense of it, I say,—

(1.) I insist principally on such things as are *not common unto them with other reformed churches*, but such as are peculiar unto the church of England. These vary the terms and practices of our communion between them and it.

(2.) The things we except against in parochial churches are not contrary to their first institution as parochial,—which, as hath been proved, is the only kind of churches that is of divine institution,—but are contrary unto what is instituted to be done and observed in such churches: which one observation makes void all that he would infer from the present suppositions; as,—

3. He inquireth hereon, "What difference there is between separating from our churches because communion in ordinances is only to be enjoyed in such churches as Christ hath instituted, and separating from them because they have things repugnant unto the first institution of churches."

The Doctor, I fear, would call this sophistry in another, or at least complain that it is somewhat oddly and faintly expressed. But we shall consider it as it is:—

(1.) Separation from parochial churches, because communion in ordinances is only to be enjoyed in such churches as Christ hath instituted, is denied by us; it is so in the assertion opposed by him, and I do not know whether it be laid down by him as that which we affirm or which we deny.

(2.) There is great ambiguity in the latter clause, of "Separating

from them because they have things repugnant unto the first institution of churches:" for it is one thing to separate from a church
because it is not of divine institution,—that is, not of that kind of
churches which are divinely instituted,—and another to do so because
of things practised and imposed in it contrary to divine institution;
which is the case in hand.

4. But he after saith, " Is not this the primary reason of separation, Because Christ hath appointed unalterable rules for the government of his church, which are not to be observed in parochial
churches ?"

I answer, No, it is not so; for there may be an omission, at least for
a season, in some churches, of some rules that Christ hath appointed
in the government of his church (and we judge his rules as unto
right unalterable), which may not be a just cause of separation.   So
the church of the Jews continued a long time in the omission of the
observance of the feast of tabernacles.   But the principal reason of
the separation we defend is the practising and imposing of sundry
things in the worship of the church not of divine institution, yea, in
our judgment contrary thereunto, and the framing of a rule of government of men's devising, to be laid on all the members of them;
this is the primary cause pleaded herein.

But because the Doctor proposeth a case on those suppositions,
whereon he seems to lay great weight,—though, indeed, however it be
determined, it conduceth nothing unto his end, but argues only some
keenness of spirit against them whom he opposeth,—I shall at large
transcribe the whole of it:—

" Let us, then," saith he, " (1.) suppose that Christ hath, by unalterable rules, appointed that a church shall consist only of such a
number of men as may meet in one congregation so qualified; and
that those, by entering into covenant with each other" (whereof we
shall treat hereafter), " become a church and choose their officers,
who are to teach, and admonish, and administer sacraments, and to
exercise discipline, by the consent of the congregation.   And let us
(2.) suppose such a church not yet gathered, but there lies fit matter
for it dispersed up and down in several parishes.   (3.) Let us suppose
Dr Owen about to gather such a church.   (4.) Let us suppose not
one thing peculiar to our church required of these members, neither
the aërial sign of the cross, nor kneeling at the communion, etc.   I
desire to know whether Dr Owen be not bound by this unalterable
rule to draw these members from communion with parochial churches,
on purpose that they might form a congregational church according
to Christ's institution ?   Either, then, he must quit these unalterable
rules and institutions of Christ" (which he will never do whilst he
lives), " or he must acknowledge, that setting up a congregational

church is the primary ground of this separation from our parochial churches," etc.

The whole design hereof is to prove that we do not withhold communion from their parochial assemblies because of the things that are practised and imposed in them in the worship of God and church-rule, but because of a necessity apprehended of setting up congregational churches. I answer,—

1. We know it is otherwise, and that we plead the true reason, and that which our consciences are regulated by, in refraining from their communion; and it is in vain for him or any man else to endeavour so to bird-lime our understandings by a multiplicity of questions, as to make us think we do not judge what we do judge, or do not do what we know ourselves well enough to do. If we cannot answer sophisms against motion, we can yet rise up and walk.

2. These things are consistent, and are not capable of being opposed one to the other,—namely, that we refrain communion on the reasons alleged, and thereon judge it necessary to erect congregational churches; which we should have no occasion to do were not we excluded from communion in parochial assemblies, as we are.

3. The case being put unto me, I answer plainly unto the Doctor's last supposition, whereon the whole depends, that if those things which we except against as being unduly practised and imposed in parochial assemblies were removed and taken away, I would hold communion with them, all the communion that any one is obliged to hold with any church, and would in nothing separate from them. This spoils the whole case. But then he will say, I am no Independent. I cannot help that; he may judge as he sees cause, for I am " nullius addictus jurare in verba magistri," designing to be the disciple of Christ alone.

4. But yet suppose that in such churches, all the things excepted against being removed, there is yet a defect in some unalterable rule that concerns the government of the churches, that they answer not in all things the strictness laid down in the Doctor's first supposition (although it is certain that if not all of them absolutely, yet the most of them, and of the most importance, would be found virtually in parochial assemblies upon the removal of the things excepted against), the inquiry is, what I would do then, or whether I would not set up a congregational church gathered out of other churches. I answer, I tell you plainly what I would do.

(1.) If I were joined unto any such church as wherein there were a defect in any of the rules appointed by Christ for its order and government, I would endeavour peaceably, according as the duties of my state and calling did require, to introduce the practice and observance of them.

(2.) In case I could not prevail therein, I would consider whether the want of the things supposed were such as to put me on the practice of any thing unlawful, or cut me short of the necessary means of edification; and if I found they do not so do, I would never for such defects separate or withdraw communion from such a church. But,—

5. Suppose that from these defects should arise not only a real obstruction unto edification, but also a necessity of practising some things unlawful to be observed, wherein no forbearance could be allowed, I would not condemn such a church, I would not separate from it, would not withdraw from acts of communion with it which were lawful, but I would peaceably join in fixed personal communion with such a church as is free from such defects; and if this cannot be done without the gathering of a new church, I see neither schism nor separation in so doing.

Wherefore, notwithstanding all the Doctor's questions, and his case founded on as many suppositions as he was pleased to make, it abides firm and unshaken, that the ground and reason of our refraining communion from parochial assemblies is the practice and imposition of things not lawful for us to observe in them. And it is unduly affirmed, p. 223, that upon my grounds, "Separation is necessary, not from the particular conditions of communion with them, but because parochial churches are not formed after the congregational way;" for what form of churches they have, be it what it will, it is after the congregational way. And it is more unduly affirmed, and contrary unto the rules of Christian charity, that this plea of ours is "a necessary piece of art to keep fair with the presbyterian party;" for as we design to "keep fair," as it is called, with no parties, but only so far as truth and Christian love require,—and so we design it with all parties whatsoever,—so the plea hath been always insisted on by us, and was the cause of nonconformity in multitudes of our persuasion, before they had any opportunity to gather any congregational churches according to the rule of the gospel. Such things will never help nor adorn any cause in the issue.

But he presseth the due consideration of this art (that, as I suppose, they may avoid the snare of it) on the Presbyterians, by minding them what was done in former times, "in the debate of the dissenting brethren, and the setting up of congregational churches in those days." For saith he, "Have those of the congregational way since altered their judgment? Hath Dr Owen yielded, that in case some terms of communion in our church were not insisted on, they would give over separation? Were not their churches first gathered out of presbyterian congregations; and if Presbytery had been settled upon the king's restoration, would they not have continued in their separation?"

Ans. 1. There is no difference, that I know of, between Presbyterians and those whom he calls Independents, about particular churches; for the Presbyterians allow them to be of divine institution, grant them *the exercise of discipline* by their own eldership, in all ordinary cases, and none to be exercised in them without them or their own consent, as also their right unto the choice of their own officers: so that there could be no separation between them on that account.

2. When they begin in good earnest to reform themselves, and to take away the unsufferable conditions of communion excepted against, they may know more of my judgment, if I am alive (which I do not believe I shall be), as unto separation; though I have spoken unto it plainly enough already.

3. It cannot be said that the churches of the Independents were gathered out of presbyterian churches, for the presbyterian government was never here established; and each party took liberty to reform themselves according to their principles, wherein there was some difference.

4. Had the presbyterian government been settled at the king's restoration, by the encouragement and protection of the practice of it, without a rigorous imposition of every thing supposed by any to belong thereunto, or a mixture of human constitutions, if there had any appearance of a schism or separation continued between the parties, I do judge they would have been both to blame: for as it cannot be expected that all churches, and all persons in them, should agree in all principles and practices belonging unto church-order,—nor was it so in the days of the apostles, nor ever since among any true churches of Christ,—so all the fundamental principles of church-communion would have been so fixed and agreed upon between them, and all offences in worship so removed, as that it would have been a matter of no great art absolutely to unite them, or to maintain a firm communion among them; no more than in the days of the apostles and the primitive times, in reference to the differences that were among churches in those days, for they allowed distinct communion upon distinct apprehensions of things belonging unto church order or worship, all keeping the unity of the Spirit in the bond of peace. If it shall be asked, then, Why did they not formerly agree in the assembly? I answer, (1.) I was none of them, and cannot tell; (2.) They did agree, in my judgment, well enough, if they could have thought so; and farther I am not concerned in the difference.

It is therefore notorious, that occasion is given unto our refraining free communion with parochial churches by the unwarrantable imposition of things not lawful for us to observe, both in church order

and worship; nor is it candid in any to deny it, though they are
otherwise minded as unto the things themselves.

His second exception is unto a saying which I quoted out of
Justice Hobart's Reports, who saith, "We know well that the primitive church in its greatest purity was but voluntary congregations of
believers, submitting themselves to the apostles and other pastors;
to whom they did minister of their temporals as God did move
them." Hereunto, with a reflection on a dead man, I know not
why, he replies, that this is "not to the purpose, or rather, quite
overthrows my hypothesis." But why so? He will prove it with
two arguments:—

The first is this: "Those voluntary congregations over which the
apostles were set were no limited congregations of any one particular
church; but those congregations over which the apostles were set
are those of which Justice Hobart speaks: and therefore it is plain
he spake of all the churches which were under the care of the
apostles, which he calls 'voluntary congregations.'"

Ans. 1. Whereas this argument seems to be cast into the form of
a syllogism, I could easily manifest how asyllogistical it is, did I delight to contend with him or any else. But,—

2. The conclusion which he infers is directly what I plead for,—
namely, that all the churches under the care of the apostles were
voluntary congregations.

3. There is a fallacy in that expression, "No limited congregations
of any one particular church." No such thing is pretended; but particular churches are congregations. Such were all the churches over
which the apostles were set; and therefore Justice Hobart speaks of
them all. This, then, is that which he seems to oppose,—namely,
that all the churches under the care of the apostles were particular
voluntary congregations, as Justice Hobart affirms; and this is that
which, in the close, he seems to grant!

His second argument, which is no less ambiguous, no less a rope
of sand, than the former, is this: "Those voluntary congregations
over whom the apostles appointed pastors, after their decease were
no particular congregations in one city. But those of whom Justice
Hobart speaks were such, for he saith they first submitted unto the
apostles and afterward to other pastors." What then? Why, "Justice
Hobart could not be such a stranger to antiquity as to believe that
the Christians in the age after the apostles amounted but to one
congregation in a city."

Ans. 1 What this is designed to prove or disprove, or how it
doth either of them, I do not understand; but I deny the proposition. The voluntary congregations over whom the apostles appointed pastors were all of them particular congregations, either

in one city or more cities, for that is nothing unto our purpose.

2. Not to engage Justice Hobart or his honour, I do confess myself such a stranger unto antiquity (if that may be esteemed the reason of it) as not to believe that the Christians in the age after the apostles amounted to any more than one church or congregation in a city, and shall acknowledge myself beholden to this reverend author if he will give me one undoubted instance where they so did. Only, let the reader observe that I intend not occasional meetings of any of the church with or without their elders, which were frequent. They met in those days in fields, in mountains, in dens and caves of the earth, in burying-places, in houses hired or borrowed, in upper rooms or cellars; whereof a large story might easily be given if it were to our present purpose. Dionysius of Alexandria sums them up briefly: Χωρίον, ἀγρὸς, ἐρημία, ναῦς, πανδοχεῖον, δεσμωτήριον—"A field, a desert, a ship, an inn, a prison, were places of our meetings," Euseb., lib. vii. cap. 22. But I speak of stated churches, with their worship, power, order, and rule. But whether there were more such churches in any one city is a matter of fact that shall be immediately inquired into. All that I here assert and confirm from the words of Justice Hobart is, that the churches in the days of the apostles were particular voluntary congregations; and the Doctor will find it a difficult task to prove that this overthrows my hypothesis.

Our author in the next place opposeth what I affirmed of the gradual deviation of the churches after the apostles from the rule of their first institution, which hath been already accounted for.

Sect. iv. p. 224. Upon an occasional expression of mine about the church of Carthage in Cyprian's time, he gives us a large account of the state of the church of Carthage at that time, wherein we are not much concerned. My words are, Vindic.[1] p. 41, " Though many alterations were before that time introduced into the order and rule of the churches, yet it appears that when Cyprian was bishop of the church of Carthage, the whole community of the members of that church did meet together to determine of things that were of their common interest, according unto what was judged to be their right and liberty in those days."

I thought no man who is so conversant in the writings of Cyprian as our author apparently is could have denied the truth hereof, nor do I say it is so done by him; only, he takes occasion from hence to discourse at large concerning the state of the church at Carthage in those days, in opposition to Mr Cotton, who affirms that there was found in that church the " express and lively lineaments of the very body of congregational discipline." Herein I am not concerned, who

---

[1] See his " Brief Vindication of the Nonconformists," etc. vol. xii. of his works.

do grant that at that time there were many alterations introduced into the order and rule of the church. But that the people did meet together unto the determination of things of their common interest, such as were the choice of their officers, and the re-admission of them into the fellowship of the church who had fallen through infirmity in time of persecution, or public offences and divisions, is so evident in the writings of Cyprian,—wherein he ascribes unto them the right of choosing worthy and of rejecting unworthy officers, and tells them that in such cases he will do nothing without their consent,—that it cannot be gainsaid. But hereon he asketh, where I had any reason to appeal to St Cyprian for the democratical government of the church; which, indeed, I did not do, nor any thing which looked like unto it. And he adds, that they have this advantage from the appeal, that we do not suppose any deviation then from the primitive institution; whereas my words are positive, that before that time there were many alterations introduced into the rule and order of the church. Such things will partiality in a cause, and aiming at success in disputation, produce.

Mr Cotton affirms that the lineaments of the congregational discipline are found in that church, that there is [not?] therein a just representation of an episcopal church; that is, I presume, diocesan, because that alone is unto his purpose. It is not lawful to make any church after the time of the apostles the rule of all church state and order, nor yet to be absolutely determined in these things by the authority of any man not divinely inspired; and yet I cannot but wish that all the three parties dissenting about church order, rule, and worship would attempt an agreement between themselves upon the representation made of the state of the church of Carthage in the days of Cyprian (which all of them lay some claim unto), although it will be an abridgment of some of their pretensions. It might bring them all nearer together, and, it may be, all of them in some things nearer to the truth; for it is certain,—

1. That the church of Carthage was at that time a particular church. There was no more church but one in that city. Many occasional meetings and assemblies in several places for divine exercises and worship there were; but stated churches, with officers of their own, members peculiarly belonging unto them, discipline among them, such as our reverend author doth afterward affirm and describe our parochial churches to be, there were none, nor is it pretended that there were.

2. That in this one church there were *many presbyters or elders*, who ruled the whole body or community of it by common advice and counsel. Whether they were all of them such as laboured in the word and doctrine, with the administration of the sacraments, or attended

unto rule only, it doth not appear; but that they were many, and such as did not stand in any peculiar relation unto any part of the people, but concurred in common to promote the edification of the whole body, as occasion and opportunity did require, is evident in the account given of them by Cyprian himself.

3. That among those elders, in that *one church*, there was one peculiarly called the *bishop*, who did constantly *preside* amongst them in all church-affairs, and without whom ordinarily nothing was done; as neither did he any thing without the advice of the elders and consent of the people. How far this may be allowed for order's sake is worth consideration; of divine institution it is not. But where there are many elders, who have equal interest in and right unto the rule of the whole church, and the administration of all ordinances, it is *necessary unto order* that one do preside in their meetings and consultations, whom custom gave some pre-eminence unto.

4. That *the people were ruled by their own consent;* and that in things of greatest importance, as the choice of their officers, the casting out and the receiving in of lapsed members, [they] had their suffrage in the determination of them.

5. That there was no *imposition* of liturgies, or ceremonies, or any human invention, in the worship of God, on the church or any members of it, the Scripture being the sole acknowledged rule in discipline and worship.

This was the state and order of the church of Carthage in those days; and although there were some alterations in it from the first divine institution of churches, yet I heartily wish that there were no more difference amongst us than what would remain upon a supposition of this state.

For what remains of the opposition made unto what I had asserted concerning congregational or particular churches, I may refer the Doctor and the reader unto what hath been farther pleaded concerning them in the preceding discourse; nor am I satisfied that he hath given any sufficient answer unto what was before alleged in the vindication, but hath passed by what was most pregnant with evidence unto the truth, and by a mistake of my mind or words diverts very much from the state of the question, which is no other but what I laid down before; yet I will consider what is material in the whole of his discourse on this subject.

Sect. v. p. 234. He says, I affirm that as to the "matter of fact concerning the institution of congregational churches, it seems evidently exemplified in the Scripture;" for which I refer the reader unto what is now again declared in the confirmation of it. And he adds, "The matter of fact is, that when churches grew too big for one

single congregation in a city, then a new congregational church was
set up under new officers, with a separate power of government;"—
that is, in that city. But this is not at all the matter of fact. I do
not say that there were originally more particular churches than one
in one city; I do grant, in the words next quoted by him, that there
is not express mention made that any such church did divide itself
into more congregations, with new officers. But this is the matter of
fact, that the apostles appointed only particular congregations; and
that therefore they did not oblige the Christians about, in a province
or diocese, to be of that church which was first erected in any town
or city, but they founded new churches, with new officers of their
own, in all places where there were a sufficient number of believers
to make up such a church. And this I prove from the instance of
the church of Jerusalem, which was first planted; but quickly after
there were churches gathered and settled in Judea, Galilee, and
Samaria. They planted churches κατὰ πόλεις καὶ χώρας, in the cities
and villages, as Clemens speaks. " But what," saith he, " is this to the
proof of the congregational way?" This it is,—namely, that the
churches instituted by the apostles were all of them congregational, not
diocesan, provincial, or national. But saith he, "The thing I desired was,
that when the Christians in one city multiplied into more congregations, they would prove that they did make new and distinct churches."
He may desire it of them who grant that the Christians did multiply
in one city into more congregations than one (which I deny) until
the end of the second century, although they might and did occasionally meet, especially in times of persecution, in distinct assemblies. Neither will their multiplication into more congregations,
without distinct officers, at all help the cause he pleadeth for; for his
diocesan church consisteth of many distinct churches, with their distinct officers, order, and power, as he afterward describes our parishes
to do under one bishop. Yet such is his apprehension of the justice
of his cause, that what hath been pleaded twenty times against it,—
namely, that speaking of one city, the Scripture still calls it the
church of that place, but speaking of a province, as Judea, Galilee,
Samaria, Galatia, Macedonia, it speaks of the *churches* of them ; which
evidently proves that it knows nothing of a diocesan, provincial, or
national church,—he produceth in the justification of it, because he
saith, that " it is evident, then, that there was but one church in one
city," which was never denied. There were, indeed, then many
bishops in one church, Phil. i. 1; Acts xx. 28. And afterward, when
one church had one bishop only, yet there were two bishops in one
city, which requires two churches, as Epiphanius affirms: Οὐ γὰρ
πότε ἡ Ἀλεξάνδρεια δύο ἐπισκόπους ἔσχεν ὡς αἱ ἄλλαι πόλεις, Hæres. lxviii.
s. 6;—" For Alexandria never had two bishops, as other cities had."

Whether he intend two bishops in one church, or two churches in one city, all is one to our purpose.

But the Doctor, I presume, makes this observation rather artificially, to prevent an objection against his main hypothesis, than with any design to strengthen it thereby; for he cannot but know how frequently it is pleaded in opposition unto any national church-state, as unto its mention in the Scripture; for he that shall speak of the churches in Essex, Suffolk, Hertfordshire, and so of other counties, without the least intimation of any general church unto which they should belong, would be judged to speak rather the independent than the episcopal dialect.

But, saith he, p. 236, " I cannot but wonder what Dr Owen means, when, after he hath produced the evidence of distinct churches in the same province, he calls this plain Scripture evidence and practice for the erecting particular, distinct congregations;—who denies that?" (I say, then, it is incumbent on him to prove, if he do any thing in this cause, that they erected churches of another sort, kind, and order also.) " But," saith he, " I see nothing like a proof of distinct churches in the same city; which was the thing to be proved, but because it could not be proved was prudently let alone."

But this was not the thing to be proved, nor did I propose it to confirmation nor assert it, but have proved the contrary unto the end of the second century. This only I assert, that every church in one city was only one church; and nothing is offered by the Doctor to the contrary, yea, he affirms the same.

But, saith he, sect. vi. p. 237, " Dr Owen saith, that the Christians of one city might not exceed the bounds of a particular church or congregation, no, although they had a multiplication of bishops or elders in them, and occasional distinct assemblies for some acts of divine worship. But then," saith he, " the notion of a church is not limited in the Scripture to a single congregation." Why so? " For," saith he, "if occasional assemblies be allowed for some acts of worship, why not for others?" I say, Because they belong unto the whole church, or are acts of communion in the whole church assembled, and so cannot be observed in occasional meetings: "Do this," saith the apostle, " when you come together into one place." " And if," saith he, " the number of elders be unlimited, then every one of those may attend the occasional, distinct assemblies for worship, and yet altogether make up the body of one church." And so, say I, they may, and yet be one church still, joining together in all acts of communion that are proper and peculiar unto the church; for as the meetings intended were occasional, so also was the attendance of the elders unto them, as they found occasion, for the edification of the whole church.

It may be the Doctor is not so well acquainted with the principles
and practice of the congregational way, and therefore thinks that
these things are contrary unto them. But those of that way do
maintain that there ought to be in every particular congregation,
unto the completeness of it, *many elders or overseers;* that the number of them ought to be increased as the increase of the church
makes it necessary for their edification; that the members of such a
church may and ought to meet occasionally in distinct assemblies,
especially in the time of persecution, for prayer, preaching of the
word, and mutual exhortation: so when Peter was in prison after
the death of James, many met together in the house of Mary to
pray, Acts xii. 12; which was not a meeting of the whole church.
And that there were such private meetings of the members of the
same church in times of persecution among the primitive churches
may be proved by a multiplication of instances; but still they continued one church, and joined together in all acts of church-communion properly so called, especially if it were possible every Lord's
day, as Justin Martyr declares that the church did in his time; "for
all the Christians," saith he, then, "in the city and villages about,"
gathered together "in one place," for the ends mentioned. But still
these distinct occasional assemblies did not constitute any *distinct
societies or corporations,* as the distinct companies do in a city.
"But," saith he, "grant one single bishop over all these elders, and
they make up that representation of a church which we have from
the best and purest antiquity." I say we would quickly grant it
could we see any warrant for it, or if he could prove that so it was
from the beginning. However, this is no part of our present contest,
—namely, whether, somewhile after the days of the apostles, in
churches that were greatly increased and many elders in them, there
was not one chosen (as at Alexandria) by those elders themselves to
preside among them, who, in a peculiar manner, was called a bishop.
But, if I mistake not, that alone which would advantage his cause
is to prove that there were in one city, or anywhere else, many, not
occasional assemblies of Christians or church-members, but many
stated, fixed churches, with officers of their own, peculiarly related
unto them, intrusted with church power and privileges, at least as
much as he afterward pleads to be in our parochial churches, all
under the government of one single bishop, making up a new church-
state beyond that of particular congregations, by their relation unto
him as their common pastor. This, I take it, is that which should
have been proved.

All the difficulty wherewith our assertion is accompanied ariseth
from the multiplication of believers and the increase of churches,
in the apostles' time or presently after; for this seems to be so great

as that those in one city could not continue in one church, notwith-standing the advantages of occasional assemblies. The church of Jerusalem had five thousand in it at the same time. The word grew and prevailed at Ephesus and other places. Whereto I shall briefly answer, as hastening unto a close of this unpleasing labour. I say, therefore,—

1. Whatever difficulty may seem to be in this matter, yet in point of fact so it was; there was no church before the end of the second century of any other species, nature, or kind, but a *particular congre-gational church* only, as hath been proved before. Let any one instance be produced of a church of one denomination, national, provincial, or diocesan, or of any other kind than that which is congregational, and I will give over this contest. But when a matter of fact is cer-tain, it is too late to inquire how it might be. And on this occasion I shall add, that if in that space of time,—namely, before the end of the second century,—any proof or undoubted testimony can be pro-duced of the imposition of the necessary use of liturgies, or of stated ceremonies of [or ?] the practice of church-discipline, consistent with that now in use in the church of England, it will go a great way in the determination of the whole controversy between us.

2. The *admirable prevalency of the gospel* in those days consisted principally in its spreading itself all the world over, and planting seminaries for farther conversions in all nations. It did, indeed, prevail more in some cities and towns than in others,—in some places many were converted, in others the tender of it was utterly rejected; howbeit it prevailed not unto the gathering of such great numbers into any church solely as might destroy or be inconsistent with its congregational institution. For not all, not, it may be, half, not sometimes a third part of them who made some profession of the truth, and attended unto the preaching of the word, and many of whom underwent martyrdom, were admitted as complete members of the church, unto all the parts of its communion. Hence there were many who upon a general account were esteemed Christians, and that justly, where the churches were but small.

3. It doth not appear that in the next age after the apostles the churches were anywhere so increased in number as to bear the least proportion with the inhabitants of the cities and towns wherein they were. The church of Smyrna, in the days of Polycarpus, may justly be esteemed one of the greatest in those days, both from the emi-nency of the place and person, who was justly accounted the great instructor of all Asia, as they called him when he was carried unto the stake. But this church giveth such an account of itself, in its epistle unto the churches of Pontus about the martyrdom of Poly-carpus, as manifests the church there to have been a very small num-

ber in comparison of the multitude of the other inhabitants, so as
that it was scarcely known who or what they were, Euseb. lib. iv.
cap. 15. So in the excellent epistle of the churches of Vienne and
Lyons unto the churches of Asia and Phrygia, concerning the persecutions that befell them, as they declare themselves to have been
particular churches only, so they make it evident that they bore in
number no proportion unto the inhabitants of the places where they
were, who could scarce discover them by the most diligent search,
Euseb. lib. v. cap. 1.

4. As for the church of Jerusalem in particular, notwithstanding
the great number of its original converts,—who probably were many
of them strangers occasionally present at the feast of Pentecost, and
there instructed in the knowledge of the truth, that they might, in
the several countries whither they immediately returned, be instruments of the propagation of the gospel,—it is certain that many years
after it consisted of no greater multitude than could come together
in one place to the management of church-affairs, Acts xv. 4, 22.
Nor is it likely that Pella, an obscure place, whose name probably
had never been known but on this occasion, was like to receive any
great multitudes; nor doth Epiphanius say, as our author pretends,
that they spread themselves from thence to Cœlo-syria, and Decapolis,
and Basanitis, for he affirms expressly that all the disciples which
went from Jerusalem dwelt at Pella. Only he says, that from thence
the sect of the Nazarenes took its original, which spread itself (afterward) in Cœlo-syria, Decapolis, and Basanitis: 'Εκεῖθεν γὰρ, ἡ ἀρχὴ
γέγονε (speaking of that sect) μετὰ τὴν ἀπὸ τῶν Ἱεροσολύμων μετάστασιν,
πάντων τῶν μαθητῶν ἐν Πέλλη οἰκηκότων,—" they dwelled all at Pella."

Sect. vii. p. 239. He quotes another saying of mine,—namely,
that I " cannot discern the least necessity of any positive rule or direction in this matter, seeing the nature of the thing and the duty
of man do indispensably require it." And hereon he attempts to
make advantage, in opposition unto another saying, as he supposeth,
of mine,—namely, " that the institution of churches, and the rules
for their disposal and government throughout the world are the same,
stated and unalterable;" from whence he makes many inferences to
countenance him in his charge of schism. But why should we contend fruitlessly about these things? Had he been pleased to read a
little farther on the same page, he would have seen that I affirm the
institution itself to be a plain command, which, considering the nature of the duties required of men in church-relation, is sufficient to
oblige them thereunto, without any new revelation unto that purpose; which renders all his queries, exceptions, and inferences of no
use. For I do not speak in that place of the *original institution of
churches*, whose laws and rules are universal and unalterable, but

our *actual gathering* into particular churches; for which I say the
necessity of duty is our warrant, and the institution itself a command. No great advantage will be made any way of such attempts.

The like I must say of his following discourse, p. 241, concerning
churches in private families, wherewith I am dismissed. I do grant
that a church may be *in a family;* there was so in the family of
Abraham before the law. And if a family do consist of such numbers as may constitute a church meet for the duties required of it,
and the privileges intrusted with it,—if it hath persons in it furnished
with gifts and graces fit for the ministerial office, and they be lawfully called and set apart thereunto,—I see no reason why they should
not be a church although they should be all in the same family.
But what is this to the imprisoning of all religious worship in private
families, that never were churches, nor can so be, with the admission
of some others which our author would justify from this concession,
I know not. But it is easy to see what our condition should always
be if some men's power did answer their desires.

But the will of God be done!

I shall not farther concern myself to consider things charged but
not proved, repeated but not confirmed, depending on a misunderstanding or misapprehension of words wherein the merit of the cause
is not concerned.

That which I first undertook, was a vindication of the Nonconformists from the charge of the guilt of schism. And this I engaged
in for no other reason but to remove, as far as in me lay, the obstruction that seemed to be cast by the Doctor's sermon unto the uniting
of all Protestants in the same common interest against Popery; for
although the design might be good, as I hope it was, and he might
judge well of the seasonableness of what he proposed unto its end,
yet we found it (it may be from the circumstances of it, as unto time
and place) to be of a contrary tendency, to the raising of new disputes,
creating of new jealousies, and weakening the hands of multitudes
who were ready and willing to join entirely in opposition unto Popery,
and [in] the defence of the protestant religion. For if a party of
soldiers (as the Doctor more than once alludes unto that sort of men)
should be drawing up in a field with others, to oppose a common
enemy, [and if] some persons of great authority and command in the
army should go unto them, and declare that they were not to be
trusted, that they themselves were traitors and enemies, fit to be
destroyed when the common enemy was despatched or reconciled; it
would certainly abate of their courage and resolution, in what they
were undertaking with no less hazard, than any others in the army.

I have here again unto the same end vindicated the principles of
the former vindication, with what brevity I could; for the truth is, I

meet with nothing material in the Doctor's large discourse, as unto what he chargeth on those of the congregational persuasion, but what is obviated in the foregoing treatise. And if any thing of the same nature be farther offered in opposition unto the same principles, it shall (if God give life and strength) be considered in and with the second part of it, concerning the matter, form, rule, polity, offices, officers, and order of evangelical churches, which is designed; and it is designed not for strife and contention with any,—which, if it be possible, and as far as in me lieth, I shall always avoid,—but for the edification of them by whom it is desired.

A BRIEF INSTRUCTION

IN THE

WORSHIP OF GOD AND DISCIPLINE OF THE CHURCHES
OF THE NEW TESTAMENT.

BY WAY OF QUESTION AND ANSWER;

WITH AN EXPLICATION AND CONFIRMATION OF THOSE ANSWERS.

PREFATORY NOTE.

THE following Catechism explains the constitution and ordinances of a Christian church, and the duties incumbent on its office-bearers and members. When it was published, in 1667, the names of the author and of the printer were withheld, and no intimation even was given of the place in which it was printed, lest danger should be incurred by the publication of a work advocating a form of polity at variance with the ecclesiastical system which the Court was at that time striving to render, as far as possible, universal in England. Dissenting congregations were, however, springing up in different parts of the country, and for the guidance of the Independents the Catechism was particularly useful. It was so much appreciated, that in the same year in which it first appeared a second edition, with some slight differences and emendations, was published; and hence certain discrepancies between the following version of it and the one which is given in Russell's edition of our author's works, printed from the first edition of the Catechism.

It came to be known as the "Independents' Catechism," and an angry attack was made upon it, in 1669, by Benjamin Camfield, rector of Whitby, in Derbyshire, in an octavo volume of 347 pages, entitled "A Serious Examination of the Independents' Catechism, and therein of the Chief Principles of Nonconformity to, and Separation from, the Church of England." The Catechism, in the estimation of the rector, was "the sink of all nonconforming and separating principles;" and he takes Owen to task for inconsistency in holding the Scriptures to be a sufficient rule of faith and duty. An attack conducted in this spirit only bespeaks the influence which this Catechism was beginning to exert in diffusing the principles and consolidating the interests of the denomination to which its author belonged. It was the occasion of another attack upon Owen, in the shape of a frivolous and bitter pamphlet with the title, "A Letter to a Friend concerning some of Dr Owen's Principles and Practices," etc., 1670. A copy of the Catechism had been sent by the "Friend" to the anonymous author of the pamphlet, who forthwith assailed Owen in a strain of pointless invective. The first charge against him is, that when vice-chancellor at Oxford, he had discountenanced some invidious distinctions in the dress of the members of the university,—"those *habits* and *formalities* by which persons of distinct qualities and degrees were distinguished in that school of learning." It was an offence, too, that "when he was brought into Westminster Hall for his witness against Mr Dutton, he refused to kiss the book, and professed it to be against his conscience to swear with any other ceremony than with eyes and hands lifted up to heaven." The pamphlet closes with "An Independent Catechism," in which the views of our author are caricatured in a style that is intended to be witty.

Certain principles laid down in Owen's Catechism, in regard to the ruling elder for example, are thought to bear some traces of affinity with Presbyterianism. Encouraged especially by the doctrine taught in it, that the elders, not the body of the church, are the primary subjects of office-power, Baxter wrote to Owen a long document of "theses," as the basis of a union between Independents and Presbyterians. The reply of the latter will be found in the Appendix to his "Life," vol. I. p. cxix. "I am still a well-wisher to these mathematics," was his remark, when he finally returned the theses to their author; and "this," says Baxter, "was the issue of my third attempt for union with the Independents." There might be ground for supposing that, on terms suggested by the Catechism, a coalition might be effected between the two denominations; and Owen himself, in a subsequent work (see p. 433 of this volume), indicated circumstances in which they could not have been in separation from each other without blame. Superior, however, in practical sagacity to his correspondent, he might see difficulties where Baxter saw none, or might feel that a formula of abstract theses was a waste of ingenuity, so long as the mutual confidence was lacking, which alone could affix upon the union the seal of permanence. Too often the victim of his own ardour and acumen, Baxter was prone to believe that the difficulty of adjusting the wayward eddies of human feeling and opinion into one smooth and onward current, should yield at once to the same treatment as would suffice to work a problem or frame a syllogism. The consummation for which he sincerely panted,—the outward unity of the church under one polity,—seems as yet reserved in providence to grace distant and happier times.—ED.

A SHORT CATECHISM:

WITH

AN EXPLICATION UPON THE SAME.

QUES. 1. *What doth God require of us in our dependence on him, that he may be glorified by us, and we accepted with him?*

ANS. That we [a]worship him [b]in and by the ways of his own appointment.—[a]Matt. iv. 10; Rev. xiv. 7; Deut vi. 13, x. 20.—[b]Lev. x. 1–3; Exod. xxiv. 3; Gen. xviii. 19; Josh. xxiii. 6–8; Zech. xiv. 16.

EXPLICATION.—By the worship of God inquired after, not that which is *natural* or *moral,* which is required in the first commandment, is intended. Such is our faith and confidence in him, our fear of him, our subjection of soul and conscience unto him, as the great sovereign Lord, First Cause, Last End, Judge, and Rewarder of all men; the law whereof was originally written in the heart of man, and hath been variously improved and directed by new revelations and institutions. And this worship is called *natural* upon a double account:—

First, Because it depends on the *nature of God,* a due perception and understanding whereof makes all this worship indispensably necessary: for none can know God but it is his duty to " glorify him as God,"—that is, to believe in him, love him, trust him, and call upon him; which all are therefore cursed that do not, Ps. lxxix. 6; 2 Thess. i. 8.

And, secondly, Because it was in the principle of it concreated with the *nature of man,* as that which suited, directed, and enabled him to answer the law of his creation, requiring this obedience of him in his dependence on God. And this worship is invariable: but it concerneth those outward ways and means whereby God hath appointed that faith, and love, and fear of him to be exercised and expressed unto his glory. And this kind of worship, though it depend not upon the nature of God, but upon his free and arbitrary disposal, and so was of old liable unto alterations, yet God did ever strictly require in the several states and conditions that his church hath gone through in the world. And this is that which most commonly in the Scripture is called by the name of "The worship of God," as that whereby all the acceptable actings of the souls of men towards him are expressed, and the only way of owning and acknowledging him in the world, as also of entertaining a visible intercourse with him. This, therefore, he calls for, and requires indispensably of all that draw nigh to him, and that because he is "the LORD our God," Rev. xiv. 6, 7; Matt. iv. 10; Deut. x. 12, 13. For his observance hereof doth he so approve of Abraham, Gen. xviii. 19; and sets it down as an everlasting law unto all others, that in a holy observation thereof "he will be sanctified in them that come nigh him," Lev. x. 1-3. His commands, also, concerning it are multiplied in the Scripture, with the approbation of all those that attend unto them. We may not think to find acceptance with God, or to inherit the promises, if, supposing ourselves to adhere unto him in worship internal and natural, we neglect that which is external and of his free appointment: for besides that we renounce thereby our inward dependence on him also, in not observing his commands, as Adam did in transgressing an institution, we become wholly useless unto all the ends of his glory in the world; which is not the way to come to an enjoyment of him. Neither do we only express and profess our inward *moral-natural worship* of God hereby, by which means it becomes the principal way and instrument of faith and trust exerting themselves in our obedience, but also it is a most effectual help and assistance unto the principle of that natural worship, strengthening the *habit* of it, and exciting it unto all suitable *actings*, unto its increase and growth.

Q. 2. *By what means do we come to know that God will thus be worshipped?*

A. That God is to be worshipped, and that according to his own will and appointment, is a principal branch of the law of our creation written in our hearts, the [b]sense whereof is renewed in the second commandment; but the ways and means of that worship depend merely on God's [c]sovereign pleasure and institution.—[a]Rom. i. 21, ii. 14, 15; Acts xiv. 16, 17, xvii. 23-31.—[b]Exod. xx. 4-6.—[c]Jer. vii. 31; Exod. xxv. 40; Heb. iii. 1-6; John i. 18.

EXPLICATION.—These two things all men saw by nature:—

First, That God, however they mistook in their apprehensions of him, would be, and was to be, worshipped with some *outward solemn* worship; so that although some are reported to have even cast off all knowledge and sense of a Divine Being, yet never any were heard of that came to an acknowledgment of any God, true or false, but they all consented that he was constantly and solemnly to be worshipped, and that not only by *individual persons*, but by *socie-ties* together; that so they might own and honour him whom they took for their God. And thus far outward worship is required in the first commandment,—namely, that the inward be exercised and expressed. When we take God for our God, we take him to worship him, Deut. x. 12, 13. Other thoughts,—namely, of inward worship without outward expression, at all or any time, or in any way,—are but a covert unto atheism. And,—

Secondly, This also they were led to an apprehension of by the same light whereby they are " a law unto themselves," Rom. ii. 14, that God would be worshipped in the *way* and by the means that he himself appointed and approved : whence none among the heathen themselves undertook to appoint ways and ceremonies of worship, but still they pretended to derive the knowledge of them from the *gods themselves;* of whom they reckoned that every one would be worshipped in his own way. And because, notwithstanding this pretence, being left of God and deluded of Satan, they did invent false and foolish ways of worship, not only not appointed of God, but such as were unsuited unto those *inbred notions* which they had of his nature and excellencies, the apostle convinces and disproves them, as men acting against *the light of nature* and principles of reason, Rom. i. 20, 21, they might have seen that in their idolatry they an-swered not their own inbred conceptions of the divine power and Godhead, so as to "glorify him as God;" and in the like manner doth he argue at large, Acts xvii. 22–31. But beyond this the inbred light of nature could not conduct any of the sons of men; this alone is con-tained in the first precept. That God was to be worshipped they knew, and that he was to be worshipped by ways and means of his own appointment they knew; but what those means were they knew not. These always depended on God's sovereign will and pleasure, and he made them known to whom he pleased, Ps. cxlvii. 19, 20. And although some of the ways which he doth appoint may seem to have a great compliance in them unto the light of nature, yet in his worship he accepts them not on that account, but merely on that of his own institution; and this as he hath declared his will about in the second commandment, so he hath severely forbidden the *addi-tion* of our own inventions unto what he hath appointed, sending us for instruction unto Him alone whom he hath endowed with *sove-reign authority* to reveal his will and ordain his worship, John i. 18; Matt. xvii. 5; 1 Chron. xvi. 7.

Q. 3. *How, then, are these ways and means of the worship of God made known unto us?*

A. In and by the written word only, which contains a full and perfect revelation of the will of God as to his whole worship and all the concernments of it.—John v. 39; Isa. viii. 20; Luke xvi. 29; 2 Tim. iii. 15–17; 2 Pet. i. 19; Deut. iv. 2, xii. 32; Josh. i. 7; Prov. xxx. 6; Rev. xxii. 18, 19; Isa. xxix. 13, 14.

EXPLICATION —The *end* wherefore God granted his word unto the church was, that thereby it might be instructed in his mind and will as to what concerns the worship and obedience that he requireth of us, and which is accepted with him. This the whole Scripture itself everywhere declares and speaks out unto all that do receive it; as 2 Tim. iii. 15–17, with the residue of the testimonies above recited, do declare. It supposeth, it declareth, that of ourselves we are ignorant how God is, how he ought to be, worshipped, Isa. viii. 20. Moreover, it manifests him to be a " jealous God," exercising that holy property of his nature in an especial manner about his worship, rejecting and despising every thing that is not according to his will, that is not of his institution, Exod. xx. 4–6.

That we may know what is so, he hath made a revelation of his mind and will in his *written* word,—that is, the Scripture. And to the end that we might expect instruction from thence alone in his worship, and act therein accordingly,—

First, *He sends us and directs us thereunto* expressly for that purpose, Isa. viii. 20; Luke xvi. 29; John v. 39; and not once intimates in the least any other way or means of instruction unto that end.

Secondly, He frequently affirms that it is sufficient, able, and perfect to guide us therein, 2 Tim. iii. 15–17; 2 Pet. i. 19; Ps. xix. 7–9. And whereas he hath expressly given it unto us for that end, if there be any want or defect therein it must arise from hence, that either God would not or could not give unto us a perfect revelation of his will; neither of which can be imagined.

Thirdly, He hath commanded us to observe all whatsoever he hath appointed therein, and not to make any addition thereunto, Josh. i. 7; Deut. iv. 2, xii. 32; Prov. xxx. 6; Rev. xxii. 18, 19. And,—

Fourthly, Peculiarly interdicted us the use of any such things as are of the institution or appointment of men, Isa. xxix. 13, 14. So that from the Scriptures alone are we to learn what is accepted with God in his worship.

Q. 4. *Have these ways and means been always the same from the beginning?*

A. No; but God hath altered and changed them at sundry seasons, according to the counsel of his own will, so as he saw necessary for his own glory and the edification of his church.—See Gen. ii. 16, 17, xvii. 10, 11; Exod. xii. 3–24, xx., xxv. 9; Heb. i 1, 2, ix. 10–12.

EXPLICATION.—The *external* worship whereof we speak being, as was showed before, not natural or moral, arising necessarily from the dependence of the rational creature on God as its first cause, chiefest good, last end, and sovereign Lord, but proceeding from the mere will and pleasure of God, determining how he will be honoured and glorified in the world, was always alterable by him by whom it was appointed. And whereas, ever since the entrance of sin into the world, God had always respect unto the promise of the Lord Christ and his mediation, in whom alone he will be glorified, and faith in whom he aimed to begin and increase in all his worship, he hath suited his institutions of the means thereof to that dispensation of light and knowledge of him which he was pleased at any time to grant. Thus, immediately after the giving of the *promise*, he appointed *sacrifices* for the great means of his worship; as to glorify himself expressly by men's offering unto him of the principal good things which he had given them, so to instruct them in the faith, and confirm them in the expectation of *the great sacrifice* for sin that was to be offered by the promised seed, Gen. iv. 3, 4; Heb. xi. 4. These were the first instituted worship of God in the world after the entrance of sin. Hereunto he nextly added *circumcision*, as an express sign of the covenant, with the grace of it, which he called Abraham and his seed unto by Jesus Christ, Gen. xvii. 10, 11. And to the same general end and purpose he afterwards superadded the *passover*, with its attendant institutions, Exod. xii. 3–24; and then the whole law of institutions contained in ordinances, by the ministry of angels on mount Sinai, Exod. xx. So by sundry degrees he built up that fabric of his *outward worship*, which was suited, in his infinite wisdom, unto his own glory and the edification of his church, until the exhibition of the promised seed, or the coming of Christ in the flesh, and the accomplishment of the work of his mediation, Heb. i. 1, 2: for unto that season were those ordinances to serve, and no longer, chap. ix. 10–12, and then were they removed by the same authority whereby they were instituted and appointed, Col. ii. 14, 18–20. So that though God would never allow that men, upon what pretence soever, should make any alteration in the worship appointed by him, by adding unto it any thing of their own, or omitting aught that he had commanded, either in matter or manner, notwithstanding that he knew that it was to abide but for a season, but commanded all men straitly to attend to the observation of it whilst it was by him continued in force, Mal. iv. 4; yet he always reserved unto himself the sovereign power of altering, changing, or utterly abolishing it at his own pleasure: which authority he exerted in the gospel as to all the mere institutions of the Old Testament. Whilst they continued he enforced them with *moral* reasons, [such] as his own holiness and authority. But those reasons prove not any of those institutions to be *moral*, unless they ensue upon those reasons alone, and are nowhere else commanded; for being once instituted and commanded, they are to be enforced with moral considerations, taken from the nature of God and our duty in reference unto his authority. So saith he, "Thou shalt reverence my sanctuary, I am the LORD;" which no more proves that a moral duty than that enjoined upon the same foundation, Lev. xi. 44, "I am the LORD your God: ye shall therefore sanctify yourselves, and ye shall be holy; for I am holy: neither shall ye defile yourselves with any manner of creeping thing that creepeth upon the earth." Not defiling ourselves with the touching or eating of creeping things is now no moral duty since the institution is ceased, although it be enforced by many moral considerations.

Q. 5. *Is there any farther alteration to be expected in or of those institutions and ordinances of worship which are revealed and appointed in the gospel?*

A. No; the last complete revelation of the will of God being made by the Son, who is Lord of all, his commands and institutions are to be observed inviolably unto the end of the world, without alteration, diminution, or addition.—Heb. i. 1, 2, x. 25–27; Matt. xxviii. 20; 1 Cor. xi. 26; 1 Tim. vi. 14.

EXPLICATION.—It was showed before that all the institutions of the Old Testament had respect unto the coming of Christ in the flesh, who was the "end of the law," Rom. x. 4; and thereupon they were subject to alteration and abolition upon a twofold account:—

1. Because that which they were appointed principally to instruct the church in, and to direct it unto the expectation of, was, upon his coming, accomplished and fulfilled; so that their end was absolutely taken away, and they could no more truly teach the mind and will of God, for they would still direct unto that which was to come, after it was past and accomplished. And this is that which the apostle Paul so variously proves and fully confirms in his Epistle to the Hebrews, especially in the seventh, eighth, ninth, and tenth chapters.

2. The Lord Christ, during their continuance, was to come as the Lord over his whole house, with more full and ample authority than *any* of those whom God had employed in the institution of his ordinances of old were intrusted withal: Heb. i. 1–3, "He spake in time past by the prophets," but now "by his Son, whom he hath appointed heir of all." Chap. iii. 6, "Christ as a son over his own house; whose house are we." And, therefore, they were all to be at his disposal, to confirm or remove, as he saw reason and occasion. And this he did,—(1.) *Virtually*, in the sacrifice of himself, or the

blood of his cross, fulfilling and finishing of them all, John xix. 30; "breaking down the middle wall of partition; abolishing in his flesh the enmity, even the law of commandments contained in ordinances;" "blotting out the hand-writing of ordinances," he " took it out of the way, nailing it to his cross," Eph. ii. 14, 15; Col. ii. 14. (2.) *Authoritatively*, by his Spirit in the apostles, and the doctrine of the gospel preached by them: Acts xv. 10, 11, " Now therefore why tempt ye God, to put a yoke upon the neck of the disciples, which neither our fathers nor we were able to bear? But we believe that through the grace of the Lord Jesus Christ we shall be saved, even as they." Gal. iii. 24, 25, " Wherefore the law was our schoolmaster to bring us unto Christ, that we might be justified by faith. But after that faith is come, we are no longer under a schoolmaster." Chap. v. 1–4. And, (3.) *Eventually* or providentially, when he caused sacrifice and offering to cease, by the prince of the people, that came with an army making desolate, to destroy both city and sanctuary, Dan. ix. 26, 27, according to his prediction, Matt. xxiv. 2. But now, under the New Testament, the worship that is appointed in the gospel is founded in and built upon what is already past and accomplished, —namely, the death and life of Jesus Christ, with the sacrifice and atonement for sin made thereby, 1 Cor. xi. 23–26; which can never be again performed; neither is there any thing else to the same purpose either needful or possible, Heb. x. 26. So that there is not any ground left for any new institution of worship, or any alteration in those that are already instituted. Nor,—

Secondly, Can any one be expected to come from God with a greater and more full authority for the revelation of his mind than that wherewith his only Son was accompanied; which yet must be, if any alterations were to be made in the appointments of worship that he hath instituted in the gospel.

For no inferior nor an equal authority can abolish or alter that which is already appointed, so as to give satisfaction unto the consciences of men in obedience unto such alterations. And, therefore, because there arose not a prophet like unto Moses under the Old Testament, there could be no alteration made in his institutions, but the church was bound severely to observe them all until the coming of Christ: Mal. iv. 4, " Remember ye the law of Moses my servant, which I commanded unto him in Horeb for all Israel, with the statutes and judgments;" and that because " there arose not a prophet afterwards in Israel like unto Moses, whom the LORD knew face to face," Deut. xxxiv. 10. And our apostle, to prove the right of Christ to alter the ordinances of the law, lays his foundation in manifesting that he was above the angels: Heb. i. 4, " Being made so much better than the angels, as he hath by inheritance obtained a more excellent name than they;" and that because the law was given by the ministry of angels, chap. ii. 2;—and so also that he was greater than Moses, chap. iii. 3, 5, " For this man was counted worthy of more glory than Moses, inasmuch as he who hath builded the house hath more honour than the house. Moses verily was faithful in all his house, as a servant, but Christ as a son over his own house;" because Moses was the lawgiver, and the mediator between God and man in the giving of the law. Now, if this be the sole foundation and warrant of the alteration made of Mosaical ordinances by Christ,—namely, that he was greater and exalted above all those whose ministry was used in the dispensation of the law,—unless some can be thought to be greater, and exalted in authority above the Son of God, there can be no alteration expected in the institutions of the gospel.

Q. 6. *May not such an estate of faith and perfection in obedience be attained in this life, as wherein believers may be freed from all obligation unto the observation of gospel institutions?*

A. No; for the ordinances and institutions of the gospel being inseparably annexed unto the evangelical administration of the covenant of grace, they may not be left unobserved, disused, or omitted, whilst we are to walk before God in that covenant, without contempt of the covenant itself, as also of the wisdom and authority of Jesus Christ.—Heb. iii. 3–6; Rom. vi. 3–6; Luke xxii. 19, 20; 1 Cor. xi. 23–26; Heb. x. 25; Rev. ii. 5, iii. 3.

EXPLICATION.—All our faith, all our obedience in this life, whatever may be obtained or attained unto therein, it all belongs unto our walking with God in the covenant of grace, wherein God dwells with men, and they are his people, and God himself is with them to be their God. Other ways of communion with him, of obedience unto him, of enjoyment of him, on this side heaven and glory, he hath not appointed nor revealed. Now, this is the covenant that God hath made with his people, " That he will put his laws into their mind, and write them in their hearts, and will be to them a God, and they shall be to him a people; and he will be merciful to their unrighteousness, and their sins and their iniquities will he remember no more," Heb. viii. 9–12. And whatever men attain unto, it is by virtue of the grace of that covenant; nor is there any grace promised in the covenant to lead men in this life, or to give them up unto a state of perfection, short of glory. Unto this covenant are the institutions of gospel-worship annexed, and unto that administration of it which is granted unto the church upon the coming and death of Christ. Without a renunciation and relinquishment of that covenant and the grace of it, these institutions cannot be omitted or deserted. If men suppose that they have attained to an estate wherein they need neither the grace of God, nor the mercy of God, nor the blood of Christ, nor the Spirit of Christ, it is not much material what they think of the ordinances of worship. Their pride and folly, without that mercy which is taught, promised, and exhibited in those ordinances, will speedily be their ruin. Besides, the Lord Christ is the absolute Lord " over his own house," Heb. iii. 3–6 ; and he hath given out the laws whereby he will have it guided and ruled whilst it is in this world. In and by these laws are his ordinances of worship established. For any persons, on what pretence soever, to plead an exemption from the obligation of those laws, it is nothing but to cast off the lordship and dominion of Christ himself. And yet farther to secure our obedience in this matter, he hath expressly commanded the continuance of them until his coming unto judgment, as in the places above quoted will appear.

Q. 7. *What are the chief things that we ought to aim at in our observation of the institutions of Christ in the gospel?*

A. [1]To sanctify the name of God ; [2]to own and avow our professed subjection to the Lord Jesus Christ ; [3]to build up ourselves in our most holy faith ; and, [4]to testify and confirm our mutual love, as we are believers.—[1]Lev. x. 3; Heb. xii. 28, 29.—[2]Deut. xxvi. 17; Josh. xxiv. 22; 2 Cor. viii. 5.—[3]Eph. iv. 11–16; Jude 20. —[4]1 Cor. x. 16, 17.

EXPLICATION.—That we may profitably and comfortably, unto the glory of God and our own edification, be exercised in the observation of the institutions and worship of God, we are always to consider what are the *ends* for which God hath appointed them and commanded our attendance unto them, that so our observance of them may be the obedience of faith. For, what end soever God hath appointed them unto, for that end are they useful and effectual, and to no other. If we come to them for any other end, if we use them for any other purpose or with any other design, if we look for any thing in them or by them, but what God hath appointed them to communicate unto us, we dishonour God and deceive our own souls. This we ought diligently to inquire into, to know not only *what* God requires of us, but *wherefore* also he requires it, and what he aims at therein; some of the principal things whereof are enumerated in this answer. And it is well known how horribly many of the institutions of the gospel have been by some (especially the Papists) abused, by a neglect of the ends of God in them, and imposing new ends of their own upon them, unto superstition and idolatry. Grace is ascribed unto the *outward observance* of them, whereas all grace is of the promise, and the promise in the covenant is given only to the faith of the right observers. The elements in the sacrament of the eucharist are turned into a god, first worshipped and then devoured, with many the like abominations.

Q. 8. *How may we sanctify the name of God in the use of gospel institutions?*

A. [1]By a holy reverence of his sovereign authority appointing of them; [2]a holy regard unto his special presence in them; [3]faith in his promises annexed to them; [4]delight in his will, wisdom, love, and grace, manifested in them; [5]constancy and perseverance in obedience unto him in their due observation.—[1]Lev. x. 3; Mal. i. 6; Rom. iv. 11; Exod. xx. 6; James iv. 12.—[2]Matt. xxviii. 20; Isa. lix. 21; Exod. xxix. 43–45.—[3]Gen. xv. 6; Heb. iv. 2, 6; Exod. xii. 27, 28; 2 Cor. vi. 16–18, vii. 1.—[4]Ps. lxxxiv. 1, 2, 4, 10, lxv. 4, xxxvi. 7, 8.—[5]Ps. xxiii. 6, xxvii. 4; Rev. ii. 3, 10; Gal. vi. 9; Heb. x. 23–25, xii. 3.

EXPLICATION.—This is the first thing that God requireth us to attend unto in the celebration of the ordinances of his worship,— namely, that we therein *sanctify his name*, the greatest duty that we are called unto in this world. This he lays down as the general rule of all we do herein: Lev. x. 3, " I will," saith he, " be sanctified in them that come nigh me, and before all the people I will be glorified." Whatever we do in his worship, we must do it that he may be sanctified, or whatever we do is an abomination to him. Now, the principal ways how we may herein sanctify the name of God are expressed; as,—

First, When in every ordinance we consider his appointment of it, and submit our souls and consciences unto his *authority* therein; which if we observe any thing in his worship but what he hath appointed we cannot do. Not formality, not custom, not the precepts of men, not any thing but the *authority* and command of God, is to be respected in this obedience. This is the first thing that faith regards in divine worship; it rests not in any thing, closeth not with any thing, but what it discerns that God hath commanded, and therein it eyes his authority as he requireth it: Mal. i. 6, " If I be a father, where is mine honour? and if I be a master, where is my fear?" Rom. xiv. 11, " As I live, saith the Lord, every knee shall bow to me, and every tongue shall confess to God." Reverence, then, unto the authority of God appointing his worship is a principal means of sanctifying the name of God therein. This was the solemn sanction of all his institutions of old: Deut. vi. 4–7, " Hear, O Israel: The LORD our God is one LORD: and thou shalt love the LORD thy God with all thine heart, and with all thy soul, and with all thy might. And these words, which I command thee this day, shall be in thy heart: and thou shalt teach them diligently unto thy children." And the observation of them he presseth on this account, that the people might fear that "glorious and fearful name, THE LORD THY GOD," Deut. xxviii. 58; which name he had so often engaged in his commands, saying, "Thou shalt do it; I am the LORD." And in the New Testament, our Lord Jesus Christ proposeth his authority as the foundation of his commanding, and our observation of all the institutions of the gospel: Matt. xxviii. 18–20, "Jesus came and spake unto them, saying, All power is given unto me in heaven and in earth. Go ye therefore, and teach all nations, baptizing them in the name of the Father, and of the Son, and of the Holy Ghost: teaching them to observe all things whatsoever I have commanded you." And he is to be considered in all our obedience as the great and only lawgiver of his church; as the "one lawgiver, who is able to save and to destroy," James iv. 12; the sovereign Lord over his "house," Heb. iii. 4–6, unto whom every knee is to bow and every conscience to be in subjection: and he who heareth not his voice is to be cut off from the people of God: Acts iii. 23, "It shall come to pass, that every soul, which will not hear that prophet, shall be destroyed from among the people."

Secondly, God hath frequently promised his *special presence* in and with his instituted ordinances of old, both unto the *things* themselves and the *places* wherein they were according to his appointment to be celebrated, those places being also his special institution. Under the New Testament, all difference of and respect unto place is taken away: John iv. 21, 23, "The hour cometh when ye shall neither in this mountain, nor yet at Jerusalem, worship the Father. But the hour cometh, and now is, when the true worshippers shall worship the Father in spirit and in truth: for the Father seeketh such to worship him." And we are commanded in *all places* equally to make our prayers and supplications. But his presence is promised and continued with the due celebration of the things themselves by him appointed for his service: Matt. xxviii. 20, "Teaching them to observe all things whatsoever I have commanded you: and, lo, I am with you alway, even unto the end of the world." In them is the "tabernacle of God with men," and he "dwells among them, and they are his people," Rev. xxi. 3; the promise of Christ being, that "where two or three are gathered together in his name, there he will be in the midst of them," Matt. xviii. 19, 20. And this promised presence of God, or Christ, consisteth,—1. In the power and efficacy which he by his Spirit implants upon his ordinances to communicate his grace and mercy unto his church, it being his covenant that his Spirit shall accompany his word for ever unto that purpose, Isa. lix. 21. 2. In the special blessing which he gives his people in those duties, both in the acceptance of them and testifying his good-will unto them: Exod. xxix. 42, 43, 45,' " At the door of the tabernacle of the congregation, there I will meet with the children of Israel, and the tabernacle shall be sanctified by my glory.   And I will dwell among the children of Israel, and will be their God;" Zech. ii. 10, 11; Ezek. xx. 40, 41, " I will accept you with your sweet savour;" chap. xliii. 27;—in both giving them intimate communion with himself by Jesus Christ, 1 John i. 3.   By all these he gives that special presence, which he requires an especial reverence and regard of faith unto, whereby his name is yet farther sanctified.

Thirdly, God hath given *special promises*, or *promises of his special grace*, unto them that attend upon him in his worship in a due manner.   And hereunto also belongs that sacred relation which, by virtue of divine institution, is between the sacramental elements and the especial graces of the covenant which they exhibit and confirm; and the mixing of these promises with faith, according as they are appropriated unto any particular institution, belongs also to the right sanctification of the mind of God.   So also,—

Fourthly, Doth our *delight* in them.   Now, this delight in the worship of God, so much commended in the Scripture, and proposed unto our example, consists not in any carnal self-pleasing, or satisfaction in the outward modes or manner of the performance of divine worship; but it is a holy, soul-refreshing contemplation on the will, wisdom, grace, and condescension of God, in that he is pleased, of his own sovereign mere will and grace, so to manifest himself unto such poor sinful creatures as we are, so to condescend unto our weakness, so to communicate himself unto us, so to excite and draw forth our souls unto himself, and to give us such pledges of his gracious intercourse with us by Jesus Christ.   By the contemplation of these things is the soul drawn forth to delight in God.

Lastly, Whereas great *opposition* lies oftentimes against the church's obedience unto God in this matter, and much persecution befalls it on that account,—great weariness also being apt, from the remainders of unbelief, carnal wisdom, indwelling sin, weakness of the flesh in believers themselves, to arise in the course thereof, and many temptations also beset them on every hand, to turn them aside from the way of truth and holiness,—constancy and perseverance in the due and orderly celebration of all the ordinances of the gospel belongs unto this duty.   And this *perseverance* respecteth both the things themselves and the manner of their performance, both which are of the highest concernment for us diligently to attend unto.

1. As to the *things themselves*.   Herein do we principally glorify God and give due honour unto Jesus Christ, when we abide in our

professed subjection unto him and observance of his commands against difficulties, oppositions, and persecutions. This he taketh notice of, Rev. ii. 13, "Thou holdest fast my name, and hast not denied my faith, even in those days wherein Antipas was my faithful martyr, who was slain among you, where Satan dwelleth." And this he requireth of us indispensably if we will be his disciples, or ever hope to obtain the reward : Matt. x. 38, 39, " He that taketh not his cross, and followeth after me, is not worthy of me ;" and it is " he that shall endure unto the end" that shall be " saved," chap. xxiv. 13. And unto them who are " faithful unto death," and them alone, doth he give the " crown of life," Rev. ii. 10; giving us caution not to "lose those things which we have wrought," that we may " receive a full reward," 2 John 8.

2. And as to the manner of their performance, two things are to be regarded in this duty of perseverance, and the sanctification of the name of God therein:—(1.) The *inward principle* of our obedience, our faith and love; which are to be preserved from decay : Rev. ii. 4, 5, " I have somewhat against thee, because thou hast left thy first love. Remember therefore from whence thou art fallen, and repent, and do the first works." Chap. iii. 3, " Remember how thou hast received and heard, and hold fast, and repent." (2.) The *outward manner* of observance; which is to be kept entire, according to the primitive institution of Christ: 1 Cor. xi. 23, "I have received of the Lord that which also I delivered unto you,"—not admitting of any corruptions in it, to avoid the greatest trouble: Gal. v. 11, " And I, brethren, if I yet preach circumcision, why do I yet suffer persecution?"

Q. 9. *How do we in our observation profess our subjection unto the Lord Jesus Christ and his gospel?*

A. In that being all of them, first, *appointed* by him as the head, lawgiver, and king of his church; and, secondly, made by him the *ensigns* and tokens of his kingdom and subjects; in their due observation principally consists that *profession* of him and his name which he so often calleth us unto, and so indispensably requireth at our hands.—Matt. xxviii. 18–20; 1 Cor. xi. 23; Heb. iii. 6, xii. 25; John xiii. 13, viii. 31, xiv. 15, 21, 23, xv. 14, 17, xiii. 35, xv. 14; Luke ix. 26; Rom. x. 10; 1 John ii. 3, 4.

EXPLICATION.—The ground and reason of this duty is evident. The Lord Jesus Christ straitly enjoins all his disciples the *profession* of his name, and lays it on them as indispensable unto salvation: Rom. x. 10, " With the heart man believeth unto righteousness, and with the mouth confession," or profession, " is made unto salvation;" John xii. 42–45. Now, this profession of the name of Christ, which is so much abused and mistaken in the world, consists in the keeping of his commandments: John xv. 14, " Ye are my friends, if ye do whatsoever I command you." So also, Matt. xxviii. 20, his disciples are to be taught to do and observe whatever he commandeth. Now, whereas he is the head and king of the church, the next immediate and special lawgiver of it, appointing unto it all his ordinances and its whole worship, as it becomes him who is lord of the house, the institutions of the gospel worship are his most especial commands; and in their observation consists that *profession* of him which he requires of us; therein doth he call them out of the world by profession whom he hath redeemed out of it by his blood, 2 Cor. vi. 15–18; Rev. v. 9. In these he exerciseth his kingly or lordly power over his church, Heb. iii. 6; and in the willing obedience of his people, gathering themselves unto the ensigns of his rule, he is glorified in the world.

Q. 10. *How do we in and by them build up ourselves in our most holy faith?*

A. By the exercise of that communion with God in Christ Jesus which, in their due observation, he graciously invites and admits us unto, for the increase of his grace in us, and the testification of his love and good-will towards us.—Gen. xvii. 10; Lev. xxvi. 11, 12; Prov. ix. 5, 6; Ezek. xxxvi. 27, 28; Zech. xiv. 16, 17; Matt. xxvi. 27, 28; Rom. vi. 3.

EXPLICATION.—The next and principal ends of all instituted worship, in respect of believers, are, the increase of the grace of God in them, their edification in their most holy faith, and the testification of the good-will of God unto them: Eph. iv. 11–16, " And he gave some, apostles; and some, prophets; and some, evangelists; and some, pastors and teachers; for the perfecting of the saints, for the work of the ministry, for the edifying of the body of Christ: till we all come in the unity of the faith, and of the knowledge of the Son of God, unto a perfect man, unto the measure of the stature of the fulness of Christ: that we henceforth be no more children, tossed to and fro, and carried about with every wind of doctrine, by the sleight of men, and cunning craftiness, whereby they lie in wait to deceive; but speaking the truth in love, may grow up into him in all things, which is the head, even Christ: from whom the whole body fitly joined together and compacted by that which every joint supplieth, according to the effectual working in the measure of every part, maketh increase of the body unto the edifying of itself in love." Whence, also, is that prayer of the apostle for the blessing of God upon the church, in the use of them: Eph. iii. 16–19, " That he would grant you, according to the riches of his glory, to be strengthened with might by his Spirit in the inner man; that Christ may dwell in your hearts by faith; that ye, being rooted and grounded in love, may be able to comprehend with all saints what is the breadth, and length, and depth, and height; and to know the love of Christ, which passeth knowledge, that ye might be filled with all the fulness of God." For these ends, and with a design to have them accomplished in and upon their souls, ought they to attend unto them: James i. 21, " Receive with meekness the engrafted word, which is able to save your souls." 1 Pet. ii. 2, " As new-born babes, desire the sincere milk of the word, that ye may grow thereby." Unto the effecting of these ends, especially the increase and establishment of our faith, are they suited and appointed of God; whereon all their efficacy doth depend. In their due observation doth God give out that supply of grace which he hath promised, Eph. iii. 16–19. And thus also is faith exercised in an especial manner; which is the only ordinary means of its growth and increase. Habits, both *acquired* and *infused*, are increased and strengthened by frequent acts on suitable objects: Hos. vi. 3, " Then shall we know, if we follow on to know the LORD." In the celebration of gospel ordinances, God in Christ proposeth himself in an intimate manner to the believing soul as his God and reward; and his love in Christ, in an especial manner, in some ordinances. So doth Christ also exhibit himself thereunto: Rev. iii. 20, " Behold, I stand at the door, and knock: if any man hear my voice, and open the door, I will come in to him, and will sup with him, and he with me." Faith, therefore, directed by the word to rest in God, to receive the Lord Christ in the observation of his ordinances, is excited, increased, strengthened, and that in answer unto the appointment and promises of God.

Q. 11. *How are mutual love and communion among believers testified and confirmed in their observation?*

A. In that they are appointed by the Lord Christ for that end, and in their own nature, as attended unto in their assemblies, are in an especial manner suited unto that purpose.—John xiii. 35; 1 Cor. x. 16, 17, xi. 18, 19; Eph. iv. 3–6.

EXPLICATION.—The principles of mutual, spiritual love among believers arise from their relation unto *one Father:* Matt. xxiii. 9, " One is your Father, which is in heaven," who giveth unto all them that believe in Christ " power to become the sons of God," John i. 12; and their being all children of the same family,—that family in heaven and earth which is called after the name of God, the Father of it, as the Father of our Lord Jesus Christ, Eph. iii. 14, 15;—and unto Christ Jesus as their elder brother, who " is not ashamed to call them brethren," Heb. ii. 11, being by him born of God;—and

from their participation of one and the self-same Spirit, which
dwelleth in them, as they are " the temple of God, and the Spirit of
God dwelleth in them," 1 Cor. iii. 16; as also in all the fruits of that
one Spirit, 1 Cor. xii. 4–8, and in that *one faith* and hope whereunto
they are called: Eph. iv. 3–6, " Endeavouring to keep the unity of
the Spirit in the bond of peace.   There is one body, and one Spirit,
even as ye are called in one hope of your calling; one Lord, one
faith, one baptism, one God and Father of all, who is above all, and
through all, and in you all."   And that love which is not built on
these principles and foundations is not evangelical, whatever other
ground it may have, or occasion it may pretend unto.   Communion
of saints consists in their mutual love, duly exercised according to
rule; and all communion is an effect of union.   In union therefore
must lie the springs of love, and this consists in a joint incorporation
of believers into Christ; " for as the body is one, and hath many
members, and all the members of that one body being many, are
one body, so also is Christ; for by one Spirit we are all baptized into
one body;"—and this they have by the means before mentioned,
namely, their adoption, faith, and inhabitation of the Spirit.   Now,
in the joint celebration of the ordinances of God's worship, they all
together make profession of these principles, and act that one faith,
hope, and love jointly, whereof they are made partakers, and thereby
grow up more and more into the head " by that which every joint
supplieth," Eph. iv. 16.   And some of them are peculiarly designed
by the Lord Christ for the testification of their love and union among
themselves: 1 Cor. x. 16, 17, " The cup of blessing which we bless,
is it not the communion of the blood of Christ? The bread which we
break, is it not the communion of the body of Christ? For we being
many are one bread, and one body: for we are all partakers of that
one bread."

Q. 12. *What is principally to be attended unto by us in the manner of the celebration of the worship of God, and observation of the
institutions and ordinances of the gospel?*

A. That we observe and do all whatsoever the Lord Christ hath
commanded us to observe, in the way that he hath prescribed; and
that we add nothing unto or in the observation of them that
is of man's invention or appointment.—Deut. iv. 2, xii. 32; Jer.
vii. 27; Matt. xv. 9, 13, xvii. 5; Col. ii. 6; Matt. xxviii. 20; Heb.
iii. 3–6; 1 Cor. xi. 23; Rev. xxii. 18, 19; 1 Chron. xvi. 7; Isa.
xxix. 13.

EXPLICATION.—This was in part spoken to before on the third
question, where it was showed that the Scripture is the only way and
means whereby God hath revealed what that worship is which he

will accept in and of the church. Here, moreover, as to the duty of
the church in this matter, three things are asserted:—

First, That we are to observe and *do all whatsoever* the Lord
Christ hath commanded us to observe. This lies plain in the command, Matt. xxviii. 20, "Teaching them to observe all things whatsoever I have commanded you." And we are directed unto it in the
injunction given us from heaven, to "hear,"—that is, to obey him in
all things, Matt. xvii. 5, he being the prophet to whose teachings and
instructions we owe obedience, on pain of extermination from among
the people of God, Deut. xviii. 15, 18, 19; Acts iii. 22, 23. Whatever
he hath appointed, commanded, revealed as the will of God to be
observed in or about the worship of God, that is to be kept and
observed by the church inviolably; for if we are his friends and
disciples, we will keep his commandments. No disuse, of what continuance soever, can discharge us from the observation of institutions.
After the feast of tabernacles had been disused from the times of
Joshua unto the return from the captivity, the restoration of it was
required of God and accepted with him, Neh. viii. 17. No abuse,
of how high a nature soever, can absolve us from obedience unto an
institution, 1 Cor. xi. 20–23. After the great abuse of the Lord's
supper in that church, the apostle recalls them again unto the observation of it, according to the institution of Christ. And after the
defilement of all the ordinances of the gospel, under the antichristian apostasy, yet the temple and the altar are to be measured again,
Rev. xi. 1, and the tabernacle of God was again to be raised amongst
men, chap. xxi. 3. No opposition, no persecution, can give the
church a dispensation wholly to omit and lay aside the use of any
thing that the Lord Christ hath commanded to be observed in the
worship of God, whilst we are under the obligation of that great rule,
Acts iv. 19, "Whether it be right in the sight of God to hearken
unto you more than unto God, judge ye." It is true, in the observation of positive institutions, we may have regard unto rules and prescriptions of prudence, as to times, places, and seasons, that by no
inadvertency or miscarriage of ours, or advantage taken by the adversaries of the truth, the edification of the church be hindered;—so
the disciples met with "the doors shut for fear of the Jews," John
xx. 19; and Paul met with the disciples in the night, in "an upper
chamber," for the celebration of all the ordinances of the church,
Acts xx. 7, 8;—yet, as to the obligation unto their observation, it
indispensably binds us, and that always, and that as to all the institutions of Christ whatever: Heb. x. 25, "Not forsaking the assembling of ourselves together, as the manner of some is; but exhorting
one another: and so much the more, as ye see the day approaching."
To dispense with Christ's commands practically is unlawful, much

more doctrinally, most of all *authoritatively*, as the pope takes on himself to do. This, then, is the church's duty, to search out all the commands of Christ recorded in the gospel, and to yield obedience unto them. We are not, in this matter, to take up merely with what we find in practice amongst others, no, though they be men good or holy. The duty of the church, and, consequently, of every member of it in his place and station, is to search the Scriptures, to inquire into the mind of Christ, and to find out whatever is appointed by him, or required of his disciples, and that with hearts and minds prepared unto a due observation of whatever shall be discovered to be his will.

Secondly, Whatever belongs unto the worship of God, in the *way or manner* whereby any of the ordinances of Christ is to be performed, comes also under the command of Christ, which is duly to be attended unto and observed. Indeed, whatever is of this nature appointed by Christ, it doth therefore belong to the worship of God; and what is not so appointed neither doth nor can be any part thereof. Of this nature is the celebration of all other ordinances with prayer, for every thing is "sanctified by the word of God and prayer," 1 Tim. iv. 5; of some of them indispensably in the assemblies of the church, 1 Cor. x. 16, 17, xi. 20, 24, 25, 33; with care in the observation of the general rules of love, modesty, condescension, and prudence, " doing all things decently and in order," 1 Cor. xi. 33, xiv. 40; gestures in some sacred actions, Matt. xxvi. 20, 26–28; John xiii. 23;—all which the church is diligently to inquire into, as things that belong to the pattern of the house of God, " the goings out thereof and the comings in thereof, the forms thereof and the ordinances thereof, with the laws thereof," promised to be showed unto it, Ezek. xliii. 11. To attend carefully to their observation is its duty, being left at liberty as to all other circumstances; which no authority of man can give any real relation to the worship of God unto. Therein lies the exercise of that spirit of wisdom and revelation in the knowledge of the mystery of the gospel, which is given unto the church, Eph. i. 17, 18. It was the wisdom of the ancient church to do and observe all that God appointed, in the way and manner that he had prescribed for their observance: Deut. iv. 5, 6, " Behold, I have taught you statutes and judgments, even as the LORD my God commanded me. Keep therefore and do them; for this is your wisdom and your understanding." And herein is the command of Christ kept inviolate and unblamable. The persuasion of some, that the Lord hath not prescribed all things wherein his worship is concerned, seems to proceed from a negligence in inquiring after what he hath so prescribed. And when once that persuasion is entertained, all farther inquiry is superseded and despised; for to what end should any one seek after that which he is satisfied cannot be found? as that which is not cannot be. But this mistake will be elsewhere more fully discovered.

Thirdly, A principal part of the duty of the church in this matter is, to take care that nothing be admitted or practised in the worship of God, or as belonging thereunto, which is not instituted and appointed by the Lord Christ. In its care, faithfulness, and watchfulness herein consists the principal part of its loyalty unto the Lord Jesus, as the head, king, and lawgiver of his church; and which to stir us up unto, he hath left so many severe interdictions and prohibitions in his word against all *additions* to his commands, upon any pretence whatever; of which afterward.

Q. 13. *Are not some institutions of the New Testament ceased as unto any obligation unto their observation, and therefore now rightly disused?*

A. [1] Some symbolical tokens of moral duties, occasionally used, only for present instruction in those duties, are mentioned in the gospel, without any intention to oblige believers unto the formal constant use and repetition of them; and [2] some temporary appointments relating unto gifts in the church, bestowed only for a season on the first plantation of the gospel, are ceased;—but [3] no institution or command of Christ, given unto the whole church, relating unto the evangelical administration of the new covenant, for the use and benefit of all believers, doth or shall cease to the end of the world, nor can be wholly omitted without a violation of the authority of Jesus Christ himself.—[1] John xiii. 12–15; Rom. xvi. 16; 1 Cor. xvi. 20; 1 Tim. v. 10.—[2] Mark vi. 13; James v. 14.—[3] Matt. xxviii. 20; 1 Tim. vi. 14; 1 Cor. xi. 26.

EXPLICATION.—Mention is made in the Scriptures of sundry things practised by the Lord Christ and his apostles, which being then in common use among men, were occasionally made by them symbolical instructions in moral duties. Such were washing of feet by one another, the holy kiss, and the like. But there being no more in them but a sanctified use directed unto the present civil customs and usages, the commands given concerning them respect not the outward action, nor appointed any continuance of them, being peculiarly suited unto the state of things and persons in those countries; as, John xiii. 12–15, "After he had washed their feet, and had taken his garments, and was set down again, he said unto them, Know ye what I have done to you? Ye call me Master and Lord: and ye say well; for so I am. If I then, your Lord and Master, have washed your feet; ye also ought to wash one another's feet. For I have given you an example, that ye should do as I have done to you."

It is evident that it is the moral duty of brotherly love, in condescension and mutual helpfulness, to be expressed in all necessary offices as occasion doth require, that is the thing which Jesus Christ here enjoineth his disciples, and leads them to by his own example in an office of love then in use in those parts. The same is to be said of the "holy kiss," Rom. xvi. 16; which was a temporary, occasional token of entire love, which may, in answer thereunto, be expressed by any sober usage of salutation amongst men to the same purpose. But the things themselves were not instituted for any continuance, nor do represent any special grace of the new covenant, which is inseparable from every institution of gospel worship properly so called. Common usages or practices, therefore, directed to be used in a due manner and unto a proper end, where they are used, make them not institutions of worship. Neither have they in them, as so commanded or directed, any one thing that concurs to the constitution of a gospel ordinance; for neither had they their rise in the authority of Christ, nor is any continuance of them enjoined, nor any promise annexed unto them, nor any grace of the new covenant represented or exhibited in them.

Besides, there were in the first churches, continued for a while, certain *extraordinary gifts,* that had their effects visible on the outward senses of men, and tended not immediately unto the edification of the churches in their faith, but unto the conviction of others, and vindication of the authority of them by whom the gospel was preached and propagated. Such was that *gift of healing* the sick: which being an especial effect of the Holy Ghost for the advantage of the church in those days, in some places it was accompanied by anointing with oil; but this being no universal practice, and used only in the exercise of a gift extraordinary, whose use and being has long since ceased, it never was appointed nor intended to be of continuance in the church, which is not tied by the Lord Christ to the empty signs and shadows of things whose substance is not enjoyed. Besides, no spiritual grace of the covenant was ever intimated, sealed, or exhibited by that usage of anointing with oil. The first mention of it is, Mark vi. 13, where its practice is reckoned among the effects of that extraordinary power which the Lord Christ committed unto his twelve disciples on their first sending out, and is referred unto the same series of miracles which they wrought in pursuit and by virtue thereof: "They cast out many devils, and anointed with oil many that were sick, and healed them." And by what is there recorded, the subsequent mention of it, James v. 14, is to be regulated. But now, unto a real evangelical institution of worship, it is required,— 1. That it be a command of Christ, manifested by his word or example proposed unto our imitation, Matt. xxviii. 20; 2. That it be given and enjoined unto the whole church, with the limitation of its administration expressed in the word, 1 Cor. xi. 25; 3. That, unto the due performance of it, gospel grace be required in them that attend unto it; 4. That it teach, or represent, or seal, or improve some grace of the covenant, and have a promise of acceptation annexed unto it. And whatever is thus appointed, the church is indispensably to continue in the observation of, unto the end of the world.

Q. 14. *May not the church find out, and appoint to be observed, such religious rites as, being adjoined unto the celebration of God's instituted worship, may further the devotion of the worshippers, and render the worship itself in its performance more decent, beautiful, and orderly, as the appointing of images, and the like?*

A. All acceptable devotion in them that worship God is the effect of faith, which respects the precepts and promises of God alone. And the comeliness and beauty of gospel worship consisteth in its relation unto God by Jesus Christ, as the merciful high priest over his house, with the glorious administration of the Spirit therein. The order also of it lieth in the due and regular observation of all that Christ hath appointed. And therefore all such inventions are in themselves needless and useless, and, because forbidden, unlawful to be observed.—Rom. i. 21, xiv. 23; Heb. iv. 2, xi. 4, 6; Deut. xiii. 4, xxvii. 10, xxx. 2, 8, 20, xi. 27; Matt. xvii. 5; Isa. xxix. 13; Eph. ii. 18; 2 Cor. iii. 7–11; Heb. x. 19–22; John iv. 21–23; 1 Cor. xiv. 25; Matt. xxviii. 20; Exod. xx. 4; Deut. iv. 2; Matt. xv. 13; Deut. xii. 32, xvii. 3.

EXPLICATION.—Three things are usually pleaded in the justification of the observance of such *rites* and ceremonies in the worship of God:—First, That they tend unto the furtherance of the *devotion* of the worshippers; secondly, That they render the worship itself *comely* and beautiful; thirdly, That they are the great preservers of *order* in the celebration thereof. And therefore on these accounts they may be instituted or appointed by some, and observed by all.

But things are indeed quite otherwise: " God is a Spirit, and will be worshipped in spirit and in truth," John iv. 24. And no devotion is acceptable unto him, but what proceedeth from and is an effect of faith; for " without faith it is impossible to please God," Heb. xi. 6. And faith in all things respects the commands and authority of God; for saith he, " In vain do they worship me, who teach for doctrines the commandments of men," Matt. xv. 9; and he rejecteth all that honour which is given him by those whose fear towards him or worship of him is " taught by the precepts of men," Isa. xxix. 13. These things, therefore, being utterly destitute of divine authority, they can no way further or promote the devotion of

the worshippers.   What natural or carnal affections may be excited
by them,—as men may "inflame themselves with idols," Isa. lvii. 5,—
or what outward, outside devotion they may direct unto or excite, is
uncertain; but that they are no means of stirring up the grace of
God in the hearts of believers, or of the increase or strengthening of
their faith,—which things alone God accepts in gospel worship,—seeing they are not appointed by him for any such purpose, is most certain: for to say that any thing will effectually stir up devotion,—that
is, excite, strengthen, or increase grace in the heart towards God,—
that is not of his own appointment, is on the one hand to reflect on his
wisdom and care towards his church, as if he had been wanting towards it in things so necessary, which he declares against, Isa. v. 4,
"What," saith he, "could have been done more to my vineyard,
that I have not done in it?" so on the other, it extols the wisdom of
men above what is meet to ascribe unto it.   Shall men find out that
which God would not, or could not, in matters of so great importance
unto his glory and the souls of them that obey him? Yea, and it cannot be but that attendance unto them and their effects must needs
divert the mind from those proper spiritual actings of faith and
grace which is its duty to attend unto.   And this is evidently seen
in them who, indulging to themselves in their observation in multiplied instances, as in the church of Rome, have changed the whole
spiritual worship of the church into a theatrical, pompous show of
carnal devotion.

Secondly, The *comeliness* and beauty of gospel worship doth not
in the least depend upon them nor their observation.   The apostle
doth in sundry places expressly compare the spiritual worship of the
gospel with that of the law, whilst the church had a *worldly sanctuary* and carnal ordinances, Heb. ix. 1.   And although it be most
evident that the worship of the Old Testament did, for the glory and
ornaments of outward ceremonies, and the splendour of their observation, far exceed and excel that worship which God commands now,
as suitable unto the simplicity of the gospel, yet doth the apostle
prefer this, for glory, comeliness, and beauty, unspeakably above the
other; which manifests that these things can have no respect unto
outward rites and ceremonies, wherein the chief admirers of them
can no way vie for glory with the old worship of the temple.   So
the apostle, 2 Cor. iii. 7-11, " If the ministration of death, written
and engraven in stones, was glorious, so that the children of Israel
could not stedfastly behold the face of Moses for the glory of his
countenance; which glory was to be done away: how shall not the
ministration of the spirit be rather glorious?   For if the ministration
of condemnation be glory, much more doth the ministration of righteousness exceed in glory.   For even that which was made glorious

had no glory in this respect, by reason of the glory that excelleth. For if that which is done away was glorious, much more that which remaineth is glorious." He compareth the two ministrations and the several worships of the law and gospel, preferring this unspeakably above the other, sufficiently manifesting that the glory of it consisteth not in any pompous observance of outward ceremonies. And elsewhere he declareth that indeed it doth consist in its relation to God in Christ, with the liberty and boldness of the worshippers to enter into the holy place, unto the throne of grace, under the ministry of their merciful and faithful high priest, being enabled thereunto by the Spirit of adoption and supplications; for therein, "through Christ, we have access by one Spirit unto the Father," Eph. ii. 18; as it is expressed, Heb. x. 19–21, "Having therefore boldness to enter into the holiest by the blood of Jesus, by a new and living way, which he hath consecrated for us, through the vail, that is to say, his flesh; and having an high priest over the house of God; let us draw near with a true heart in full assurance of faith, having our hearts sprinkled from an evil conscience, and our bodies washed with pure water." This is the glory of gospel worship and the beauty of it; whose consideration whilst the minds of men are diverted from, to look for beauty in the outward preparation of ceremonies, they lose the privilege purchased for believers by the blood of Christ. Instead, then, of furthering the beauty and comeliness of gospel worship, they are apt to lead men into a dangerous error and mistake,— namely, that the beauty and excellency of it consists in such things as, upon a due consideration, will appear to be mean and carnal, and far beneath those ceremonies and ordinances of the Old Testament, which yet, in comparison of the worship of the gospel, are called "worldly, carnal, beggarly," and are said to have "no glory."

Thirdly, They do not in the least tend unto the preservation of due *order* in the celebration of divine worship. All *order* consists in the due observation of *rule*. The rules of actions are either natural or of his special appointment. Both these take place in religious worship; the institutions or commands of Christ containing the substance thereof, in their observation principally consists the order of it. Whatever is of circumstance in the manner of its performance, not capable of especial determination, as emerging or arising only *occasionally*, upon the doing of that which is appointed at this or that time, in this or that place, and the like, is left unto the rule of *moral prudence*, in whose observation their order doth consist. But the superaddition of ceremonies necessarily belonging neither to the institutions of worship nor unto those circumstances whose disposal falls under the rule of moral prudence, neither doth nor can add any thing unto the due order of gospel worship; so that they are altogether needless and useless in the worship of God. Neither is this the whole of the inconvenience wherewith their observance is attended; for although they are not in particular and expressly in the Scripture forbidden, —for it was simply impossible that all instances wherein the wit of man might exercise its invention in such things should be reckoned up and condemned,—yet they fall directly under those severe prohibitions which God hath recorded to secure his worship from all such *additions* unto it, of what sort soever. Yea, the main design of the second precept is to forbid all making unto ourselves any such things in the worship of God, to add unto what he hath appointed; whereof an instance is given in that of *making and worshipping images,* the most common way that the sons of men were then prone to transgress by against the institutions of God. And this sense and understanding of the commandment is secured by those ensuing prohibitions against the adding any thing at all unto the commands of God in his worship: Deut. iv. 2, "Ye shall not add unto the word which I command you, neither shall ye diminish ought from it, that ye may keep the commandments of the LORD your God." Chap. xii. 32, "What thing soever I command you, observe to do it: thou shalt not add thereto, nor diminish from it;" chap. xvii. 3. To the same purpose were the places before mentioned, Matt. xv. 9, etc.; as also is that severe rule applied by our Saviour unto the additions of the Pharisees, verse 13, "Every plant, which my heavenly Father hath not planted, shall be rooted up."

And there is yet farther evidence contributed unto this intention of the command, from those places where such evils and corruptions as were particularly forbidden in the worship of God are condemned, not on the special account of their being so forbidden, but on that more general, of being introduced without any warrant from God's institutions or commands: Jer. vii. 31, "They have built the high places of Tophet, which is in the valley of the son of Hinnom, to burn their sons and their daughters in the fire; which I commanded not, neither came it into my heart." Chap. xix. 5, "They have built also the high places of Baal, to burn their sons with fire for burnt-offerings unto Baal, which I commanded not, nor spake it, neither came it into my mind." These things were particularly forbidden; but yet God here condemns them as coming under the general evil of making additions unto his commands,—doing that which he commanded not, nor did it ever enter into his heart.

The Papists say, indeed, that all *additions corrupting* the worship of God are forbidden, but such as further, adorn, and preserve it are not so; which implies a contradiction, for whereas every *addition* is principally a *corruption* because it is an addition, under which notion it is forbidden (and that in the worship of God which is forbidden is a corruption of it), there can be no such preserving, adorning addition, unless we allow a preserving and adorning corruption. Neither is it of more force which is pleaded by them, that the additions which they make belong not unto the *substance* of the worship of God, but unto the *circumstances* of it; for every circumstance observed religiously, or to be observed in the worship of God, is of the substance of it, as were all those ceremonious observances of the law, which had the same respect in the prohibitions of adding with the most weighty things whatsoever.

Q. 15. *Whence may it appear that the right and due observation of instituted worship is of great importance unto the glory of God, and of high concernment unto the souls of men?*

A. This is fully taught in the Scriptures; as, [1]God would never accept in any state of the church, before or since the fall, moral obedience without the observation of some institutions as trials, tokens, and pledges of that obedience. And [2]in their use and signification by his appointment they nearly concern the principal mysteries of his will and grace; and [3]by their celebration is he glorified in the world. And, therefore, [4]as he hath made blessed promises to his people, to grant them his presence and to bless them in their use; so, [5]being the tokens of the marriage relation that is between him and them, with respect unto them alone he calls himself "a jealous God," and [6]hath actually exercised signal severity towards the neglecters, corrupters, or abusers of them.—[1]Gen. ii. 16, 17, iv. 3–5, xvii. 9–11; Exod. xii. 21, xx.; Matt. xxviii. 19, 20, xxvi. 26, 27; Eph. iv. 11, 12; Rev. i. 13, xxi. 3.—[2]Gen. xvii. 10; Exod. xii. 23, 24; Rom. vi. 3–5; Matt. xxvi. 26–28; 1 Cor. xi. 23–26.—[3]See questions the eighth and ninth.—[4]Exod. xxix. 42, 43, 45; Deut. xiv. 23, 24; Ps. cxxxiii. 3; Matt. xviii. 20; Rev. xxi. 3.—[5]Exod. xx. 5; Deut. iv. 23, 24; Josh. xxiv. 19; Ezek. xvi.—[6]Lev. x. 1, 2; Num. xvi. 1–40; 1 Sam. ii. 27–34; 2 Sam. vi. 6, 7; 2 Chron. xxvi. 16–21; 1 Cor. xi. 30.

EXPLICATION.—For the most part, the instituted worship of God is neglected and despised in the world. Some are utterly regardless of it, supposing that if they attend, after their manner, unto moral obedience, that neither God nor themselves are much concerned in this matter of his worship. Others think the disposal and ordering of it to be so left unto men, that, as to the manner of its performance, they may do with it as it seems right in their own eyes; and some follow them therein, as willingly walking after their commandments, without any respect unto the will or authority of God. But the whole Scripture gives us utterly another account of this matter. The *honour* of God in this world, the *trial* of our faith and obedience, the *order* and beauty of the church, the *exaltation* of Christ in our professed subjection to him, and the *saving* of our souls in the ways of his appointment, are therein laid upon the due and right observance of instituted worship; and they who are negligent about these things, whatever they pretend, have no real respect unto any thing that is called religion. First, therefore, in every state and condition of the church, God hath given his ordinances of worship as the touchstone and trial of its faith and obedience; so that they by whom they are neglected do openly refuse to come unto God's trial. In the state of innocency, the trial of Adam's obedience, according to the law of nature, was in and by the institution of the *tree of life, and of the knowledge of good and evil:* Gen. ii. 16, 17, "And the LORD God commanded the man, saying, Of every tree of the garden thou mayest freely eat: but of the tree of the knowledge of good and evil, thou shalt not eat of it: for in the day that thou eatest thereof thou shalt surely die." This was the first institution of God, and it was given unto the church in the state of innocency and purity. And in our first parents' neglect of attending thereunto did they transgress the whole law of their creation, as failing in their duty in that which was appointed for their trial in the whole: Chap. iii. 11, "Hast thou eaten of the tree, whereof I commanded thee that thou shouldest not eat?" etc. And the church in his family after the fall, built upon the promise, was tried also in the matter of instituted worship. Nor was there any discovery of the wickedness of Cain, or approbation of the faith of Abel, until they came to be proved in their *sacrifices;* a new part of God's instituted worship, the first in the state and condition of sin and the fall whereinto it was brought: Gen. iv. 3–5, " In process of time it came to pass, that Cain brought of the fruit of the ground an offering unto the LORD. And Abel, he also brought of the firstlings of his flock and of the fat thereof. And the LORD had respect unto Abel and to his offering: but unto Cain and his offering he had not respect." The ground whereof the apostle declares, Heb. xi. 4, " By faith Abel offered unto God a more excellent sacrifice than Cain, by which he obtained witness that he was righteous, God testifying of his gifts." In the observation of that first institution, given to the church in the state of the fall, did Abel receive a testimony of his being justified and accepted with God. Afterward, when Abraham was called, and peculiarly separated to bear forth the name of God in the world, and to become the spring of the church for future ages, he had the institution of *circumcision* given him for the trial of his obedience; the law and condition whereof was, that he who observed it not should be esteemed an alien from the covenant of God, and be cut off from his people: Gen. xvii. 9–11, " God said unto Abraham, Thou shalt keep my covenant, thou, and thy seed after thee in their generations. This is my covenant, which ye shall keep, between me and you and thy seed after thee; Every man-child among you shall be circumcised." Verse 14, " And the uncircumcised man-child whose flesh of his foreskin is not circumcised, that soul shall be cut off from his people; he hath broken my covenant." And in like manner, so soon as ever his posterity were to be collected into a new church state and order, God gave the ordinance of the *passover:* Exod. xii. 24, " Ye shall observe this thing for an ordinance to thee and to thy sons for ever;" and that upon the same penalty with that of circumcision. To these he added many more on mount Sinai, Exod. xx.; all as the trials of their faith and obedience unto succeeding generations. How he hath dealt with his church under the New Testament we shall afterward declare. In no state or condition, then, of the church did God ever accept of moral obedience without the observation of some instituted worship, accommodated in his wisdom unto its various states and conditions; and not only so, but, as we have seen, he hath made the observation of them, according unto his mind and appointment, the means of the trial of men's whole obedience, and the rule of the acceptance or rejection of them. And so it continues at this day, whatever be the thoughts of men about the worship which at present he requires.

Besides, God hath appointed that his ordinances of worship shall be an *effectual means,* as to instruct us in the mysteries of his will and mind, so of communicating his love, mercy, and grace unto us; as also of that communion or intercourse with his holy Majesty, which he hath graciously granted unto us by Jesus Christ. And this, as it is sufficiently manifested in the Scriptures quoted in answer unto this question, so it is at large declared in the writings of those holy and good men who have explained the nature of gospel ordinances; and therefore, in particular, we need not here insist much in the farther proof of it. Thus, Abraham was instructed in the nature of the covenant of grace by circumcision, Gen. xvii. 10, which is often explained in the Old Testament by applying it in particular to *the grace of conversion,* called the " circumcision of the heart," Deut. x. 16, xxx. 6, Jer. iv. 4; as also in the New Testament, Col. ii. 11. And by the passover were the people taught not only the mercy of their present deliverance, Exod. xii. 23, 24, but also to look for the Lamb of God who was to take away the sin of the world, John i. 29, the true Passover of the people of God, which was sacrificed for them, 1 Cor. v. 7. How our insition or implanting into Christ is represented and signified by our baptism, the apostle declares, Rom. vi. 3–5; as also our communion with him in his death, by the supper of the Lord, Matt. xxvi. 26, 27, 1 Cor. xi. 24, 25. And all these graces which they teach they also exhibit, and are the means of the communication of them unto believers. Moreover, the experience of all believers who have conscientiously waited upon God in their due observance may be produced in the confirmation of it. The instruction, edification, consolation, spiritual strength, courage, and resolution, which they have received in and by them, hath been witnessed unto in their lives and ends; and they to whom these things are not of the greatest importance do but in vain pretend a regard unto God in any thing whatever.

Furthermore; God hath appointed our duty in the observation of his instituted worship to be the means of our *glorifying him* in the world. Nor can we otherwise give glory to God but as we own his authority over us, and yield obedience to what he requires at our hands. And what we do herein is principally evident in those duties which lie under the eye and observation of men. Some duties of obedience there are which the world neither doth nor can discern in believers; such are their faith, inward holiness, purity of heart, heavenly-mindedness, sincere mortification of indwelling sin; some whose performance ought to be hid from them, as personal prayer and alms, Matt. vi. 2–6; some there are which are very liable to misconstruction amongst men, as zeal in many of the actings of it; but this conscientious observation of instituted worship, and therein avowing our subjection unto the authority of God in Christ, is that which the world may see and take notice of, and that which, unless in case of persecution, ought not to be hid from them, and that which they can have no pretence of scandal at: and therefore hath God appointed that by this means and way we shall honour and glorify him in the world; which if we neglect, we do evidently cast off all regard unto his concernments in this world. Herein it is that we manifest ourselves not to be ashamed of the gospel of Christ, of him and his words, which he so indispensably requireth at our hands: Mark viii. 38, " For," saith he, " whosoever shall be ashamed of me and of my words in this adulterous and sinful generation; of him also shall the Son of man be ashamed, when he cometh in the glory of his Father with the holy angels." Hereby do we keep the commandments of Christ, as his " friends," John xv. 14, for these peculiarly are his commands (and if we suffer for them, then we do most properly suffer as Christians, which is our glory), that, 1 Pet. iv. 14–16, " If ye be reproached for the name of Christ, happy are ye; for the spirit of glory and of God resteth upon you: on their part he is evil spoken of, but on your part he is glorified. But let none of you suffer as a murderer, or as a thief, or as an evil-doer, or as a busy-body in other men's matters. Yet if any man suffer as a Christian, let him not be ashamed; but let him glorify God on this behalf." And a happy and a blessed thing it is to suffer for the observation of the special commands of Christ.

Farther; to encourage us in our duty, the holy faithful God hath given us many *great and precious promises* that he will graciously afford unto us his especial, sanctifying, blessing presence, in our attendance on his worship according to his appointment; for as he promised of old that he would make glorious "the place of his feet," or abode amongst his people, Isa. lx. 13,—that he would meet them in his sanctuary, the place of his worship, and there dwell amongst them, and bless them, and be their God, Exod. xxix. 42–45, Deut. xiv. 23, 24,—so the Lord Jesus Christ hath promised his presence to the same ends and purposes, unto all them that assemble together in his name for the observation of the worship which in the gospel he hath appointed: Matt. xviii. 20, "For where two or three are gathered together in my name, there am I in the midst of them." And therein is the tabernacle of God, his gracious dwelling-place, with men, Rev. xxi. 3. Now, when God offereth unto us his presence, his gracious, blessing, sanctifying, and saving presence, and that in and by promises which shall never fail, what unspeakable guilt must we needs contract upon our own souls if we neglect or despise the tenders of such grace!

But because we are apt to be slothful, and are slow of heart in admitting a due sense of spiritual things, that fall not in with the light and principles of nature, to stir us up unto a diligence in our attendance unto the will of God in this matter, he hath declared that he looks upon our obedience herein as our *whole loyalty* unto him in that *conjugal covenant* which he is pleased in Christ Jesus to take believers into with himself: Jer. iii. 14, 15, "Turn, O backsliding children, saith the LORD; for I am married unto you: and I will take you one of a city, and two of a family, and I will bring you unto Zion: and I will give you pastors according to mine heart, which shall feed you with knowledge and understanding." Coming unto Zion, in the worship of God, under the leading and conduct of pastors according to the heart of God, is our answering the relation wherein we stand unto him as he is married unto us; and thereupon he teacheth us that as a husband he is jealous of our discharge of our duty in this matter, accounting our neglect of his worship, or profanation of it by inventions and additions of our own, to be spiritual disloyalty, whoredom and adultery, which his soul abhorreth, for which he will cast off any church or people, and that for ever. See Exod. xx. 5; Deut. iv. 23, 24; Josh. xxiv. 19; Ezek. xvi. Whatever he will bear withal in his church, he will not bear with that which his jealousy is exercised about. If it transgress therein, he will give it a bill of divorce; which repudiated condition is the state of many churches in the world, however they please and boast themselves in their meretricious ornaments and practices.

To give yet farther strength unto all these considerations, that we may not only have rules and precepts, but examples also for our instruction, God hath given many signal instances of his *severity* against persons who, by ignorance, neglect, or regardlessness, have miscarried in not observing exactly his will and appointment in and about his worship.   This was the case of Nadab and Abihu, the sons of Aaron, Lev. x. 1, 2; of Korah, Dathan, and Abiram, Num. xvi. 1–40; of the sons of Eli,—a sin not to be " expiated with sacrifice nor offering for ever," 1 Sam. ii. 27–34, iii. 14; of Uzza in putting the ark into a cart, when he should have borne it upon his shoulders, 1 Chron. xiii. 7–10; of Uzziah the king in offering incense contrary to God's institution, that duty being appropriated unto the priests of the posterity of Aaron, 2 Chron. xxvi. 16–21.   These are sufficient intimations of what care and diligence we ought to use in attending unto what God hath appointed in his worship; and although now, under the New Testament, he doth not ordinarily proceed to the inflicting of temporal judgments in the like cases of neglect, yet he hath not wholly left us without instances of his putting forth tokens of his displeasure in temporal visitations on such miscarriages in his church: 1 Cor. xi. 30, "For this cause," saith the apostle, "many are weak and sickly among you, and many sleep."   From all which it appears of what concernment it is unto the glory of God, and the salvation of our own souls, to attend diligently unto our duty in the strict and sincere observation of the worship of the gospel; for he lets us know that now a more severe punishment is substituted against such transgressions in the room of that which he so visibly inflicted under the Old Testament, Heb. x. 25–29.

Q. 16. *Is there yet any other consideration that may stir up believers to a holy and religious care about the due observation of the institutions of the gospel?*

A. Yea; namely, that the great apostasy of the church in the last days, foretold in the Scripture, and which God threateneth to punish and revenge, consists principally in false worship and a departure from the institutions of Christ.—Rev. xiii. 4, 5, xvii. 1–5.

EXPLICATION.—That there is an apostasy of the church foretold in the book of the Revelation is acknowledged by all who with sincerity have inquired into the mind of God therein.   The state of things at this day, and for many ages past in the world, sufficiently confirm that persuasion.   And herein sundry things in general are obvious unto every sober consideration thereof:—

First, The horrible evils, troubles, and confusions that are to be brought into and upon the world thereby.

Secondly, The high guilt and provocation of God that is contained in it and doth accompany it.

Thirdly, The dreadful vengeance that God in his appointed time will take upon all the promoters and obstinate maintainers of it. These things are at large all of them foretold in the Revelation; and therein also the apostasy itself is set forth as the cause of all the plagues and destructions that, by the righteous judgment of God, are to be brought upon the world in these latter days. Now, as God doth earnestly call upon all that fear him not to intermeddle nor partake in the sins of the apostates, lest they should also partake in their judgments,—chap. xviii. 4, " I heard a voice from heaven, saying, Come out of her, my people, that ye be not partakers of her sins, and that ye receive not of her plagues;"—so he doth plainly declare wherein the apostasy and sin itself should principally consist; and that is in the corrupting and contaminating of the ordinances of his worship, or the introduction of false worship, joined with the persecution of them who refused to submit thereunto. For this cause is the sin itself set out under the name of " fornication" and " whoredom," and the church that maintains it is called " The mother of harlots," chap. xvii. 5. That by fornication and whoredom in the church, the adulterating of the worship of God, and the admission of false, self-invented worship in the room thereof, whereof God is jealous, is intended, the Scripture everywhere declares. It is easy, then, to gather of how great concernment unto us it is, especially in these latter days, wherein this so heinous and provoking sin is prevalent in the world, carefully to attend unto the safe, unerring rule of worship, and diligently to perform the duties that are required therein.

Q. 17. *Which are the principal institutions of the gospel to be observed in the worship of God?*

A. [1]The *calling*, gathering, and settling of churches, with their officers, as the seat and subject of all other solemn instituted worship; [2]*prayer*, with thanksgiving; [3]*singing* of psalms; [4]*preaching* the word; [5]administration of the *sacraments* of baptism and the supper of the Lord; [6]*discipline* and rule of the church collected and settled; most of which have also sundry particular duties relating unto them, and subservient unto their due observation.—[1]Matt. xxviii. 19, 20; Acts ii. 41, 42; 1 Cor. xii. 28; Eph. iv. 11, 12; Matt. xviii. 17, 18; 1 Cor. iv. 17, vii. 17; Acts xiv. 23; Titus i. 5; 1 Tim. iii. 15.— [2]1 Tim. ii. 1; Acts vi. 4, xiii. 2, 3.—[3]Eph. v. 19; Col. iii. 16.—[4]2 Tim. iv. 2; Acts ii. 42; 1 Cor. xiv. 3; Acts vi. 4; Heb. xiii. 7.—[5]Matt. xxviii. 19, xxvi. 26, 27; 1 Cor. xi. 23.—[6]Matt. xviii. 17–19; Rom. xii. 6–8; Rev. ii., iii.

EXPLICATION.—These things, being all of them afterward to be

spoken unto severally and apart, need not here any particular explication. They are the principal heads wherein gospel worship consisteth, and whereunto the particular duties of it may be reduced.

Q. 18. *Whereas sundry of these things are founded in the light
and law of nature, as requisite unto all solemn worship, and are,
moreover, commanded in the moral law, and explications of it in
the Old Testament, how do you look upon them as evangelical
institutions, to be observed principally on the authority of Jesus
Christ?*

A. Neither their general suitableness unto the principles of right
reason and the dictates of the light and law of nature, nor the practice of them in the worship of God under the Old Testament, does at
all hinder them from depending on the mere institution of Jesus
Christ, as to those especial ends of the glory of God in and by himself, and the edification of his church in the faith which is in him,
whereunto he hath appointed them, nor as unto that especial manner
of their performance which he requireth; in which respects they are
to be observed on the account of his authority and command only.
—Matt. xvii. 5, xxviii. 20; John xvi. 23, 24; Heb. iii. 4–6; Eph. i.
22, ii. 20–22; Heb. xii. 25.

EXPLICATION.—The principal thing we are to aim at, in the whole
worship of God, is the discharge of that duty which we owe to Jesus
Christ, the king and head of the church: Heb. iii. 6, "Christ as a
son over his own house, whose house are we." 1 Tim. iii. 15, "That
thou mayest know how thou oughtest to behave thyself in the house
of God, which is the church of the living God." This we cannot do unless we consider his authority as the formal reason and
cause of our observance of all that we do therein. If we perform
any thing in the worship of God on any other account, it is no part
of our obedience unto him, and so we can neither expect his grace
to assist us, nor have we his promise to accept us therein; for that
he hath annexed unto our doing and observing whatever he hath
commanded, and that because he hath commanded us: Matt. xxviii.
20, "Teaching them to observe all things whatsoever I have commanded you: and, lo, I am with you alway, even unto the end of
the world." This promised presence respects only the observance of
his commands. Some men are apt to look on this authority of
Christ as that which hath the least influence into what they do. If
in any of his institutions they find any thing that is suited or agreeable unto the light of nature,—as ecclesiastical societies, government
of the church, and the like, they say, are,—they suppose and contend
that that is the ground on which they are to be attended unto, and
so are to be regulated accordingly. The interposition of his autho-

rity they will allow only in the *sacraments*, which have no light in reason or nature; so desirous are some to have as little to do with Christ as they can, even in the things that concern the worship of God! But it would be somewhat strange, that if what the Lord Christ hath appointed in his church to be observed in particular, in an especial manner, for especial ends of his own, hath in the general nature of it an agreement with what in like cases the light of nature seems to direct unto, therefore, his authority is not to be considered as the sole immediate reason of our performance of it. But it is evident,—

First, That our Lord Jesus Christ being the king and head of his church, the lord over the house of God, nothing is to be done therein but with respect unto his authority: Matt. xvii. 5, "This is my beloved Son, in whom I am well pleased; hear ye him." Eph. iv. 15, 16, "Speaking the truth in love, may grow up into him in all things, which is the head, even Christ: from whom the whole body fitly joined together and compacted by that which every joint supplieth, according to the effectual working in the measure of every part, maketh increase of the body unto the edifying of itself in love." Chap. ii. 20–22, "Ye are built upon the foundation of the apostles and prophets, Jesus Christ himself being the chief corner-stone; in whom all the building fitly framed together groweth unto an holy temple in the Lord: in whom ye also are built together for a habitation of God through the Spirit."

Secondly, And that, therefore, the suitableness of any thing to right reason or the light of nature is no ground for a church-observation of it, unless it be also appointed and commanded in especial by Jesus Christ.

Thirdly, That being so appointed and commanded, it becomes an especial institution of his, and as such is to be observed. So that in all things that are done, or to be done, with respect unto the worship of God in the church, the authority of Christ is always principally to be considered, and every thing to be observed as commanded by him, without which consideration it hath no place in the worship of God.

Q. 19. *What is an instituted church of the gospel?*

A. A society of persons called out of the world, or their natural worldly state, by the administration of the word and Spirit, unto the obedience of the faith, or the knowledge and worship of God in Christ, joined together in a holy band, or by special agreement, for the exercise of the communion of saints, in the due observation of all the ordinances of the gospel.—Rom. i. 5, 6; 1 Cor. i. 2, iv. 15; Heb. iii. 1; James i. 18; Rev. i. 20; 1 Pet. ii. 5; Eph. ii. 20–22; 2 Cor. vi. 16–18.

EXPLICATION.—The church whose nature is here inquired after is not the *catholic* church of elect believers of all ages and seasons, from the beginning of the world unto the end thereof, nor of any one age, nor the *universality of professors* of the gospel; but a *particular church*, wherein, by the appointment of Christ, all the ordinances of the worship of God are to be observed and attended unto according to his will. For although it be required of them of whom a particular church is constituted that they be true believers, seeing that unless a man be born again he cannot enter into the kingdom of God, and so on that account they be members of the church catholic, as also that they make *visible profession* of faith and obedience unto Jesus Christ, yet moreover it is the will, command, and appointment of Christ, that they should be joined together in particular societies or churches, for the due observation of the ordinances of the gospel, which can alone be done in such assemblies. For as the members of the catholic church are not known unto one another merely on the account of that faith and union with Christ which make them so,—whence the whole society of them is, *as such, invisible* to the world, and themselves *visible* only on the account of their profession, and therefore cannot, merely as such, observe the ordinances of the gospel, which observation is their profession;—so the visible professors that are in the world, in any age, cannot at any time assemble together; which, from the nature of the thing itself, and the institution of Christ, is indispensably necessary for the celebration of sundry parts of that worship which he requires in his church: and therefore particular churches are themselves an ordinance of the New Testament, as the *national church* of the Jews was of old; for when God of old erected his worship, and enjoined the solemn observation of it, he also appointed a church as his institution for the due celebration of it. That was the people of Israel, solemnly taken into a church relation with him by covenant; wherein they took upon themselves to observe all the laws, and ordinances, and institutions of his worship: Exod. xx. 19, " Speak thou with us, and we will hear." Chap. xxiv. 3, " And Moses came and told the people all the words of the LORD, and all the judgments: and all the people answered with one voice, and said, All the words which the LORD hath said will we do." Deut. v. 27, " All that the LORD our God shall speak unto thee, we will hear it, and do it." And God accordingly appointed them ordinances to be observed by the whole congregation of them together, at the same time, in the same place: Exod. xxiii. 17, " Three times in the year all thy males shall appear before the Lord GOD." Deut. xvi. 16, " Three times in a year shall all thy males appear before the LORD thy God in the place which he shall choose."

Neither would God allow any stranger, any one not of the church so instituted by him, to celebrate any part of his instituted worship, until he was solemnly admitted into that church as a member thereof: Exod. xii. 47, 48, " All the congregation of Israel shall keep it. And when a stranger shall sojourn with thee, and will keep the passover to the LORD, let all his males be circumcised, and then let him come near and keep it; and he shall be as one that is born in the land: for no uncircumcised person shall eat thereof."

To the same end and purpose, when the knowledge of God was to be diffused all the world over by the preaching of the gospel, and believers of all nations under heaven were to be admitted unto the privilege of his worship, Eph. ii. 13–18, the national church of the Jews with all the ordinances of it being removed and taken away, the Lord Christ hath appointed *particular churches*, or united assemblies of believers, amongst and by whom he will have all his holy ordinances of worship celebrated. And this institution of his, at the first preaching of the gospel, was invariably and inviolably observed by all that took on them to be his disciples, without any one instance of questioning it to the contrary in the whole world, or the celebration of any ordinances of his worship amongst any persons, but only in such societies or particular churches. And there is sufficient evidence and warranty of this institution given us in the Scripture; for,—

First, They are appointed and approved by Christ: Matt. xviii. 15–20, " If thy brother shall trespass against thee, go and tell him his fault between thee and him alone: if he shall hear thee, thou hast gained thy brother. But if he will not hear thee, then take with thee one or two more, that in the mouth of two or three witnesses every word may be established. And if he shall neglect to hear them, tell it unto the church: but if he neglect to hear the church, let him be unto thee as a heathen man and a publican. Verily I say unto you, Whatsoever ye shall bind on earth shall be bound in heaven: and whatsoever ye shall loose on earth shall be loosed also in heaven. Again I say unto you, That if two of you shall agree on earth as touching any thing that they shall ask, it shall be done for them of my Father which is in heaven. For where two or three are gathered together in my name, there am I in the midst of them."

Such a church he supposeth and approveth as his disciples had relation unto, and as any one of them could have recourse unto, as a brother, in obedience to his commands and directions. This could not be the church of the Jews, neither in its whole body nor in any of its judicatories; for as at that time there was a solemn decree of excommunication against all and every one that should profess his name,—John ix. 22, "The Jews had agreed already, that if any man did confess that he was Christ, he should be put out of the synagogue,"—which was executed accordingly upon the man that was born blind, verse 34, which utterly disabled them from making any use of this direction, command, or institution of his for the present; so afterward the chief business of the rulers of those assemblies, from the highest court of their sanhedrim to the meanest judicatory in their synagogues, was to persecute them and bring them unto death: Matt. x. 17, "They will deliver you up to the councils, and they will scourge you in their synagogues;" John xv. 20, 21. And it is not likely that the Lord Christ would send his disciples for direction and satisfaction in the weighty matters of their obedience unto him, and mutual love towards one another, unto them with whom they neither had, nor could, nor ought to have, any thing to do withal; and if they were intended, they were all already made as heathens and publicans, being cast out by them for refusing to hear them in their blasphemies and persecutions of Christ himself. Such a society, also, is plainly intended as whereunto Christ promiseth his presence by his Spirit, and whose righteous sentences he takes upon himself to ratify and confirm in heaven.

Moreover, such a church doth he direct unto as with which his disciples were to have familiar, brotherly, constant converse and communion, with whom they were so to be joined in society as to be owned or rejected by them according to their judgment; as is apparent in the practice enjoined unto them, and without relation whereunto no duty here appointed could be performed. As, therefore, the very name of the church and nature of the thing bespeak a society, so it is evident that no society but that of a particular church of the gospel can be here intended.

Secondly, These churches he calls his "candlesticks," Rev. i. 20, in allusion unto the candlesticks of the temple; which, being an institution of the Old Testament, doth directly declare these churches to be so under the New. And this he speaks in reference unto those seven principal churches of Asia, every one of which was a candlestick or an institution of his own.

Thirdly, In pursuit of this appointment of Christ, and by his authority, the apostles, so soon as any were converted unto the faith at Jerusalem, although the old national church-state of the Jews was yet continued, gathered them into a *church* or society for celebration of the ordinances of the gospel: Acts ii. 41, 42, "They that gladly received his word were baptized. And they continued stedfastly in the apostles' doctrine and fellowship, and in breaking of bread, and in prayers." Verse 47, "The Lord added to the church daily such as should be saved." And this company is expressly called "The church at Jerusalem," Acts viii. 1. This church, thus called and collected out of the church of the Jews, was the rule and pattern of the disposing of all the disciples of Christ into church-societies, in obedience unto his command, throughout the world, Acts xi. 26, xiv. 23, 27.

Fourthly, They took care for the forming, completing, and establishing them in *order* according to his will, under the rule of them given and granted unto them by himself for that purpose; all in a steady pursuit of the commands of Christ: Acts xiv. 23, "They ordained them elders in every church;" Titus i. 5, "For this cause left I thee in Crete, that thou shouldest set in order the things that are wanting, and ordain elders in every city, as I had appointed thee;" 1 Cor. xii. 28; Eph. iv. 11, 12.

Fifthly, They do everywhere, in the name and authority of Christ, give unto these churches rules, directions, and precepts, for the due ordering of all things relating to the worship of God, and according to his mind, as we shall see afterward in particular; for,—

1. There is no charge given unto the officers, ministers, guides, or overseers that he hath appointed, but it is in reference unto the discharge of their duty in such churches. That ministers or officers are of Christ's appointment is expressly declared, Eph. iv. 11, 12, "He gave some, apostles; and some, prophets; and some, evangelists; and some, pastors and teachers; for the perfecting of the saints, for the work of the ministry, for the edifying of the body of Christ." 1 Cor. xii. 28, "God hath set some in the church, first apostles, secondarily prophets, thirdly teachers." These are of Christ's institution, but to what end? Why, as they were ordained in every church, Acts xiv. 23, Titus i. 5, so their whole charge is limited to the churches: Acts xx. 17, 18, 28, "He sent to Ephesus, and called the elders of the church, and said to them, Take heed therefore unto yourselves, and to all the flock, over the which the Holy Ghost hath made you overseers, to feed the church of God, which he hath purchased with his own blood;" 1 Pet. v. 1, 2, "The elders which are among you I exhort: feed the flock of God which is among you, taking the oversight thereof;" 1 Tim. iii. 15; Col. iv. 17, "And say to Archippus, Take heed to the ministry which thou hast received in the Lord, that thou fulfil it." They were the churches of Christ wherein they ministered; which Christ, appointing them to take care of, manifests to be his own institution and appointment. And this is fully declared, Rev. ii., iii., where all the dealings of Christ with his angels, or ministers, are about their behaviour and deportment among his candlesticks, each of them, the candlestick whereunto he was related, or the particular churches that they had care of and presided in, the candlesticks being no less of the institution of Christ than the angels. And

they were distinct particular churches, which had their distinct particular officers, whom he treateth distinctly withal about his institutions and worship, especially about that of the state of the churches themselves, and their constitution according to his mind.

2. There is no instruction, exhortation, or reproof given unto any of the disciples of Christ after his ascension, in any of the books of the New Testament, but as they were collected into and were members of such particular churches. This will be evidenced in the many instances of those duties that shall afterward be insisted on. And the Lord Christ hath not left that as a matter of liberty, choice, or conveniency, which he hath made the foundation of the due manner of the performance of all those duties whereby his disciples yield obedience unto his commands, to his glory in the world.

Sixthly, The principal writings of the apostles are *expressly* directed unto such churches, and all of them intentionally, 1 Cor. i. 1, 2; 2 Cor. i. 1; Gal. i. 1, 2; Phil. i. 1; Col. i. 1, 2, iv. 16; 1 Thess. i. 1; 2 Thess. i. 1; Eph. i. 1, compared with Acts xx. 17; 1 Pet. v. 2;— or unto particular persons, giving directions for their behaviour and duty in such churches, 1 Tim. iii. 15; Titus i. 5. So that the great care of the apostles was about these churches, as the principal institution of Christ, and that whereon the due observance of all his other commands doth depend. Of what nature or sort these churches were shall be afterward evinced; we here only manifest their institution by the authority of Christ.

Seventhly, Much of the writings of the apostles, in those epistles directed to those churches, consists in rules, precepts, instructions, and exhortations for the guidance and preservation of them in purity and order, with their continuance in a condition of due obedience unto the Lord Christ. To this end do they so fully and largely acquaint the rulers and members of them with their mutual duty in that especial relation wherein they stand to each other; as also all persons in particular in what is required of them by virtue of their membership in any particular society; as may be seen at large in sundry of Paul's epistles. And to give more strength hereunto, our Lord Jesus Christ, in the revelation that he made of his mind and will personally after his ascension into heaven, insisted principally about the condition, order, and preservation of particular churches, not taking notice of any of his disciples not belonging to them or joined with them. These he warns, reproves, instructs, threatens commands; all in order to their walking before him in the condition of particular churches, Rev. ii. and iii. at large.

Besides, as he hath appointed them to be the seat and subject of all his ordinances, having granted the right of them unto them alone, 1 Tim. iii. 15, intrusting them with the exercise of that authority which he puts forth in the rule of his disciples in this world, he hath also appointed the most holy institution of his supper to denote and express that union and communion which the members of each of these churches have by his ordinance among themselves: 1 Cor. x. 16, 17, " The cup of blessing which we bless, is it not the communion of the blood of Christ? The bread which we break, is it not the communion of the body of Christ? For we being many are one bread, and one body: for we arc all partakers of that one bread." And also he gives out unto them the gifts and graces of his Spirit, to make every one of them meet for and useful in that place which he holds in such churches; as the apostle discourseth at large, 1 Cor. xii. 15–26; Col. ii. 19; Eph. iv. 16. It is manifest, then, that no ordinance of Christ is appointed to be observed by his disciples, no communication of the gifts of the Holy Ghost is promised to them, no especial duty is required of them, but with respect unto these churches of his institution.

In the answer to this question four things are declared tending to the explication of the nature of a particular church or churches: —1. The *subject-matter* of them, or the persons whereof such a church doth or ought to consist. 2. The *means* whereby they are brought into a condition capable of such an estate, or qualified for it. 3. The *general ends* of their calling. 4. The *especial means* whereby they are constituted a church; which last will be spoken unto in the next question.

For the first, all men are by nature the children of wrath, and do belong unto the world, which is the kingdom of Satan, and are under the power of darkness, as the Scripture everywhere declares. In this state men are not subjects of the kingdom of Christ, nor meet to become members of his church. Out of this condition they cannot deliver themselves. They have neither will unto it nor power for it; but they are called out of it. This calling is that which effectually delivers them from the kingdom of Satan, and translates them into the kingdom of Christ. And this work or effect, the Scripture, on several accounts, variously expresseth; sometimes by *regeneration*, or a new birth; sometimes by *conversion*, or turning unto God; sometimes by *vivification*, or quickening from the dead; sometimes by *illumination*, or opening of the eyes of the blind;—all which arc carried on by *sanctification* in holiness, and attended with justification and adoption. And as these are all distinct in themselves, having several formal reasons of them, so they all concur to complete that effectual vocation or calling that is required to constitute persons members of the church. For besides that this is signified by the typical holiness of the church of old, into the room whereof real holiness was to succeed under the New Testament,—Exod. xix. 6; Ps.

xxiv. 3–6, xv. 1, 2; Isa. xxxv. 8, 9, liv. 13, 14, lx. 21; 1 Pet. ii. 9,—our Lord Jesus Christ hath laid it down as an everlasting rule, that " except a man be born again, he cannot enter into the kingdom of God," John iii. 3, 5, requiring regeneration as an indispensable condition in a member of his church, a subject of his kingdom : for his temple is now to be built of living stones, 1 Pet. ii. 5,—men spiritually and savingly quickened from their death in sin, and by the Holy Ghost, whereof they are partakers, made a meet habitation of God, Eph. ii. 21, 22; 1 Cor. iii. 16; 2 Cor. vi. 16; which receiving vital supplies from Christ its head, increaseth in faith and holiness, edifying itself in love, Eph. iv. 15, 16. And as the apostles in their writings do ascribe unto all the churches, and the members of them, a participation in this effectual vocation, affirming that they are " saints, called, sanctified, justified," and accepted with God in Christ,—Rom. i. 5, 6; 1 Cor. i. 2, iv. 15; Heb. iii. 1; James i. 18; 1 Pet. ii. 5; 2 Cor. vi. 17, 18; 1 Cor. vi. 11,—so many of the duties that are required of them in that relation and condition are such as none can perform unto the glory of God, their own benefit, and the edification of others (the ends of all obedience), unless they are partakers of this effectual calling, 1 Cor. x. 16, 17, xii. 12; Eph. iv. 16. Add hereunto that these churches, and the members of them, are not only commanded to separate themselves, as to their worship of God, from the world,—that is, men in their worldly state and condition,—but are also required, when any amongst them transgress against the rules and laws of this holy calling above described, to cast them out of their society and communion, 1 Cor. v. 13. From all which it appears who are the subject-matter of these churches of Christ; as also, secondly, the means whereby they come to be so,—namely, the administration of the Spirit and word of Christ; and, thirdly, the general ends of their calling, which are all spoken to in this answer.

Q. 20. *By what means do persons so called become a church of Christ?*

A. They are constituted a church, and interested in the rights, power, and privileges of a gospel church, by the will, promise, authority, and law of Jesus Christ, upon their own voluntary consent and engagement to walk together in the due subjection of their souls and consciences unto his authority, as their king, priest, and prophet, and in a holy observation of all his commands, ordinances, and appointments.—Matt. xviii. 20, xxviii. 19, 20; Acts ii. 41, 42; Exod. xxiv. 3; Deut. v. 27; Ps. cx. 3; Isa. xliv. 5, lix. 21; Eph. iv. 7–10; 2 Cor. viii. 5.

EXPLICATION.—That the Lord Christ hath constituted such a church-state as that which we inquire about hath been proved already. Unto a church so constituted he hath also, by his word and promise, annexed all those privileges and powers which we find a church to be intrusted withal. This he hath done by the standing and unalterable law of the gospel, which is the charter of their spiritual society and incorporation. Neither are nor can any persons be interested in the rights of a church any otherwise but by virtue of this law and constitution. This, therefore, is first to be laid down, that the sole moral foundation of that church-state which we inquire after is laid in the word, law, and appointment of Christ. He alone hath authority to erect such a society; he is the builder of this house as well as the lord over it, Heb. iii. 3–6. Neither without it can all the authority of men in the world appoint such a state or erect a church; and all acceptable actings of men herein are no other but acts of pure obedience unto Christ.

Furthermore, we have declared that the Lord Christ, by the dispensation of his word and Spirit, doth prepare and fit men to be subjects of his kingdom, members of his church. The work of sending forth the means of the conversion of the souls of men, of translating them from the power of darkness into light, he hath taken upon himself, and doth effectually accomplish it in every generation. And by this means he builds his church, for unto all persons so called he gives command that they shall do and observe whatever he hath appointed them to do, Matt. xxviii. 20; in particular, that they profess their subjection to him, and their obedience, in joining themselves in that state wherein they may be enabled to observe all his other laws and institutions, with the whole worship of God required therein. Being converted unto God by his word and Spirit, they are to consider how they may now obey the Lord Christ in all things. Amongst his commands, this of joining themselves in church-societies, wherein he hath promised his presence with them, Matt. xviii. 20,—that is, to dwell amongst them by his word and Spirit, Isa. lix. 21,—is the very first. This, by virtue of that command and promise of his, they are warranted and enabled to do; nor do they need any other warrant. The authority of Christ is sufficient to bear men out in the discharge of their duty to him. Being then made willing and ready in the day of his power, Ps. cx. 3, they consent, choose, and agree to walk together in the observation of all his commands. And hereby do they become a church; for their becoming a church is an act of their willing obedience unto Christ. This is an act of their wills, guided by rule; for this also is necessary, that they proceed herein according to the rules of his appointment, afterward to be unfolded. And herein, upon their obedience unto the commands of Christ, and faith in his promises, do believers, by virtue of his law and constitution, become a gospel church, and are really and truly interested in all the power, rights, and privileges that are granted unto any church of Christ; for in this obedience they do these two things, which alone he requires in any persons for the obtaining of an interest in these privileges:—First, They *confess* him, his person, his authority, his law, his grace; secondly, They take upon themselves the observance of all his commands.

Thus did God take the children of Israel into a church-state of old. He proposed unto them the church-obedience that he required of them, and they voluntarily and freely took upon themselves the performance of it: Exod. xxiv. 3, " And Moses came and told the people all the words of the LORD, and all the judgments: and all the people answered with one voice, and said, All the words which the LORD hath said will we do:" so Deut. v. 27. And hereby they had their solemn admission into their church-state and relation unto God. And the like course they took whenever there was need of renewing their engagements: Josh. xxiv. 18–22, " And the people said, We will serve the LORD; for he is our God. And Joshua said unto the people, Ye are witnesses against yourselves that ye have chosen the LORD, to serve him. And they said, We are witnesses." This was the covenant that was between God and that people, which was solemnly renewed so often as the church was eminently reformed. Now, although the outward solemnity and ceremonies of this covenant were peculiar unto that people, yet as to the substance and nature of it, in a sacred consent for the performance of all those duties towards God and one another which the nature and edification of a church do require, it belongs to every church as such, even under the gospel.

And this is the way whereby believers, or the disciples of Christ, do enter into this state, the formal constituting cause of any church, this account doth the apostle give of the churches of the Macedonians: 2 Cor. viii. 5, " And this they did, not as we hoped, but first gave their own selves to the Lord, and unto us by the will of God," before the performance of other duties; and in order thereunto, they first gave themselves to the Lord Jesus Christ, or took upon themselves the observance of his commands and institutions, which is the intendment of that expression. Among these commands one was, that they should give up themselves to the apostles' doctrine, rule, and government, in the order by Christ prescribed,—that is, in church-order. This, therefore, they did by *the will of God*, according to his will and appointment. This description doth the apostle give of the way whereby the believers of Macedonia were brought into churches. It was by their own obedience unto the will of God; consenting, agreeing, and taking upon themselves the observation of all the commands and institutions of Christ, according to the direction and guidance of the apostles. So did the believers at Jerusalem, Acts ii. 41, 42. Being converted by the word, and making profession of that conversion in their baptism, they gave up themselves to a steadfast continuance in the observation of all other ordinances of the gospel.

Besides, the church is a house, a temple,—the " house of God," 1 Tim. iii. 15; the " house of Christ," Heb. iii. 6; the " temple of the Lord,"Eph. ii. 21, 22. Believers, singly considered, are "stones, living stones," 1 Pet. ii. 5. Now, how shall these " living stones" come to be a house, a temple? Can it be by occasional occurrences, civil cohabitation in political precincts, usage, or custom of assembling for some parts of worship in any place? These things will never frame them into a house or temple. This can be no otherwise done but by their own voluntary consent and disposition: Eph. ii. 19–22, " Ye are fellow-citizens with the saints, and of the household of God; and are built upon the foundation of the apostles and prophets, Jesus Christ himself being the chief corner-stone; in whom all the building fitly framed together groweth unto a holy temple in the Lord: in whom ye also are builded together for an habitation of God through the Spirit." Chap. iv. 16, " From whom the whole body fitly joined together and compacted by that which every joint supplieth, according to the effectual working in the measure of every part, maketh increase of the body unto the edifying of itself in love." From these and sundry other places it is manifest that the way and means of believers' coalition into a church-state is their own obedience of faith, acting itself in a joint voluntary consent to walk together in a holy observation of the commands of Christ; whence the being and union of a particular church is given unto any convenient number of them by his law and constitution.

Q. 21. *Seeing the church is a society or spiritual incorporation of persons under rule, government, or discipline, declare who or what are the rulers, governors, or officers therein under Jesus Christ?*

A. They have been of two sorts:—1. *Extraordinary*, appointed for a season only; and, 2. *Ordinary*, to continue unto the end of the world.

Q. 22. *Who are the extraordinary officers, or rulers, or ministers of the church, appointed to serve the Lord Jesus Christ therein for a season only?*

A. [1]The apostles of our Lord Jesus Christ, with [2]the evangelists and prophets, endowed with extraordinary gifts of the Holy Ghost, associated with them and employed by them in their works and

ministry.—[1]Matt. x. 2–4; Acts i. 26; 1 Cor. xii. 28; Eph. iv. 11.—
[2]Luke x. 1; 2 Tim. iv. 5; Titus i. 5; Acts xi. 27, 28, xxi. 9–11;
2 Cor. i. 1.

EXPLICATION.—That the church is a spiritual corporation, attended
with rule and government, is evident from the nature of the thing
itself and testimonies of Scripture. Only, as the kingdom of Christ
is not of this world or worldly, so this rule and government of the
church is not merely external and secular, but spiritual. Neither
doth this rule at all belong unto it merely as *materially* considered,
in men yielding obedience unto the call which is the foundation of
the church; nor *absolutely*, as it is formally constituted a church by
the consent and agreement described; but, moreover, it is required
that it be *organically* complete, with officers or rulers. Now, to the
constitution of such a society or corporation there is required,—

First, That the persons whereof it is constituted do *consent* together into it for the attaining of the ends which they design. Without this no society of any kind can exist. This is the form of men's
coalescency into societies; and that there is in the church such
consent and agreement hath been showed.

Secondly, That there be rules or laws for the guidance and direction of all the members of the society, in order to their pursuit of
the proper ends of it. That such rules or laws are given and prescribed by the Lord Christ unto the church will afterward appear, in
our consideration of them in particular; so that the church is a society of men walking according unto rule or law for the attaining of
the ends of the society.

Thirdly, That there be authority instituted to see to the due observation of these rules and laws of the society, which consists in
this:—1. That some be appointed to rule and govern in the church;
2. Others to obey and be ruled or governed; both according to the
laws of the society, and not otherwise. And both these are eminently
found in this church-state, as we shall see in the ensuing questions,
with their answers and explications.

Now, that these officers or rulers should be of two sorts, both the
nature of the thing itself required and so hath our Lord Jesus Christ
appointed; for when the church was first to be called, gathered, and
erected, it was necessary that some persons should be extraordinarily
employed in that work, for ordinary officers antecedent unto the
calling and erection of the church there could be none. And, therefore, these persons were in an extraordinary manner endowed with
all that power which afterward was to reside in the churches themselves; and, moreover, with that which was peculiarly needful unto
the discharge and performance of that special duty and work that
they were appointed unto. But when churches were called, gathered,

erected, and settled for continuance, there was need of officers suited to their state and condition, called in an ordinary way,—that is, in a way appointed for continuance unto the end of the world; and to be employed in the ordinary work of the church,—that is, the duties of it which were constantly incumbent on it by virtue of the command and appointment of Christ.

Q. 23. *Who are the ordinary officers or ministers of Christ in the church, to be always continued therein?*

A. Those whom the Scripture calls pastors and teachers, bishops, elders, and guides.—Acts xiv. 23, xx. 17, 28; 1 Cor. xii. 28; Eph. iv. 11; Phil. i. 1; 1 Tim. iii. 1, 2, v. 17; Titus i. 5, 7; Heb. xiii. 7, 17; 1 Pet. v. 1.

EXPLICATION.—Several names are, on several accounts, partly designing their authority, partly their duty, and partly the manner of their discharge thereof, assigned in the Scripture to the ordinary ministers of the churches. Sometimes they are called " pastors and teachers," Eph. iv. 11 ; 1 Cor. xii. 28;—sometimes " bishops" or " overseers," Phil. i. 1; Acts xx. 28;—sometimes " elders," Titus i. 5; 1 Pet. v. 1; 1 Tim. v. 17; Acts xiv. 23, xx. 17;—sometimes "guides," Heb. xiii. 7, 17. By all which names, and sundry others whereby they are expressed, the same sort, order, and degree of persons is intended. Nor is any one of these names applied or accommodated unto any, but all the rest are also in like manner; so that he who is a pastor or a teacher is also a bishop or overseer, a presbyter or elder, a guide or ruler, a minister, a servant of the church for the Lord's sake. And of all other names assigned to the ministers of the church, that of bishop can least of all be thought to have designed any special order or degree of pre-eminence amongst them; for whereas it is but four times, or in four places, used in the New Testament as denoting any officers of the church, in each of them it is manifest that those expressed by the other names of elders and ministers are intended. So, Acts xx. 28, the bishops are the elders of the particular church of Ephesus, verse 17. Phil. i. 1, there were many bishops in that one particular church, who had only deacons joined with them; that is, they were the elders of it, Titus i. 7. The bishops were the elders to be ordained, verse 5; which persons are also directly intended, 1 Tim. iii. 2, as is evident from the coincidence of the directions given by the apostle about them, and the immediate adjoining of deacons unto them, verse 8; so that no name could be fixed on with less probability, to assert from it a special supreme order or degree of men in the ministry, than this of bishops. Neither is there any mention in any place of Scripture of any such pre-eminence of one sort of these church-officers or ministers over another, not in particular in those places where the officers of the church are in an especial manner enumerated, as 1 Cor. xii. 28; Eph. iv. 11; Rom. xii. 5–8.   Nor is there any mention of any special office that should be peculiar unto such officers; or of any gifts or qualifications that should be required in them; or of any special way of calling or setting apart to their office; nor of any kind of church that they should relate unto, different from the churches that other elders or pastors do minister in; nor of any special rule or direction for their trial; nor any commands for obedience unto them but what are common to all ministers of the churches of Christ duly discharging their trust and performing their duty; no intimation is given unto either elders or ministers to obey them, or directions how to respect them, nor unto them how to behave themselves towards them: but all these things are spoken and delivered promiscuously and equally concerning all ministers of the gospel.   It is evident, then, that these appellations do not belong unto one sort of ministers, not one more than another.   And for what is pleaded by some from the example of Timothy and Titus, it is said that when any persons can prove themselves to be evangelists, 2 Tim. iv. 5, to be called unto their office upon antecedent prophecy, 1 Tim. i. 18, and to be sent by the apostles, and in an especial manner to be directed by them in some employment for a season, which they are not ordinarily to attend unto, Titus i. 5, iii. 12, it will be granted that they have another duty and office committed unto them than those who are only bishops or elders in the Scripture.

Q. 24. *What are the principal differences between these two sorts of officers or rulers in the church, extraordinary and ordinary?*

A. [1]The former were called to their office immediately by Jesus Christ in his own person, or revelation made by the Holy Ghost in his name to that purpose; the latter by the suffrage, choice, and appointment of the church itself.   [2]The former, both in their office and work, were independent on, and antecedent unto, all or any churches, whose calling and gathering depended on their office as its consequent and effect; the latter, in both, consequent unto the calling, gathering, and constituting of the churches themselves, as an effect thereof, in their tendency unto completeness and perfection. [3]The authority of the former being communicated unto them immediately by Jesus Christ, without any intervenient actings of any church, extended itself equally unto all churches whatever; that of the latter being derived unto them from Christ by the election and designation of the church, is in the exercise of it confined unto that church wherein and whereby it is so derived unto them.   [4]They differ also in the gifts, which were suited unto their several distinct

works and employments.—¹Matt. x. 1; Luke x. 1; Gal. i. 1; Acts i.
26, vi. 3, xiv. 23.—²John xx. 21–23; Gal. i. 1; Eph. ii. 20; Rev.
xxi. 14; Acts xiv. 23; Titus i. 5, 7.—³Matt. xxviii. 18–20; 2 Cor.
xi. 28; Acts xx. 28; 1 Pet. v. 2; Col. iv. 17.—⁴1 Cor. xii. 28–33.
The answer hereunto is such as needs no farther explication.

Q. 25. *What is required unto the due constitution of an elder,
pastor, or teacher of the church?*

A. ¹That he be furnished with the gifts of the Holy Spirit for the
edification of the church, and the evangelical discharge of the work
of the ministry; ²that he be unblamable, holy, and exemplary in
his conversation; ³that he have a willing mind to give up himself
unto the Lord in the work of the ministry; ⁴that he be called and
chosen by the suffrage and consent of the church; ⁵that he be
solemnly set apart by fasting and prayer, and imposition of hands,
unto his work and ministry.—¹Eph. iv. 7, 8, 11–13.—²Titus i. 7–9;
1 Tim. iii. 2–7.—³1 Pet. v. 1–3.—⁴Acts xiv. 23.—⁵Acts xiii. 2, 3;
1 Tim. iv. 14, v. 22.

EXPLICATION.—Five things are here said to be required unto the
due and solemn constitution of a minister, guide, elder, pastor, or
teacher of the church, which, as they do all equally belong unto
the essence of the call, so they are all indispensably necessary unto
him that would be accounted to have taken that office upon him
according to the mind of Christ; and they are plainly expressed in
the Scripture.

The first is, That they be furnished with the *gifts* of the Holy
Ghost for the discharge of the ministry. The communication of
the gifts of the Holy Ghost is the foundation of the ministry, as
the apostle declares, Eph. iv. 7, 8, 11–13, " But unto every one of
us is given grace according to the measure of the gift of Christ.
Wherefore he saith, When he ascended up on high, he led captivity
captive, and gave gifts unto men. And he gave some, apostles; and
some, prophets; and some, evangelists; and some, pastors and teachers;
for the perfecting of the saints, for the work of the ministry, for the edifying of the body of Christ: till we all come in the unity of the faith,
and of the knowledge of the Son of God, unto a perfect man." And
if this were not continued, if the Lord Christ did not continue to
give gifts unto men for that end, the ministry must and would cease
in the church, and all church order and administrations thereon.
The exercise, also, of the gifts is required in all them that are called
unto sacred offices: 1 Tim. iv. 14, " Neglect not the gift that is in
thee." Hence, persons destitute of these gifts of the Spirit, as they
cannot in a due manner discharge any one duty of the ministry, so,
wanting an interest in that which is the foundation of the office, are

not esteemed of God as ministers at all, whatever their outward call may be: Hos. iv. 6, "Because thou hast rejected knowledge, I will also reject thee, that thou shalt be no priest to me."

Secondly, Their unblamableness and holiness of conversation is previously required in them that are to be set apart unto the ministry. This the apostle expressly declares, and lays down many particular instances whereby it is to be tried: Tit. i. 7–9, "For a bishop must be blameless, as the steward of God; not self-willed, not soon angry, not given to wine, no striker, not given to filthy lucre; but a lover of hospitality, a lover of good men, sober, just, holy, temperate; holding fast the faithful word as he hath been taught, that he may be able by sound doctrine both to exhort and convince the gainsayers." 1 Tim. iii. 2–7, "A bishop must be blameless, the husband of one wife, vigilant, sober, of good behaviour, given to hospitality, apt to teach; not given to wine, no striker, not greedy of filthy lucre; but patient, not a brawler, not covetous; one that ruleth well his own house, having his children in subjection with all gravity; (for if a man know not how to rule his own house, how shall he take care of the church of God?) not a novice, lest being lifted up with pride he fall into the condemnation of the devil. Moreover he must have a good report of them which are without; lest he fall into reproach and the snare of the devil." Not that the particulars here mentioned by the apostle are only to be considered in the conversation of the person to be called to the ministry, but that, in a universal holy conversation, these things he requires that he should be eminent in amongst believers, as those which have an especial respect to his work and office. And a failure in any of them is a just cause or reason to debar any person from obtaining a part and lot in this matter; for whereas the especial end of the ministry is to promote and further faith and holiness in the church by the edification of it, how unreasonable a thing would it be if men should be admitted unto the work of it who in their own persons were strangers both unto faith and holiness! And herein are the elders of the churches seriously to exercise themselves unto God, that they may be an example unto the flock, in a universal labouring after conformity in their lives unto the great bishop and pastor of the church, our Lord Jesus Christ.

Thirdly, It is required that such a person have a *willing mind* to give up himself unto God in this work: 1 Pet. v. 1–3, "The elders which are among you, I exhort: feed the flock of God which is among you, taking the oversight thereof, not by constraint, but willingly; not for filthy lucre, but of a ready mind; neither as being lords over God's heritage, but being ensamples to the flock." Willingness and readiness of mind are the things here required as a previous qualification unto any man's susception of this office; and two things doth the apostle declare to be contrary hereunto:—

1. The undertaking of it by *constraint*, which compriseth every antecedent external impression upon the mind of the undertaker; such are personal outward necessities, compulsions of friends and relations, want of other ways of subsistence in the world,—all which, and the like, are condemned by the apostle as bringing some constraint on the mind, which on other accounts ought to be free and willing; as also, all tergiversation and backwardness in persons duly qualified and called, on the consideration of difficulties, temptations, straits, persecutions, is here condemned.

2. An eye and regard unto *filthy lucre* or profit in the world is proposed as opposite unto the readiness of mind which is required in them that are called to this work. An aim in this employment for men by it to advantage themselves in the outward things of this world,—without which it is evident that the whole work and office would lie neglected by the most of them who now would be accounted partakers of it,—is openly here condemned by the apostle.

Fourthly, *Election*, by the suffrage and consent of the church, is required unto the calling of a pastor or teacher; so that without it formally or virtually given or obtained, the call, however otherwise carried on or solemnized, is irregular and defective. There are but two places in the New Testament where there is mention of the manner whereby any are called in an ordinary way unto any ministry in the church, and in both of them there is mention of their election by the community of the church; and in both of them the apostles themselves presided with a fulness of church-power, and yet would not deprive the churches of that which was their liberty and privilege. The first of these is Acts vi., where all the apostles together, to give a rule unto the future proceeding of all churches in the constitution of officers amongst them, do appoint the multitude of the disciples, or community of the church, to look out from among themselves, or to choose the persons that were to be set apart therein unto their office; which they did accordingly: Verses 2, 3, 5, "Then the twelve called the multitude of the disciples unto them, and said, It is not reason that we should leave the word of God, and serve tables. Wherefore, brethren, look ye out among you seven men of honest report, full of the Holy Ghost and wisdom. And the saying pleased the whole multitude: and they chose Stephen," etc. This was done when only deacons were to be ordained, in whom the interest and concernment of the church is not to be compared with that which it hath in its pastors, teachers, and elders. The same is mentioned again, Acts xiv. 23, where Paul and Barnabas are said to ordain elders in the churches by their election and suffrage; for the word there used will admit of no other sense, however it be ambiguously expressed in our translation. Neither can any instance be given of the use of that word, applied unto the communication of any office or power to any person or persons in an assembly, wherein it denoteth any other action but the suffrage of the multitude; and this it doth constantly in all writers in the Greek tongue. And hence it was that this right and privilege of the church, in choosing of those who are to be set over them in the work of the Lord, was a long time preserved inviolate in the primitive churches, as the ancients do abundantly testify. Yea, the show and appearance of it could never be utterly thrust out of the world, but is still retained in those churches which yet reject the thing itself. And this institution of our Lord Jesus Christ by his apostles is suited to the nature of the church, and of the authority that he hath appointed to abide therein; for, as we have showed before, persons become a church by their own voluntary consent. Christ makes his subjects willing, not slaves; his rule over them is by his grace in their own wills, and he will have them every way free in their obedience. A church-state is an estate of absolute liberty under Christ, not for men to do what they will, but for men to do their duty freely, without compulsion. Now, nothing is more contrary to this liberty than to have their guides, rulers, and overseers imposed on them without their consent. Besides, the body of the church is obliged to discharge its duty towards Christ in every institution of his; which herein they cannot, if they have not their free consent in the choice of their pastors or elders, but are considered as mute persons or brute creatures. Neither is there any other ordinary way of communicating authority unto any in the church, but by the voluntary submission and subjection of the church itself unto them ; for as all other imaginable ways may fail, and have done so, where they have been trusted unto, so they are irrational and unscriptural as to their being a means of the delegation of any power whatever.

Fifthly, Unto this election succeeds the solemn setting apart of them that are chosen by the church unto this work and ministry, by fasting, prayer, and imposition of the hands of the presbytery, before constituted in the church wherein any person is so to be set apart.

Q. 26. *May a person be called to, or be employed in, a part only of the office or work of the ministry; or may he hold the relation and exercise the duty of an elder or minister unto more churches than one at the same time?*

A. Neither of these has either warrant or precedent in the Scripture; nor is the first of them consistent with the authority of the ministry, nor the latter with the duty thereof, nor either of them with the nature of that relation which is between the elders and the church.—Acts. xiv. 23; 1 Pet. v. 2; Acts xx. 28.

EXPLICATION.—There are two parts of this question and answer, to be spoken unto severally. The first is concerning a person to be called or employed in any church in a part only of the office or work of the ministry;—as suppose a man should be called or chosen by the church to administer the sacraments, but not to attend to the work of preaching, or unto the rule or guidance of the church; or, in like manner, unto any other part or parcel of the work of the ministry, with an exemption of other duties from his charge or care. If this be done by consent and agreement, for any time or season, it is unwarrantable and disorderly (what may be done occasionally upon an emergency, or in case of weakness or disability befalling any elder as to the discharge of any part of his duty, is not here inquired after); for,—

First, If the person so called or employed have received gifts fitting him for the whole work of the ministry, the exercise of them is not to be restrained by any consent or agreement, seeing they are given for the edification of the church to be traded withal: 1 Cor. xii. 7, "The manifestation of the Spirit is given to every man to profit withal;" and this he who hath received such gifts is bound to attend unto and pursue.

Secondly, If he have not received such gifts as completely to enable him unto the discharge of the whole work of the ministry in the church wherein he is to administer, it is not lawful for the church to call him unto that work wherein the Lord Christ hath not gone before them in qualifying him for it; yea, to do so would be most irregular, for the whole power of the church consists in its attendance unto the rule given unto it: and therefore the office and work of the ministry being constituted by the law of Christ, it is not in the power of the church to enlarge or straiten the power or duty of any one that is called unto the office thereof. Neither can or ought any person that is called unto the work of the ministry to give his consent to the restraint of the exercise of that gift that he hath received, in a due and orderly manner, nor to the abridgment of the authority which the Lord Christ hath committed unto the ministers of the gospel.

As it is incumbent upon them to take care to preserve their whole authority, and to discharge their whole duty, so [it follows] that arbitrary constitutions of this nature are irregular, and would bring in confusion into churches.

The second part of the question is concerning the relation of the same person to more churches than one at the same time, and his undertaking to discharge the duty of his relation unto them, as an elder or minister. And this also is irregular and unwarrantable. Now, a man may hold the relation of an elder, pastor, or minister unto more churches than one, two ways:—1. Formally and directly, by an equal formal interest in them, undertaking the pastoral charge equally and alike of them, being called alike to them, and accepting of such a relation. 2. Virtually, when, by virtue of his relation unto one church, he puts forth his power or authority in ministerial acts in or towards another. The first way is unlawful, and destructive both of the office and duty of a pastor; for as elders are ordained in and unto the churches respectively that they are to take care of, Acts xiv. 23, Titus i. 5, and their office-power consists in a relation unto the church that they are set over, so they are commanded to attend unto the service of the churches wherein and whereunto they are so ordained, Acts xx. 28, 1 Pet. v. 2, and that with all diligence, care, and watchfulness, as those that must give an account, Heb. xiii. 17, which no man is able to do towards more churches than one, the same duty being at all times to be performed towards all. And because the whole authority of the elders, pastors, or bishops of churches, is ministerial, 1 Cor. iv. 1, consisting in a power of acting upon the command of Christ, they are bound in their own persons to the discharge of their duty and office, without the least pretence of authority to delegate another, or others, to act their part or to do their duty; which would be an effect of autocratorical authority, and not of obedience or ministry. The latter way, also, of relation unto many churches is unwarrantable: for,—1. It hath no *warrant* in the Scripture; no law nor constitution of Christ or his apostles can be produced to give it countenance; but elders were ordained to their own churches, and commanded to attend unto them. 2. No *rule* is given unto any elders how they should behave themselves in reference unto more churches than one, in the exercise of their ministerial power, as there are rules given unto every one for the discharge of that duty in the church whereunto he is related. 3. There is no *example* to give it countenance recorded in the Scripture. 4. The authority to be put forth hath no foundation. (1.) Not in the *gifts* they have received; for the ministerial power is not an absolute ability or faculty of doing what a man is able, but a *right*, whereby a man hath power to do that rightly and lawfully which before he could not do. This, gifts will not give to any; for if they did, they would do it to all that have received them. (2.) Not in their *election;* for they are chosen in and by that church whereunto they stand in especial relation, whose choice cannot give ministerial power over any but themselves. (3.) Not in their *setting apart* by fasting, prayer, and imposition of hands; for this is only unto that office-work and power whereunto they are chosen. They are not chosen for one end, and set apart for another. (4.) Not from the communion of churches; for that gives no new power, but only a due exercise of that which was before received.

Q. 27. *What are the principal duties of the pastors or teachers of the church?*

A. [1]To be examples unto the flock in faith, love, knowledge, meekness, patience, readiness to suffer for the name and gospel of Christ, with constancy therein; [2]to watch for the souls and take care of all the spiritual concernments of the whole flock committed to them; [3]to preach the word diligently, dividing it aright; [4]to preserve and contend for the truth; [5]to administer all the ordinances of the gospel duly and orderly; [6]to stir up and exercise the gifts they have received in the discharge of their whole work and administration of all ordinances; [7]to instruct, admonish, cherish, and comfort all the members of the church, as their conditions, occasions, and necessities do require; [8]to attend with diligence, skill, and wisdom unto the discharge of that authority which in the rule of the church is committed unto them.—[1]1 Tim. iii. 1–7, iv. 12; 2 Tim. ii. 3; Col. i. 24; Phil. ii. 17, iii. 17.—[2]Heb. xiii. 17; Acts xx. 28.—[3]2 Tim. ii. 15, iv. 2; Rom. xii. 6–8.—[4]1 Tim. vi. 20; Acts xx. 28; Jude 3.—[5]1 Cor. iv. 1, 2; 1 Tim. iii. 15.—[6]1 Tim. iv. 14–16. —[7]Acts xx. 18–20, 25, 27; 1 Thess. iii. 5; 2 Tim. ii. 24, 25.—[8]Rom. xii. 7, 8; 1 Tim. v. 17.

The answer is full and plain.

Q. 28. *Wherein principally doth the authority of the elders of the church consist?*

A. [1]In that the rule of the church and the guidance thereof, in things appertaining unto the worship of God, is committed unto them. And, therefore, [2]whatever they do as elders in the church, according unto rule, they do it not in the name or authority of the church by which their power is derived unto them, nor as members only of the church by their own consent or covenant, but in the name and authority of Jesus Christ, from whom, by virtue of his law and ordinance, their ministerial office and power are received. So that, [3]in the exercise of any act of church-power, by and with the consent of the church, there is an obligation thence proceeding, which ariseth immediately from that authority which they have received of Jesus Christ, which is the spring of all rule and authority in the church.— [1]Acts xx. 28; Heb. xiii. 7, 17; 1 Pet. v. 2; 1 Cor. xii. 28.—[2]1 Tim. iii. 5; Col. iv. 17; 2 Cor. x. 4, 8.—[3]1 Tim. iv. 11; Titus ii. 15; 1 Pet. v. 2–5.

EXPLICATION.—The answer unto this question explains the power or authority of the elders of the church, from whom they do receive it, and how it is exercised by them; the right stating whereof is of great importance in the whole discipline of the church, and must, therefore, here be farther explained. To this end we may consider,—

First, That all church-power is originally vested in Jesus Christ, the sole head and monarch thereof. God the Father hath committed it unto him, and intrusted him with it for the accomplishment of his work of mediation, Matt. xxviii. 18.

Secondly, That he doth communicate of this authority by way of trust, to be exercised by them in his name, unto persons by him appointed, so much as is needful for the ordering and disposing of all things in his churches unto the blessed ends for which he hath instituted and appointed them; for no man can have any power in his church, for any end whatever, but by delegation from him. What is not received from him is mere usurpation. And whoever takes upon himself the exercise of any rule, or authority, or power in the church, not granted unto them by him, or not rightly derived from him, is an oppressor, a " thief and a robber." This necessarily follows upon the absolute investiture of all power in him alone, 1 Cor. xii. 28; Eph. iv. 11, 12.

Thirdly, The means whereby the Lord Christ communicates this power unto men is by his law and constitution, whereby he hath granted, ordained, and appointed, that such and such powers shall be exercised in his church, and that by such and such persons, to be derived unto them in such a way and manner; so that the word of the gospel, or the laws and constitutions of the Lord Christ therein, are the first recipient seat and subject morally of all church-power whatever, Matt. xvi. 19, xviii. 17–20.

Fourthly, The way and means whereby any persons come to a participation of this power regularly, according to the mind of Christ, is by the obedience unto, and due observation of, his laws and commands in them unto whom they are prescribed; as when an office, with the power of it, is constituted and limited by the law of the land, there is no more required to invest any man in that office, or to give him that power, than the due observance of the means and way prescribed in the law to that end. The way, then, whereby the elders of the church do come to participate of the power and authority which Christ hath appointed to be exercised in his church is by their and the church's due observance of the rules and laws given by him for their election and setting apart unto that office, Heb. v. 4, 5; Acts xiv. 23.

Fifthly, On this account they receive their power from Christ himself alone, and that immediately; for the means used for their participation of it are not recipient of the power itself formally, nor do

authoritatively collate or confer it, only the laws of Christ are executed in a way of obedience. So that though they are chosen and
set apart to their office by the church, yet they are made overseers
by the Holy Ghost, Acts xx. 28. Though they have their power *by*
the church, yet they have it not *from* the church; nor was that
power whereof they are made partakers, as was said, formally resi-
dent in the body of the church, before their participation of it, but
really in Christ himself alone, and *morally* in his word or law. And
thence is the rule and guidance of the church committed unto them
by Christ, Heb. xiii. 7, 17; 1 Pet. v. 2; 1 Tim. iii. 5.

Sixthly, This authority and power, thus received from Christ, is that
which they exert and put forth in all their ministerial administrations, in all which they do as ministers in the house of God, either
in his worship or in the rule of the church itself. They exercise that
authority of Christ which he hath in his law appointed to be exercised in his church; and from that authority is due order given unto
the administration of all the ordinances of worship, and an obligation
unto obedience to acts of rule doth thence also ensue; so that they
who despise them despise the authority of Christ.

Seventhly, When, as elders, they do or declare any thing in the
name of the church, they do not, as such, put forth any authority
committed unto them from and by the church, but only declare the
consent and determination of the church in the exercise of their own
liberty and privilege; but the authority which they act by, and which
they put forth, is that which is committed to themselves, as such, by
Jesus Christ.

Eighthly, This authority is comprised in the law and constitution
of Christ, which themselves exert only *ministerially;* and therefore,
whenever they act any thing *authoritatively*, which they are not
enabled for or warranted in by the word of the gospel, or do any
thing without or contrary unto rule, all such actings, as to any spiritual effect of the gospel, or obligation on the consciences of men, are
" ipso facto" null, and are no way ratified in heaven, where all their
orderly actings are made valid,—that is, by Christ himself in his
word.

Ninthly, The reason, therefore, why the *consent* of the church is
required unto the authoritative acting of the elders therein is, not
because from thence any authority doth accrue unto them anew,
which virtually and radically they had not before, but because by the
rule of the gospel this is required to the orderly acting of their power,
which without it would be contrary to rule, and therefore ineffectual;
as also it must needs be from the nature of the thing itself, for no
act can take place in the church without or against its own consent,
whilst its obedience is voluntary and of choice.

But if it be asked, " What, then, shall the elders do in case the church refuse to consent unto such acts as are indeed according to rule, and warranted by the institution of Christ?" it is answered, that they are,—1. Diligently to *instruct* them from the word in their duty, making known the mind of Christ unto them in the matter under consideration ; 2. To declare unto them the *danger* of their dissent in obstructing the edification of the body, to the dishonour of the Lord Christ and their own spiritual disadvantage; 3. To *wait patiently* for the concurrence of the grace of God with their ministry in giving light and obedience unto the church; and, 4. In case of the church's continuance in any failure of duty, to seek for advice and *counsel* from the elders and brethren of other churches;—all which particulars might be enlarged, would the nature of our present design and work permit it.

Q. 29. *What is the duty of the church towards their elders, pastors, or teachers?*

A. [1] To have them in reverence and honour for their office and work's sake; [2] to obey them conscientiously in all things wherein they speak unto them in the name of the Lord; [3] to pray earnestly for them, that they may, and to exhort them, if need require, to fulfil the work of the ministry; [4] to communicate unto them of their temporals, for their comfortable subsistence in the world and usefulness unto others; [5] wisely to order things by their direction, so as that they may be amongst them without fear; [6] to abide with and stand by them in their sufferings for the gospel, and service of Christ among them.—[1]1 Thess. v. 12, 13; 1 Tim. v. 17.—[2]Heb. xiii. 17; 1 Cor. xvi. 16.—[3]Eph. vi. 18, 19; Col. iv. 3; 2 Thess. iii. 1; Col. iv. 17.—[4]Gal. vi. 6; 1 Cor. ix. 14.—[5]1 Cor. xvi. 10.—[6]2 Tim. i. 16–18, iv. 16.

Q. 30. *Are there any differences in the office or offices of the guides, rulers, elders, or ministers of the church?*

A. The office of them that are teachers is one and the same among them all; but where there are many in the same church, it is the will of Christ that they should be peculiarly assigned unto such especial work, in the discharge of their office-power, as their gifts received from him do peculiarly fit them for and the necessities of the church require.—Rom. xii. 4–8; 1 Cor. xii. 4–6, 8; 1 Pet. iv. 10, v. 2.

EXPLICATION.—The office of them that are to instruct the church in the name and authority of Christ is one and the same, as hath been showed before. And there are many names that are equally accommodated unto all that are partakers of it, as elders, bishops, guides; they are all alike elders, alike bishops, alike guides,—have the one office in common amongst them, and every one the whole entire unto himself. But there are names also given unto them, whereby they are distinguished, not as to office, but as to their work and employment in the discharge of that office: such are " pastors and teachers," Eph. iv. 11, which are placed as distinct persons in their work, partakers of the same office. Now, the foundation of this distinction and difference lies,—

First, In the different gifts that they have received; for although it be required in them all that they have received all those gifts, abilities, and qualifications which are necessary for the work of the ministry, yet as to the degrees of their participation of their gifts, some may more excel in one, others in another: 1 Cor. xii. 4–6, 8, " There are diversities of gifts, but the same Spirit. And there are differences of administrations, but the same Lord. And there are diversities of operations, but it is the same God which worketh all in all. For to one is given by the Spirit the word of wisdom; to another the word of knowledge by the same Spirit," etc. And all these gifts are bestowed upon them to be exercised and laid out for the profit and benefit of the church: Verse 7, " The manifestation of the Spirit is given to every man to profit withal." And therefore every one is in an especial manner to attend unto the exercise and use of that gift wherein he doth excel, or which tends most to the edification of the church, every man being to minister according as he hath received, 1 Pet. iv. 10.

Secondly, It lies in the nature of the work of the ministry in the church, which in general may be referred unto two heads or ends:—

1. The *instruction* of it in the knowledge of God in Christ, and the mysteries of the gospel, that it might grow in grace, wisdom, saving light, and knowledge.

2. The *exhortation* of it to walk answerable unto light received, in holiness and universal obedience. Now, though these several ends of the ministry cannot be divided or separated, yet they may be dis‑ tinguished, and so carried on distinctly, that in the one, knowledge or light may be firstly and principally intended, so as to lead unto obedience; in the other, holiness may be firstly designed, as spring- ing from gospel light or knowledge. Hence, therefore, are the elders of the church principally to attend unto that work, or that end of the ministry, which by the Holy Ghost they are most suited unto. And, therefore, the church following the intimations of the Holy Ghost, in communicating his gifts in variety as he pleaseth, and attending to their own edification, may and ought, amongst those whom they choose to the office of elders or ministers, withal design them in particular unto that especial work which they are especially fitted and prepared for; and this, upon their being chosen and set

apart, they are accordingly to attend unto : " He that teacheth, on teaching; he that exhorteth, on exhortation," Rom. xii. 7, 8. Their office, then, is the same; but their teaching work and employment, on the grounds mentioned, distinct and different.

Q. 31. *Are there appointed any elders in the church whose office and duty consist in rule and government only?*

A. Elders not called to teach ordinarily or administer the sacraments, but to assist and help in the rule and government of the church, are mentioned in the Scripture.—Rom. xii. 8; 1 Cor. xii. 28; 1 Tim. v. 17.

EXPLICATION.—This office of *ruling elders* in the church is much opposed by some, and in especial by them who have least reason so to do: for, first, they object against them that they are *lay elders*, when those with whom they have to do deny that distinction of the church into the clergy and laity; for although they allow the distribution of it into officers and the multitude of the brethren, yet they maintain that the whole church is God's clergy, his lot, and portion, 1 Pet. v. 3. Again, they affirm them to be elders, and therein not merely of the members of the church, but officers set apart unto their office according to rule, or the appointment of Christ. And if by laity, the people distinct from the officers of the church are to be understood, the very term of a *lay elder* implies a contradiction, as designing one who is and is not a church-officer. Besides, themselves do principally govern the church by such whom they esteem laymen, as not in holy orders, to whom the principal part of its rule, at least in the execution of it, is committed; which renders their objection to this sort of church-officers unreasonable. Others, also, have given advantage by making this office *annual* or *biennial* in them that are chosen unto it; which, though they plead the necessity of their churches for, as not having persons meet for this work and duty who are willing to undertake it constantly during their lives, without such a contribution for their maintenance as they are not able to afford, yet the wisest of them do acknowledge an irregularity in what they do, and wish it remedied. But this hinders not but that such church-officers are indeed designed in the Scripture, and of whom frequent mention is made in the ancient writers, and footsteps also yet remain in most churches of their institution, though wofully corrupted; for besides that some light in this matter may be taken from the church of the Jews, wherein the elders of the people were joined in rule with the priests, both in the sanhedrim and all lesser assemblies, there is in the gospel express mention of persons that were assigned peculiarly for rule and government in the church, as 1 Cor. xii. 28. And it is in vain pretended that those words, "helps, governments," do denote gifts only, seeing the apostle expressly enumerates the persons in office, or officers, which the Lord Christ then used in the foundation and rule of the churches as then planted. He that *ruleth*, also, is distinguished from him that *teacheth* and him that *exhorteth*, Rom. xii. 8; and is prescribed diligence as his principal qualification in the discharge of his duty. And the words of the apostle to this purpose are express: 1 Tim. v. 17, " Let the elders that rule well be counted worthy of double honour, especially those who labour in the word and doctrine." For the words expressly assign two sorts of elders, whereof some only attend unto rule; others, moreover, labour in the word and doctrine. Neither doth that word, as some would have it, " labour in the word," intend any other labour but what is incumbent on all the pastors and teachers of the church as their constant duty. See Rom. xvi. 12; Acts xx. 35; 1 Thess. v. 12. Now, can we suppose that the apostle would affirm them to be worthy of double honour, whom, comparing with others, he notes as remiss and negligent in their work? for it seems that others were more diligent in the discharge of that duty, which was no less theirs, if only one sort of elders be here intended. The Scripture is not wont to commend such persons as worthy of double honour, but rather to propose them as meet for double shame and punishment, Jer. xlviii. 10; 1 Cor. ix. 16. And they are unmindful of their own interest who would have bishops that attend to the rule of the church to be distinctly intended by the elders that rule well, seeing the apostle expressly preferreth before and above them those that attend constantly to the word and doctrine. And besides what is thus expressly spoken concerning the appointment of this sort of elders in the church, their usefulness, in the necessity of their work and employment, is evident; for whereas a constant care in the church that the conversation of all the members of it be such as becometh the gospel, that the name of our Lord Jesus Christ be not evil spoken of, is of great concernment and importance, and the pastors and teachers, being to give up themselves continually unto prayer and the ministry of the word, cannot attend unto the constant and daily oversight thereof, the usefulness of these elders, whose proper and peculiar work it is to have regard unto the holy walking of the church, must needs be manifest unto all. But whereas in most churches there is little or no regard unto the *personal holiness* of the members of them, it is no wonder that no account should be had of them who are ordained by the Lord Christ to look after it and promote it.

The qualification of these elders, with the way of their call and setting apart unto their office, being the same with those of the teaching elders before insisted on, need not be here again repeated.

Their authority, also, in the whole rule of the church, is every way the same with that of the other sort of elders; and they are to act in the execution of it with equal respect and regard from the church. Yea, the business of rule being peculiarly committed unto them, and they required to attend thereunto with diligence in an especial manner, the work thereof is principally theirs, as that of labouring in the word and doctrine doth especially belong unto the pastors and teachers of the churches. And this institution is abused when either unmeet persons are called to this office, or those that are called do not attend unto their duty with diligence, or do act only in it by the guidance of the teaching officers, without a sense of their own authority, or due respect from the church.

Q. 32. *Is there no other ordinary office in the church but only that of elders?*
A. Yes, of deacons also.

Q. 33. *What are the deacons of the church?*
A. Approved men chosen by the church to take care for the necessities of the poor belonging thereunto, and other outward occasions of the whole church, by the collection, keeping, and distribution of the alms and other supplies of the church; set apart and commended to the grace of God therein by prayer.—Acts vi. 3, 5, 6; Phil. i. 1; 1 Tim. iii. 8–13.

EXPLICATION.—The office of the deacon, the nature, end, and use of it, the qualifications of the persons to be admitted unto it, the way and manner of their election and setting apart, are all of them plainly expressed in the Scripture: Acts vi. 1–3, 5, 6, "There arose a murmuring of the Grecians against the Hebrews, because their widows were neglected in the daily ministration. Then the twelve called the multitude of the disciples unto them, and said, It is not reason that we should leave the word of God, and serve tables. Wherefore, brethren, look ye out among you seven men of honest report, full of the Holy Ghost and wisdom, whom we may appoint over this business. And the saying pleased the whole multitude: and they chose Stephen," etc., "whom they set before the apostles: and when they had prayed, they laid their hands on them." 1 Tim. iii. 8–13, "Likewise must the deacons be grave, not double-tongued, not given to much wine, not greedy of filthy lucre; holding the mystery of the faith in a pure conscience. And let these also first be proved; then let them use the office of a deacon, being found blameless; the husbands of one wife, ruling their children and their own houses well. For they that have used the office of a deacon well purchase to themselves a good degree, and great boldness in the faith which is in Christ Jesus." These things are thus plain and express in the Scripture. But whereas many have grown weary of the observation of the institutions of the gospel, this office hath for a long time been lost amongst the most of Christians. By some the name is retained, but applied to another work, duty, and employment, than this to which it is peculiarly appropriated in the Scripture. Their proper and original work of taking care for the poor, they say, is provided for by others; and therefore that office being needless, another, unto another purpose, under the same name, is erected. Such are deacons that may read service, preach, and baptize, when they have licence thereunto. But this choice, to reject an office of the appointment of Christ, under pretence of provision made for the duties of it another way, and the erecting of one not appointed by him, seems not equal. But whereas it is our duty in all things to have regard to the authority of Christ and his appointments in the gospel, if we claim the privilege of being called after his name, some think that if what he hath appointed may be colourably performed another way without respect unto his institutions, that is far the best; but omitting the practice of other men, the things that concern this office in the church are, as was said, clear in the Scripture.

First, The persons called unto it are to be of *honest report*, furnished with the gifts of the Holy Ghost, especially with wisdom, Acts vi. 3, and those other endowments useful in the discharge of their duty mentioned, 1 Tim. iii. 8–13.

Secondly, The way whereby they come to be made partakers of this office is by the choice or *election* of the church, Acts vi. 2, 3, 5, whereupon they are solemnly to be set apart by prayer.

Thirdly, Their work or duty consists in a daily ministration unto the necessities of the poor *saints*, or members of the church, verses 1, 2.

Fourthly, To this end, that they may be enabled so to do, it is ordained that every *first day* [*of the week*] the members of the church do contribute, according as God enables them, of their substance for the supply of the wants of the poor, 1 Cor. xvi. 2; and also occasionally, as necessity shall require, or God move their hearts by his grace.

Fifthly, Hereunto is to be added whatever by the providence of God may be conferred upon the church for its outward advantage, with reference unto the end mentioned, Acts iv. 34, 35.

Sixthly, These supplies of the church being committed to the care and charge of the *deacons*, they are from thence to minister with diligence and wisdom unto the necessities of the poor; that so the needy may be supplied, that there may be none that lack, the rich may contribute of their riches according to the mind of Christ, and in obedience unto his command; that they which minister well in this office "may purchase to themselves a good degree and great boldness in the faith," and that in all the name of our Lord Jesus Christ may be glorified with praise and thanksgiving.

It belongs, therefore, unto persons called unto this office,—

First, To acquaint themselves with the *outward condition* of those that appear to be poor and needy in the church, whether by the addresses of such poor ones, who are bound to make known their wants, occasions, and necessities unto them, or by the information of others, or their own observation.

Secondly, To acquaint the elders and the church, as occasion requireth, with the necessities of the poor under their care, that those who are able may be stirred up by the elders to a free supply and contribution.

Thirdly, To dispose of what they are intrusted with *faithfully*, cheerfully, tenderly, without partiality or preferring one before another, for any outward respect whatever.

Fourthly, To keep and give an account unto the church, when called for, of what they have received, and how they have disposed of it; that so they may be known to have well discharged their office, —that is, with care, wisdom, and tenderness,—whereby they procure to themselves a good degree, with boldness in the faith, and the church is encouraged to intrust them farther with this sacrifice of their alms, which is so acceptable unto God.

Q. 34. *Wherein consists the general duty of the whole church, and every member thereof, in their proper station and condition?*

A. In performing, doing, and keeping inviolate all the commands and institutions of Jesus Christ, walking unblamably and fruitfully in the world, holding forth the word of truth, and glorifying the Lord Christ in and by the profession of his name, and keeping his testimony unto the end.—Matt. xxviii. 20; Acts ii. 42; Phil. ii. 15, 16, iv. 8, 9; 1 Thess. iii. 8; 1 Pet. iv. 10–14; 1 Tim. iii. 15; Heb. x. 23.

EXPLICATION.—Besides the general duties of Christianity incumbent on all believers or disciples of Christ, as such, there are sundry especial duties required of them as gathered into church-societies, upon the account of an especial trust committed unto them in that state and condition; for,—

First, The church being appointed as the *seat* and subject of all the institutions of Christ and ordinances of gospel worship, it is its duty,—that is, of the whole body, and every member in his proper place,—to use all care, watchfulness, and diligence that all the commands of Christ be kept inviolate, and all his institutions observed according to his mind and will. Thus, those "added to the church," Acts ii. 42, together with the whole church, "continued steadfastly" (which argues care, circumspection, and diligence) " in the apostles' doctrine and fellowship, and breaking of bread, and in prayers;" which principal duties are enumerated to express their respect towards all. This is their " standing fast in the Lord," which was a matter of such joy to the apostle when he found it in the Thessalonians, 1 Epist. iii. 8, " For now we live, if ye stand fast in the Lord;"—that order and steadfastness which he rejoiced over in the Colossians, chap. ii. 5, " For though I be absent in the flesh, yet am I with you in the spirit, joying and beholding your order, and the steadfastness of your faith in Christ." And where this duty is despised, men contenting themselves with what is done by others, there is a great neglect of that faithfulness in obedience which the church owes unto Jesus Christ.

Secondly, The *glory* of the Lord Christ, and the doctrine of the gospel, to be manifested in and by the power of a holy, exemplary conversation, is committed unto the church and all the members of it. This is one end wherefore the Lord Christ calls them out of the world, separates them to be a peculiar people unto himself, brings them forth unto a visible profession, and puts his name upon them,— namely, that in their walking and conversation he may show forth the holiness of his doctrine, and power of his Spirit, grace, and example, to effect in them all holiness, godliness, righteousness, and honesty in the world. Hence are they earnestly exhorted unto these things: Phil. iv. 8, " Brethren, whatsoever things are true, whatsoever things are honest, whatsoever things are just, whatsoever things are pure, whatsoever things are lovely, whatsoever things are of good report; if there be any virtue, and if there be any praise, think on these things;" and that to this end, that the doctrine of the gospel may be adorned, and Christ glorified in all things, Tit. ii. 10. And those who fail herein are said to be " enemies of the cross of Christ," Phil. iii. 18, as hindering the progress of the doctrine thereof, by rendering it undesirable in their conversation. This also, therefore, even the duty of universal holiness, with an especial regard unto the honour of Christ and the gospel, which they are called and designed to testify and express in the world, is incumbent on the church, and every member of it, namely, as the apostle speaks, " that they may be blameless and harmless, the sons of God, without rebuke, in the midst of a crooked and perverse nation," among whom they are to " shine as lights in the world," Phil. ii. 15.

Thirdly, The care of *declaring* and manifesting the truth is also committed unto them. Christ hath made the church to be the " pillar and ground of the truth," 1 Tim. iii. 15; where the truth of the gospel is to be firmly seated, founded, fixed, established, and then lifted up in the ways of Christ's appointment, to be seen, discerned, and known by others. And as this is done principally in the preaching of the gospel by the elders of the church, and in their "contending for the faith once delivered unto the saints," Jude 3, so it is also the duty of the whole church to "hold forth the word of life," Phil. ii. 16, by ministering of "the gift that every man hath received," 1 Pet. iv. 10, in the way of Christ's appointment. In these and the like instances doth our Lord Jesus Christ require of his church that they express in the world their subjection unto him and his authority; and that they abide therein unto the end against all opposition whatever.

The sinful neglect of churches in the discharge of their duty herein was one great means of that apostasy from the rule of the gospel which they generally of old fell into. When the members of them began to think that they had no advantage by their state and condition, but only the outward participation of some ordinances of worship, and no duty incumbent on them but only to attend and follow the motions and actings of their guides, the whole societies quickly became corrupt, and fit to be disposed of according to the carnal interest of those that had by their neglect and sin gotten dominion over them. And at all times, as the people were negligent in their duty, the *leaders* of them were apt to usurp undue authority. When the one sort will not do that which they ought, the other are ready to take upon them what they ought not. It is a circumspect performance of duty on all hands alone that will keep all sorts of persons in the church within those bounds and limits, and up to those rights and privileges, which Christ hath allotted and granted unto them. And herein alone doth the order, honour, and beauty of the church consist. Church-members, therefore, are to search and inquire after the particular duties which, as such, are incumbent on them; as also to consider what influence their special state and condition, as they are church-members, ought to have into all the duties of their obedience as they are Christians: for this privilege is granted unto them for their edification; that is, their furtherance in their whole course of walking before God. And if this be neglected,— if they content themselves with a name to live in this or that church, to partake of the ordinances that are stated and solemnly administered only,—that which would have been to their advantage may prove to be a snare and temptation unto them. What these especial duties are, in the particular instances of them, is of too large a consideration here to be insisted on. Besides, it is the great duty of the' guides of the church to be inculcating of them into the minds of those committed to their charge; for the church's due performance of its duty is their honour, crown, and reward.

Q. 35. *Whence do you reckon prayer, which is a part of moral and natural worship, among the institutions of Christ in his church?*

A. On many accounts; as,—[1]because the Lord Christ hath commanded his church to attend unto the worship of God therein; [2]because he bestows on the ministers of the church gifts and ability of prayer for the benefit and edification thereof; [3]he hath appointed that all his other ordinances should be administered with prayer, whereby it becomes a part of them; [4]because himself ministers in the holy place, as the great high priest of his church, to present their prayers unto God at the throne of grace; [5]because in all the prayers of the church there is an especial regard had unto himself and the whole work of his mediation.—[1]Luke xviii. 1, xxi. 36; Rom. xii. 12; 1 Tim. ii. 1, 2.—[2]Eph. iv. 8, 12, 13; Rom. viii. 15, 16; Gal. iv. 6.—[3]Acts ii. 42; 1 Tim. iv. 5.—[4]Rev. viii. 3, 4; Heb. iv. 14–16, vi. 20, x. 19–22.—[5]John xiv. 13, xv. 16, xvi. 23, 26; Eph. iii. 14, 15.

Q. 36. *May not the church, in the solemn worship of God, and celebration of the ordinances of the gospel, make use of and content itself in the use of forms of prayer in an unknown tongue composed by others, and prescribed unto them?*

A. So to do would be [1]contrary to one principal end of prayer itself, which is, that believers may therein apply themselves to the throne of grace for spiritual supplies according to the present condition, wants, and exigencies of their souls; [2]to the main end that the Lord Jesus Christ aimed at in supplying men with gifts for the discharge of the work of the ministry, tending to render the promise of sending the Holy Ghost, which is the immediate cause of the church's preservation and continuance, needless and useless. Moreover, [3]it will render the discharge of the duty of ministers unto several precepts and exhortations of the gospel, for the use, stirring up, and exercise of their gifts, impossible; and [4]thereby hinder the edification of the church, the great end of all ordinances and institutions. —[1]Rom. viii. 26; Phil. iv. 6; Heb. iv. 16; 1 Pet. iv. 7.—[2]Eph. iv. 8, 12, 13.—[3]1 Tim. iv. 14; 2 Tim. i. 6, 7; Col. iv. 17; Matt. xxv. 14–17.—[4]1 Cor. xii. 7.

Q. 37. *Is the constant work of preaching the gospel by the elders of the church necessary?*

A. It is so, both on the part of the elders or ministers themselves, of whom that duty is strictly required, and who principally therein labour and watch for the good of the flock, and on the part of the church, for the furtherance of their faith and obedience, by instruction, reproof, exhortation, and consolation.—Matt. xxiv. 45–51;

Rom. xii. 7, 8; 1 Cor. ix. 17, 18; Eph. iv. 11–13; 1 Tim. iv. 15, 16, v. 17; 2 Tim. ii. 24, 25, iii. 14–17, iv. 2.

Q. 38. *Who are the proper subjects of baptism?*
A. Professing believers, if not baptized in their infancy, and their infant seed.—Matt. xxviii. 19; Acts ii. 38, 39, xvi. 33; 1 Cor. i. 16, vii. 14; Col. ii. 12–14, with Gen. xvii. 10–12.

Q. 39. *Where and to whom is the ordinance of the Lord's supper to be administered?*
A. In the church, or assembly of the congregation, to all the members of it, rightly prepared and duly assembled, or to such of them as are so assembled.—1 Cor. xi. 20–22, 28, 29, 33; Acts ii. 46.

Q. 40. *How often is that ordinance to be administered?*
A. Every first day of the week, or at least as often as opportunity and conveniency may be obtained.—1 Cor. xi. 26; Acts xx. 7.

Q. 41. *What is the discipline of the church?*
A. It consists in the due exercise of that authority and power which the Lord Christ, in and by his word, hath granted unto the church, for its continuance, increase, and preservation in purity, order, and holiness, according to his appointment.—Matt. xvi. 19; Rom. xii. 8; 2 Cor. x. 4–6; Rev. ii. 2, 20.
EXPLICATION.—Sundry things are to be considered about this discipline of the church; as,—

First, The *foundation* of it, which is a grant of power and authority made unto it by Jesus Christ as mediator, head, king, and lawgiver of his church; for all discipline being an act of power, and this being exercised in and about things internal and spiritual, no men can of themselves, or by grant of any others, have any right or authority to or in the exercise thereof. Whoever hath any interest herein or right hereunto, it must be granted unto him from above by Jesus Christ, and that as mediator and head of his church; for as all church-power is in an especial manner, by the authority and grant of the Father, vested in him alone, Matt. xxviii. 18, Eph. i. 20–23, so the *nature* of it, which is spiritual, the *objects* of it, which are the consciences and gospel privileges of believers, with the *ends* of it,—namely, the glory of God in Christ, with the spiritual and eternal good of the souls of men,—do all manifest that it can have no other right nor foundation. This in the first place is to be fixed, that no authority can be exercised in the church but what is derived from Jesus Christ· as was spoken before.
Secondly, The *means* whereby the Lord Christ doth communicate

this power and authority unto his church is his word or his law and constitution concerning it in the gospel; so that it is exactly limited and bounded thereby. And no power or authority can be exercised in the church but what is granted and conveyed unto it by the word, seeing that Christ communicates no power or authority any other ways. Whatever of that nature is beside it or beyond it is mere usurpation, and null in its exercise. Herein is the commission of the guides and rulers of the church expressed, which they are not to exceed in any thing. Herein are bounds and limits fixed to the actings of the whole church, and of every part and member of it.

Thirdly, This power or authority, thus granted and conveyed by Jesus Christ, is to be exercised, as to the *manner* of the administration of discipline, with skill and diligence, Rom. xii. 8; 1 Cor. xii. And the skill required hereunto is a gift, or an ability of mind, bestowed by the Holy Ghost upon men, to put in execution the laws of Christ for the government of the church in the way and order by him appointed, or a spiritual wisdom, whereby men know how to behave themselves in the house of God in their several places, for its due edification in faith and love, 1 Tim. iii. 15. And this ability of mind to make a due application of the laws of the gospel unto persons, times, and actions, with their circumstances, is such a gift of the Holy Ghost as whereof there are several degrees, answering to the distinct duties that are incumbent on the rulers of the church on the one hand, and the members on the other. And where this skill and wisdom is wanting, there it is impossible that the discipline of the church should be preserved or carried on. Hereunto also diligence and watchfulness are to be added, without which ability and power will never obtain their proper end in a due manner, Rom. xii. 6–8.

Fourthly, The *end* of this discipline is the continuance, increase, and preservation of the church, according to the rule of its first institution, 1 Cor. v. 7. This power hath Christ given his church for its conservation, without which it must necessarily decay and come to nothing. Nor is it to be imagined that where any church is called and gathered according to the mind of Christ, he hath left it destitute of power and authority to preserve itself in that state and order which he hath appointed unto it. And that which was one principal cause of the decays of the Asian churches was the neglect of this discipline, the power and privilege whereof the Lord had left unto them and intrusted them withal, for their own preservation in order, purity, and holiness. And, therefore, for the neglect thereof they were greatly blamed by him, Rev. ii. 14, 15, 20, iii. 1, 2; as is also the church of Corinth by the apostle, 1 Cor. v. 2; as they are

commended who attended unto the diligent exercise of it, Rev.
ii. 2, iii 9. The disuse, also, of it hath been the occasion of all the
defilements, abominations, and confusions that have spread themselves over many churches in the world.

Q. 42 *Unto whom is the power and administration of this discipline committed by Jesus Christ?*

A As to the authority to be exerted in it, in the things wherein
the whole church is concerned, unto the elders; as unto trial, judgment, and consent in and unto its exercise, unto the whole brotherhood; as unto love, care, and watchfulness in private and particular
cases, to every member of the church.—Matt. xxiv. 45; Eph.
iv. 11, 12; Acts xx. 28; 1 Tim. iii. 5, v. 17; Heb. xiii. 7, 17; 1 Pet.
v. 2; 1 Thess. v. 12; Gal. vi. 1, 2; 1 Cor. iv 14, v. 2, 4, 5; 2 Cor. ii.
6–8; 2 Tim. iv. 2.

EXPLICATION.—It hath been showed that this power is granted
unto the church by virtue of the *law* and constitution of Christ.
Now, this law assigns the means and way whereby any persons do
obtain an interest therein, and makes the just allotments to all concerned in it. What this law, constitution, or word of Christ assigns
unto any, as such, that they are the first seat and subject of, by what
way or means soever they come to be intrusted therein. Thus, that
power or authority which is given unto the elders of the church doth
not first formally reside in the body of the church unorganized or
distinct from them, though they are called unto their office by their
suffrage and choice; but they are themselves, as such, the first subject
of office-power, for so is the will of the Lord Christ. Nor is the
interest of the whole church in this power of discipline, whatever it
be, given unto it by the elders, but is immediately granted unto it
by the will and law of the Lord Jesus.

First, In this way and manner the authority above described is
given in the first place, as such, unto the *elders* of the church. This
authority was before explained, in answer unto the 28th question; as
also was the way whereby they receive it. And it is that power of
office whereby they are enabled for the discharge of their whole duty,
in the teaching and ruling of the church, called the " power of the
keys," from Matt. xvi. 19; which expression being metaphorical, and
in general liable unto many interpretations, is to be understood according to the declaration made of it in those particular instances
wherein it is expressed. Nor is it a twofold power or authority that
the elders of the church have committed unto them,—one to teach
and another to rule, commonly called the power of order and of
jurisdiction; but it is one power of office, the duties whereof are of
several kinds, referred unto the two general heads, first of teaching, by

preaching the word and celebration of the sacraments, and secondly, of rule or government. By virtue hereof are they made rulers over the house of God, Matt. xxiv. 45; stewards in his house, 1 Cor. iv. 1; overseers of the church, Acts xx. 28, 1 Pet. v. 2; guides unto the church, Heb. xiii. 7, 17. Not that they have a supreme or *autocratorical* power committed unto them, to enable them to do what seems right and good in their own eyes, seeing they are expressly bound up unto the terms of their commission, Matt. xxviii. 19, 20, *to teach men to do and observe all and only what Christ hath commanded;* nor have they by virtue of it any dominion in or over the church,— that is, the laws, rules, or privileges of it,—or the consciences of the disciples of Christ, to alter, change, add, diminish, or bind by their own authority, 1 Pet. v. 3, Mark x. 42–44. But it is a power merely *ministerial*, in whose exercise they are unto the Lord Christ accountable servants, Heb. xiii. 17, Matt. xxiv. 45, and servants of the church for Jesus' sake, 2 Cor. iv. 5. This authority, in the discipline of the church they exert and put forth by virtue of their office, and not either as declaring of the power of the church itself, or acting what is delegated unto them thereby, but as ministerially exercising the authority of Christ committed unto themselves.

Secondly, The body of the church, or the multitude of the brethren (women being excepted by especial prohibition, 1 Cor. xiv. 34, 35, 1 Tim. ii. 11, 12), is, by the law and constitution of Christ in the gospel, interested in the administration of this power of discipline in the church, so far as,—

1. To consider, try, and make a judgment in and about all persons, things, and causes, in reference whereunto it is to be exercised. Thus, the brethren at Jerusalem joined in the consideration of the observation of Mosaical ceremonies with the apostles and elders, Acts xv. 23; and the multitude of them to whom letters were sent about it likewise did the same, verses 30–32; and this they thought it their duty and concernment to do, chap. xxi. 22. And they are blamed who applied not themselves unto this duty, 1 Cor. v. 2–6. Thence are the epistles of Paul to the churches to instruct them in their duties and privileges in Christ, and how they ought to behave themselves in the ordering of all things amongst them according to his mind. And these are directed unto the churches themselves, either jointly with their elders, or distinctly from them, Phil. i. 1. And the whole preservation of church-order is, on the account of this duty, recommended unto them. Neither can what they do in compliance with their guides and rulers be any part of their obedience unto the Lord Christ, unless they make previously thereunto a rational consideration and judgment, by the rule, of what is to be done. Neither is the church of Christ to be ruled without its know-

ledge or against its will; nor in any thing is blind obedience acceptable to God.

2. The brethren of the church are intrusted with the privilege of giving and testifying their consent unto all acts of church-power, which, though it belong not formally unto the authority of them, is necessary unto their validity and efficacy; and that so far forth as that they are said to do and act what is done and effected thereby, 1 Cor. v. 4, 5, 13; 2 Cor. ii. 6–8. And they who have this privilege of consent, which hath so great an influence into the action and validity of it, have also the liberty of dissent, when any thing is proposed to be done, the warrant whereof from the word and the rule of its performance are not evident unto them.

Q. 43. *Wherein doth the exercise of the authority for discipline committed unto the elders of the church consist?*

A. [1]In personal private admonition of any member or members of the church, in case of sin, error, or any miscarriage known unto themselves; [2]in public admonition in case of offences persisted in, and brought orderly to the knowledge and consideration of the church; [3]in the ejection of obstinate offenders from the society and communion of the church; [4]in exhorting, comforting, and restoring to the enjoyment and exercise of church-privileges such as are recovered from the error of their ways;—all according to the laws, rules, and directions of the gospel.—[1]Matt. xviii. 15; 1 Thess. v. 14; 1 Cor. iv. 14; Titus i. 13, ii. 15; 2 Tim. iv. 2.—[2]1 Tim. v. 19, 20; Matt. xviii. 16, 17.—[3]Titus iii. 10; 1 Tim. i. 20; Matt. xviii. 17; 1 Cor. v. 5; Gal. v. 12.—[4]2 Cor. ii. 7, 8; Gal. vi. 1; 2 Thess. iii. 15.

Q. 44. *May the church cast any person out of its communion without previous admonition?*

A. It may in some cases, where the offence is notorious and the scandal grievous, so that nothing be done against other general rules.—1 Cor. v.

Q. 45. *Wherein doth the liberty and duty of the whole brotherhood in the exercise of discipline in the church in particular consist?*

A. [1]In a meek consideration of the condition and temptations of offenders, with the nature of their offences, when orderly proposed unto the church; [2]in judging with the elders, according to rule, what, in all cases of offence, is necessary to be done for the good of the offenders themselves, and for the edification and vindication of the whole church, [3]in their consent unto, and concurrence in, the admonition, ejection, pardoning, and restoring of offenders, as the matter shall require.—Gal. vi. 1, 2; 1 Cor. v. 2, 4, 5, 12, vi. 2; 2 Cor. ii. 6–8.

Q. 46. *What is the duty of private members in reference unto the discipline appointed by Christ in his church?*

A. It is their duty, in their mutual watch over one another, to exhort each other unto holiness and perseverance; and if they observe any thing in the ways and walkings of any of their fellow-members not according unto the rule and the duty of their profession, which, therefore, gives them offence, to admonish them thereof in private, with love, meekness, and wisdom; and in case they prevail not unto their amendment, to take the assistance of some other brethren in the same work; and if they fail in success therein also, to report the matter, by the elders' direction, unto the whole church.—Matt. xviii. 16–18; 1 Thess. v. 14.

EXPLICATION.—In these questions an inquiry is made after the exercise of discipline in the church,—as to that part of it which belongs unto the reproof and correction of miscarriages, according to the distribution of right, power, and privilege before explained.

The first act hereof consists in *private admonition;* for so hath our Lord ordained, that in case any brother or member of the church do in any thing walk disorderly, and not according to the rule of the gospel, he or they unto whom it is observed, and who are thereby offended, may and ought to admonish the person or persons so offending of their miscarriage and offence; concerning which is to be observed,—

First, What is previously required thereunto; and that is,—

1. That in all the members of the church there ought to be " love without dissimulation." They are to " be kindly affectioned one to another with brotherly love," Rom. xii. 9, 10; which as they are taught of God, so they are greatly exhorted thereunto, Heb. xiii. 1. This love is the bond of perfection, the most excellent way and means of preserving church-order, and furthering the edification thereof, 1 Cor. xiii., without which, well seated and confirmed in the hearts and minds of church-members, no duty of their relation can ever be performed in a due manner.

2. This love is to exert and put forth itself in tender care and watchfulness for the good of each other; which are to work by mutual exhortations, informations, instructions, according as opportunities do offer themselves, or as the necessities of any do seem to require, Heb. iii. 13, x. 24.

Secondly, This duty of admonishing offenders privately and personally is common to the elders with all the members of the church; neither doth it belong properly unto the elders as such, but as brethren of the same society. And yet, by virtue of their office, the elders are enabled to do it with more authority morally, though office-power properly be not exercised therein. By virtue, also, of their constant general watch over the whole flock in the discharge of their office, they are enabled to take notice of and discern miscarriages in any of the members sooner than others: but as to the exercise of the discipline of the church in this matter, this duty is equally incumbent on every member of it, according as the obligation on them to watch over one another, and to exercise especial love towards each other, is equal; whence it is distinguished from that private pastoral admonition, which is an act of the teaching office and power, not directly belonging unto the rule or government inquired after. But this admonition is an effect of love; and when it proceedeth not from thence it is irregular, Matt. xviii. 16–18; Rom. xv. 14.

Thirdly, This duty is so incumbent on every member of the church, that in case of the neglect thereof, he both sinneth against the institution of Christ and makes himself partaker of the sin of the party offending, and is also guilty of his danger and ruin thereby, with all that disadvantage which will accrue to the church by any of the members of it continuing in sin against the rule of the gospel. They have not only liberty thus to admonish one another, but it is their express and indispensable duty so to do; the neglect whereof is interpreted by God to be "hatred of our brother," such as wherewith the love of God is inconsistent, Lev. xix. 17; 1 John iii. 15, iv. 20.

Fourthly, Although this duty be personally incumbent on every individual member of the church, yet this hinders not but if the sin of an offender be known to more than one at the same time, and they jointly take offence thereat, they may together in the first instance admonish him, which yet still is but the first and private admonition; which is otherwise when others are called into assistance who are not themselves acquainted with the offence, but only by information, and join in it, not upon the account of their own being offended, but of being desired according unto rule to give assistance to them that are so.

Fifthly, The way and manner of the discharge of this duty is, that it be done with prudence, tenderness, and due regard unto all circumstances; whence the apostle supposeth a spiritual ability to be necessary for this work: Rom. xv. 14, "Ye also are full of goodness, filled with all knowledge, able also to admonish one another." Especially four things are to be diligently heeded:—

1. That the whole duty be so managed that the person *offending* may be convinced that it is done out of love to him and affectionate, conscientious care over him, that he may take no occasion thereby for the exasperation of his own spirit.

2. That the persons admonishing others of their offence do make it appear that what they do is in obedience unto an institution of Christ, and therein to preserve their own souls from sin, as well as to benefit the offenders.

3. That the admonition be grounded on a rule; which alone gives it authority and efficacy.

4. That there be a readiness manifested by them to receive satisfaction,—either (1.) in case that, upon trial, it appeareth the information they have had of the miscarriage whence the offence arose was undue or not well grounded; or, (2.) of acknowledgment and repentance.

Sixthly, The ends of this ordinance and institution of Christ are,—

1. To keep up love without dissimulation among all the members of the church; for if offences should abide unremoved, love, which is the bond of perfection, would not long continue in sincerity, which tends to the dissolution of the whole society.

2. To gain the offender, by delivering him from the guilt of sin, that he may not lie under it, and procure the wrath of God against himself, Lev. xix. 17.

3. To preserve his person from dishonour and disreputation, and thereby to keep up his usefulness in the church. To this end hath our Lord appointed the discharge of this duty in private, that the failings of men may not be unnecessarily divulged, and themselves thereby exposed unto temptation.

4. To preserve the church from that scandal that might befall it by the hasty opening of all the real or supposed failings of its members. And,—

5. To prevent its trouble in the public hearing of things that may be otherwise healed and removed.

Seventhly, In case these ends are obtained, either by the supposed offending persons *clearing of themselves* and manifesting themselves innocent of the crimes charged on them, as Josh. xxii. 21–29, 2 Cor. vii. 11, or by their *acknowledgment*, repentance, and amendment, then this part of the discipline of the church hath, through the grace of Christ, obtained its appointed effect.

Eighthly, In case the persons offending be not humbled nor reformed, nor do give satisfaction unto them by whom they are admonished, then hath our Lord ordained a second degree of this private exercise of discipline:—that the persons who, being offended, have discharged the foregoing duty themselves according unto rule, shall take unto them others,—two or three, as the occasion may seem to require, —to join with them in the same work and duty, to be performed in the same manner, for the same ends, with that before described, Matt.

xviii. 15–17. And it is the duty of these persons so called in for assistance,—

1. To judge of the crime, fault, or offence reported to them, and not to proceed unless they find it to consist in something expressly contrary to the rule of the gospel, and attested in such manner and with such evidence as their mutual love doth require in them with respect unto their brethren. And they are to judge of the testimony that is given concerning the truth of the offence communicated unto them, that they may not seem either lightly to take up a report against their brother or to discredit the testimony of others.

2. In case they find the offence pretended not to be a real offence, indeed contrary to the rule of the gospel, or that it is not aright grounded as to the evidence of it, but taken up upon prejudice or an over-easy credulity, contrary to the law of that love which is required amongst church-members, described 1 Cor. xiii., and commanded as the great means of the edification of the church and preservation of its union, then to convince the brother offended of his mistake, and with him to satisfy the person pretended to be the offender, that no breach or schism may happen among the members of the same body.

3. Being satisfied of the crime and testimony, they are to associate themselves with the offended brother in the same work and duty that he himself had before discharged towards the offender.

Ninthly, Because there is no determination how often these private admonitions are to be used in case of offence, it is evident from the nature of the thing itself that they are to be reiterated, first the one and then the other, whilst there is any ground of hope that the ends of them may be obtained, through the blessing of Christ,—the brother gained, and the offence taken away. Neither of these, then, is to be deserted or laid aside on the first or second attempt, as though it were performed only to make way for somewhat farther; but it is to be waited on with prayer and patience, as an ordinance of Christ appointed for attaining the end aimed at.

Tenthly, In case there be not the success aimed at obtained in these several degrees of private admonition, it is then the will of our Lord Jesus Christ that the matter be reported unto the church, that the offended may be publicly admonished thereby and brought to repentance; wherein is to be observed,—

1. That the persons who have endeavoured in vain to reclaim their offending brother by private admonition are to acquaint the elders of the church with the case and crime, as also what they have done according to rule for the rectifying of it; who, upon that information, are obliged to communicate the knowledge of the whole matter to the church. This is to be done by the elders, as to whom the pre-

servation of order in the church and the rule of its proceeding do belong, as we have showed before.

2. The report made to the church by the elders is to be,—(1.) Of the *crime*, guilt, or offence; (2.) Of the *testimony* given unto the truth of it; (3.) Of the *means* used to bring the offender to acknowledgment and repentance; (4.) Of his *deportment* under the private previous admonitions, either as to his rejecting of them, or as to any satisfaction tendered; all in order, love, meekness, and tenderness.

3. Things being proposed unto the church, and the offender heard upon the whole of the offence and former proceeding, the whole church or multitude of the brethren are, with the elders, to consider the nature of the offence, with the condition and temptation of the offender, with such a spirit of meekness as our Lord Jesus Christ, in his own person, set them an example of in his dealing with sinners, and which is required in them as his disciples, Gal. vi. 1, 2; 2 Cor. ii. 8.

4. The elders and brethren are to judge of the offence and the carriage of the offender according to rule; and if the offence be evident and persisted in, then,—

5. The offender is to be *publicly admonished* by the elders, with the consent and concurrence of the church, 1 Thess. v. 14; 1 Tim. v. 20; Matt. xviii. 17. And this admonition consists of five parts: —(1.) A declaration of the *crime* or offence, as it is evidenced unto the church. (2.) A conviction of the *evil* of it, from the rule or rules transgressed against. (3.) A declaration of the *authority* and duty of the church in such cases. (4.) A rebuke of the offender in the name of Christ, answering the nature and circumstances of the offence. (5.) An exhortation unto *humiliation*, and repentance, and acknowledgment.

Eleventhly, In case the offender despise this admonition of the church, and come not upon it unto repentance, it is the will and appointment of our Lord Jesus Christ that he be *cut off* from all the privileges of the church, and cast out from the society thereof, or be excommunicated; wherein consists the last act of the discipline of the church for the correction of offenders. And herein may be considered,—

1. The *nature* of it, that it is an *authoritative act*, and so principally belongs unto the elders of the church, who therein exert the power that they have received from the Lord Christ, by and with the consent of the church, according to his appointment, Matt. xvi. 19, xviii. 18; John xx. 23; 1 Cor. v. 4, 5; Titus iii. 10; 1 Tim i. 20; 2 Cor. ii. 6. And both these, the authority of the eldership and the consent of the brethren, are necessary to the validity of the sentence, and that according to the appointment of Christ, and the practice of the first churches.

2. The *effect* of it, which is the cutting off or casting out of the person offending from the communion of the church, in the privileges of the gospel, as consequently from that of all the visible churches of Christ in the earth, by virtue of their communion one with another; whereby he is left unto the visible kingdom of Satan in the world.—Matt. xviii. 17; 1 Cor. v. 2, 5, 13; 1 Tim. i. 20; Titus iii. 10; Gal. v. 12.

3. The *ends* of it, which are,—

(1.) The *gaining* of the party offending, by bringing him to repentance, humiliation, and acknowledgment of his offence, 2 Cor. ii. 6, 7, xiii. 10.

(2.) The *warning* of others not to do so presumptuously.

(3.) The *preserving* of the church in its purity and order, 1 Cor. v. 6, 7; all to the glory of Jesus Christ.

4. The *causes* of it, or the grounds and reasons on which the church may proceed unto sentence against any offending persons. Now, these are no other but such as they judge, according to the gospel, that the Lord Christ will proceed upon in his final judgment at the last day; for the church judgeth in the name and authority of Christ, and are to exclude none from its communion but those whom they find by the rule that he himself excludes from his kingdom; and so that which they bind on earth is bound by him in heaven, Matt. xviii. 18. And their sentence herein is to be declared, as the declaration of the sentence which the Head of the church and Judge of all will pronounce at the last day; only with this difference, that it is also made known that this sentence of theirs is not final or decretory, but in order to the prevention of that which will be so unless the evil be repented of. Now, although the particular evils, sins, or offences that may render a person obnoxious unto this censure and sentence are not to be enumerated, by reason of the variety of circumstances, which change the nature of actions, yet they may in general be referred unto these heads:—

(1.) *Moral evils*, contrary to the light of nature and express commands or prohibitions of the moral law, direct rules of the gospel, or of evil report in the world amongst men walking according to the rule and light of reason. And, in cases of this nature, the church may proceed unto the sentence whereof we speak without previous admonition, in case the matter of fact be notorious, publicly and unquestionably known to be true, and no general rule (which is not to be impeached by particular instances) lie against their procedure, 1 Cor. v. 3–5; 2 Tim. iii. 2–5.

(2.) Offences against that *mutual love* which is the bond of perfection in the church, if pertinaciously persisted in, Matt. xviii. 16, 17.

(3.) *False doctrines* against the fundamentals in faith or worship, especially if maintained with contention, to the trouble and disturb-ance of the peace of the church, Gal. v. 12; Titus iii. 9–11; 1 Tim. vi. 3–5; Rev. ii. 14, 15.

(4.) Blasphemy or evil speaking of the ways and worship of God in the church, especially if joined with an intention to hinder the prosperity of the church or to expose it to persecution, 1 Tim. i. 20.

(5.) Desertion, or total causeless relinquishment of the society and communion of the church; for such are self-condemned, having broken and renounced the covenant of God, that they made at their entrance into the church, Heb. x. 25–31.

5. The *time* or season of the putting forth the authority of Christ in the church for this censure is to be considered, and that is ordi-narily after the admonition before described, and that with due waiting, to be regulated by a consideration of times, persons, tempta-tions, and other circumstances; for,—

(1.) The church in proceeding to this sentence is to express the patience and long-suffering of Christ towards offenders, and not to put it forth without conviction of a present resolved impenitency.

(2.) The event and effect of the preceding ordinance of admoni-tion is to be expected; which though not at present evident, yet, like the word itself in the preaching of it, may be blessed to a good issue after many days.

6. The person offending thus cut off, or cast out from the present actual communion of the church, is still to be looked on and account-ed as a brother, because of the nature of the ordinance which is in-tended for his amendment and recovery,—2 Thess. iii. 15, "Count him not as an enemy, but admonish him as a brother,"—unless he manifest his final impenitency by blasphemy and persecution: 1 Tim. i. 20, "Whom I have delivered unto Satan, that they may learn not to blaspheme."

7. The church is, therefore, still to perform the duties of love and care towards such persons,—

(1.) In *praying* for them, that they "may be converted from the error of their way," James v. 19, 20. 1 John v. 16, "If any man see his brother sin a sin which is not unto death, he shall ask, and he shall give him life for them that sin not unto death."

(2.) In *withdrawing* from them even as to ordinary converse, for their conviction of their state and condition, 1 Cor. v. 11, "With such an one no not to eat;" 2 Thess. iii. 14.

(3.) In *admonishing of* him: 2 Thess. iii. 15, "Admonish him as a brother:" which may be done,—[1.] *Occasionally,* by any member of the church; [2.] *On set purpose,* by the consent and appointment of the whole church : which admonition is to contain,—1*st,* A *press-ing of his sin* from the rule on the conscience of the offender; 2*dly,*

A *declaration* of the nature of the censure and punishment which he lieth under; 3*dly*, A *manifestation* of the danger of his impenitency, in his being either hardened by the deceitfulness of sin or exposed unto new temptations of Satan.

8. In case the Lord Jesus be pleased to give a blessed effect unto this ordinance, in the repentance of the person cut off and cast out of the church, he is,—

(1.) To be *forgiven* both by those who in an especial manner were offended at him and by him, and by the whole church, Matt. xviii. 18; 2 Cor. ii. 7.

(2.) To be *comforted* under his sorrow, 2 Cor. ii. 7, and that by,— [1.] The *application of the promises* of the gospel unto his conscience; [2.] A *declaration of the readiness* of the church to receive him again into their love and communion.

(3.) *Restored*,—[1.] By a *confirmation* or testification of the love of the church unto him, 2 Cor. ii. 8; [2.] A *re-admission* unto the exercise and enjoyment of his former privileges in the fellowship of the church; all with a spirit of meekness, Gal. vi. 1.

Q. 47. *The preservation of the church in purity, order, and holiness, being provided for, by what way is it to be continued and increased?*

A. The way appointed thereunto is by adding such as, being effectually called unto the obedience of faith, shall voluntarily offer themselves unto the society and fellowship thereof, Acts ii. 41; 2 Cor. viii. 5.

EXPLICATION.—The means appointed by our Lord Jesus Christ for the continuance and increase of the church are either *preparatory* unto it or *instrumentally efficient of it.* The principal means subservient or *preparatory* unto the continuance and increase of the church is the preaching of the word to the conviction, illumination, and conversion of sinners, whereby they may be made meet to become living stones in this spiritual building, and members of the mystical body of Christ. And this is done either ordinarily, in the assemblies of the church, towards such as come in unto them and attend to the word dispensed according to the appointment of Christ amongst them,—1 Cor. xiv. 24, 25, "If there come in one that believeth not, or one unlearned, he is convinced of all, he is judged of all: and thus are the secrets of his heart made manifest; and so falling down on his face he will worship God,"—or occasionally, amongst the men of the world, Acts viii. 4.

Secondly, The *instrumentally efficient cause* is that which is expressed in the answer,—namely, the adding in due order unto it such as, being effectually called unto the obedience of the faith and profession of the gospel, do voluntarily, out of conviction of their duty and resolution to walk in subjection to all the ordinances and commands of Christ, offer themselves to the society and fellowship thereof, whereby they may be laid in this spiritual building as the stones were in the temple of old, which were hewed and fitted elsewhere.

Q. 48. *What is required of them who desire to join themselves unto the church?*

A. [1]That they be free from blame and offence in the world; [2]that they be instructed in the saving truths and mysteries of the gospel; [3]sound in the faith; [4]that, the Lord having called them unto faith, repentance, and newness of life by Jesus Christ, they give up themselves to be saved by him, and to obey him in all things; and, therefore, [5]are willing and ready, through his grace, to walk in subjection to all his commands, and in the observation of all his laws and institutions, notwithstanding any difficulties, oppositions, or persecutions, which they meet withal.—[1]Phil. i. 10, ii. 15; 1 Cor. x. 32; 1 Thess. ii. 11, 12; Tit. ii. 10.—[2]John vi. 45; Acts xxvi. 18; 1 Pet. ii. 9; 2 Cor. iv. 3, 4, 6.—[3]1 Tim. i. 19, 20; 2 Tim. iv. 3, 4; Tit. i. 13; Jude 3.—[4]Eph. iv. 20–24.—[5]2 Cor. viii. 5.

Q. 49. *What is the duty of the elders of the church towards persons desiring to be admitted unto the fellowship of the church?*

A. [1]To discern and judge by the rule of truth, applied in love, between sincere professors and hypocritical pretenders; [2]to influence, direct, comfort, and encourage in the way, such as they judge to love the Lord Jesus in sincerity; [3]to propose and recommend them unto the whole church, with prayers and supplications to God for them; [4]to admit them, being approved, into the order and fellowship of the gospel in the church.—[1]Acts viii. 20, 23; Tit. i. 10; Rev. ii. 2; Jer. xv. 19.—[2]Acts xviii. 26; 1 Thess. ii. 7, 8, 11.—[3]Acts ix. 27, 28.—[4]Rom. xiv. 1.

Q. 50. *What is the duty of the whole church in reference unto such persons?*

A. To consider them in love and meekness, according as their condition is known, reported, or testified unto them; to approve of and rejoice in the grace of God in them; and to receive them in love without dissimulation, 1 Cor. xiii.

EXPLICATION.—What in general is required, unto the fitting of any persons to be members of a visible church of Christ, was before declared; and that is that which the Lord Jesus hath made the indispensable condition of entering into his kingdom,—namely, of being " born again," John iii. 3, 5. This work, being secret, hidden, and invisible, the church cannot judge of directly and in its own form or nature, but in the means, effects, and consequents of it; which are to be testified unto it, concerning them who are to be admitted unto its fellowship and communion.   It is required, therefore, of them,—

First, That they be of a conversation free from blame in the world; for whereas one end of the gathering of churches is to hold forth and express the holiness of the doctrine of Christ, and the power of his grace in turning men from all ungodliness unto sobriety, right-eousness, and honesty, it is required of them that are admitted into them that they answer this end.   And this the principle of grace, which is communicated unto them that believe, will effect and pro-duce; for although it doth not follow that every one who hath at-tained an unblamable honesty in this world is inwardly quickened with a true principle of saving grace, yet it doth that they who are endowed with that principle will be so unblamable.   And although they may on other accounts be evil spoken of, yet their good conver-sation in Christ will justify itself.

Secondly, Competent knowledge in the mysteries of the gospel is another means whereby the great qualification inquired after is testi-fied unto the church; for as without this no privilege of the gospel can be profitably made use of, nor any duty of it rightly performed, so saving light is of the essence of conversion, and doth inseparably accompany it: 2 Cor. iv. 6, "God, who commanded the light to shine out of darkness, hath shined in our hearts, to give the light of the knowledge of the glory of God in the face of Jesus Christ." Where this is wanting, it is impossible for any person to evidence that he is delivered from that blindness, darkness, and ignorance, which all men are under the power of in the state of nature.   Such a measure, then, of light and knowledge, as whereby men are enabled to apprehend aright of the person and offices of Christ, of the nature of his mediation, the benefits thereof, and the obedience that he re-quires at the hands of his disciples, is expected in them who desire to be admitted into the fellowship of the church.

Thirdly, Hereunto is to be added soundness in the faith; for the unity of faith is the foundation of love and all the duties thereof, which in an especial manner are to be performed towards the church, called, therefore, "The household of faith."   There is among the mem-bers of the church "one faith," Eph. iv. 5; the "common faith," [Tit. i. 4;] the "faith once delivered unto the saints," Jude 3; which is the "sound doctrine," 1 Tim. i. 10, which those that will not endure must be turned from, 2 Tim. iii. 5; the "faithful word," that is to be "held fast," Tit i. 9, 1 Tim. i. 19, and which we are to be "sound in," Tit. i. 13; contained in a "form of sound words," as to the profession of it, 2 Tim. i. 13.   And this soundness in the unity of faith, as it should be improved unto oneness of mind and oneness of accord in all the things of God, Phil. ii. 2, though it may admit of some different apprehensions in some things, wherein some may have more clear and distinct discoveries of the mind and will of God than others, which hinders not but that all may walk according to the same rule, Phil. iii. 15, 16; so it is principally to be regarded in the fundamental truths of the gospel, in and by the faith whereof the church holdeth on the head, Jesus Christ, Col. ii. 19; and in the fundamental principles of gospel worship, the joint celebration whereof is the next end of the gathering the church: for without a consent of mind and accord herein, no duty can be performed unto edification, nor the peace of the church be preserved. And these principles are those which we have explained.

Fourthly, It is required that these things be testified by them unto the church, with the acknowledgment of the work of God's grace towards them, and their resolution, through the power of the same grace, to cleave unto the Lord Christ with full purpose of heart, and to live in all holy obedience unto him. They come to the church as disciples of Christ, professing that they have learnt the truth as it is in Jesus: which what it infers the apostle teacheth at large, Eph. iv. 20–24; see also Acts xi. 23, xiv. 22. And this by themselves [is] to be testified unto the church:—

1. That they may be received in love without dissimulation, as real partakers in the same faith, hope, and salvation with themselves, as living members of the mystical body of Christ.

2. That on all ensuing occasions they may be minded of their own profession and engagements, to stir them up thereby unto faithfulness, steadfastness, and perseverance. Hereupon are the elders of the church to judge by the rule of truth, in love and meekness, concerning their condition and meetness to be laid as living stones in the house of God; so as that they may,—

(1.) Reject false, hypocritical pretenders, if in or by any means their hypocrisy be discovered unto them, Acts viii. 20–23; Tit. i. 10; Jer. xv. 19.

(2.) That they may direct and encourage in the way such as appear to be sincere, instructing them principally in the nature of the way whereinto they are engaging, the duties, dangers, and benefits of it, Acts xviii. 26, xiv. 22; 1 Cor. iii. 22, 23.

(3.) To propose them, their condition, their desires, their resolutions, unto the church, after their own expressions of them, to be considered of in love and meekness, Acts ix. 26, 27. Whereupon those that are approved do give up themselves unto the Lord, to walk in the observation of all his commands and ordinances; and to the church for the Lord's sake, 2 Cor. viii. 5, abiding in the fellowship thereof, whereunto they are admitted, Acts ii. 41, 42.

Q. 51. *Wherein doth the especial form of a particular church, whereby it becomes such, and is distinguished as such from all others, consist?*

A. In the special consent and agreement of all the members of it to walk together in the observation of the same ordinances numerically; hence its constitution and distinction from other churches doth proceed.—Exod. xix. 5, 8, xxiv. 3, 7; Deut. xxvi. 17; 2 Cor. viii. 5; Acts xiv. 23, xx. 28; Heb. xiii. 17.

EXPLICATION.—It hath been before declared what especial agreement or covenant there ought to be among all the members of the same church, to walk together in a due subjection unto and observance of all the institutions of the Lord Christ. And this is that which gives it its special *form* and distinction from all other churches. In the general nature of a church, all churches do agree and equally partake. There is the same law of the constitution of them all; they have all the same rule of obedience, all the same Head, the same end; all carry it on by the observation of the same ordinances in *kind.* Now, besides these things, which belong unto the nature of a church in general, and wherein they all equally participate, they must also have each one its proper difference, that which doth distinguish it from all other churches; and this gives it its special form as such. Now, this cannot consist in any thing that is accidental, occasional, or extrinsical unto it, such as is cohabitation (which yet the church may have respect unto, for conveniency and furthering of its edification); nor in any civil or political disposal of its members into civil societies for civil ends, which is extrinsical to all its concernments as a church; nor doth it consist in the relation of that church to its present officers, which may be removed or taken away without the dissolution of the form or being of the church: but it consisteth, as was said, in the agreement or covenant before mentioned. For,—

First, This is that which constitutes them a *distinct body,* different from others; for thereby, and no otherwise, do they coalesce into a society, according to the laws of their constitution and appointment.

Secondly, This gives them their *especial relation* unto their own elders, rulers, or guides, who watch over them as so associated by their own consent, according unto the command of Christ. And,—

Thirdly, From hence they have their mutual especial relation unto one another; which is the ground of the especial exercise of all church duties whatsoever.

Q. 52. *Wherein consists the duty of any church of Christ towards other churches?*

A. [1]In walking circumspectly, so as to give them no offence; [2]in prayer for their peace and prosperity; [3]in communicating supplies to their wants according to ability; [4]in receiving with love and readiness the members of them into fellowship, in the celebration of the ordinances of the gospel, as occasion shall be; [5]in desiring and making use of their counsel and advice in such cases of doubt and difficulty as may arise among them; [6]in joining with them to express their communion in the same doctrine of faith.—[1]1 Cor. x. 32. —[2]Ps. cxxii. 6; Eph. vi. 18; 1 Tim. ii. 1.—[3]2 Cor. viii. 1–15; Acts xi. 29, 30; Rom. xv. 26, 27.—[4]Rom. xvi. 1, 2; 3 John 8, 9.—[5]Acts xv. 2, 6.—[6]1 Tim. iii. 15.

EXPLICATION.—Churches being gathered and settled according to the mind of Christ, ought to preserve a mutual holy communion among themselves, and to exercise it in the discharge of those duties whereby their mutual good and edification may be promoted; for whereas they are all united under one head, the Lord Christ, Eph. i. 22, 23, in the same faith and order, chap. iv. 5, and do walk by the same rule, they stand in such a relation one to another as is the ground of the communion spoken of. Now, the principal ways whereby they exercise this communion are the acts and duties enumerated in the answer unto this question; as,—

First, Careful walking, so as to give no offence unto one another; which, although it be a moral duty in reference unto all, yet therein especial regard is to be had unto other churches of Christ, that they be not in any thing grieved or tempted: 1 Cor. x. 32, " Give none offence, neither to the Jews, nor to the Gentiles, nor to the church of God."

Secondly, In constant prayer for the peace, welfare, edification, and prosperity one of another, Rom. i. 9 ; Col. i. 9 ; Eph. vi. 18. And this because of the special concernment of the name and glory of our Lord Jesus Christ in their welfare.

Thirdly, In communicating of supplies for their relief according unto their ability, in case of the outward wants, straits, dangers, or necessities of any of them.—Acts xi. 29, 30; Rom. xv. 26, 27; 2 Cor. viii. 1–15.

Fourthly, The receiving of the members of other churches to communion, in the celebration of church-ordinances, is another way whereby this communion of churches is exercised, Rom. xvi. 1, 2; 3 John 8, 9; for whereas the personal right of such persons unto the ordinances of the church, and their orderly walking in the observation of the commands of Christ, are known by the testimony of the church whereof they are members, they may, without farther inquiry or satisfaction given, be looked on " pro tempore" as members of the church wherein they desire fellowship and participation of the ordinances of Christ.

Fifthly, In desiring or making use of the counsel and advice of one another, in such cases of doubt and difficulty, whether *doctrinal* or *practical*, as may arise in any of them, Acts xv. 2, 6. And from hence it follows, that in case any church, either by error in doctrine, or precipitation, or mistake in other administrations, do give offence unto other churches, those other churches may require an account from them, admonish them of their faults, and withhold communion from them in case they persist in the error of their way; and that because in their difficulties, and before their miscarriages, they were bound to have desired the advice, counsel, and assistance of those other churches, which being neglected by them, the other are to recover the end of it unto their utmost ability, Gal. ii. 6–11. And hence, also, it follows that those that are rightly and justly censured in any church ought to be rejected by all churches whatever; both because of their mutual communion, and because it is and ought to be presumed, until the contrary be made to appear, that, in case there had been any difficulty or doubt in the procedure of the church, they would have taken the advice of those churches, with whom they were obliged to consult.

Lastly, Whereas the churches have all of them one *common faith*, and are all obliged to hold forth and declare it to all men as they have opportunity, 1 Tim. iii. 15, to testify this their mutual communion, their interest in the same faith and hope, for the more open declaration and proposition of the truths of the gospel which they profess, and for the vindication both of the truth and themselves from false charges and imputations, they may, and, if God give opportunity, ought to join together in declaring and testifying their joint consent and fellowship in the same doctrine of faith, expressed in a " form of sound words."

Q. 53. *What are the ends of all this dispensation and order of things in the church?*

A. The glory of God, the honour of Jesus Christ the mediator, the furtherance of the gospel, the edification and consolation of believers here, with their eternal salvation hereafter.—Rev. iv. 9–11, v. 12, 13; 1 Cor. iii. 22, 23; Eph. iv. 11–16.

END OF VOL. XV.